.972
33cr
2009

Croatia

Vesna Marić

Anja Mutić

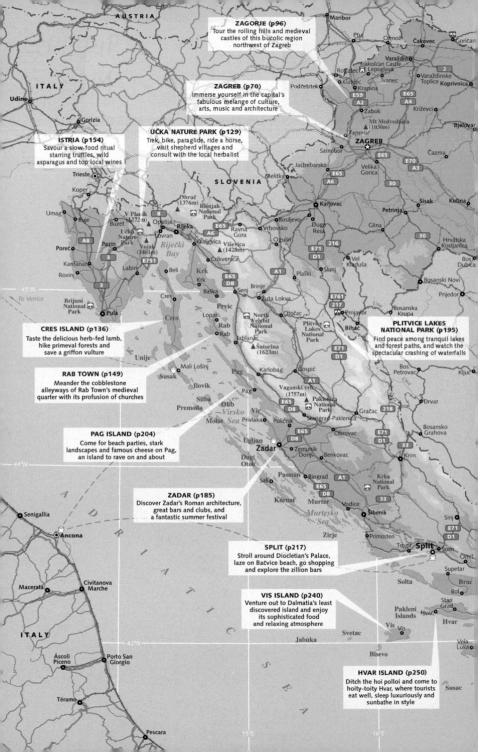

ZAGORJE (p96)
Tour the rolling hills and medieval castles of this bucolic region northwest of Zagreb

ZAGREB (p70)
Immerse yourself in the capital's fabulous melange of culture, arts, music and architecture

UČKA NATURE PARK (p129)
Trek, bike, paraglide, ride a horse, visit shepherd villages and consult with the local herbalist

ISTRIA (p154)
Savour a slow-food ritual starring truffles, wild asparagus and top local wines

CRES ISLAND (p136)
Taste the delicious herb-fed lamb, hike primeval forests and save a griffon vulture

PLITVICE LAKES NATIONAL PARK (p195)
Find peace among tranquil lakes and forest paths, and watch the spectacular crashing of waterfalls

RAB TOWN (p149)
Meander the cobblestone alleyways of Rab Town's medieval quarter with its profusion of churches

PAG ISLAND (p204)
Come for beach parties, stark landscapes and famous cheese on Pag, an island to rave on and about

ZADAR (p185)
Discover Zadar's Roman architecture, great bars and clubs, and a fantastic summer festival

SPLIT (p217)
Stroll around Diocletian's Palace, laze on Bačvice beach, go shopping and explore the zillion bars

VIS ISLAND (p240)
Venture out to Dalmatia's least discovered island and enjoy its sophisticated food and relaxing atmosphere

HVAR ISLAND (p250)
Ditch the hoi polloi and come to hoity-toity Hvar, where tourists eat well, sleep luxuriously and sunbathe in style

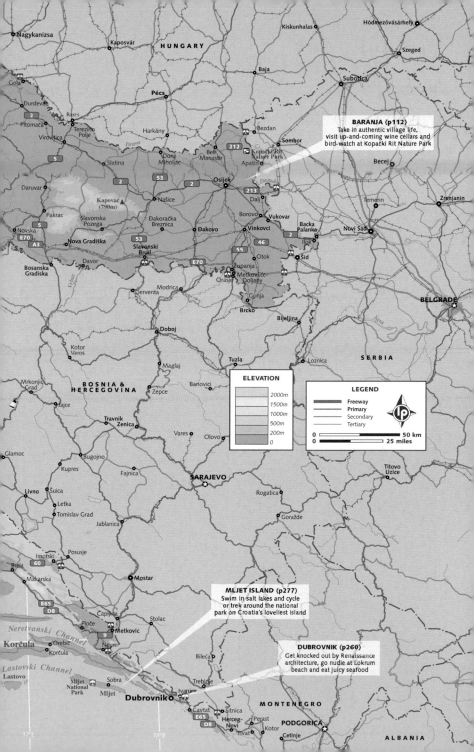

BARANJA (p112)
Take in authentic village life,
visit up-and-coming wine cellars and
bird-watch at Kopački Rit Nature Park

MLJET ISLAND (p277)
Swim in salt lakes and cycle
or trek around the national
park on Croatia's loveliest island

DUBROVNIK (p260)
Get knocked out by Renaissance
architecture, go nude at Lokrum
beach and eat juicy seafood

ELEVATION

2000m
1500m
1000m
500m
200m
0

LEGEND

Freeway
Primary
Secondary
Tertiary

0   50 km
0   25 miles

HUNGARY

BOSNIA &
HERCEGOVINA

SERBIA

MONTENEGRO

ALBANIA

Nagykanizsa
Kaposvár
Kiskunhalas
Hódmezővásárhely
Szeged
Baja
Subotica
Gola
Pécs
Durdevac
Rarcs
Pitomača
Terezino
Polje
Harkány
Bezdan
Sombor
Becej
Virovitica
Drava
Belí
Manastir
Kopački Rit
Nature Park
Apatino
Temerin
Zrenjanin
Slatina
Donji
Miholjac
Osijek
Dali
Daruvar
Našice
Borovo
Vukovar
Novi Sad
Pakrac
Kapovac
(790m)
Slavonska
Požega
Đakovačka
Breznica
Đakovo
Vinkovci
Backa
Palanka
Ilok
Novska
Nova Gradiška
Slavonski
Brod
Otok
Šid
Bosanska
Gradiska
Davor
Zupanja
Metković
Doljany
Orašje
Modrica
Derventa
Grnja
Brcko
Bijeljina
BELGRADE
Kotor
Varos
Doboj
Maglaj
Tuzla
Loznica
Mrkonjic
Grad
Žepce
Banovici
Jajce
Travnik
Zenica
Vares
Olovo
Glamoc
Bugojno
Kupres
Fajnica
SARAJEVO
Titovo
Uzice
Livno
Šuica
Rogatica
Letka
Tomislav Grad
Goražde
Jablanica
Posusje
Imotski
Brela
Makarska
Mostar
Korčula
Orebić
Korčula
Čapljina
Ploče
Metković
Stolac
Neum
Bileća
Mljet
National
Park
Sobra
Mljet
Trebinje
Dubrovnik
Cavtat
Sitnica
Herceg-
Novi
Perast
Kotor
Cetinje
PODGORICA
Ivanica
Neretvanski Channel
Lastovski Channel
Lastovo

On the Road

VESNA MARIĆ Coordinating Author
No matter how many times I see Dubrovnik, I can't get enough of it. On this day I was walking around the Ploče area and I stopped to look at the beach and the beautiful old town (p264) below.

ANJA MUTIĆ I'm pondering the meaning of life and taking a rare and precious moment to relax. The back terrace of Kamene Priče (Stone Tales; see boxed text, p174) in Istria's town of Bale is the perfect place for it. Surrounded by ancient stone and filled with a plethora of cool objects, it's the type of place where you can sink into a chair and spend endless hours thinking, writing, talking, scribbling, eating, drinking, dreaming, listening to music… Anything goes here.

For author biographies, see p326.

Croatia Highlights

Croatia is the word on everybody's lips at the moment, and everyone who's been there has their own favourite haunt. We asked Lonely Planet staff and travellers for their top picks.

MARTIN MOOS

1 THE GEM IN THE VALLEY: PLITVICE

In a valley between mountains lie the Plitvice Lakes (p195), 16 crystal-blue lakes with roaring waterfalls. Crossing the many small wooden pathways between the lakes, find your favourite spot away from the tourists to marvel at this hidden gem.

Snjezana Pruginic, traveller, Canada

ANDREW BURKE

MLJET: ODYSSEUS' RETREAT

Odysseus reputedly spent seven years on Mljet (p277) under the spell of Calypso. Once you arrive you'll understand its enchanting power. Wander through the pine forest, swim in the emerald salt-water lake and feel like part of a legend.

Colleen Kerney, traveller, USA

3

2

HVAR ISLAND

The luscious green flora, rocky beaches and rugged beauty of Hvar (p250) are best appreciated from the Venetian fortress on the hill above the medieval town.

Lisa Vitaris, traveller, Australia

HOLGER LE

4

ALL THAT IS DUBROVNIK

Walking around Dubrovnik on the city's walls (p267) offers beautiful views of rocky islands, grassy mountains and shimmering seas, along with real-life views of women pegging out their washing and winding it along on lines between buildings.

Lisa Vitaris, traveller, Australia

THE MANY FLAVOURS OF ZAGREB

Croatia's capital is a crossroads for central Europe to the Adriatic coast and the rest of the Balkans. With an upper and lower town, there are many flavours to Zagreb (p70). Croatia's largest metropolis has great architecture and museums, beautiful parks and magnificent views of the city from the hillside.

Michael Sabelli, traveller, Canada

5

ANDREW BURKE

ISTRIAN TREATS

The daily feasts in Istria are a real treat. The truffles, olive oil and wine stand out, as do myriad regional specialities. Slow food is a hit here – you can sample the ritual in upmarket restaurants, traditional taverns and converted olive mills.

Anja Mutić, Lonely Planet author, USA

6

WAYNE WALTON

7 **POREČ**

The islands surrounding Poreč range from the wild and undisturbed to those catering for large hotels. Poreč itself has an ornate, World Heritage–listed Byzantine church (p171).

Lisa Vitaris, traveller, Australia

WAYNE WALTON

ANDREW BURKE

9 WINDSURFING ON BOL

Beaches, sun, Zlatni Rat, wind-surfing: Bol (p247) is an island paradise. Oh, and try the cocktail bar with the bamboo umbrellas by the harbour!

Kevin Toogood, traveller, UK

8 INDULGE YOUR SWEET TOOTH

You absolutely must not miss the pastry shops (*slastičarna*). In the summertime head straight for the ice-cream counters, which commonly display 10 to 20 flavours of fresh, homemade ice cream. *Sladoled*, ice cream in Croatian, gives Italian gelato a run for its money.

Andreja Zebic, traveller, Canada

MARTIN MO

10 KRKA NATIONAL PARK

Skradinski Buk (p213), with its clear, fast-flowing water and falls, is a magical place. My jaw hit the floor as we crossed stream after stream flowing through woods, emerging by the most beautiful cascades I've ever seen. I wasn't the only one who couldn't resist a dip followed by a picnic and a snooze in the sun.

Tom Hall, Lonely Planet staff, UK

PICTURESQUE CAVTAT

A short drive south from Dubrovnik lies the beautiful town of Cavtat (p280). Set around a picturesque harbour, the pace of life slows as you approach the town from the main road. There are numerous pebbly beaches, cafés and restaurants overlooking the sea, and it is a great setting for evening visits to Dubrovnik.

Maja Thompson, traveller, UK

11

JON DAVISON

VISIT VARAŽDIN

Varaždin (p97) is a city famous for its castle, its old city, the baroque evenings held every year in September, its cemetery – the most beautiful place to be buried in Europe – and for its spirit, which makes every tourist feel like they're at home.

Željka Banicek, traveller, Croatia

12

WILMAR PHOTOGRAPHY / ALAMY

WAYNE WALT

13

CAFÉ CHAIRS & THE PALACE AT SPLIT

Nuns dart in and out of Diocletian's Palace (p220), also a favourite of many travellers. Palm trees and café swing chairs line the water's edge, offering respite from the summer heat or a well-deserved break after climbing nearby Marjan Hill.

Lisa Vitaris, traveller, Australia

ZADAR

Zadar (p185): a great medieval town in a carless fortress. There are many interesting sites from all periods of time. On a corner of this town stuck into the Adriatic, there's a wind chime (called the Sea Organ; p189) built into the steps going down to the water where it seems everyone goes at least once a day to relax.

Michael Sabelli, traveller, Canada

ANDREW BURKE

15

IMPACT PHOTOS / ALAMY

14 NORTHERN CRES

I fell in love with the Tramuntana region on northern Cres Island. The labyrinth of eco-trails from the ancient town of Beli (p138) takes you through virgin old-growth forests and abandoned villages, where you almost expect an elf to jump out from behind one of the giant oak trees.

Anja Mutić, Lonely Planet author, USA

TIM HUGHES

16 TAKING THE FERRY

The overnight ferry along the Croatian coast (see p311) is a great way to see the country, with a lot more room than a cramped bus. It's a wonderful opportunity to wake up to the sunshine and relax while taking in the scenery of one of the world's most beautiful coastlines.

Kate West, traveller, Australia

ANNE DOWIE

SIP THE 'SLJIVO'

Unless otherwise indicated, you can drink alcohol almost anywhere. Plum brandy *(šljivovica)* is served by locals for toasting. Remember that even if your drink is served in a common shot glass, you should sip it.

Andreja Zebic, traveller, Canada

RICHARD I'AN'

18

17 KORČULAN AMBIENCE

Korčula (p282) surprised and impressed. This protuberant town, with alleys built high and narrow for wind protection, has so much ambience that the locals could bottle it and make a fortune. The ice cream is unbelievable.

Iisad, traveller

JAN STROM

19 CRYSTAL WATERS OF MAKARSKA

Most of the coastline east and west of Makarska is considered sensational, but the Makarska Riviera (p236) would have to have the most pristine water ever seen. No pretence, just an exquisite presence.

Branka King, traveller, Australia

Contents

Regional Map Contents

Hrvatsko
Zagorje p97

Zagreb
pp74-5

Istria
p156

Kvarner
Region
p119

Slavonia p107

Northern
Dalmatia
p185

Central
Dalmatia
p217

Southern
Dalmatia
pp260-1

Destination Croatia

Sitting on a see-saw between the Balkans and Central Europe, Croatia has been suffering from something of a love-hate-love affair with the EU and its neighbours. Invited to join the UN Security Council in January 2008, its NATO membership was poised for 2009, but its dispute with the EU over its fishing laws saw displeased finger-wagging from the European officials and the already slightly elusive EU joining date (is it 2010? 2011? Perhaps 2012?) caught on yet another hurdle. March 2008 saw the beginning of the trial of Ante Gotovina, Croatia's wartime general whose arrest was the main prerequisite for the beginning of Croatia's talks for joining the EU back in 2005. Gotovina stands accused of 'joint criminal enterprise' for the expulsion of Serbs from Krajina in 1995. Revered and still seen as a hero by many in his native Zadar region, Gotovina's trial is sure to bring home some controversial elements of Croatia's Homeland War.

Still in progress at the time of writing were the judicial reforms, the struggle against corruption and the improvement of conditions for the setting up of private businesses in the country, all of which have to be fulfilled before Croatia can get its foot in the door of the desirable European club. Life for the average Croat remains on the tough side, however – the average salary of 6000KN per month is often too low to support a family – and there is a declining but still substantial rate of unemployment (11.18%). Statistics show that the support for joining the EU, which was once vast and palpable, is lately hovering around the 50% mark and is only threatening to sink further. Many Croats feel their progress is being scrutinised more carefully than that of other, recently joined, EU members, and while this may well be the case, it's an unsurprising sign of caution after the large EU expansions of 2004 and 2007.

Croatia's economy is looking brighter, however, with a steady GDP growth over recent years. This is, of course, thanks to the continuing growth of tourism and the ensuing development. The country has, with few exceptions, managed to keep massive development at bay and maintain Croatia's beauty – the very ingredients that keep the punters coming for more. New luxury hotels are sprouting up every year, especially on Hvar and in Dubrovnik, but smaller, budget-oriented and agritourism options are increasing, too, especially in Istria.

Croatia has also been doing well at sport, one of its most successful endeavours. The country won the World Handball Championship in 2007 (just don't ask 'What's handball?'), and the national football team reached the quarter finals in the 2008 Euro Cup, beating Germany but sadly losing to Turkey on penalties.

With its economic growth, sporting successes and great bars, restaurants, films and music festivals, plus a desire to further improve its infrastructure and sustainable development, Croatia seems to be saying 'never mind the EU, we're comin' atcha'.

FAST FACTS

Population: 4.5 million

Area: 56,538 sq km

Head of state: President Stjepan Mesić

GDP growth rate: 5%

Inflation: 2.9%

Average net monthly salary: 6000KN

Unemployment rate: 11.18%

Primary trading partner: Italy

Population growth rate: -0.04%

Life expectancy: male 71, female 78.5

Getting Started

It may not surprise you to learn that Croatia is at its most popular in the summer months. Its luxurious hotels, modest family-owned *pensions* (guest houses) or beachfront camping grounds all get busy with guests, local and international, especially in the peak season (July through August). It's a good idea to book a place to stay in advance during these two months, especially if you'll be staying on one of the islands. Spring and autumn are less busy and more attractive – think entire beaches to yourself, a plentiful choice of places to stay, and museums and churches serenely empty.

The high season does have its advantages, however: everything stays open later, there is more transport, the ferries and catamarans have extra and speedy service, and if you're into beach parties and lots of summer fun, this is the best time to visit. Out of season, be aware that taking ferries from island to island can be tricky; there isn't always a daily ferry connection. You may have more flexibility than you think in July and August, but less from September to June.

WHEN TO GO

Although Croatia's peak season is in July and August, the coast is gorgeous in spring and early autumn: the Adriatic is still too cool for plunging into in April, but it can be good during a warm May, especially in Central and Southern Dalmatia, and in September it is almost guaranteed that the sea's temperatures will climb up to 23°C! Unlike the sea's temperature, accommodation prices pleasantly drop during the off-season months.

See Climate Charts (p297) for more information.

Cities such as Zagreb are in full cultural swing during spring and autumn – you can attend the Zagreb Biennial of Contemporary Music, the Zagreb Film Festival, various street festivals or the Queer Zagreb FM Festival (see p83). May and June are great months for most outdoor activities (skiing aside, of course); during this time accommodation prices are also reasonable and you'll enjoy long, sunny days. This being the end-of-term-excursion season in Croatia, you may come across lively battalions of school students at the end of May and beginning of June; hotels and transport around cultural highlights can fill up with boisterous youngsters and their harried chaperones.

July and August are the most expensive months to visit Croatia: accommodation prices skyrocket, popular cities, sights, hotels and restaurants get super-packed, and the beaches can get noisy and crowded. The main advantages of high-season travel are the extra boat lines to whisk you to the islands.

September is perhaps the best month in Croatia. The sea is warm (the weather too), the crowds are sparse and everything becomes cheaper. If you're a fan of Mediterranean fruit, you'll find figs and pomegranates in abundance. October is popular with some, and locals and foreigners alike use this month to really relax – it may be too cool for camping, but the weather should still be fine along the coast, and private rooms will be plentiful and inexpensive.

COSTS & MONEY

Croatia isn't a cheap country. This means that unless you stay in hostels and private accommodation or go camping, hotels – especially the new, refurbished and glitzy ones – can compare with those in any European destination, both in terms of price and comfort. Accommodation prices, boat fares and anything else relating to tourism skyrocket in summer, reaching a peak in

---

DON'T LEAVE HOME WITHOUT...

■ Rubber shoes to wade into the water along Croatia's rocky coast.

■ High protection sunscreen.

■ Valid travel insurance (p300).

■ Anti-seasickness medicine just in case the Adriatic gets choppy.

■ A small rucksack for any day trips you might take.

July and August. In the high season, a double room costs between 250KN and 300KN in a private residence, from 500KN to 1000KN in a three-star hotel, and anything from 2000KN in a boutique hotel. The premium prices are in Dubrovnik and Hvar, where the most luxurious hotels are and where most tourists tend to go. Rooms in Zagreb and continental Croatia cost about the same all year, and you'll find that accommodation in the Slavonia and Zagorje regions is less pricey than on the coast and in the capital. Note that private owners usually add a 30% surcharge for private rooms rented for less than three nights and some insist on a seven-night minimum in the high season – always check in advance. Hotels usually have no minimum-stay requirements. Car rental in Croatia is always incredibly expensive when compared with its EU neighbours, but also Montenegro and Bosnia and Hercegovina. Prices start from around 325KN for a day and go down for longer rentals.

Concert and theatre tickets and museums are reasonably cheap (concert and theatre tickets run from about 60KN to 200KN and museums are between 15KN and 35KN); boat transport is also cheap unless you take a car on board. The average intercity bus fare ranges from 40KN to 80KN. You can easily get a pizza for 30KN, and a plate of pasta costs about 50KN to 60KN even in the more expensive restaurants. Fish, meat and produce are about the same price as elsewhere in Europe.

Backpackers who stay in one place can plan on spending about 350KN a day. Staying in nicely appointed private rooms, eating in moderate restaurants and travelling along the coast costs about 500KN per day; it's more than double that to stay in the best hotels and eat at the best restaurants. Families and a bunch of friends travelling together are better off renting an apartment than staying in a hotel. A one-bedroom apartment sleeping three costs up to 600KN per night along the coast.

In a good, moderate restaurant expect to pay about 35KN to 55KN for a starter and 80KN to 120KN for a meat or fish main course. Bread usually costs extra and a few restaurants tack on a service charge, which is supposed to be indicated on the menu. Fish and shellfish are more expensive and usually charged by the kilogram. An average portion is about 250g, but sometimes you'll be expected to choose a whole fish from a selection – feel free to ask the waiter to weigh the fish so that you can better estimate the final cost. Squid runs at about 300KN per kilogram, but for fish and shrimp you'll pay from 320KN to 380KN per kilogram.

HOW MUCH?

Cross-country bus fare 150-300KN

Coffee in a café 10KN

Pizza 30KN

Museum visit 15-35KN

Island ferry 25-50KN

See also Lonely Planet Index, on the inside front cover.

TRAVELLING RESPONSIBLY

Since our inception in 1973, Lonely Planet has encouraged our readers to tread lightly, travel responsibly and enjoy the magic of independent travel. International travel is growing at a jaw-dropping rate, and we still firmly believe in the benefits it can bring – but, as always, we encourage you to consider the impact your visit will have on both the global environment and the local economies, cultures and ecosystems.

Getting There & Away

Being a continental country, Croatia is easy to reach by land. Zagreb is connected to the rest of Europe by rail, while the coast can be reached by ferry from Italy. Ferry travel, however, is a major pollutant to sea life, which makes it unappealing in eco terms.

Slow Travel

There's no need to fly within Croatia – trains and especially buses cross every corner of the country. The recent building of a motorway from Zagreb to the coast makes travelling by bus or car faster than before. It's a small country, too, so the maximum a trip will ever last is a few hours (unless you decide to head all the way from Zagreb to Dubrovnik in one go). It's a good idea to base yourself in one place and take day trips – on the coast, many opt to island hop by sailing and the really sturdy grab some oars and cram themselves into a kayak. Others walk and explore – a gorgeous option in spring and autumn.

Accommodation & Food

Considering Croatia's ever-growing appeal, some of the coastal places are gravitating towards resort-style accommodation and aiming their developments at large groups. This, however appealing it may seem to big hotel owners, is damaging to the smaller, family-run hotels, guest houses and restaurants that give each destination its uniqueness and appeal, especially for the individual traveller. If you can, opt to stay in smaller-scale hotels or guest houses, or even at some of the eco-friendly campsites, such as Natural Holiday (p243), off Vis Island.

Croatia's small restaurants almost always offer better quality food than popular places with menus that feature hundreds of dishes. The rule of thumb is that the more selective the daily menu, the fresher the ingredients are bound to be. Eating at small, family-run restaurants and sleeping in independent accommodation mean you'll be contributing to the local economy and helping create a more sustainable future.

> "The rule of thumb is that the more selective the daily menu, the fresher the ingredients are bound to be"

READING UP

There are plenty of excellent pickings from Croatia for bookworms, both written about Croatia and by Croatian authors.

We have to start with the classic travel book on Yugoslavia: Rebecca West's *Black Lamb and Grey Falcon*. Written in 1941 as the world was becoming enmeshed in WWII, West recounts her journeys through Croatia, Serbia, Bosnia, Macedonia and Montenegro, weaving her observations into a seamless narrative. Tony White, a British writer, retraced West's journey in *Another Fool in the Balkans* (2006), juxtaposing modern life in Serbia and Croatia with the region's political history.

White also co-edited and contributed to *Croatian Nights* (2005), together with Borivoj Radaković and Matt Thorne, an excellent anthology of 19 short stories by prominent Croatian and British writers such as Gordan Nuhanović, Vladimir Arsenijević, Zoran Ferić, Toby Litt, Edo Popović and the editors themselves.

Two important Croatian writers to look out for are Dubravka Ugrešić and Slavenka Drakulić. Ugrešić (www.dubravkaugresic.com) published *Nobody's Home* in 2007, a book that is part memoir, part travelogue, with stories of travels across Europe and the US, and essays on literature, geopolitics, the East and the West. Drakulić's *Café Europa – Life After Communism* (1999) is an excellent read, wittily detailing the pervasive infiltration of Western

TOP 10

Slovenia • Zagreb
CROATIA

NATURAL WONDERS

Croatia owes more than half of its beauty to its nature – the waterfalls, forests, mountains and, of course, the gorgeous Adriatic coast.

1 Plitvice Lakes National Park (p195)
2 Istria's truffle season (see boxed text, p179)
3 Krka National Park (p212)
4 Kornati Islands (p214)
5 Fresh fish and seafood (p51)

6 Paklenica National Park (p198)
7 Mljet Island (p277)
8 The Elafiti Islands (p276)
9 Cres Island (p136)
10 Susak Island (p134)

FAVOURITE FESTIVALS

Croats love to party and show off their culture. For an overview of national and major regional festivals, see p299.

1 Rijeka Carnival, Rijeka, February (p122) – dress up and party on the Kvarner.
2 Holy Week, Korčula, week before Easter (p285) – witness ancient religious rites.
3 Strossmartre, Zagreb, June (p83) – a quirky street festival.
4 The Garden Festival, Zadar, 4–6 July (p190)
5 Rab Fair, Rab Town, 25–27 July (p151) – religious rituals and folk fun.
6 Motovun Film Festival, late July/early August (p181) – Croatia's finest film festival.

7 Pag Carnival, Pag Town, 31 July (p207) – more dressing up and dancing.
8 Dubrovnik Summer Festival, Dubrovnik, July and August (p268) – culture and live performances galore in Croatia's most glorious city.
9 Full Moon Festival, Zadar, August (p190) – an all-nighter for moon lovers.
10 Varaždin Baroque Evenings, Varaždin, September (p100) – baroque music and culture feast.

TOP BEACHES

Get your kit off or don the latest designer bikini on one of these gorgeous beaches.

1 Brela (p239) – watch the sunset from this long beach with perfectly round pebbles.
2 Pakleni Islands (p254) – pine-shaded beaches for naturists and bikini-wearers alike.
3 Lokrum Island (p276) – a rocky beach that is a haven for nudies; it's always peaceful and the waters are crystalline.
4 Mljet Island's Veliko Jezero (p277) – it's not so much the beach here as it is the swimming location: a lovely salt lake in the middle of an island.
5 Split's Bačvice (p222) – active, fun and full of local life.

6 Baška on Krk Island (p146) – knockout crescent of fine pebbles with a mountain backdrop.
7 Lubenice on Cres Island (p140) – small, secluded, sensational and difficult to reach.
8 Beli on Cres Island (p138) – cosy, crystal-clear cove you won't have to share with crowds.
9 Paradise Beach in Lopar, Rab Island (p152) – sandy stunner with shallow waters and the shade of pine trees.
10 Rt Kamenjak (p160) Thirty virgin kilometresof inlets, coves, pebbles and rocks.

culture in Eastern Europe, and highlighting the reluctance with which the West handles Eastern European culture.

Gold, Frankincense and Myrrh by Slobodan Novak, originally published in Yugoslavia in 1968, has recently been translated into English. The book is set on the island of Rab, where an elderly Madonna is dying, and her carer – the narrator – reminisces about his life, love, the state, religion, duty and memory. It's considered to be one of the pivotal works of 20th-century literature and Novak's writing is compared to that of Chekhov, Borges, Beckett and Kiš.

Croatia: Travels in Undiscovered Country (2003), by Tony Fabijančić, recounts the life of rural folks in a new Croatia.

"Novak's writing is compared to that of Chekhov, Borges, Beckett and Kiš"

INTERNET RESOURCES

Adriatica.net (www.adriatica.net) Cumbersome navigation, but allows you to book rooms, apartments, hotels and lighthouses all along the coast.

Balkanology (www.balkanology.com/croatia) Lots of good information on travel in Croatia and the wider region.

Croatia Homepage (www.hr) Hundreds of links to everything you want to know about Croatia.

National Tourist Board (www.croatia.hr) The best starting point to plan your Croatian holiday.

Itineraries
CLASSIC ROUTES

CONTINENT TO COAST: ESSENTIAL CROATIA
Two Weeks/Zagreb to Dubrovnik

Start at the capital, **Zagreb** (p70), and delve into its simmering nightlife, fine restaurants and choice museums over a long weekend. Head south to the World Heritage–listed **Plitvice Lakes National Park** (p195), a verdant maze of lakes and waterfalls. After spending the day here, head down to **Zadar** (p185), one of Croatia's most underrated cities. It's a real find: historic, modern, active and off the well-trodden track. Take a day trip to the island of **Pag** (p204) and try some of that famous cheese, or go partying on one of its beaches if it's the height of summer. Head over for a swim under the falls at **Krka National Park** (p212) or chill out at the gorgeous **Kornati Islands** (p214). Stroll through lovely **Trogir** (p232) and then meander around the Roman ruins of **Solin** (p231). Next, prepare for one of the region's best sights: Diocletian's Palace in **Split** (p220) is a living part of this exuberant seafront city. Take it easy down the winding coastal road to **Dubrovnik** (p260), a magnificent city whose beauty will blow you away.

From the urban and continental delights of Zagreb, the cascading waterfalls and tranquil lakes of Croatia's national parks, down to the coastal treasures of cities such as Zadar, Trogir, Split and Dubrovnik, this 600km-long itinerary gives you the cream of Croatia's aesthetic crop.

THE CREAM OF THE COAST   Two Weeks/Poreč to Dubrovnik

Start your journey in the town of **Poreč** (p169), admiring the World Heritage–listed Euphrasian Basilica. Head south to the Venetian-inspired architecture of **Rovinj** (p164) and splash in the waters off **Crveni Otok** (p169).

Wander Rovinj's cobblestone streets for a day, then go on to **Pula** (p155), where you can tour the evocative Roman ruins and amphitheatre before heading to the beach for some R&R. After two days in Pula, head north, stopping for a night in the old Austrian resort of **Opatija** (p125) for a healthy stroll along the seaside promenade and gorgeous views of the Kvarner coast. From nearby **Rijeka** (p118) you can take a catamaran to tranquil **Rab** (p149). After wandering the ancient town, relax on the aptly named **Paradise Beach** (p152) at Lopar. Next, head to historic **Zadar** (p185) for its wealth of museums and churches, promenade strolls, café life and bar scene. Head on south to **Split** (p217), an excellent city and great base to explore the beaches of **Brela** (p239), and the nearby islands. On Brač, head over to pretty **Bol** (p247) and hop over to **Hvar** (p250) and the offshore **Pakleni Islands** (p254) for some bikini-clad or nudie sunbathing. If you want a few days of real rest and escape, head over to **Vis Island** (p240). From Split, drive down to **Dubrovnik** (p260), where you can explore the gleaming marble streets, vibrant street life and fine architecture. Don't miss a hop to the gorgeous island of **Mljet** (p277), where the verdancy, salt lakes and tranquillity heal the soul.

Get your sunscreen, sunglasses and sunhat for there'll be sun-soaking galore along this 660km route that covers old-school fishing villages, ancient towns, a dramatic and rugged coastline, spectacular islands and the sparkling waters of the Adriatic.

ROADS LESS TRAVELLED

BEAUTY'S ON THE INSIDE: INLAND CROATIA   Two Weeks/Zagreb to Osijek

Start off in Croatia's dynamic capital, **Zagreb** (p70). Enjoy the museums, art and nightlife, then head to charming little **Samobor** (p93) for some top class cakes and countryside treks. Go forth and explore where not many tourists have gone before in **Zagorje** (p96), a bucolic landscape of forests, pastures and farms. Start with **Klanjec** (p105) and discover the art of Antun Augustinčić in the town museum. You can't not see the birthplace of Croatia's most famous son – Josip Briz Tito – at **Kumrovec** (p104). It's not a communist site but a fascinating examination of traditional village life. If you have a thing for the mysterious aroma of times past, you'll revel in **Trakošćan Castle** (p102), and if you don't have enough there, head forth to the beautifully restored castle-fortress at **Varaždin** (p97). Immerse yourself in the baroque architecture before you dive into the waters at the **Varaždinske Toplice** (p101). On the way south, stop at the pilgrimage site of **Marija Bistrica** (p105) for heady views of the surrounding region. The green rolling hills of Zagorje flatten out as you head east to Slavonia. On the edge of Croatia is the Hungarian-influenced town of **Osijek** (p108) on the Drava River. Enjoy Osijek's unique architecture and take a day trip to the **Kopački Rit Nature Park** (p112), with its profusion of bird life. To finish, take a ride on one of the majestic Lipizzaner horses in **Đakovo** (p112).

Had enough of the sun, sea and crowds? You're in luck: Croatia's unspoiled interior is a real find. From the gentle hills of Zagorje to the wide-open landscape of Slavonia, you'll find castles, spas, villages, an unusual park and a refreshing absence of crowds on this 660km itinerary.

TAILORED TRIPS

FOOD, GLORIOUS FOOD

Gastronomes, prepare for glorious gorging. **Zagreb** (p70) and continental Croatia are influenced by neighbouring Hungary and Austria, and excel at goulash and *paprikaš* (a pepper and beef stew with wine and herbs), as well as pork knuckle served with eye-watering horseradish. Move over to **Samobor** (p93) for some spectacular *kremšnite* (custard cakes) and follow your belly into **Zagorje** (p96) for *štrukle* (dough rolls with cottage cheese) and spit-roast suckling pig or lamb. Zagorje and **Slavonia** (p106) like their game served with buckwheat, and turkey comes with *mlinci* (baked noodles). Sausages, from *kulen* (paprika-flavoured) to blood or garlic ones, are much loved, too.

Moving down towards the coast, the cuisine changes markedly and looks upon its marine creatures with lip-licking glee. **Istria** (p154) carries the foodie region crown, with its delicate truffles, air-dried ham, gorgeous olives and excellent wines. Northern Dalmatia's island of **Pag** (p204) has the country's most famous cheese. **Split** (p217) does a mean *brodet* (fish stew with wine and herbs) and the unmistakeably Mediterranean seafood *na buzaru* (wine, garlic and parsley sauce). The southern island of **Mljet** (p277) prepares the juiciest octopus, kid or lamb by putting it in a clay or metal pot and baking it from all sides. The **Pelješac Peninsula** (p288) is home to some of Croatia's best seafood, with farms of mussels and oysters that are sold by the kilo at little kiosks when in season.

CLIMB, DIVE, SURF 'N' HIKE

Hikers, bikers, windsurfers and divers have no shortage of options in Croatia. The hills around **Samobor** (p93) are favourite weekend hiking spots for Zagreb's urbanites, but real nature lovers head to the less-visited **Risnjak National Park** (p128) for gentle walks and demanding hikes. **Rovinj** (p164) is known for its many dives, especially the wreck of the *Baron Gautsch,* one of the Adriatic's most fascinating shipwrecks. From Lovran, hiking up Vojak in the **Učka Nature Park** (p129) provides unforgettable views of the Kvarner coast. **Mali Lošinj** (p131) is criss-crossed with bike paths, and nearby **Susak** (p134) is known for its reef, accessible to even rookie divers. **Paklenica National Park** (p198) is popular for its rock climbing and provides a good base for

hikes in the Velebit Range. **Dugi Otok** (p201) has a spectacular underwater landscape for experienced cave divers and the **Pakleni Islands** (p254) off Hvar have an underwater reef and canyon to explore. **Makarska Riviera** (p236) has great rock climbing, while the dramatic **Mount Biokovo** (p237) is a treat for hikers. **Bol** (p247) on the island of Brač, is the windsurfing capital of Croatia, while **Viganj** (p289), a small village on Pelješac, is fast catching up as the windsurfers' favourite. **Mljet National Park** (p277) is excellent for biking.

History

Croatia has a long and torrid history. Since time immemorial, people have come and gone, invading, trading and settling. For long periods, the Croats have been ruled by and have fought off others – Venetians, Ottomans, Hungarians, Habsburgs. This troubled history has helped define the Croats and contributed much to the fabric of the country.

EARLY INHABITANTS

Around 30,000 years ago, Croatia was the haunt of Neanderthals, who lumbered through the hills of Slavonia. The Croatian Natural History Museum (p77) in Zagreb displays relics of this distant era, and the outdoor 'prehistoric park' at Krapina (p103) offers a general picture of Neanderthal life.

During the third millennium BC, Vučedol, near Vukovar, became the base for a relatively advanced culture, which eventually spread throughout Central Europe. Around the same time, Hvar saw the rise of an early, distinctively Mediterranean culture.

The Illyrians took centre stage in what is now Croatia, Serbia and Albania by around 1000 BC. Historians debate the origins of the Illyrians and whether they were a culturally homogenous people or a loose conglomeration of tribes. Whatever the case, the Illyrians had to contend with Greeks who established trading colonies on the Adriatic coast at Vis and elsewhere by the 4th century BC, and Celts who pushed down from the north.

In 231 BC an uppity Illyrian, Queen Teuta, committed a fatal tactical error in seeking to conquer various Greek colonies. The put-upon Greeks asked the Romans for military support. Thereafter the Romans pushed their way into the region. By 168 BC, they defeated Gentius, the last Illyrian king, and the Illyrians were gradually Latinised.

> The Adriatic is derived from the name of the ancient Illyrian tribe Ardeioi.

ROME, THEN BYZANTIUM

The Romans swiftly established the province of Illyricum, then broadened their control along the Dalmatian coast. By 11 BC, Rome had conquered the Pannonian tribes, which inhabited the interior, thus extending their empire's reach to the Danube. The realm was later reorganised into the provinces of Dalmatia (the former Illyricum), and Upper and Lower Pannonia, thus covering much of the interior of modern Croatia.

Roman rule centred on the administrative headquarters of Salona (now Solin). Other important Roman towns included Jadera (Zadar), Parentium (Poreč) and Polensium (Pula). The amphitheatre at Pula (p159) remains an evocative reminder of the glory – and lust for blood – of the Roman era.

TIMELINE

300 BC	11 BC	AD 257
Illyrian tribes achieve supremacy in the Balkans founding city states – including Histri (from which the Istrian Peninsula takes its name) and Liburnia – and establishing themselves as maritime powers in the Adriatic.	The Roman province of Illyricum, covering present-day Dalmatia, is extended to the Danube after the defeat of Pannonian tribes. The new province takes in much of modern-day Croatia.	Salona, the Roman capital, with a population of about 10,000, becomes the first diocese in Roman Dalmatia, thus creating a toehold for Catholicism in the region; within 30 years the Bishop of Salona has become pope.

WHO ARE THE CROATS?

A conundrum surrounds the exact origins of the Croats. While they are clearly related to other Slavic nations, the name by which they know themselves – Hrvat – is not a Slavic word. One theory posits that Hrvat is in fact a Persian word, and the Croats are a Slavic tribe who were briefly ruled – and named – by a ruling cast of Persian-speaking Alans from Central Asia.

The Romans constructed a series of roads reaching to the Aegean and Black seas and the Danube, thus facilitating trade and the spread of Roman culture. The roads also accelerated the spread of Christianity, a religion initially persecuted by the Romans.

In the late 3rd century AD, two strong Dalmatian emperors emerged. Diocletian became emperor in AD 285, and in an effort to simplify the unwieldy empire, he divided it into two administrative halves. In so doing he sowed the seeds for the later division into the Eastern and Western Roman Empires. In AD 305, Diocletian retired to his palace in Spalato (Split; see p220), today the greatest Roman remnant in Eastern Europe.

The last Roman leader to rule a united empire was Theodosius the Great, who adeptly staved off threats from the northern Visigoths. On Theodosius' death in AD 395, the empire was formally divided into eastern and western realms along the perforation created earlier by Diocletian. The eastern half became the Byzantine Empire, which persisted until 1453. Visigoth, Hun and Lombard invasions marked the fall of the Western Roman Empire in the 5th century.

ARRIVAL OF THE SLAVS

In the wake of these 'barbarian' tribes, the Croats and other Slavic groups headed south from their original territory north of the Carpathians to fill the vacuum left by the disintegrating Roman Empire. No definitive historical records exist, but it appears that early in the 7th century they moved south across the Danube. Around the same time, the Avars (Eurasian nomads) were sallying around the Balkan fringes of the Byzantine Empire. The Avars were responsible for ravaging the former Roman towns of Salona and Epidaurus, whose inhabitants took refuge in Spalato and Ragusa (Dubrovnik) respectively.

By the middle of the 7th century, the Slavs in the Western Balkans had divided into two distinct groups: the Croats, who settled in Pannonia and Dalmatia forming communities around the Dalmatian towns of Jadera, Aeona (Nin) and Tragurium (Trogir); and the Serbs, who settled the central Balkans. By the 8th century the Dalmatian and Pannonian Croats organised themselves into two powerful tribal entities, each led by a duke (*knez*). The Avars, meanwhile, faded into history.

Clearly explaining centuries of complicated events, Marcus Tanner's *Croatia: A Nation Forged in War* sallies from the Roman era to President Tudman, presenting in a lively, readable style the trials and tribulations of Croatian history.

395	614	845–64
On the death of Theodosius the Great, the Roman Empire is split in two. Present-day Slovenia, Croatia and Bosnia fall into the Western Roman Empire, with modern Serbia, Kosovo and Macedonia in the Byzantine Empire.	Central Asian marauders, the Avars, sack Salona and Epidaurus. Some contend that Slavic tribes, including the Croats, followed in their wake; others say the Croats were invited into the region by Emperor Heraclius to fend off the Avars.	Trpimir establishes the first Croatian royal line. He fights and defeats the powerful Bulgarian state, as well as inflicting major defeats on the Byzantines. Under Trpimir's rule Croatian territory expands well into what is now Bosnia.

CHRISTIANITY & THE CROAT KINGS

Charlemagne's Franks, who had gradually encroached on Central Europe, seized Dalmatia in AD 800, which led to mass baptisms of the previously pagan Croats. After Charlemagne's death in AD 814, the Pannonian Croats revolted unsuccessfully against Frankish rule without the support of the Dalmatian Croats, whose major coastal cities remained under the influence of the Byzantine Empire.

Trpimir, *knez* from 845 to 864, is widely considered to have founded the first Croatian dynasty. Trpimir's successors held their own among the jostling Adriatic powers of the time until Branimir revolted against Byzantine control and in so doing won recognition for the Croats from Pope John VIII. This brought the Croats into the Vatican's sphere of influence and ensured that Catholicism became a defining feature of Croatian national identity.

Tomislav was the first ruler to unite Pannonian and Dalmatian Croatian entities. He rewarded himself in 925 by crowning himself king, whereas all of his predecessors had worn the mantle of *knez*. Tomislav's realm included virtually all of modern Croatia as well as parts of Bosnia and the coast of Montenegro.

However, the vagaries of history saw the Byzantines and Venetians reimpose themselves on the Dalmatian coast during the 11th century, while new adversaries, the Hungarians, emerged in the north and advanced into Pannonia. Krešimir IV (r 1058–74) turned the tables and regained control of Dalmatia, but Croatia was on the rebound only temporarily. Krešimir was succeeded by Zvonimir and Stjepan, neither of whom produced an heir, and the Hungarians, by stealth and outright invasion, terminated the era of the Croat kings at the end of the 11th century.

Dalmatian dogs are thought to be one of the oldest breeds; however, there is no conclusive evidence that they originated in Dalmatia. Some experts on the breed believe the dogs may have been brought to Dalmatia by the Roma.

COVETOUS NEIGHBOURS: HUNGARY & VENICE

The Hungarian King Koloman imposed the *Pacta conventa* in 1102. This ostensibly stated that Hungary and Croatia were separate entities under a single – Hungarian – monarchy, but in practice, while Croatia maintained a *ban* (viceroy or governor) and *sabor* (parliament), the Hungarians steadily marginalised the Croatian nobility.

Under the Hungarians, Pannonia became known as Slavonia, and the interior towns of Zagreb, Vukovar and Varaždin became thriving centres of trade and culture. In 1107, Koloman talked around the Dalmatian nobility, thus bringing the coast, long coveted by land-locked Hungarian kings, into his realm. However, Koloman's very eagerness for sea access meant he was willing to grant Dalmatian cities more autonomy than others in the kingdom. But the Venetians, who had tarried a while, returned soon enough. Upon Koloman's death in 1116, Venice launched new assaults on Biograd and the islands of Lošinj, Pag, Rab and Krk.

869	910–28	1000
At the behest of Byzantium, Macedonian monks Methodius and Cyril create the Cyrillic alphabet, specifically with a view to speeding the spread of Christianity among the Slavic peoples.	Tomislav proclaims himself king while making territorial expansion at the expense of the Hungarians and defeating Bulgarian Tsar Simeon in modern Bosnia. During his reign, Tomislav unites Pannonian and Dalmatian Croats.	Venice capitalises on a lack of stability in Croatia to begin encroaching on the Dalmatian coast. So begins what is to become a recurring theme: the tussle between Venice and other powers for control of Dalmatia.

THE VENETIAN YOKE

For nearly 800 years the doges of Venice sought to control, colonise and exploit the Croatian coast. Coastal and island towns from Rovinj in the north to Korčula in the south still show a marked Venetian influence in architecture, cuisine and culture, but, as in Venice's other dominions, the period was not a happy time.

Venetian rule in Dalmatia and Istria was a record of virtually unbroken economic exploitation. The Venetians systematically denuded the landscape in order to provide timber for their ships. State monopolies set artificially low prices for olive oil, figs, wine, fish and salt, thus ensuring cheap commodities for Venetian buyers, while local merchants and producers were impoverished and threadbare. Shipbuilding was effectively banned, since Venice tolerated no competition with its own ships. No roads or schools were built, and no investment was made in local industry.

In the meantime, Zadar had grown to be the largest and most prosperous Dalmatian city. It succeeded in fending off two Venetian naval expeditions in the 1190s. A vengeful Venetian doge in 1202 paid the soldiers of the Fourth Crusade to attack and sack Zadar; this they did before rumbling on to turn Constantinople on its ear.

But there was more trouble on the horizon. In 1242, the Mongol juggernaut in Central Europe inevitably rolled through Hungary. King Bela IV of Hungary fled the onslaught taking refuge in Trogir, but the Croatian interior was ravaged. As ever, the opportunistic Venetians hovered on the periphery and took advantage of the confusion to consolidate their hold on Zadar. The death of King Bela in 1270 led to another power struggle among the Croatian nobility, which allowed Venice to add Šibenik and Trogir to its possessions.

King Ludovic (Louis) I of Hungary (r 1342–82) re-established control over the country and even persuaded Venice to relinquish Dalmatia. But the Hungarian victory was short-lived. New conflicts emerged upon Ludovic's death and the Croatian nobility rallied around Ladislas of Naples who was crowned king in Zadar in 1403. Short of funds, Ladislas then sold Zadar to Venice in 1409 for a paltry 100,000 ducats and renounced his rights to Dalmatia. In the early 15th century, Venice solidified its grip on the Dalmatian coastline south from Zadar and remained in control until the Napoleonic invasion of 1797. Only the wily citizens of Ragusa (Dubrovnik) managed to retain their independence.

The Balkans, by noted historian Mark Mazower, is a highly readable short introduction to the region. It offers clearly discussed overviews of geography, culture and the broad historical sweep of the Balkans in general.

HOVERING OTTOMANS

As if Croatia hadn't had enough to contend with as Venetians, Hungarians, Mongols and others picked at the remnants of the original Croatian state, another threat loomed from the east during the 14th century. The Ottoman Turks had emerged out of Anatolia in the early 1300s and rapidly swallowed up the Balkans. The Serbs were rolled at Kosovo Polje in 1389, a hastily

---

1058–74	1091–1102	1242
Krešimir IV is recognised by the pope as king of Dalmatia and Croatia. Coming soon after the Great Schism of 1054, which split the church into Orthodox and Catholic realms, this places Croatia squarely within the Catholic sphere.	Hungarian King Ladislas, related by marriage to the late King Zvonimir, claims the Slavonian throne; his successor, Koloman, defeats the last Croatian king, Petar, and cements Hungarian control of Croatia with the *Pacta conventa*.	The Mongols rumble through, devastating Hungary and Croatia and their royal houses. Nobility, including the Šubić and Frankopan families, steps into the breach to assume a degree of political and economic power that persists for centuries.

THE REPUBLIC OF RAGUSA

While most of the Dalmatian coast struggled under Venetian rule for many years, Ragusa (now Dubrovnik) led a charmed life, existing as a republic in its own right. A ruling class, abounding in business acumen and diplomatic skill, ensured that this miniscule city-state punched well above its weight and played a significant role in the immediate region and beyond.

The Ragusans asked the pope for permission to trade with the Turks in 1371 and subsequently established trade centres throughout the Ottoman Empire. Burgeoning trade led to a flowering in the arts and sciences. The Ragusans, once described as 'mild and noble', were extremely liberal for the time, abolishing the slave trade in the 15th century, and advanced in the realms of science, establishing a system of quarantine in 1377.

However, they had to maintain a perilous position sandwiched between Ottoman and Venetian interests. An earthquake in 1667 caused a great deal of damage, and Napoleon finally swallowed up the republic in 1808.

Šibenik-born Faust Vrančić (1551–1617) made the first working parachute.

The neck tie is a descendant of the cravat, which originated in Croatia as part of military attire and was adopted by the French in the 17th century. The name 'cravat' is a corruption of Croat and Hrvat.

choreographed anti-Turkish crusade was garrotted in Hungary in 1396, Bosnia was despatched in 1463 and when the Croatian nobility finally faced up to the Ottomans in 1493 in Krbavsko Polje, they too were pummelled.

Despite a sudden show of unity among the remaining noble families, one city after another fell to the Ottoman sultans. The important bishopric at Zagreb heavily fortified the cathedral in Kaptol, which remained untouched, but the gateway town of Knin fell in 1521. Five years later, the Ottomans engaged the Hungarians in Mohács. Again the Turks were victorious, the might of the Hungarian army was annulled and by knock-on effect the era of Hungarian domination of Croatia was ended. The Croats then turned to the Austrians for protection and were duly absorbed into the Habsburg Empire, ruled from Vienna. Nevertheless, by the end of the century only a narrow strip of territory around Zagreb, Karlovac and Varaždin was under Habsburg control. The Adriatic coast was threatened by the Turks but never captured, and Ragusa maintained its independence throughout the turmoil.

Turkish assaults on the Balkans caused massive disruptions. Cities and towns were destroyed, people were enslaved and commandeered to the Ottoman war machine, and movements of refugees created havoc in the region. The Habsburgs sought to build a buffer against the Ottomans, creating the Vojna Krajina (Military Frontier), a string of forts south of Zagreb, and a region in which a standing army, largely of Vlachs and Serbs, faced down the Ottomans.

Exactly a century after their defeat by the Ottomans, the Croats managed to turn the tables on the Turks. At Sisak in 1593 the Habsburg army, including Croat soldiers, finally inflicted a defeat on the Ottomans. In 1699 in Sremski Karlovci the Ottomans sued for peace for the first time and the Turkish stranglehold on Central Europe was loosened. The Habsburgs

1300s	1358	1409
The Hungarian Anjou dynasty under Carl (Charles) and Louis (Ludovic) reasserts royal authority in Croatia and endeavours to expel the Venetians who had recently taken Dalmatian territory. Venice is ejected, albeit temporarily.	Ragusa (modern Dubrovnik) prises itself from the clutches of Venice and establishes itself as a city republic. It grows to become an advanced and liberal society, while cannily fending off Venetians and Ottomans.	Ladislas of Naples assumes the throne of Croatia but dynastic squabbling puts him to flight. He sells Dalmatia to Venice for 100,000 ducats. Within a decade Venetian control extends along the coast from Zadar to Ragusa.

reclaimed Slavonia soon after, thus expanding the Krajina. And while the Turkish threat may have been eliminated, the Hungarians reasserted their authority over the Croats within the pecking order of the Habsburg Empire. This period's rule saw a return to stability and advances in agricultural production, but Croatian culture and language were neglected. Meanwhile, the Venetians, no longer troubled by Ottoman navies, pestered the Dalmatian coast again.

NAPOLEON & THE ILLYRIAN PROVINCES

Habsburg support for the restoration of the French monarchy provoked Napoleon to invade Italian states in 1796. After conquering Venice in 1797 he agreed to transfer Dalmatia to Austria in the Treaty of Campo Formio in exchange for other concessions. Croatian hopes that Dalmatia would be united with Slavonia were soon dashed as the Habsburgs made it clear that the two territories would retain separate administrations.

Austrian control of Dalmatia only lasted until Napoleon's 1805 victory over Austrian and Prussian forces at Austerlitz, which forced Austria to cede the Dalmatian coast to France. Ragusa quickly surrendered to French forces, which also swallowed up Kotor in Montenegro. Napoleon renamed his conquest the 'Illyrian provinces' and moved with characteristic swiftness to reform the neglected territory. A tree-planting program was implemented to reforest the barren hills. Since almost the entire population was illiterate, the new government set up primary schools, high schools and a college at Zadar. Roads and hospitals were built and new crops introduced. Yet the French regime remained unpopular, partly because the anticlerical French were staunchly opposed by the clergy and also because the population was heavily taxed to pay for the reforms.

The fall of the Napoleonic empire after Napoleon's Russian campaign led to the 1815 Congress of Vienna, which recognised Austria's claims to Dalmatia and placed the rest of Croatia under the jurisdiction of Austria's Hungarian province. For the Dalmatians the new regime meant a return to the status quo, since the Austrians restored the former Italian elite to power. For the northern Croats the agreement meant they remained hobbled, as the Hungarians imposed the Hungarian language and culture on the population.

Napoleon, flush with Enlightenment fervour, had aimed to create a south Slavic consciousness. This sense of a shared identity eventually manifested itself in an 'Illyrian' movement in the 1830s that centred on the revival of the Croatian language. Napoleon's grand plan was to foster Serbian culture, too, but since Serbia remained under Ottoman occupation, Croatia first took the baton. Traditionally, upper-class Dalmatians spoke Italian, and northern Croats spoke German or Hungarian. The establishment of the first Illyrian newspaper in 1834, written in Zagreb dialect, prompted the Croatian *sabor* to call for the teaching of Slavic languages in schools.

Misha Glenny's *The Balkans: Nationalism, War & the Great Powers, 1804–1999* explores the history of outside interference in the Balkans. His *The Fall of Yugoslavia* deciphers the complex politics, history and cultural flare-ups that led to the wars of the 1990s.

The ballpoint pen and fountain pen were invented in 1906 by the Croatian Slavoljub Penkala (1871–1922), who also introduced the hot-water bottle and a laundry blueing agent.

1493	1526–27	1537–40
At Krbavsko Polje a joint Croatian-Hungarian army engages the Turks but is obliterated, leaving Croatia open to Turkish raids. The Turkish advance in the region brings turmoil, as populations flee and famine ensues.	At the Battle of Mohács, the all-powerful Ottoman Turks annihilate the Hungarian nobility, thus ending Hungarian control of Croatia. Hungarian King Louis dies without an heir, allowing the Austrian Habsburgs to assume control of Hungary.	The Turks, under Sultan Suleyman, take Klis, the last Croatian bastion in Dalmatia. The Turkish advance continues to Sisak, just south of Zagreb. For reasons unknown, the Turks never push on to Zagreb.

In the wake of the 1848 revolution in Paris, the Hungarians began agitating for reform within the Habsburg Empire. The Croats, in turn, saw this as a way of reclaiming their autonomy and unifying Dalmatia, the Krajina and Slavonia. The Habsburgs paid lip service to Croatian sentiments and appointed Josip Jelačić *ban* of Croatia. Jelačić promptly called elections, claimed a mandate and declared war on Hungarian agitators in order to curry favour with the Habsburgs. Jelačić is immortalised in a martial pose in the heart of Zagreb (p79), but the Habsburgs quietly ignored his demands for autonomy.

Nikola Tesla (1856–1943), the father of the radio and alternating electric current technology, was born in Croatia. The Tesla unit for magnetic induction was named after him.

DREAMS OF YUGOSLAVIA

Disillusionment spread after 1848, and was amplified after the birth of the Austro-Hungarian Dual Monarchy in 1867. The monarchy placed Croatia and Slavonia within the Hungarian administration, while Dalmatia remained within Austria. Whatever limited form of self-government the Croats enjoyed under the Habsburgs disappeared.

The river of discontent forked into two streams that dominated the political landscape for the next century. The old 'Illyrian' movement became the National Party, dominated by the brilliant Bishop Josif Juraf Strossmayer. Strossmayer believed that the differences between Serbs and Croats were magnified by the manipulations of the Habsburgs and the Hungarians, and that only through Jugoslavenstvo (south Slavic unity) could the aspirations of both peoples be realised. Strossmayer supported the Serbian independence struggle in Serbia but favoured a Yugoslav (ie south Slavic) entity within the Austro-Hungarian Empire rather than complete independence.

By contrast, the Party of Rights, led by the militantly anti-Serb Ante Starčević, envisioned an independent Croatia made up of Slavonia, Dalmatia, the Krajina, Slovenia, Istria, and part of Bosnia and Hercegovina. At the time, the Eastern Orthodox Church was encouraging the Serbs to form a national identity based upon their religion. Until the 19th century, Orthodox inhabitants of Croatia identified themselves as Vlachs, Morlachs, Serbs, Orthodox or even Greeks, but with the help of Starčević's attacks, the sense of a separate Serbian Orthodox identity within Croatia developed.

Under the theory of 'divide and rule', the Hungarian-appointed *ban* of Croatia blatantly favoured the Serbs and the Orthodox Church, but his strategy backfired. The first organised resistance formed in Dalmatia. Croat representatives in Rijeka and Serb representatives in Zadar joined together in 1905 to demand the unification of Dalmatia and Slavonia with a formal guarantee of Serbian equality as a nation. The spirit of unity mushroomed, and by 1906 Croat-Serb coalitions had taken over local government in Dalmatia and Slavonia, forming a serious threat to the Hungarian power structure. During the Balkan wars of 1912–13, newly independent Serbia won considerable prestige in advancing into Ottoman territory in Europe.

1593	1671	1699
At Sisak, previously the Ottoman high-tide mark, the Habsburgs inflict the first major defeat on the Ottomans, thus proving the Turks were not invincible and prefiguring the long, slow Turkish retreat from Central Europe.	A deputation led by Franjo Frankopan and Petar Zrinski, with the aim of ridding Croatia of Hungarian domination, is cut short. Frankopan and Zrinksi are hanged and their lands confiscated by the Habsburgs.	At the Treaty of Karlovci, the Ottomans renounce all claims to Croatia. However, rather than allowing Croatia to assume control of its territory, Venice and Hungary reclaim all freed lands over the next 20 years.

THE KINGDOM OF SERBS, CROATS & SLOVENES

With the outbreak of WWI, Croatia's future was again up for grabs. Sensing that they would once again be pawns to the Great Powers, a Croatian delegation, the 'Yugoslav Committee', convinced the Serbian government to agree to the establishment of a parliamentary monarchy that would rule over the two countries. The Yugoslav Committee became the National Council of Slovenes, Croats and Serbs after the collapse of the Austro-Hungarian Empire in 1918 and it quickly negotiated the establishment of the Kingdom of Serbs, Croats and Slovenes to be based in Belgrade. Although many Croats were unsure about Serbian intentions, they were very sure about Italian intentions, since Italy lost no time in seizing Pula, Rijeka and Zadar in November 1918. Effectively given a choice between throwing in their lot with Italy or Serbia, the Croats chose Serbia.

Problems with the kingdom began almost immediately. As under the Habsburgs, the Croats enjoyed scant autonomy. Currency reforms benefited Serbs at the expense of the Croats. A treaty between Yugoslavia and Italy gave Istria, Zadar and a number of islands to Italy. The new constitution abolished Croatia's *sabor* and centralised power in Belgrade, while new electoral districts severely under-represented the Croats.

Opposition to the new regime was led by the Croat Stjepan Radić, who favoured the idea of Yugoslavia but wished to transform it into a federal democracy. His alliance with the Serb Svetozar Pribićević proved profoundly threatening to the regime and Radić was assassinated in 1928. Exploiting fears of civil war, on 6 January 1929 King Aleksandar in Belgrade proclaimed a royal dictatorship, abolished political parties and suspended parliamentary government, thus ending any hope of democratic change. Meanwhile, during the 1920s the Yugoslav communist party arose; Josip Broz Tito was to become leader in 1937.

Ivan Vučetić (1858–1925), the man who developed dactyloscopy (fingerprint identification), was born on the island of Hvar.

THE RISE OF USTAŠE & WWII

One day after the proclamation, a Bosnian Croat, Ante Pavelić, claiming inspiration from Mussolini, set up the Ustaše Croatian Liberation Movement in Zagreb with the stated aim of establishing an independent state, by force if necessary. Fearing arrest, he fled to Sofia in Bulgaria and made contact with anti-Serbian Macedonian revolutionaries before fleeing to Italy. There, he established training camps for his organisation under Mussolini's benevolent eye. After organising various disturbances, in 1934 he and the Macedonians succeeded in assassinating King Aleksandar in Marseilles while he was on a state visit. Italy responded by closing down the training camps and imprisoning Pavelić and many of his followers.

When Germany invaded Yugoslavia on 6 April 1941, the exiled Ustaše were quickly installed by the Germans with the support of the Italians who hoped to see their own territorial aims in Dalmatia realised. Within days the

1780s	1797–1815	1830–50
The Habsburgs begin a process of Germanisation, ordering all administration be conducted in German. This creates 'blowback' in the form of rising nationalist feelings among the Habsburg's non-German subjects.	Napoleon brings the Venetian Republic to an end; Venetian dominions are initially given to the Habsburgs, but in 1806 Napoleon gains the Adriatic coast, which he dubs the 'Illyrian provinces'. He begins a program of reform.	The south Slavic consciousness is awakened, aiming to reverse the processes of Hungarianisation and Germanisation under the Habsburgs. An offshoot is the Croatian National Revival.

Independent State of Croatia (NDH; Nezavisna Država Hrvatska), headed by Pavelić, issued a range of decrees designed to persecute and eliminate the regime's 'enemies', a thinly veiled reference to the Jews, Roma and Serbs. The majority of the Jewish population was rounded up and packed off to extermination camps between 1941 and 1945.

Serbs fared little better. The Ustaše program explicitly called for 'one-third of Serbs killed, one-third expelled and one-third converted to Catholicism', an agenda that was carried out with appalling brutality. Villages conducted their own personal pogroms against Serbs and extermination camps were set up, most notoriously at Jasenovac (south of Zagreb), where Jews, Roma and antifascist Croats were killed. The exact number of Serb victims is uncertain and controversial, with Croat historians tending to minimise the figures and Serbian historians tending to maximise them. In all, around one in six Serbs was killed.

> For a quirky, or perhaps reverent (who can tell?) look at Tito, visit his home page: www .titoville.com. Enjoy pictures of him in statesmanlike poses, scripts from his speeches, lists of his 'wives' and jokes about him.

TITO & THE PARTISANS

Not all Croats supported these policies, and some spoke out against them. The Ustaše regime drew most of its support from the Lika region southwest of Zagreb and western Hercegovina, but Pavelić's agreement to cede a good part of Dalmatia to Italy was highly unpopular and the Ustaše had almost no support in that region.

Armed resistance to the regime took the form of Serbian 'Četnik' formations led by General Draža Mihailović. The Četniks began as an antifascist rebellion but soon retaliated against the Ustaše with in-kind massacres of Croats in eastern Croatia and Bosnia.

The most effective antifascist struggle was conducted by National Liberation Partisan units and their leader, Josip Broz, known as Tito (see opposite). With their roots in the outlawed Yugoslavian Communist Party, the Partisans attracted long-suffering Yugoslav intellectuals, Croats disgusted with Četnik massacres, Serbs disgusted with Ustaše massacres, and antifascists of all kinds. The Partisans gained wide popular support with their early manifesto, which, although vague, appeared to envision a postwar Yugoslavia that would be based on a loose federation.

Although the Allies initially backed the Serbian Četniks, it became apparent that the Partisans were waging a far more focused and determined fight against the Nazis. With the diplomatic and military support of Churchill and other Allied powers, the Partisans controlled much of Croatia by 1943. They established functioning local governments in the territory they seized, which later eased their transition to power. On 20 October 1944, the Partisans entered Belgrade alongside the Red Army. When Germany surrendered in 1945, Pavelić and the Ustaše fled and the Partisans entered Zagreb.

The remnants of the NDH army, desperate to avoid falling into the hands of the Partisans, attempted to cross into Austria. A small British contingent

1867	**1905**	**1908**
The Habsburg throne devolves to become the Dual Monarchy of Austria-Hungary. Croatian territory is divided between them: Dalmatia is awarded to Austria, and Slavonia is under Hungarian control.	Burgeoning Croatian national consciousness is clearly visible in the Rijeka Resolution, which, aside from making demands for increased democracy, calls for the reunification of Dalmatia and Slavonia. A Serb-Croatian coalition forms soon after.	Austria-Hungary assumes control of Bosnia and Hercegovina, thus bringing the Slavic Muslims of the Balkans within its sphere of responsibility, and unwittingly creating the nucleus of the future Yugoslav federation.

TITO

Josip Broz was born in Kumrovec in 1892 to a Croat father and Slovene mother. When WWI broke out, Tito was drafted into the Austro-Hungarian army and was taken prisoner by the Russians. He escaped just before the 1917 revolution, became a communist and joined the Red Army. He returned to Croatia in 1920 and became a union organiser while working as a metalworker.

As secretary of the Zagreb committee of the outlawed Communist Party, he worked to unify the party and increase its membership. When the Nazis invaded in 1941, he adopted the name Tito and organised small bands of guerrillas, which formed the core of the Partisan movement. His successful campaigns attracted military support from the British and Americans, but the Soviet Union, despite sharing his communist ideology, repeatedly rebuffed his requests for aid.

In 1945 he became prime minister of a reconstituted Yugoslavia. Although retaining a communist ideology, and remaining nominally loyal to Russia, Tito had an independent streak. In 1948 he fell out with Stalin and adopted a conciliatory policy towards the West.

Yugoslavia's rival nationalities were Tito's biggest headache, which he dealt with by suppressing all dissent and trying to ensure a rough equality of representation at the upper echelons of government. As a committed communist, he viewed ethnic disputes as unwelcome deviations from the pursuit of the common good.

Yet Tito was well aware of the ethnic tensions that simmered just below the surface of Yugoslavia. Preparations for his succession began in the early 1970s as he aimed to create a balance of power among the ethnic groups of Yugoslavia. He set up a collective presidency that was to rotate annually but the system proved unworkable. Later events revealed how dependent Yugoslavia was on its wily, charismatic leader.

When Tito died in May 1980, his body was carried from Ljubljana (Slovenia) to Belgrade (Serbia). Thousands of mourners flocked the streets to pay respects to the man who had united a difficult country for 35 years. It was the last communal outpouring of emotion that Yugoslavia's fractious nationalities were able to share.

met the 50,000 troops and promised to intern them outside Yugoslavia. It was a trick. The troops were forced into trains that headed back into Yugoslavia where the Partisans awaited them. The ensuing massacre claimed the lives of at least 30,000 men (although the exact number is in doubt) and left a permanent stain on the Yugoslav government.

YUGOSLAVIA

Tito's attempt to retain control of the Italian city of Trieste and parts of southern Austria faltered in the face of Allied opposition, but Dalmatia and most of Istria were made a permanent part of postwar Yugoslavia. In creating the Federal People's Republic of Yugoslavia, Tito was determined to forge a state in which no ethnic group dominated the political landscape. Croatia became one of six republics – along with Macedonia, Serbia, Montenegro, Bosnia and Hercegovina, and Slovenia – in a tightly configured federation.

1918	1920	1941
The Kingdom of Serbs, Croats and Slovenes is created after the Serbs and others break away from Austria-Hungary. Serbian Prince Aleksander Karađorđević assumes the throne. Montenegrin and Macedonian territory is included in his domains.	Stjepan Radić establishes the Croatian Republican Peasant Party. It becomes the primary voice for Croatian interests in the face of Serb domination. In the same year, the communist party, later led by Tito, is established.	Ante Pavelić proclaims the Independent State of Croatia (NDH), a Nazi puppet state. Pavelić's Ustaše begins a brutal persecution of Serbs, Roma and Jews; the Serbs respond by forming the Četniks, who harass Croatian populations.

However, Tito effected this delicate balance by creating a one-party state and rigorously stamping out all opposition.

During the 1960s, the concentration of power in Belgrade was an increasingly testy issue as it became apparent that money from the more prosperous republics of Slovenia and Croatia was being distributed to the poorer autonomous province of Kosovo and the republic of Bosnia and Hercegovina. The problem seemed particularly blatant in Croatia, which saw money from its prosperous tourist business on the Adriatic coast flow into Belgrade. At the same time, Serbs in Croatia were over-represented in the government, armed forces and police.

Croatia Through History by Branka Magaš is a highly detailed doorstopper of a history, focusing on pivotal events and clearly delineating the gradual development of Croatian national identity.

In Croatia the unrest reached a crescendo in the 'Croatian Spring' of 1971. Led by reformers within the Communist Party of Croatia, intellectuals and students called for greater economic autonomy and constitutional reform to loosen Croatia's ties to Yugoslavia, but nationalistic elements manifested themselves as well. Tito fought back, clamping down on the liberalisation that had gradually been gaining momentum in Yugoslavia. Serbs viewed the movement as the Ustaše reborn; in turn, jailed reformers blamed the Serbs for their troubles. The stage was set for the rise of nationalism and the war of the 1990s, even though Tito's 1974 constitution afforded the republics more autonomy.

THE COLLAPSE OF YUGOSLAVIA

Tito left a shaky Yugoslavia upon his death in May 1980. The economy was in a parlous state and a presidency rotating among the six republics could not compensate for the loss of his steadying hand at the helm. The authority of the central government sank along with the economy, and long-suppressed mistrust among Yugoslavia's ethnic groups resurfaced.

In 1989 repression of the Albanian majority in Serbia's Kosovo province sparked renewed fears of Serbian hegemony and precipitated the end of the Yugoslav Federation. With political changes sweeping Eastern Europe, Slovenia embarked on a course for independence and many Croats felt the time had come for them to also achieve autonomy. In the Croatian elections of April 1990, Franjo Tuđman's Croatian Democratic Union (HDZ; Hrvatska Demokratska Zajednica) secured 40% of the vote, to the 30% won by the Communist Party, which retained the loyalty of the Serbian community as well as voters in Istria and Rijeka. On 22 December 1990, a new Croatian constitution was promulgated, changing the status of Serbs in Croatia from that of a 'constituent nation' to a national minority.

The constitution's failure to guarantee minority rights, and the mass dismissals of Serbs from the public service, stimulated the 600,000-strong ethnic Serb community within Croatia to demand autonomy. In early 1991, Serb extremists within Croatia staged provocations designed to force federal military intervention. A May 1991 referendum (boycotted by the Serbs)

1943	1945–48	1960s
Tito's communist Partisans achieve military victories and build a popular antifascist front. They reclaim territory from retreating Italian brigades. The British and US lend military support.	The Federal People's Republic of Yugoslavia is founded. In time, Tito breaks with Stalin and steers a careful course between Eastern and Western blocs, building the economic middle way of syndicalism and founding the nonaligned movement.	Croatian unrest about the centralisation of power in Belgrade builds. The use of Croatian money to support poorer provinces is resented, along with the over-representation of Serbs in the Croatian government, armed forces and police.

produced a 93% vote in favour of Croatian independence, but when Croatia declared independence on 25 June 1991, the Serbian enclave of Krajina proclaimed its independence from Croatia.

THE WAR FOR CROATIA

Under pressure from the EU, Croatia declared a three-month moratorium on its independence, but heavy fighting broke out in Krajina, Baranja and Slavonia, initiating what Croats refer to as the Homeland War. The Yugoslav People's Army, dominated by Serbs, began to intervene on its own authority in support of Serbian irregulars under the pretext of halting ethnic violence. When the Croatian government ordered a blockade of federal military installations in the republic, the Yugoslav navy blockaded the Adriatic coast and laid siege to the strategic town of Vukovar on the Danube. During the summer of 1991, a quarter of Croatia fell to Serb militias and the Serb-led Yugoslav People's Army.

In late 1991, the federal army and Montenegrin militia moved against Dubrovnik (see boxed text, p263, for more), and the presidential palace in Zagreb was hit by rockets fired by Yugoslav jets in an apparent assassination attempt on President Tuđman. When the three-month moratorium on independence ended, Croatia declared full independence. Soon after, Vukovar finally fell when the Yugoslav army moved in, in one of the more bloodthirsty acts in all of the wars in the former Yugoslavia (see boxed text, p115). During six months of fighting in Croatia, 10,000 people died, hundreds of thousands fled and tens of thousands of homes were destroyed.

Beginning on 3 January 1992, a UN-brokered ceasefire generally held. The federal army was allowed to withdraw from its bases inside Croatia and tensions diminished. At the same time, the EU, succumbing to pressure from Germany, recognised Croatia. This was followed by US recognition and in May Croatia was admitted to the UN.

The UN peace plan in Krajina was intended to bring about the disarming of local Serb paramilitary formations, the repatriation of refugees and the return of the region to Croatia. Instead, it only froze the existing situation and offered no permanent solution. In January 1993, the Croatian army suddenly launched an offensive in southern Krajina, pushing the Serbs back in some areas and recapturing strategic points. The Krajina Serbs vowed never to accept rule from Zagreb and in June 1993 they voted overwhelmingly to join the Bosnian Serbs (and eventually Greater Serbia); continued 'ethnic cleansing' left only about 900 Croats in Krajina out of an original population of 44,000. A comprehensive ceasefire in early 2004 substantially reduced the violence in the region and established demilitarised 'zones of separation' between the parties.

In the meantime, neighbouring Bosnia had been subjected to similar treatment at the hands of the Yugoslav army and Serbian paramilitaries.

Blanka Raguz' *Labyrinth* is a coming-of-age story set during the tragic fall of Vukovar, painting a stark yet humane representation of tragic events little-known to the outside world.

1971	1980	1989
In the 'Croatian Spring' Communist Party reformers, intellectuals, students and nationalists call for greater economic and constitutional autonomy for Croatia.	President Tito dies. There is a genuine outpouring of grief, and tributes are paid from around the world; however, Yugoslavia is beset by inflation, unemployment and foreign debt, setting the scene for the difficulties to come.	The communist system begins to collapse in Eastern Europe; Franjo Tuđman establishes the Croatian Democratic Union (HDZ), the first noncommunist party in Yugoslavia. Early in 1990 Tuđman is sworn in as president.

Richard Holbrooke's *To End A War* recounts the events surrounding the Dayton Accords. As the American diplomat who prodded the warring parties to the negotiating table to hammer out a peace accord, Holbrooke was in a unique position to evaluate the personalities and politics of the region.

Initially, in the face of Serbian advances, Bosnia's Croats and Muslims had banded together but in 1993 the two sides fell out and began fighting each other. The Bosnian Croats, with tacit support from Zagreb, were responsible for several horrific events in Bosnia, including the destruction of the old bridge in Mostar. This conflagration was extinguished when the US fostered the development of the Muslim-Croatian federation in 1994 while the world looked on in horror at the Serb siege of Sarajevo.

While these grim events unfolded in Bosnia and Hercegovina, the Croatian government quietly began procuring arms from abroad. On 1 May 1995, the Croatian army and police entered occupied western Slavonia, east of Zagreb, and seized control of the region within days. The Krajina Serbs responded by shelling Zagreb in an attack that left seven people dead and 130 wounded. As the Croatian military consolidated its hold in western Slavonia, some 15,000 Serbs fled the region despite assurances from the Croatian government that they were safe from retribution.

Belgrade's silence throughout this campaign showed that the Krajina Serbs had lost the support of their Serbian sponsors, encouraging Croats to forge ahead. On 4 August the military launched a massive assault on the rebel Serb capital of Knin. The Serb army fled towards northern Bosnia, along with 150,000 civilians whose roots in the Krajina stretched back centuries. The military operation ended in days, but was followed by months of terror. Widespread looting and burning of Serb villages seemed designed to ensure the permanence of this huge population shift.

The Dayton Accords signed in Paris in December 1995 recognised Croatia's traditional borders and provided for the return of eastern Slavonia. The transition proceeded relatively smoothly, but the two populations still regard each other with suspicion and hostility.

POSTWAR MOVES TOWARDS EUROPE

Hostilities over, a degree of stability returned to Croatia. A key provision of the agreement was the promise by the Croatian government to facilitate the return of Serbian refugees, a promise that is far from being fulfilled. Although the central government in Zagreb made the return of refugees a priority in accordance with the demands of the international community, its efforts have often been subverted by local authorities intent on maintaining the ethnic purity of their regions. In many cases, Croat refugees from Bosnia and Hercegovina have occupied houses abandoned by their Serb owners. Serbs intending to reclaim their property face a forbidding array of legal impediments in establishing a claim to their former dwellings, plus substantial obstacles in finding employment in what are now economically precarious regions. Twelve years after the cessation of hostilities, only about half have returned.

On the political scene, Franjo Tuđman, the strong man of the war era, rapidly declined in popularity once the country was no longer under threat.

1991	1992	1995
The Croatian *sabor* (parliament) proclaims the independence of Croatia; Krajina Serbs declare independence from Croatia, with support of Slobodan Milošević who is pursuing a dream of Greater Serbia. War breaks out between Croats and Serbs.	A first UN-brokered ceasefire takes effect temporarily. The EU recognises Croatian independence and Croatia is admitted into the UN in the (unrealised) hope that official recognition will halt fighting. War breaks out in neighbouring Bosnia.	The 'Bljesak' (Lightning) military campaign sees Croatian forces reclaiming lost Croatian territory and expelling Serbs from Krajina. This reversal of military fortunes leads to the Dayton Accords, bringing peace and establishing Croatia's borders.

His combination of authoritarianism and media control, resurrection of old NDH symbolism, and tendency to be influenced by the far right no longer appealed to the weary Croatian populace. By 1999 opposition parties united to work against Tuđman and the HDZ. Tuđman was hospitalised and died suddenly in late 1999, and planned elections were postponed until January 2000. Still, voters turned out in favour of a centre-left coalition, ousting the HDZ and voting the centrist Stipe Mesić into the presidency.

The 2000 election results illustrated that Croatia had made a distinct turn towards the West and integration in modern Europe. The country gradually began welcoming foreign tourists again, and the economy opened up to foreign competition. This westward lilt lost some momentum when the International War Crimes Tribunal indicted two Croatian generals for crimes against the Serbian populations of Krajina. The handing over of General Norac to the Hague in 2001 proved a divisive issue among Croats, and perhaps explains the return of the HDZ to power in the elections of late 2003. However, by this time the HDZ had pragmatically abandoned the hardline stance of the Tuđman era and was, like the centrist parties, focused on economic reform and attaining membership of the EU and NATO. Above all, the peaceful transition of power was interpreted by Europe as evidence of the maturity of Croatian democracy. The handover of General Ante Gotovina to the Hague in 2005 was the main condition for the beginning of Croatia's negotiations to join the EU, though these discussions have been slowed down by various hurdles, such as the reforms of the country's judiciary system and the fight against corruption. The proposed joining date is anywhere between 2009 and 2012.

Dubrovnik: A History by Robin Harris is a thoughtful and thorough look at the great city, investigating events, individuals and movements that have contributed to the architectural and cultural fabric of the 'pearl of the Adriatic'.

1999	2003	2005
Croatia's first president, Franjo Tuđman, dies; elections the following January are convincingly won by a coalition of anti-Tuđman parties. The centrist coalition is led by Ivica Račan (prime minister) and Stipe Mesić (president).	The HDZ returns to power, having abandoned the nationalistic baggage it had borne under Tuđman. This time it has an agenda of economic reform and a goal of UN and NATO membership.	War crimes suspect Ante Gotovina is captured and handed to the International War Crimes Tribunal. The arrest of Gotovina, considered by some Croats as a war hero, is controversial in Croatia but is regarded positively by the EU.

The Culture

THE NATIONAL PSYCHE

Like in all countries in the world, a collective 'national psyche' is subject to a variety of nuances, regional differences and historical heritage. With its capital on the continent and the majority of its big cities on the coast, Croatia is torn between a more serious and *mitteleuropean* mindset in Zagreb and northern Croatia (with meaty food, Austrian architecture and a strong interest in personal advancement over pleasure) and the coastal, more relaxed, Mediterranean character. The Istrians, bilingual in Italian and Croatian, have a strong Italian influence, while the Dalmatians are generally a relaxed and easygoing bunch: many offices empty out at 3pm, allowing people to enjoy the long hours of sunlight on a beach or at an outdoor café. Most people involved in the tourist industry speak German, English and Italian, though English is the most widely spoken language among the young.

The vast majority of Croats have a strong cultural identification with Western Europe and like to think of themselves as especially more Western than their 'Eastern' Bosnian or Serbian neighbours. The idea that Croatia is the last stop before the Ottoman East is prevalent in all segments of the population, though this idea is questionable when considering the recently overwhelming popularity of Serbian turbo folk in Croatia (see p48), a type of music frowned upon and avoided during the 1990s war. It seems that with the national tensions of the 1990s easing up, the connecting Balkan elements are again being embraced in some parts of Croatia's society.

For a thorough rundown of cultural events in Croatia, check www.culturenet.hr.

Attitudes towards Croatia joining the EU are divided. Most people are enthusiastic, though the enthusiasm is starting to droop with, according to some locals, 'an endless list of rules' presented to the country, and the date for joining – anywhere between 2009 and 2012 – edging out of reach. Predictably, it's the younger generations who are more geared towards joining the EU, while the older generations lament the loss of industrial and agricultural independence that will inevitably happen when the country joins up.

The word 'normal' pops up frequently in Croatian conversations about themselves. 'We want to be a normal country', they might say. Croats will frequently make a distinction between rabid, flag-waving nationalists and 'normal people' who only wish to live in peace. International isolation is exceedingly painful for most Croats, which is why Croatia reluctantly bowed to international pressure to turn over its war criminals.

Attitudes towards the 1990s 'Homeland War' or 'Patriotic War' vary by region. The destruction of Vukovar, the shelling of Dubrovnik and Osijek, and the ethnic cleansing of and by the Krajina Serbs has traumatised the surrounding regions. Comments questioning the assumption that Croats were wholly right and Serbs were wholly wrong are not likely to be appreciated. In other parts of the country, Croats are more open to a forthright discussion of the last decade's events.

Croats are united by a common religion, Catholicism, though there are small Muslim, Serb Orthodox and Jewish minorities.

DAILY LIFE

Croats like the good life and take a lot of pride in keeping up appearances. Streets are tidy and clothes are stylish. Even with a tight economy, people will cut out restaurants and films in order to afford a shopping trip to Italy or Austria for some new clothes. Lounging in cafés and bars for much of the day is an important part of life here and you often wonder how the country's wheels are turning with so many people at leisure rather than work. But perhaps it's all that coffee that makes them work twice as fast once they're back in the office?

Most people own their homes, bought in the post-communist years when previously state-owned homes were sold to the tenants for little money. It's traditional and perfectly normal for children to live with their parents well into their adult life. The tradition extends particularly to sons, who often bring their wives to the family home where they'll continue to live – this is, however, mostly the case in rural and small-town areas. Family is very important to the Croats and extended family links are strong.

Although attitudes are slowly changing towards homosexuality, Croatia is an overwhelmingly Catholic country with highly conservative views of sexuality. In a recent survey only 58% of those surveyed said they regarded gays as 'normal people with a different sexual orientation'. The rest consider it a perversion. Most homosexuals are highly closeted, fearing harassment if their sexual orientation were revealed.

In Croatia 32% of women and 34% of men are smokers.

ECONOMY

Croatia has emerged from a rocky period that reached its height with a series of corruption and privatisation scandals in the late 1990s. While corruption remains a problem, the government has made progress in investigating and prosecuting corruption cases, which reassures international investors. Croatia's prospective entry into the EU has also brought increased investment, especially from Austria and Italy in banking, Germany in telecommunications and Hungary in the oil industry. Several Croatian companies have high brand-recognition throughout former Yugoslavia. Pliva (pharmaceuticals), Podravka (food processing) and Croatia Osiguranje (insurance) are valuable exports. Naturally, there's tourism, which accounts for about 20% of GDP.

From the point of view of the average Croat, life is tough. Unemployment, though decreasing, is still high (11.18%), pensions for retirees are ridiculously low, unemployment compensation isn't much better and the cost of living continues to rise. About 11% of Croats, mostly in rural areas, live below the poverty line.

POPULATION

According to the most recent census (2001), Croatia had a population of roughly 4.5 million people, a decline from the prewar population of nearly five million. Some 59% live in urban areas. About 280,000 Serbs (50% of the Serbian population) departed in the early 1990s; an estimated 110,000 have returned. In the postindependence economic crunch, 120,000 to 130,000 Croats emigrated, but a roughly equal number of ethnic Croat refugees arrived from Bosnia and Hercegovina and another 30,000 or so came from the Vojvodina region of Serbia. The current breakdown after the census is: Croat 89.6%, Serb 4.5%, Bosniak 0.5%, Hungarian 0.4%, Slovene 0.3%, Czech 0.2%, Roma 0.2%, Albanian 0.1%, Montenegrin 0.1% and others 4.1%. The Serb population is highest in eastern Slavonia, which also includes a significant number of Hungarians and Czechs. Italians are concentrated in Istria, while Albanians, Bosniaks and Roma can be found in Zagreb, Istria and some Dalmatian towns.

War and a discouraging economic outlook are responsible for a steady decline in Croatia's population as educated young people leave in search of greater opportunities abroad. Some experts predict that in 50 years only 13% of the population will be children under 14, and adults between 25 and 64 will drop to only 54%. There are no easy solutions, but the

The literacy rate in Croatia is 98.5%.

government is hoping to encourage the children of expats working abroad to return to Croatia.

About one million Croats live in the other states of former Yugoslavia, mainly Bosnia and Hercegovina, northern Vojvodina and around the Bay of Kotor in Montenegro. Some 2.3 million ethnic Croats live abroad, including almost 1.5 million in the USA, 270,000 in Germany, 240,000 in Australia, 150,000 in Canada and 150,000 in Argentina. Pittsburgh and Buenos Aires have the largest Croatian communities outside Europe. Croatians outside of the country retain the right to vote in national elections and many do. Many of these voting expatriates take a hard nationalistic line and tend to vote for right-wing parties.

SPORT

Football, tennis and skiing are enormously popular and sporty Croatia has contributed a disproportionate number of world-class players in each sport.

Basketball

The most popular Croatian sport after football, basketball is followed with some reverence. The teams of Split, Zadar and Cibona from Zagreb are known across Europe, though no one has yet repeated the star team of the 1980s, when players such as Dražen Petrović, Dino Rađa and Toni Kukoč formed Cibona and became European champions. For the thorough low-down on Croatian basketball, go to www.kos arka.hr.

> Croatia has fielded national teams at every Olympic Games (summer and winter) since 1992.

Football

By far the most popular spectator sport in Croatia is football (soccer), which frequently serves as an outlet for Croatian patriotism and, occasionally, as a means to express political opposition. When Franjo Tuđman came to power he decided that the name of Zagreb's football club, 'Dinamo', was 'too communist', so he changed it to 'Croatia'. Waves of outrage followed the decision, led by angry young football fans who used the controversy to express their opposition to the regime. Even though the following government restored the original name, you will occasionally see *Dinamo volim te* (Dinamo I love you) graffiti in Zagreb. Dinamo's frequent rival is Hajduk of Split, named after ancient resisters to Roman rule. Hajduk and Dinamo supporters are infamous rivals, often causing brawls when the two teams meet.

The national team did well in the 2008 European Championships, coached by Croatia's own and formerly West Ham's Slaven Bilić, reaching the quarter finals, and beating strong teams such as Germany, but finally losing to Turkey. It also performed outstandingly to finish third in the 1998 World Cup in France, following stunning victories over teams of the calibre of Germany and Holland. In addition, Davor Šuker won the prestigious 'Golden Boot' award for being the tournament's leading goal scorer with six goals. By career end Šuker scored 46 international goals, 45 of them for Croatia; he is the Croatian national team's all-time goal-scoring leader. Football great Pelé named him one of the top 125 greatest living footballers in March 2004.

Tennis

'I don't know what's in the water in Croatia, but it seems like every player is over 7ft tall' (Andy Roddick).

Not quite. Yet Croatia is producing some mighty big players, in every sense of the word.

The 2001 victory of 6ft 4in Goran Ivanišević at Wimbledon provoked wild celebrations throughout the country, especially in his home town of Split.

The charismatic serve-and-volley player was much loved for his engaging personality and on-court antics, and dominated the top 10 rankings during much of the 1990s. Injuries forced his retirement in 2004, but Croatia stayed on the court with a 2005 Davis Cup victory led by Ivan Ljubičić and Mario Ančić. Born in Bosnia and Hercegovina, Ljubičić fled to Croatia with the outbreak of war and built his rocketlike serve in Rijeka. Split-born Mario Ančić is dubbed 'Baby Goran' by Ivanišević himself.

On the women's side, Zagreb-born Iva Majoli won the French Open in 1997 with an aggressive baseline game, but failed to follow up with other Grand Slam victories.

Tennis is more than a spectator sport in Croatia. The coast is amply endowed with clay courts and they are rarely empty. The biggest tournament in Croatia is the Umag Open in Istria, held in July.

Skiing

If Croatia had a national god it would be Janica Kostelić. Born in Zagreb to a family of winter-sports nuts, Kostelić is the most accomplished skier to have emerged from Croatia. After winning the Alpine Skiing World Cup in 2001, Kostelić won three gold medals and a silver in the 2002 Winter Olympics – the first Winter Olympic medals ever for an athlete from Croatia. At the age of 20 she became the first female skier ever to win three gold medals at one Olympics. Since 2002, Kostelić was plagued by a knee injury and the removal of her thyroid, but this didn't stop her from winning a gold medal in the women's combined and a silver in the Super-G at the 2006 Winter Olympics in Torino.

Maybe it's in the genes. Brother Ivica Kostelić took the men's slalom World Cup title in 2002 and brought home a silver medal in the men's combined in Torino 2006.

Keep up with Croatian football by following the fortunes of Dinamo Zagreb at www.nk-dinamo.hr.

MEDIA

The media landscape in Croatia has changed considerably from the days of tight censorship. Now the only state-owned newspaper is *Vjesnik,* the most respected daily in Croatia with a loyal but relatively small readership. Croatian newspapers and magazines have discovered that fighting for advertisers is not much easier than fighting censorship. The two largest private dailies, *Večernji List* and *Jutarnji List*, are trying to lure advertisers with a mix of politics, show biz and scandal, while the glossy news magazines *Globus* and *Nacional* struggle for readers. Newspapers and magazines in Croatia are independently owned, usually by Croatians, except for *Večernji List*, which is Austrian owned.

The Croatian edition of *Metro,* called *Metro Express,* was launched in 2006 and has had a reasonable readership, though it has run into financial difficulties more than once in its short life – the daily newspaper changed to a weekly publication in August 2007, then went back to being a daily before firing all 20 of its reporters in July 2008 and announcing yet another return to being published weekly!

There are two government-owned radio stations (HRT1 and HRT2) that broadcast nationally, plus about 150 commercial radio stations that broadcast locally and nationally. There are three national TV networks: the government-owned HRT and the privately owned Nova and RTL. (RTL is the Croatian extension of the German RTL channel.) Nova and RTL entered the arena amid high hopes for improving Croatia's TV landscape, but they have seen their viewers and profits decline dramatically as each searches for a winning format. In contrast, the government-owned HRT, which broadcast state propaganda during the Tuđman years, has turned into a respectable public station, financed by a tax on all TV-owning households.

RELIGION

According to the most recent census, 87.8% of the population identified itself as Catholic, 4.4% Orthodox, 1.3% Muslim, 0.3% Protestant, and 6.2% others and unknown. Croats are overwhelmingly Roman Catholic, while all Serbs belong to the Eastern Orthodox Church, a division that has its roots in the fall of the Roman Empire. In fact, religion is the only factor separating the ethnically identical populations. In addition to various doctrinal differences, Orthodox Christians venerate icons, allow priests to marry and do not accept the authority of the pope.

It would be difficult to overstate the extent to which Catholicism shapes the Croatian national identity. The Croats pledged allegiance to Roman Catholicism as early as the 9th century and were rewarded with the right to conduct Mass and issue religious writings in the local language, which eventually became the Glagolitic script. The popes supported the early Croatian kings who in turn built monasteries and churches to further promote Catholicism. Throughout the long centuries of domination by foreign powers, Catholicism was the unifying element in forging a sense of nationhood.

Tragically, the profound faith that had animated Croatian nationalism was perverted into a murderous intolerance under the wartime Ustaše regime. The complicity of local parishes in 'cleansing' the population of Jews and Serbs prompted Tito to suppress religion – and, he hoped, nationalism – when he took power. Although religion was not officially forbidden, it was seen as 'politically incorrect' for ambitious Croats to attend Mass. Small wonder that the Vatican was the first entity to recognise an independent Croatia in 1991.

The Church enjoys a respected position in Croatia's cultural and political life and Croatia is the subject of particular attention from the Vatican. Nearly 76% of Croatian Catholics answering a poll said they considered themselves religious and about 30% attended services weekly. The Church is also the most trusted institution in Croatia, rivalled only by the military. Also Croats, both within Croatia and abroad, provide a stream of priests and nuns to replenish the ranks of Catholic clergy.

Former president Tuđman cultivated a close relationship with the Church, signing a series of treaties with the Vatican that codified the relationship between the Church and state in Croatia. The most important provisions deal with the equivalency of a church marriage and a civil wedding, the introduction of obligatory religious instruction in the state school system, and restitution of Church property nationalised under Tito's communists. The state also agreed to give financial support to Church activities.

Croatia's special relationship with the Vatican is a mutual one. In 2003, Pope John Paul II made his third trip to Croatia since independence. As the Catholic Church loses ground in much of secular Europe, Croatia's strong identity as a Catholic country has become increasingly important to the Vatican. Religious holidays are celebrated with fervour and Sunday Mass is strongly attended.

WOMEN IN CROATIA

Eva Sköld Westerlind's *Carrying the Farm on Her Back* traces the lives of three generations of Croatian farm women in mountain villages.

Women face special hurdles in Croatia. Under Tito's brand of socialism, women were encouraged to become politically active and their representation in the Croatian *sabor* (parliament) increased to 18%. Since independence, however, it has fallen to a mere 8%. Because of the overwhelming 'maleness' of politics, some 80% of men and women find it highly unlikely that a woman would be head of state.

More and more wives and mothers must work outside the home to make ends meet (48% of women are in the workforce), but they still perform most household duties and are under-represented at the executive levels. Only 66% of women and 42% of men unequivocally accept the idea of a female boss.

Women fare worse in traditional villages than in urban areas and were hit harder economically than men after the Homeland War. Many of the factories that closed, especially in eastern Slavonia, had a high proportion of women workers. Both domestic abuse and sexual harassment at work are common in Croatia and the legal system is not yet adequate for women to seek redress.

ARTS
Arts are of major importance to the Croats, from the more classical forms – classical music, theatre, dance and fine art – to modern stuff such as pop, rock or electronic music, avant garde and experimental theatre and dance, fashion and spoken word. Folk music and crafts are also very popular.

Literature
The Croatian language developed in the centuries following the great migration into Slavonia and Dalmatia. In order to convert the Slavs to Christianity, Greek missionaries Cyril and Methodius learned the language and Cyril put the language into writing. This became known as Glagolitic script. The earliest known example of Glagolitic script is an 11th-century inscription in a Benedictine abbey on the island of Krk. Ecclesiastical works in Glagolitic continued to appear until the Middle Ages.

Ivan Gundulić (1589–1638) from Ragusa (Dubrovnik) is widely considered to be the greatest Croatian poet.

POETS & PLAYWRIGHTS
The first literary flowering in Croatia, however, took place in Dalmatia, which was strongly influenced by the Italian Renaissance. The works of the scholar and poet Marko Marulić (1450–1524), from Split, are still venerated in Croatia. His play *Judita* was the first work produced by a Croatian writer in his native tongue. Ivan Gundulić's (1589–1638) epic poem *Osman* celebrated the Polish victory over the Turks in 1621 – a victory that the author saw as heralding the destruction of the detested Ottoman rule. The plays of Marin Držić (1508–67), especially *Dundo Maroje*, express humanistic Renaissance ideals and are still performed, especially in Dubrovnik.

The most towering figure in the post-1990s-war period was the lyrical and sometimes satirical Vesna Parun. Although Parun was often harassed by the government for her 'decadent and bourgeois' poetry, her *Collected Poems* have reached a new generation who find solace in her vision of wartime folly.

NOVELISTS
Croatia's towering literary figure is 20th-century novelist and playwright Miroslav Krleža (1893–1981). Always politically active, Krleža broke with Tito in 1967 over the writer's campaign for equality between the Serbian and Croatian literary languages. Depicting the concerns of a changing Yugoslavia, his most popular novels include *The Return of Philip Latinovicz* (1932), which has been translated into English, and *Banners* (1963–65), a multivolume saga about middle-class Croatian life at the turn of the 20th century.

Mention should also be made of Ivo Andrić (1892–1975), who won the 1961 Nobel Prize in Literature for his Bosnian historical trilogy *The Bridge on the Drina, Bosnian Story* and *Young Miss*. Born as a Catholic Croat in Bosnia, the writer used the Serbian dialect and lived in Belgrade, but identified himself as a Yugoslav.

Some contemporary writers have been strongly marked by the implications of Croatian independence. Alenka Mirković is a journalist who wrote a powerful memoir of the siege of Vukovar. Goran Tribuson uses the thriller genre to explore the changes in Croatian society after the war. In *Oblivion*, Pavao Pavličić uses a detective story to explore the problems of collective historical memory. American-based Josip Novakovich's work stems from

Vedrana Rudan's novel *Night* (2004) perfectly illustrates the strong language and controversial, antipatriarchal themes that are often ruffling feathers in the literary establishment. Rudan was born in Rijeka.

nostalgia for his native Croatia. His most popular novel, *April Fool's Day* (2005), is an absurd and gritty account of the recent wars that gripped the region. Slavenka Drakulić is another worthy name, with books that are often politically and sociologically provocative, and always witty and intelligent.

Expat writer Dubravka Ugrešić has been a figure of controversy in Croatia and acclaimed elsewhere. Now living in the Netherlands in self-imposed exile, she is best known for her novels *The Culture of Lies* (1998) and *The Ministry of Pain* (2006). Ugrešić (www.dubravkaugresic.com) also published *Nobody's Home* in 2007, a collection of stories and essays on travel across Europe and the US, and the relationship between East and West. Slavenka Drakulić's *Café Europa – Life After Communism* (1999) is another excellent book to look out for.

Miljenko Jergović, Sarajevo-born but living in Croatia, is a witty, poignant writer whose *Sarajevo Marlboro* (1994) and *Mama Leone* (1999) powerfully conjure up the atmosphere in prewar Yugoslavia.

A great introduction to contemporary Croatian writers is the collection of short stories, *Croatian Nights* (2005), edited by Tony White, Borivoj Radaković and Matt Thorne. The excellent anthology of 19 short stories features prominent Croatian writers such as Gordan Nuhanović, Vladimir Arsenijević, Jelena Čarija, Zoran Ferić, Miljenko Jergović and Zorica Radaković, and British writers including Toby Litt, Anna Davis, Tony White, Ben Richards, Niall Griffiths and others.

> Award-winning writer Dubravka Ugrešić and four other female writers were accused of being 'witches' by a Croatian magazine for not wholeheartedly supporting the Croatian war for independence.

Cinema

Yugoslav cinema was dominated by Serbian directors, but Croatia had two important names to call their own: Krešo Golik (1922–98), who directed popular comedies such as *Plavi 9* (Blue 9; 1950) and *Tko pjeva zlo ne misli* (He Who Sings Never Means Harm; 1970); and Branko Bauer (1921–), who directed thrillers, war dramas and adventure films. Croatia excelled at more experimental and 'intellectual' filmmaking (which wasn't necessarily very popular), with prominent names being Branko Babaja, Zvonimir Berković, Lordan Zafranović and Vatroslav Mimica, among others.

Franjo Tuđman's rule brought about a crisis in Croatian cinema, and the 1990s are considered to be the lowest point of Croatian filmmaking since WWII.

Some notable names in recent Croatian cinema are Vinko Brešan (1964–) and Goran Rušinović (1968–). Brešan's *Kako je počeo rat na mom otoku* (How the War Started on My Island; 1996) and *Maršal* (Marshal Tito's Spirit; 1999) were massively popular hits in Croatia. Goran Rušinović's film *Mondo Bobo* (1997) is a stylish black-and-white criminal drama inspired by the films of Jim Jarmusch and Shinya Tsukamoto, and the first independent feature film in Croatia.

Dalibor Matanić's *Fine Mrtve Djevojke* (Fine Dead Girls; 2002) was a popular thriller, while Rajko Grlić's *Karaula* (2006) recalled Yugoslav army days with much hilarity.

> Hrvoje Hribar's *What's a Man Without a Moustache?* (2005) sees a young widow, an ageing widower and returnee, and a priest from a bankrupt parish struggling to come to terms with the postwar environment and unrequited love.

Music

FOLK

Although Croatia has produced many fine classical musicians and composers, its most original musical contribution lies in its rich tradition of folk music. This music reflects a number of influences, many dating back to the Middle Ages when the Hungarians and Venetians vied for control of the country. Franz Joseph Haydn (1732–1809) was born near a Croat enclave in Austria and his classical music pieces were strongly influenced by Croatian folk songs.

RECOMMENDED FOLK RECORDINGS

■ *Croatie: Music of Long Ago* is a good starting point as it covers the whole gamut of Croatian music.

■ *Lijepa naša tamburaša* is a selection of Slavonian chants accompanied by *tamburica* (a three- or five-string mandolin).

■ *Omiš 1967–75* is an overview of *klapa* (an outgrowth of church-choir singing) music.

■ *Pripovid O Dalmaciji* is an excellent selection of *klapa* in which the influence of church choral singing is especially clear.

The instrument most often used in Croatian folk music is the *tamburica*, a three- or five-string mandolin that is plucked or strummed. Introduced by the Turks in the 17th century, the instrument rapidly gained a following in eastern Slavonia and came to be closely identified with Croatian national aspirations. *Tamburica* music remained the dominant kind played at weddings and local festivals during the Yugoslav period, too.

Vocal music followed the *klapa* tradition. Translated as 'group of people', *klapa* is an outgrowth of church-choir singing. The form is most popular in Dalmatia, particularly in Split, and can involve up to 10 voices singing in harmony about love, tragedy and loss. Traditionally the choirs were all-male, but now women are getting into the act, although there are very few mixed choirs. For an insight into a *klapa*, see p225.

Yet another popular strain of folk music emanates from the region of Međimurje in northeastern Croatia. Strongly influenced by music in neighbouring Hungary, the predominant instrument is a *citura* (zither). The tunes are slow and melancholic, frequently revolving around love-lost themes. New artists have breathed life into this traditional genre, including Lidija Bajuk and Dunja Knebl, female singers who have done much to resuscitate the music and gained large followings in the process.

In dance, look for the *drmeš*, a kind of accelerated polka danced by couples in small groups. The *kolo*, a lively Slavic round dance in which men and women alternate in the circle, is accompanied by Roma-style violinists. In Dalmatia, the *poskočica* is also danced by couples creating various patterns. Like the music, Croatian traditional dances are kept alive at local and national festivals. The best is the International Folklore Festival (p83) in Zagreb in July, but if you can't make it to that, not to worry: music and folklore groups make a circuit in the summer, hitting most coastal and island towns at one point or another. Ask at local tourist offices for the schedule.

POP, ROCK & THE REST

There's a wealth of home-grown talent in Croatia's pop and rock music scene. One of the most prominent bands is Hladno Pivo (Cold Beer), which plays energetic punky music with witty, politically charged lyrics. Then there's the ridiculously named indie-rock band Pips, Chips & Videoclips, whose breakthrough single 'Dinamo ja te volim' (Dinamo, I Love You) referred to Tuđman's attempts to rename Zagreb's football team (see p42), but whose music has generally been apolitical since. Vještice (The Witches) is a Zagreb-based band that mixes folk music from Međimurje, South African jive and punk rock.

The band Gustafi sings in the Istrian dialect and mixes Americana with local folk sounds, while the deliciously insane Let 3 from Rijeka is (in)famous for its nutty tunes and live performances at which the band members often show up naked, with only a piece of cork up their backsides (yes, really). TBF

BROTHERHOOD & UNITY OR DUMB & DUMBER?

Turbo folk, a supercharged, techno version of Serbian folk music, is notoriously difficult to cat-
egorise as anything but itself. Widely listened to in Croatia, Serbia, Montenegro, Macedonia, and
Bosnia and Hercegovina, it's possibly one of the biggest unifying contemporary factors across
former Yugoslavia. The undisputed queen of turbo folk is Svetlana Ražnatović 'Ceca', widow of
the Serbian Arkan, who was indicted by the UN for crimes against humanity. Ceca has produced
numerous albums and performed at sell-out concerts at all the biggest stadiums across the region.
Turbo folk started out and flourished under the Milošević regime and is widely associated with
mafia types – Ceca herself was arrested (but later cleared of all charges) in connection with her ties
to members of the Zemun clan, responsible for the murder of the Serbian prime minister Zoran
Đinđić in 2003. Some *folkotekas* – the clubs where turbo folk is played – have metal detectors
at their entrances and, particularly in Bosnia and Hercegovina, are subject to occasional bomb
attacks associated with 'unfinished business' among the local mafia members. The intellectual
elite sees turbo folk as a sort of 'dumbing down' of the current generation, but its ever-growing
popularity is an undeniable fact.

(The Beat Fleet) is Split's answer to hip hop, using Split slang to talk about
current issues, family troubles, heartbreak, happy times and so on. Bosnian-
born but Croatia-based, hip-hop singer Edo Maajka is another witty voice.

The fusion of jazz and pop with folk tunes has been a popular musical
direction in Croatia for a while. Two of the more prominent names in
this scene are Tamara Obrovac, a talented singer from Istria, and Mojmir
Novaković, formerly the singer of the popular band Legen.

The Croatian queen of pop is Severina, famous for her good looks and
eventful personal life, which is widely covered by local celebrity and gossip
magazines. Gibonni is another massively popular singer from Dalmatia,
and his major influence is Oliver Dragojević, a legendary singer of loveable
schmaltz. All three (Severina, Gibonni and Dragojević) are from Split.

If anything unifies the fractious former republics of Yugoslavia, it's music.
Bosnian Goran Bregović teamed up with filmmaker Emir Kusturica for some
remarkable scores and his music remains loved throughout the region.

Architecture

Examples of Roman architecture are abundant in Dalmatia, and the
Euphrasian Basilica (p171) in Poreč is an outstanding example of Byzantine
art; however, the first distinctively Croatian design also appeared along the
coast. *Pleter* (plaited ornamentation) appeared around AD 800 on the baptismal font of Duke Višeslav of Nin in the Church of the Holy Cross (Nin). This
ornamentation appears frequently on church entrances and church furniture
from the early medieval period. Around the end of the 10th century, the lat-
tice-work began to acquire leaves and tendrils. The design is so linked with the
country's culture that ex-president Franjo Tuđman used it on a poster during
his first election campaign to signal a return to traditional Croatian culture.

The best example of pre-Romanesque architecture is found on the
Dalmatian coast, beginning with the 11th-century Church of the Holy
Cross in Nin, built in the shape of a cross with two apses and a dome
above the centre point. There are remains of circular pre-Romanesque
churches in Split, Trogir and Ošalj, but the most impressive is the Church
of St Donat (p188) in Zadar, dating from the 9th century. Its round central structure and three semicircular apses make it most unusual. Other
smaller churches in Šipan and Lopud from the 10th and 11th centuries are
built with a cross-shaped ground plan indicating the growing influence of
Byzantine culture at that time.

The Romanesque tradition persisted along the coast long after the Gothic style had swept the rest of Europe. In the 13th century the earliest examples of Gothic style usually appeared still mixed with Romanesque forms. The most stunning work from this period is the portal on the Cathedral of St Lovro (p233) in Trogir, carved by the master artisan Radovan. Depicting human figures performing everyday chores was a definite break with traditional Byzantine reliefs of saints and apostles. The unusual wooden portal on Split's Cathedral of St Domnius (p223), made up of 28 square reliefs by Andrija Buvina, is another masterpiece from the Gothic period. The Cathedral of the Assumption of the Blessed Virgin Mary (formerly St Stephen's; p73) in Zagreb was the first venture into the Gothic style in northern Croatia. Although reconstructed several times, the sacristy has remnants of 13th-century murals.

Late-Gothic building was dominated by the builder and sculptor Juraj Dalmatinac, who was born in Zadar in the 15th century. His most outstanding work was Šibenik's Cathedral of St James (p209), which marks a transition from the Gothic to the Renaissance period. In addition to constructing the church entirely of stone, without timber, Dalmatinac adorned the apses with a wreath of realistically carved local people.

The Renaissance flourished especially in independent Ragusa (Dubrovnik), and by the second half of the 15th century, Renaissance influences were appearing on late-Gothic structures. The Sponza Palace (p266), formerly the Customs House, is a fine example of this mixed style. By the mid-16th century, Renaissance features began to supplant the Gothic style in the palaces and summer residences built in and around Ragusa by the wealthy nobility. Unfortunately, much was destroyed in the 1667 earthquake and now Dubrovnik is more notable for the mixed Gothic-Romanesque Franciscan Monastery (p265), the 15th-century Orlando Column (p266), the Onofrio Fountain (p265), the baroque St Blaise's Church (p266), the Jesuit St Ignatius Church (p267) and the Cathedral of the Assumption of the Blessed Virgin Mary.

Northern Croatia is well known for the baroque style that was introduced by Jesuit monks in the 17th century. The city of Varaždin was a regional capital in the 17th and 18th centuries and, because of its location, it enjoyed a steady interchange of artists, artisans and architects with northern Europe. The combination of wealth and a creatively fertile environment led to Varaždin becoming Croatia's foremost city of baroque art. You'll notice the style in the elaborately restored houses, churches and especially the impressive castle.

In Zagreb, good examples of the baroque style are found in the Upper Town. Notice the Jesuit Church of St Catherine (p73) and the restored baroque mansions that are now the Croatian History Museum (p78) and the Croatian Museum of Naïve Art (p78). Wealthy families built baroque mansions around Zagreb, including at Brezovica, Milyana, Lobor and Bistra.

Zagreb was the backdrop for scenes in Orson Welles' masterpiece *The Trial*.

Painting & Sculpture

The painter Vincent of Kastav was producing lovely church frescoes in Istria during the 15th century. The small church of St Maria near Beram contains his frescoes, most notably the *Dance of Death*. Another notable Istrian painter of the 15th century is Ivan of Kastav, who has left frescoes throughout Istria, mostly in the Slovenian part.

Many artists born in Dalmatia were influenced by, and in turn influenced, Italian Renaissance style. The sculptors Lucijan Vranjanin and Frano Laurana, the miniaturist Julije Klović and the painter Andrija Medulić left

Dalmatia while the region was under threat from the Ottomans in the 15th century and worked in Italy. Museums in London, Paris and Florence contain examples of their work, but few of their creations are in Croatia.

Vlaho Bukovac (1855–1922) was the most notable Croatian painter in the late 19th century. After working in London and Paris, he came to Zagreb in 1892 and produced portraits and paintings on historical themes in a lively style. Early-20th-century painters of note include Miroslav Kraljević (1885–1913) and Josip Račić (1885–1908), but the most internationally recognised artist was the sculptor Ivan Meštrović (1883–1962), who created many masterpieces on Croatian themes. Antun Augustinčić (1900–79) was another internationally recognised sculptor whose *Monument to Peace* is outside New York's UN building. A small museum of his work can be visited in the town of Klanjec (p105), north of Zagreb.

Post-WWI artists experimented with abstract expressionism, but this period is best remembered for the naïve art that began with the 1931 *Zemlja* (Soil) exhibition in Zagreb, which introduced the public to works by Ivan Generalić (1914–92) and other peasant painters. Committed to producing art that could be easily understood and appreciated by ordinary people, Generalić was joined by painters Franjo Mraz (1910–81) and Mirko Virius (1889–1943), and sculptor Petar Smajić (1910–85), in a campaign to gain acceptance and recognition for naïve art.

Abstract art also infiltrated the postwar scene. The most celebrated modern Croatian painter is Edo Murtić (1921–2005), who drew inspiration from the countryside of Dalmatia and Istria. In 1959, a group of artists – Marijan Jevšovar (1922–88), Ivan Kožarić (1921–) and Julije Knifer (1921–2004) – created the Gorgona group, which pushed the envelope of abstract art. Dubrovnik-born Đuro Pulitika (1922–2006) was well known for his colourful landscapes, and together with Antun Masle (1919–67) and Ivo Dulčić (1916–75) formed a trio of Dubrovnik painters.

The post-WWII trend to avant-garde art has evolved into installation art, minimalism, conceptualism and video art. Contemporary Croatian artists worth seeing include Lovro Artuković (1959–), whose highly realistic style is contrasted with surreal settings; on the video scene look for Sanja Iveković (1949–) and Dalibor Martinis (1947–). The multimedia works of Andreja Kulunčić (1968–) and the installations of Sandra Sterle (1965–) are attracting international attention, while the performances of Slaven Tolj (1964–) could be called 'extreme art'. Lana Šlezić (1973–) is a New York-based photographer, whose excellent work is often shot in Croatia.

The Gallery of Modern Art (p79) in Zagreb gives an excellent overview of the last 200 years of Croatian art.

Art Treasures of Croatia by Radovan Ivančević is a great summary of the history of Croatian art.

Food & Drink

If thoughts of Croatian cuisine conjure up images of greasy steaks with a side of boiled potatoes and sauerkraut, think again. While it still holds firm to its Eastern European roots and positively pleases meat-happy Balkan palates, Croatian food is a savoury smorgasbord of taste, echoing the varied cultures that have influenced the country over the course of its history. You'll find a sharp divide between the Italian-style cuisine along the coast and the flavours of Hungary, Austria and Turkey in the continental parts. From grilled sea bass smothered in olive oil in Dalmatia to a robust paprika-heavy meat stew in Slavonia, there's something for every taste. Each area proudly touts its very own speciality, but regardless of the region you'll be surprised by the generally good food made from fresh, seasonal ingredients.

The price and quality of meals varies little in the midrange category, but if you're willing to splurge you can spend hours feasting on slow food delicacies or savouring forward-thinking concoctions created by up-and-coming young chefs. There is a limit to what the local crowd can afford to pay, so restaurants still cluster in the middle of the price spectrum – few are unbelievably cheap and few are exorbitantly expensive. Whatever your budget, it's hard to get a truly bad meal anywhere in Croatia. Another plus is that food is often paired with plenty of alfresco dining in warm weather.

Even though Croatians are not overly experimental when it comes to food, they're particularly passionate about it. They'll spend hours discussing the quality of the lamb or the first-grade fish, and why it overshadows all food elsewhere. Foodie culture is on the rise in Croatia, inspired largely by the slow food movement (p52), which puts the emphasis on fresh seasonal ingredients and the joy of dining for hours.

Istria and Kvarner have quickly shot up to the top of the gourmet ladder but other places aren't lagging far behind. There is a new generation of chefs updating traditional Croatian dishes and joining the cult of celebrity chefs – yes, this movement has even made it to Croatia! Wine and olive oil production have been revived, and there's now a network of signposted roads around the country celebrating these precious nectars.

STAPLES & SPECIALITIES

Zagreb and northwestern Croatia favour the kind of hearty meat dishes you might find in Vienna. Juicy *pečenje* (spit-roasted and baked meat) features *janjetina* (lamb), *svinjetina* (pork) and *patka* (duck), often accompanied by *mlinci* (baked noodles) or *pečeni krumpir* (roast potatoes). Meat slow-cooked under a *peka* (domed baking lid) is especially delicious, but needs to be ordered in advance at many restaurants. *Purica* (turkey) with *mlinci* is practically an institution on Zagreb and Zagorje menus, along with *zagrebački odrezak* (veal steak stuffed with ham and cheese, then fried in breadcrumbs) – another calorie-ridden speciality. Another mainstay is *sir i vrhnje* (fresh cottage cheese and cream) bought from the locals at markets. If you have a sweet tooth, *palačinke* (thin pancakes) with various fillings and toppings are a common dessert.

Spicier than in other regions, cuisine in Slavonia uses liberal amounts of paprika and garlic. The Hungarian influence is most prevalent here, as many typical dishes, such as *čobanac* (a meat stew), are in fact a version of *gulaš* (goulash). The nearby Drava River provides fresh fish such as carp, pike and perch, which is stewed in a paprika sauce and served with noodles in a dish known as *fiš paprikaš*. Another speciality is *šaran u rašljama* (carp

The salt extracted at the Pag and Ston saltpans is the cleanest in the Mediterranean.

SLOW FOOD

With its plastic industrialised approach to the eating experience, it was only a matter of time before fast food got an enemy. It was – surprise, surprise! – 'slow food' that stood up to the fast-food trend that was taking over the world. Originally started in Italy in the 1980s, this movement now exists in over 120 countries in an attempt to preserve the culture of particular cuisines. The emphasis is placed on indigenous plants, seeds and animals, all raised and grown in a traditional way.

While there are countless interpretations of slow food, Croatia has its very own version that focuses on promoting local, fresh and seasonal ingredients. There's much attention placed on the ritual of eating as well as the presentation of food. The courses are served in small portions and brought out in a certain order. There's a longish break between the dishes, and they're all paired with fitting wines. The experience is about the joy of eating and understanding where your food comes from.

When Nenad Kukurin, the owner of Kukuriku restaurant (p123) in Rijeka introduced the concept over a decade ago, they called him a 'gastro-terrorist'. Kukuriku is now a destination, and reason enough to make it to the Kvarner Gulf. All bread and pasta is handmade, the herbs picked from the restaurant's garden, and the ingredients market fresh. The owner frequents the Rijeka market daily, consults the chef by phone and together, on the spot, they create that day's menu according to what's in the stalls. Whether you savour wild asparagus from Učka, truffles from the Motovun forest or lamb from a nearby village, you're guaranteed pure ingredients, without much elaboration. As Nenad Kukurin says, 'the point of a good meal is to walk away feeling light and happy'.

on a forked branch), roasted in its own oils over an open fire. The region's sausages are particularly renowned, especially *kulen*, a paprika-flavoured sausage cured over a period of nine months and usually served with cottage cheese, peppers, tomatoes and often *turšija* (pickled vegetables).

Coastal cuisine is typically Mediterranean, using a lot of olive oil, garlic, fresh fish and shellfish, and herbs. Along the coast, look for lightly breaded and fried *lignje* (squid) as a main course; Adriatic squid is generally more expensive than squid from further afield. Meals often begin with a first course of pasta such as spaghetti or *rižoto* (risotto) topped with seafood. For a special appetiser, try *paški sir* (Pag cheese; p206), a pungent hard cheese from the island of Pag. Dalmatian *brodet* (stewed mixed fish served with polenta; also known as *brodetto*) is another regional treat, but it's often only available in two-person portions. Dalmatian *pašticada* (beef stewed in wine and spices and served with gnocchi) appears on menus on the coast as well as in the interior. Lamb from Cres and Pag is deemed Croatia's best, as it's fed on fresh herbs, which makes the meat delicious.

The secret behind the pungent taste of *paški sir* (Pag cheese) is the diet of wild herbs that the sheep feast on while producing their milk.

Istrian cuisine has been attracting international foodies in recent years for its long gastronomic tradition, fresh foodstuffs and unique specialities. Typical dishes include *maneštra*, a thick vegetable-and-bean soup similar to minestrone, *fuži*, hand-rolled pasta often served with *tartufi* (truffles) or *divljač* (game meat), and *fritaja* (omelette often served with seasonal veggies, such as wild asparagus). Thin slices of dry-cured Istrian *pršut* (prosciutto) – also excellent in Dalmatia – are often on the appetiser list; it's expensive because of the long hours and personal attention involved in smoking the meat. Istrian olive oil is highly rated and award-winning; the tourist board has marked an olive oil route along which you can visit local growers, tasting oils from the source. The best seasonal ingredients include white truffles (see boxed text, p179), picked in autumn, and wild asparagus, harvested in spring.

Pizza is often a good choice in Croatia. These range from thin crispy pizzas to those with a puffy crust, and the toppings are fresh. For fast food, you can usually snack on *ćevapčići* (small spicy sausages of minced beef, lamb or pork), *pljeskavica* (an ex-Yugo version of a hamburger), *ražnjići* (small chunks of pork grilled on a skewer) or *burek* (pastry stuffed with ground meat or cheese).

DRINKS

Croatia is famous for its *rakija* (brandy), which comes in different flavours. The most commonly drunk are *loza* (grape brandy), *šljivovica* (plum brandy) and *travarica* (herbal brandy). Istrian grappa is particularly excellent, and ranges in flavour from *medica* (honey) to *biska* (mistletoe) and various berries. The island of Vis is famous for its delicious *rogačica* (carob brandy). It's customary to have a small glass of brandy before a meal. Other popular drinks include *vinjak* (cognac), maraschino (cherry liqueur made in Zadar), *prosecco* (sweet dessert wine) and *pelinkovac* (herbal liqueur).

The two top types of Croatian *pivo* (beer) are Zagreb's Ožujsko and Karlovačko from Karlovac. The small-distribution Velebitsko has a loyal following among in-the-know beer drinkers but only some bars and shops carry it, and they're mostly in continental Croatia. You'll want to practise saying *živjeli!* (cheers!).

Wine is an important part of Croatian meals but oenophiles will be dismayed to see Croats diluting their wine with water. This is called *bevanda* (red wine with water) in Dalmatia, and *gemišt* (white wine with mineral water) in continental Croatia, especially Zagorje. This watering down is hardly necessary. Although not world-class, Croatian wines are eminently drinkable and occasionally distinguished. Virtually every region produces its own wine but Istrian wines are the most acclaimed, with the main grape varieties being the white *malvazija*, red *teran* and sweet *muškat*. The tourist board has marked wine trails across the peninsula, so you can visit the growers in their cellars. The top winemakers include Coronica, Kozlović, Matošević, Markežić, Degrassi and Sinković.

The Kvarner region is known for its *žlahtina* of Vrbnik on Krk Island; Katunar is the best-known producer. Dalmatia has a long wine-producing tradition – look for *pošip*, *rukatac* and *grk* on Korčula, *dingač* and *postup* from the Pelješac Peninsula, *mali plavac* on Hvar (Plenković winery is tops) and *brač* and *vugava* on Vis. Slavonia produces excellent white wines such as *graševina*, Rhine riesling and *traminac* (see p114).

Strongly brewed *kava* (espresso-style coffee) served in tiny cups is popular throughout Croatia. You can have it diluted with milk (macchiato) or order a cappuccino. Although some places have decaf options this is considered somewhat of a sacrilege, as Croatians love their coffee. Herbal teas are widely available but regular tea *(čaj)* is apt to be too weak for aficionados. Tap water is drinkable.

Research shows that the prized oysters in the Ston area on Pelješac have been farmed since Roman times.

CELEBRATIONS

Croatians love to eat and take any excuse to feast, so holidays and special celebrations such as weddings and christenings are party time if you like food.

As in other Catholic countries, most Croats don't eat meat on *Badnjak* (Christmas Eve); instead they eat fish. In Dalmatia, the traditional Christmas Eve dish is *bakalar* (dried salted cod). Christmas dinner may be roast suckling pig, turkey with *mlinci* or another meat. Also popular at Christmas is *sarma* (sauerkraut rolls stuffed with minced meat). Fresh Christmas Eve bread, also known as *Badnji Kruh*, is the centrepiece; it's made with honey, nuts and dried fruit. Another tradition is the Christmas braid, glazed dough made with nutmeg, raisins and almonds and shaped into a braid. It's often decorated with wheat and candles and left on the table until the Epiphany (6 January), when it is cut and eaten. *Orahnjača* (walnut cake), *fritule* (fritters) and *makovnjača* (poppy seed cake) are popular desserts at celebrations.

The most typical Easter dish is ham with boiled eggs, served with fresh veggies. *Pinca*, a type of hard bread, is another Easter tradition, especially in Dalmatia.

THE OLIVE OIL BOOM OF ISTRIA *Anja Mutić*

There's an olive tree on Veli Brijun in the Brijuni Islands proven to be 1600 years old. Even the early Greek and Roman manuscripts praised the quality of Istrian olive oil. Now there's a revival of this ancient agricultural activity, with 94 listed growers on the Istrian Peninsula and a network of signposted olive oil roads. In Istria, the plant is cultivated with special attention, and each tree given love and care. Several growers have received prestigious international awards and top marks for their fruity nectars, which is no small feat in the competitive world olive oil market.

Duilio Belić is a relative newbie on the scene. The son of a miner, he grew up in Raša and went on to become a successful Zagreb businessperson before starting Croatia's newest gastronomic trend – olive oil tastings. With his wife Bosiljka, an agriculture specialist, he bought an old grove near Fažana seven years ago and started what has become a real hit among gourmets. He now has five olive groves in three locations in Istria, with a total of 5500 trees. Under the brand name Oleum Viride, they produce eight single-sort, extra virgin olive oils, four of which are made of indigenous varietals – Buža, Istarska Bjelica, Rosulja and Vodnjanska Crnica. Their showcase oil is Selekcija Belić, a blend of six mono-sorts with a flavour of vanilla and chicory.

Over a coffee at a Fažana café, Duilio reminds me of a simple fact most people forget: olive is a fruit and olive oil is a fruit juice. Just like with wine, certain oils can be combined with certain dishes to enhance the flavours. Selekcija Belić, for example, is a great accompaniment to lamb and veal under a *peka* (domed baking lid), or a wild asparagus omelette. The highly prized Buža oil pairs wonderfully with raw fish and meat, as well as mushrooms and grilled vegetables. The golden-green Istarska Bjelica with its scent of mown grass and a hint of radicchio goes well with chocolate ice cream or a dark-chocolate hazelnut cake.

It's all sounding quite abstract to me so we move on to Vodnjanka (p161), a restaurant in Pula, where Duilio pulls out a box with a selection of his oils and orders a range of hors d'oeuvres. There, I learn to taste olive oil. A small sample is poured into a wine glass, which you warm up with your hand in order for the oil to reach body temperature. You then cover the glass with your hand to release the oil's natural aroma. Next, you place a small sip of the oil at the front of your mouth, mix it gently and then swallow in one go.

Such tastings have become a trend among Croatian foodies. Duilio organises the gatherings for his wider circle of friends and hopes to offer them at his olive grove in the future. In the meantime, his oils can be sampled at Croatia's top restaurants: Bevanda (p127) in Opatija, Valsabbion (p162) and Milan (p162) in Pula, Kukuriku (p123) in Rijeka, Foša (p192) in Zadar and Damir i Ornella (p174) in Novigrad. At 650KN per litre (400KN from the producer), they don't come cheap but the experience is worth every lipa.

I ask Duilio my last questions as we sample Vodnjanska Crnica in *maneštra* (a thick vegetable-and-bean soup similar to minestrone). I wonder what makes Istria such prime territory for growing olives. 'It's the microlocation,' Duilio says. 'Plus we harvest the olives early, unlike in Dalmatia, to preserve the natural antioxidants and nutrients. The oils may taste more bitter but they're also healthier.'

As we're parting ways, fascinated by the man's passion for olive oil, I wonder what made him enter this whole new world. 'It's simple – I love food, I love wine, I love all good things in life,' he replies. 'Olive oil is one of them.'

WHERE TO EAT & DRINK

A *restauracija* or *restoran* (restaurant) is at the top of the food chain, generally presenting a more formal dining experience and an elaborate wine list. A *gostionica* or *konoba* is usually a traditional family-run tavern – the produce may come from the family garden. A *pivnica* is more like a pub, with a wide choice of beer; sometimes there's a hot dish or sandwiches available. A *kavana* is a café, where you can nurse your coffee for hours and, if you're lucky, have cakes and ice cream. A *slastičarna* (pastry shop) serves ice cream, cakes, strudels and sometimes coffee, but you usually have to gobble your food standing up or take it away. Self-service *samoposluživanje* (cafeterias) are good for a quick meal. Even if the quality varies, all you need to do is point to what you want.

If you're on your own, an elaborate breakfast is difficult as all you can get easily is coffee at a café and pastries from a bakery. Otherwise, you can buy some bread, cheese and milk at a supermarket and have a picnic. If you're staying in a hotel you'll be served a buffet breakfast that includes cornflakes, bread, yoghurt, a selection of cold meat, powdered 'juice' and cheese. More upmarket hotels have better buffets that include eggs, sausages and homemade pastries.

Fruit and vegetables from the market and a selection of cheese, bread and ham from a grocery store can make a healthy picnic lunch. If you ask nicely, the person behind the deli counter at supermarkets or grocery stores will usually make a *sir* (cheese) or *pršut* (prosciutto) sandwich and you only pay the regular price of the ingredients.

VEGETARIANS & VEGANS

A useful phrase is *Ja ne jedem meso* (I don't eat meat), but even then you may be served soup with bits of bacon swimming in it. That is slowly changing and vegetarians are making inroads in Croatia, but this is mostly felt in the larger cities. Zagreb, Rijeka, Split and Dubrovnik now have vegetarian restaurants, and even standard restaurants are beginning to offer vegetarian menus in the big cities. Vegetarians may have a harder time in the north (Zagorje) and the east (Slavonia) where traditional fare has meat as its main focus. Specialities that don't use meat include *maneštra od bobića* (bean and fresh maize soup) and *juha od krumpira na zagorski način* (Zagorje potato soup). If that's not enough, go on to *štrukli* (dumplings filled with cottage cheese) or *blitva* (Swiss chard boiled and often served with potatoes, olive oil and garlic). Along the coast you'll find plenty of pasta dishes and risottos with various vegetable toppings and delicious cheese. If fish and seafood are part of your diet, you'll eat royally nearly everywhere.

EATING WITH KIDS

Croats are kid-friendly and the relaxed dining scene means that you can bring the kids nearly everywhere. Even the more upmarket restaurants will have a kid-friendly pasta or rice dish on the menu. Children's portions are easily arranged. However, you won't often find high chairs for the tinier tots and dining establishments are rarely equipped with nappy-changing facilities. Baby food and powdered baby milk formulas are easily found at most supermarkets and pharmacies, and are sold according to age group. For more information on travelling with children, see p297.

HABITS & CUSTOMS

Throughout former Yugoslavia, the *doručak* (breakfast) of the people was *burek*. Modern Croats have opted for a lighter start to their day, usually just coffee and a pastry with yoghurt and fresh fruit.

Restaurants open for *ručak* (lunch) around noon and usually serve continuously until midnight, which can be a major convenience if you're arriving in town at an odd hour or just feel like spending more time at the beach. Croats tend to eat either an earlier *marenda* or *gablec* (cheap filling lunch) or a large, late lunch. *Večera* (dinner) is typically a much lighter affair, but most restaurants have adapted their schedules to the needs of tourists who tend to load up at night. Few Croatians can afford to eat out regularly; when they do, it's likely to be a large family outing on Saturday night or Sunday afternoon.

Croats are proud of their cuisine and vastly prefer it to all others (except Italian). Outside the main cities there are few restaurants serving international cuisine (mostly Chinese and Mexican) and few variations on the basic Croatian themes.

The history of wine-making in Istria goes back to ancient Phoenicians and Greeks, but it really flourished during the Roman times (177 BC–AD 476).

COOKING COURSES

Cooking courses in Croatia are becoming increasingly popular but mainly for the affluent crowd, as they don't come cheap. British-based operation **My Croatia** (☎ in the UK 44-118-961 1554; www.mycroatia.co.uk) offers upmarket gourmet holidays in Zagreb, Lovran and Istria. They start at £895 per person based on two people and include upmarket accommodation for seven nights, private tours, gourmet meals, wine tastings and cooking classes. The cheapest option is a three-day Zagreb fling for £595 per person. A Zagreb-based company, **Delicija 1001** (www.1001delicija.com) organises a variety of cooking courses and gourmet events. Options and pricing vary greatly. A one-day cooking course in Zagreb or Istria (with a visit to the market, a cooking lesson and the meal with wine) starts at €125 per person. A weekend cooking course in Istria or Dalmatia – with accommodation, meals with wine and cooking lessons – ranges from €260 to €360 per person. Such a weekend in Istrian *agroturizmi* (rural retreats) starts at €190 per person.

EAT YOUR WORDS

Get behind the cuisine scene by getting to know the language. For pronunciation guidelines see p318.

Useful Phrases

I'm hungry.	*Ja sam gladan/gladna.* (m/f)	ya sam *gla*·dan/*glad*·na
I'm a vegetarian.	*Ja sam vegetarijanac/ vegetarijanka.* (m/f)	ya sam ve·ge·ta·ree·*ya*·nats/ ve·ge·ta·*ree*·yan·ka
I don't eat meat.	*Ja ne jedem meso.*	ya ne *ye*·dem *me*·saw
Waiter!	*Konobar!*	*kaw*·naw·bar
The menu, please.	*Molim vas jelovnik.*	*maw*·leem *ye*·lawv·neek
What's the speciality of the house?	*Što je vaš specijalitet kuće?*	shtaw ye vash spe·tsee·ya·*lee*·tet *koo*·che
What would you recommend?	*Što biste nam preporučili?*	shtaw *bee*·ste nam pre·paw·*roo*·tchee·lee
Please bring the bill.	*Molim vas donesite račun.*	*maw*·leem vas daw·*ne*·see·te *ra*·tchoon
Enjoy your meal!	*Dobar tek!*	*daw*·bar tek

Food Glossary

BASICS

čaša	*tcha*·sha	glass
doručak	*daw*·roo·tchak	breakfast
kavana	ka·*va*·na	café
mlijeko	mlee·*ye*·ko	milk
nož	nawzh	knife
papar	*pa*·par	pepper
pivnica	*peev*·nee·tsa	pub
račun	*ra*·tchoon	bill/cheque
restoran	re·*staw*·ran	restaurant
ručak	*roo*·tchak	lunch
šećer	*she*·cher	sugar
sol	sawl	salt
tvečera	*ve*·tche·ra	dinner
viljuška	vee·*lyoosh*·ka	fork
voda	*vaw*·da	water
žlica	*zhlee*·tsa	spoon

The Zadar sour cherry liqueur maraschino was conjured up in the early 16th century by pharmacists working in Zadar's Dominican monastery.

DRINKS

biska	*bee*·ska	mistletoe brandy
pelinkovac	pe·*lin*·ko·vats	herbal liqueur
pivo	*pee*·vo	beer
prosecco	pro·*se*·ko	sweet dessert wine
rogačica	*ro*·ga·tchee·tsa	carob brandy
šljivovica	*shlyee*·vo·vee·tsa	plum brandy
travarica	*tra*·va·ree·tsa	herbal brandy
vinjak	*vee*·nyak	cognac

FISH

bakalar	ba·*ka*·lar	codfish
brancin	bran·*tseen*	sea bass
dagnja	*dag*·nya	mussel
lignje	*leeg*·nye	squid
losos	*law*·saws	salmon
oslić	*aw*·sleech	hake
pastrva	*pas*·tr·va	trout
prstaci	prs·*ta*·tsee	shellfish
rak	rak	crab
riba	*ree*·ba	fish
šaran	sharan	carp
škamp	shkamp	shrimp

MEAT

govedina	*gaw*·ve·dee·na	beef
guska	*goo*·ska	goose
janjetina	*ya*·nye·tee·na	lamb
patka	*pat*·ka	duck
piletina	*pee*·le·tee·na	chicken
pršut	*pr*·shoot	prosciutto
purica	*poo*·ree·tsa	turkey
šunka	*shoon*·ka	ham
svinjetina	*svee*·nye·tee·na	pork

VEGETABLES & FRUIT

artičoka	ar·tee·*tchaw*·ka	artichoke
breskva	*bres*·kva	peach
jabuka	*ya*·boo·ka	apple
krumpir	kroom·*peer*	potato
kukuruz	koo·*koo*·rooz	corn
kupus	*koo*·poos	cabbage
luk	look	onion
naranča	*na*·ran·tcha	orange
paprika	*pa*·pree·ka	fresh pepper
rajčica	*rai*·tchee·tsa	tomato
riža	*ree*·zha	rice
tartufi	tar·*too*·fee	wild truffle

STARTERS

brodet	braw·*det*	mixed stewed fish, served with polenta; also called *brodetto*
burek	*boo*·rek	heavy pastry stuffed with meat or cheese
buzara	boo·*za*·ra	sauce of tomatoes, onions, herbs, white wine and bread crumbs, usually served with shellfish

juha od krumpira	yoo·ha awd krawm·pee·ra	Zagorje potato soup
na zagorski način	na za·gawr·skee na·tcheen	
klipići	klee·pee·chee	Varaždin's finger-shaped bread
kulen	koo·len	paprika-flavoured sausage
maneštra	ma·nesh·tra	vegetable-and-bean soup similar to minestrone
maneštra od bobića	ma·nesh·tra awd baw·bee·cha	bean and fresh maize soup
miješana salata	mee·ye·sha·na sa·la·ta	mixed salad
paški sir	pash·kee seer	sheep's milk cheese from the island of Pag
pršut	pr·shoot	dry-cured ham
štrukli	shtroo·klee	dumplings filled with cottage cheese
turšija	toor·shee·ya	pickled vegetables

MAIN COURSES

blitva	bleet·va	Swiss chard boiled and often served with potatoes, olive oil and garlic
ćevapčići	che·vap·tchee·chee	small spicy sausages of minced beef, lamb or pork
crni rižoto	tsr·nee ree·zho·to	'black risotto' usually with cuttlefish, squid, olive oil, onion, garlic, parsley and red wine
fiš paprikaš	fish pap·ree·kash	fish stew with paprika
fuži	foo·zhee	Istrian hand-rolled pasta tubes
gulaš	goo·lash	goulash
hrvatska pisanica	hr·vat·ska pee·sa·nee·tsa	beef steak in a spicy mushroom, onion, tomato and red wine sauce
husarska pečenka	hoo·sar·ska pe·tchen·ka	steak with onions and bacon
lignje na žaru	leeg·nye na zha·roo	grilled squid
mlinci	mleen·tsee	baked noodles
pašticada	pash·tee·tsa·da	beef stewed in wine and spices and served with gnocchi
pečenje	pe·tche·nye	roasted meat
pileći ujušak	pee·le·chee oo·yoo·shak	chicken stew
pljeskavica	plye·ska·vee·tsa	a hamburger of minced pork, beef or lamb
prženi krumpir	pr·zhe·nee kroom·peer	fried potatoes
punjene paprike	poo·nye·ne pa·pree·ke	peppers stuffed with minced beef or pork and rice in tomato sauce
purica s mlincima	poo·ree·tsa s mleen·tsee·ma	turkey with mlinci
ražnjići	razh·nyee·chee	small chunks of pork grilled on a skewer
riblji rižoto	reeb·lyee ree·zhaw·taw	fish risotto usually with tomato sauce
rižoto	ree·zhaw·taw	risotto
šurlice	shoor·lee·tse	homemade noodles from Krk island, topped with goulash or seafood
zagrebački odrezak	za·gre·batch·ki od·rez·ak	veal steak stuffed with ham and cheese, then fried in breadcrumbs

DESSERTS

amareta	a·ma·re·ta	round, rich cake with almonds
cukarini	tsoo·ka·ree·nee	sweet biscuit
klajun	kla·yoon	pastry stuffed with walnuts
kremšnite	krem·shnee·te	custard pie
palačinke	pa·la·tcheen·ke	thin pancakes, often filled with jam, chocolate or walnut paste
palačinke sa sirom	pa·la·tcheen·ke sa see·rawm	pancakes filled with cottage cheese, sugar, raisins, egg and sour cream and then oven baked

Environment

THE LAND

Croatia is shaped like a boomerang: from the Pannonian plains of Slavonia between the Sava, Drava and Danube Rivers, across hilly central Croatia to the Istrian peninsula, then south through Dalmatia along the rugged Adriatic coast. The unusual geography makes it tricky to circle the country. If you're touring the country from Zagreb, when you get to Dubrovnik you can either fly back to Zagreb to catch a flight out, double back by land through Split, or drive up through Bosnia and Hercegovina to enter Croatia from the east.

The narrow Croatian coastal belt at the foot of the Dinaric Alps is only about 600km long as the crow flies, but it's so indented that the actual length is 1778km. If the 4012km of coastline around the offshore islands is added to the total, the length becomes 5790km. Most of the 'beaches' along this jagged coast consist of slabs of rock sprinkled with naturists. Don't come expecting to find sand, but the waters are sparkling clean, even around large towns.

Croatia's offshore islands are every bit as beautiful as those off the coast of Greece. There are 1185 islands and islets along the tectonically submerged Adriatic coastline, 66 of them inhabited. The largest are Cres, Krk, Mali Lošinj, Pag and Rab in the north; Dugi Otok in the middle; and Brač, Hvar, Korčula, Mljet and Vis in the south. Most are barren and elongated from northwest to southeast, with high mountains that drop right into the sea.

> The fine weather on Hvar is so reliable that hotels give a discount on cloudy days and a free stay should you ever see snow.

WILDLIFE
Animals

Deer are plentiful in the dense forests of Risnjak National Park (p128), as are brown bears, wild cats and *ris* (lynx), from which the park gets its name. Occasionally a wolf or wild boar may appear but only rarely. Plitvice Lakes National Park (p195), however, is an important refuge for wolves. A rare sea otter is also protected in Plitvice, as well as in Krka National Park (p212).

The griffon vulture, with a wingspan of 2.6m, has a permanent colony on Cres (see p138), and Paklenica National Park (p198) is rich in peregrine falcons, goshawks, sparrow hawks, buzzards and owls. Krka National Park is an important migration route and winter habitat for marsh birds, such as herons, wild duck, geese and cranes, and rare golden eagles and short-toed eagles. Kopački Rit Nature Park (p112), near Osijek in eastern Croatia, is an extremely important bird refuge.

> Croatia is home to about 400 bears.

KARST CAVES & WATERFALLS

The most outstanding geological feature of Croatia is the prevalence of the highly porous limestone and dolomitic rock called karst. Stretching from Istria to Montenegro and covering large parts of the interior, karst is formed by the absorption of water into the surface limestone, which then corrodes and allows the water to seep into the harder layer underneath. Eventually the water forms underground streams, carving out fissures and caves before resurfacing, disappearing into another cave and finally emptying into the sea. Caves and springs are common interior features of karstic landscapes, which explains Croatia's Pazin Chasm (p177), Plitvice Lakes (p195) and the Krka waterfalls (p213), as well as the Manita Peć cave (p199) in Paklenica. The jagged, sparsely vegetated exterior landscape is dramatic, but deforestation, wind and erosion have made the land unsuitable for agriculture. When the limestone collapses, a kind of basin (known as *polje*) is formed, which is then cultivated despite the fact that this kind of field drains poorly and can easily turn into a temporary lake.

Two venomous snakes are endemic in Paklenica – the nose-horned viper and the European adder. The nonvenomous leopard snake, four-lined snake, grass snake and snake lizard species can be found in both Paklenica and Krka National Parks.

Plants

The richest plant life is found in the Velebit Range, part of the Dinaric Range that provides the backdrop to the central Dalmatian coast. Botanists have counted 2700 species and 78 endemic plants there, including the increasingly threatened edelweiss. Risnjak National Park is another good place to find edelweiss, along with black-vanilla orchids, lilies and hairy alpenroses, which look a lot better than they sound. The dry Mediterranean climate along the coast is perfect for maquis, a low brush that flourishes all along the coast but especially on the island of Mljet. You'll also find oleander, jasmine and juniper trees along the coast, and lavender is cultivated on the island of Hvar. Typically, Mediterranean olive and fig trees are also abundant.

NATIONAL PARKS

When the Yugoslav federation collapsed, eight of its finest national parks ended up in Croatia. These cover 7.5% of the country and have a total area of 994 sq km, of which 235 sq km is water. Risnjak National Park (p128), southwest of Zagreb, is the most untouched forested park, partly because the climate at its higher altitudes is somewhat inhospitable – an average temperature of 12.6°C in July. The winters are long and snowy, but when spring finally comes in late May or early June everything blooms at once. The park has been kept deliberately free of tourist facilities, with the idea that only mountain-lovers need apply. The main entrance point is the motel and information facility at Crni Lug.

The dramatically formed karstic gorges and cliffs make Paklenica National Park (p198) along the coast a rock-climbing favourite and the scene of a European rock-climbing competition held each year in early May. Large grottoes and caves filled with stalactites and stalagmites make it an interesting park for cave explorers, and there are many kilometres of trails for hiking. Tourist facilities are well developed here. More rugged is the mountainous Northern Velebit National Park, a stunning patchwork of forests, peaks, ravines and ridges that backs northern Dalmatia and the Šibenik-Knin region.

The waterfalls of Plitvice Lakes National Park (p195) were formed by mosses that retain calcium carbonate as river water rushes through the karst. Travertine or tufa builds up, sprouting plants that grow on top of each other to create barriers to the river. The park has been named a Unesco World

Croatia's currency, the kuna, is named for the pelt of the stone marten *(kuna)*, which was used as the medium of exchange under the Venetians.

(Continued on page 69)

THE ADRIATIC

Touted as the 'new this' and the 'new that' for years upon its re-emergence on the world tourism scene, it is now obvious that Croatia is a unique destination that can hold its own, and then some. The Adriatic coast is a knockout: its limpid sapphire-blue waters pull visitors to remote islands, hidden coves and traditional fishing villages, while touting the glitzy beach and yacht scene. Istria is captivating with its gastronomic and wine offerings, and the bars, clubs and festivals of Zadar and Split remain little-explored delights. Punctuate all this with Dubrovnik in the south and a country couldn't wish for a better finale.

Island Hopping

Croatia's coast is speckled with dozens of magnificent islands that range from tiny, verdant and unpopulated, to massive, arid and sporting ancient towns and villages. One of the chief delights on any visit to Croatia is hopping between the islands on the numerous ferries, catamarans and taxi boats, or, if you're thus blessed, your own sailing boat.

1 The Elafiti Islands
An easy hop away from Dubrovnik, the Elafiti Islands (p276) range from totally unpopulated swimming spots to small villages on little-explored islands. They can be reached by a taxi boat from Dubrovnik or via a fishing picnic tour.

2 Hvar
Croatia's most popular island, Hvar (p250), draws more tourists than any other Adriatic atoll thanks to its gorgeous hub (also called Hvar). Stari Grad and Jelsa, the island's two other towns, are emerging as popular alternatives thanks to their quieter, more discerning charms.

3 Cres
Long, hardly populated and undeveloped, this wild island (p136) is perfect for wandering around primeval forests, visiting ageing hilltop towns, admiring Venetian mansions, swimming in hidden coves and sampling some of Croatia's most delicious lamb.

4 Mljet
The northwestern half of Mljet (p277) is a national park. There are two salt lakes in the middle of the island, remote sandy beaches, only one conventional hotel and the food is magnificent. Need we say more?

5 Brač
The biggest of the Adriatic islands, Brač (p243) sports Croatia's most famous beach, the lasciviously alluring Zlatni Rat in the pretty town of Bol. Windsurf and sunbathe here, but don't forget to explore the island's gorgeous interior.

6 Vis
Off-limits to foreign visitors for around four decades, Vis (p240) is a mysterious island that's truly off the trodden path. With its three small fishing villages and one of Croatia's few real eco-holiday options, Vis is well worth exploring.

Activities

There's tonnes to do for active and outdoorsy types. Starting with vigorous swimming in the clear Adriatic waters and exertive sunbathing, you can progress on to mountain hiking, windsurfing, trekking, kayaking, climbing, sailing and more.

1

① Sailing

Possibly the most popular activity on the Adriatic, the privileged and much-envied owners of sailing boats or those renting can exercise their biceps while gliding between the beautiful Croatian islands. The most popular place to dock is Hvar (p250), but use your chance to discover some of the more difficult-to-reach islands such as Kornati (p214) or Elafiti (p276).

② Hiking

The numerous national parks – Plitvice (p195), Paklenica (p198) and Krka (p212) among others – are fantastic for hikers. If you want something more challenging, head for Mt Biokovo (p237), near Makarska. The islands of Cres (p136) and Mljet (p277) are perfect for light walking among nature.

③ Windsurfing

Bol's gorgeous Zlatni Rat must be one of the most picturesque places to hurl yourself into the wind and water, which explains why so many do each year (see p248). The village of Viganj, near Dubrovnik, is a close contender for favourite, with the majority of visitors being windsurfing enthusiasts (see boxed text, p289).

④ Diving

The islands are prime diving spots with dozens of marine beauties to be discovered off Hvar (p250), Brač (p243), Krk (p141), Kornati (p214) and others. Most coastal towns have diving opportunities, too, so make sure you plunge and explore Croatia underwater at least once.

⑤ Naturism

Yes, you read it right. Croatia has a venerable naturist history, its founders being Edward VIII and Wallis Simpson, who skinny-dipped along the Rab coast in 1936 (see boxed text, p157). Istria is now Croatia's number-one place for going starkers, though the rest of the coast reserves numerous nudist beaches, too. Just look for the FKK sign!

Architecture & Landscape

It's all here – Renaissance, Venetian and Gothic architecture, sweeping green fields and breezy forests, and the impressive, rugged Dinaric Alps, not to mention the enchanting Adriatic Sea. Wherever you look, you're bound to swoon.

❶ Dubrovnik

You didn't think we'd forget the star of the show? Dazzling all with its heart-stopping beauty, Dubrovnik (p260) is packed with five-star hotels, high-class restaurants and countless tourists, but move away from the main streets and there's still much to discover.

❷ Kornati Islands

Imagine this: 147 mostly uninhabited islands and reefs, carved with cracks, caves and cliffs, and dotted with tufts of evergreen forest (see p214). The Kornati National Park (p215) is a delight for any lover of stark and unspoilt nature, limpid waters and solitude.

❸ Plitvice Lakes National Park

A verdant maze of paths, woods and meadows revolves around 16 sparkling lakes and crashing waterfalls at Plitvice (p195). It's a World Heritage site and Croatia's most popular national park – also much loved by its resident bears and wolves and over 120 species of birds.

❹ Trogir

A pocket-size town that brims with Romanesque and Renaissance architecture, and one of the loveliest cathedrals on the coast, Trogir's (p232) illustrious history has left it with a fantastic Venetian heritage.

❺ Zadar

An up-and-coming city destination, Zadar (p185) has one of Dalmatia's prettiest old town centres, with marble, traffic-free streets that follow the old Roman street plan. Zadar's Roman ruins and medieval churches dazzle, as does its nightlife.

❻ Adriatic Sea

It may be obvious, but it's hard to over-emphasise the beauty of the Adriatic. It's smooth, silky and pellucid, and the colour (in turn electric blue, jade green and steely) is unmatched. Fish will tickle your calves as you step in, but watch out for sea urchins!

❼ Diocletian's Palace

One of the world's most impressive Roman ruins, these Unesco-protected remains still serve the very purpose they were built for: life is lived inside them. Split's heart, soul and most of its arteries, Diocletian's Palace (p220) is packed with shoppers, bar-hoppers, workers, kids and tourists. It's a real beauty.

Food & Drink

Gastro culture is on the rise in Croatia, particularly in the northern Adriatic region of Istria. Making the most of its Mediterranean ingredients, you'll find it producing fantastic olive oil, incredible truffles, seafood and fish, and some great wine. But the southern Dalmatian region isn't holding back either, with its cheese, brandy, wine and fabulous smoked ham.

❶ Slow Food

Check out Croatia's own version of slow food, which is all about promoting local, fresh and seasonal ingredients, and enjoying the ritual of eating. Not only that, but each course is paired with fitting wines (see p52 for more). Go on, get proficient in the joy of eating.

❷ Olive Oil

Istria leads the way on the path to Croatia's olive oil perfection (see p54). A sophisticated small-business industry has rooted itself in the region, making olive oil tasting sessions one of the more popular activities around.

❸ Wine

Go to Istria for its excellent white *malvazija*, red *teran* and sweet *muškat*. You can even follow a wine trail across the peninsula, visiting the growers and their cellars. Dalmatia's *pošip*, *rukatac* and *grk* from Korčula are corkers, while *dingač* and *postup* from the Pelješac Peninsula are some of Croatia's best (see p53 for more).

(Continued from page 60)

Heritage site and is easily accessible from either Zagreb or Zadar. The falls are at their watery best in the spring.

Krka National Park (p212) is an even more extensive series of lakes and waterfalls than Plitvice. The Zrmanja, Krka, Cetina and Neretva Rivers form waterfalls, but Manojlovac's power plant upstream can interfere with the flow, which can slow considerably in July or August. The main access point is in Skradinski Buk, with the largest cascade covering 800m.

The Kornati Islands (p214) consist of 140 islands, islets and reefs scattered over 300 sq km. They are sparsely inhabited and sparsely vegetated, but the great indented form of the islands and extraordinary rock formations make them an Adriatic highlight. Unless you have your own boat, however, you'll need to join an organised tour from Zadar.

The northwestern half of the island of Mljet (p277) has been named a national park due to its two highly indented salt-water lakes surrounded by lush vegetation. Maquis is thicker and taller on Mljet than nearly anywhere else in the Mediterranean, which makes it a natural refuge for many animals. Snakes nearly overran the island until the Indian mongoose was introduced in 1909. This idyllic island is accessible by regular boats from Dubrovnik.

The Brijuni Islands (p163) are the most cultivated national park since they were developed as a tourist resort in the late 19th century. They were the getaway paradise for Tito and now attract glitterati, their helpers and their yachts. Most of the exotic animals and plants were introduced (elephants are not normally found in the Adriatic), but the islands are lovely. Access to the islands is restricted, however, and you must visit on an organised tour.

ENVIRONMENTAL ISSUES

The lack of heavy industry in Croatia has had the happy effect of leaving its forests, coasts, rivers and air generally fresh and unpolluted, but, as ever, an increase in investment and development brings forth problems and threats to the environment. With the tourist boom, the demand for fresh fish and shellfish has risen exponentially. As it is no longer possible to fish their way out of the problem, the only alternative for Croats is to grow their own seafood. The production of farmed sea bass, sea bream and tuna (for export) is rising substantially with all the resulting environmental pressure along the coast. It's particularly disturbing that Croatian tuna farms capture the young fish for fattening before they have a chance to reproduce and replenish the fish population.

Although 23% of Croatia is covered by forests, they are under serious threat. It's estimated that about 50% of the forests are imperilled as a result of acid rain, mostly from neighbouring countries. Logging and building projects are cutting into forested land at the rate of about 1000 hectares a year.

Coastal and island forests face particular problems. First logged by Venetians to build ships, then by local people desperate for fuel, centuries of neglect have left many island and coastal mountains barren. The dry summers and brisk *maestrals* (strong, steady westerly winds) also pose substantial fire hazards along the coast. In the last 20 years, fires have destroyed 7% of Croatia's forests.

The Adriatic's temperature ranges from 7°C in December up to 23°C in September.

Although the sea along the Adriatic coast is among the cleanest in the world, overfishing has greatly reduced the fish population.

The website of the Ministry of Environmental Protection (www.mzopu .hr) is the place for the latest news on Croatia's environment.

Zagreb

Everyone knows about Croatia, its coast, beaches and islands, but a mention of the country's capital still draws confused questions: 'Is it nice?' 'Worth going to for a weekend?' Well, here it is, once and for all: yes, Zagreb is a great destination, weekend or week-long. There's lots of culture, arts, music, architecture, gastronomy and all the other things that make a quality capital. Admittedly, it doesn't register highly on a nightlife Richter scale, but it does have an ever-developing art and music scene, and a growing influx of fun-seeking travellers.

Zagreb is made for strolling the streets, drinking coffee in the almost permanently full cafés, popping into museums and galleries, and enjoying the theatres, concerts, cinema and music. It's a year-round outdoor city: in spring and summer everyone scurries to Jarun Lake in the southwest to swim, boat or dance the night away at a lakeside disco, while in autumn and winter Zagrebians go skiing at Mt Medvednica, only a tram ride away, or hiking in nearby Samobor.

Visually, Zagreb is a mixture of straight-laced Austro-Hungarian architecture and rough-around-the-edges socialist structures. Its character is a sometimes uneasy combination of these two elements: try hard as they may, frequenters of Zagreb's elegant galleries, high-class restaurants and alternative art and music venues cannot quite ignore the vast turbo folk crowds, attesting to the city's – and the country's – lasting struggle between its perceived Central European sophistication and Balkan 'savagery'. But perhaps therein lies much of its charm – the mixture of and the schism between these two characteristics have given Zagreb a personality all of its own.

HIGHLIGHTS

- Sipping coffee and cocktails alfresco along **Tkalčićeva** (p87)
- Strolling along the winding streets of Zagreb's **Upper Town** (p73)
- Gorging on *štrukli* (dumplings filled with cottage cheese) in **Samobor** (p93), after a day's hiking
- Coveting the paintings at the **Museum Mimara** (p80)
- Picnicking in **Maksimir Park** (p81)
- Contemplating mortality amid the trees and tombs in **Mirogoj** (p80)

- TELEPHONE CODE: 01

HISTORY

Zagreb's known history begins with two hills. Kaptol, now the site of Zagreb's cathedral, was a thriving canonical settlement in the 11th century while another small settlement was developing on nearby Gradec hill. Both were devastated by the Mongol invasion of 1242.

In order to attract foreign artisans to the ruined region, King Bela walled Gradec and turned it into a sort of royally controlled 'fiscal paradise' (tax haven) with numerous privileges. Kaptol remained unprivileged, unwalled and under the church's jurisdiction. As the centuries rolled on, a ruinous rivalry developed between the two towns that frequently descended into violence and near-warfare.

On a number of occasions, the bishops of Kaptol excommunicated the entire town of Gradec, which responded by looting and burning Kaptol. The two communities were finally united by their common commercial interests, such as the three annual fairs that brought merchants and money to the neighbourhood.

In the middle of the 15th century, the Ottomans reached the Sava River, prompting the bishop to finally fortify Kaptol. By the mid-16th century, they had taken much of the surrounding territory, but not the two hill towns, which, having lost their economic importance by the beginning of the 17th century, decided to merge into one town. Thus Zagreb was born.

Zagreb emerged as the capital of the tiny Croatian state largely because there were few towns left standing after the Turkish onslaught. The commercial life of the city stagnated during the ensuing two centuries of warfare, fires and plague, and in 1756 the seat of Croatian government fled from Zagreb to Varaždin, where it remained until 1776. By the end of the 18th century, Zagreb had a mere 2800 residents, the majority of whom were German or Hungarian.

Meanwhile, the space now known as Trg Josipa Jelačića grew as a commercial centre and became the site of Zagreb's lucrative trade fairs, spurring construction around its edges. In the 19th century the economy expanded with the development of a prosperous clothing trade, a steam mill and tannery, and a rail link connecting Zagreb with Vienna and Budapest, and the city's cultural and educational life blossomed, too.

Zagreb also became the centre for the Illyrian movement that was pressing for south-Slavic unification, greater autonomy within the Austro-Hungarian Empire and recognition of the Slavic language. Count Janko Drašković, lord of Trakošćan Castle, published a manifesto in Illyrian in 1832 and his call for a national revival resounded throughout Croatia.

Drašković's dream came to fruition when Croatia and its capital joined the Kingdom of Serbs, Croats and Slovenes after WWI. Between the two world wars, working-class neighbourhoods emerged in Zagreb between the railway and the Sava River, and new residential quarters were built on the southern slopes of Mt Medvednica. In April 1941, the Germans invaded Yugoslavia and entered Zagreb without resistance. Ante Pavelić and the Ustaše moved quickly to proclaim the establishment of the Independent State of Croatia (Nezavisna Država Hrvatska), with Zagreb as its capital (see p33 for more on Pavelić and the Ustaše). Although Pavelić ran his fascist state from Zagreb until 1944, he never enjoyed a great deal of support within the capital, which consistently maintained support for Tito's Partisans.

In postwar Yugoslavia, Zagreb (to its chagrin) took second place to Belgrade but continued to expand, with the development of Zagreb Airport and the Zagreb fairgrounds.

Zagreb was made the capital of Croatia in 1991, the same year that the country became independent.

ORIENTATION

Lying between the southern slopes of Mt Medvednica and the Sava River, Zagreb covers 631 sq km. Most of the city's highlights lie within the Upper Town (Gornji Grad), which includes the neighbourhoods of Gradec and Kaptol, and the Lower Town (Donji Grad), which runs between the Upper Town and the train station. The majestic central square of the Lower Town is Trg Josipa Jelačića, which is the hub for most of Zagreb's trams. Radiating west from the square is Ilica, the main commercial street; north of the square are the medieval Gradec and Kaptol neighbourhoods. Many streets in the Upper and Lower Towns are closed to cars.

The train station is in the southern part of the city. As you come out of the train station, you'll see a series of parks and pavilions directly in front of you, which lead into the centre of town.

The bus station is 1km east of the train station. Trams 2, 3 and 6 run from the bus station to the train station. Tram 6 goes to Trg Josipa Jelačića.

See p293 for more information on the use of street names in Zagreb.

INFORMATION
Bookshops
Algoritam (Gajeva 1; ☺ 8am-7pm Mon-Fri, 9am-5pm Sat) This shop off Trg Josipa Jelačića has a wide selection of books and magazines in English, French, German, Italian and Croatian to choose from. It's inside the Hotel Dubrovnik but accessed through a separate entrance.
Knjižara Ljevak (Ilica 1; ☺ 8am-7pm Mon-Fri, 9am-5pm Sat) Has an excellent selection of maps as well as English translations of destination guides and Croatian cookbooks.

Emergency
Police station (☎ 45 63 311; Petrinjska 30) Assists foreigners with visa problems.

Internet Access
In addition to the place listed here, there are a number of smaller internet cafés along Preradovićeva.
Sublink (☎ 48 11 329; www.sublink.hr; Teslina 12; per hr 15KN; ☺ 9am-10pm Mon-Sat, 3-10pm Sun) It was the city's first cybercafé and it remains its best.

Laundry
If you're staying in private accommodation you can usually ask the owner to do your laundry, which would be cheaper than the two options listed here. Both charge about 60KN for 5kg of laundry.
Petecin (Kaptol 11; ☺ 8am-8pm Mon-Fri)
Predom (Draškovićeva 31; ☺ 7am-7pm Mon-Fri)

Left Luggage
Garderoba bus station (per hr 1.20KN; ☺ 5am-10pm Mon-Sat, 6am-10pm Sun); train station (per hr 1.20KN; ☺ 24hr)

Libraries
British Council (☎ 48 13 700; Ilica 12; ☺ 10am-4.30pm Mon, Tue, Thu & Fri, 1.30-6.30pm Wed) Has a library where you can read British and American newspapers, books and periodicals, watch BBC news and borrow books and DVDs. It also sponsors plays, concerts and exhibitions.
French Cultural Institute (☎ 48 10 745; Preradovićeva 40; ☺ media centre 10am-5pm Mon-Thu, to 4pm Fri, library 10am-5pm Mon-Fri) Has a reading room

and media centre. Enter at 5 Preradovićeva to listen to French tapes or watch French news in the media centre. The institute's library has a selection of French books, magazines and newspapers. Both the media centre and library are closed for five or six weeks in the summer.

Medical Services
Dental Emergency (☎ 48 28 488; Perkovčeva 3; ☺ 24hr)
KBC Rebro (☎ 23 88 888; Kišpatićeva 12; ☺ 24hr) East of the city, it provides emergency aid.
Pharmacy (☎ 48 16 198; Trg Josipa Jelačića 3; ☺ 24hr)

Money
There are ATMs at the bus and train stations, the airport, and at numerous locations around town. There are banks in the train and bus stations that accept travellers cheques, and exchange offices can be found in the Importanne Centar, Zagreb's main shopping centre, on Starčevićev Trg. Atlas Travel Agency (below) is the Amex representative in Zagreb.

Post
Main post office (☎ 48 11 090; Jurišićeva 13; ☺ 8am-7pm Mon-Fri, 9am-5pm Sat) Has a telephone centre.
Post office (☎ 49 81 300; Branimirova 4; ☺ 24hr Mon-Sat, 1pm-midnight Sun) Holds poste restante mail. This post office is also the best place to send packages.

Tourist Information
Main tourist office (☎ 48 14 051; www.zagreb-tourist info.hr; Trg Josipa Jelačića 11; ☺ 8.30am-8pm Mon-Fri, 9am-5pm Sat, 10am-2pm Sun) Distributes city maps and free leaflets. It also sells the Zagreb Card (see p77).
Plitvice National Park Office (☎ 46 13 586; Trg Kralja Tomislava 19; ☺ 9am-5pm Mon-Fri) Has details on Croatia's national parks.
Tourist office annexe (☎ 49 21 645; Trg Nikole Šubića Zrinjskog 14; ☺ 9am-6pm Mon-Fri) Same services as the main tourist office but less documentation.
Zagreb County Tourist Association (☎ 48 73 665; www.tzzz.hr; Preradovićeva 42; ☺ 8am-4pm Mon-Fri) Has information about attractions in the region outside Zagreb.

Travel Agencies
Atlas Travel Agency (☎ 48 07 300; Zrinjevac 17; ☺ 8am-7pm Mon-Fri, 9am-5pm Sat) Amex representative.
Croatia Express (☎ 49 22 237; www.zug.hr; Trg Kralja Tomislava 17; ☺ 9.30am-7pm Mon-Fri, 9am-3pm Sat) At this office opposite the train station you can change money, make train reservations, rent cars, buy air and ferry tickets, and book hotels around the country.
Dali Travel (☎ 48 47 472; travelsection@hfhs.hr; Dežmanova 9; ☺ 9am-5pm Mon-Fri) The travel branch

of the Croatian YHA can provide information on HI hostels throughout Croatia and make advance bookings. **Dalmacijaturist** (☎ 48 73 073; Zrinjevac 16; ⏰ 8am-7pm Mon-Fri, 9am-3pm Sat) Next to the tourist office annexe. Specialises in the Dalmatian coast; also books excursions and air tickets and is a good source of information on boat and ferry routes along the coast. **Generalturist** (☎ 48 10 033; www.generalturist.com; Praška 5; ⏰ 9.30am-7pm Mon-Fri, 9am-3pm Sat) Has branches throughout Croatia and books excursions to the coast, cruises and plane tickets. Bookings are done at the office on Petrićeva. **Marko Polo** (☎ 48 15 216; Masarykova 24; ⏰ 9am-6.30pm Mon-Fri, to 2pm Sat) Handles information and ticketing for Jadrolinija's coastal ferries.

SIGHTS

As the oldest part of Zagreb, the Upper Town has landmark buildings and churches from the earlier centuries of Zagreb's history. The Lower Town has the city's most interesting art museums and fine examples of 19th- and 20th-century architecture.

Keep track of the latest special exhibitions in the Zagreb tourist office's monthly *Zagreb Events & Performances* guide, but bear in mind that nearly everything is closed on Monday.

Upper Town

DOLAC FRUIT & VEGETABLE MARKET
Zagreb's colourful **Dolac fruit & vegetable market** (⏰ 6am-3pm) is just north of Trg Josipa Jelačića. It's the buzzing centre of Zagreb's daily activity, with traders coming from all over Croatia to sell their products here. The Dolac has been heaving since the 1930s when the city authorities set up a market space on the 'border' between the Upper and Lower towns. The main part of the market is on an elevated square; the street level has indoor stalls selling meat and dairy products and, a little further towards the square, flowers. The stalls at the northern end of the market are packed with locally produced honey, handmade ornaments and super-cheap food.

KAPTOL SQUARE
The medieval Upper Town centres on Kaptol Sq. Most of the buildings here date from the 17th century. Make sure you take a peek at the **Stone Gate**, the eastern gate to medieval Gradec Town, now a shrine. According to legend, a great fire in 1731 destroyed every part of the wooden gate except for the painting of the Virgin and Child

by an unknown 17th-century artist. People believe that the painting possesses magical powers and come regularly to pray before it, light candles and leave flowers. Square stone slabs are engraved with thanks and praise to the Virgin.

On the western facade of the Stone Gate you'll see a **statue of Dora**, the hero of an 18th-century historical novel who lived with her father next to the Stone Gate.

CATHEDRAL OF THE ASSUMPTION OF THE BLESSED VIRGIN MARY
Kaptol Sq is dominated by this **cathedral** (Katedrala Marijina Uznešenja; ☎ 48 14 727; Kaptol; admission free; ⏰ 7am-7.30pm), formerly known as St Stephen's. Its twin spires – seemingly permanently under repair – soar over the city. Construction of this cathedral (on the site of an earlier Romanesque cathedral, which had been destroyed by the Tartar invasion in 1242) began in the second half of the 13th century. It followed the prototype of the Church of St Urban in Troyes, France.

Although the cathedral's original Gothic structure has been transformed many times over, the sacristy still contains a cycle of **frescoes** that date from the second half of the 13th century. As the furthest outpost of Christianity in the 15th century, the cathedral was surrounded by walls with towers, one of which is still visible on the eastern side. An earthquake in 1880 badly damaged the cathedral and reconstruction in a neo-Gothic style began around the turn of the 20th century.

Despite the scars inflicted on the structure, there is much to admire on the inside. Notice the **triptych** by Albrecht Dürer on the side altar; the baroque marble altars, statues and pulpit; and the **tomb of Cardinal Alojzije Stepinac** by Ivan Meštrović.

To the north of the cathedral, an **Archbishop's Palace** was built in the 18th century in a baroque style, but little remains. Under the northeastern wing of the cathedral is a **19th-century park** with a sculpture of a female nude by Antun Augustinčić.

JESUIT CHURCH OF ST CATHERINE
This fine baroque **church** (Crkva Svete Katarine; ☎ 48 51 959; Katarinin Trg; ⏰ 7am-noon) was built between 1620 and 1632. Although battered by fire and earthquake, the facade still gleams and the interior contains a fine altar dating from 1762. The interior stucco work dates

ZAGREB

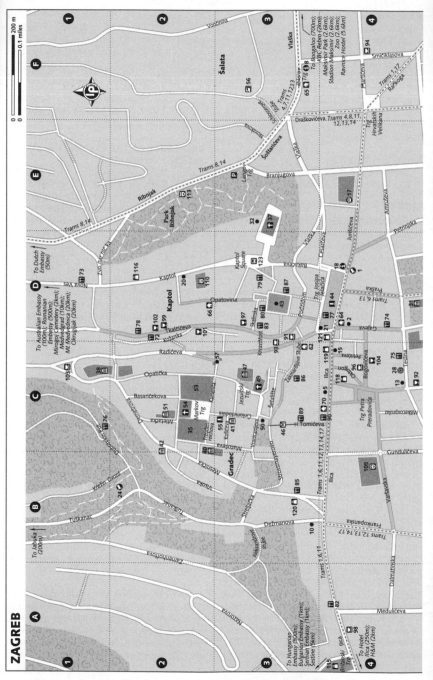

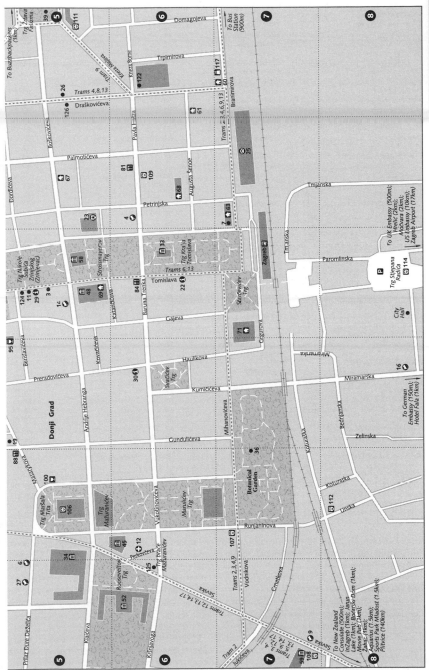

ZAGREB

from 1720 and there are 18th-century medallions depicting the life of St Catherine on the ceiling of the nave.

GALERIJA KLOVIĆEVI DVORI

This **gallery** (☎ 48 51 926; www.galerijaklovic.hr; Jezuitski Trg 4; adult/student 40/20KN; ☺ 11am-7pm Tue-Sun) is housed in a former Jesuit monastery and is the city's most prestigious space for exhibiting modern Croatian and international art, presented in a series of changing exhibitions.

Some of the more noted exhibitions have included Picasso and, more recently, Chagall, as well as collections of Croatia's prominent fine artists, such as Lovro Artuković and Ivan Lovrenčić. If you're looking for an unusual, arty souvenir, try the gallery's gift shop. There's also a nice café attached to the gallery.

Opposite the gallery is the 18th-century **Dverce mansion**, which was restored in the 19th century and is now used for official receptions.

Before leaving the square, note the **fountain** with the statue *Fisherman with Snake*, which was created by Simeon Roksandić in 1908.

SABOR

The eastern side of Markov Trg is taken up by the Croatian **sabor** (parliament), built in 1910 on the site of baroque 17th- and 18th-century townhouses. Its neoclassical style is quite incongruous on the square, but the historical (and present) importance of this building is undeniable – Croatia's secession from the Austro-Hungarian Empire was proclaimed from its balcony in 1918, and it is the centre of Croatian politics today.

ST MARK'S CHURCH

This **church** (Crkva Svetog Marka; ☎ 48 51 611; Markov Trg; ☽ 11am-4pm & 5.30-7pm) is one of Zagreb's most emblematic buildings. Its colourful tiled roof was constructed in 1880 and the tiles on the left side depict the medieval coat of arms of Croatia, Dalmatia and Slavonia, while the emblem of Zagreb is on the right side. The 13th-century church was named for the annual St Mark's fair, which was held in Gradec at the time, and it retains a 13th-century Romanesque window on the southern side. The Gothic portal composed of 15 figures in shallow niches was sculpted in the 14th century. The present bell tower replaces an earlier one that was destroyed by an earthquake in 1502. The interior contains sculptures by Meštrović.

It is unfortunate that the church's courtyard (ie the square itself) is used as a car park for government members.

CROATIAN NATURAL HISTORY MUSEUM

This **museum** (Hrvatski Prirodoslovni Muzej; ☎ 48 51 700; Demetrova 1; adult/concession 15/7KN; ☽ 10am-5pm Tue-Fri, to 1pm Sat & Sun) houses a collection of prehistoric tools and bones excavated from the Krapina cave as well as exhibits showing the evolution of animal and plant life in Croatia. Temporary exhibits often focus on specific regions.

BANSKI DVORI

The **Banski Dvori** (Ban's Palace; Markov Trg) was once the seat of Croatian viceroys and is now the presidential palace. The building is composed of two baroque mansions and houses courts, archives and other government offices. In October 1991 the palace was bombed by the

federal army, in what some believe to have been an assassination attempt on President Franjo Tuđman. From April to September there is a guard-changing ceremony every Friday, Saturday and Sunday at noon.

Leaving Markov Trg by Ćirilometodska, you'll come across a **sculpted stone head** representing Matija Gubec, the leader of a celebrated peasant rebellion who was allegedly beheaded on the square.

MEŠTROVIĆ ATELIER

Croatia's most recognised artist is Ivan Meštrović. His former home, a 17th-century building where he worked and lived from 1922 to 1942, is now the **Meštrović Atelier** (☎ 48 51 123; Mletačka 8; adult/concession 30/15KN; ☽ 10am-6pm Tue-Fri, to 2pm Sat & Sun). The excellent collection has some 100 sculptures, drawings, lithographs and furniture from the first four decades of his artistic life. Meštrović, who also worked as an architect (see boxed text, p80), designed many parts of the house himself.

CITY MUSEUM

The **City Museum** (Muzej Grada Zagreba; ☎ 48 51 364; www.mdc.hr/mgz; Opatička 20; adult/concession 20/10KN; ☽ 10am-6pm Tue-Fri, to 1pm Sat & Sun) sits in the 17th-century Convent of St Clair, which is built along the eastern wall of the town. Since 1907 the convent has housed a historical museum presenting the history of Zagreb in documents, artwork and crafts, plus interactive exhibits that fascinate kids. Most interesting is a scale model of old Gradec. Summaries of the exhibits are posted in English and German in each room and evocative music accompanies your visit.

ZAGREB

ZAGREB IN...

Two Days

Start your day with a stroll through Strossmayerov Trg, Zagreb's oasis of greenery. While you're there, take a look at the **Strossmayer Gallery of Old Masters** (opposite) and then walk to **Trg Josipa Jelačića** (below), the city's centre.

Head up to **Kaptol Square** (p73) for a look at the **Cathedral of the Assumption of the Blessed Virgin Mary** (p73), the centre of Zagreb's (and Croatia's) religious life. While you're in the Upper Town, pick up some fruit at the **Dolac fruit & vegetable market** (p73) or, better, have lunch at **Kerempuh** (p85). Then get to know the work of Croatia's best sculptor at **Meštrović Atelier** (p77) and see its naïve art legacy at the **Croatian Museum of Naïve Art** (below) or take in a contemporary art exhibition at **Galerija Klovićevi Dvori** (p76). See the lay of the city from the top of **Lotršćak Tower** (below). The evening is best spent having a drink at **Škola** (p87) or bar-crawling along **Tkalčićeva** (p87).

On the second day, tour the Lower Town museums, reserving a good two hours for the **Museum Mimara** (p80). Lunch at **Tip Top** (p85) and digest in the **Botanical Garden** (p80). Early evening is best at Trg Petra Preradovića before dining at one of the Lower Town restaurants and sampling some of Zagreb's nightlife.

Four Days

Your third day should take in the lovely **Mirogoj cemetery** (p80), with maybe a stop at **Medvedgrad** (p81) or **Maksimir Park** (p81).

On your last day, make a trip out to **Samobor** (p93) for a heavy dose of small-town charm. Eat, drink and then take a nice walk to digest it all.

CROATIAN HISTORY MUSEUM

Located in a gorgeous baroque building, the **Croatian History Museum** (Hrvatski Povijesni Muzej; ☎ 48 51 900; www.hismus.hr; Matoševa 9; adult/concession 10/5KN; ☼ 10am-5pm Mon-Fri, to 1pm Sat & Sun) displays an interesting collection of flags, stones, fine art, photos, documents and maps tracing Croatia's history.

CROATIAN MUSEUM OF NAÏVE ART

If you like Croatia's naïve art, a form that was highly fashionable locally and worldwide during the 1960s and 1970s and has declined somewhat since, the **Croatian Museum of Naïve Art** (Hrvatski Muzej Naivne Umjetnosti; ☎ 48 51 911; www.hmnu.org; Ćirilometodska 3; adult/student 10/5KN; ☼ 10am-6pm Tue-Fri, to 1pm Sat) will be a feast. The small museum houses over 1000 paintings, drawings and some sculpture by the discipline's most important artists, such as Generalić, Mraz, Virius and Smaljić. For more on these artists, see p105.

Don't miss the fun and technicolour sculptures produced by Sofija Naletilić Penavuša (1913–94), an illiterate Hercegovinian woman who first started making wooden sculptures to amuse her grandson and then became massively popular during the 1980s and 1990s.

LOTRŠĆAK TOWER

The **Lotršćak Tower** (Kula Lotršćak; ☎ 48 51 926; Strossmayerovo Šetalište; admission 10KN; ☼ 11am-8pm Tue-Sun) was built in the middle of the 13th century in order to protect the southern city gate. For the last hundred years a cannon has been fired every day at noon commemorating an event from Zagreb's history. According to legend, a cannon was fired at noon one day at the Turks camped across the Sava River. On its way across the river, the cannonball happened to hit a rooster. The rooster was blown to bits and, the story goes, that's why the Turks became so demoralised and failed to attack the city. A less fanciful explanation is that the cannon shot allows churches to synchronise their clocks.

The tower may be climbed for a sweeping 360-degree view of the city. Near the tower is a **funicular railway** (3KN), which was constructed in 1888 and connects the Lower and Upper Towns.

Lower Town
TRG JOSIPA JELAČIĆA

Zagreb's main orientation point and the geographic heart of the city is Trg Josipa Jelačića. This is where most people arrange to meet up, and if you want quality people-watching you can sit in one of the cafés and watch the tram-loads of people getting out, greeting each other and dispersing among the newspaper and flower sellers.

The square's name comes from Ban Jelačić, the 19th-century *ban* (viceroy or governor) who led Croatian troops into an unsuccessful battle with Hungary in the hope of winning more autonomy for his people. The **equestrian statue** of Jelačić stood in the square from 1866 until 1947, when Tito ordered its removal because it was too closely linked with Croatian nationalism. Franjo Tuđman's government then dug it up out of storage in 1990 and returned it to the square.

Most of the buildings date from the 19th century; note the reliefs by sculptor Ivan Meštrović at No 4.

ARCHAEOLOGICAL MUSEUM

The **Archaeological Museum** (Arheološki Muzej; ☎ 48 73 101; www.amz.hr; Trg Nikole Šubića Zrinjskog; adult/concession 20/10KN; ☺ 10am-5pm Tue-Fri, to 1pm Sat & Sun) has artefacts that stem from prehistoric times onwards. Among the most interesting are the 'Vučedolska golubica' (Vučedol Dove), a 4000-year-old ceramic censer found near the town of Vukovar. The 'bird' has since become a symbol of Vukovar and peace. Also fascinating are the **Egyptian mummies**, with ambient sounds and light designed to provoke pondering. The **coin collection** is one of the most important in Europe, containing some 260,000 coins, medals, medallions and decorations.

The courtyard has a collection of **Roman monuments** dating from the 5th to 4th centuries BC and functions as an open-air café in summer.

STROSSMAYER GALLERY OF OLD MASTERS

This **museum** (Strossmayerova Galerija Starih Majstora; ☎ 48 95 115; www.mdc.hr/strossmayer; Zrinjevac 11; adult/concession 10/5KN; ☺ 10am-1pm & 5-7pm Tue, 10am-1pm Wed-Sun) is housed in the 19th-century neo-Renaissance Croatian Academy of Arts and Sciences. This lovely building showcases the impressive fine-art collection donated to the city by the illustrious Bishop Strossmayer in 1884.

The museum includes Italian masters from the 14th to 19th centuries such as G Bellini, Tintoretto, Veronese and Tiepolo; Dutch and Flemish painters such as J Brueghel the Younger; French and Spanish artists Proudhon, Carpeaux and El Greco;

and the classic Croatian artists Medulić and Benković.

The interior courtyard contains the **Baška Slab** (Bašćanska ploča), a stone tablet from the island of Krk, which contains the oldest example of Glagolitic script, dating from 1102. There is also a **statue of Bishop Strossmayer** by Ivan Meštrović.

GALLERY OF MODERN ART

West of the Strossmayer Gallery is the **Gallery of Modern Art** (Moderna Galerija; ☎ 49 22 368; Andrije Hebranga 1; adult/concession 20/10KN; ☺ 10am-6pm Tue-Fri, to 1pm Sat), which has a glorious display of Croatian artists of the last 200 years, including such 19th- and 20th-century Croatian masters as Bukovac, Mihanović and Račić. It's an excellent overview of the vibrant Croatian arts scene.

ART PAVILION

The yellow **Art Pavilion** (Umjetnički Paviljon; ☎ 48 41 070; www.umjetnicki-paviljon.hr; Trg Kralja Tomislava 22; adult/concession 20/10KN; ☺ 11am-7pm Mon-Sat, 10am-1pm Sun) presents changing exhibitions of contemporary art. Constructed in 1897 in stunning art nouveau style, the pavilion is the only space in Zagreb that was specifically designed to host large exhibitions.

ARTS & CRAFTS MUSEUM

Built between 1882 and 1892, this **museum** (Muzej za Umjetnost i Obrt; ☎ 48 82 111; www.muo.hr, in Croatian; Trg Maršala Tita 10; adult/student 30/15KN; ☺ 10am-6pm Tue-Fri, to 1pm Sat & Sun) exhibits furniture, textiles, metal, ceramic and glass dating from the Middle Ages to contemporary times. You can see Gothic and baroque sculptures from northern Croatia as well as paintings, prints, bells, stoves, rings, clocks, bound books, toys, photos and industrial designs. The museum also contains an important library and there are frequent temporary exhibitions.

ETHNOGRAPHIC MUSEUM

This **museum** (Etnografski Muzej; ☎ 48 26 220; www.emz.hr; Trg Mažuranićev 14; adult/concession 15/10KN, free Thu; ☺ 10am-6pm Tue-Thu, to 1pm Fri-Sun) is worth a visit, especially on Thursdays when admission is free. It's housed in a domed building dating from 1903 and contains some 70,000 items that catalogue the ethnographic heritage of Croatia. Only about 2750 exhibits are on display, including ceramics, jewellery, musical instruments, tools and weapons, as well

ZAGREB

ART VERSUS HISTORY

The **Croatian Association of Fine Artists** (Hrvatsko Društvo Likovnih Umjetnika; ☎ 46 11 818; www .hdlu.hr; Trg Žrtava Fašizma; admission free; ❂ 11am-7pm Tue-Fri, 10am-2pm Sat & Sun) is one of the few architectural works by Ivan Meštrović and a building that's had several fascinating incarnations that reflect the region's history in a nutshell.

Originally designed by Meštrović in 1938 as an exhibition pavilion, the structure honoured King Petar Karađorđević – the ruler of the Kingdom of Serbs, Croats and Slovenes – which grated against the sensibilities of Croatia's nationalists. With the onset of Croatia's fascist government, the building was renamed The Zagreb Artists' Centre in May 1941, but several months later Ante Pavelić, Croatia's fascist leader, gave orders for the building to be evacuated of all artwork and turned into a mosque. This was, according to him, so that the local Muslim population would feel at home in Croatia (there was no other mosque at the time to serve the needs of these people). There were murmurs of disapproval from the artists, but the building was significantly restructured and eventually surrounded by three minarets.

With the establishment of Socialist Yugoslavia, however, the mosque was promptly closed and the building's original purpose restored, although the government renamed it the Museum of the People's Liberation. A permanent exhibition was set up and, in 1949, the government had the minarets knocked down. In 1951, an architect called V Richter set about returning the building to its original state according to Meštrović's design. The building has remained an exhibition space ever since, with a nonprofit, nongovernment association of Croatian artists making use of it. Despite being renamed the Croatian Association of Fine Artists in 1991 by the country's new government, everyone in Zagreb still knows it as 'the old mosque'.

as Croatian folk costumes, gold-embroidered scarves from Slavonia and lace from the island of Pag. Thanks to donations from the Croatian explorers Mirko and Stevo Seljan, there are also interesting artefacts from South America, the Congo, Ethiopia, China, Japan, New Guinea and Australia. Fascinating temporary exhibitions are often held on the 2nd floor.

MUSEUM MIMARA

Zagreb's best art collection is at the **Museum Mimara** (Muzej Mimara; ☎ 48 28 100; Roosveltov Trg 5; adult/concession 20/15KN; ❂ 10am-5pm Tue, Wed, Fri & Sat, to 7pm Thu, to 2pm Sun). This is the diverse private collection of Ante Topić Mimara, who donated over 3750 priceless objects to his native Zagreb, even though he spent much of his life in Salzburg, Austria.

Housed in a neo-Renaissance former school building (1883), the collection spans a wide range of periods and regions. There is an archaeological collection with 200 items from Egypt, Mesopotamia, Persia, Greece, Rome and early medieval Europe; exhibits of ancient Far Eastern artworks; a glass, textile and furniture collection that spans centuries; and 1000 European art objects.

In painting, Italian artists Raphael, Veronese, Caravaggio and Canaletto are represented. Dutch artists Rembrandt and Ruisdael are also present, and there are Flemish paintings from Bosch, Rubens and Van Dyck. Spanish painters Velázquez, Murillo and Goya, German and English painters, and French masters de la Tour, Boucher, Delacroix, Corot, Manet, Renoir and Degas are also in the collection.

BOTANICAL GARDEN

If you need a change from museums, galleries and/or shopping and schlepping, take a break in this lovely **garden** (Botanički Vrt; http://hirc.botanic .hr; Mihanovićeva bb; admission free; ❂ 7am-9pm Apr-Oct). Laid out in 1890, the garden has 10,000 species of plant, including 1800 tropical flora specimens. The landscaping has created restful corners and paths that seem a world away from bustling Zagreb.

North of the Centre

MIROGOJ

A 10-minute ride north of the city centre on bus 106 from the cathedral (or a 30-minute walk through leafy streets) takes you to **Mirogoj cemetery** (❂ 6am-10pm), at the base of Mt Medvednica. This is without a doubt one of the most beautiful cemeteries in Europe – one wag commented that the people here are better housed in death than they ever were in life. The cemetery was designed in 1876 by one of Croatia's finest architects, Herman Bollé, who also created numerous buildings around Zagreb. In Mirogoj he built a majestic arcade topped by a string of cupolas, which looks like a fortress from the outside but is calm and graceful on the inside. The cemetery is lush and green and the paths are interspersed with sculpture and artfully designed tombs. Highlights include the graves of poet Petar Preradović and the political leader Stjepan Radić, the bust of Vladimir Becić by Ivan Meštrović and the sculpture by Mihanović for the Mayer family. The newest addition at Mirogoj is a **memorial cross** in honour of the fallen soldiers in Croatia's Homeland War.

MEDVEDGRAD

The medieval fortress of **Medvedgrad** (admission free; ⊗ 7am-10pm), on the southern side of Mt Medvednica just above the city, is Zagreb's most important medieval monument. Built from 1249 to 1254, it was erected to protect the city from Tartar invasions and is itself well protected by high rocks. The fortress was owned by a succession of aristocratic families but fell into ruin as a result of an earthquake and general neglect. Restoration began in 1979, but was pursued with greater enthusiasm in 1993 and 1994 when the country was looking to honour monuments from its past. Today you can see the rebuilt thick walls and towers, a small **chapel** with frescoes and the **Shrine of the Homeland**, which pays homage to those who have died for a free Croatia. On a clear day, it also offers a beautiful view of Zagreb and surrounds.

East of the Centre
MAKSIMIR PARK

This **park** (Maksimirska; ⊗ 9am-dusk) is a peaceful wooded enclave covering 18 hectares; it is easily accessible by trams 4, 7, 11 and 12. Opened to the public in 1794, it was the first public promenade in southeastern Europe and is landscaped like an English garden-style park with alleys, lawns and artificial lakes. The most photographed structure in the park is the exquisite **Bellevue Pavilion**, which was constructed in 1843, but there is also the **Echo Pavilion** and a house built to resemble a rustic Swiss cottage. There's also a modest **zoo** (adult/under 8yr 20/10KN; ⊗ 9am-8pm), which came up with the novel idea of installing 'cages' for humans to educate the big-brained wonders about their impact on the environment.

ACTIVITIES

The **Sports Park Mladost** (☎ 36 58 541; Jarunska 5, Jarun; family day ticket 60KN; ⊗ 11am-3pm & 4-8pm Mon, Tue, Thu & Fri, 11am-3pm Wed, 1-5pm Sat, 10am-2pm Sun) has outdoor and indoor Olympic-sized swimming pools, as well as smaller pools for children and a gym. To get to Jarun, take tram 5 or 7.

The **Sports & Recreational Centre Šalata** (☎ 46 10 300; www.salata.hr; hr Croatian, Schlosserove Stube 2, admission 25KN; ⊗ 1.30-6pm Mon-Fri, 11am-7pm Sat & Sun) offers outdoor and indoor tennis courts, a gym, a winter ice-skating rink and two outdoor swimming pools. There's also an indoor ice-skating rink that rents skates.

Although Zagreb is not normally associated with winter sports, if the snow lasts long enough you can ski right outside town at Sljeme, the main peak of Mt Medvednica. It has four ski runs, three ski lifts and a triple chairlift; call the **ski centre** (☎ 45 55 833) for information on snow conditions.

Jarun Lake in south Zagreb is a popular getaway for residents at any time of the year, but especially in summer when the clear waters are ideal for swimming. Although part of the lake is marked off for boating competitions, there is more than enough space to enjoy a leisurely swim. Take tram 5 or 17 to Jarun and follow signs to the *jezero* (lake). When you come to the lake you can head left to Malo Jezero for **swimming** and **canoe** or **pedal-boat** rental, or right to Veliko Jezero, where there's a **pebble beach** and **windsurfing**.

ZAGREB WALKING TOUR

You can pick up a copy of *City Walks* free from any tourist office. It suggests two walking tours around the town centre exploring both the Upper and Lower Towns.

The natural starting point of any walk in Zagreb is the buzzing **Trg Josipa Jelačića** (1; p78). Climb the steps up to **Dolac fruit & vegetable market** (2; p73) and pick up some fruit or a quick snack and head for the **cathedral** (3; p73). Cross **Kaptol Square** (4; p73), walk down Skalinska and come out at Tkalčićeva. Wander up the street and climb the stairs next to the bar **Melin** (5; p87), which will take you up to **Stone Gate** (6; p73), a fascinating shrine. Next, go up Kamenita and you'll come out at Markov Trg, the site of **St Mark's Church** (7; p77), Zagreb's most emblematic place, the **sabor** (8; p77), the country's parliament, and **Banski Dvori** (9; p77), the presidential palace. Wander

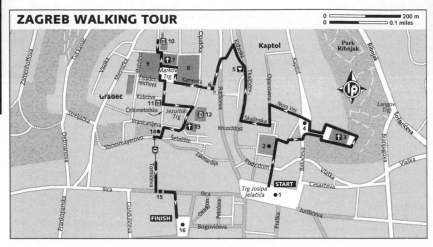

WALK FACTS

Start Trg Josipa Jelačića
End Trg Petra Preradovića
Duration 1½ hours

about the winding streets of the Upper Town and take in different aspects of Croatia's art world in **Meštrović Atelier** (**10**; p77). Walk back across Markov Trg and down Ćirilometodska, stepping into one of the country's most particular museums, the **Croatian Museum of Naïve Art** (**11**; p78). Cross Jezuitski Trg and enter **Galerija Klovićevi Dvori** (**12**; p76), where local and international contemporary art exhibitions await. When you're finished with art, gaze up at the gorgeous **Jesuit Church of St Catherine** (**13**; p73), before finally emerging at **Lotrščak Tower** (**14**; p78). Take in the cityscape, and, if you fancy, go down in the funicular. Otherwise descend the verdant stairway – both will leave you on the side of **Ilica** (**15**), Zagreb's commercial artery.

Cross Ilica and walk to **Trg Petra Preradovića** (**16**), where you can take a break at any of the (many) alfresco cafés.

ZAGREB FOR CHILDREN

Zagreb has some wonderful attractions for kids but getting around with small children can be a challenge. Between the tram tracks, high kerbs and cars, manoeuvring a stroller on the streets is not easy. Buses and trams are usually too crowded to accommodate strollers

even though buses have a designated stroller spot. Up to the age of seven, children travel free on public transport. If you choose taxis, be aware that few have working seat belts for either you or junior.

After checking out the bug collection at the Croatian Natural History Museum (p77), take your kids to the **Technical Museum** (Tehnički Muzej; ☎ 48 44 050; Savska 18; admission 15KN; ⏰ 9am-5pm Tue-Fri, to 1pm Sat & Sun), which has a planetarium, a steam-engine locomotives, scale models of satellites and space ships, and a replica of a mine within the building, as well as departments of agriculture, geology, energy and transport.

For a little open-air activity, the best place for tots to work off some steam is **Bočarski Dom** (☎ 61 95 713; Prisavlje 2). The park has the best in playground equipment, playing fields and a rollerblading ramp. There's also a relaxing path along the Sava River for parents to enjoy. To get there, take tram 17 west to the Prisavlje stop.

There are two playgrounds (as well as a zoo) inside Maksimir Park (p81), but these are smaller than those at Bočarski Dom and usually more crowded. Aquatically minded kids will like the pools in the Sports Park Mladost (p81) or Jarun Lake (p81).

TOURS

The tourist office sells tickets for two-hour walking tours (95KN) and three-hour combination bus and walking tours (150KN), which operate daily. The walking tours leave from in front of the main tourist office on Trg Josipa Jelačića and the combination tours leave from in front of the Arcotel Allegra hotel. Tickets are on sale in tourist offices, travel agencies and most hotels, and should be purchased at least one day in advance.

FESTIVALS & EVENTS

For a complete listing of Zagreb events, see www.zagreb-convention.hr. Open air events are free but admission is usually charged for the indoor concerts. Prices depend upon the concert, but tickets for most musical events can be purchased from **Koncertna Direkcija Zagreb** (☎ 45 01 200; www.kdz.hr; Kneza Mislava 18; ☉ 9am-6pm Mon-Fri). Highlights on Zagreb's calendar include the following:

Zagreb Biennial of Contemporary Music (www .biennale-zagreb.hr) Croatia's most important classical music event is held during odd-numbered years in April.

Queer Zagreb FM Festival (www.queerzagreb.org) Camp out and party during the last week of April.

Žedno Uho (Thirsty Ear) An excellent festival (held 24 to 29 April) that promotes contemporary international music with a focus on electronic sounds.

Urban Festival (www.urbanfestival.hr) A contemporary art fest with specific themes every year (5 to 15 May).

Vip INmusic Festival (www.vipinmusicfestival.com) A two-day extravaganza, this is Zagreb's highest-profile music festival. Nick Cave fronted the 2008 line-up and previous years have seen Franz Ferdinand, Iggy Pop and Morrissey take the Jarun Lake main stage. There are four stages, a camping ground and 48 sleepless, party-packed hours (from 3 to 4 June).

Animafest (www.animafest.hr) A festival of animated film is held during even-numbered years in June.

Strossmartre (www.kraljeviulice.com) An oddball's feast, this festival lasts the whole of June and stages free outdoor film screenings, concerts and things such as best-in-show mongrel dog competitions. All along the Strossmayer Promenade.

International Folklore Festival This festival has been taking place in Zagreb for over 30 years, usually for six days in July. The program includes folk dancers and singers from Croatia and other European countries dressed in traditional costumes. There are free workshops in dance, music and art that are designed to introduce you to Croatian folk culture.

Zagreb Summer Festival In July and August this festival presents a cycle of concerts and theatre performances in the Upper Town. The atrium of Galerija Klovićevi Dvori on Jezuitski Trg, the Jesuit Church of St Catherine, St Mark's Church and the Cathedral of the Assumption of the Blessed Virgin Mary are often used, and sometimes the concerts are held in squares in the Upper Town.

Zagreb Film Festival (www.zagrebfilmfestival.com) This is a major cultural event in town, so if you're in Zagreb between 19 and 24 October, don't miss the screenings or the parties that accompany them. International directors compete for the Golden Pram award.

Croatia's largest international fairs are the Zagreb spring (mid-April) and autumn (mid-September) grand trade fairs.

SLEEPING

Zagreb's accommodation scene has been undergoing a small but noticeable change with the arrival of some of Europe's budget airlines; the budget end of the market (so far rather fledgling) is consequently starting to get a pulse. Although the new hostels cater mainly to the backpacker crowd, it's a good start. For midrangers and those wanting more privacy and a homely feel, there are private rooms and apartments, arranged through agencies. The city's business and high-end hotels are in full flow, thanks to Zagreb's role as an international conference hot spot. This means that if you want to splash out, you should have plenty of choice.

Prices usually stay the same in all seasons, but be prepared for a 20% surcharge if you arrive during a festival, especially in the autumn fair. The rates of the budget and midrange hotels listed here include breakfast.

If you intend to stay in a private house or apartment, try not to arrive on Sunday because most of the agencies will be closed. Prices for doubles run from about 300KN and apartments start at 400KN per night for a studio. There's usually a surcharge for staying only one night. Some agencies worth trying include the following:

Evistas (☎ 48 39 554; evistas@zg.htnet.hr; Augusta Šenoe 28; s from 200KN, d 250KN; ☉ 9am-1.30pm & 3-8pm Mon-Fri, 9.30am-5pm Sat) This agency is recommended by the tourist office; it's closest to the train station and finds private accommodation.

InZagreb (☎ 65 23 201; www.inzagreb.com; Remetinečka 13; apt €65-86) Great apartments, centrally located, with a minimum two-night stay. The price includes bike rental and pick up/drop off from the railway or bus station. Book through the website or over the phone.

Never Stop (Nemoj Stati; ☎ 48 73 225; www.nest.hr; Boškovićeva 7a; ☉ 9am-5pm Mon-Fri) Great apartments in the centre of town, but note the minimum three-night stay. Check the website for details and contact for prices.

ZAGREB

Budget

Fulir Hostel (☎ 48 30 882; www.fulir-hostel.com; Radićeva 3a; dm low-high 100-140KN; 🖳) Right in the centre of town, seconds away from the bustle of Jelačića and bars on Tkalčićeva, the Fulir has 16 beds, friendly owners, self-catering (its proximity to Dolac market is perfect), a DVD-packed common room, satellite TV and free internet. Opened in summer 2006, it's a popular spot for shoestring travellers, so book in advance.

Omladinski Hostel (☎ 48 41 261; www.hfhs.hr; Petrinjska 77; 6-/3-bed dm per person 103/113KN, s/d 193/256KN) Although recently renovated, this place still maintains a bit of its old gloomy feel. The rooms are sparse and clean; it's relatively central and the cheapest in town.

Buzzbackpackers (☎ 23 20 267; www.buzzback packers.com; Babukićeva 1b; dm/d from 120/400KN; 🎮 🖳) More slick and bright than Fulir, but a bit further out, Buzzbackpackers is another great-value newcomer. It's clean, the rooms are bright, there's wi-fi access, free internet, a shiny kitchen, laundry service (at a charge) and a BBQ area for the summer months. Take tram 4 or 9 from the main train station to the Heinzelova stop; it's a short walk from there (check the website for detailed directions).

Ravnice Hostel (☎ /fax 23 32 325; www.ravnice-youth -hostel.hr; Ravnice 38d; dm 125KN; 🖳) This place is possibly the weakest link in Zagreb's hostel choices due to its location – it's a good 45-minute hike from the centre or a 20-minute tram ride (take 4, 7, 11 or 12 and get off at the Ravnice stop). Having said that, the quiet residential area, past Maksimir Park, is quite lovely. The rooms are clean but spartan, there's a big kitchen downstairs where tea and coffee are free, and the nice garden has ping pong tables for your entertainment. The internet is charged at 16KN per hour, laundry 50KN per load and, oddly, you have to pay 7KN for your locker.

Krovovi Grada (☎ 48 14 189; Opatovina 33; s/d/tr 200/300/400KN) Possibly the most charming of Zagreb's central budget options, this place is right in the Upper Town. The restored old house is set back from the street; rooms have creaky floors, vintage furniture and grandma blankets. There are also two large apartments with shared bathrooms that can sleep eight. The amenities may be one-star but it's a five-star location within spitting distance of the restaurants and nightlife of Tkalčićeva.

Midrange

Hotel Fala (☎ /fax 61 94 498; www.hotel-fala-zg.hr; Trnjanska 18; s/d 350/495KN; 🅿 🎮) The rooms are small and frill-free, and it takes a tram ride or a 20-minute walk to get to the centre, but it's all neat and clean. Take tram 5 or 13 to Lisinski.

Hotel Ilica (☎ 37 77 522; www.hotel-ilica.hr; Ilica 102; s/d/tr/apt 399/499/599/849KN; 🅿 🎮) A great central option, with rooms ranging from super-kitsch to lushly decorous – there are gilded motifs, plush beds, wall-long paintings and lots of reds. The bathrooms are well equipped and the setting is quiet. Trams 6, 11 and 12 stop right outside the entrance, or walk down buzzy Ilica for 15 minutes.

Hotel Jadran (☎ 45 53 777; www.hup-zagreb.hr; Vlaška 50; s/d 517/717KN; 🎮) This six-storey hotel has a superb location only minutes from Trg Josipa Jelačića. The 48 rooms are laid out in a cheery, modern style and the service is good and friendly.

Pansion Jägerhorn (☎ 48 33 877; www.hotel-pan sion-jaegerhorn.hr; Ilica 14; s/d/apt 590/690/890KN; 🎮) A great little hotel that sits right underneath Gradec and Lotrščak Tower, the 'Hunter's Horn' (don't snigger!) has friendly service and spacious, classic rooms with good views (you can gaze over Gradec from the top-floor attic rooms). The downstairs restaurant serves wild game.

Hotel Central (☎ 48 41 122; www.hotel-central.hr; Branimirova 3; s/d 600/780KN; 🎮) The best place to stay if you have a train to catch, the Central is right opposite the train station. It's in a square cement building and the rooms are modern if a little pokey. The top-floor rooms facing the leafy courtyard are larger, so ask to stay in one of those.

Top End

Palace Hotel (☎ 49 20 530; www.palace.hr; Strossmayerov Trg 10; s/d from 810/1050KN; 🅿 ✖ 🎮 🖳) This hotel oozes European charm and is the oldest in Zagreb. Built in 1891, it's both aristocratic and outfitted with the latest modern comforts. Try to get a front room for the fantastic views over the park.

Hotel Dubrovnik (☎ 48 73 555; www.hotel-dubrovnik .hr; Gajeva 1; s/d from 875/1350KN; 🎮) Right in the centre of town, this glass New York–wannabe building is a real city landmark. It buzzes with business travellers who love being at the centre of the action. The 260 rooms are elegant and have all you need, and the style is old-school classic. Try to get a view of Jelačića and watch Zagreb pass by under your window.

ourpick Arcotel Allegra (☎ 46 96 000; www.arcotel.at/allegra; Branimirova 29; d €152-162; P ⊠ ✣ 💻) The Arcotel Allegra is Zagreb's first designer hotel, with airy, elegant rooms and a plush, marble-and-exotic-fish reception. The bed linen is covetable and soft, and the bed throws are printed with faces of Kafka, Kahlo, Freud, Lorca and numerous other iconic personalities. There's a DVD player in each room and the hotel has movies you can borrow. The top floor has a gym, sauna and great views of the city. The on-site Radicchio restaurant is good and Joe's Bar's hot on Latino music.

ourpick Regent Esplanade Zagreb (☎ 45 66 666; www.regenthotels.com; Mihanovićeva 1; s/d 1660/2025KN; P ⊠ ✣ 💻) Sprawling and drenched with history, this six-storey, 215-room hotel was built next to the train station in 1924 to welcome the *Orient Express* crowd in grand style. It has hosted kings, journalists, artists and politicians since. It's an art deco masterpiece, replete with walls of swirling marble, immensely wide staircases and wood-panelled lifts. Even if you're not staying here, take a peek at the magnificent Emerald Ballroom or eat at Zinfandel's Restaurant (p86), one of the finest dining experiences in Croatia.

EATING

You'll have to love Croatian and (below par) Italian food to enjoy Zagreb's restaurants, but new places are branching out to include Japanese and other world cuisines. The biggest move is towards elegantly presented *haute cuisine* at *haute* prices.

Budget

Nocturno (☎ 48 13 394; Skalinska 4; mains 20-50KN) Right on the sloping street underneath the cathedral, this place is very popular for its Italian menu and lively outdoor terrace. There are all the usual pizzas, and some good salads, too, which will gladden vegetarian hearts. The risottos are pretty huge, so order one of those if you're starving.

Rubelj (☎ 48 18 777; www.rubelj-grill.hr; Tržnica Mala Terasa; mains from 25KN) One of the many Rubeljs across town, this Dolac branch is a great place for a quick portion of *ćevapi* (small spicy sausage of minced beef, lamb or pork). Though none is as tasty as those in neighbouring Bosnia and Hercegovina (the spiritual home of the *ćevap*), these are Zagreb's best.

Vallis Aurea (☎ 48 31 305; Tomićeva 4; mains from 30KN) This is a true local eatery that has some of the best home cooking you'll find in town, so it's no wonder that it's chock-a-block at lunchtime. Taste the Dalmatian staple, *pašticada* (beef stew with wine and spices), or the slightly spicy beans, accompanying either with some house red. Right by the lower end of the funicular.

ourpick Tip Top (☎ 40 30 349; Gundulićeva 18; mains from 35KN) Oh how we love Tip Top and its waiting staff, who still sport old socialist uniforms and scowling faces that eventually turn to smiles. But we mostly love the excellent Dalmatian food. Every day has its own set menu (in addition to à la carte); Thursdays are particularly delicious with octopus *brodet* (octopus stewed in red wine, garlic and herbs). Owned and run by Korčulans, you'll find that island's wines on offer – wines that were no doubt enjoyed by Tin Ujević, once Tip Top's most loyal customer.

Ivica i Marica (☎ 48 17 321; Tkalčićeva 70; mains from 40KN) Based on the Brothers Grimm story *Hansel & Gretel*, this little restaurant/cake shop is made to look like the gingerbread house from the tale, with waiting staff clad in traditional costumes. It's not exactly veggie, but it does have a decent range of veggie and fish dishes plus meatier fare. The ice creams and cakes are good, too.

Boban (☎ 48 11 549; Gajeva 9; mains 40-60KN) Italian is the name of the game in this cellar restaurant that's owned by the Croatian World Cup star Zvonimir Boban. Devised by an Italian chef (who hasn't quite instilled the concept of pasta al dente into the local chefs), the menu is a robust range of pastas, salads and meats. It's a popular lunch and dinner spot; the upstairs café's terrace attracts Zagreb's youngsters.

ourpick Kerempuh (☎ 48 19 000; Kaptol 3; mains 50-70KN) Overlooking Dolac market, this is a fabulous place to taste: a) Croatian cuisine cooked well and simply, and b) the market's ingredients on your plate. The set menu changes daily and the dishes are decided in the morning, when the chef gets that day's freshest ingredients from Dolac. Get an outside table and enjoy the excellent food and market views.

Konoba Čiho (☎ 48 17 060; Pavla Hatza 15; mains from 55KN; 🕑 Mon-Sat) An old-school Dalmatian *konoba* (simple family-run establishment), where, downstairs, you can get fish and seafood grilled or stewed just the way the

ZAGREB

regulars like it. Try the wide range of *rakija* (grape brandy).

Midrange

Pivnica Stari Fijaker 900 (☎ 48 33 829; www.stari fijaker.hr; Mesnička 6; mains 50-80KN) This was once the height of dining out in Zagreb, and its decor, comprised of banquettes, wood and white linen, still has a certain staid sobriety. Tradition reigns in the kitchen, so try the homemade sausages, beans and *štrukli* (dumplings filled with cottage cheese).

Kaptolska Klet (☎ 48 14 838; Kaptol 5; mains from 70KN) This friendly restaurant is comfortable for everyone from solo diners to groups of noisy backpackers. There's a huge outdoor terrace and a brightly lit beer-hall-style interior. Although famous for its Zagreb specialities such as grilled meats and homemade sausages, it also turns out a nice platter of grilled vegetables and a vegetable loaf.

Okrugljak (☎ 46 74 112; Mlinovi 28; mains from 80KN) This is a popular spot on Mt Medvednica for city people celebrating a special occasion. Dining is casual; you can sit at wooden tables in carved-out wine barrels or on the terrace. There is usually music on weekends, and the occasional wedding reception can make the ambience more than lively. The spit-roasted meat, especially lamb or duck, is unusually juicy and served with delicious *mlinci* (baked noodles).

Cantinetta (☎ 48 11 315; Teslina 14; mains 80-120KN) The perfect environment to end an affair. No one would think of making a scene in such elegant surroundings and the exquisitely prepared cuisine would go a long way towards mending a broken heart.

Makronova (☎ 48 47 115; www.makronova.com; Ilica 72; mains 80-120KN; ☯ Mon-Sat) This macrobiotic restaurant is elegant and peaceful, and more than welcoming for those of the vegan persuasion. It's part of a whole healthy emporium – there's a health food shop downstairs, shiatsu treatment, yoga classes and feng shui courses.

Pod Gričkim Topom (☎ 48 33 607; Zakmardijeve Stube 5; mains from 90KN) Tucked away by a leafy path below the Upper Town, this restaurant has a somewhat self-conscious charm, along with an outdoor terrace and good Croatian meat-based specialities. It's a great place to hole up on a snowy winter evening or dine under the stars in summer.

Agava (☎ 48 29 826; Tkalčićeva 39; mains 100-120KN) Right on Tkalčićeva, this is a smart and sophisticated place for smart and sophisticated people. The food ranges from starters such as swordfish carpaccio (50KN) to mains of steak and truffle, while the delectable risottos and pastas feature seafood seared in cognac (60KN). The wine list is good, with plenty of Istrian and Slavonian choices.

Baltazar (☎ 46 66 999; www.restoran-baltazar.hr; Nova Ves 4; mains from 120KN; ☯ Mon-Sat) Meats – duck, lamb, pork, beef and turkey – are grilled and prepared the Zagorje and Slavonia way in this upmarket old-timer, and there's a good choice of local wines. The summer terrace is a great place to dine under the stars.

Top End

Dubravkin Put (☎ 48 34 975; Dubravkin Put 2; mains 90-150KN) In a woodsy area northwest of the town centre, this is an upmarket restaurant with a light and modern decor and outstanding fish specialities that attract the crowds. The owner is from Dubrovnik and the cuisine is inspired by Dalmatia, with risottos as starters and main courses of perfectly grilled fish.

Zinfandel's Restaurant (☎ 45 66 666; www.regent hotels.com; Mihanovićeva 1; mains 90-200KN; ☯ Mon-Sat) The tastiest, most creative dishes in town are served with polish in the dining room of the Regent Esplanade Zagreb. For a simpler but still delicious dining experience, head to Le Bistro, also in the Esplanade. Don't miss the *štrukli*.

Quick Eats

The town's main shopping street, Ilica, is lined with fast-food joints and inexpensive snack bars.

Pekarnica Dora (Strossmayerov Trg 7; ☯ 24hr) Close to the train station, this bakery is open round the clock for those late-night pastry needs.

Vincek (☎ 48 33 612; Ilica 18) This *slastičarna* (pastry shop) serves the best ice cream in town. The long lines as soon as summer starts attest to its popularity.

Self-Catering

Right in the centre of town, there's **Gavrilović** (☯ Mon-Sat) for excellent local cheese, smoked meat and cold cuts. On Ilica, there's a daily fruit and vegetable **market** (Britanski Trg; ☯ 6am-3pm), which sells farm-fresh produce. There's also the Dolac fruit and vegetable market (p73). Don't hesitate to bargain.

DRINKING

In the Upper Town, the chic Tkalčićeva is throbbing with bars. In the Lower Town, there's bar-lined Bogovićeva, just south of Trg Josipa Jelačića, which turns into prime meet-and-greet territory on sunny spring and summer days and balmy nights. Trg Petra Preradovića is the most popular spot in the Lower Town for street performers and occasional bands in mild weather. With half a dozen bars and footpath cafés between Trg Preradovića and Bogovićeva, the scene on some summer nights resembles a vast outdoor party. Things do close by midnight though.

Cafés

Café culture is alive and well in Zagreb and probably one of the nicest ways to see the city is to experience *špica* – the Saturday morning and pre-lunch coffee drinking on the many terraces along Preradovićeva and Tkalčićeva.

our pick Booksa (☎ 46 16 124; www.booksa.hr; Martićeva 14d; ☑ 9am-11pm Tue-Sun) Bookworms and poets, writers and performers, oddballs and artists, basically anyone on the creative side of things in Zagreb comes to chat and drink coffee, buy books and hear readings at this lovely bookshop. There are English-language readings here, too, so check the website.

Eli's Café (☎ 091 527 9990; www.eliscaffe.com; Ilica 63; ☑ 8am-9pm Mon-Sat, 9am-3pm Sun) You'll see why this tiny place was given the 'Best Coffee in Croatia' award in 2008 when you try the excellent espresso or smooth cappuccino. There are also breakfast pastries for dipping.

Bulldog Café (☎ 49 17 393; Bogovićeva 6) It's easy to sit for hours outside, watching the activity on this busy pedestrian street. At night, it's a good place to meet and have a few drinks before clubbing.

Palainovka (☎ 48 51 357; Ilirski Trg 1) Claiming to be the oldest café in Zagreb (dating from 1846), this Viennese-style place serves delicious coffee, tea and cakes under pretty frescoed ceilings.

Bars

Most of the places following open around noon and serve drinks all day but the action heats up at night.

our pick Škola (☎ 48 28 197; www.skolaloungebar .com; Bogovićeva 7) This has to be the best designed bar in the whole of Zagreb with its huge, differently themed rooms, lounge sofas, an olive tree in the middle of the main room, and notebook-style menus (it's called 'School', you see?). There are DJ nights, various 'after-school' parties and it's packed with the trendiest people (and, of course, students).

Cica (Tkalčićeva 18) The size of an east London bedsit, and with a similar vibe, this underground place has a massive choice of *rakija*. Herbal, nutty, fruity – you think it, they've got it. Lovers of hedonistic pleasures, Cica is your place.

Apartman (☎ 48 72 168; Preradovićeva 7) A 1st-floor space decked out with large cushions and an unpretentious, relaxed crowd, Apartman gets going with DJ music on weekends. You can also come and lounge around during the day.

Melin (☎ 48 28 966; Tkalčićeva 47) This is rock'n'roll as it used to be, with grotty seats, oddly painted walls, smoke curtains and music that bursts ear drums. A corner of grungy old Zagreb on a fast-gentrifying street.

Hemingway (☎ 48 34 956; Trg Maršala Tita) The main accoutrements you'll need here are black sunglasses and a mobile phone glued to your ear. This is an upmarket cocktail bar where you come to pose and be seen.

BP Club (☎ 48 14 444; Teslina 7; ☑ 10pm-2am) One of a couple of cafés and music shops that share the lively complex at the corner of Teslina and

---

TKALČIĆEVA DAY-LONG BAR CRAWL

Start your day with a healthy shot of fresh juice or a cool smoothie at **100% Liquid Health** (No 5), then go on to **Argentina** (No 9) for an energy boost of excellent coffee. Pop over to **Cica** (No 18) for a dizzying array of artisanal *travarica* (herbal brandy). Do some serious people-watching from the sprawling outdoor terrace of **Oliver Twist** (No 60). If the weather is uncooperative, you can hide out inside where a British pub has been perfectly reproduced for the benefit of Zagreb's trendies. Grab some pub grub and settle in until the DJ arrives (Friday and Saturday nights). If nothing's happening, try **Funk** (No 52) a few steps away, which combines a gallery with an eclectic music scene.

Gajeva streets. In the basement, check it out for jazz, blues and rock bands.

Žabac (☎ 36 95 792; Jarunska bb) The booze is cheap, the scene is rowdy and you're only steps away from Aquarius (below).

Movie Pub (☎ 60 55 045; www.the-movie-pub.com, in Croatian; Savska 141) This immensely popular pub has posters of movie stars on the walls, staring with bemusement as their fans sample 30 varieties of beer. The Thursday karaoke night starts at 10pm, so come and belt out all the tunes you know.

ENTERTAINMENT

Zagreb's theatres and concert halls present a great variety of programs throughout the year. Many (but not all) are listed in the monthly brochure *Zagreb Events & Performances,* which is available from the main tourist office. The daily newspapers *Jutarnji List* and *Večernji List* show the current offerings on the concert, gallery, museum, theatre and cinema circuit on the back page.

Nightclubs

Nightclub entry ranges from 40KN to 80KN, depending on the evening and the event. Clubs open around 9pm but most people show up around midnight.

KSET (☎ 61 29 999; www.kset.org; Unska 3; ☯ 8pm-midnight Mon-Fri, to 3am Sat) Zagreb's best music venue, with anyone who's anyone performing here. Saturday nights are dedicated to DJ music, when hundreds of young Zagrebians drink, dance and stay up late. You'll find gigs and events to suit most tastes.

Aquarius (☎ 36 40 231; Jarun Lake) A truly fab place to party, this enormously popular spot has a series of rooms that opens onto a huge terrace on the lake. House and techno are the standard fare here.

Močvara (☎ 60 55 599; www.mochvara.hr, in Croatian; Trnjanski Nasip bb) Unfortunately closed down in May 2008 until further notice, do keep an eye on the website as this club may open again. In a former factory, it is one of the best venues in town and has hosted the cream of alternative music.

Boogaloo (☎ 63 13 021; www.boogaloo.hr; OTV Dom, Vukovarska 68) A great venue that hosts DJ nights and live music. It's a 15-minute walk from Jelačića square.

Purgeraj (☎ 48 14 734; Park Ribnjak) This is a funky, relaxed space to listen to live rock, blues, rock-blues, blues-rock, country rock and avant-garde jazz. There's a daily two-drinks-for-one happy hour from 9pm to 11pm.

Jabuka (☎ 48 34 397; Jabukovac 28) This is a bit of an old-time favourite, with 1980s hits played to a 30-something crowd that reminisces about the good old days. It's a fun place and much loved by Zagrebians.

Gay & Lesbian Venues

The gay and lesbian scene in Zagreb is finally becoming more open than it had previously been, although 'freewheeling' it isn't. Many gays discreetly cruise the south beach around Jarun Lake and are welcome in most discos.

David (☎ 091 533 7757; Marulićev Trg 3) This sauna, bar and video room is a popular spot on Zagreb's gay scene.

G Bar (www.gprojekt.com; Mesnička) Still under wraps at the time of writing, G Bar promises to be at the forefront of Zagreb's gay community, with events, parties and great drinks.

Theatre

Theatre tickets are usually available, even for the most in-demand shows. A small office marked **Kazalište Komedija** (☎ 48 12 657; ☯ 8am-5.30pm Mon-Fri, to 1pm Sat) in the Oktogon sells theatre tickets (look for the posters). It's in a passage connecting Trg Petra Preradovića to Ilica near Trg Josipa Jelačića.

Croatian National Theatre (☎ 48 28 532; Trg Maršala Tita 15) This neobaroque theatre, established in 1895, stages opera and ballet performances. You have a choice of *parket* (orchestra), *lože* (lodge) or *balkon* (balcony) seats. Check out Ivan Meštrović's sculpture *The Well of Life* (1905) standing in front. The theatre was designed in 1894 by Herman Helmer and Ferdinand Fellner, the same team that designed the Art Pavilion.

Komedija Theatre (☎ 48 14 566; Kaptol 9) Close to the Zagreb cathedral, this theatre stages a good range of operettas and musicals.

Vatroslav Lisinski Concert Hall (☎ 61 21 166; www.lisinski.hr; Trg Stjepana Radića 4) This is the city's most prestigious venue in which to hear symphony concerts and attend theatrical productions.

Croatian Music Institute (☎ 48 30 822; Gundulićeva 6a) Another good venue for classical music concerts, which often feature Croatian composers performed by Croatian musicians.

Sport

Jarun Lake hosts competitions in rowing, kayaking and canoeing in the summer. See the schedule at www.jarun.hr or phone ☎ 0800 300 301. There's a racetrack in south Zagreb, across the Sava River. For information on sporting events dial ☎ 9841.

Basketball is popular in Zagreb, and from September to April Zagreb's basketball team, Cibona, plays at the **Dražen Petrović Basketball Centre** (☎ 48 43 333; Savska 30; tickets from 35KN), next to the Technical Museum. Games are usually on Saturdays at 7.30pm. Tickets are available at the door.

Dinamo is Zagreb's most popular football (soccer) team and it plays matches at **Stadion Maksimir** (☎ 23 86 111; Maksimirska 128; tickets from 30KN), on the eastern side of Zagreb. Games are played on Sunday afternoons between August and May. Take trams 4, 7, 11 or 12 to Bukovačka. If you arrive too early for the game, Zagreb's zoo is across the street. For more information check out www.nk-dinamo.hr.

SHOPPING

Ilica is Zagreb's main shopping street with fashionable international brands peeking out from the staid buildings.

our pick **Prostor** (☎ 48 46 016; www.multiracionalna kompanija.com; Mesnička 5; ☼ noon-8pm Mon-Fri, 10am-3pm Sat) A fantastic little art gallery and clothes shop, featuring some of the city's best independent artists and young designers. Check out the website for exhibition openings, when you can go and hang out with interesting people and take a closer look at Zagreb's arty crowd. In a little courtyard off Mesnička.

Croata (☎ 48 12 726; www.croata.hr; Oktogon Passage, Ilica 5) Since the necktie originated in Croatia, nothing could make a more authentic gift, and this is the place to get one. The locally made silk neckties are priced from 175KN to 380KN.

Rukotvorine (☎ 48 31 303; Trg Josipa Jelačića 7) Sells traditional Croatian handicrafts such as

dolls, pottery and red-and-white embroidered tablecloths.

Bornstein (☎ 48 12 361; Kaptol 19) If Croatia's wine and spirits have gone to your head, get your fix here. This shop presents an astonishing collection of brandy, wine and gourmet products.

If shopping centres are your thing, head to the following:

Branimir Centar (Draškovićeva 51) With a giant cinema, bars, cafés and restaurants to help you relax after a good shop.

Nama (Ilica 4) Zagreb's immortal department store.

GETTING THERE & AWAY
Air

Zagreb Airport (☎ 62 65 222; www.zagreb-airport.hr), 17km southeast of Zagreb, is one of the country's major airports, offering a range of international and domestic services. International and domestic flights to and from Zagreb are operated by **Croatia Airlines** (☎ 48 19 633; www .croatiaairlines.hr; Zrinjevac 17; ☼ 8am-8pm Mon-Fri, 9am-noon Sat).

Bus

Zagreb's big, modern **bus station** (☎ 61 57 983; www.akz.hr, in Croatian; Avenija M Držića) has a large enclosed waiting room where you can stretch out while waiting for your bus (but be warned – there's no heating in winter).

Buy most international tickets at windows 11 and 12. Eurolines operates bus services between Vienna and Zagreb (€35, six hours, two daily), a twice-weekly service all year between Brussels and Zagreb (€115, 22 hours) and three daily buses between Sarajevo and Zagreb (€18, eight hours). There are six daily buses from Zagreb to Belgrade (€20, six hours); at Bajakovo on the border, a Serbian bus takes you on to Belgrade. There are also buses between Ljubljana and Zagreb (110KN, three hours, two daily).

MARKET DAYS

Zagreb doesn't do many markets, but those that it does do, it does well. The Sunday **antiques market** (☼ 9am-2pm) on Britanski Trg is one of central Zagreb's joys, but to see a flea market that's unmatched in the whole of Croatia, you have to make it to **Hrelić** (☼ 7am-3pm Sun). It's a huge space that's packed with everything – and we mean everything – from car parts, cars and antique furniture to clothes, records, kitchenware, you name it. All goods are, of course, second-hand, and you can bargain if you find something you want. Apart from the shopping, it's a great experience in itself and a side of Zagreb you probably won't see anywhere else – expect lots of Roma, music, general liveliness and grilled meat smoking in the food section. If you're going in the summer months, take a hat and put on some sunscreen – there's no shade. Take bus 295 (8KN, 20 minutes) to Sajam Jakuševac from behind the railway station.

The following domestic buses depart from Zagreb:

Destination	Fare (KN)	Duration (hr)	Daily services
Dubrovnik	250	11	7-8
Korčula	224	11	1
Krk	160-190	4-5	4
Makarska	210	8	10
Mali Lošinj	260-280	6½	2
Osijek	125-160	4	8
Plitvice	80	2½	19
Poreč	170-210	5	6
Pula	170-230	4-5	6
Rab	195	5	2
Rijeka	125-150	2½-3	14
Rovinj	170-190	5-8	8
Šibenik	165	6½	15
Split	195	5-9	27
Varaždin	69	2	20
Zadar	120-140	3½-5	20

Train

The following domestic trains depart from the Zagreb **train station** (☎ 060 333 444; www.hznet.hr):

Destination	Fare (KN)	Duration (hr)	Daily services
Osijek	113	4	5
Pula	131	6½	2
Rijeka	96	5	5
Šibenik	149	6½-10	3
Split	160	6-8½	6
Varaždin	59	3	13
Zadar	156	7-9¾	5

Trains to Zadar stop at Knin. It's advisable to book in advance because of limited seating (the trains can be quite small).

There are two daily and two overnight trains between Vienna and Zagreb (€69, 6½ to 13 hours), and daily train services connecting Zagreb with Banja Luka (200KN, five hours), Sarajevo (260KN, eight hours), Mostar (290KN, 11 hours 40 minutes) and Ploče (310KN, 10 hours). There are three trains daily from Munich to Zagreb (€88, nine hours) via Salzburg and Ljubljana. Reservations are required southbound but not northbound.

There are four daily trains from Zagreb to Budapest (€60, 5½ to 7½ hours). Between Venice and Zagreb (€60, 6½ to 7½ hours) there are two daily direct connections and several more that run through Ljubljana. Five daily trains connect Zagreb with Belgrade (€25, seven hours). There are up to 11 trains daily between Zagreb and Ljubljana (€16, 2¼ hours).

GETTING AROUND

Zagreb is a fairly easy city to navigate, whether by car or public transport. Traffic isn't bad, there's sufficient parking and the efficient tram system should be a model for more polluted, traffic-clogged European capitals. Walking is, of course, always the best way to see a city.

To/From the Airport

The Croatia Airlines bus to the airport (one way 50KN) leaves from the bus station every half-hour or hour from about 4am to 8.30pm depending on flights, and returns from the airport on about the same schedule. A taxi would cost about 300KN.

Car

Zagreb is a fairly easy city to navigate by car (boulevards are wide and garage parking only costs 5KN per hour), but watch out for trams buzzing around. The **Hrvatski Autoklub** (HAK; Croatian Auto Club; ☎ 46 40 800; www.hak.hr; Draškovićeva 25) helps motorists in need.

The following international car-hire companies are represented in Zagreb:

Avis (☎ 46 73 603; www.avis.com.hr; Hotel Sheraton, Kneza Borne 2)

Budget Rent-a-Car (☎ 45 54 936; www.budget.hr; Hotel Sheraton, Kneza Borne 2)

Hertz (☎ 48 46 777; www.hertz.hr; Vukotinovićeva 1)

Bear in mind that local companies will usually have lower rates. Try **H&M** (☎ 37 04 535; www.hm -rentacar.hr; Grahorova 11), which also has an office at the airport.

Taxi

Zagreb's taxis all have meters, which begin at 20KN and then ring up 7KN per kilometre. On Sunday and at night from 10pm to 5am there's a 20% surcharge. Waiting time is 40KN per hour. The baggage surcharge is 2KN per suitcase. At these rates, you'll have no trouble finding idle taxis, usually at blue-marked taxi signs, or you can call ☎ 970 to reserve one.

Tram

Public transport is based on an efficient network of trams, although the city centre is compact enough to make them unnecessary. Tram maps have been posted at most stations, making the system easier to navigate. Trams 3 and 8 don't run on weekends. Buy tickets at newspaper kiosks for 8KN. You can use your ticket for transfers within 90 minutes, but only in one direction. A *dnevna karta* (day ticket), valid on all public transport until 4am the next morning, is available for 25KN at most newspaper kiosks. Make sure you validate your ticket when you get on the tram by inserting it in the yellow box.

AROUND ZAGREB

The area around Zagreb is rich with quick getaways from the city, from picturesque Karlovac to Samobor with its peaceful hillside walks (and great cakes).

MOUNT MEDVEDNICA

Mt Medvednica to the north of Zagreb offers excellent **hiking** opportunities. There are two popular routes. You can take tram 14 to the last stop and then change to tram 15 and take it to its last stop. Here you'll be near the funicular that goes to the top of the mountain; next to the funicular there is a clearly marked footpath that also takes you to the top. Or you can take bus 102 from Britanski Trg, west of the centre on Ilica, to the church in Šestine and take the hiking route from there. Allow about three hours (return) for each of these hikes and remember that this is a heavily wooded mountain with ample opportunities to become lost. Take warm clothes and water, and make sure to return before sundown. There is

AROUND ZAGREB

also a danger of disease-carrying ticks in the summer, so wear trousers and long sleeves, and examine your body after the hike for ticks (for information on tick-borne infections, see p316). For more information about hiking on the mountain, contact the Zagreb tourist office (p72).

You can also go skiing at the **Sljeme ski resort** (www.sljeme.hr), where there are five slopes of varying difficulty – the website provides an up-to-date status on each slope. Lunch is available at one of the local restaurants and you can rent equipment on site.

BANIJA-KORDUN REGION

South of Zagreb and bound by the Sava River basin in the north, the Una and Kupa Rivers in the east and west, and Mala Kapela mountain range in the south, the Banija-Kordun region is trying to recapture some of the tourism it had before the war. Until 1991 the region's many rivers were popular with local anglers, and hunters combed the woods for prey. The large Serbian majority made it a tempting target for Serbian expansion in the early days of the war and large parts of the region remained under Serbian control until 1995. The many mines laid in the countryside have curtailed the hunting and fishing that made the area famous, but as de-mining proceeds, anglers and hunters are returning.

Karlovac

☎ 047 / pop 49,000

Lying at the confluence of four rivers – the Kupa, Korana, Mrežnica and Dobra – it's not surprising that Karlovac and its surrounds have become a haven for city folk looking for waterside relaxation. The town itself is unique in that its historical centre is shaped in the form of a six-point star, divided into 24 almost rectangular blocks. It lies on the main road that links Zagreb with Rijeka and was constructed in 1579 as a military stronghold against the Turks. Although only the moats remain from the original fortifications, the town centre retains its tidy geometric streets of baroque buildings.

ORIENTATION & INFORMATION

The Kupa River divides the town along an east–west axis. The main road through town is Prilaz Vece Holjevca, which runs north–south. The old town is east of Prilaz Vece Holjevca

and lies on the southern bank of the Kupa River. The main square in the old town is Trg Josipa Jelačića. The bus station is on Prilaz Vece Holjevca, about 500m south of the town centre, and the train station is 1.5km north of the town centre also along Prilaz Vece Holjevca. The **tourist office** (☎ /fax 615 115, www.karlovac-touristinfo.hr; Petra Zrinskog 3; ☺ 8am-5pm Mon-Fri, to 1pm Sat & Sun) has a limited amount of documentation available but finds private accommodation.

SIGHTS & ACTIVITIES

The main attraction of Karlovac is the **Zvijezda** (Star), the old town. The 17th-century **Church of the Holy Trinity**, with its altar of black marble, and the adjacent **Franciscan monastery**, are the highlights of Trg Jelačića. The 17th- and 18th-century merchant and military residences on the surrounding streets are being restored to emphasise their fine features. Merchants' houses are recognisable by their inscriptions showing the year of construction and the owner's initials. Military houses are often distinguished by stone carvings and wrought-iron work. Particularly attractive is a stroll down Radićeva, which features the house of Count Janko Drašković.

One block north of Trg Jelačića is Strossmayerov Trg, a semicircular baroque-style square that contains the **Town Museum** (Gradski Muzej; ☎ 615 980; Strossmayerov Trg; adult/student 10/7KN; ☺ 7am-3pm Mon-Fri, 10am-noon Sat & Sun). The museum is in a Frankopan palace and features scale models of old Karlovac among its displays of local handicrafts and historical exhibits.

A 30-minute walk north along the banks of the Kupa River and then uphill takes you to **Dubovac** (Zagrad 10), a medieval fortress that now contains a restaurant and affords an excellent view of Karlovac.

SLEEPING & EATING

The tourist office can help you find private accommodation (about 90KN per person) and there is one hotel in the town centre.

Carlstadt Hotel (☎ /fax 611 111; www.carlstadt.hr; Vranicanijeva 1; s/d 317/462KN; P ⌘) Carlstadt is a business travellers' favourite, with beige and brown rooms, each with TVs and phones. The location is excellent.

Mirna (☎ 654 172; Rakovačko Šetalište bb; mains from 70KN) After an aperitif at the Carlstadt, head here for fresh and saltwater fish served up on a pretty terrace overlooking the Korana River.

GETTING THERE & AWAY

Karlovac is well connected to Zagreb by bus (36KN to 40KN, 50 minutes, 20 daily). There are also frequent trains to Zagreb (35KN, 50 minutes, 18 daily) and Rijeka (81KN, three hours, six daily).

Samobor

☎ 01 / pop 14,000

Samobor is Zagrebians' version of the Hamptons for New Yorkers, only it doesn't have a beach and it's much smaller. OK, we may be stretching it with this comparison, but this is where stressed-out city dwellers come to wind down and get their fix of hearty food, creamy cakes and pretty scenery. A shallow stream stocked with trout curves through a town centre that is composed of trim pastel houses and several old churches, while the verdant woods of Samoborsko Gorje are perfect for hiking.

In keeping with its mission to preserve a little piece of the past, the main economic activity centres on small family businesses involved in handicrafts, restaurants and the production of mustard and spirits. The town's literary and musical traditions, which produced the poet Stanko Vraz and the composer Ferdo Livadić, are reflected in a number of annual festivals, most famously the **Fašnik** (Samobor Carnival) on the eve of Lent.

ORIENTATION & INFORMATION

The bus station (no left-luggage office) is on Šmidhenova, about 100m uphill from the town, which centres on Trg Kralja Tomislava.

In the town centre, the **tourist office** (☎ 33 60 044; www.samobor.hr, in Croatian; Trg Kralja Tomislava 5; ☽ 8am-7pm Mon-Fri, 9am-7pm Sat, 10am-7pm Sun) has limited documentation but you can purchase hiking maps.

SIGHTS & ACTIVITIES

The **Town Museum** (Gradski Muzej; ☎ 33 61 014; Livadićeva 7; adult/student 8/5KN; ☽ 8am-3pm Tue-Sat, 9am-1pm Sun) has vaguely interesting exhibits on regional culture. It's housed in Livadićev Dvor Villa, which once belonged to composer Ferdo Livadić and was an important centre for the 19th-century nationalist cause. Stop by the **Museum Marton** (☎ 33 64 160; admission 15KN; ☽ 10am-1pm & 3-6pm Sat & Sun) for a look at a private art collection that centres on paintings from the Biedermeier period as well as porcelain, glass and furniture.

SLEEPING & EATING

Most people come to Samobor on a day trip from Zagreb but you can also stay here and commute into Zagreb.

Hotel Livadić (☎ 33 65 850; www.hotel-livadic .hr; Trg Kralja Tomislava 1; s 360KN, d low-high 465-530KN) This atmospheric place is decorated in 19th-century style and provides spacious, comfortable rooms with TV and phone. Since cuisine is a major draw for Samobor, you can count on the quality of the restaurant and café.

Samoborska Pivnica (☎ 33 61 623; Šmidhena 3; mains 35-90KN) An excellent array of local specialities is served in this vaulted space, with a variety of sausages, eye-watering horseradish and delicious, cheesy štrukli. It's a beer house

---

TAKE A HIKE

Samobor is a good jumping-off point for hikes into the **Samoborsko Gorje**, a mountain system (part of the Žumberak Range) that links the high peaks of the Alps with the karstic caves and abysses of the Dinaric Range. Carpeted with meadows and forests, the range is the most popular hiking destination in the region. Most of the hikes are easy and there are several mountain huts that make pleasant rest stops. Many are open weekends only (except in the high season).

The range has three groups: the Oštrc group in the centre, the Japetić group to the west and the Plešivica group to the east. Both the Oštrc and the Japetić groups are accessible from Šoićeva Kuća, a mountain hut 10km west of Samobor, only reachable by foot. From there, it's an easy 30-minute climb to the hill fort of Lipovac and an hour's climb to the peak of Oštrc (753m). Another popular hike is the 1½-hour climb from Šoićeva Kuća to Japetić (780m). You can also follow a path from Oštrc to Japetić, which will take about two hours. If you want to explore the Plešivica group, head east to the hunting cabin Srndać on Poljanice (12km), from where it's a 40-minute climb to the peak of Plešivica (780m). The tourist office in town has maps and information on hikes in the region.

LONJSKO POLJE NATURE PARK

Lonjsko Polje is a fascinating mix of several diverse delights. It's packed with Croatia's 19th-century wooden architecture, bird-watchers (well, stork-lovers) can have a field day here, as can those who appreciate all things equestrian, and if you're a WWII history buff, the area holds one of ex-Yugoslavia's most poignant monuments. Pronounced a nature park in 1990 and nominated for World Heritage site status in January 2008, **Lonjsko Polje** (☎ 044-715 115; www pp-lonjsko-polje hr; Čigoć; adult/child 20/5KN; ☒ 8am-4pm) is a 506-sq-km stretch of swampland (*polje* is literally 'field') in the Posavina region, between the Sava River and Mt Moslavačka Gora. Seated along Lonja River, a Sava tributary that gives the park its name, this huge Sava River retention basin is famed for the diversity of its flora and fauna.

The area is divided into several villages. The most interesting is **Čigoć**, a world-famous 'stork meeting point' (though you're forgiven if you weren't aware of this fact), most of whom nest on top of Čigoć's lovely wooden houses. The baby-bringing birds flock here in late March and early April, hanging around and munching on the swampland insects all the way until the end of August, when they start their two- to three-month flight back towards southern Africa. If you're here during autumn and winter, you might catch sight of a few year-round storks, who are content to hang out and be fed by the villagers. Čigoć is home to the park's information point and ticket office and a small ethnographic collection owned by the Sučić family.

The next village is **Mužilovčica**, another place rich with wooden architecture. Nearby is **Retencisko Polje**, where the meadows turn into a massive lake from autumn to spring and waterfowl descend to bathe and eat. Look out for the *posavski* horse, a local breed that grazes in the oak forests of Lonjsko Polje. You can go horse riding here – ask at the information office in Čigoć.

After Mužilovčica is **Jasenovac**, the site of a notorious WWII concentration camp. Run by the Ustaše and Croatia's pro-Nazi WWII government, the estimated number of Serbs, Jews, gypsies and antifascist Croats who died here ranges from 30,000 to one million, depending on who came up with the statistics. Some modern historians estimate the number of victims at between 85,000 and 90,000. The camp, now a monument (undergoing refurbishment at the time of research), is a touching reminder of the horrors of war.

Lonjsko Polje is 50km southeast of Zagreb. The best way to visit is with your own transport – public transport is poor and makes moving around the park quite difficult.

(*pivnica*), so accompany your food with a glass of crisp local beer.

Pri Staroj Vuri (☎ 33 60 548; Giznik 2; 2-course meal 90-110KN) About 50m uphill from Trg Kralja Tomislava, this restaurant serves traditional dishes in a cosy cottage, and sometimes hosts poetry readings. The specialities of the house are *hrvatska pisanica* (beef steak in a spicy mushroom, onion, tomato and red wine sauce) and *štruklova juha* (soup with *štrukli*).

our pick **U Prolazu** (☎ 83 66 420; Trg Kralja Tomislava 5) This eatery on the main square serves the best *kremšnite* (custard pie) in town.

SHOPPING

The local aperitif is a delicious, woody red drink called *bermet*, which Samobor has been producing for centuries according to a top-secret recipe. It's not for every taste so try it in town first with lemon and ice before deciding to buy a bottle, which will cost about 120KN.

Samoborska muštarda (Samobor mustard) is from another age-old recipe. The 60KN price tag may seem rather expensive for mustard, but it comes in attractive (and reusable) clay pots.

GETTING THERE & AWAY

Samobor is easy to reach by public transport. Get a **Samoborček bus** (www2.samoborcek.hr, in Croatian) from the main bus station in Zagreb (one way 12KN, 30 minutes, half-hourly).

STUBIČKE TOPLICE

As the spa closest to Zagreb, **Stubičke Toplice** (www.bolnicastubicketoplice.com) steams away the stress of a devoted band of Zagreb habitués. There was talk of the spa going into private hands, with sharp protests from the staff and regulars, so it remains to be seen what will become of this socialist-era remnant.

The hot-spring water (69°C) rising from the subterranean rock layers has spurred tourism since the 18th century. The pools – eight outdoor and one indoor – have a temperature of between 32°C and 36°C, and are used to treat a variety of muscular and rheumatic conditions. The services range from the most basic – 15KN for an hour in the pools and 30KN for a 15-minute massage – to a whole array of elaborate therapies. Check the website for an exhaustive rundown.

The bus drops you off in the centre of town near the **tourist office** (☎ 282 727; Šipeka 24; ☷ 9am-5pm Mon-Fri, to 1pm Sat), which can help you find private accommodation.

Hotel Matija Gubec (☎ 282 630; www.hotel-mgubec .com; Šipeka 27; s/d 340/540KN; ☒) has modest rooms with TVs and phones, plus use of swimming pools, a sauna and a gym. If you don't stay in the hotel, it costs 30KN to use its outdoor pools and 50KN to use the pool, sauna and massage facilities.

Buses from Zagreb's main bus station go to the spa (37KN, one hour, eight daily).

Hrvatsko Zagorje

Despite its proximity to Zagreb, the bucolic region of Hrvatsko Zagorje in the country's north receives few tourists even at the height of the summer season. This is especially surprising given that it is blissfully crowd-free (slightly less so on weekends, when day-tripping families from Zagreb storm the area), and delightful villages, medieval castles and thermal springs speckle its green rolling hills. These leafy landscapes with Austrian-influenced food and architecture (and the same prices year-round) present a nice alternative to the busy Mediterranean south and offer a good escape from the summer heat.

The Zagorje region (as it's commonly known) begins north of Mt Medvednica, near Zagreb, and extends west to the Slovenian border, and as far north as Varaždin, the area's largest city. With its surface largely covered with forests – mostly beech, oak, chestnut and fir – this agricultural zone also features endless vineyards, gardens, orchards, and corn and wheat fields.

Whether you want to feast on hearty Zagorje cuisine at rustic restaurants, dip into the hot springs at Varaždinske or Krapinske Toplice, get a taster of village life at Staro Selo Museum in Kumrovec or tour ancient castles, you're in for an offbeat treat.

Many of the region's inhabitants speak a local dialect called Kajkavski, named after their word for 'what?' *(kaj?)* After Croatian or Kajkavski, the second language is likely to be German; few speak English and those who do will mostly be from younger generations. Although the cities and attractions are linked to Zagreb by bus and train, the connections are sporadic so it helps to have your own wheels to fully appreciate the area. Renting a car for a day or two and setting off along its twisting country roads is the best way to take in Zagorje's rustic charms.

HIGHLIGHTS

- Admiring the immaculately preserved baroque architecture of **Varaždin** (opposite)
- Experiencing the life of Croatian nobility at **Trakošćan Castle** (p102)
- Getting an insight into traditional village life at **Staro Selo Museum** (p104) in Kumrovec
- Sampling Croatian culinary specialities at **Vuglec Breg** (p103) near Krapinske Toplice
- Learning about our Neanderthal ancestors at the **Museum of Evolution** (p103) in Krapina
- Catching the international **Tabor Film Festival** (p104) in Veliki Tabor

- TELEPHONE CODE: 042, 049

VARAŽDIN

☎ 042 / pop 49,000

Varaždin, 81km north of Zagreb, is a largely
overlooked destination that's often used as
a mere transit point on the way to or from
Hungary. However, the town is worth a visit in
its own right as its centre is a showcase of scru-
pulously restored baroque architecture and
well-tended gardens and parks. It was once
Croatia's capital and most prosperous city,
which explains the extraordinary refinement
of its buildings. Topping off the symphony is
the gleaming white, turreted Stari Grad (Old
City), which contains a city museum.

History

The town of Garestin (now Varaždin) played
an important role in Croatia's history. It first
became a local administrative centre in 1181
under King Bela III, and in 1209 it was raised
to the status of a free royal borough by King
Andrew II, receiving its own seal and coat of
arms. The 800-year anniversary of this event
will be celebrated in 2009.

When Croatia was under siege by the Turks,
Varaždin was the most powerful stronghold

and the residence of choice for generals. Once
the Ottoman threat receded, Varaždin prospered as the cultural, political and commercial
centre of Croatia. Its proximity to northern
Europe facilitated the boom of baroque architecture, which flourished in Europe during
this period. Top artisans and builders flocked
to Varaždin, designing mansions, churches
and public buildings.

The town was made the capital of Croatia in
1756, a position it held until a disastrous fire in
1776, when the Croatian *ban* (viceroy) packed
up and moved his administration to Zagreb.
The still-thriving town was quickly rebuilt in
the baroque style, which is still visible today.

The pleasant town is a centre for textiles,
shoes, furniture and agricultural products.
It's also an increasingly popular day-trip destination – its historic core is currently being
spruced up, with plans to complete the renovations by 2010.

Orientation

The bus station lies just to the southwest of the
town centre, while the train station is to the east,
at the opposite end of town. About 1km apart,

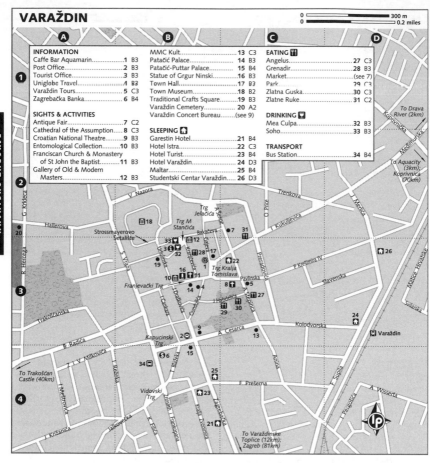

VARAŽDIN

INFORMATION		
Caffe Bar Aquamarin.................1 B3	MMC Kult.........................13 C3	EATING
Post Office.............................2 B3	Patačić Palace....................14 B3	Angelus..............................27 C3
Tourist Office.........................3 B3	Patačić-Puttar Palace........15 B4	Grenadir.............................28 B3
Uniglobe Travel.....................4 B2	Statue of Grgur Ninski......16 B3	Market..............................(see 7)
Varaždin Tours.......................5 C3	Town Hall..........................17 B3	Park.................................29 C3
Zagrebačka Banka...................6 B4	Town Museum...................18 B2	Zlatna Guska......................30 B3
	Traditional Crafts Square.....19 B3	Zlatne Ruke.......................31 C2
SIGHTS & ACTIVITIES	Varaždin Cemetery.............20 A2	
Antique Fair..........................7 C2	Varaždin Concert Bureau....(see 9)	DRINKING
Cathedral of the Assumption.....8 C3		Mea Culpa.........................32 B3
Croatian National Theatre.......9 B3	SLEEPING	Soho..................................33 B3
Entomological Collection........10 B3	Garestin Hotel...................21 B4	
Franciscan Church & Monastery	Hotel Istra.........................22 C3	TRANSPORT
of St John the Baptist..........11 B3	Hotel Turist.......................23 B4	Bus Station.........................34 B4
Gallery of Old & Modern	Hotel Varaždin...................24 D3	
Masters............................12 B3	Maltar...............................25 B4	
	Studentski Centar Varaždin.....26 D3	

---

the stations are linked by a minibus (5KN) that serves the town and nearby villages. The pedestrian zone of attractive 18th-century buildings centres on Trg Kralja Tomislava, with the old streets radiating from this square. One of these is the main commercial street, Ivana Gundulića.

Information

Caffe Bar Aquamarin (☎ 311 868; Gajeva 1; per hr 15KN; ☽ 7am-midnight Mon-Thu, to 1am Fri-Sun) Popular student hangout with internet terminals.

Garderoba bus station (per bag 7KN; ☽ 5am-8.30pm); train station (per day 15KN; ☽ 24hr) Left luggage.

Post office (Trg Slobode 9; ☽ 7am-7pm Mon-Fri, to 2pm Sat) The usual gamut of postal services.

Tourist office (☎ 210 987; www.tourism-varazdin.hr, in Croatian; Ivana Padovca 3; ☽ 8am-6pm Mon-Fri, 9am-

1pm Sat Apr-Oct, 8am-4pm Mon-Fri Nov-Mar) Plenty of colourful brochures and a wealth of information available.

Uniglobe Travel (☎ 210 989; Ivana Gundulića 2; ☽ 8.30am-7pm Mon-Fri, to 12.30pm Sat) Offers package tours around Croatia, and has a small souvenir shop.

Varaždin Tours (☎ 320 400; www.varazdintours.com; Alojzija Stepinca 1; ☽ 8am-7.30pm Mon-Fri, to 1pm Sat) Books domestic and international bus tickets.

Zagrebačka Banka (Kapucinski Trg 5) Diagonally opposite the bus station; there's also an ATM in the bus station.

Sights

Varaždin offers a fine ensemble of baroque buildings in the town centre, a number of which have been turned into museums. Many of its aristocratic mansions and elegant churches are being restored as part of the town's bid to be included in Unesco's list of World Heritage sites. Conveniently, most buildings have plaques with architectural and historical explanations in English.

The **Town Museum** (Gradski Muzej; ☎ 658 754; www .gmv.hr; Strossmayerovo Šetalište 7; adult/student 20/12KN; ☺ 10am-6pm Tue-Sun May-Sep, 10am-5pm Tue-Fri, 10am-1pm Sat & Sun Oct-Apr) is housed inside the Stari Grad (Old City), a gem of medieval defensive architecture surrounded by a lovingly manicured park. Construction of this whitewashed fortress began in the 14th century and shaped up into the present Gothic-Renaissance structure by the 16th century, when it was the regional fortification against the encroaching Turks. In private hands until 1925, today it's a museum that houses furniture, paintings, decorative objects, insignia and weapons amassed over centuries and now divided into 10 exhibition rooms. Far more interesting than the historic collections is the architecture: enter via a drawbridge and wander around archways, courtyards, chapels and towers of this sprawling castle-fortress.

A 10-minute stroll west takes you to the serene **Varaždin Cemetery** (Hallerova Aleja; ☎ 7am-9pm May-Sep, to 5pm Oct-Apr), a horticultural masterpiece designed in 1905 by Viennese architect Hermann Helmer. A meander amid tombstones, avenues, promenades and over 7000 trees, including magnolia, beech and birch, reveals some superb landscaping.

Just south of Stari Grad is the **Gallery of Old & Modern Masters** (Galerija Starih i Novih Majstora; ☎ 214 172; Trg Miljenka Stančića 3; adult/student 20/12KN; ☺ 10am-6pm Tue-Sun May-Sep, 10am-5pm Tue-Fri, 10am-1pm Sat & Sun Oct-Apr), housed in the Rococo-style Sermage Palace built in 1759. Note the carved medallions on the facade and then pay a quick visit to the museum, with a display of portraits and landscapes from Croatian, Italian, Dutch, German and Flemish schools. Note that the permanent exhibition occasionally shuts down in favour of temporary shows.

The fascinating **Entomological Collection** (Entomološka Zbirka; ☎ 658 760; Franjevački Trg 6; adult/student 20/12KN; ☺ 10am-6pm Tue-Sun May-Sep, 10am-5pm Tue-Fri, 10am-1pm Sat & Sun Oct-Apr), housed in the classicist Hercer Palace, comprises nearly 4500 exhibits of the bug world, including 1000 different insect species. The examples of insect nests, habitats and reproductive habits are informative and well displayed, with interactive stations and free audio guides.

Built in 1650 in baroque style on the site of an earlier structure, the **Franciscan Church & Monastery of St John the Baptist** (Crkva Svetog Ivana Krstitelja; ☎ 213 166; Franjevački Trg 8; ☺ 6.30am-noon & 5.30-7.30pm) contains the town's tallest tower (at 54.5m). It also houses an ancient pharmacy ornamented with 18th-century ceiling frescoes depicting the continents and natural elements. Next to the church is a copy of the bronze **statue of Grgur Ninski** that Ivan Meštrović created for Split. If you're needing a little extra luck, touch the statue's big toe and good luck will come you way…or so the story goes.

One of the town's most striking buildings is the **Town Hall** (Gradska Vijećnica; Trg Kralja Tomislava 1), a handsome Romanesque-Gothic structure that has had this civic function since the 16th century. Notice the town's coat of arms at the foot of the tower and the carved portal dating from 1792. There's a guard-changing ceremony every Saturday from 11am to noon.

The town's newest attraction is the **Traditional Crafts Square** (Trg Tradicijskih Obrta; ☺ 10am-6pm Mon-Sat Apr-Oct). Here, the town blacksmith forges 'Varaždin Medallions' and there are demonstrations of pottery, weaving and hat-making to recreate the olden times.

Just to the south of Trg Kralja Tomislava is the **Cathedral of the Assumption** (Katedrala Uznesenja Marijina; ☎ 210 688; Pavlinska 5; ☺ 7am-noon & 4-7.30pm), formerly a Jesuit church built in 1646. The facade is distinguished by an early baroque portal bearing the coat of arms of the noble Drašković family. Occupying the central nave is the altar with elaborate engravings, marble columns and the gilded painting of the Assumption of the Virgin Mary. Famous for its great acoustics, it's the site of concerts during the Baroque Evenings (see p100).

Other highlights in Varaždin (to be admired from the outside) include the **Patačić Palace** (Palača Patačić; Franjevački Trg 4), an exquisitely restored rococo palace dating from 1764 with a finely carved stone portal, and the **Patačić-Puttar Palace** (Palača Patačić-Puttar; Zagrebačka 2), an eye-catching mixture of baroque and classical styles with a richly decorated stone portal featuring the coat of arms of the Patačić family. The **Croatian National Theatre** (Hrvatsko Narodno Kazalište; ☎ 214 688; Augusta Cesarca 1) was built in 1873 in neo-Renaissance style, following the designs of Hermann Helmer.

A 15-minute walk northeast of the town centre takes you to the verdant **Drava River waterfront**. This wide, tranquil river is bordered by footpaths and several outdoor cafés in which to kick back. For some water fun, head 3km out of town to **Aquacity** (☎ 350 555; Motičnjak bb, Trnovec Bartolomečki), Varaždin's version of a city beach on the road to Koprivnica, with a lake, tennis courts and a restaurant.

Festivals & Events

Varaždin is famous for its baroque music festival, **Varaždin Baroque Evenings** (www.vbv.hr), which takes place over two to three weeks each September. Local and international orchestras play in the cathedral, churches and theatres around town. Tickets range from 75KN to 150KN, depending on the event, and become available one hour before the concert at travel agencies or the **Varaždin Concert Bureau** (☎ /fax 212 907; Croatian National Theatre, Augusta Cesarca 1).

In late August, the eclectic **Špancirfest** (www .spancirfest.com) enlivens the town's parks and squares with world music (from Afro-Cuban to tango), acrobats, theatre, traditional crafts and illusionists.

A more offbeat event is the annual **Trash Film Fest** (☎ /fax 390 925; www.trash.hr; MMC Kult, Anina 2), an extravaganza of low-budget action flicks that takes place in MMC Kult over a few days in mid-September.

Between April and October, the town market is transformed into an **antique fair** (🕙 9am-noon) the second Saturday of every month.

Sleeping

Generally less expensive than in Zagreb, most hotels in Varaždin are clean, well maintained and offer decent value for money. The clientele consists mostly of visiting businesspeople from Zagreb and neighbouring countries – this means hotels are likely to be busy on weekdays and empty on weekends.

If you're looking for private accommodation, turn to the tourist office, which has listings of single/double rooms from about 150/250KN. There is generally no supplement for a single night's stay and prices remain the same year-round.

Studentski Centar Varaždin (☎ 332 910, 332 911; hostel@scvz.hr; Julija Merlića bb; s low-high 180-225KN, d 310KN; 🖵) This student hall/hostel has 12 newly renovated single rooms available for rent year-round, each with TV, cable internet and fridge. Doubles can be booked in summer only, when students leave. There's laundry service for 23KN.

Maltar (☎ 311 100; www.maltar.hr; F Prešerna 1; s/d 220/405KN; P 🐾) Good value for money can be had at this cheerful little family-run *pension* (guest house) near the centre. Rooms are well kept and complete with satellite TV and air-con. Four suites (two/three people 465/595KN) have kitchenettes.

Garestin Hotel (☎ /fax 214 314; Zagrebačka 34; s/d 308/341KN; P) Locals frequent the popular restaurant of this establishment a stone's throw from the centre, while visitors kick back in comfy rooms upstairs, each outfitted with a minibar and other standard trimmings.

Hotel Turist (☎ 395 395; www.hotel-turist.hr; Kralja Zvonimira 1; s/d from 353/546KN; P 🐾 🖵) A lack of character at this six-storey hotel is balanced by 35 years of service, solid facilities and functional rooms. The hotel has a freshly painted facade and is a stroll away from the centre. The pricier and slightly larger 'business class' rooms come with minibars.

our pick **Hotel Varaždin** (☎ 290 720; www.hotel varazdin.com; Kolodvorska 19; s/d from 388/576KN; P 🐾 🖵) Sparkling contemporary rooms at the city's newest hotel, opposite the train station, are jam-packed with amenities such as internet and minibars. On the premises is a restaurant with a bar and terrace.

Hotel Istra (☎ 659 659; www.istra-hotel.hr; Ivana Kukuljevića 6; s/d from 570/860KN; P 🐾 🖵) The unbeatable location in the heart of town hardly justifies the hefty room costs at Varaždin's only four-star property. The expected facilities and in-room perks are all in place, but wowed you won't be.

Eating & Drinking

While it doesn't stand out as a gourmet destination, Varaždin offers plentiful opportunities to try Croatia's continental cuisine, for various budgets. There is a daily **market** (Augusta Šenoe 12), open until 2pm. Many bakeries sell Varaždin's savoury finger-shaped bread, *klipić*.

Angelus (☎ 303 868; Alojzija Stepinca 3; pizzas/mains from 25/45KN) Housed in a vaulted basement, this cosy pizzeria-trattoria churns out excellent pizza, pasta (from gnocchi to tagliatelle), risottos and meat mainstays.

Grenadir (☎ 211 131; Kranjčevića 12; mains from 32KN) No-frills but great-value *gableci* (cheap filling lunches) are popular with locals at this traditional town centre eatery.

Park (☎ 211 499; Jurja Habdelića 6; mains from 35KN) The grilled meats and salad buffets are pretty standard here; what's special are the terrace with leafy views, the old-school vibe and cheap lunches.

Zlatne Ruke (☎ 320 650; Ivana Kukuljevića 13; mains 49-116KN) The latest outpost by the owners of Zlatna Guska, this subterranean spot is the town's most design-conscious choice, with white-stone walls and creative dishes, such as deer tartare steak and goose liver with peaches.

ourpick Zlatna Guska (☎ 213 393, Jurja Habdelića 4, mains 57-119KN) A medieval theme runs through this basement restaurant, which evokes a knights' dining hall with plenty of armour. Portions are copious and the dishes are well prepared and imaginatively named, including 'the last meal of the inquisitions victims' (a hearty bread-and-sausage soup).

Mea Culpa (☎ 300 868; Ivana Padovca 1) Get your caffeine or cocktail fix at this swanky lounge-bar with two floors inside and, on sunny days, tables extending out on Trg Miljenka Stančića.

Soho (Trg Miljenka Stančića 1) Just like Mea Culpa, this café-bar has tables on the square but the interior is more intimate and toned down.

Getting There & Away

Varaždin is a major transport hub in north Croatia, with bus and train lines running in all directions. For information on long-haul buses to Germany and northern Europe, see p309. Remember that northbound buses originate in Zagreb, stop at Varaždin and cost the same whether you buy the ticket in Zagreb or Varaždin.

There's a daily bus to Vienna, Austria (210KN, six hours) and two daily buses to Munich, Germany (345KN, eight hours). There's a twice weekly bus to Berlin (773KN, 15 hours) and to Zurich, Switzerland (509KN, 13 hours). Most buses to the coast go through Zagreb. There are also weekday buses to Trakošćan Castle (25KN, four to six daily), Varaždinske Toplice (15KN, 30 minutes, 18 daily) and Zagreb (69KN, 1¾ hours, hourly). Note that service is greatly reduced on weekends to Trakošćan and Varaždinske Toplice (only one bus on Saturday, none on Sunday).

There are 11 to 14 daily trains to Zagreb (53KN, 2½ hours); connect in Zagreb for trains to the coast. One direct train runs daily to Budapest, Hungary (205KN, six hours).

VARAŽDINSKE TOPLICE
☎ 042 / pop 6973

Sulphurous thermal springs at a steaming temperature of 58°C have been attracting weary visitors to Varaždinske Toplice since the Romans first established a health settlement here in the 1st century AD. Gentle, wooded hills surround this appealing spa town with an assortment of churches and historic buildings, including the baroque castle of **Stari Grad** (Trg Slobode 16). Behind its neo-Gothic facade hides the **tourist office** (☎ 633 133; www.toplice -vz.hr, in Croatian; ☻ 7.30am-7.30pm Mon-Fri, 9am-1pm & 4-7pm Sat & Sun Jul & Aug, 7.30am-3.30pm Mon-Fri Sep-Jun), which distributes brochures and info about relaxing health therapies and can help you find private accommodation.

Adjacent is the **city museum** (☎ 633 339), which showcases a sculpture of Minerva from the 3rd century AD; the museum was closed for renovations at the time of research, but should reopen soon. History buffs should stroll around **Aqua Iasae**, the remains of the Roman spa built between the 1st and 4th centuries AD, located just a quick stroll from Stari Grad.

Hotel Minerva (☎ 630 831; www.minerva.hr; Trg Slobode 1; s/d 340/520KN; P ᴁ) is built around the thermal pools, which are said to have curative powers, especially for rheumatic ailments. The unsightly concrete building features rooms with balconies, an indoor and outdoor pool, an aqua park and a fitness center. Guests have free access to the pools, while day visitors pay 40/45KN on weekdays/weekends. There is also a sauna (45KN per hour), massages (120KN per 40 minutes) and various antistress programs.

An infinitely more pleasant overnight option is the family-run guest house **Ozis** (☎ 250 130; Zagrebačka 7; s/d 180/300KN; P) at the town entrance. It has 10 spick-and-span rooms and three suites, plus a lovely courtyard. Breakfast is additional and there's a 10% surcharge for stays under three nights.

If you have your own wheels, stop for lunch at **Zlatne Gorice** (☎ 666 054; www.zlatne-gorice.com; Banjščina 104, Gornji Kneginec; mains from 36KN), 3km from Toplice along the old road to Varaždin. This sparklingly restored mansion among vineyards serves Central European fare (think schnitzels, stews and veal medallions) in the four interior salons or on a terrace with pastoral views. There's a wine trail, a garden labyrinth, wine tastings (45KN with cheese, fruit and bread) and three cosy doubles (300KN) upstairs.

EN ROUTE TO HUNGARY: MEĐIMURJE

The undulating landscapes of Međimurje stretch northeast of Varaždin towards the borders with Hungary and Slovenia. Fertile, scenic and packed with vineyards, orchards, wheat fields and gardens, this area sees few tourists. That is slowly changing, however, as its attractions, such as up-and-coming wine cellars and the spa village of Sveti Martin, become uncovered.

To sample the region's top wines in an authentic family environment, head to **Lovrec vineyard** (☎ 040-830 171; www.hotel.hr/vino-lovrec; Sveti Urban 133, Štrigova; ☉ by appointment) in the village of Sveti Urban, 20km northwest of Čakovec, the region's capital. The guided tour (available in English, French and German) of this country estate tells you about the boutique wine production and its fascinating history, which spans six generations of winemakers. You'll peek into the 300-year-old wine cellar with ancient wine presses and barrels, rest in the shade of two towering plane trees once used as air-conditioning for the cellar, take in the vistas of the 6-hectare vineyards, and top it off with tasting about 10 wine varieties, from chardonnay and pinot gris to local *graševina*. The whole experience lasts up to two hours and costs 80KN (20KN extra for tasty cheese, salami and bread snacks), with a bottle of wine to take home. You're encouraged to buy another bottle.

A few kilometres away along verdant hilly roads, the pleasant village of Sveti Martin Na Muri showcases a recently renovated spa resort, **Toplice Sveti Martin** (☎ 040-371 111; www.toplicesveti martin.hr; Grkaveščak bb; s/d 428/656KN). It has a series of outdoor, indoor and thermal pools, a water park, tennis courts, forest trails, shops, restaurants and a golf course in the works. Accommodation consists of swanky apartment-style units, each with a living room, kitchen and balcony. For nonguests, day tickets to the pools start at 50KN (60KN on weekends); the price drops by 10KN after 1pm. Other facilities include a fitness room (25KN per day), sauna (60KN per day) and various body therapies, including mud wraps (160KN per 30 minutes) and chocolate massages (300KN for 45 minutes).

At **Goričanec farm** (☎ 040-868 288; Dunajska 26), about 4km from the village, you can try horse riding, fishing or hunting. **Potrti Kotač** (☎ 040-868 318; Jurovčak 79; mains from 35KN), 1km uphill from the spa, serves good local food and has double rooms for rent (250KN).

The spa is 12km southeast of Varaždin and 69km northeast of Zagreb. There are numerous buses from Varaždin (see p101).

TRAKOŠĆAN CASTLE
☎ 042

Among continental Croatia's most impressive castles, **Trakošćan Castle** (☎ 796 281; www.trakoscan .hr; adult/student 30/15KN; ☉ 9am-6pm Apr-Oct, to 4pm Nov-Mar), 80km northwest of Zagreb, is worth a visit for its well-presented museum and attractive grounds. The exact origin of its construction is unknown but the first official mention dates to 1334. Not many of its original Romanesque features were retained when the castle was restored in neo-Gothic style in the mid-19th century and the 215-acre castle grounds landscaped into a romantic English-style park with exotic trees and an artificial lake.

Occupied by the aristocratic Drašković family until 1944, the castle features three floors of exhibits that display the family's original furniture and a plethora of portraits. The series of rooms ranges in style from neo-Renaissance to Gothic and baroque. There's also an armaments collection of swords and firearms, and a period kitchen in the basement. After soaking up the history, wander along the verdant paths down to the wooden jetty at the lake, where you can rent a two-person paddleboat (50KN per hour) in warm weather.

No buses operate between Zagreb and Trakošćan but there are weekday connections from Varaždin, making a day trip possible (see p101).

KRAPINA
☎ 049 / pop 4647

The main reason to visit Krapina, a busy provincial town at the heart of a pretty rural region, is one of Europe's largest Neanderthal excavation sites, which is now a museum. In 1899, an archaeological dig on the Hušnjakovo hill unearthed findings of human and animal bones from a Neanderthal tribe that lived in the cave from 100,000 BC to 35,000 BC. Alongside stone tools and weapons from the Palaeolithic Age, 876 human remains were found, including 196 single teeth belonging to several dozen individuals.

Once you've connected to our long-gone ancestors and briefly meandered around town, Krapina offers little to keep you entertained.

Orientation & Information
The main road that runs through town is Zagrebačka Ulica, which becomes Ljudevita Gaja in the centre and Magistratska at the northern end. The town centre is Trg Stjepana Radića between Zagrebačka and Ljudevita Gaja. The train station is about 300m to the south; the new bus terminal is another 600m away along the same street, at Frana Galovića 15.

The **tourist office** (☎ 371 330; tzg-krapina@ kr.htnet.hr; Magistratska 11; � 8am-3pm Mon-Fri, to noon Sat) keeps sporadic hours and offers scant information.

Sights
Krapina's highlight is the **Museum of Evolution** (☎ 371 491; www.krapina.com; Šetalište Vilibalda Sluge bb; adult/student 20/10KN; ☺ 9am-5pm May-Oct, 9am-3pm Tue-Sun Nov-Apr), just west of the centre. The current museum has a limited display while the newly built 1200-sq-metre exhibition space gears up to open (by the end of 2009), with prehistoric artefacts and interactive exhibits tracing the history and geology of the region. The nearby park remains unchanged, with sculpted life-sized models of Neanderthals engaged in everyday activities such as wielding clubs and throwing stones.

Worth peeking at in the otherwise unremarkable town of Krapina is the baroque **Franciscan monastery**, which once housed a philosophy and theology school, and the adjoining **St Catherine church**, with evocative frescoes by Pauline monk Ivan Ranger in the sacristy. The **City Art Gallery** (☎ 370 810; Magistratska 25; admission free; ☺ 10am-1pm Mon, Fri & Sat, 10am-1pm & 5-7pm Tue-Thu) has rotating exhibits of Croatian artists.

Festivals & Events
At the beginning of September, the annual **Festival of Kajkavian Songs** (Festival Kajkavske Popevke) features folkloric performances, poetry readings and traditional Zagorje food.

Sleeping & Eating
There's no private accommodation, but **Pod Starim Krovovima** (☎ 370 536; Trg Ljudevita Gaja 15;

s/d 210/340KN), the one pleasant *pension* in the town centre, has eight plain but clean units, each with a bathroom. Cheap and tasty *gablec* (lunch) – for 23KN – can be had at the restaurant downstairs. For a coffee break in the sun, grab an outside table at loungey **Ilir** (☎ 371 444; Trg Ljudevita Gaja 3), or soak up the old-fashioned vibe inside.

Getting There & Away
There are four weekday buses daily from Zagreb to Krapina (39KN, one hour) but only two on Saturday and one on Sunday. There are up to 13 trains on weekdays from Zagreb (33KN, 1½ hours), changing at Zabok; trains run less frequently on weekends.

KRAPINSKE TOPLICE
☎ 049 / pop 1265
This spa town, about 17km southwest of Krapina, is located amid the rolling hills of the Zagorje countryside. The showpieces are the four thermal springs, rich in magnesium and calcium and never below 39°C. The town itself isn't particularly attractive and nor is its atmosphere upbeat, as the visitor pool mainly consists of ageing patients in various rehabilitation programs. That may change with the unveiling of the new spa centre currently under construction, which will feature indoor pools, saunas and various other fitness and wellness facilities.

The bus station is in the centre of town, a stone's throw from most facilities, as is the **tourist office** (☎/fax 232 106; tzo-krapinske-toplice@ kr.t-com.hr; Zagrebačka 4; ☺ 8am-3pm Mon-Fri, to 1pm Sat), which gives out brochures and information.

The smallish rooms at **Hotel Aquae Vivae** (☎ 202 202; www.aquae-vivae.hr; Antuna Mihanovića 2; s/d 320/500KN; ℗ ☒) have outdated decor, so it's worth paying 30KN or 60KN extra for a superior version with a newer bathroom. Request a room that overlooks the verdant backyard. Rates include the use of outdoor and indoor swimming pools and the fitness centre.

A far more scenic option is **Vuglec Breg** (☎ 345 015; www.vuglec-breg.hr; Škarićevo 151; s/d 405/540KN; ℗ ☒), a delightful rural hotel in the village of Škarićevo, 4km from Krapinske Toplice. The four traditional cottages (with seven renovated rooms and three suites) sit amid hills, vineyards and forests, while the restaurant (mains 70KN to 140KN) serves fantastic Zagorje specialities such as *purica s mlincima* (slow-roasted turkey with baked noodles) on a terrace with panoramic vistas. The grounds feature tennis courts, hiking trails, a wine cellar, and a playground and pony riding to keep the little ones busy. Vuglec Breg is best reached with your own wheels. Drive through town in the direction of Krapina following the signs to Vuglec Breg, at hilltop Hršak Breg, take a left and continue to the end of the road.

Located 46km northwest of Zagreb, the spa is well connected to the capital by bus (36KN, 1¼ hours, seven to 12 daily), making it an easy day trip option.

VELIKI TABOR CASTLE
☎ 049

As you approach the hilltop castle of Veliki Tabor, 57km northwest of Zagreb, what unfolds is a pleasing panorama of hills, corn fields, vineyards and forests. The rural vistas alone make a visit worthwhile, as does good traditional dining nearby.

The Croatian aristocracy began building fortified castles in the region to stave off the Turkish threat at the end of the 16th century. The pentagonal **Veliki Tabor Castle** (☎ 343 963; Košnički Hum 1, Desinić; adult/student 20/10KN; ◷ 9am-5pm) was built on the grounds of an earlier medieval structure in the early 16th century, with the four semicircular towers added later. Strategically perched on top of a hill, the golden-yellow castle-fortress has everything a medieval master could want – towers, turrets and holes in the walls for pouring tar and hot oil on the enemy.

Recently renovated, it now features three levels of galleries around the central courtyard, with a collection of medieval weaponry, period furniture and miscellaneous objects showcased in glass cabinets. Bilingual explanations illuminate the display, but far more interesting than the exhibits is wandering around the castle with its towers, staircases and the 1st-floor chapel that houses the skull of Veronika Desinić. According to local lore, this poor village girl was punished for her romance with the castle owner's son and bricked up in the walls; what's on display is a woman's skull found in the walls during the renovations in the 1980s.

Consider timing your castle visit around two annual events: the **Tabor Film Festival** (www.taborfilmfestival.com) in July, an extravaganza of international short films with screenings in the atrium, and a **medieval fair** in September,

which is a one-day celebration featuring sword battles, falcon-hunting tournaments and Renaissance dancing.

To admire the castle from a distance, grab an alfresco table at **Grešna Gorica** (☎ 343 001; www.gresna-gorica.com; Taborgradska Klet 3, Desinić; mains from 42KN), a rustic eatery often stomped over on weekends by day-tripping families from Zagreb. The place is a tad gimmicky but great for kids, with farm animals roaming around, a playground and lots of open space. Adults will appreciate the countryside views and well-prepared Zagorje staples, such as *štrukle* (dough rolls with cottage cheese) and *srneći gulaš* (venison goulash). The restaurant can be found about 2km east of Veliki Tabor; a marked trail leads from the back of the castle to the restaurant (40 minutes on foot).

There are eight daily buses from Zagreb to Desinić (52KN, 1½ hours) from Monday to Saturday and four on Sunday, but you will have to walk 3km northwest to Veliki Tabor.

KUMROVEC
☎ 049 / pop 304

The Zagorje region was the birthplace of several celebrated Croats, most notably Tito, who was born as Josip Broz in Kumrovec. Nestled in the Sutla River valley near the Slovenian border, this pretty village has been thoughtfully transformed into an open-air ethnographic museum. A re-creation of a 19th-century village, the **Staro Selo Museum** (☎ 225 830; www.mdc.hr/kumrovec; Kumrovec bb; adult/student 20/10KN; ◷ 9am-7pm Apr-Sep, to 4pm Oct-Mar) features 40 restored houses and barns made of pressed earth and wood. These *hiže* (Zagorje huts) are now filled with furniture, mannequins, toys, wine presses and baker's tools (all accompanied by English captions) in order to evoke the region's traditional arts, crafts and customs.

With a stream bubbling through the idyllic setting, the museum presents a vivid glimpse of peasant traditions and village life. Note the life-sized bronze sculpture of Marshal Tito outside his humble place of birth, with the original furniture, letters from foreign leaders and random memorabilia inside. On weekends from April to September, the museum hosts demonstrations of blacksmithing, candle-making, pottery-making and flax-weaving.

There are four daily buses between Zagreb and Kumrovec (39KN, 1¼ hours) on weekdays,

CROATIAN NAÏVE ART

Croatia is the birthplace of its own version of naïve art, a distinct style of 20th-century painting that features fantastical and colourful depictions of rural life.

It was the painter Krsto Hegedušić (1901–75) who founded the Hlebine School in the village of the same name in Podravina region, 13km east of the provincial centre of Koprivnica. Upon his return from studying in Paris in the 1930s, he gathered a pocket of self-taught artists with no formal art education and gave them a chance to shine. This first generation of Croatian naïve painters included Ivan Generalić (1914–92), now the most internationally acclaimed, Franjo Mraz (1910–81) and Mirko Virius (1889–1943). All were amateur artists portraying vibrantly coloured and vividly narrated scenes of village life.

Today, a clutch of painters and sculptors still works in Hlebine. Their work can be seen on display in **Hlebine Gallery** (☎ 048-836 075; Trg Ivana Generalića 15, Hlebine; adult/student 10/5KN; ☼ 10am-4pm Mon-Fri, to 2pm Sat). Also in Hlebine is **Galerija Josip Generalić** (☎ 048-836 071; Gajeva 75-83; adult/student 10/5KN; ☼ by appointment), named after the son of the famous Ivan, also a renowned painter, in the Generalić family home.

Other places to see naïve art in Croatia are the Croatian Museum of Naïve Art (p78) in Zagreb and the **Koprivnica Gallery** (☎ 048-622 564; Zrinski Trg 9; ☼ 10am-1pm & 5-8pm Tue-Fri, 10am-1pm Sat & Sun).

one on Saturday and none on Sunday. There are six daily trains (30KN, 1½ to two hours) from Monday to Saturday (five on Sunday), with a change in Sutla.

KLANJEC
☎ 049 / pop 562

Apart from Tito, another notable Croat from Zagorje was sculptor Antun Augustinčić (1900–79), who created the *Monument to Peace* in front of the UN building in New York. Klanjec, his pleasant home town, has a **gallery** (☎ 550 343; www.mdc.hr/augustincic; Trg Antuna Mihanovića 10; adult/student 20/10KN; ☼ 9am-5pm Apr-Sep, to 3pm Tue-Sun Oct-Mar) devoted to his opus, plus lots of headless bronze torsos and a huge replica of the *Peace* statue. There's a small sculpture garden outside and the sculptor's memorial to fallen Partisans nearby.

Once you've seen the gallery, you'll be strapped for more sightseeing, but do stroll around the charming town to see the 17th-century **baroque church** and the **Franciscan monastery** opposite the gallery, and to take in the views of surrounding hills.

The four daily buses running from Zagreb to Kumrovec stop in Klanjec (36KN, one hour).

MARIJA BISTRICA
☎ 049 / pop 1107

Croatia's largest pilgrimage centre is in Zagorje at Marija Bistrica, a village 37km north of Zagreb on the slopes of Mt Medvednica. What steals the show here is the **Marija Bistrica Church** (Hodočasnička Crkva Marije Bistričke), which contains a wooden Gothic statue of the Black Madonna created in the 15th century. The statue's alleged miraculous power dates back to the 16th-century Turkish invasions when it was saved from destruction; it was further proven when a disastrous 1880 fire destroyed everything but the statue. Behind the church is the **Way of the Cross**, a path leading up Calvary Hill, with 14 stations marked with works by Croatian sculptors and paired with excellent vistas. The church attracts 600,000 pilgrims a year, but there were even more in 1998 when Pope John Paul II arrived to beatify Cardinal Alojzije Stepinac. To witness a display of serious religious devotion, visit on 15 August for the most popular pilgrimage of Velika Gospa (Assumption of the Virgin Mary).

There are up to 20 buses a day from Zagreb to Marija Bistrica (30KN to 45KN, 40 minutes to one hour) on weekdays, less on weekends.

Slavonia

As locals say, 'the highest mountain is a cabbage' in pancake-flat Slavonia. While it can't boast much geographical diversity, this fertile region has quite an impressive cultural mix, having blended Hungarian, Serbian and German influences over the centuries. Bounded by three major rivers, the Sava, Drava and Danube, it borders Hungary in the north, Bosnia and Hercegovina in the south and Serbia in the east.

For visitors, Slavonia provides a landscape nearly untouched by tourism, with unique natural wonders and tasty regional cuisine. The wetlands of Kopački Rit are one of Europe's finest ornithological reserves, and you can take a boat tour along its lakes. Osijek, Slavonia's largest town, is well worth a visit for its riverfront setting, a remarkable fortress quarter and Secessionist architecture. The Baranja region to the northeast, with its up-and-coming wine country, has developed 'ethnotourism' in an attempt to preserve traditional village life and make it accessible to tourists. Further east, Vukovar is still healing its war wounds but rising out of the ashes and calling visitors to its war memorials. Ilok, on the Serbian border, with its ancient wine cellars and a preserved old town, gives a glimpse of where East meets West.

Slavonia was once Croatia's breadbasket, its plains yielding wheat, corn, beets, sunflowers and clover, plus some of Croatia's finest wines. Although the 1990s war put a serious dent in the agricultural industry, you'll still see plenty of grain fields and few industrial landscapes. Traces of the war remain, but the peaceful villages, laid-back people and steady year-round prices make Slavonia an ideal destination for those who want to skip the standard experience.

HIGHLIGHTS

- Touring the ancient wine cellars of **Ilok** (p116)
- Sampling the restaurants of Osijek's fortress quarter **Tvrđa** (p110)
- Bird-watching in **Kopački Rit Nature Park** (p112), one of Europe's largest wetlands
- Visiting the war memorials in **Vukovar** (p115)
- Experiencing village life in **Karanac Ethno-Village** (p113)
- Travelling the wine roads of **Baranja** (see boxed text, p114)

- TELEPHONE CODE: 031, 032, 034, 035

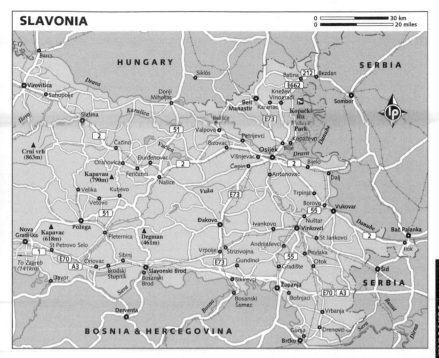

History

Before the 1991 war displaced tens of thousands of inhabitants, Slavonia contained one of the most ethnically diverse populations in Europe. Settled by Slavic tribes in the 7th century, the region was conquered by the Turks in the 16th century. Catholic residents fled and Serbian Orthodox settlers, who were better received by the Turks, arrived en masse.

In 1690, Serb supporters of Vienna, in their battles with the Turks, left Kosovo and settled in the Srijem region around Vukovar. The Turks ceded the land to Austria in 1699 and the Habsburgs turned a large part of the region into a Military Frontier (Vojna Krajina).

The Muslim population left but more Serbs arrived, joined by German merchants, Hungarian, Slovak and Ukrainian peasants, Catholic Albanians and Jews. Much land was sold to German and Hungarian aristocrats who built huge baroque and classical mansions around Osijek, Vukovar and Ilok. Many Germans were killed or expelled after WWI and WWII and their homesteads occupied by Serbs and Montenegrins from southern Yugoslavia.

The large Serbian community prompted Serbian president Slobodan Milošević's attempt to incorporate the region into 'Greater Serbia'. This assault began with the destruction of Vukovar and the shelling of Osijek in 1991. A ceasefire prevailed in 1992, but it wasn't until January 1998 that the region was returned to Croatia as part of the Dayton peace agreement. The scars of war remain clearly visible but the region has been hard at work to revive its economy and inject new life into its landscapes.

Dangers & Annoyances

Osijek and its surrounds were heavily laid with land mines during the 1990s war. Although the city and its outskirts along the main road have been de-mined and are completely safe, it would be unwise to wander through the swampland north of the Drava River, which leads to Kopački Rit. Most mined areas are marked, so watch out for the skeleton head signs.

In summer, the mosquitoes are bloodthirsty little devils, chewing through every bit of flesh they can find. Wear long sleeves and trousers or slather on plenty of repellent after dark.

OSIJEK

☎ 031 / pop 90,411

Photographs of Osijek before the 1990s reveal a relaxed river city of wide avenues, leafy parks and grand 19th-century Secessionist mansions. Sadly, the shells that fell during the 1991 offensive scarred the pretty image of this lively university town.

Although many buildings along the avenues have been restored to their former lustre, the pits and pock-marks on other structures are grim reminders of the war that ravaged eastern Slavonia in the early 1990s. However, the economy is kicking back, with a healthy number of people returning to their home town after years of exile, new hotels and restaurants popping up and tourists slowly trickling in. A new highway extension from Zagreb shortened the travel time by some 40 minutes, while direct flights from Germany also make access easier.

A pleasant waterfront promenade along the Drava River, an imposing 18th-century fortress and the resilient spirit of this relaxed city all make excellent reasons to visit Osijek.

History

Osijek's location on the Drava River, near its junction with the Danube (Dunav in Croatian), has made it strategically important for more than two millennia. It was the Slavic settlers that gave Osijek its name; by the 12th century it was a thriving market town. In 1526, the Turks destroyed Osijek, rebuilt it in Ottoman style and made it into an administrative centre.

The Austrians chased the Turks out in 1687, the Muslims fled into Bosnia, and the city was repopulated with Serbs, Croats, Germans and Hungarians. Still wary of Turkish attacks, the Austrians built the fortress that still stands, Tvrđa, in the early 18th century.

Until the recent 1990s war, Osijek was a powerful industrial centre of former Yugoslavia. When the war broke out in 1991, the federal Yugoslav army and Serbian paramilitary units overran the Baranja region north of Osijek. The first shells began falling in July 1991 from Serbian positions across the Drava River. When Vukovar fell in November of that year, federal and Serbian forces made Osijek the object of their undivided attention, pounding it with artillery as thousands of terrified residents poured out of the city. This devastating shelling continued until May 1992, but the city never fell.

The economy was seriously hurt by the costs of reconstruction and of housing refugees, as well as the loss of markets for its products. In the last couple of years, the city has awoken from its postwar slumber and a new optimism is in the air.

Orientation

Stretching along the southern bank of the Drava River, Osijek is composed of three boroughs: the Upper Town (Gornji Grad), the Lower Town (Donji Grad) and the 18th-century fortress, Tvrđa. The bus station (a new one is being built just to the west) and train station are adjacent in the southern part of the Upper Town. Most of the sights, hotels, cafés and shops are located between the train and bus stations and the river.

The main shopping street is Kapucinska, which becomes the wide Europska Avenija in the east, bordered by a series of parks planted with chestnut and linden trees. A pleasant riverfront promenade stretches all the way to the city's outskirts.

Information

INTERNET ACCESS

Press Café (☎ 212 313; Lorenza Jägera 24; per hr 15KN; ⏲ 7am-11pm Mon-Sat, 8am-11pm Sun)

MEDICAL SERVICES

Hospital (☎ 511 511; Josipa Huttlera 4)

MONEY

Privredna Banka (Stjepana Radića 19)
Slavonska Banka (Kapucinska 29)

POST

Post office (Kardinala Alojzija Stepinca 17; ⏲ 7.30am-7pm Mon-Sat) You can make phone calls and get cash advances on MasterCard.

TOURIST INFORMATION

Tourist office (☎ /fax 203 755; www.tzosijek.hr; Županijska 2; ⏲ 9am-5pm Mon-Fri, to 4pm Sat) Distributes plentiful brochures, booklets and maps.

TRAVEL AGENCIES

OK Tours (☎ 212 815; www.ok-tours.hr; Trg Slobode 7; ⏲ 9am-7pm Mon-Fri, to noon Sat) Good source of local information and some private accommodation.
Panturist (☎ 214 388; www.panturist.hr; Kapucinska 19; ⏲ 8am-8pm Mon-Fri, to 1pm Sat) Slavonia's largest

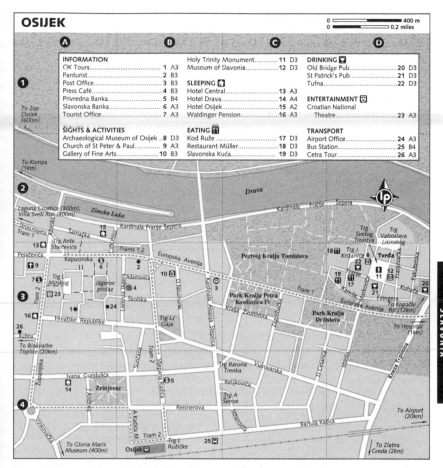

OSIJEK

0 _____ 400 m
0 _____ 0.2 miles

INFORMATION
OK Tours............................... 1 A3
Panturist.............................. 2 B3
Post Office............................ 3 B3
Press Café............................ 4 B3
Privredna Banka.................... 5 B4
Slavonska Banka................... 6 A3
Tourist Office....................... 7 A3

SIGHTS & ACTIVITIES
Archaeological Museum of Osijek ..8 D3
Church of St Peter & Paul........... 9 A3
Gallery of Fine Arts.................. 10 B3

Holy Trinity Monument............ 11 D3
Museum of Slavonia................. 12 D3

SLEEPING
Hotel Central......................... 13 A3
Hotel Drava........................... 14 A4
Hotel Osijek.......................... 15 A2
Waldinger Pension.................. 16 A3

EATING
Kod Ruže 17 D3
Restaurant Müller................... 18 D3
Slavonska Kuća...................... 19 D3

DRINKING
Old Bridge Pub...................... 20 D3
St Patrick's Pub..................... 21 D3
Tufna.................................. 22 D3

ENTERTAINMENT
Croatian National
    Theatre............................ 23 A3

TRANSPORT
Airport Office........................ 24 A3
Bus Station........................... 25 B4
Cetra Tour............................ 26 A3

agency, it runs buses to the coast as well as to Germany, Switzerland and Bosnia and Hercegovina.

Zlatna Greda (☎ 565 180; www.zlatna-greda.org; Opatijska 26F; ☻ 8am-4pm Mon-Fri) An offshoot of the Zeleni Osijek (www.zeleni-osijek.hr) environmental nonprofit group, which runs an ecocentre in the wetlands of Baranja, this agency organises hiking trips, photo safaris, boat and canoe rides along the Danube, and bike tours.

Sights
TVRĐA
Built under Habsburg rule as a defence against Turkish attacks, the 18th-century citadel was relatively undamaged during the recent war. This baroque complex of cobblestone streets, spacious squares and stately mansions reveals

a remarkable architectural unity, lending it an open-air museum feel.

The main square, Trg Svetog Trojstva, is marked by the elaborate **Holy Trinity Monument**, a baroque pillar erected in 1729 to commemorate the victims of the 18th-century plague that swept the city.

The **Museum of Slavonia** (Muzej Slavonije Osijek; ☎ 250 730; Trg Svetog Trojstva 6; adult/student 15/10KN; ☻ 8am-2pm Tue-Fri, 10am-1pm Sat & Sun) traces Slavonia's long history, beginning with implements from the Bronze Age and displays of coins, pottery and utensils from the Roman colony of Mursa.

Diagonally opposite is the city's newest museum, the **Archaeological Museum of Osijek** (Arheološki Muzej Osijek; ☎ 232 132; Trg Svetog Trojstva 2;

adult/student 15/8KN; ☺ 10am-3pm Tue-Fri, to 1pm Sat & Sun). In the renovated city guard building with a glass dome over an arcaded patio, it showcases finds – from Roman stones to Celtic helmets – unearthed during the building of the new highway.

UPPER TOWN

The towering **Church of St Peter & Paul** (☎ 310 020; ☺ 8am-7.30pm) looms over Trg Ante Starčevića with its 90m-high tower, surpassed in height only by the cathedral in Zagreb. Built in the 1890s, this red-brick neo-Gothic structure features an interior with 40 elaborate stained-glass windows in Viennese style, and vividly coloured frescoes by Croatian painter Mirko Rački.

Housed in an elegant neoclassical mansion, the **Gallery of Fine Arts** (Galerija Likovnih Umjetnosti; ☎ 251 280; Europska Avenija 9; adult/student 10/5KN; ☺ 10am-6pm Tue-Fri, to 1pm Sat & Sun) contains a collection of paintings and sculptures by Slavonian artists from the 18th century onwards.

BEYOND THE CENTRE

As an escape from museums and churches, take a free ride on the emblematic *kompa* (a wooden pedestrian ferry propelled by the water current) from the shore of Gornji Grad to **Zoo Osijek** (☎ 285 234; Tvrđavica 1; adult/child 7/3KN; ☺ 9am-7pm Mar-Aug, to 5pm Sep-Feb) on the other side of the Drava. Croatia's largest zoo spreads over 11 verdant riverside hectares, with 80 animal species and a reptile-filled aquarium. The *kompa* operates from 8am to midnight, June to September, and from 9am to 6pm, October to May.

Worth a trek to the semi-industrial zone of Bosutsko Naselje is Osijek's most offbeat sight: the **Gloria Maris Museum** (☎ 273 008; Svetog Josipa Radnika 35; adult/child 20/15KN; ☺ 10am-1pm & 4-7pm Tue-Sat, 10am-1pm Sun) of sea shells and marine life. This private collection of over 250,000 items – from the giant mammoth tooth found in the Sava River to pearl shells from the Indian Ocean – has been gathered over a lifetime by avid collector Ivan Filipović. Ivan also shares a million fascinating titbits on an educational guided tour (request in advance for an English speaker).

Festivals & Events

Extreme sports fans should make it here in August, when the **Pannonian Challenge** (www .pannonian.org) event attracts an international following of adrenaline junkies who compete in skateboarding, BMX skills, in-line skating and mountain biking.

Sleeping

Osijek recently got a fresh crop of hotels, and a few more are in the works. There are no hostels and limited private accommodation. For private rooms (from 165KN per person), ask at the tourist office or OK Tours (p108).

our pick Waldinger Pension (☎ 250 450; www .waldinger.hr; Županijska 8; s/d 290/440KN; P ❄ 🖥) In the quiet backyard of Osijek's boutique Waldinger Hotel, this three-star annexe – with a pond and garden – offers plain but gracious rooms. The hotel rooms (single/double 650/950KN) in the elegant Secessionist building come with jacuzzis. The lovely tearoom showcases rotating exhibits and fantastic cakes.

Hotel Central (☎ 283 399; www.hotel-central-os.hr; Trg Ante Starčevića 6; s/d 335/514KN; P 🖥) While it no longer holds its status as the grandest of Osijek hotels, this old-fashioned property still has a prime location on the main square. The room decor is out of date, but perks include wireless internet and nice panoramas from the square-facing units.

Hotel Drava (☎ 250 500; www.hotel-drava.com; Ivana Gundulića 25a; s/d 380/680KN; P ❄ 🖥) Tucked away from the busy street, a hop and a skip from the train and bus stations, this small family-run hotel has colourful rooms, each slightly different but all with modern furnishings.

Villa Sveti Rok (☎ 310 490; www.villa-sveti-rok.hr; Svetog Roka 13; s/d 585/785KN; P ❄ 🖥) Hole up in one of the plush rooms at this swanky little guest house on a leafy residential street a stone's throw from the centre. You may not want to leave – there are DVD players, hydromassage showers, wireless internet and piped music in the bathrooms.

Hotel Osijek (☎ 230 333; www.hotelosijek.hr; Šamačka 4; s/d 760/950KN; P ❄ 🖥) While your next-door neighbours are busy making business deals, you can indulge in the luxury facilities and in-room trappings of this 14-storey riverfront hotel. There's a top-floor wellness centre and gourmet restaurant, and delicious cakes and ice cream at the pastry shop.

Eating

Osijek is the place to sample hearty and spicy Slavonian cuisine, which is strongly influenced by neighbouring Hungary. Paprika is sprinkled on almost every dish and, as else-where in continental Croatia, meat is promi-nent. Freshwater fish features highly, often in a delicious stew called *fiš paprikaš*, served with noodles. Note that all restaurants listed here are closed on Sunday evening.

Laguna Croatica (☎ 369 203; Dubrovačka 13; mains 35-75KN) Once you've studied the extensive and varied menu, you can admire the bric-a-brac on the walls of this dark basement restaurant a short walk from the centre. Try the uniquely Slavonian version of calamari – filled with *kulen* (spicy pork sausage) and cheese!

Slavonska Kuća (☎ 369 955; Kamila Firingera 26a; mains from 40KN) This rustic old house on the edge of Tvrđa serves mean *fiš paprikaš* and venison *perkelt* (a goulash-like stew), as well as other regional specialities. Wash your meal down with *graševina*, a fruity white wine.

Restaurant Müller (☎ 204 770; Trq Jurja Križanića 9; mains 45-70KN) Conveniently located at the heart of Tvrđa, this place is perfectly pleasant and a decent choice for its well-prepared if unin-spired Croatian and international standards. Frog legs à la Parisienne anyone?

ourpick Kod Ruže (☎ 206066; Kuhačeva 25a; mains from 45KN) Clad in wood and villagey knick-knacks, one of the city's newest restaurants has quickly become a locals' favourite for its excellent re-gional mainstays. Try the *čobanac* stew with game and don't miss the homemade cakes.

Drinking & Entertainment
BARS & NIGHTCLUBS
On warm evenings, everyone socialises at the outdoor cafés that line the riverfront around Hotel Osijek. Stjepana Radića has a cluster of cafés and bars catering to the local student population.

In winter, the coffee-sipping moves in-doors to *kavanas*, as cafés are known locally. Waldinger, Central and Osijek are particu-larly popular. Most nightlife is in Tvrđa where nobody minds the noise.

ourpick Old Bridge Pub (☎ 211611; www.oldbridge pub.hr; Franje Kuhača 4) You'll catch anything from karaoke to *tamburica* (a small stringed instru-ment popular in Slavonian folk music) con-certs at this classy pub-bar. There's tasty finger food, a huge menu of drinks and an upstairs restaurant with a country club vibe.

St Patrick's Pub (Franje Kuhača 15) With tables spilling out on Tvrđa's main square, this Irish-style pub is a simple but popular affair where lads and lasses chug their Osječko brews.

Tufna (www.tufna.hr; Franje Kuhača 10) The old popular Posh club has been turned into Tufna, Osijek's hottest nightclub with two floors, DJs spinning anything from disco to electro, and two-for-one happy hours from 10pm till midnight every weekend.

THEATRE
Croatian National Theatre (Hrvatsko Narodno Kazalište; ☎ 220 700, Županijska 9) Designed in 1866 in his-toricist style, the theatre features a regular program of drama, ballet and opera perform-ances from September to May.

Getting There & Away
Osijek is a major transport hub with buses and trains arriving and departing in all directions.

AIR
Klisa Airport (☎ 514 451, 060 339 338; Vukovarska 67, Klisa) is 20km from Osijek on the road to Vukovar. Its city office is at Vijenac J Gotovca 4. Germanwings has a direct flight from Cologne twice weekly. Croatia Airlines has weekly flights to Zagreb, Dubrovnik, Split, Pula and Zadar.

BUS
Following are some of the international buses that depart from Osijek. Many more buses leave for Germany than can be listed here.

Destination	Fare (KN)	Duration (hr)	Daily/weekly services
Belgrade	107	3½	5 daily
Tuzla	112	4	1 daily
Vienna	302	10	2 weekly
Zürich	675	7½	1 weekly

The following domestic buses depart from Osijek:

Destination	Fare (KN)	Duration (hr)	Daily services
Bizovačke Toplice	22	½	3 (weekdays only)
Đakovo	32	¾	17
Dubrovnik	300	14	1
Požega	78	2¼	5 (2 on Sun)
Rijeka	235	7	1
Slavonski Brod	67	1¾	20
Split	283	11	1
Vukovar	31	¾	11
Zagreb	128	4	9

ĐAKOVO CATHEDRAL & HORSES

The peaceful provincial town of Đakovo is just 35km to the south of Osijek and makes for an easy day trip. There are three major reasons to visit: its impressive cathedral, the Lipizzaner horses and a wonderful folk festival every summer.

The town's pride and glory is the red-brick **cathedral** (☎ 031-802 200; Trg Strossmayera 6; ⏰ 6amnoon & 3-7pm), which dominates the town centre with its two 84m-high belfries. Commissioned by Bishop Strossmayer in 1862, this neo-Romanesque structure features a three-nave interior colourfully painted with biblical scenes.

Đakovo is famous for its Lipizzaner horses, a noble pure breed with a lineage that can be traced back to the 16th century. They are bred on a farm outside town and trained at **Ergela** (☎ 031-813 286; www.ergela-djakovo.hr; Augusta Šenoe 45; adult/student 20/10KN; ⏰ 7am-5.30pm Mon-Fri), a short walk from the cathedral. About 50 horses undergo daily training for their eventual work as high-class carriage horses.

Đakovački Vezovi (Đakovo Embroidery) in early July each year features a display by the Lipizzaner horses and a folklore show complete with folkloric dancing and traditional songs.

TRAIN

There's one train a day in either direction between Peés and Osijek (56KN, two hours). The train from Osijek connects to Budapest (207KN, six hours). There is a daily train to Sarajevo (138KN, seven hours).

The following domestic trains depart from Osijek:

Destination	Fare (KN)	Duration (hr)	Daily services
Bizovačke Toplice	17	¼	12
Đakovo	23	½	8
Požega	53	2½	3
Rijeka	200	9-10	2
Šibenik	242	14	1 (change in Perković)
Slavonski Brod	45	1½	7 (only 2 direct)
Zagreb	130	4-5	7

Getting Around

A shuttle bus takes people from the airport to the city centre for 25KN. It also departs from the bus station 2½ hours before each flight.

Osijek has a tram line that dates from 1884 and makes transportation within the city easy. The fare is 8KN each way from the driver, or 7KN from a *tisak* (newsstand). On Saturday, a **tourist tram** (tickets 10KN; ⏰ 10am-1pm) with a guide makes an hour-long circuit of the city centre (for an English-speaking guide, contact the tourist office in advance).

For visitors, the most useful tram lines are 2, which connects the train and bus station with Trg Ante Starčevića in the centre, and 1, which goes to Tvrđa.

There is a bus line that connects Osijek to Bilje in Baranja. Take bus 6 (route 24, 25 or 27) with the sign Darda–Bilje.

BARANJA
☎ 031

A small triangle in the far northeast of Croatia at the confluence of the Drava and Danube Rivers, Baranja ('wine mother' in Hungarian) stretches east of Osijek towards Serbia, north towards the town of Beli Manastir and southwest towards Đakovo. The Hungarian influence is strongly felt in this largely agricultural area; even all the towns have bilingual names.

In the last few years, this scenic area of swamps, vineyards, orchards and wheat fields (without a single street light) has been on the rise as eastern Croatia's most interesting tourist destination. That's thanks in part to its star attraction, the bird sanctuary of Kopački Rit, but also to a clutch of authentic farm stays, regional restaurants and up-and-coming wineries.

Kopački Rit Nature Park

Only 12km northeast of Osijek, **Kopački Rit Nature Park** (Park Prirode Kopački Rit; www.kopacki-rit.com; adult/child 10/5KN) is one of the largest wetlands in Europe, home to 141 bird species throughout its 23,000 hectares. Formed by the meeting of the Drava and Danube Rivers, this vast floodplain has two main lakes, Sakadaško and Kopačevo, surrounded by a remarkable variety of vegetation – from aquatic and grassland flora to willow, poplar and oak forests. Depending on the season, you can find water lilies, sedges, water ferns, duckweeds, reeds and ryegrass.

Beneath the waters lie 44 species of fish, including carp, bream, pike, catfish and perch. Above the water buzz 21 kinds of mosquito (bring a tonne of repellent!) and roam red deer, wild boar, pine marten and red foxes. But it's really about the birds here – look for the rare black storks, white-tailed eagles, great crested grebes, mallard ducks, purple herons, cormorants, falcons and wild geese. The best time to come is during the spring and autumn migrations, when hundreds of thousands of birds rest here before continuing their flight.

The park was heavily mined during the war and closed for many years as a result. Most mines have now been cleared, safe trails have been marked, and the park has a spanking new **visitor centre** (☎ 752 320; ☻ 9am-5pm), located at the main entrance along the Bilje–Kopačevo road.

You can walk the two educational trails nearby, but the best way to take in the wetlands is on a **boat tour** (adult/child Apr-Jun & Sep-Nov 60/45KN, Jul & Aug 40/25KN). These one-hour trips around the southern section of Sakadaško depart several times daily from an embarkation point about 1km from the visitor centre. Although the boat fits 54, book in advance, especially during spring and autumn.

At the northern end of the park, 12km from the visitor centre, is an Austro-Hungarian castle complex, Dvorac Tikveš. It's home to the renovated **bio-ecological research station** (☎ 752 320; s/d 200/400KN), the park's only lodging. The ground floor has labs used by scientists; accessed from the verandah upstairs are seven pleasant en suite rooms with leafy views. Once used by Tito as a hunting lodge, the castle was occupied by the Serbian paramilitary leader Arkan in the early 1990s, and used as the training centre for his infamous troops. The forests around the complex are still mined, so don't wander off by yourself. Don't miss lunch at the restaurant (mains 42KN to 86KN) where carp is roasted on a forked branch and *fiš paprikaš* slow-cooked in the open-fire kitchen.

There is no public transport to the park, but you can take a local Osijek bus to Bilje and walk the remaining 3km. Alternatively, rent a bike in Osijek at **CetraTour** (☎ 031-372 920; www.cetratour.hr; Ružina 16; ☻ 8.30am-3.30pm Mon-Fri, 9am-1pm Sat) or take a day trip with Zlatna Greda (p109).

AROUND KOPAČKI RIT

The low-key town of Bilje, just 5km north of Osijek, is a good alternative base for Kopački Rit. The prime source of information here is **Bilje Plus** (☎ 750 264; www.biljeplus.hr), an association of five rural B&Bs that rents rooms and bikes (70KN per day). One of those is **Crvendać** (☎ 750 264; www.crvendac.com; Biljske Satnije ZNG RH 5; s/d 155/310KN), run by two outgoing women, Ankica and Marija. As biking enthusiasts, they will inform you of the cycle paths in the area, such as the 80km **Pannonian Peace Trail**, which connects Osijek and the Serbian city of Sombor. The three rooms inside this red-themed house are simple and clean, with one shared bathroom; there's also an internet kiosk (1KN per minute).

The quiet village of Kopačevo on the edge of Kopački Rit is home to an outstanding regional restaurant, **Zelena Žaba** (☎ 752 212; Ribarska 3; mains from 40KN), or 'green frog', after the thousands of squatters bellowing in the backyard swamp. The specialities are *fiš paprikaš* and *fiš perkelt*, a fish stew with homemade noodles, soft cheese and bacon.

Karanac Ethno-Village

Located in the far north of Baranja, 8km east of Beli Manastir, the ethno-village of Karanac provides an authentic slice of Slavonian village life. In fact, 95% of its inhabitants still work in agriculture. Lined with cherry trees and lovingly tended gardens, home to three churches (Reformist, Catholic and Orthodox) and proud of its well-preserved Pannonian architecture, it's a success story of 'ethnotourism'.

Several accommodation options are available, but the man who started it all still offers the real-deal experience at his restored 1910 farmhouse, **Sklepić** (☎ 720 271; www.sklepic.hr, in Croatian; Kolodvorska 58; s/d 230/338KN). The en suite rooms here are small, rustic and charming, and breakfast is a delicious affair of homemade jams, *kulen* and free-range eggs.

Sklepić also has an **ethno-museum** (☎ 720 271; admission 15KN; ☻ by appointment) in an 1897 rural estate at the end of the village. He greets groups on a horse and with his family shows off 2000 traditional objects in the string of old-fashioned rooms, workshops, a wine cellar and stables. For an extra 10KN, you get homemade snacks thrown in.

Karanac has one of Baranja's best restaurants, **Baranjska Kuća** (☎ 720 180; Kolodvorska 99; mains from 45KN). The owners say they'll accept only as many guests as they can bake bread for – so reserve ahead, especially on weekends. You can sample traditional dishes, such as

---

A SIP OF SLAVONIAN WINE

Known mainly for its whites such as *graševina* and *traminac*, the viticulture of Slavonia is undergoing a serious renaissance, so let's take a walk down the wine roads of eastern Croatia. You should call ahead at all these cellars to make sure somebody is there to receive you and show you around.

Kutjevo (☎ 034-255 002; www.kutjevo.com, in Croatian; Kralja Tomislava 1, Kutjevo; ⊗ by appointment) is home to a medieval wine cellar dating from 1232, formerly of the Cistercian Abbey; you can visit on a guided tour (20KN). Nearby are two of Slavonia's top wineries: **Krauthaker** (☎ 034-315 000; www.krauthaker.hr; Ivana Jambrovića 6, Kutjevo; tasting & tour 40KN), famous for its fruity *graševina*, and **Enjingi** (☎ 034-267 201; www.enjingi.hr; Hrnjevac 87, Vetovo; tasting & tour 50KN), which has an award-winning ecological production and 51 years of winemaking experience.

In Baranja, grape cultivation has been revived on the gentle hills around Kneževi Vinogradi, long known for its wine production. A smattering of up-and-coming winegrowers, mainly in the villages of Zmajevac and Suza, work along these well-marked wine trails. Traditionalist in its approach to winemaking, **Gerstmajer** (☎ 031-735 276; Šandora 31, Zmajevac) offers tasting tours of its 11 vineyard hectares and the cellar. Just down the hill is the area's biggest producer, **Josić** (☎ 031-734 410; www.josic.hr; Planina 194, Zmajevac), which also has a restaurant on site. More commercial **Kolar** (☎ 031-733 006; Maršala Tita 141; ⊗ 9am-5pm) offers wine tastings at the cellar and shop on the main road in Suza.

Slavonia also boasts the ancient cellars in Ilok (p116) as well as Croatia's first wine hotel, **Zdjelarević** (☎ 035-427 775; www.zdjelarevic.hr), located in Brodski Stupnik near Slavonski Brod. The hotel has marked educational paths through the vineyards, which you can visit with an agronomist who will teach you about pedology (soils) and the difference between grape varieties. At the hotel's restaurant, the chefs use Zdjelarević's wines in cooking and promote the many edible plants that grow here; for instance, they'll serve nettle soup, which is full of iron and was once used for cleaning people's organs. The owner, Višnja Zdjelarević, says that each winemaker in Croatia has a story and a philosophy – and they all think theirs is the right approach. The smell, taste and structure of wine from the same sort of grape can be entirely different. The great thing is, you can feel the hand of the winemaker in each wine that you sample.

---

catfish *perkelt* stew, and more offbeat ones, including snails in nettle sauce. Check out the chestnut-tree-shaded backyard with traditional barns, a blacksmith's workshop and a natural ice house.

BIZOVAČKE TOPLICE
☎ 031

In the town of Bizovac, this vast **spa resort** (☎ 685 100; www.bizovacke-toplice.hr; Sunčana 39) comprises more than 10 pools, six of which are fed by thermal springs at 96°C, including a mineral-rich salt spring. The water park has a series of interconnected indoor and outdoor pools, as well as whirlpools, jacuzzis, a music cave and water slides. It's best tackled as a day trip from Osijek (30KN per day to use the pools), but should you decide to stay there are two options. The rooms at **Hotel Termia** (☎ 685 100; www.bizovacke-toplice.hr; Sunčana 39; s/d 294/478KN; 🖫) could use a freshening up but are clean and adequate. A nearby annexe, Hotel Toplice, has units with shared bathrooms for 144/238KN per single/double.

The spa, 20km west of Osijek, is connected to Osijek by train (17KN, 15 minutes, 12 daily); the train station is about 1km from the spa. There are buses from Osijek (22KN, 30 minutes, three daily) on weekdays only.

VUKOVAR
☎ 032 / pop 31,670

When you visit Vukovar today, it's a challenge to visualise this town as it was before the war. A pretty place on the Danube, with historical roots that stretch back to the 10th century and a series of elegant baroque mansions, it once bustled with art galleries and museums. All that changed with the brutal siege of 1991 that destroyed its economy, culture, physical infrastructure and civic harmony.

Since the return of Vukovar to Croatia in 1998, there has been much progress in repairing the damage. In the centre, there are new buildings, but many pock-marked and blasted facades remind you of the violent past. The former water tower on the road to Ilok has been left as a living testament to destruction.

Less progress has been made in restoring civic harmony. Local Serbs and Croats live in parallel and hostile universes, socialising in separate spheres. Even their children attend separate Serb or Croat schools. A bevy of international organisations is trying to encourage harmony and integration, but forgiveness comes hard to those who have lost family members and livelihoods.

The city needs a boost to its economy so consider making a contribution – you can do so by visiting, spending and paying homage.

Orientation & Information

The bus station is at the northern end of town, opposite the daily market and a block south of the town's main street, Strossmayera. Leading into the town centre, Strossmayera turns into Ulica Dr Franje Tuđmana once you've crossed the Vuka River. There are ATMs at several locations along Strossmayera.

The **tourist office** (☎ /fax 442 889; www.turizam vukovar.hr; J J Strossmayera 15; ☻ 7am-fri Mon-Fri) has few brochures but can be a useful source of information. For biking tours, kayaking on the Danube and various activities in Vukovar and Ilok, turn to **Danubium Tours** (☎ /fax 445 455; www.danubiumtours .hr; Trg Republike Hrvatske 1; ☻ 8am-3pm Mon-Sat).

Sights

The **Town Museum** (Gradski Muzej; ☎ 441 270; Županijska 2; adult/child 10/5KN; ☻ 7am-3pm Mon-Fri) is lodged in the 18th-century Eltz Palace at the end of Strossmayera. Badly damaged and looted during the war, it currently has temporary exhibits on the 2nd floor and a tiny permanent display on the ground floor.

However emotionally wrenching an experience it may be, it's important to visit the war memorial sites in and around town. At **Place of Memory: Vukovar Hospital** (☎ 452 011; www.ob -vukovar.hr/mjesto-sjecanja; Županijska 37; admission 10KN; ☻ 1-3pm Mon-Fri, by appointment), a ground-floor section has been turned into a multimedia museum recreating the tragic events that took place in the hospital during the 1991 siege (see boxed text, below). The stirring tour takes you through a series of sandbag-protected corridors with video projections of war footage, bomb holes and the claustrophobic atomic shelter where newborn babies and the nurses' children were kept. There are small cubicles where you can listen to interviews and speeches by the victims and survivors.

About 3.5km out of town along the main road to Ilok is the **Memorial War Cemetery**, a heartbreaking place with 938 white crosses that symbolise the victims of the siege.

A further 2.5km en route to Ilok is the turn-off to the **Ovčara Memorial** (☻ 10am-5pm), which is another 4km down the road. This is the hangar where the 200 victims from the hospital were tortured. Inside the dark room are projections of the victims' photos, with a single candlelight burning in the middle. The memorial is free, but consider buying a souvenir at the shop to support the project. The victims met their death in a cornfield

---

THE SIEGE OF VUKOVAR

Before the war, Vukovar had a multiethnic population of about 44,000, of which Croats constituted 44% and Serbs 37%. As Croatia edged away from former Yugoslavia in early 1991, tensions mounted between the two groups. In August 1991, the federal Yugoslav force launched a full-scale artillery and infantry assault in an attempt to seize the town.

By the end of August all but 15,000 of Vukovar's original inhabitants had fled. Those who remained cowered in bomb-proof cellars, living on tinned food and rationed water while bodies piled up in the streets above them. For several months of the siege, the city held out as its pitifully outnumbered defenders warded off the attacks.

After weeks of hand-to-hand fighting, Vukovar surrendered on 18 November. On 20 November, Serb-Yugoslav soldiers entered Vukovar's hospital and removed 400 patients, staff and their families. Two hundred of those people were massacred near the village of Ovčara (see above), their bodies dumped in a mass grave nearby. In 2007 at the War Tribunal in The Hague, two Yugoslav army officers, Mile Mrkšić and Veselin Šljivančanin, were sentenced to 20 and five years in prison respectively for their role in this massacre.

It's estimated that 2000 people – including 1100 civilians – were killed in the defence of Vukovar. There were 4000 wounded, several thousand who disappeared, presumably into mass graves, and 22,000 who were forced into exile.

another 1.5km down the road, now marked with a black marble gravestone, covered with candles and flowers.

Festivals & Events
A good time to visit is during the annual **Vukovar Film Festival** (www.vukovarfilmfestival.com) in July, which shows features, docos and shorts from Danubian countries.

Sleeping & Eating
Hotel Dunav (☎ 441 285; Trg Republike Hrvatske 1; s/d 250/420KN; **P**) On the Danube, this place has basic rooms, some with river views.

Hotel Lav (☎ 445 100; www.hotel-lav.hr; JJ Strossmayera 18; s/d 590/900KN; **P** **⌨**) This more luxurious four-star option is in a modern structure with all the expected trappings, such as wireless internet and a restaurant.

Vrške (☎ 441 788; Parobrodarska 3; mains from 35KN) The interior here is nondescript, but the meat and river-fish specialities are tasty and the location on a tree-shaded terrace along the river is particularly lovely.

Getting There & Away
Vukovar has good bus connections to Osijek (31KN, 45 minutes, 16 daily) and all around Croatia, including Zagreb (151KN, five hours, four to five daily). There's a bus that runs from Vukovar to Belgrade (92KN, 2¾ hours, five daily) in Serbia. There's also a recently introduced direct train from Vukovar to Zagreb (114KN, four hours).

ILOK
☎ 032 / pop 8350
The easternmost town of Croatia, 37km from Vukovar, Ilok sits perched on a hill overlooking the Danube and the Serbian region of Vojvodina across the river. Surrounded by the gentle wine-growing hills of Fruška Gora, famous for wine production since Roman times, and with a pleasant riverfront below, this preserved medieval town is where East meets West.

Occupied by Serbia in the early 1990s, it was reintegrated into Croatia in 1998. Wine production has since been revived – the area now has 15 wineries you can tour – and the fortified town centre is being renovated following recent archaeological excavations. Even though it currently looks like a construction site (with plans to finish by 2010), the remote town is well worth a visit.

Orientation & Information
The bus stops in the town centre, at Nazorova, just steps from the medieval town. The **tourist office** (☎ 590 020; www.turizamilok.hr; Trg Nikole Iločkog 2; ☷ 8am-4pm Mon-Fri) has many excellent brochures, but call ahead as it has sporadic hours. **Danubium Tours** (p115) organises biking trips and wine tours (140KN for a three-hour tour, with lunch and a wine cellar visit).

Sights & Activities
The medieval town is a leafy place surrounded by the remains of the city walls. It has two rare specimens of Ottoman heritage: a 16th-century **hammam** and a **turbe**, the grave of a Turkish nobleman.

The centrepiece is the **Odescalchi Castle** (Šetalište Oca Mladena Barbarića bb), built on the foundations of a 15-century structure by King Nikola Iločki. In the late 17th century, it was given to the noble Italian family Odescalchi as a reward for their help in liberating Ilok from the Turks. They restored the medieval castle in the baroque-classicist style and built the wine cellars beneath it.

From spring 2009, the castle will house the **city museum** (Muzej Grada Iloka; ☎ 590 065), with a permanent exhibition of archaeological, ethnographic and art items, from old wine equipment to folk costumes. The ancient winery is now run by **Ilok Wine Cellars** (Iločki Podrumi; ☎ 590 088; www.ilocki-podrumi.hr; Dr Franje Tuđmana 72; tours 5KN; ☷ 8am-6pm) next door. It's famous for its *traminac*, a dry white wine served at the coronation of Queen Elizabeth II. The 20-minute tour takes you to the atmospheric underground cellar with its oak barrels; tours in English need to be arranged in advance.

Sleeping & Eating
Hotel Dunav (☎ 596 500; www.hoteldunavilok.com; Julija Benešića 62; s/d 300/500KN; **P** **⌨**) Ilok has its own excellent three-star Hotel Dunav on the Danube, featuring a set of recently renovated rooms with verdant views and a lovely riverfront café terrace. Danubium Tours has a branch here.

Odescalchi Castle (☎ 590 126; Šetalište Oca Mladena Barbarića 5; mains from 45KN) This is the town's best restaurant, serving regional specialities under a domed ceiling.

Getting There & Away
Ilok is connected to Vukovar by 14 daily buses (31KN, 45 minutes).

Kvarner Region

Protected by soaring mountains, covered with luxuriant forests, lined with beaches and dotted with islands, the Kvarner Gulf (Quarnero in Italian) abounds in holiday options. You can explore the urban fabric of Rijeka, Croatia's third-largest city and biggest port, swim in clear seas off secluded bays, hike in the dense woods of Učka and Risnjak parks, feast on fresh seafood in the foodie mecca of Volosko, wander about medieval Rab Town on the eponymous island, and tour the ancient hilltop villages of Cres.

Covering 3300 sq km between Rijeka in the north and Pag in the south, Kvarner is a microcosm of the many influences that have formed Croatian culture. Rijeka owes its architecture to Hungary, and echoes of the Venetian era pervade the islands of Cres, Lošinj and Rab, while Krk was the seat of Croatia's native nobility, the Frankopan dukes. The mild weather explains the wealth of vegetation: the islands of Cres, Lošinj and Krk feature some 1300 plant species; Rab is known for its evergreen forests; and the lush greenery around Opatija helped establish its reputation as a health resort.

From the gateway city of Rijeka, you can easily connect to the 19th-century elegance of Opatija or Baška's sandy beach on Krk. The picture-perfect old towns of Krk, Rab, Mali Lošinj and Cres are just a ferry ride away, as are plenty of remote coves for scenic swimming. Krk is the largest and most developed island, with excellent tourist infrastructure and summer hordes that make use of it. Mali Lošinj is also packed but prettier, and you're within easy reach of wild unspoiled Cres with its virgin woods and medieval villages. Rab has the most striking old town and enough hidden coves to easily escape the shoulder-to-shoulder summer crowds.

KVARNER REGION

HIGHLIGHTS

- Sampling seafood specialities in the foodie mecca of **Volosko** (p128)
- Taking in the panoramic views from Rijeka's **Trsat Castle** (p122)
- Enjoying a verdant hike in **Učka Nature Park** (p129)
- Learning about Adriatic dolphins at **Blue World** (p136) on Veli Lošinj
- Hiking the primeval forests of Tramuntana on **Cres** (p138)
- Wandering the cobbled streets of medieval **Rab Town** (p149)

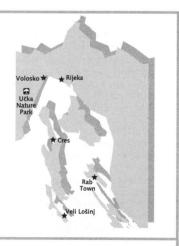

- TELEPHONE CODE: 051

Climate

The region's mild climate has played an important part in the growth of tourism. The Kvarner Gulf is protected from harsh weather by the mountain range running from Vojak (1401m) on Mt Učka in the northwest to Gorski Kotar in the east and the Velebit Range in the southeast. Summers here are long and cooled by the *maestral* (strong, steady westerly wind). In winter, the *bura* (cold northeasterly wind) brings sudden rushes of cold air, but temperatures rarely drop below freezing.

KVARNER COAST

RIJEKA

pop 147,700

While Rijeka (Fiume in Italian) doesn't fit the bill as a tourist destination per se, it does offer an insightful glimpse into the workaday life of Croatia's third-largest city. Most people rush through en route to the islands or Dalmatia, but for those who pause, a few assets await. Blend in with the coffee-sipping locals on the bustling Korzo pedestrian strip, stroll along the tree-lined promenade that fronts the harbour, and visit the imposing hilltop fortress of Trsat. Rijeka also boasts a burgeoning nightlife and, every year, Croatia's biggest and most colourful carnival celebration.

Despite some regrettable architectural ventures in the outskirts, much of the centre contains the ornate, imposing public buildings you would expect to find in Vienna or Budapest, evidence of the strong Austro-Hungarian influence. It's a surprisingly verdant city once you've left its concrete core, which contains Croatia's largest port. The industrial aspect is evident from the boats, cargo and cranes that line the waterfront, but there's a seedy beauty to it. There's rumour of redeveloping the harbour, building a new ferry terminal, banning traffic along the seaside and revitalising the city.

As one of Croatia's most important transportation hubs, Rijeka has buses, trains and ferries that connect Istria and Dalmatia with Zagreb. There's no real beach in the city so it's assumed most visitors will pass through. Tourist resources are limited and hotel options few, as most people base themselves in Opatija.

History

Following their successful conquest of the indigenous Illyrian Liburnian tribe, the Romans established a port here called Tarsaticae. It was the Slavic tribes who migrated to the region in the 7th century and built a new settlement within the old Roman town.

The town changed feudal masters – from German nobility to the Frankopan dukes of Krk – before becoming part of the Austrian empire in the late 15th century. Rijeka was an important outlet to the sea for the Austrians and a new road was built in 1725 connecting Vienna with the Kvarner coast. This spurred economic development, especially shipbuilding, the industry that has remained the centrepiece of Rijeka's economy ever since.

With the birth of the Austro-Hungarian Dual Monarchy in 1867, Rijeka was given over to the jurisdiction of the Hungarian government. The urban landscape acquired a new look as Hungarian architects descended upon the city to erect municipal buildings. A new railway was built linking the city to Zagreb, Budapest and Vienna, and bringing the first tourists to the Kvarner Gulf.

Between 1918, when Italian troops seized Rijeka and Istria under the leadership of Gabriele d'Annunzio, and 1942 when Rijeka became part of postwar Yugoslavia, it changed hands several times, with sporadic periods as a free city. In 1991, Rijeka became part of independent Croatia but still retains a sizable, well-organised Italian minority who have their own newspaper, *La Voce del Popolo*.

Orientation

Korzo runs through the city centre, roughly parallel to Riva, towards Mrtvi Kanal and the Rječina River in the east. The intercity bus station is on Trg Žabica at the western edge of Riva. Local buses and the airport shuttle run from Jelačićev Trg. The train station is a five-minute walk west of the intercity bus station.

Information

INTERNET ACCESS

There's free wireless access along Korzo and in parts of Trsat.

Cont (☎ 371 630; Andrije Kačića Miošića 1; per hr 15KN; ☽ 7am-10pm) This café inside Hotel Continental has a full bank of computers.

Erste Club (☎ 320 072; Korzo 22; ☽ 7am-11pm Mon-Sat, 8am-10pm Sun) Four terminals where you can surf for free, up to 30 minutes.

KVARNER REGION

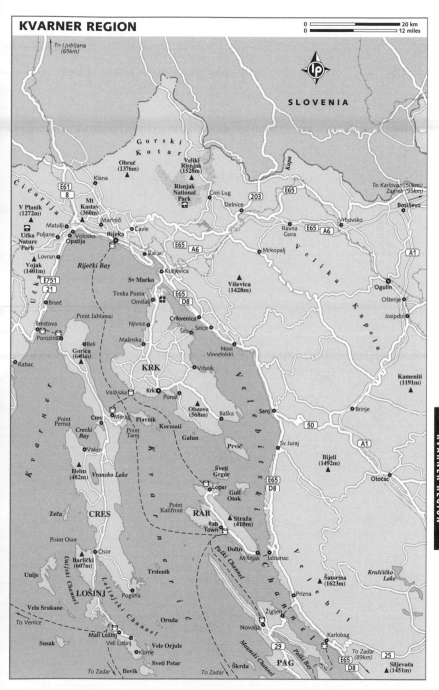

RIJEKA

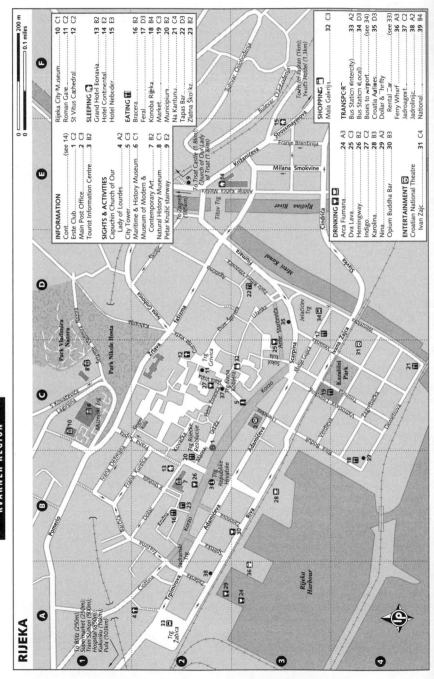

To Trsat Castle (1.8km);
Church of Our Lady
of Trsat (1.8km)

To Zagreb
(185km)

Milana Smokvine

Franje Brentinija

Rječina River

Cindrića

Bulevar Oslobođenja

To Hotel Jadran (1km);
YouGH Hostel (1.3km)

Park Vladimira
Nazora

Park Nikole Hosta

Rijeka Harbour

Trsat Castle

0   200 m
0   0.1 miles

LAUNDRY
Blitz (Krešimirova 3a; per small load 51KN; ⊗ 7am-8pm Mon-Fri, to 2pm Sat) Between the intercity-bus and train stations.

LEFT LUGGAGE
Garderoba intercity bus station (per day 13KN; ⊗ 5.30am-10.30pm); train station (per day in locker 15KN; ⊗ 4.30am-10.30pm) The bus station *garderoba* is at the café next door to the ticket office.

MEDICAL SERVICES
Hospital (☎ 658 111; Krešimirova 42)

MONEY
There are two ATMs at the train station and a number of them along Korzo and around the city centre. The exchange offices adjacent to the train and bus stations keep long hours.

POST
Main post office (Korzo 13; ⊗ 7am-8pm Mon-Fri, to 2pm Sat) Has a telephone centre and an exchange office.

TOURIST INFORMATION
Tourist Information Centre (☎ 335 882; www.tz -rijeka.hr; Korzo 33a; ⊗ 8am-8pm Mon-Sat, 9am-2pm Sun Jun-Aug, 8am-8pm Mon-Fri, 8am-2pm Sat Sep-May) This spiffy centre has plentiful free materials and info about private accommodation.

Sights
A devastating earthquake struck Rijeka in 1750 and destroyed much of its original architecture. The city was almost entirely rebuilt in the grand Habsburg style that prevails today. **Korzo**, the main pedestrian promenade and these days the focal point of social coffee drinking, was built as a commercial avenue on the site of the demolished town walls.

The maze of streets and squares in the ancient core of Rijeka is excellently marked with multilingual plaques explaining the history of each sight. The tourist office distributes maps of this **walking route**, called Turistička Magistrala.

MONUMENTS
One of the few buildings to have survived the earthquake, the distinctive yellow **City Tower** (Gradski Toranj) was originally a gate from the seafront to the city. The Habsburgs added the baroque decorations after the disaster, including the portal with coats of arms and busts of emperors. The still-functioning clock was mounted in 1873.

Pass under the City Tower, continue through Trg Ivana Koblera and take an alley to the north to find the oldest architectural monument in Rijeka, the **Roman Gate** (Stara Vrata). This plain archway marks the former entrance to Praetorium, an ancient military complex, the remains of which you can see in a small excavation area.

ST VITUS CATHEDRAL
North of the Roman Gate is the **cathedral** (Katedrala Svetog Vida; Trg Grivica 11; ⊗ 7am-noon & 4.30-7pm Mon-Sat, 7am-noon Sun Jun-Aug, 6.30am-noon Sep-May), built by the Jesuit order in 1638 on the site of an older church and dedicated to Rijeka's patron saint. Massive marble pillars support the central dome under which are housed baroque altars and a 13th-century Gothic crucifix. According to legend, a man named Petar Lončarić threw a stone at the crucifix and blood began to flow from Christ's body. The man was swallowed by the ground and the blood is still held in a vial.

CAPUCHIN CHURCH OF OUR LADY OF LOURDES
Looming over the intercity bus station, this **church** (Crkva Gospe Lurdske; Kapucinske Stube 5; ⊗ 8am-noon & 4-6pm), with its ornate neo-Gothic facade, dates from 1904. The Capuchin sponsors of the project ran into financing problems midway through construction and enlisted the aid of a 'St Johanca', who allegedly sweated blood in front of the credulous masses. Gifts and money poured into the coffers and the building was finally completed in 1929. ('St Johanca' was arrested for fraud in 1913.)

MARITIME & HISTORY MUSEUM
This **museum** (Pomorski i Povijesni Muzej Hrvatskog Primorja; ☎ 553 666; www.ppmhp.hr; Muzejski Trg 1; adult/student 10/5KN; ⊗ 9am-8pm Tue-Fri, to 1pm Sat) is housed in the Governor's Palace, a splendid showcase of Hungarian architecture. Pick up the small leaflet in English for a self-guided tour that gives a vivid picture of life among seafarers, with model ships, sea charts, navigation instruments and portraits of captains.

RIJEKA CITY MUSEUM
Just to the west of the palace is the **Rijeka City Museum** (Muzej Grada Rijeke; ☎ 336 711; Muzejski Trg 1/1; adult/student 10/5KN, admission free Mon; ⊗ 10am-1pm &

KVARNER REGION

5-8pm Mon-Fri, 10am-1pm Sat). Housed in a 1970s cubicle structure, it hosts temporary exhibits and events, ranging from retrospectives by local photographers and architects, to visiting shows from Serbia and Italy.

NATURAL HISTORY MUSEUM

In the same area, the **Natural History Museum** (Prirodoslovni Muzej; ☎ 553 669; Lorenzov Prolaz 1; adult/student 10/5KN; ⏱ 9am-7pm Mon-Sat, to 3pm Sun) is devoted to the geology and botany of the Adriatic. In addition to a multimedia centre with an aquarium, there are exhibits on bugs, snakes and frogs on the three floors of this 19th-century villa. The adjacent botanical garden with over 2000 native plant species is a great place to unwind.

MUSEUM OF MODERN & CONTEMPORARY ART

Just up from the Korzo on the 2nd floor of the University Library, this **museum** (Muzej Moderne i Suvremene Umjetnosti; ☎ 334 280; www.mmsu.hr; Dolac 1; adult/student 10/5KN; ⏱ 10am-1pm & 6-9pm Tue-Sun Jun-Aug, 10am-1pm & 5-8pm Sep-May) puts on rotating shows, be it an opus of a contemporary Croatian artist or a display of multi-artist works curated around a single theme.

TRSAT CASTLE & CHURCH

High on a hill overlooking Rijeka and the Rječina River, **Trsat Castle** (☎ 217 714; adult/student 15/5KN; ⏱ 9am-8pm May-Oct, to 5pm Nov-Apr) is a 13th-century fortress that has occupied this strategic position since Illyrian times. The present structure was built by the Frankopan dukes of Krk, but the latest facelift was done in 1824 when Irish-born count Laval Nugent, a commander in the Austrian army, bought the castle and had it restored in a romantic Classicist-Biedermeier style. The ancient Greek-style Nugent family mausoleum houses a gallery, while underground a former dungeon hosts occasional exhibits. During summer, the fortress features concerts, theatre performances and fashion shows. The open-air café is a wonderful spot to take in the vistas.

The other hill highlight is the **Church of Our Lady of Trsat** (Crkva Gospe Trsatske; ☎ 452 900; Frankopanski Trg; ⏱ by appointment), a centuries-old magnet for believers. According to legend, the angels carrying the house of the Virgin Mary from Nazareth rested here in the late 13th century before moving it to Loreto in

TOP FIVE BEACHES IN THE KVARNER REGION

- Baška (p146; Krk Island) – a gorgeous sweep of pebble beach with a glorious mountain backdrop

- Beli (p138; Cres Island) – this cosy cove has calm, crystal water and no crowds

- Lopar (p152; Rab Island) – a strip of sandy beaches bordered by pine groves

- Sunčana Uvala (p132; Lošinj Island) – plenty of rocky and pebbly coves with pine-tree shade

- Lungomare (p126; Opatija) – rock formations create dozens of private beaches along the promenade

Italy. Pilgrims started trickling in to the chapel erected on the site, and then pouring in when the pope donated an icon of Mary in 1367. The famous painting is on the main altar behind a magnificent wrought-iron gate. Check out the offerings of votive gifts across the baroque cloister and make an appointment to see the valuable sacral art collection in the treasury, where they'll play a 15-minute film about the church.

To follow in the pilgrims' steps, climb the **Petar Kružić stairway** from Titov Trg, built in 1531 for the faithful on their way to Our Lady of Trsat. The steep stairs are lined with chapels dedicated to saints, once used as rest stops for the pilgrims. For an easier way up, take a quick ride on city bus 1 or 1A to Trsat Castle.

Festivals & Events

The **Rijeka Carnival** (www.ri-karneval.com.hr) is the largest and most elaborate in Croatia, with two weeks of partying that involves pageants, street dances, concerts, masked balls, exhibitions and an international parade. Check out the *zvončari*, masked men clad in animal skins who dance and ring loud bells to frighten off evil spirits. The festivities take place anywhere between late January and early March, depending on when Easter falls.

Concerts are held at the Croatian National Theatre (p124) during **Rijeka Summer Nights** (Riječke Ljetne Noći) in June and July.

Sleeping

Prices in Rijeka hotels generally stay the same year-round except at Carnival time, when you

KVARNER REGION

can expect to pay a surcharge. You should book well in advance if you want to visit during this time. There are few private rooms in Rijeka itself; the tourist office lists these on its website. Opatija is a much better choice for accommodation (see p126).

Youth Hostel (☎ 406 420; rijeka@hfhs.hr; Šetalište XIII Divizije 23; dm/s/d 130/235/310KN; 🖳) Five bus stops east of the centre (on bus 2) in the leafy residential area of Pećine, this renovated 19th-century villa has clean and snug units and a communal TV room. Breakfast is available (15KN); reservations are advisable in summer.

Hotel Continental (☎ 372 008; www.jadran-hoteli .hr; Andrije Kačića Miošića 1; s/d 384/449KN; P 🖳) At the time of writing, more than half of the rooms inside this grand building were being revamped. Once they're primped up, the rating will go up to three stars and the prices will increase by 15%. The location is great, just northeast of the centre.

Hotel Neboder (☎ 373 538; www.jadran-hoteli.hr; Strossmayerova 1; s/d 440/550KN; P 🖳) Fantastic city and harbour views make up for the small rooms in this recently refurbished high-rise on a gentle hill near Hotel Continental. Superior units have air-con and balconies.

ourpick Hotel Jadran (☎ 216 600; www.jadran-ho teli.hr; Šetalište XIII Divizije 46; s/d 672/793KN; P 🔀 🖳) The four-star upgrade of this longstanding hotel produced airy rooms with huge glass windows or balconies offering sea vistas. Perks include a restaurant, a small gym and a private beach below. It's worth the 1km trip east of the city centre.

Grand Hotel Bonavia (☎ 357 100; www.bonavia .hr; Dolac 4; s/d from 945/1135KN; P 🔀 🔀 🖳) Bet on highbrow luxury at this top hotel, one of Croatia's best. Slick rooms are equipped with all top-of-the-line amenities. The restaurant serves outstanding creative cuisine, while the spa offers treats such as aromatherapy showers.

Eating

If you want a meal on a Sunday, you'll be relegated to either fast food, pizza or a hotel restaurant, as nearly every other place in Rijeka is closed. There are a number of cafés on Korzo that serve light meals.

Konoba Rijeka (☎ 312 084; Riva Boduli 7c; mains from 25KN) Tasty and cheap fish meals can be had at this restaurant right on the harbour, with high ceilings, stone walls and plenty of

fish nets. Try the dried octopus omelette, a house speciality.

Tapas Bar (☎ 315 313; Pavla Rittera Vitezovića 5; tapas around 25KN) One of Rijeka's newest openings, this small and stylish spot on a quiet city centre block churns out Croatian-inspired tapas. Delicious *bruschette* are topped with anchovies, truffles, fresh tuna and so on, and cost 9KN per piece. Portions are small and the bill adds up.

ourpick Na Kantunu (☎ 313 271; Demetrova 2; mains from 35KN) If you're lucky to grab a table at this tiny lunchtime spot on an industrial stretch of the port, you'll be treated to the superlative daily catch. Just point to your fish of choice or let the staff prepare it house style. Friday lunches are the busiest, when many locals don't eat red meat.

Feral (☎ 212 274; Matije Gupca 5b; mains from 60KN) It may be past its glory as one of Rijeka's best restaurants but this city classic, around since 1964, still does great black risotto and *šurlice* (homemade pasta from Krk) in its exposed brick interior. The fish *marenda* (lunch) served till 1pm costs just 30KN.

Zlatna Školjka (☎ 213 782; Kružna 12; mains 65-95KN) Savour the superbly prepared seafood and choice Croatian wines at this classy maritime-themed restaurant. The mixed-fish starter, Conco d'Oro, is pricey (100KN) but worth it. The adjacent Bracera, by the same owners, serves crusty pizza, even on a Sunday.

Municipium (☎ 213 000; Trg Riječke Rezolucije 5; mains from 70KN) What comes out of the kitchen at this fancy restaurant in a historic building are updated versions of Croatian classics. The food is light and well prepared and the crowd busy making business deals.

Kukuriku (☎ 691 417; www.kukuriku.hr; Trg Matka Laginje 1a, Kastav; 6-course meals 370-510KN; ☺ closed Mon Nov-Easter) Among the pioneers of the slow food movement in Croatia (see p52), this gastronomic destination in the old town of Kastav, Rijeka's hilltop suburb, offers delectable meals amid lots of rooster-themed decoration. It's worth the splurge and the trek out of town on bus 18. The restaurant is set to move to a new nearby location soon; check the website for updates.

For self-caterers, there's a large supermarket in between the intercity bus and train stations, and a **city market** (btwn Vatroslava Lisinskog & Trninina) open till 2pm daily (noon on Sundays).

MORČIĆI

The *morčići* is a traditional symbol of Rijeka, and its official mascot. The image of a black person topped with a colourful turban is made into ceramic brooches and earrings, and is a popular disguise at the Rijeka Carnival (p122).

There are a few legends about Rijeka's most recognisable symbol. According to one story, during the 16th-century Turkish invasions, the women and children prayed for a rain of stones to bury their enemy. An arrow struck and killed the Turkish pasha in the temple as a result of their prayers. The terrified Turks scattered as the skies opened and stones hailed down, burying them. The men were so grateful for their wives' assistance that they presented them with the colourful earrings. Another tale tells of an Italian baron who was so fond of her black slave that she granted the woman her freedom and had earrings made in her image.

More mundanely, it appears that the *morčići* was a spin-off from the Venetian *moretto* design that was part of a 17th- and 18th-century fad. The gem-encrusted Venetian Moor was simplified by Rijeka jewellers and sold to poorer women as simple B&W ceramic earrings. Men also picked up on the fashion; a single earring was worn by only sons, sailors and fishermen for good luck.

In the late 19th century, Rijeka jewellers improved the quality of the artisanship and branched out into rings, brooches and necklaces. Upper-class women snatched up the pieces and, with a display at the Vienna International Exhibition of 1873, *morčići* became popular throughout Europe.

Drinking

With several recent openings, Rijeka's nightlife got a boost of energy. Bar-hoppers cruise the bars and cafés along Riva and Korzo for the liveliest social hubbub. A couple of these are housed in boats on Adamićev Gat: the downstairs of *Arca Fiumana* is frequented by the rock crowd, while *Nina* next door hops with *narodnjaci* (folk music). Many of the bars double as clubs on weekends.

Dva Lava (☎ 332 390; Ante Starčevića 8) The two alfresco terraces of this popular den, one on a tree-shaded square, are always packed during the day. DJs spin on weekend nights and the two floors with futuristic decor hop till late.

Hemingway (☎ 211 696; Korzo 28) This stylish venue for coffee-sipping, cocktail-drinking and people-watching pays homage to its namesake with large B&W photos and drinks named after him. It's part of a fashionable chain.

Indigo (☎ 315 174; Stara Vrata 3) On weekends, the owner likes to lay tracks at this snazzy hang-out next to an archaeological dig. Salsa dancing and after-work parties take place on weeknights. There's a restaurant that, atypically, serves brunch.

Karolina (☎ 211 447; Gat Karoline Riječke bb) Trendy but not self-conscious about it, this waterfront bar-café is a relaxed place for a daytime coffee. At night, crowds spill out onto the wharf in a huge outdoor party. There are live DJ acts on summer nights.

Opium Buddha Bar (Riva 12a) The decor is wannabe Asian, the sounds are electronic and the weekends jump at this dark and sprawling lounge bar with an outdoor terrace.

Entertainment

Croatian National Theatre Ivan Zajc (☎ 355 900; www.hnk-zajc.hr; Verdieva 5a) In 1885, the inaugural performance at this imposing theatre was lit by the city's first light bulb. These days, you can catch mostly dramas in Croatian and Italian, as well as opera and ballet. Gustav Klimt painted some of the ceiling frescoes.

Shopping

Look for the traditional Rijeka design known as *morčići*, a ceramic jewellery piece of a Moor wearing a turban (see boxed text, above). You can pick one up at **Mala Galerija** (☎ 335 403; www.mala-galerija.hr, in Croatian; Užarska 25).

Getting There & Away

AIR

Croatia Airlines (☎ 330 207; www.croatiaairlines.hr; Jelačićev Trg 5; ⏰ 8am-4pm Mon-Fri, 9am-noon Sat) operates international and domestic flights.

BOAT

Jadrolinija (☎ 211 444; www.jadrolinija.hr; Riva 16; ⏰ 8am-8pm Mon-Fri, 9am-5pm Sat & Sun) sells tickets for the large coastal ferries that run all year between Rijeka and Dubrovnik on their way to Bari in Italy, via Split, Hvar and Korčula.

KVARNER REGION

Other ferry routes include Rijeka–Cres–Mali Lošinj and Rijeka–Rab–Pag. Schedules and fares change so check Jadrolinija's website. All ferries depart from Rijeka's wharf (Adamićev Gat).

Jadroagent (☎ 211 626; www.jadroagent.hr; Trg Ivana Koblera 2) has information on all boats around Croatia.

BUS

If you fly into Zagreb, there is a Croatia Airlines van that goes directly from Zagreb airport to Rijeka twice daily (145KN, two hours, 3.30pm and 9pm). It goes back to Zagreb from Rijeka at 5am and 11am. There are six daily buses to Trieste (60KN, 2½ hours) and one daily bus to Plitvice (130KN, four hours), with a change in Otočac.

The **intercity bus station** (☎ 060 302 010; Trg Žabica 1) is in the town centre. For international connections, see p308. Following are some of the more popular domestic routes:

Destination	Fare (KN)	Duration (hr)	Daily services
Baška	71	2¼	4-8
Dubrovnik	340-485	12-13	2-3
Krk	50	1-2	14
Poreč	72-114	1-3	7-11
Pula	78-88	2¼	8-10
Rab	125	3	2
Rovinj	81-112	2-3	4-5
Split	241-327	8	6-7
Zadar	153-202	4-5	6-7
Zagreb	95-174	2½-3	13-17

CAR

Dollar & Thrifty Rental Car (☎ 325 900; www.subrosa .hr), with a booth inside the intercity bus station, has cars from 466KN per day (2500KN per week) with unlimited kilometres. You can also try **National** (☎ 212 452; www.nationalcar .hr; Demetrova 18b).

TRAIN

The **train station** (☎ 213 333; Krešimirova 5) is a five-minute walk from the city centre. Seven daily trains run to Zagreb (96KN, 3½ to five hours). There's a daily train to Split (160KN, 10 hours) that changes at Ogulin, where you wait for two hours. Two direct daily services head to Ljubljana (93KN, three hours) and one daily train goes to Vienna (307KN to 498KN, nine hours). Reservations are compulsory on some *poslovni* (business-class) trains.

Getting Around

TO/FROM THE AIRPORT

Rijeka Airport (☎ 842 040; www.rijeka-airport.hr; Hamec 1, Omišalj) is on Krk Island, 30km from town. An airport bus meets all flights for a 30-minute ride to Jelačićev Trg; it leaves from this same square for the airport two hours and 20 minutes before flight times. You can buy the ticket (22KN) on the bus. Taxis cost about 300KN; call ☎ 332 893 or ☎ 335 138.

BUS

Rijeka has an extensive network of city buses that run from the central station at Jelačićev Trg. Buy two-trip tickets for 14KN at any *tisak* (newsstand). A single ticket from the driver costs 10KN.

Rijeka also has a sightseeing bus that shuttles tourists between major sights in Rijeka, Trsat and Opatija. The one-day ticket, available for hopping on and off wherever and whenever you please, costs 70KN. For tickets and detailed schedules, visit the tourist office (p121).

OPATIJA

pop 9073

Just 15km west of Rijeka, Opatija (Abbazia in Italian) is one of Croatia's most spectacular sights. On this stretch of coast, the forested hills slope down to the sparkling sea, enhanced by the peak of Vojak (1401m), west of Opatija and the highest point on the Istrian peninsula. The best vantage point for this vista is Lungomare, a waterfront promenade that stretches for 12km along the Opatija Riviera from Volosko to Lovran.

It was this breathtaking location and the agreeable year-round climate that made Opatija the most fashionable seaside resort for the Viennese elite during the Austro-Hungarian Empire. Between the world wars and during the Yugoslav period, however, the belle époque villas went into decline and Opatija lost its former lustre.

The good news is that the grand residences of the wealthy have since been revamped and turned into upmarket hotels, with a particular accent on spa and health holidays. Foodies have been flocking from afar, too, for the clutch of fantastic restaurants in the nearby fishing village of Volosko. Good food, coastal scenery, clear waters and many parks attract a steady flow of tourists, especially in the summer months and around Christmas.

KVARNER REGION

History

Until the 1840s, Opatija was a humble fishing village with 35 houses and a church, but the arrival of wealthy Iginio Scarpa from Rijeka turned things around. He built Villa Angiolina (named after his wife) and surrounded it with species of exotic plants from Japan, China, South America and Australia. The villa hosted some of Europe's finest aristocrats, including the Austrian queen Maria Anna, wife of Ferdinand. The town's reputation as a retreat for the elite was born.

Opatija's development was also assisted by the construction of a rail link on the Vienna–Trieste line in 1873. Construction of Opatija's first hotel, the Quarnero (today the Hotel Kvarner), began and wealthy visitors arrived en masse. It seemed everyone who was anyone was compelled to visit Opatija, including kings from Romania and Sweden, Russian tsars and the celebrities of the day such as Isadora Duncan, Gustav Mahler, Giacomo Puccini and Anton Chekov.

Although Opatija has never acquired the glitter of the French Riviera, it has become a favoured holiday spot for sleek, bronzed Italians in the summer. The mild winters attract a sizable number of elderly Austrians who come to nibble on cakes in the Hotel Kvarner and take a healthy saunter by the sea.

Orientation

Opatija sits on a narrow strip of land sandwiched between the sea and the foothills of the Učka mountain range. Ulica Maršala Tita is the main road that runs through town; it's lined with travel agencies, restaurants, shops and hotels. The bus from Rijeka stops first at the Hotel Belvedere, then near the market and finally at the bus station at the foot of town on Trg Vladimira Gortana.

Information

Ulica Maršala Tita has numerous ATMs and travel agencies eager to change money.

Da Riva (☎ 272 990; www.da-riva.hr; Ulica Maršala Tita 170; ☽ 8am-8pm Jun–mid-Sep, shorter hr rest of year) Finds private accommodation and offers excursions around Croatia.

GI Turizam (☎ 273 030; www.tourgit.com; Ulica Maršala Tita 65; ☽ 9am-10pm summer, to 8pm rest of year) Finds private accommodation, books excursions, rents cars and changes money.

Katarina Line (☎ 603 400; www.katarina-line.hr; Ulica Maršala Tita 71; ☽ 8am-10pm Mon-Sat, 8am-9pm Sun summer, 8am-4pm Mon-Sat rest of year) Known for its cruises around the Adriatic, it also books accommodation and day trips.

Linea Verde (☎ 701 107; www.lineaverde-croatia.com; Andrije Štangera 42, Volosko; ☽ 8am-10pm Mon-Sat, 8am-9pm Sun summer, 8am-4pm Mon-Sat rest of year) Hiking excursions to Risnjak (p128), gourmet tours to Istria (p154) and shepherd's picnics to Učka Nature Park (p129).

Post office (☎ 271 733; Eugena Kumičića 4; ☽ 7am-9pm Mon-Fri, to 2pm Sat) Behind the market.

Tourist office (☎ 271 310; www.opatija-tourism.hr; Ulica Maršala Tita 101; ☽ 8am-10pm Mon-Sat, 5-9pm Sun Jul & Aug, 8am-7pm Mon-Sat Apr-Jun & Sep, 8am-4pm Mon-Sat Oct-Mar) Distributes maps, leaflets and brochures.

Sights & Activities

Restored to its former neoclassical splendour, the exquisite Villa Angiolina now houses the **Croatian Museum of Tourism** (Park Angiolina 1; ☽ 9am-1pm & 4.30-9.30pm Tue-Sun summer, shorter hr rest of year). The collection of old photographs, postcards, brochures and posters tracing the history of travel is interesting enough, but the real highlight is the villa's interior – a marvel of trompe l'œil frescoes, Corinthian capitals and geometric floor mosaics. Don't miss a stroll around the lush park, overgrown with gingko trees, sequoias, holm oaks and Japanese camellia, Opatija's symbol. At the time of writing, admission to the museum and grounds was free; however, there will soon be an entrance fee.

The pretty **Lungomare** is the region's showcase. Lined with plush villas and ample gardens, this shady promenade winds along the sea for 12km from Volosko to Lovran via the small villages of Ičići and Ika. Along the way are innumerable rocky outgrowths providing places to throw down a towel and jump into the sea – a better option than Opatija's concrete beach.

Opatija and the surrounding region offer some wonderful opportunities for hiking and biking around Učka Nature Park (see p129).

Sleeping

There are no real budget hotels in Opatija, but the midrange and top-end places offer surprisingly good value for money considering Opatija's overall air of chic. **Liburnia Hotels** (☎ 710 444; www.liburnia.hr) manages 15 hotels in the area and is a good bet for getting a room. Note that Opatija gets booked up over the Christmas holidays, so reserve ahead for this time.

Private rooms are abundant and reasonably priced. The travel agencies listed on opposite all find private accommodation. In the high season, rooms cost between 80KN and 115KN per person, depending on the amenities; two-person apartments range from 255KN to 575KN. A 30% surcharge applies for stays under three nights.

HOTELS

Hotel Opatija (☎ 271 388; www.hotel-opatija.hr; Trg Vladimira Gortana 2/1; s low-high 280-361KN, d 678-1002KN; P ⊠) The setting in a Habsburg-era mansion is the forte of this hilltop three-star with pleasant rooms. Facilities include a fantastic terrace, an indoor seawater pool and tennis courts.

Hotel Residenz (☎ 271 399; www.liburnia.hr; Ulica Maršala Tita 133; s low-high 293-524KN, d 354-816KN) While rooms boast no frills – unless you pay extra for a unit with a balcony – the building is a classic, right on the seafront with a private beach below.

Villa Ariston (☎ 271 379; www.villa-ariston.com; Ulica Maršala Tita 179; s low-high 350-480KN, d 600-800KN; P ⊠) Plush furnishings, gilt-edged mirrors and ornate chandeliers adorn this imperial villa that has hosted celebrities including Coco Chanel and the Kennedys. A fragrant garden of cypress and pine trees drops down to the sea.

Hotel Kvarner (☎ 271 233; www.liburnia.hr; Pave Tomašića 1-4; s low-high 462-578KN, d 653-1039KN; ⊠) Feel like part of the jet set from a bygone era in Opatija's oldest hotel. Splash in an indoor-outdoor pool, walk through plush hallways and recline on period furniture in high-ceilinged rooms that, despite the fame, could use an update.

Hotel Mozart (☎ 718 260; www.hotel-mozart.hr; Ulica Maršala Tita 138; s low-high 660-920KN, d 1095-1530KN; P ⊠ 🖥 ⊠) Light-flooded rooms feature old-school style and Secessionist furniture, the stars add up to five, and the spiffy new spa offers saunas and steam baths. Most rooms come with sea-facing balconies.

CAMPING

There are two camping grounds in the area: **Medveja** (☎ 291 191; ac-medveja@liburnia.hr; per adult/ tent 41/29KN; ❄ Easter–mid-Oct), on a pretty cove 10km south of Opatija, and **Camping Opatija** (☎ 704 836; www.rivijera-opatija.hr; Liburnijska 46, Ičići; adult/tent 36/27KN; ❄ Apr-Oct), in a pine forest 5km south of town before you reach Lovran.

Eating

Maršala Tita is lined with serviceable restaurants that offer pizza, grilled meat and fish. The better restaurants are off the main strip.

Vongola (☎ 711 854; Ulica Maršala Tita 113; mains from 30KN) For cheap chow, head to this simple spot on Slatina city beach, at the eastern end of Maršala Tita. Expect pizzas, pastas, grilled meats and fish.

Kaneta (☎ 712 222; Nova Cesta 64; mains from 40KN) At the top of Maršala Tita, this family restaurant specialises in goulash, pasta with truffles, steak with gorgonzola and other hearty delicacies.

Istranka (☎ 271 835; Bože Milanovića 2; mains from 45KN) Graze on flavourful Istrian mainstays, such as *maneštra* (vegetable and bean soup similar to minestrone) and *fuži* (hand-rolled pasta tubes), at this rustic-themed tavern in a small street just up from Maršala Tita.

Bevanda (☎ 493 888; Zert 8; mains from 80KN) It recently changed ownership from that which built its reputation, but this elegant restaurant on the Lido still delivers terrific fresh fish and shellfish. Get a table at the all-white terrace right on the sea.

For self-catering types, there's a **supermarket-deli** (Ulica Maršala Tita 80).

Drinking

Opatija used to be the playground of Rijeka's partygoers, but it took a hit when the police started cracking down on drunk drivers. Viennese-style coffeehouses and hotel terraces still dominate the scene, while a few stylish bars add the extra punch.

The ever-popular **Hemingway** (Zert 2) on the harbour is an enjoyable place for a seaside drink. For a cocktail on the beach, head to **Tantra** (Lido) just around the corner, a lounge bar with chill-out music and unbeatable coastal views. The trendiest place in town is still **Monokini** (☎ 703 888; Ulica Maršala Tita 96), the watering hole of choice for Opatija's scenesters. Chocolate lovers should head next door for a sweet fix at **Choco Bar** (☎ 603 562; Ulica Maršala Tita 94), with elegant chocolate cocktails, ice cream and cakes. **Disco Seven** (www.discoseven.hr; Ulica Maršala Tita 125) is Opatija's only club with a typical roster of electronic tunes and a seaside terrace.

Getting There & Away

Bus 32 stops in front of the train station in Rijeka (15KN, 15km) and runs along the Opatija Riviera west of Rijeka to Lovran every 20 minutes daily until late in the evening.

AROUND OPATIJA
Volosko

Volosko, 2km east of Opatija, is an old fishing village rising up on a gentle hill in a warren of narrow alleyways, stone townhouses and flower-laden balconies. In addition to its Mediterranean allure, a chief reason to visit is a set of stellar restaurants that has sprouted around the small harbour of this otherwise quiet village. Volosko is now a mecca for foodies, with several fine choices, however deep your pockets.

You can come from Rijeka by bus or walk along the coastal promenade from Opatija, a 20-minute stroll past bay trees, palms, figs and oaks, behind which you can glimpse magnificent villas.

EATING

Konoba Ribarnica Volosko (☎ 701 483; Štangerova 5; mains from 20KN; ☾ closed Sun dinner) No cash to splash? This tiny shopfront has Volosko's cheapest fresh fish. Point to your desired sea creature – calamari, sardines, scampi – and eat the well-prepared dish in a small downstairs dining room around the corner. It's on the main road parallel to the harbour.

our pick **Skalinada** (☎ 701 109; Put Uz Dol 17; mains from 25KN) One of Volosko's best-kept secrets, this small, colourful and artsy restaurant hides behind a stone vault entrance just below the second bus stop on the road from Rijeka. Appetising food is made with seasonal ingredients from nearby villages.

Tramerka (☎ 701 707; Andrije Mohorovičića 15; mains from 30KN) Locals in the know flock to the stonewall interior of this *konoba* (tavern) named after an uninhabited island in the Zadar archipelago. Expect creatively prepared and well-priced seafood dishes. It's just up a set of stairs to the left of Plavi Podrum.

Plavi Podrum (☎ 701 223; Supilova Obala 12; mains from 60KN) The decor is on the maritime-kitsch side, but the seafood is consistently top-rated and paired with select wines. The owner is one of Croatia's top sommeliers and wine columnists.

Le Mandrać (☎ 701 357; Supilova Obala 10; mains from 60KN) The forward-thinking Mediterranean food at Le Mandrać is innovative and full of flavour, but locals appear to prefer Plavi Podrum next door. It could be that the over-designed swanky interior is a tad intimidating. Splurge on a tasting menu (270KN to 490KN).

RISNJAK NATIONAL PARK

Relatively isolated, rarely visited and certainly underappreciated by foreign tourists, this majestic park only 35km northeast of Rijeka deserves to be much better known. Part of the wooded Gorski Kotar region, it covers an area of 63 sq km and rises up to 1528m at its highest peak, Veliki Risnjak. The landscape is thickly forested with beech and pine trees, carpeted with meadows and wildflowers, and pock-marked by karst formations: sinkholes, cracks, caves and abysses. The bracing alpine breezes make it the perfect hideaway when the coastal heat and crowds below become overpowering. Wildlife includes brown bears, lynx (*ris* in Croatian, after which the park is named), wolves, wild cats, wild boar, deer, chamois and 500 species of butterfly.

Most of the park is unspoiled virgin forest, with only a few settlements. The largest is Crni Lug at the park's edge where you'll find the **park information office** (☎ 836 133; ☾ 9am-4pm Mon-Fri, to 6pm Sat & Sun) in the park's only hotel, **Pension Risnjak** (☎ 836 133; Bijela Vodica 48, Crni Lug; d low-high 240-260KN; ℗). The **park entrance** (adult/concession 30/15KN) is a few hundred metres behind the *pension* (guest house).

The best way to discover the park is to walk the **Leska Path**, a delightful 4.5km trail that begins at the park's entrance. It's an easy and shady walk punctuated by several dozen explanatory panels (in English) telling you all about the park's history, topography, geology, flora and fauna. You'll pass crystal-clear streams, forests of tall fir trees, bizarre rock formations, a feeding station for the deer, and a mountain hut with a picnic table.

There's no public transport to the park. To get there by car, exit the main Zagreb–Rijeka motorway at Delnice and follow the signs to Crni Lug.

LOŠINJ & CRES ISLANDS

Separated by only an 11m-wide canal, these two serpentine islands in the Kvarner archipelago are often treated as a single entity. Although their topography is different, the islands' identities are blurred by a shared history and close transportation links. On Lošinj (Lussino in Italian), the fishing villages of Mali Lošinj and Veli Lošinj attract tourist hordes in summer, especially from Italy. The more deserted Cres (Crepsa in Italian) has remote

UČKA NATURE PARK

One of Croatia's best-kept nature secrets, this 160-sq-km park lies just 30 minutes from Lovran on the Opatija Riviera. Comprised of the Učka mountain massif and the adjacent Ćićarija plateau, it's officially split between Kvarner and Istria. Its highest peak is Vojak (1401m), which, on a clear day, affords views of the Italian Alps and the Bay of Trieste.

Much of the area is covered by beech forests but there are also sweet chestnut trees, oaks and hornbeam. Sheep peacefully graze on alpine meadows, griffon vultures and golden eagles fly overhead, brown bears roam and endemic bellflowers blossom.

The enthusiastic staff at the **park office** (293 733; www.pp-ucka.hr; Liganj 42; 8am–4pm Mon–Fri) in Lovran have info on all the activities listed following. The office also has two seasonal info points: one at **Poklon** (9am–7pm mid-Jun–mid-Sep) and one at **Vojak** (9am–7pm mid-Jun–mid-Sep).

Don't miss **Mala Učka**, a half-abandoned village at over 995m above sea level, where a few shepherds live from May to October. You can buy delicious sheep's cheese from the house with green windows by the stream at the village's end. Just ask for *sir* (cheese).

Organised activities in the park include **mountain biking** and **trekking** on 150km of trails, incorporating two marked educational paths, Slap and Vela Draga. Pick up a map for 55KN from the park office or the tourist office in Opatija (p126). There's also **free-climbing** in the Vela Draga canyon, **horseback riding** (around 80KN per hour) and **bird-watching**. Paragliding and hang-gliding can be organised through **Homo Volans Free Flying Club** (www.homo-volans.hr) in Opatija.

The park has several sleeping options but the standout is **Učka Lodge** (091 762 2027; www .uckalodge.com; d 360KN), a traditional house at 600m above sea level, deep in the woods. The English owners, Frank and Alice, had it beautifully converted into an eco-B&B. The electricity comes from solar panels, the rainwater is filtered and there's a natural sewage treatment plant. There are two charming rooms with shared bathroom, and the breakfast is made of local ingredients (jam from forest fruits and sheep's cheese from the neighbours). Frank will take you out in his 4WD upon request and they'll arrange any tour in the area.

Another highlight is **Dopolavoro** (299 641; www.dopolavoro.hr; Učka 9; mains from 40KN; closed Mon), which serves excellent game dishes featuring deer, wild boar and bear prepared under *peka* (domed baking lids). Bikes are available for rent beside the restaurant (20/90KN per hour/ day), and there's a herbalist across the street who sells curative teas and creams made from local plants.

camping grounds and pristine beaches, especially outside Cres Town, and a handful of medieval hilltop villages. Both islands are criss-crossed by hiking and biking trails.

History

Excavations indicate that a prehistoric culture spread out over both islands from the Stone Age to the Bronze Age. The ancient Greeks called the islands the Apsyrtides, which were in turn conquered by the Romans, then put under Byzantine rule and settled by Slavic tribes in the 6th and 7th centuries.

The islands subsequently came under Venetian rule, followed by that of the Croatian-Hungarian kings, then back to the Venetians. By the time Venice fell in 1797, Veli Lošinj and Mali Lošinj had become important maritime centres, while Cres devoted itself to wine and olive production. During the 19th century, shipbuilding flourished in

Lošinj, but with the advent of steamships it was replaced by health tourism as a major industry. Meanwhile, Cres had its own problems in the form of a phylloxera epidemic that wiped out its vineyards. Both islands were poor when they were annexed to Italy as part of the 1920 Treaty of Rapallo. They became part of Yugoslavia in 1945 and, most recently, Croatia in 1991.

Today, apart from a small shipyard in Nerezine in north Lošinj and some olive cultivation, sheep farming and fishing on Cres, the main activity on both islands is tourism.

Getting There & Away
BOAT

The main maritime port of entry for the islands is Mali Lošinj, which is connected to Rijeka, Pula, Zadar, Venice and Koper in the summer. Jadrolinija (see p134) runs a daily ferry between Zadar and Mali Lošinj

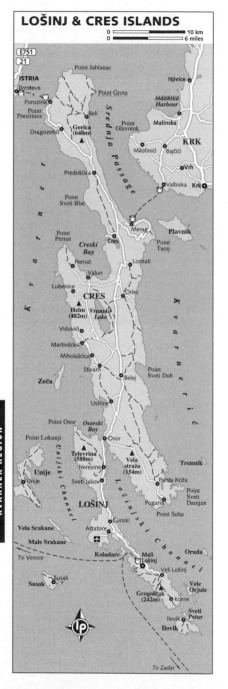

LOŠINJ & CRES ISLANDS

(47KN, seven hours) from June through September. In July and August, it also runs a daily catamaran from Mali Lošinj to Cres (28KN, 2½ hours) and Rijeka (40KN, four hours). There is also an hourly Jadrolinija car ferry from Brestova in Istria to Porozina at the tip of Cres (passenger/car 17/113KN, 20 minutes).

In July and August, **Venezia Lines** (☎ 052-422 896; www.venezialines.com) runs catamarans from Venice to Mali Lošinj via Pula twice weekly (465KN, five hours). **Split Tours** (☎ 021-352 533; www.splittours.hr) runs a catamaran service from Zadar to Pula via Mali Lošinj five times weekly during July and August (50KN, two hours); in June and September, the service is reduced to twice weekly.

BUS

All buses travelling to and from the islands originate in Veli Lošinj and stop in Mali Lošinj before continuing to Cres and the mainland. There are six to nine daily buses from Veli Lošinj to Cres Town (50KN, 1½ hours); four daily to Merag (62KN, two hours) and Valbiska on Krk (99KN, 2½ hours); three per day to Porozina on Cres (82KN, 2½ hours) and Brestova in Istria (90KN, three hours); five daily buses to Rijeka (146KN, 4¼ hours); three to Zagreb (260KN to 275KN, seven hours); and one daily to Ljubljana (295KN, 6¼ hours) in Slovenia.

LOŠINJ ISLAND

The more populated and touristy of the twin islands, the 31km-long Lošinj also has a more indented coastline than Cres, especially in the south. The towns of Mali Lošinj and Veli Lošinj in the southeast are ringed by natural pine forests interspersed with tall Aleppo pines planted in the 19th century. The vegetation on the island is particularly lush and varied, with 1100 plant species, 230 medicinal herbs and some atypical growths such as lemon, banana, cedar and eucalyptus brought from exotic lands by sea captains.

The island is known for its dolphin population; in fact, its waters are the first protected marine area for dolphins in the entire Mediterranean. The Blue World NGO (p136) based in Mali Lošinj has done much to protect these graceful sea creatures with an educational centre and various activities.

CYCLING THE KVARNER REGION

An increasingly popular cycling destination, Kvarner offers a variety of options for biking enthusiasts, from gentle rides to heart-pumping climbs on steep island roads. There are several trails around Opatlja; two easier paths depart from Mt Kastav (360m), while a challenging 4½-hour adventure goes from Lovran to Učka Nature Park (p129). Lošinj offers a moderately difficult 2½-hour route that starts and ends in Mali Lošinj. On Krk, a leisurely two-hour ride from Krk Town shows you meadows, fields and hamlets of the little-visited island's interior. A biking route from Rab Town on Rab explores the virgin forests of the Kalifront Peninsula. On Cres, a 50km trail takes you from the marina at Cres Town past the medieval hilltop village of Lubenice (p140) and the seaside gem of Valun (p140).

For details on these itineraries, ask at any tourist office for the *Kvarner by Bicycle* brochure, which outlines 19 routes across the region. A great source of info is www.pedala.hr, which focuses on trails mainly around Zagreb but also has good practical info about biking in Croatia.

Mali Lošinj
pop 6500

Mali Lošinj sits at the foot of a protected V-shaped harbour on the southeast coast of Lošinj. Vestiges of its 19th-century prosperity can still be seen in the stately sea captains' houses that line up along the seafront of the pretty old town. Even with the summer tourist commotion, this ancient quarter still retains the charm of a small Mediterranean town. That's partly due to the fact that most large hotels sit out of town, leading up from the harbour to Sunčana Uvala in the south and Čikat in the southwest.

This leafy area started to flourish in the late 19th century, when the wealthy Vienna and Budapest elite, who gravitated to the 'healthy air' of Mali Lošinj, started building villas and luxurious hotels around Čikat. Some of these grand residences remain, but most of the current hotels are modern developments surrounded by pine forests that blanket the cove and its fantastic beaches.

More relaxed to visit in spring and autumn, even in the hectic summer months Mali Lošinj can serve as a good base for excursions around Lošinj and Cres or to the small islands of Susak, Ilovik and Unije nearby.

ORIENTATION
The Jadrolinija ferry dock for all large boats is in the northeastern part of town, a 500m walk along the harbour from the town centre; catamarans stop a few metres closer to town. The bus station is further down, on the edge of the seafront.

Most shops, travel agencies and cafés are on Riva Lošinjskih Kapetana, which runs along the harbour to Trg Republike Hrvatske and its fountain. When you cross over to the other end of the harbour, there are roads to the hotels and beaches of Sunčana Uvala and Čikat.

INFORMATION
With the town's long history of tourism, there is no shortage of travel agencies to arrange private accommodation, handle air tickets, change money and book excursions.

Cappelli (☎ 231 582; www.cappelli-tourist.hr; Kadin bb; ⊗ 9am-9pm) Books private accommodation on Cres and Lošinj and sells tickets for Venezia Lines.

Erste Banka (Riva Lošinjskih Kapetana 4) There's an ATM outside.

Garderoba (☎ 231 110; Riva Lošinjskih Kapetana 19; ⊗ 6am-10pm) Left-luggage facilities (10KN per piece).

Hospital (☎ 231 824; Dinka Kozulića 1)

Internet Point F1 (☎ 231 129; Giuseppe Garibaldi 39; per hr 25KN; ⊗ 8am-1pm & 5-10pm) Internet access.

Manora Lošinj (☎ 520 100; www.manora-losinj.hr; Priko 29; ⊗ 8.30am-9pm Mon-Sat, 9am-1pm & 6-9pm Sun) Friendly agency with a full gamut of services.

Post office (Vladimira Gortana 4; ⊗ 8am-9pm Mon-Fri, to noon Sat)

Tourist office (☎ 231 884; www.tz-malilosinj.hr; Riva Lošinjskih Kapetana 29; ⊗ 8am-8pm Mon-Sat, 9am-1pm Sun Jun-Sep, 8am-5pm Mon-Fri, 9am-1pm Sat Oct-May) This treasure trove of useful information distributes spiffy brochures and maps of hiking trails on the two islands.

SIGHTS
The main attraction of Mali Lošinj is the attractive port and the greenery of the surrounding hills tumbling into the sea. There are a few monuments that recall the island's history. In the graveyard around the 15th-century **Church of St Martin** are the tombstones of the town's former inhabitants – sailors, fortune-seekers

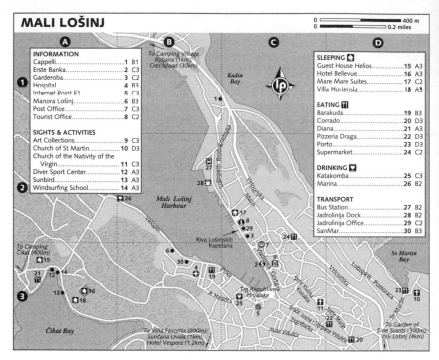

MALI LOŠINJ

0 — 400 m
0 — 0.2 miles

INFORMATION
Cappelli.....................................1 B1
Erste Banka...............................2 C3
Garderoba.................................3 C2
Hospital....................................4 B3
Internet Point E1......................5 C3
Manora Lošinj..........................6 B3
Post Office................................7 C3
Tourist Office...........................8 C2

SIGHTS & ACTIVITIES
Art Collections.........................9 C3
Church of St Martin.................10 D3
Church of the Nativity of the
  Virgin...................................11 C3
Diver Sport Center..................12 A3
Sunbird...................................13 A3
Windsurfing School.................14 A3

SLEEPING
Guest House Helios.................15 A3
Hotel Bellevue.........................16 A3
Mare Mare Suites....................17 C2
Villa Hortensia........................18 A3

EATING
Barakuda..................................19 B3
Corrado....................................20 D3
Diana.......................................21 D3
Pizzeria Draga.........................22 D3
Porto.......................................23 D3
Supermarket............................24 C2

DRINKING
Katakomba...............................25 C3
Marina.....................................26 B2

TRANSPORT
Bus Station...............................27 B2
Jadrolinija Dock.......................28 B2
Jadrolinija Office......................29 C2
SanMar....................................30 B3

To Camping Village Poljana (1km); Cres Island (30km)

Kadin Bay

Mali Lošinj Harbour

Riva Lošinjskih Kapetana

To Camping Čikat (400m)

Čikat Bay

To Villa Favorita (800m); Sunčana Uvala (1km); Hotel Vespera (1.2km)

Trg Republike Hrvatske

Sv Martin Bay

To Garden of Fine Scents (300m); Veli Lošinj (4km)

---

from Italy and Austria, Italian royalty and 19th-century Austrian children sent here in the hopes that the mild climate would cure their tuberculosis or respiratory problems.

In the town centre, peek into the parish **Church of the Nativity of the Virgin** (Župna Crkva Male Gospe) either before or after Sunday Mass at 10am. Inside are some notable artworks, including a painting of the Nativity of the Blessed Virgin by an 18th-century Venetian artist and relics of St Romulus.

Mali Lošinj's arts scene centres on the **art collections** (Umjetničke Zbirke; ☎ 233 892; Vladimira Gortana 35; admission 10/5KN; ☑ 10am-1pm & 7-10pm Tue-Sun) of the Mihičić and Piperata families. There are modern Croatian works, as well as the old masters with emphasis on Italian, French and Dutch painting.

For a whiff of enchanting Adriatic smells, head to the **Garden of Fine Scents** (Miomirisni Otočki Vrt; ☎ 233 638; Braće Vidulić bb; admission free; ☑ 10am-noon & 6-9pm Jul & Aug, 10am-noon Sep-Jun), just out of town. This fragrant paradise has over 250 native plant varieties plus 100 exotic species, all framed with *gromače*, traditional stone fences. There are special events on summer

Wednesday nights, from traditional drink tastings to guest lectures.

The town's unofficial icon is the antique statue of **Apoksiomen**, found on the sea bed near Lošinj in 1999. At 192m, this 2000-year-old bronze athlete is one of few such well-preserved pieces in the world. After years of meticulous restoration, the statue is expected to move into its very own exhibition space inside Mali Lošinj's restored Kvarner Palace some time in the future; contact the tourist office to find out whether the statue is on display yet.

ACTIVITIES

Sunčana Uvala offers the best pebble beaches, excellent for swimming. With its long, narrow pebble beach and great wind exposure, **Čikat** is *the* spot for windsurfing. You can take a course at the **Windsurfing School** (☎ 231 222) or at **Sunbird** (☎ 091 792 5926; www.sunbird.de), near Hotel Bellevue. Sunbird also offers courses in cat-sailing and rents mountain bikes (75KN per day).

Cycling and **hiking** have become increasingly popular on Lošinj, and these activities are much promoted by the local tourist board. Pick up the free brochure *Promenades & Footpaths*, with maps of 220km of trails that criss-cross the five islands of the archipelago (Lošinj, Cres, Ilovik, Susak and Unije). Options include climbing up to the highest peak of Televrina (588m) or a steep hike to Sveti Nikola (557m) for the nicest views.

The waters surrounding Lošinj offer good **diving**. Who knows, you may uncover the next Apoksiomen! There's a wreck dating from 1917, a large, relatively shallow cave suitable for beginners and the wonderful Margarita Reef off the island of Susak. The main dive operation is **Diver Sport Center** (☎ 233 900; www .diver.hr) on Čikat, which offers courses and dive packages from 320KN.

SLEEPING

Mali Lošinj offers a range of accommodation options. The travel agencies listed under Information (p131) find rooms and apartments around Mali Lošinj, although there's little available in the town itself. The tourist office has a detailed brochure with listings of private accommodation. Expect to pay between 90KN and 140KN per person for a room in the high season. Two-person apartments start at 320KN. In summer, you're likely to pay a penalty for a stay under four nights.

Most hotels are in the pine forest on the hill over in Čikat, with some in Sunčana Uvala. The majority falls under the umbrella of **Lošinj Hotels & Villas** (www.losinj-hotels.com). Most of these package resorts are bland and nearly indistinguishable tourist developments, despite recent facelifts and renovations. The leafy beachside location is the main draw of staying here. Most hotels close between November and Easter; in summer, they impose a surcharge for stays under three or four nights.

Budget

Camping Čikat (☎ 232 125; www.camps-cres-losinj.com; Dražica 1, Čikat bb; per adult/site 62/47KN; ❧ Apr–mid-Oct) Near a concrete beach, this large camping ground has a full spectrum of facilities.

Camping Village Poljana (☎ 231 726; www.poljana .hr; Poljana bb; per site low-high 87-166KN) Surrounded by a pine forest, this spiffy spot has perks such as wireless internet (for a fee), a restaurant and a supermarket.

Guest House Helios (☎ 232 124; www.losinj-hotels .com; Čikat bb; s low-high 158-270KN; d 315-540KN; ℗) Bland and screaming for a renovation, but

boasting a brilliant location amid greenery, and just steps from the beaches.

Midrange

Hotel Vespera (☎ 231 304; www.losinj-hotels.com; Sunčana Uvala bb; s low-high 233-420KN, d 360-735KN; ℗ 💻) Tennis courts, volleyball, hiking paths and water sports nearby make this three-star a great option for families and active types. It's a stone's throw from a pretty beach in Sunčana Uvala.

Hotel Bellevue (☎ 231 222; www.losinj-hotels.com; Čikat bb; s low-high 233-420KN, d 390-765KN; ℗ 💻 ☎) The pine forest location, wellness centre and refurbished rooms can help you forget the package tour groups that frequent this place. The lower priced annexe, Villa Hortensia (single low-high season 132KN to 315KN; double 263KN to 630KN), is right on the beach.

Top End

Mare Mare Suites (☎ 232 010; www.mare-mare.com; Riva Lošinjskih Kapetana 36; s low-high 600-900KN; d 750-1050KN; ℗ ✗ ✗ 💻) This chic little B&B occupies a historic townhouse on the seafront. No two rooms or suites are alike but all have sea vistas and stylish decor. There's a jacuzzi terrace, an à la carte pillow service, and free wireless internet, bikes and beach transfers in summer.

Villa Favorita (☎ 520 640; www.villafavorita.hr; Sunčana Uvala; d low-high 660-1150KN; ℗ ✗ 💻 ☎) Set in an intimate Habsburg mansion, the eight deluxe rooms here are named after flowers; four face the sea. There's a sauna, massage and a seawater pool in a well-kept garden. The annexe, Villa Jelena (single low-high season 330KN to 575KN; double 610KN to 850KN), has slightly smaller rooms with no air-con.

EATING

Catering to the tremendous influx of Italian tourists in summer has lent the island's cuisine a decidedly Italian flavour. As on many islands, there is not a wide variety in price or quality and the menus tend to be more or less the same, with an accent on seafood, grilled fish, pasta and risotto. You'll generally eat better at places away from the main harbour area in the old town.

Pizzeria Draga (☎ 231 132; Braće Ivana i Stjepana Vidulića 77; pizzas from 35KN) The owner has received many awards for the pizzas that come out of the brick oven at this friendly place. No wonder the terrace gets packed with locals and tourists in summer.

Corrado (☎ 232 487; Svete Marije 1; mains from 50KN) No farmed seafood is served at this *konoba* with a covered terrace, owned by a deep-sea fisher. The oven-baked fish with veggies is delicious, as is the peasant specialty, *verze na pofrih*, a squid and kale stew (order two hours ahead).

our pick **Porto** (☎ 231 956; Sveti Martin 35; mains from 60KN) A fish fillet with sea urchins is the signature dish at this lovely little spot on a small quiet bay near the Church of St Martin. Slightly off the tourist track, its covered terrace by the sea doesn't get too crowded.

Diana (☎ 232 055; Čikat bb; mains from 65KN) Part of a small four-star hotel complex in Čikat, this restaurant is particularly notable for its cypress-tree-shaded terrace on the sea and its lamb medallions with asparagus. The fish dishes are good, too.

Barakuda (☎ 233 309; Priko 31; mains from 70KN) The charcoal-grilled seafood and the nautically themed decor make this harbour restaurant stand out. However, tourist crowds can detract from your eating pleasure in summer months.

Self-caterers can head to the large supermarket on Trg Zagazinjine, just north of the harbour's edge.

ENTERTAINMENT

The terraces of café-bars along the harbour get packed with tourists and locals in the summer months. Riva Lošinjskih Kapetana and Ulica Vladimira Gortana are chock-a-block with choices, although they're not widely varied. For live music and a fun atmosphere, head to the town's most popular spot, **Katakomba** (Del Conte Giovanni 1), in an alleyway on the other side of the harbour. To party on the water, check out **Marina** (Velopin bb), a floating cocktail bar docked on the southwest side of the harbour, with DJs and live music on summer nights.

GETTING THERE & AWAY

There are nine buses a day between Mali Lošinj and Veli Lošinj (15KN, 10 minutes). For other bus and boat connections, see p129. The **Jadrolinija** (☎ 231 765; www.jadrolinija.hr; Riva Lošinjskih Kapetana 22) office has ferry information and tickets.

GETTING AROUND

From late April to October there is an hourly shuttle bus (10KN) that runs from the centre of town to the hotels in Sunčana Uvala and Čikat, till 11pm.

You can zip around the island on a scooter, available at **SanMar** (☎ /fax 233 571; www.sanmar .hr; Priko 24; per day 200KN; ⏰ 8.30am-2.30pm & 6-10pm), which also rents bikes (80KN per day).

Islands Around Mali Lošinj

The nearby car-free islands of Susak, Ilovik and Unije are the most popular day trips from Mali Lošinj. Tiny **Susak** (population 188; area 3.8 sq km) is unique for the thick layer of fine sand that blankets the underlying limestone and creates delightful beaches. It's the island's unusual culture that makes it particularly interesting. Islanders speak their own dialect, which is nearly incomprehensible to other Croats. On feast days and at weddings, you can see the local women outfitted in traditional multicoloured skirts and red leggings. When you see the old stone houses on the island, consider that each stone had to be brought over from Mali Lošinj and carried by hand to its destination. No wonder the island has steadily lost its population, with many of its citizens settling in Hoboken, New Jersey.

In contrast to flat Susak, **Ilovik** (population 145; area 5.8 sq km) is a hilly island known for its profusion of flowers. Overgrowing with oleanders, roses and eucalyptus trees, it's popular with boaters and has some secluded swimming coves.

The largest of the islands in the Lošinj archipelago, **Unije** (population 273; area 18 sq km) has an undulating landscape that abounds in Mediterranean shrubs, pebble beaches and numerous coves and inlets. The island's only settlement is a picturesque fishing village of gabled stone houses.

Many travel agencies sell excursions to Susak, Ilovik and Unije but it's easy enough to get there on your own. Jadrolinija makes a daily summer circuit from Mali Lošinj to Susak (13KN, 2½ hours) and Ilovik (13KN, one hour), with a boat departing in the morning (some days at the crack of dawn) and one returning in late afternoon. You can do a day trip to Unije (13KN, 1½ hours) any day but Monday or Wednesday. Note that the boat schedule for all islands is tricky on Sundays.

Veli Lošinj

Despite the name (in Croatian, *veli* means big and *mali* means small), Veli Lošinj is smaller, more languid and somewhat less crowded than Mali Lošinj, only 4km to the northwest. It's also managed to retain more of its fishing-village character. Pastel-coloured baroque houses cluster around a narrow bay that protrudes like a thumb into the island's southeastern coastline. Narrow cobblestone alleyways lead uphill from the central square past foliage-buried cottages to the rocky coast. The absence of cars in the centre is refreshing, but the presence of summer tourist hordes takes away from the pleasure of walking the traffic-free streets.

Like its neighbour, Veli Lošinj had its share of rich sea captains who built villas and surrounded them with gardens of exotic plants they brought back from afar. You can glimpse these villas on a walk up the steep streets. Sea captains also furnished the churches in town, most notably St Anthony's on the harbour.

ORIENTATION
The bus station is on a hill at the entrance to town, by the main parking lot. Vladimira Nazora takes you down to the harbour, which is the town centre. The bank, post office, tourist agencies and a number of cafés are on Obala Maršala Tita, which wraps around the bay. A coastal route leads north up to the Hotel Punta beach and east to the bay of Rovenska, a 10-minute walk away.

INFORMATION
Erste Banka (Obala Maršala Tita) Has a foreign-exchange counter. There are a few other ATMs in town.
Post office (Obala Maršala Tita 33; 🕙 8am-9pm Mon-Fri, to noon Sat)
Turist (☎ 236 256; www.island-losinj.com; Obala Maršala Tita 17; 🕙 8am-2pm & 5-9pm summer, shorter hr rest of year) Finds private accommodation, changes money, rents bikes (50KN per six hours) and scooters (80KN per hour) and offers excursions to Susak and Ilovik (115KN).
Val (☎ /fax 236 352; www.val-losinj.hr; Vladimira Nazora 29; 🕙 9am-8pm Jul & Aug) In addition to booking private accommodation, this travel agency has internet access (30KN per hour).

SIGHTS & ACTIVITIES
You can't miss the tall bell tower of the **Church of St Anthony the Hermit** (Crkva Svetog Antuna) on the right side of the harbour. Built in baroque style in 1774, thanks to wealthy sea captains it is elaborately decked out with marble altars, a rich collection of Italian paintings, a pipe organ and relics of St Gregory. It's only open for Sunday Mass

but you can catch a glimpse of the interior through a metal gate.

The striking **tower** (kula; Kaštel 2) in the maze of streets set back from the harbour was built by the Venetians in 1455 to defend the town from the notorious Uskoks (a community of pirates that once lived in Senj). It now contains a small **museum & gallery** (☎ 236 594; admission 10KN; 🕙 10am-1pm & 7-10pm Tue-Sun mid-Jun–mid-Sep, 10am-1pm Tue-Sat mid-Sep–Oct & Apr–mid-Jun), which centres on the island's maritime history, explaining it with English captions.

The town's most enlightening attraction is the **Lošinj Marine Education Centre** (☎ 236 406; Kaštel 24; adult/student 10/7KN; 🕙 9am-1pm & 6-10pm Jul & Aug, 9am-1pm & 6-8pm Jun & Sep, shorter hr rest of year), dedicated to sensitising visitors to the local marine life, particularly its endangered population of bottlenose dolphins. The centre is a project of Blue World (see p136).

Stop by **Ultramarin art gallery** (☎ 236 117; www.ultramarin.hr; Obala Maršala Tita 7; 🕙 9am-10pm Jun-Aug), signposted from the harbour. You can peek inside this family-run atelier where a wife and husband make colourful decorative boats, vases and candleholders out of driftwood collected from the island.

SLEEPING
Both Val and Turist travel agencies (left) will find private accommodation for about the same price as in Mali Lošinj. Pension Saturn on the harbour is a good choice; you can book through Val. At the time of writing, a new hostel was in the works, which should be up and running shortly.

Youth Hostel (☎ 236 234; www.hfhs.hr; Kaciol 4; dm low-high 110-135KN; 🕙 Jun-Oct; 🖳) You can bunk for peanuts in the decently clean and comfy rooms of this slightly rundown 1884 Habsburg villa in the middle of a shady pine forest. Book in advance, as school groups sometimes take over.

Hotel Punta (☎ 662 000; www.losinj-hotels.com; s low-high 285-487KN, d 420-827KN; 🅿 🖳 🐾) There's not much character at this standard package resort on a hill, but the balconied rooms are adequate, and there's easy access to the beach and a full array of facilities, including a small wellness centre.

EATING
The restaurants along the harbour serve generic seafood and meat dishes. The two spots following are worth sampling.

BLUE WORLD

The **Blue World Institute of Marine Research & Conservation** (☎ 236 406; www.blue-world.org; Kaštel 24) is a Veli Lošinj–based NGO founded in 1999 to promote environmental awareness in the Lošinj–Cres archipelago, Croatia and the Adriatic. It raises public awareness through lectures, media presentations and the organisation of **Dolphin Day** in Veli Lošinj on the first Saturday of August, which sees photography exhibitions, street performances, treasure hunts and children's competitions in drawing and painting.

As part of the Adriatic Dolphin Project, Blue World studies bottlenose dolphins that frequent the Lošinj–Cres area. Each dolphin is named and catalogued by photos taken of the natural marks that can be seen on their dorsal fin. Since the community of resident bottlenose dolphins in the Lošinj–Cres archipelago has dropped by a dramatic 40% in the last 15 years – only about 100 dolphins frequent the area today – Blue World has managed to establish the **Lošinj Dolphin Reserve**, the first marine protected area in the Mediterranean dedicated to bottlenose dolphins.

We stole a few minutes with Peter Mackelworth, Conservation Director of Blue World. When asked about the steady drop of dolphin numbers in these waters, Peter explained: 'Overfishing and the busy summer season bring a lot of disturbing noise and boat traffic. Dolphins leave for calmer waters to the north and south in the summer months, but each year it takes them a little longer to return.'

We asked Peter what people can do. 'For now, visit the centre and get informed,' he said. Want to do more? You can adopt a dolphin, for only 150KN! By doing so, you are supporting the activities of the Adriatic Dolphin Project. You even get a personalised adoption certificate and a photo of your chosen dolphin. At the time of writing, four friendly dolphins were up for adoption – Sonja, Debbie, Meta and Mush.

If you want to do something even more active, you can join an eco-volunteer holiday. Blue World offers these from June through September – 12-day programs start at €700 per person with accommodation, food, lectures and activities.

Ribarska Koliba (☎ 236 235; Obala Maršala Tita 1; mains from 55KN) Just around the corner from St Anthony's church, this pleasant place serves lamb and suckling pig on a spit, as well as good *buzara* (scampi and mussel stew) on a sea-facing terrace.

ourpick Bora Bar (☎ 867 544; www.borabar.com; Rovenska Bay 3; mains from 70KN) Truffle specialities conjured up by Italian-born chef Marko Sasso are reason enough to come to Veli. Delicacies include truffle-topped saffron risotto and *panna cotta* (a creamy Italian dessert) with truffle honey. On scenic Rovenska Bay, it's cheerful, colourful and friendly, with wireless internet and a book exchange. All dishes – many without the fungus, too – are made from scratch and with love, so don't mind a longish wait.

GETTING THERE & AWAY
There are nine buses a day between Veli Lošinj and Mali Lošinj (15KN, 10 minutes).

CRES ISLAND
Stretching 68km from tip to tip, Cres is longer, less populated and more undeveloped than Lošinj. On this wild island, you can wander around primeval forests, swim in hidden coves, sample some of Croatia's most delicious lamb, and visit ageing hilltop towns.

The northern half of the island, known as Tramuntana, is covered with dense oak, hornbeam, elk and chestnut forests. It's also home to the protected griffon vulture (see p138) in the hilltop village of Beli, on the eastern coast. The 6km-long Vrana Lake (Vransko Jezero) in the centre of the island, with its bottom about 60m below sea level, is the source of drinking water for both islands. The main seaside settlements lie on the western shore of Cres, while the mountainous interior southwest of Valun features the astounding medieval town of Lubenice (see p140).

Cres Town
pop 2234
Wandering around sun-drenched Cres Town, with old ladies chattering away in Italian, you may wonder if you've accidentally strayed across the border to Italy. Pastel-coloured terrace houses and Venetian mansions hug the medieval harbour, Mandrać, which is

jam-packed with small fishing boats. The town is popular with Italian boaters, who come here in droves come summer.

The Italian influence dates from the 15th-century Venetians who relocated their headquarters to Cres Town after Osor fell victim to plague and pestilence. Public buildings and patricians' palaces were built along the harbour and a town wall added in the 16th century. As you stroll along the seaside promenade and the maze of old town streets, you'll notice reminders of Italian rule, including coats of arms of powerful Venetian families and Renaissance loggias.

ORIENTATION

The bus stop (there is no left-luggage office) is on the southeastern side of the harbour next to the tourist office and bank. The old town stretches from the harbour promenade, Riva Creskih Kapetana, inland to Šetalište 20 Travnja. Most of the monuments and churches are concentrated within this area. If you continue around the harbour to Lungomare Sveti Mikule, after about 1km you'll reach the rocky beaches around Hotel Kimen and Autocamp Kovačine.

INFORMATION

Autotrans (☎ 572 050; www.autotrans-turizam.com; Zazid 4; ☷ 7am-9pm Jun-Aug, 8am-noon & 5.30-7.30pm Mon-Sat Sep-May) Arranges private accommodation, bike rental (20KN per hour), excursions and bus tickets.

Cresanka (☎ 571 161; www.cresanka.hr; Cons 11; ☷ 7.30am-10pm Jul & Aug, 7.30am-9pm Jun & Sep, 7.30am-noon & 3.30-8pm Oct-May) Books private accommodation and changes money.

Erste Banka (Cons 8) Changes money. There's another ATM at Riva Creskih Kapetana 3.

Post office (Cons 3; ☷ 7.30am-7pm Mon-Fri, to 1pm Sat)

Tourist Agency Croatia (☎ 573 053; www.cres-travel .com; Melin 2/33; ☷ 8am-9pm summer, shorter hr rest of year) Can arrange private accommodation and has internet access (1KN per minute).

Tourist office (☎ 571 535; www.tzg-cres.hr; Cons 10; ☷ 8am-8pm Mon-Sat, 9am-1pm Sun Jul & Aug, 8am-2pm Mon-Fri Sep-Jun) Has maps and brochures.

SIGHTS

At the end of Riva Creskih Kapetana is Trg Frane Petrića with the graceful 16th-century **municipal loggia**, the scene of public announcements, financial transactions and festivals under Venetian rule. It's now the site of a morning fruit and vegetable market.

Behind the loggia is the 16th-century gate that leads to **St Mary of the Snow Church** (Sv Marije Snježne; Pod Urom; ☷ Mass only). The facade is notable for the Renaissance portal with a relief of the Virgin and Child. It's worth checking out the serene interior before or after Mass for the carved wooden pietà from the 15th century (now under protective glass) at the left altar.

Stop by **Ruta** (☎ 571 835; www.ruta-cres.hr; Zazid 4A; ☷ sporadic or by appointment), a local collective that promotes the island's cultural and ecological identity by preserving old traditions such as weaving and felting of sheep wool. Using the discarded wool of the indigenous Pramenka sheep, the craftspeople make wonderful slippers, hats, handbags and clothes. You can see the workshop, learn about felting or even try it yourself (three-hour workshops are available for 150KN).

ACTIVITIES

For the best beaches, head to the area around Hotel Kimen. Diving is offered by **Diving Cres** (☎ /fax 571 706; www.divingcres.de, in German) in Autocamp Kovačine. **Cres-Insula Activa** (☎ 091 738 9490; www.cres-activa.hr, in Croatian) is an ecologically minded association that can organise biking, climbing and kite-surfing trips. Hiking has become increasingly popular on Cres and Lošinj; the tourist office (left) distributes a map of footpaths and trails around the island.

SLEEPING

All the agencies listed under Information (left) can find private rooms. Prices vary greatly according to season (August being the peak), comfort level and location (in the old town or on the outskirts). Rooms with shared bathroom start from 175KN per person in a single; doubles start at 235KN. Two-person apartments go for about 365KN.

Autocamp Kovačine (☎ 573 150; www.camp -kovacine.com; Melin 1/20; per person low-high 34-70KN; ☷ Easter–mid-Oct) There's no tent charge at this 18-hectare camping ground about 1km southwest of town. There are solar-powered bath facilities, a restaurant and activities galore, including basketball, volleyball and diving.

Kovačine Rooms (☎ 573 150; www.camp-kova cine.com; Melin 1/20; s low-high 225-348KN; d 406-624KN; ☷) Part of Autocamp Kovačine, this small building has 13 efficient en suite rooms with phones, satellite TV and even air-con. Some feature balconies with views over Valun Bay.

Hotel Kimen (☎ 573 305; www.hotel-kimen.com; Melin 1/16; s low-high 240-485KN, d 334-610KN; P ✗ ⌨) The shady pine forest location, about 1km from the centre, and the beaches are the highlight of this otherwise unremarkable hotel. The recently touched-up rooms all have balconies. There's also an older annexe (single low-high 174KN to 304KN; double 290KN to 507KN).

EATING

Luna Rossa (☎ 572 207; Palada 4b; pizzas from 18KN, mains from 32KN) This small Italian spot on the harbour churns out excellent pizza and pasta on a small terrace. The risottos and the gnocchi are also yummy.

our pick Bukaleta (☎ 571 606; Loznati bb, Loznati; mains from 40KN) Don't miss the famous Cres lamb, deliciously prepared at this longstanding family restaurant in the hamlet of Loznati, 5km from Cres Town. Start with the sheep ricotta and continue with the herb-fed lamb (from 80KN) – breaded, grilled or from the spit. It's worth the taxi ride.

Santa Lucia (☎ 573 222; Lungomare Sveti Mikule 4; mains from 40KN) Don't be turned off by the fancy look of this good-value restaurant on the coastal promenade towards Hotel Kimen. Sit on the terrace by the sea and savour the speciality – salty oven-baked fish.

Restaurant Riva (☎ 571 107; Riva Creskih Kapetana 13; mains from 50KN) The fish is prepared with care and the terrace on the harbour is a great place to watch the sun disappear over the pastel-coloured townhouses across the way. Order the barbecued scampi.

The **supermarket** (Trg Frane Petrića) can be found right across from the loggia.

GETTING THERE & AWAY

There are three buses a day to Opatija (61KN, two hours) and five to Rijeka (84KN, 2½ hours). Three daily buses go to Porozina (29KN, one hour) and Brestova in Istria (with ferry ticket 66KN, 1½ hours).

For more information on buses between Cres and Mali and Veli Lošinj, see p130.

Beli

Lying at the heart of the Tramuntana region on the island's northern tip, with ancient virgin forests, abandoned villages, lone chapels and myths of good elves, Beli is one of the

---

THE THREATENED GRIFFON VULTURE

Of all Croatia's birds, the Eurasian griffon vulture is the most majestic. With a wingspan of almost 3m, measuring about 1m from end to end, and weighing 7kg to 9kg, the bird looks big enough to take on passengers. They cruise comfortably at 40km/h to 50km/h, reaching speeds of up to 120km/h. The vulture's powerful beak and long neck are ideally suited for rummaging around the entrails of its prey, which is most likely to be a dead sheep.

Finding precious sheep carcasses is a team effort for griffon vultures. Usually a colony of birds will set out and fly in a comb formation of up to a kilometre apart. When one of the vultures spots a carcass, it circles as a signal for its neighbours to join in the feast. Shepherds don't mind griffons, reasoning that the birds prevent whatever disease or infection killed the sheep from spreading to other livestock.

The total known number of griffon vultures in Croatia is 150, most of them living on the coastal cliffs of Cres and in small colonies on Krk and Prvić islands. The birds' dietary preferences mean that griffons tend to follow sheep although they will eat other dead mammals, to their peril. The last remaining birds in Paklenica National Park recently died after eating poisoned foxes. Fewer local farmers are raising sheep but shepherding is still active on Cres, supported by the Eco-Centre Caput Insulae in Beli (opposite).

Breeding habits discourage a large population, as a griffon couple produces only one fledgling a year and it takes five years for the young bird to reach maturity. During that time, the growing griffons travel widely: one griffon tagged in Paklenica National Park was found in Chad, 4000km away.

The griffon population enjoys legal protection as an endangered species in Croatia. Killing a bird or disturbing them while nesting carries a €5000 fine. Intentional murder is rare but because the young birds cannot fly more than 500m on a windless day, tourists on speedboats who provoke them into flight often end up killing them. The exhausted birds drop into the water and drown.

island's oldest settlements. Perched on a 130m hill above a lovely pebble beach, its 4000-year history can still be felt in its twisting lanes and stone townhouses overgrown with plants.

The highlight is **Eco-Centre Caput Insulae** (☎ /fax 840 525; www.caput-insulae.com; Beli 4; adult/concession 25/10KN; ♈ 9am-8pm summer, to 4pm spring & autumn), part nature park, part sanctuary for the endangered Eurasian griffon (see boxed text, opposite). The eco-centre is devoted to caring for and maintaining the habitat of these majestic birds. It works with local farmers to ensure a supply of sheep needed for the griffons' survival and with local fishers to rescue drowning vultures. It saves about 10 young griffons each summer; these young birds cannot fly more than 500m and if provoked to fly, many fall into the sea and drown.

A visit to the centre, inside an old mansion at the town entrance, starts with exhibits explaining the biology and habits of the vulture, but the highlight is the vultures themselves. There are usually about four birds in residence flapping around in a caged-in area behind the centre. Keep an eye on the sky and you may spot one of the birds swooping overhead. The best time to see one is after their morning and afternoon meals. The eco-centre also offers a well-established volunteer program that runs throughout the year, as well as a griffon adoption program (what's 200KN to save a griffon?).

Admission to the centre includes access to the 50km network of seven educative **eco-trails** that connects the abandoned villages of Tramuntana, each clearly marked with a different colour. There are also **stone labyrinths** dedicated to ancient Croatian and Slavic gods, designed to connect walkers to nature's spirit. Pick up an informative booklet and maps from the centre, explaining the history, culture, and flora and fauna of the region.

Down on the beach about 1km from town, the small **Brajdi campsite** (☎ /fax 840 532; Beli bb; per person & site 54KN; ♈ May-Sep) has a diving centre (www.diving-beli.com) and a beach bar offering snacks.

In summer, there are two daily buses from Cres Town to Beli (27KN, 30 minutes), except on Sundays.

Osor

pop 70

When crossing from Lošinj to Osor, you may have to wait at the drawbridge spanning the Kavuada Canal, as the bridge is raised twice a day (at 9am and 5pm) to allow boats to move from the Lošinjski Channel to the Kvarner Gulf and back. It's a treat to watch the yachts, sailboats and motorboats file through the narrow canal that separates the two islands.

The channel is thought to have been dug by the Romans, and because of it Osor was able to control a key navigational route. In the 6th century, a bishopric was established in Osor, which controlled both Cres and the largely unpopulated Lošinj throughout the Middle Ages. Until the 15th century, Osor was a strong commercial, religious and political presence in the region, but a combination of plague, malaria and new sea routes devastated the town's economy and it slowly decayed.

Now it's gaining a new life as a museum-town of churches, open-air sculptures and country lanes that meander off from its 15th-century town centre. Despite obvious investment in bringing Osor back to life, there's still no tourist office but it's an easy day trip from Mali Lošinj and Cres Town.

SIGHTS

Entering through the gate on the canal, you walk right into the centre of town. First you'll pass the remains of an old castle and then, on your right, the **Archaeological Museum** (☎ 237 346; admission 10KN; ♈ 10am-1pm & 7-10pm Tue-Sun Jun-Sep, 10am-1pm Tue-Sat Oct-May) on the main square in the 15th-century town hall. It contains a collection of stone fragments and reliefs from the Roman and early Christian periods.

Next door is the **Church of the Assumption** (Crkva Uznesenja; ♈ 10am-noon & 7-9pm Jun-Sep) built in the late 15th century, with a rich Renaissance portal on the facade. The baroque altar inside has relics of St Gaudencius, Osor's patron saint. Gaudencius was an 11th-century bishop who, according to local legend, took it upon himself to castigate the townspeople for their sins and corruption. The bitter bishop was in turn expelled from town, became a hermit in a cave and put a curse upon all the poisonous snakes on the island (the curse is still on – there are no poisonous snakes on Cres).

Before leaving the square, notice the Ivan Meštrović statue **Daleki Akordi** (Distant Chords), one of the town's many modern sculptures on a musical theme.

KVARNER REGION

FESTIVALS

During **Musical Evenings of Osor** (Osorske Glazbene Večeri) from mid-July to late August, high-calibre Croatian artists perform classical music in the cathedral and on the main square. The tourist offices in Mali Lošinj and Cres Town have details.

SLEEPING & EATING

There are no hotels in Osor, but private accommodation is available and there are two camping grounds in the area. The tourist offices in Mali Lošinj and Cres Town have listings of private rooms and apartments.

Bijar (☎ /fax 237 027; www.camps-cres-losinj.com; Osor bb; per person low-high 40-60KN) This camping ground is 500m from Osor, on the way to the town of Nerezine, and twice the size of Preko Mosta. The location on a remote cove with pebble and rocky beaches makes it a tranquil hideaway.

Preko Mosta (☎ 237 350; www.jazon.hr; Osor bb; per person/site 52/41KN) Overlooking the bridge to Lošinj, this small camping ground sits in a nice pine forest.

Konoba Bonifačić (☎ 237 413; Osor 64; mains from 50KN) The cuisine at this down-home restaurant features dependable risottos, with asparagus, scampi, prosciutto and plenty of fish. You can enter through the lush garden in the back or from the old town. Have a shot of elderflower grappa while you're there.

GETTING THERE & AWAY

All buses travelling between Cres and Mali Lošinj stop at Osor (24KN, 45 minutes).

Valun

pop 68

In a country with numerous idyllic coves, Valun is a standout. The little hamlet, 14km southwest of Cres Town, is buried at the foot of steep cliffs and surrounded by shingle beaches. You leave the car on top of the hill and go down steep steps to the old town that drops to the cove. The relative inaccessibility means that the narrow cove with a handful of restaurants is rarely crowded, and there are no souvenir stalls blocking your view of the old stone town clinging to the hills.

The **tourist bureau** (☎ 525 050; ⏰ 8am-9pm Jul & Aug), a branch of Cresanka (see p137), is in the centre a few steps up from the harbour. It

---

LUBENICE

Time seems to stand still at this medieval hilltop hamlet atop a rocky ridge on the western side of Cres. Semi-abandoned (with a permanent population of 17) and swept by strong winds at 378m above sea level, this small maze of ancient stone houses and churches provides one of the last vestiges of traditional island life.

The experience of getting there, along a narrow road lined with stone walls, wildflowers and meadows, is just as spectacular as the settlement itself. At the end of the 10km drive (from the main road to Valun), this breathtaking place awaits. **Ekopark Pernat** (☎ 513 010; www.ekoparkpernat .org), a Rijeka-based centre for sustainable development, has done much to keep Lubenice alive. It runs a **cultural-educational space** (☎ 840 406; suggested donation 7KN; ⏰ 9am-10pm Easter-Oct) in the old school building at the village's end, with a small permanent exhibition about sheep-raising. Other projects are in the works, such as restoring the parsonage building and organising various workshops.

Lubenice lies above one of Kvarner's most remote and beautiful **beaches**, in a secluded cove accessible by a steep path through the underbrush. The 45-minute descent is a breeze, but coming up is more of a challenge so you could consider taking a taxi boat from Valun or Cres.

Another reason to visit Lubenice is for the annual **Lubeničke Glazbene Večeri** (Lubenice Music Nights), with alfresco classical concerts every Friday night in July and August. The tourist office in Cres Town (p137) has schedules and info on organised transportation.

The only way to stay in Lubenice is to rent private accommodation. The tourist office in Cres Town has private room listings, although there aren't many to choose from.

The only place to eat is **Konoba Hibernicia** (☎ 840 422; Lubenice 17; mains from 45KN), notable for its lamb dishes served in a cool stone interior or on the handful of tables outside.

In summer, there are two daily buses from Cres Town (27KN, 50 minutes), except on Sunday. It's possible to visit on a day trip on Tuesday, Thursday and Saturday, which are the only days when there is a same-day return bus.

books private accommodation (scarce in tiny Valun and usually reserved way in advance), but it's better to go through the main office in Cres Town. Expect to pay the same price as for private accommodation in Cres Town.

The main sight is the 11th-century **Valun Tablet**, kept in the parish Church of St Mary (whose opening hours are sporadic). Inscribed in both Glagolitic and Latin, this tombstone reflects the ethnic composition of the island, which was inhabited by Roman descendants and newcomers who spoke Croatian.

Valun's natural showcase is its series of lovely **beaches**. To the right of the harbour, a path leads to a beach and camping ground. West of the hamlet, about 700m further on, there's another lovely pebble beach bordered by pines.

Zdovice campsite (per person 95KN; ☽ May-Sep) is a small camping ground on the eastern cove, but it doesn't accept reservations. Call the tourist bureau to find out if there's space.

Of the town's restaurants, **Konoba Toš-Juna** (☎ 525 084; Valun bb; mains from 35KN) stands out. It's inside a converted olive mill with lots of wood, exposed stone and a nice terrace on the harbour. Try the fresh tuna in olive oil as a starter and continue with lamb or scampi.

There are two daily buses from Cres Town (24KN, 20 minutes), but none on Sunday. The problem is the return: there's a morning bus back only twice a week (on Monday and Wednesday). If you come by car, you'll have to pay the 15KN parking charge.

KRK ISLAND

pop 16,402

Croatia's largest island, connected to the mainland by a bridge, 409-sq-km Krk (Veglia in Italian) is also one of the busiest in summer, as Germans and Austrians stream over to its holiday houses, autocamps and hotels. It may not be the lushest or most beautiful island in Croatia (in fact, it's largely overdeveloped and stomped over), but its decades of experience in tourism make it an easy place to visit, with good transport connections and a well-organised infrastructure.

The northwestern coast of the island is rocky and steep with few settlements because of the fierce *bura* that whips the coast in winter. The climate is milder in the south, with more vegetation and beaches, coves and inlets. The major towns – Krk, Punat and Baška – are found on the forested southwestern coast.

Centrally located Krk Town makes a good base for exploring the island. Nearby Punat is an alternative place to stay and the gateway for the unique Košljun Island and monastery. Baška, on a wide sandy bay at the foot of a scenic mountain range, is the island's prime beach destination. On the east coast and off the beaten trail, Vrbnik is a cliff-top medieval village known for its *žlahtina* wine.

History

The oldest-known inhabitants of Krk were the Illyrian Liburnian tribe, followed by the Romans who settled on the northern coast. With the decline of the Roman Empire, Krk was incorporated into the Byzantine Empire, then passed between Venice and the Croatian-Hungarian kings.

In the 11th century, Krk became the centre of the Glagolitic language – the old Slavic language put into writing by the Greek missionaries Cyril and Methodius. The oldest preserved example of the script was found in a former Benedictine abbey in Krk Town. A later tablet with the script was found near Baška and is now exhibited in Zagreb. The script was used on the island up to the first decades of the 19th century.

In 1358, Venice granted rule over the island to the Dukes of Krk, later known as the Frankopans, who became one of the richest and most powerful families in Croatia. Although vassals of Venice, they ruled with a measure of independence until 1480, when the last member of the line put the island under the protection of Venice.

Although tourism is the dominant activity on the island, there are two shipyards in Punat and Krk for small-ship repairs, and some agriculture and fishing.

Getting There & Away

Krk is home to Rijeka Airport (p125), the main hub for flights to the Kvarner region, which consist mostly of low-cost and charter flights during summer.

The Krk toll bridge links the northern part of the island with the mainland and a regular car ferry links Valbiska with Merag (passenger/car 17/113KN, 30 minutes) on

KVARNER REGION

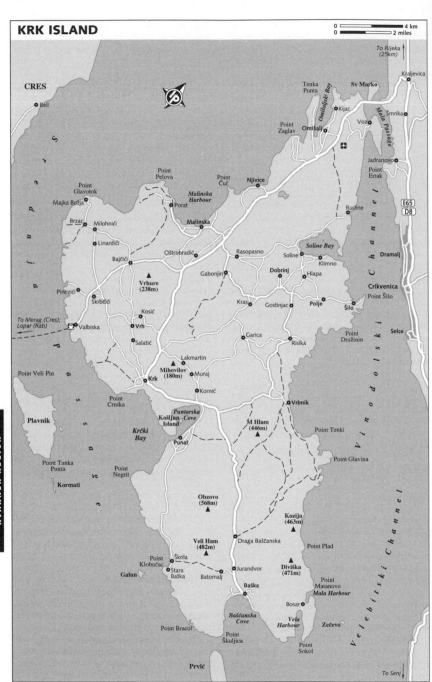

KRK ISLAND

0 ——— 4 km
0 ——— 2 miles

CRES

Beli

To Rijeka
(25km)

Kraljevica

Tenka
Punta

Sv Marko

Smrika

Point
Zaglav

Omišalj

Kijac

Voz

Jadranovo

Point
Ertak

E65
D8

Point
Glavotok

Majka Božja

Point
Pelova

Point
Čuf

Njivice

Malinska
Harbour

Porat

Malinska

Rudine

Brzac

Milohnići

Linardići

Oštrobradić

Rasopasno

Soline

Soline Bay

Dramalj

Bajčići

Gabonjin

Dobrinj

Klimno

Hlapa

Vrhure
(238m)

Crikvenica

Point Šilo

Pinezići

Skrbčići

Kosić

Kras

Gostinjac

Polje

Šilo

Selce

To Merag (Cres);
Lopar (Rab)

Valbiska

Vrh

Salatić

Garica

Risika

Point
Družinin

Lakmartin

Mihovilov
(180m)

Muraj

Krk

Kornić

Vrbnik

Point Veli Pin

Point
Crnika

Puntarska
Cove

Košljun
Island

M Hlam
(446m)

Point Tenki

Plavnik

Krčki
Bay

Punat

Point Glavina

Point Tanka
Punta

Point
Negrit

Kormati

Obzovo
(568m)

Kozija
(463m)

Point Plad

Veli Ham
(482m)

Draga Baščanska

Galun

Point
Klobučac

Škrila

Stara
Baška

Batomalj

Jurandvor

Diviška
(471m)

Baška

Bosar

Point
Matanovo

Mala Harbour

Zečevo

Baščanska
Cove

Point
Bracol

Vela
Harbour

Point
Škuljica

Point
Sokol

Prvić

To Senj

Omišaljke Bay

Mala passage

Vinodolski Channel

Velebitski Channel

e r s k i   j u r u p   s   s a   P

Cres. Another ferry, run by Split Tours, operates between Valbiska and Lopar (37KN, 1½ hours) on Rab four times daily.

About 14 buses per weekday travel between Rijeka and Krk Town (50KN, one to two hours). About 11 of those go via Punat (56KN to 64KN, one to two hours). Two daily buses continue on to Vrbnik (23KN, 35 minutes) from Monday to Friday. There are 10 daily buses to Baška from Krk Town (27KN, 45 minutes). All services are reduced, if running at all, on weekends.

There are six daily buses from Zagreb to Krk Town (163KN to 183KN, three to four hours). Note that some bus lines are more direct than others, which will stop in every village en route. Make sure to ask about travel time before deciding which bus to take. Out of the summer season, bus services are reduced.

To go from Krk to Cres and Lošinj, change buses at Malinska for the Lošinj-bound bus that comes from Rijeka or Zagreb, but check the departure and arrival times carefully (at www.autotrans.hr) as the connection only works four times a day.

Getting Around

Bus connections between towns are frequent because the many buses to and from Rijeka pick up passengers in all the island's main towns.

KRK TOWN

On the island's southwestern coast, Krk Town clusters around a medieval walled centre and, spreading out into the surrounding coves and hills, a modern development that includes a port, beaches, camping grounds and hotels. The seafront promenade can get seriously crowded in summer with tourists and weekending Croats from the mainland, who spill into the narrow cobbled streets that make up the pretty old quarter.

Minus the crowds, this stone labyrinth is the highlight of Krk Town. The former Roman settlement still retains sections of the ancient city walls and gates, as well as the Romanesque cathedral and a 12th-century Frankopan castle.

You won't need more than a couple of hours to see these sights, but from a base in Krk Town it's easy to hop on a bus to other island towns and beaches or take a boat trip around the island.

Orientation

The bus station (no left-luggage office) is on the harbour, only a few minutes' walk north to the historic town centre along the seafront. The main strip in the ancient quarter is JJ Strossmayera, lined with souvenir and ice-cream shops. Most hotels are east of the town centre, dotting the pine forests around the small sandy beach at Dražica cove.

Information

You can change money at most travel agencies; there are 13 in town.

Aurea (☎ 221 777; www.aurea-krk.hr; Vršanska 26l; ⏰ 8am-2pm & 3-8pm) Books private accommodation and excursions on the agency's very own boats.

Autotrans (☎ 222 661; www.autotrans-turizam.com; Šetalište Svetog Bernardina 3; ⏰ 8am-9pm Mon-Sat, 9am-1.30pm & 6-9pm Sun) Conveniently placed in the bus station, this agency finds private accommodation and sells bus tickets.

Erste Banka (Trg Bana Josipa Jelačića 4) Changes money and has an ATM.

Hospital (☎ 221 224; Vinogradska bb)

Krk Sistemi (☎ 222 999; Šetalište Svetog Bernardina 3; per 20min 10KN; ⏰ 9am-2pm & 5-10pm Mon-Sat, 5-10pm Sun) Free wireless internet plus terminals for those without a laptop.

Post office (Bodulska bb; ⏰ 7.30am-9pm Mon-Fri, to 2.30pm Sat) You can get cash advances on your credit cards.

Tourist offices (☎ 220 226; www.tz-krk.hr, in Croatian) Obala Hrvatske Mornarice (Obala Hrvatske Mornarice bb; ⏰ 8am-9pm Jun-Sep); Vela Placa (Vela Placa 1; ⏰ 8am-3pm Mon-Fri) The seasonal tourist office distributes brochures and materials, including a map of hiking paths. Out of season, go to the main tourist office nearby.

Sights

On the site of the 1st-century Roman baths and an earlier basilica, the **Cathedral of the Assumption** (Katedrala Uznesenja; Trg Svetog Kvirina; ⏰ morning & evening Mass) is a Romanesque structure from the 12th century. Note the rare early Christian carving of two birds eating a fish on the first column next to the apse. The left nave features a Gothic chapel from the 15th century, with the coats of arms of the Frankopan princes who used it as a place of worship.

The 18th-century campanile topped with an angel statue is shared between the cathedral and the adjoining **St Quirinus** (Trg Svetog Kvirina), an early Romanesque church built of white stone and dedicated to the town's patron saint. The **church museum** (Trg Svetog Kvirina;

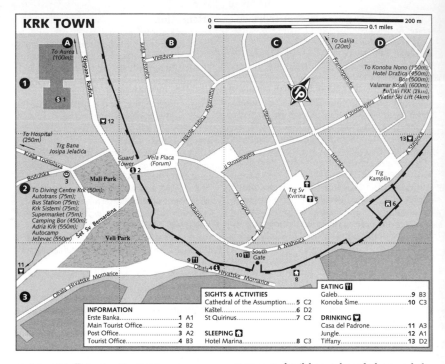

admission 5KN; 9am-1pm Mon-Sat) is a treasury of sacral art, with a silver altarpiece of the Virgin Mary from 1477 and a polyptych by Paolo Veneziano.

The fortified **Kaštel** (Trg Kamplin) facing the seafront on the northern edge of the old town has a 12th-century tower once used as a Frankopan courtroom and another round Venetian tower. The castle is now used as an open-air venue for summer concerts and plays.

Activities

A number of outfits organise diving trips around the island. Try **Diving Centre Krk** (222 563; www.fun-diving.com; Braće Juras 3) or **Adria Krk** (604 248; Creska 12). Popular dive sites include a sunken Greek cargo vessel and a variety of underwater caves, tunnels and coral walls around the island of Plavnik and as far as Cres.

Adrenaline junkies can get their fix at the **water ski lift** (091 272 7302; www.wakeboarder.hr; 5 rounds 50KN; mid-Apr–Sep), a 650m-long cableway for wakeboarding and waterskiing, running at a speed of 32km/h. Located between Krk Town and Punat, it has a restau-

rant, a cocktail bar, a board shop and the surfer crowd.

Festivals & Events

Every July and August the **Krk Summer Festival** hosts concerts, plays and dances in the Kaštel (the otherwise closed Franciscan monastery northwest of the harbour) and on the squares of the old town. The tourist office has schedules. The **Krk Fair** is a Venetian-inspired event that takes over the town for three days in mid-August with concerts, people dressed in medieval costumes, and stalls selling traditional food.

Sleeping

There are three camping grounds and a range of hotel options in and around Krk Town. The old town has only one hotel, on the seafront; a large complex east of the town centre has all the others. The travel agencies listed under Information (p143) can find private accommodation. Prices are fixed by the tourist association and range from 210KN to 250KN for a double room in the high season (130KN to 170KN for a single). Two-person studios go for between 210KN and 310KN in the high season.

Camping Bor (☎ 221 581; www.camp-bor.hr; Crikvenička 10; per adult/site 36/25KN; ❤ Apr-Oct) On a hill of olive groves and pine forests a 10-minute walk west of the seafront.

Autocamp Ježevac (☎ 221 081; camping@valamar .com; Plavnička bb; per adult/site 44/56KN; ❤ mid-Apr–mid-Oct) The beachfront ground offers shady sites and places to swim. It's just a 10-minute walk southwest of town.

Politin FKK (☎ 221 351; camping@valamar.com; per adult/site 46/56KN; ❤ mid-Apr–Sep) Be happily nude at this recently expanded naturist camp on the wooded Prniba Peninsula, a short distance from town, with views of Plavnik and Cres islands. There's free wireless internet.

Bor (☎ /fax 220 200; www.hotelbor.hr; Šetalište Dražica 5; s low-high 152-369KN, d 231-564KN; P) The rooms are modest and without trimmings at this low-key hotel right below the Dražica complex, but the seafront location amid pine forests makes it a worthwhile stay.

Hotel Dražica (☎ 655 755; www.hotelikrk.hr; Ružmarinska 6; s low-high 188-608KN, d 290-840KN; P ✕ 🖳 🖾) If you don't mind the package tour experience, this large central hotel of the Dražica complex delivers quality and facilities – two outdoor pools, tennis courts and a fitness centre. The two annexes nearby, Tamaris and Villa Lovorka (same prices), are a touch more intimate.

Valamar Koralj (☎ 655 400; www.valamar.com; Vlade Tomašića bb; d low-high 420-912KN; P ✕ 🖳 🖾) Book a standard room and you may wonder why this hotel on a peaceful cove is marketed as 'romantic', but pay extra for one of the 19 new suites and it becomes clear. Each suite has a terrace or balcony and a living room, while the outdoor pool has a jacuzzi.

Hotel Marina (☎ 221 357; www.hotelikrk.hr; Obala Hrvatske Mornarice 6; s/d 760/1168KN; P ✕ 🖳) The most recent overhaul of this old town hotel boosted it to four stars. Now each of the 10 deluxe units sports sea vistas and modern trappings such as LCD TVs.

Eating

Konoba Nono (☎ 222 221; Krčkih Iseljenika 8; mains from 40KN) Savour local specialities such as *šurlice* topped with goulash or scampi, just a hop and a skip from the old town. The arched rustic interior covered with fishing nets houses a small olive oil production plant in the winter months.

Galija (☎ 221 250; Frankopanska 38; mains from 45KN) If you don't mind forgoing sea vistas, make a climb to this cavernous place on the northwestern tip of the old town. Open year-round, it's popular with locals for its bread-oven pizzas, as well as risottos, meat mainstays and fish.

Konoba Šime (☎ 221 426; Antuna Mahnića 1; mains from 45KN) While it's nothing to write home about, this popular *konoba* by the harbour serves a good selection of pastas and local meaty treats such as *ćevapčići* (small spicy sausages of minced beef, lamb or pork). Dine inside in a medieval-type environment or out on the alfresco tables.

Galeb (☎ 221 261; Obala Hrvatske Mornarice 3; mains from 60KN) You'll pay mostly for the location here – the seafront terrace is a great place to linger and people-watch. The food is unimaginative but decent; expect standard mainstays and pizzas.

You can pick up picnic supplies at the large supermarket across from the bus station, or at one of the small grocery stores on JJ Strossmayera in the old town.

Drinking & Entertainment

Casa del Padrone (Šetalište Svetog Bernardina bb) Krk partygoers crowd the two floors of this faux-Renaissance bar-club that hosts DJs on summer weekends. Daytime fun consists of lounging on the seaside tables while nibbling on cakes and sipping espresso.

Jungle (☎ 221 503; Stjepana Radića bb; ❤ May-Sep) The only veritable club in town draws a youngish set to its tropically themed dance floor where house music is king. The cocktail bar outside is more low-key.

Tiffany (Stepinca 2) Perch on the town walls right outside this pub, beer in hand, and bop to the sound of old disco and pop hits. The views from the terrace are spectacular.

PUNAT

Eight kilometres southeast of Krk is the small town of Punat, frequented by yachters for its marina. The main attraction here is the monastery on the islet of Košljun, only a 10-minute boat ride away. The tiny island contains a 16th-century **Franciscan monastery** (admission 15KN; ❤ 9.30am-6pm Mon-Sat, to 12.30pm Sun) built on the site of a 12th-century Benedictine abbey. Highlights include a large, appropriately chilling *Last Judgment,* painted in 1653 and housed in the monastery church, and the small museum with a display of other religious paintings, an ethnographic collection and a rare copy of Ptolemy's *Atlas* printed in Venice in the late 16th century. Take a little extra time to stroll around the forested island with 400 plant species. Although agencies in Krk Town organise excursions to Košljun, it's cheaper to take one of the frequent buses to Punat and then a taxi boat from the harbour (20KN return). These are more expensive if you're hiring the boat solo or as a couple, but there'll be plenty of interested parties in summer who you can share the costs with. Boats go regularly; try **More** (☎ 854 127; www.more-punat .com; Kovačića 49).

With decent beaches on the outskirts, Punat can also serve as an alternative place to stay. There are two camping grounds: **Campsite Pila** (☎ 854 020; www.hoteli-punat.hr; Šetalište Ivana Brusića 2; per adult/site 51/98KN; ☼ Apr–mid-Oct), just south of the town centre, and the naturist **FKK Konobe** (☎ 854 049; www.hoteli-punat.hr; Obala 94; per adult/site 51/98KN; ☼ mid-Apr–Sep), about 3km south down the coast. The 90-bed **youth hostel** (☎ 854 037; www.hfhs.hr; Novi Put 8; dm low-high 75-85KN; d 95-110KN; ☼ May-Sep) was recently spruced up, so book ahead.

VRBNIK

Perched on a 48m cliff overlooking the sea on the east coast of the island, Vrbnik is a beguiling medieval village of steep, arched streets. It was once the centre of the Glagolitic language and repository for many Glagolitic manuscripts. The language was kept alive by priests, who were always plentiful in the town since many young men entered the priesthood to avoid serving on Venetian galleys.

Now the town is a terrific place to soak up the vistas and sample the *žlahtina* white wine produced in the surrounding region. After wandering the tight-packed cobbled alleyways where local women sell wine, descend to the town beach for some swimming. The small **tourist office** (☎ 857 479; Placa Vrbničkog Statuta 4; ☼ 8am-3pm Mon-Fri, 9am-1pm Sat & Sun Jul & Aug) has limited info. If you get enchanted and wish to stay, **Mare Tours** (☎ 604 400; www.mare-vrbnik .com; Pojana 4) has details about private rooms, although many get snatched up ahead of the summer season.

Restaurant Nada (☎ 857 065; Glavača 22; mains from 55KN), with a covered terrace upstairs, is a good place to sample *šurlice* topped with meat goulash or scampi. At its dark rustic *konoba*

downstairs, you can snack on sheep's cheese, wine, prosciutto and olive oil.

Only two daily weekday buses travel the 12km from Krk Town to Vrbnik (23KN, 35 minutes) and back. Weekends are tricky, as there's only one evening bus from Vrbnik on Sunday.

BAŠKA
pop 816

At the southern end of Krk Island, Baška has the island's most beautiful beach, a 2km-long crescent set below a dramatic, barren range of mountains. It's no wonder that it's turned into an immensely popular resort. The location is indeed spectacular, and the swimming and scenery better than at Krk Town. However, there's one caveat should you visit in summer – tourists are spread towel-to-towel and what's otherwise a pretty pebble beach turns into a fight for your place under the sun.

The 16th-century core of Venetian townhouses is pleasant enough for a stroll, but what surrounds it is a bland tourist development of modern apartment blocks and generic restaurants. Facilities are plentiful, however, and there are nice hiking trails into the surrounding mountains, two recently added rock-climbing sites and more secluded beaches to the east of town, reachable on foot or by water taxi.

Information

Just down the street from the bus station, between the beach and the harbour, is the **tourist office** (☎ 856 817; www.tz-baska.hr; Zvonimirova 114; ☼ 7am-9pm Mon-Sat, 8am-1pm Sun Jun–mid-Sep, 8am-3pm Mon-Fri mid-Sep–May). It distributes a wealth of brochures and a map of hiking trails around the island's southern tip.

Sights & Activities

One of the hiking trails leads to the Romanesque **St Lucy Church** (Sveta Lucija; admission 10KN; ☼ 8am-noon & 2-8pm) in the village of Jurandvor, 2km away; this is where the 11th-century Baška tablet was found. What's inside is a replica, as the original is now in the Archaeological Museum (p79) in Zagreb.

Several popular trails begin around Camping Zablaće, including an 8km walk to **Stara Baška**, a restful little village on a bay surrounded by stark, salt-washed limestone hills.

There are also two **rock climbing** sites in the area; the tourist office has maps and information.

Sleeping

Private accommodation can be arranged by most agencies in town, such as **PDM Guliver** (☎ /fax 856 004; www.pdm-guliver.hr; Zvonimirova 98; 7am-9pm Mon-Sat, 8am-1pm Sun Jun–mid-Sep, shorter hr rest of year) and **Primaturist** (☎ 856 132; www.primaturist.hr; Zvonimirova 98; 8am-7pm Mon-Fri, to 2pm Sat Jun-Aug) next door. There's a four-night minimum stay in summer (or a hefty surcharge) and rooms get filled up fast. Prices are a touch higher than in Krk Town.

Most hotels and the town's two camping grounds are managed by **Hoteli Baška** (☎ 656 111; www.hotelibaska.hr). During summer it is essential to arrange accommodation well in advance as the town swarms with Austrian, German and Czech tourists. Hotel space is booked solid by late spring, and accommodation is tight in the shoulder seasons as well.

The hotels managed by Hoteli Baška include the town's newest and fanciest – Atrium Residence Baška on the beach, with swanky rooms and all the upmarket trimmings. The tourist settlement about 1km southwest of town comprises a spa and fitness centre with an indoor and outdoor pool, as well as the four-star Hotel Zvonimir and the midrange Hotel Corinthia and Villas Corinthia, a small complex of villa apartments suitable for families. During the low season, singles range from 614KN to 768KN, while doubles hover between 494KN and 648KN. High season prices in single units start at 1304KN and go up to 1596KN; doubles range from 1184KN to 1476KN. There's a 20% surcharge if you stay under three nights.

Camping Zablaće (☎ 856 909; www.campzablace.info; per adult/site 45/95KN; Apr–mid-Oct) spreads along a long pebble beach. The shady naturist **FKK Camp Bunculuka** (☎ 856 806; www.bunculuka.info; per adult/site 45/95KN; Apr-Oct) is a 15-minute walk over the hill east of the harbour.

Eating

Restaurants are plentiful but there's not much variety.

Bistro Forza (☎ 856 611; Zvonimirova 98; mains from 38KN) A good cheap-bite option, this place dishes out pizza and the usual shebang of grilled meat, pasta and salads.

Cicibela (☎ 856 013; Emila Geistlicha bb; mains from 60KN) This seafront restaurant still rules the roost, especially for fish, seafood and excellent vistas.

RAB ISLAND

Rab (Arbe in Italian), between the islands of Krk and Pag, is the most enticing island in Kvarner when it comes to landscape diversity. The more densely populated southwest is pock-marked with pine forests, beaches and coves, while the northeast is a windswept region with few settlements, high cliffs and a barren look. In the interior is fertile land protected by mountains from cold winds, allowing the cultivation of olives, grapes and vegetables. The island's northeast tip is taken over by the Lopar Peninsula, which offers the best sandy beaches, while the northwest peninsula, which emerges from Supetarska Draga, is fringed with coves and lagoons that continue on to the Kalifront cape and the Suha Punta resort.

The cultural and historical showcase of the island is the enchanting Rab Town, characterised by four elegant bell towers rising from the ancient stone streets. Even at the peak of the summer season, when the island is overrun with visitors, you can still have a sense of discovery wandering around its old quarter and escaping to nearly deserted beaches just a quick boat ride away. In spring and autumn, Rab Island is a lovely place to visit, as the climate is famously mild – there are 2470 sunny hours per year – and visitors are scarce.

History

Originally settled by Illyrians, Rab underwent periods of Roman, Byzantine and Croatian rule before being sold to Venice, along with Dalmatia, in 1409. Farming, fishing, vineyards and salt production were the economic mainstays, but most income ended up in Venice. Two plague epidemics in the 15th century nearly wiped out the population and brought the economy to a standstill.

When Venice fell in 1797, there was a short period of Austrian rule until the French arrived in 1805. After the fall of Napoleon in 1813, the power went back to the Austrians who favoured the Italianised elite and it was not until 1897 that Croatian was made an 'official' language. The tourism industry

KVARNER REGION

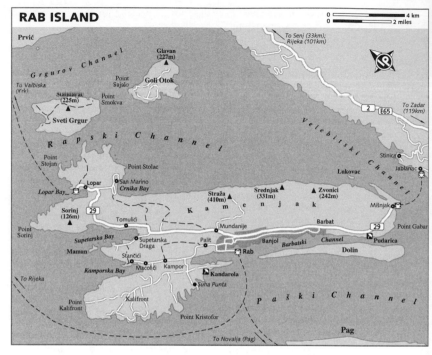

began flourishing among the Viennese elite at the turn of the 20th century. After the fall of Austria in 1918, Rab eventually became part of the Kingdom of Yugoslavia. Occupied by Italian and then German troops in the early 1940s, it was finally liberated in 1945. In the late 1940s, Goli Otok, off the Lopar Peninsula, served as a notorious prison camp under Tito's rule; Stalinist supporters were secretly shipped off to the islet and kept in dire conditions.

These days, tourism is the bread and butter of Rab, with several purpose-built settlements and faithful visitors who return year after year. Even during the 1990s war, Rab managed to hold onto its German and Austrian tourists.

Getting There & Away

The Split Tours ferry between Valbiska on Krk and Lopar (passenger/car 37/225KN, 1½ hours) operates four times daily, year-round. A car ferry by Rapska Plovidba shuttles back and forth nonstop in the summer months between Mišnjak on the island's southeastern edge and Jablanac (passenger/car 15/105KN, 15 minutes) on the mainland.

Rab Town has a daily connection with Lun (55KN, 40 minutes) on Pag; this Rapska Plovidba ferry departs daily, but day trips are only possible on Tuesday, Thursday and Friday. Jadrolinija has a daily catamaran service between Rijeka and Rab (40KN, two hours); it continues on to Novalja on Pag, from where you can proceed to Zadar.

The most reliable way to come and go is on one of the two daily buses between Rab and Rijeka (120KN, three hours). In the high season there are three direct daily buses from Zagreb to Rab (188KN, four to five hours). These services can fill up, so book ahead if possible. There's no direct bus from Rab to Zadar, but there are several daily buses that connect at Senj with Rijeka buses travelling to Zadar (195KN, five hours).

Getting Around

In addition to island tours operated from Rab Town (see p151), there's a water-taxi service between Rab Town and Suha Punta resort (25KN) that operates four times daily in July and August, leaving from the front of Hotel Padova. Private taxi boats will take you to any island beach, including the nudist Kandarola (30KN per person), Pudarica (400KN return, up to five people) and anywhere else for 150KN per hour (up to five people).

From Lopar to Rab Town (23KN, 15 minutes, 13km) there are 11 daily buses (a few less on weekends) in either direction; some are timed to meet the Valbiska–Lopar ferry.

RAB TOWN
pop 592

Medieval Rab Town is among the northern Adriatic's most instantly sights. Crowded onto a narrow peninsula, its four instantly recognisable bell towers rise like exclamation points from a red-roofed huddle of stone buildings. Uphill from the harbour leads a maze of streets dotted with richly endowed churches and lovely lookout points. It's a pure delight to meander through the narrow old alleys and shady Komrčar Park just to the west of the old town. In summer, a dose of culture can be had, too, as the churches often host concerts and art exhibitions. Once you've soaked up the town, there are excursion and taxi boats to whisk you off to plentiful beaches and coves scattered around the island.

Orientation

The old town lies directly across the bay from the marina. Narrow side streets climb up from the three main streets parallel to the harbour – Donja, Srednja and Gornja *ulica* (literally, lower, middle and upper roads). Trg Municipium Arba by the harbour is the old town's focal point.

A five-minute walk north of the old town is the new commercial centre, Palit, with the Merkur department store, some travel agencies and the bus station. The northwestern portion of the peninsula is given over to the 100-year-old Komrčar Park, bordered by the town's beaches. There are also beaches around the Padova complex on the other side, but better swimming can be found away from town.

Information

There is free wireless internet around Hotel Padova and in the commercial centre.

Digital X (☎ 777 010; Donja bb; per hr 30KN; ⏱ 10am-2pm & 6pm-midnight Mon-Sat, 6pm-midnight Sun) Internet access.

Erste Banka (Mali Palit bb) Changes money and has an ATM.

Garderoba (Mali Palit bb; per hr 0.70KN; ⏱ 5.30am-7.30pm) Left-luggage at the bus station.

Katurbo (☎ 724 495; www.katurbo.hr; Šetalište Markantuna Dominisa 5; ⏱ 8am-10pm Jun-Aug, to 9pm May & Sep) Private accommodation, money exchange, bike rental (per hour 20KN) and tours.

Kristofor (☎ 725 543; www.kristofor.hr; Mali Palit 70; ⏱ 8am-1pm & 5-9pm Mon-Fri & Sun, 8am-10pm Sat) Next to the bus station, this friendly and efficient agency offers the full gamut of services.

Numero Uno (☎ /fax 724 688; www.numero-uno .hr; Šetalište Markantuna Dominisa 5; ⏱ 6am-midnight Mon-Sat, 8am-11pm Sun) Books private accommodation, has boat tours and rents bikes (55KN per half day).

Post office (Mali Palit 67; ⏱ 7am-8pm Mon-Fri, to 2pm Sat).

Tourist office (☎ 771 111; www.tzg-rab.hr; Trg Municipium Arba 8; ⏱ 8am-10pm Jul-Sep, 8am-9pm May, Jun & Oct, 8am-2pm Mon-Fri Nov-Apr) An excellent source for maps, brochures and leaflets about the entire island. There's an annexe (open 8am to 10pm June to September) round the corner from the bus station.

Sights

Most of Rab's famous churches and towers are along Gornja Ulica, the upper road that turns into Ivana Rabljanina in the Kaldanac section of the old town. The churches are mostly open only for morning and evening Mass but, even when closed, most have metal grates over the front door, so you can have a glimpse of the interior.

Start your exploration from Trg Svetog Kristofora near the harbour. On the right side of the square as you face the old town is a **fountain** with sculptures of the two mythical figures Kalifront and Draga. Legend says the passionate Kalifront attempted to seduce the shepherdess Draga, who had taken a vow of chastity. Goddess Diana, to whom Draga had pledged purity, turned her into a stone statue to save her from the seducer.

Go up Bobotine and pause at the corner of Srednja to admire **Dominis Palace** on the left. Built at the end of the 15th century for a prominent patrician family who taught the public to read and write here, the facade has Renaissance windows and a striking portal decorated with the family coat of arms. Continue up Bobotine and at the top bear to the right to reach the Chapel of St Christopher (Svetog Kristofora), which houses a small collection of ancient stones inside its **lapidarium** (admission by donation; ⏱ 10am-12.30pm & 7.30-9pm Mon-Sat, 7.30-9pm Sun summer).

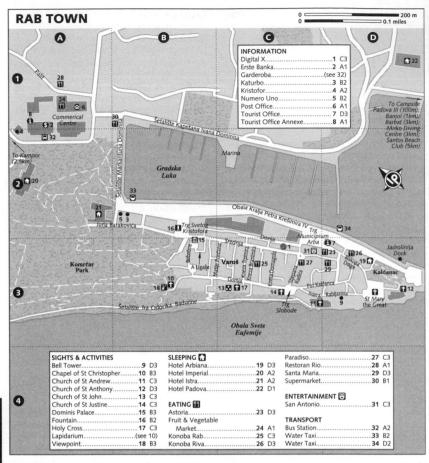

RAB TOWN

0 _____ 200 m
0 _____ 0.1 miles

INFORMATION	
Digital X	1 C3
Erste Banka	2 A1
Garderoba	(see 32)
Katurbo	3 B2
Kristofor	4 A2
Numero Uno	5 B2
Post Office	6 A1
Tourist Office	7 D3
Tourist Office Annexe	8 A1

SIGHTS & ACTIVITIES	
Bell Tower	9 D3
Chapel of St Christopher	10 B3
Church of St Andrew	11 C3
Church of St Anthony	12 D3
Church of St John	13 C3
Church of St Justine	14 C3
Dominis Palace	15 B3
Fountain	16 B2
Holy Cross	17 C3
Lapidarium	(see 10)
Viewpoint	18 B3

SLEEPING	
Hotel Arbiana	19 D3
Hotel Imperial	20 A2
Hotel Istra	21 A2
Hotel Padova	22 D1

EATING	
Astoria	23 D3
Fruit & Vegetable Market	24 A1
Konoba Rab	25 C3
Konoba Riva	26 D3

Paradiso	27 C3
Restoran Rio	28 A1
Santa Maria	29 C3
Supermarket	30 B1

ENTERTAINMENT	
San Antonio	31 C3

TRANSPORT	
Bus Station	32 A2
Water Taxi	33 B2
Water Taxi	34 D2

A nearby passage leads to the beautifully landscaped **Komrčar Park**, a great place for a cool walk on a hot summer's day. For a fine vista of the church spires and mighty Velebit mountain range in the distance, take the stairs to the right before the park entrance to reach the **viewpoint** on top of the ramparts.

Continuing south along Gornja, you'll come to the **Church of St John** (Svetog Ivana), which probably dates to the pre-Christian era. Little survives of this Romanic basilica except the 13th-century bell tower next to it, which can be climbed for 5KN (although opening hours are sporadic). Next to the bell tower is the 13th-century **Holy Cross Church** (Svetog Križa), with a cross that Christ allegedly wept upon because of the town

residents' immoral conduct. Today it's the venue for summer concerts during Rab Musical Evenings (opposite).

Further along Gornja is Trg Slobode, with the **Church of St Justine** (Svete Justine) on the right-hand side. The church (currently under renovation) has a bell tower dating from 1572 and a collection of religious artefacts. The mighty oak tree in the middle was planted as a sign of liberation from the Italians in 1921. Pause at this beautiful little piazza and soak up the sea vistas stretching ahead.

Pass Trg Slobode bearing right and on your right you'll see the Benedictine monastery founded in the 11th century and the adjacent Romanesque **Church of St Andrew** (Svetog Andrije), which has Rab's oldest bell tower.

KVARNER REGION

The tallest tower – and one of the most beautiful on the entire Croatian coast – is coming up on the right. Dating to the 13th century, the 26m-tall **bell tower** (admission 5KN; ☯ sporadic) is topped with an octagonal pyramid surrounded by a Romanesque balustrade and features a cross with five small globes and reliquaries of several saints. Climb it for views of the old town rooftops and the sea.

The extreme end of the cape accommodates the baroque **Church of St Anthony** (Svetog Antuna), with 17th-century inlaid marble and a painting of St Anthony decorating the altar. Adjacent is a working convent of Franciscan nuns who tend the garden, make lace tablecloths out of agave threads and live a quiet life by the sea.

Activities

Rab is criss-crossed with 100km of marked **hiking trails** and 80km of **biking trails**, several of which can be accessed from Rab Town. Pick up the map from the tourist office. From behind Hotel Istra, there's a trail that leads northeast to the mountain peak of Svcti Ilija. It only takes about 30 minutes on foot and the view is great. Bikes can be rented from several travel agencies listed under Information (p149).

Diving sites include various submarine caves and tunnels, as well as a protected amphora field off the cape of Sorinj. The small island of Čutin nearby is popular with divers for its submarine beauty. You can arrange to dive or take a course at **Mirko Diving Centre** (☎ 721 154; www.mirkodivingcenter.com; Barbat 710), in nearby Barbat.

Tours

Most travel agencies offer day tours of the island by boat, which include plenty of swim stops around Rab and at nearby islands such as Sveti Grgur and the infamous Goli Otok. These range between 100KN and 200KN, depending on the itinerary and trip length. Alternatively, take one of the taxi boats that depart from the harbour outside Hotel Istra and opposite Trg Municipium Arba (see p148). Travel agencies also offer excursions to other islands, such as Lošinj (160KN) and Krk (160KN), as well as to Plitvice (360KN).

Festivals & Events

For a few days each summer, Rab goes back to the Middle Ages during **Rab Fair** (Rapska Fjera), when residents dress in period garb and the town comes alive with drumming, processions, fireworks, medieval dancing and crossbow competitions. Celebrated between 25 and 27 July, this tradition commemorates Rab's liberation from Venetian rule in 1364 and honours its patron saint, St Christopher.

Rab Musical Evenings take place from June to September and revolve around Thursday-night concerts (9pm) in the Holy Cross Church. Tickets (30KN) are available an hour before the concert.

Sleeping

Everything from camping to expensive hotels can be found in and around Rab Town. Most of the hotels and camping grounds on the island are managed by **Imperial** (www.imperial .hr). The travel agencies can organise private rooms, with prices starting at 145KN (up to 245KN) per double room in the high season. There's a surcharge for stays of less than three nights in summer.

Campsite Padova III (☎ 724 355; www.rab-camp ing.com; Banjol bb; per adult/tent 43/30KN; ☯ Apr-Oct) To sleep cheap, carry your tent around the bay and walk south along the waterfront to this camping ground about 2km from the old town. It's right on a sandy beach and has extensive facilities.

Hotel Istra (☎ 724 134; www.hotel-istra.hr; Šetalište Markantuna Dominisa bb; s low-high 300-420KN, d 458-696KN; P) From the outside, this freshly painted yellow building looks inviting, but inside the outdated rooms are calling for a facelift. The location, right on the harbour, is a serious bonus.

Hotel Imperial (☎ 724 522; www.imperial.hr; Palit bb; s low-high 370-505KN, d 560-760KN; P) Set back from town in shady Komrčar Park, some newer rooms have air-con, others balconies with sea views. The café terrace is lovely, bar the cheesy piano tunes.

Hotel Padova (☎ 724 444; www.imperial.hr; Banjol bb; s low-high 405-635KN, d 590-870KN; P ☒ ☎) Facilities are the forte at this oversized concrete hotel complex across the bay in Banjol. There's a well-equipped wellness centre and balconies grace each of the recently renovated rooms.

Hotel Arbiana (☎ 724 444; www.arbianahotel.com; Obala Kralja Petra Krešimira IV 12; s 876KN, d 978-1300KN; P ☒ ☐) Understated luxury seekers have gotten lucky with this recently refurbished boutique hotel on the harbour. Most of the 28 colourful rooms and suites have balconies; each boasts wireless internet, LCD TV and bathrobes. There's a slow-food restaurant with a candlelit terrace.

Eating

Rab cuisine revolves around fresh fish, seafood and pasta. The quality and prices are generally uniform, with restaurants catering mainly to summer tourists.

Konoba Riva (☎ 725 887; Biskupa Drage 3; mains 40-90KN) Riva has tables on the harbour, an atmospheric terrace covered with fish nets and a small stone interior. The menu features fish and seafood, with some meat dishes thrown in.

Santa Maria (☎ 724 196; Dinka Dokule 6; mains from 55KN) The cool stone patio and upstairs terrace are the highlights at Santa Maria, and the food is decent, too. Try the tuna or shark steaks, seafood lasagne or one of the many meat dishes. There's a cocktail bar right next door, open till 2am.

Restoran Rio (☎ 725 645; Palit 57; mains from 57KN) This place is in the new part of town, at the back of the commercial centre, with a pleasant leafy terrace and a fish theme running through the decor and menu.

our pick Konoba Rab (☎ 725 666; Kneza Branimira 3; mains from 65KN; ☺ closed Sun lunch) Some of the scrumptious specialities at this cosy *konoba,* such as lamb baked under *peka,* must be ordered in advance. Others don't need to be, including *rapska grota,* a beef steak with cheese and prosciutto in a sweet fruit sauce (190KN for two).

Paradiso (☎ 771 109; Stjepana Radića 1; mains 70-130KN) Bundle art, wine and good food, offer it all in an ancient stone townhouse and you're close to paradise. This art gallery/winery/boutique restaurant-café has a patio out the back and a Venetian loggia up front. Try the dentex fillet in *traminac.*

Astoria (☎ 774 844; Trg Municipium Arba 7; mains 85-140KN) The classiest of the old town restaurants gets you a view of the harbour from the terrace. The *buzara* is superb, as is the Barbat beef fillet in red wine and thyme sauce.

There's a supermarket at the entrance to town on Šetalište Markantuna Dominisa. Another one is in the basement of the Merkur department store in the new part of town, where there's also a fruit and vegetable market.

Entertainment

San Antonio (www.sanantonio-club.com; Trg Municipium Arba 4) It has tables on the square filled with daytime crowds sipping cocktails, plus a popular disco that stays open till 6am.

Santos Beach Club (www.sanantonio-club.com; Pudarica Beach; ☺ 10am-dawn Jul & Aug) The owners of San Antonio are behind this seasonal beach club affair about 10km from Rab Town near Barbat (shuttles run at night). It's reminiscent of Zrće (see boxed text, p208) on Pag, with DJs spinning tunes to a party crowd. There are live concerts, foam parties and fashion shows, as well as beach volleyball during the day.

AROUND RAB TOWN

The **Franciscan Monastery of St Euphemia** (Samostan Svete Eufemije; ☎ 724 951; Kampor; admission 10KN; ☺ 10am-noon & 4-6pm Mon-Sat) and adjacent baroque church of St Bernardine are well worth the 2.5km walk northwest from Palit to Kampor. The Franciscan monks have a small museum here with old parchment books, stones and religious paintings, but it's the peaceful ambience that makes the monastery special. Check out the pleasant cloister and, inside the church, the ethereal painted ceiling, a stark contrast to the agony depicted on the late-Gothic wooden crucifix. Note also the 15th-century polyptych by the Vivarini brothers.

LOPAR

The tourist development on Lopar Peninsula occupying the northern tip of Rab Island has little charm, but there is a compelling reason to come here – a series of 22 sandy beaches that fringe the cape bordered by shady pine groves. Central European families flock here in droves in the summer months, as the sea is shallow and perfect for small children; this is particularly so on the 1500m-long **Paradise Beach** (Rajska Plaža) on Crnika Bay, right at the heart of town. As the island's most famous beach, it gets crowded, so head to nearby **Livačina Beach** for a quieter option.

If you wish to strip out of your bikini, **Sahara Beach** is a popular nudist spot in a delightful northern cove. It's accessible along a marked trail through pine forests; pass the San Marino hotel complex and pick up the trail from there. The beach is pretty remote – it takes about 45 minutes to get there. A closer nudist option is **Stolac Beach**, a 15-minute walk from Paradise Beach.

The town centre has a **tourist office** (☎ 775 508; www.lopar.hr; Lopar bb; ☺ 8am-9.30pm Jul & Aug, 8am-8pm Mon-Sat, 8am-2pm Sun Jun & Sep), which offers information about town and the beaches. For private accommodation, go to **Sahara Tours** (☎ 775 444; www.sahara-tours.hr; Lopar bb), which has double rooms from 230KN and two-person apartments from 360KN in the high season.

The unattractive settlement centred on Crnika Bay is comprised of **Camping San Marino** (☎ 775 133; www.imperial.hr; Lopar bb; adult/tent 43/30KN; ☺ Apr-Oct), fronting Paradise Beach, the San Marino Hotel complex, a small commercial centre and several cookie-cutter restaurants. Should you wish to stay, book a room at **Epario Hotel** (☎ 777 500; www.epario.net; Lopar 456a; s low-high 160-232KN, d 362-593KN; P ⊗ ⊑), within spitting distance of Paradise Beach. Rooms are clean, comfy and come with wireless internet; most also have balconies.

If you get hungry, pick **Fortuna** (☎ 775 387; Lopar bb; mains from 50KN), slightly out of town opposite Hotel Lopar, which has a nice leafy terrace with palm trees. **Laguna** (☎ 775 177; Lopar 547; mains 40-120KN) is a more central choice, with an extensive menu of run-of-the-mill food such as grilled meats, pizzas and fish staples.

The ferry from Valbiska stops 1km from the town centre; there's a small train for foot passengers (adult/child 10/5KN).

Istria

Continental Croatia meets the Adriatic in Istria (Istra to Croats), the heart-shaped 3600-sq-km peninsula just south of Trieste in Italy. While the bucolic interior of rolling hills and fertile plains attracts artsy visitors to its hilltop villages, rural hotels and farmhouse restaurants, the verdant indented coastline is enormously popular with the sun 'n' sea set. Vast hotel complexes line much of the coast and its rocky beaches are not Croatia's best, but the facilities are wide-ranging, the sea is clean and secluded spots still plentiful.

Pazin, in the interior, is the administrative capital of the region, while coastal Pula, with its thriving shipyard and Roman amphitheatre, is the economic and cultural centre. Tourism along the coast centres on the fetching fishing village of Rovinj and the ancient Roman town of Poreč, surrounded by a modern sprawl. Inland, the medieval towns of Motovun, Buzet, Labin and Grožnjan perch on hill crests in atmospheric clusters.

The northern part of the peninsula belongs to Slovenia, while the Ćićarija mountains (an extension of the Dinaric Range) in the northeastern corner separate Istria from the continental mainland. Just across the water is Italy, but the pervasive Italian influence makes it seem even closer. Italian is, in fact, a second language in Istria, while many Istrians have Italian passports, and each town name has an Italian counterpart.

The coast, or 'Blue Istria', as the tourist board calls it, gets flooded by tourists in summer, but you can still feel alone and undisturbed in 'Green Istria', even in the mid-August. Add acclaimed gastronomy (starring fresh seafood, prime truffles, wild asparagus and award-winning wines), sprinkle it with historical charm and you have a little slice of heaven.

HIGHLIGHTS

- Admiring the mosaics at **Euphrasian Basilica** (p171) in Poreč
- Truffle-hunting and feasting in the forests around **Buzet** (p178)
- Taking in Rovinj's fishing history at **Batana House** (p166)
- Walking the trails of the legendary **Pazin Cave** (p177)
- Catching alfresco screenings during the summer film festival of **Motovun** (p181)
- Soaking up communist chic at Tito's playground of **Brijuni** (p163)
- Exploring the wild landscapes of **Rt Kamenjak** (p160) near Pula

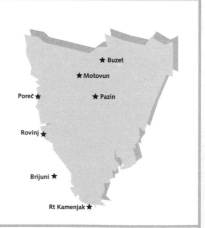

- TELEPHONE CODE: 052

History

Towards the end of the 2nd millennium BC, the Illyrian Histrian tribe settled the region and built fortified villages on top of the coastal and interior hills. The Romans swept into Istria in the 3rd century BC and began building roads and more hill forts as strategic strongholds.

From 539 to 751, Istria was under Byzantine rule, the most impressive remnant of which is the Euphrasian Basilica (p171) in Poreč, with its stunning mosaics. In the period that followed, power switched between Slavic tribes, the Franks and German rulers until an increasingly powerful Venice wrested control of the Istrian coast in the early 13th century. Treaties signed in 1374 and 1466 gave continental Istria to the Habsburgs.

Misery, famine and warfare haunted the peninsula. Bubonic plague first broke out in 1371 and regularly ravaged Istrian cities until the 17th century. Although the Turks never reached Istria, the peninsula lay in the path of the fearsome Uskok pirates from Senj who repeatedly attacked Istrian cities throughout the 16th and 17th centuries.

With the fall of Venice in 1797, Istria came under Austrian rule, followed by the French (1809–13) and the the Austrians again. During the 19th and early 20th centuries, most of Istria was little more than a neglected outpost of the Austro-Hungarian Empire.

When the empire disintegrated at the end of WWI, Italy moved quickly to secure Istria. Italian troops occupied Pula in November 1918, and, in the 1920 Treaty of Rapallo, the Kingdom of Serbs, Croats and Slovenes ceded Istria along with Zadar and several islands to Italy, as a reward for joining the Allied powers in WWI.

A massive population shift followed as 30,000 to 40,000 Italians arrived from Mussolini's Italy and many Croats left, fearing fascism. Their fears were not misplaced as Istria's Italian masters attempted to consolidate their hold by banning Slavic speech, printing, education and cultural activities.

Italy retained the region until its defeat in WWII when Istria became part of Yugoslavia, causing another mass exodus, as Italians and many Croats fled Tito's communists. Trieste and the peninsula's northwestern tip were points of contention between Italy and Yugoslavia until 1954, when the region was finally awarded to Italy. As a result of Tito's reorganisation of Yugoslavia, the northern part of the peninsula was incorporated into Slovenia, where it has remained.

THE ISTRIAN COAST

At the tip of the Istrian peninsula is Pula, the coast's largest city. The Brijuni Islands, the former playground of Tito, are an easy day trip from here. The east coast of Istria centres on the modern seaside resort of Rabac, just below the ancient hilltop town of Labin. The west coast is the tourist showcase, with Rovinj the most enchanting town and Poreč the easiest – and cheaper – holiday choice, with plenty of lodging and entertainment options.

PULA
pop 65,000

The wealth of Roman architecture makes otherwise workaday Pula (ancient Polensium) a standout among Croatia's larger cities. The star of the Roman show is the remarkably well-preserved Roman amphitheatre, smack in the heart of the city, which dominates the streetscape and doubles as a venue for summer concerts and performances.

Historical attractions aside, Pula is a busy commercial city on the sea that has managed to retain a friendly small-town appeal. Just a short bus ride away, a series of beaches awaits at the resorts that occupy the Verudela Peninsula to the south. Although marred with residential and holiday developments, the coast is dotted with fragrant pine groves, seaside cafés and a clutch of fantastic restaurants. Further south along the indented shoreline, the Premantura Peninsula hides a spectacular nature park, the protected cape of Kamenjak.

History

In the 1st century BC, the Illyrian Pola (now Pula) was conquered by the Romans and used as their administrative headquarters for the region that stretched from the Limska Draga Fjord to the Raša River. The Romans cleverly exploited Pula's terrain, using Kaštel Hill, which now contains the citadel, as a vantage point to protect the bay. The ancient town developed in concentric circles around the hill, with the amphitheatre placed outside the fortified city centre. Pula joined the powerful Venetian empire in 1150 to protect itself

ISTRIA

ISTRIA

0 — 10 km
0 — 6 miles

ITALY

To Trieste (19km)

To Ljubljana

SLOVENIA

Koparski Bay

Koper

A8

Point Savudrija

Portorož

Camp Kanegra

Piranski Bay

Savudrija

Umag

Volpia

Momjan

Brest

Point Umaški

Buje

Buzet

Roč

Mirna

Glagolitic Alley

To Rijeka (11km); Zagreb (171km)

Krasica

Grožnjan

Oprtalj

V Planik (1272m)

Brtonigla

Istarske Toplice

Kotli

Hum

Opatija

Point Dajla

Mirna

E751

Livade

21

A8

Motovun

Sovinjsko Polje

Boljun

Lovran

Novigrad

Kaštelir

Karojba

Mirna Harbour

Baredine Cave

Cerovlje

3

Vojak (1401m)

E751

Point Basuja

Gedići

Višnjan

21

Riječki Bay

Naturist Centre Ulika

Nova Vas

Beram

Sušnjevica

Naturist Solaris Residence

Pazin

Moščenice

Poreč

Brulo

Gračišće

Pićan

Plava Laguna

Brseč

Zelena Laguna

Sv Petar u Šumi

Brestova

Funtana

Medaki

Katun Lindarski

Vozilići

Porozina

Naturist Camping Istra

Point Prestinice

Cres

Vrsar

Koversada

Žminj

Raša

Naturist Resort

Valalta

A8

Liburna Reserve

Labin

Dragozetići

Limska Draga Fjord

Kanfanar

Rovinj

Smoljanci

Raša

Rabac

Point Kurent

Svetvinčenat

Bale

3

Barban

Point Gustinja

E751

Valalta Naturist Camp

21

Trget

E751

Barbariga

21

Adriatic

Fažana Channel

Vodnjan

Marčana

Koromačno

Point Crna

Point Pernat

Mali Brijun

Fažana

Raški Bay

Cres

Brijuni National Park

Veli Brijun

Kavran

Point Kumpar

Pula

Kvarner

Stoja

Verudela Peninsula

Banjole

Medulin

Camp Kažela

Premantura

Medulinski Bay

Point Marlera

Rt Kamenjak

Zeča

Sea

Lošinj

Unije

ISTRIA

TAKING IT OFF IN ISTRIA

Naturism in Croatia enjoys a long and venerable history that began on Rab Island around the turn of the 20th century. It quickly became a fad among Austrians influenced by the growing German Freikörperkultur movement, loosely translated as 'free body culture'. Later, Austrian Richard Ehrmann opened the first naturist camp on Paradise Beach in Lopar (on Rab), but the real founders of Adriatic naturism were Edward VIII and Wallis Simpson, who popularised it by going skinny-dipping along the Rab coast in 1936.

The coast of Istria now has many of Croatia's largest and most well-developed naturist resorts. Naturist camping grounds are marked as FKK, an acronym for Freikörperkultur.

Start in the north at **Camp Kanegra** (www.istraturist.com), north of Umag, a relatively small site on a long pebble beach. Continuing south along the coast, you'll come to **Naturist Centre Ulika** (www.plavalaguna.hr) just outside Poreč, with 559 pitches, as well as caravans and mobile homes available for rent. If you prefer to stay in an apartment, **Naturist Solaris Residence** (www.valamar .hr) is the ideal choice. Only 12km north of Poreč on the wooded Lanterna Peninsula, the complex also includes a naturist camping ground. South of Poreč, next to the fishing village Funtana, is the larger **Naturist Camping Istra** (www.valamar.hr), which sleeps up to 3000 people. Continue south past Vrsar and you come to the mother ship of naturist resorts, **Koversada** (www.maistra .hr). In 1961, Koversada islet went totally nude and the colony soon spread to the nearby coast. Now this behemoth can accommodate 6000 people in campsites, villas and apartments. If that seems a little overwhelming, keep going south 7km past Rovinj to **Valalta Naturist Camp** (www .valalta.hr), near the Lim Channel. It has a manageable number of apartments, bungalows, caravans, mobile homes and campsites. If you prefer to be within easy reach of Pula, travel down the coast to Medulin and **Camp Kažela** (www.kampkazela.com), which also has mobile homes for rent, plus campsites right on the sea.

against piracy, but the city suffered badly under Venetian rule.

The fall of Venice in 1797 brought in the Habsburgs as the new rulers. Pula stagnated until the Austro-Hungarian monarchy chose it as the empire's main naval centre in 1853. The construction of the port and the 1886 opening of its large shipyard unleashed a demographic and economic expansion that transformed Pula into a military and industrial powerhouse. The city fell into decline once again under Italian fascist rule, which lasted from 1918 to 1943, when the city was occupied by the Germans. At the end of WWII, Pula was administered by Anglo-American forces until it became part of postwar Yugoslavia in 1947. Pula's industrial base weathered the recent war relatively well and the city remains an important centre for shipbuilding, textiles, metals and glass.

Orientation

The oldest part of the city follows the ancient Roman plan of streets circling the central citadel, while the city's newer portions follow a rectangular grid pattern. Most shops, agencies and businesses are clustered in and around the old town as well as on Giardini, Carrarina, Istarska and Riva, which runs along the harbour. With the exception of a few hotels and restaurants in the old town, most others, as well as the beaches, are 4km to the south on the Verudela Peninsula; these can be reached by walking south on Arsenalska, which turns into Tomasinijeva and then Veruda. The bus station is 500m northeast of the town centre; the harbour is west of the bus station. Less than a kilometre north of town, the train station is near the sea along Kolodvorska.

Information
INTERNET ACCESS
Cafe-Bar Etna (Sergijevaca 3; per hr 20KN; 🕑 6am-11pm Mon-Fri, 8am-11pm Sat & Sun)
MMC Luka (☎ 224 316; Istarska 30; per hr 20KN; 🕑 8am-midnight Mon-Fri, 8am-3pm Sat)

LAUNDRY
Mika (☎ 210 692; Trinajstićeva 16; 🕑 8am-2pm Mon-Fri, to noon Sat)

LEFT LUGGAGE
Garderoba (per hr 2.20KN; 🕑 4am-10.30pm Mon-Sat, 5am-10.30pm Sun) Left-luggage at the bus station.

MEDICAL SERVICES
Hospital (☎ 376 548; Zagrebačka 34)

ISTRIA

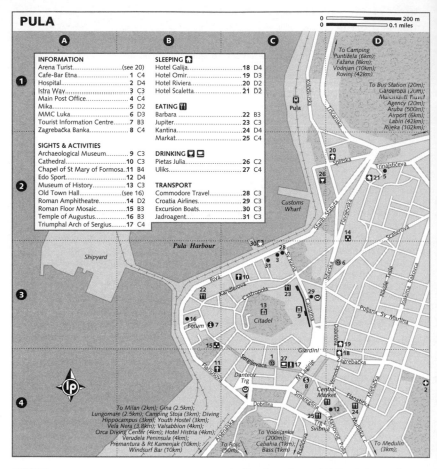

PULA

MONEY

You can exchange money in banks, travel agencies or at the post office. **Zagrebačka Banka** (M Laginje 1) has an ATM.

POST

Main post office (Danteov Trg 4; 7.30am-7pm Mon-Fri, to 2.30pm Sat) You can make long-distance calls here. Check out the cool staircase inside!

TOURIST INFORMATION

Tourist information centre (212 987; www .pulainfo.hr; Forum 3; 8am-9pm Mon-Fri, 9am-9pm Sat & Sun summer, 8am-7pm Mon-Fri, 9am-7pm Sat, 10am-4pm Sun rest of year) Knowledgeable and friendly, staff here provide maps, brochures and schedules of events in Pula and around Istria. Pick up two useful

booklets: *Domus Bonus*, which lists the best-quality private accommodation in Istria, and *Istra Gourmet*, with a list of all restaurants.

TRAVEL AGENCIES

Arena Turist (529 400; www.arenaturist.hr; Splitska 1a; 8am-8pm Mon-Fri, to 6pm Sat) In the Hotel Riviera, Arena Turist books rooms in the network of hotels it manages. It also offers guide services and excursions.
Istra Way (214 868; www.istraway.hr; Riva 14; 9am-9pm Jul–mid-Sep) On the harbour, it books private accommodation, offers excursions to Brijuni, Rovinj and Lim, and has bikes for rent (100KN per day).
Maremonti Travel Agency (384 000; www.mare monti-istra.hr; Trg I Istarske Brigade 1; 9am-8pm Mon-Fri, 9am-2pm Sat Jul & Aug, 9am-2pm & 5-8pm Mon-Fri, 9am-2pm Sat Sep-Jun) At this agency inside the

bus station, you can book accommodation and rent cars and scooters (from 100KN to 180KN per day).

Sights

ROMAN RUINS

Pula's most famous and imposing sight is the 1st-century **Roman amphitheatre** (☎ 219 028; Flavijevska bb; adult/concession 40/20KN; ☻ 8am-9pm summer, 9am-8pm spring & autumn, 9am-5pm winter) overlooking the harbour northeast of the old town. Built entirely from local limestone, the amphitheatre with seating for up to 20,000 spectators was designed to host gladiatorial contests. On the top of the walls is a gutter that collected rainwater and you can still see the slabs used to secure the fabric canopy, which protected spectators from the sun. In the chambers downstairs is a small **museum** with a display of ancient olive oil equipment. Every summer, **Pula Film Festival** is held here, as are pop and classical concerts.

Along Carrarina are **Roman walls**, which mark the eastern boundary of old Pula. Follow these walls south and continue down Giardini to the **Triumphal Arch of Sergius**. This majestic arch was erected in 27 BC to commemorate three members of the Sergius family who achieved distinction in Pula. Until the 19th century, the arch was backed by the city gate and was surrounded by walls that were pulled down to allow the city to expand beyond the old town.

The pedestrian street beyond the arch, Sergijevaca, winds right around old Pula. Follow it to the ancient **Forum**, the town's central meeting place from antiquity through the Middle Ages. It used to contain temples and public buildings, but today the only visible remnant from the Roman era is the **Temple of Augustus** (☎ 218 603; Forum; adult/concession 10/5KN; ☻ 9am-8pm Mon-Fri, 10am-3pm Sat & Sun summer, by appointment other times), erected from 2 BC to AD 14. When the Romans left, the temple became a church and then a grain warehouse. Reconstructed after a bomb hit it in 1944, it now houses a small historical museum with captions in English. Also in the Forum, notice the **old town hall**, which was built in 1296 as the seat of Pula's municipal authorities. With its mixture of architectural styles – from Romanesque to Renaissance – it's still the seat of Pula's mayor.

Just off Sergijevaca is a **Roman floor mosaic** dating from the 3rd century. In the midst of remarkably well-preserved geometric motifs is the central panel, which depicts bad-girl Dirce from Greek mythology being punished for the attempted murder of her cousin.

CHURCHES

Pula's **cathedral** (Katedrala; Kandlerova; ☻ 10am-5pm mid-Jun–mid-Sep, Mass only mid-Sep–mid-Jun) dates back to the 5th century; the main altar is even older, being a Roman sarcophagus with relics of saints from the 3rd century. The floor reveals fragments of 5th- and 6th-century mosaics. The late-Renaissance facade was added in the early 16th century and the 17th-century bell tower was made of stones from the amphitheatre.

The **Chapel of St Mary of Formosa** (Kapela Marije Formoze; Flaciusova) is all that remains of the 6th-century Benedictine abbey that once stood here. This Byzantine structure was adorned with mosaics, which are now in the city's Archaeological Museum. The chapel is only open for occasional art exhibitions in summer or by prior arrangement through the Archaeological Museum.

MUSEUMS

The **Archaeological Museum** (Arheološki Muzej; ☎ 218 603; Carrarina 3; adult/concession 20/10KN; ☻ 9am-8pm Mon-Sat, 10am-3pm Sun May-Sep, 9am-2pm Mon-Fri Oct-Apr) presents finds from all over Istria. The permanent exhibits cover prehistory to the Middle Ages, but the accent is on the period from the 2nd century BC to the 6th century AD. Even if you don't enter the museum, be sure to visit the large **sculpture garden** around it, and the **Roman theatre** behind. The garden, entered through 2nd-century twin gates, is the site of concerts in summer.

The **Museum of History** (Povijesni Muzej Istre; ☎ 211 566; Gradinski Uspon 6; adult/concession 15/7KN; ☻ 8am-9pm Jun-Sep, 9am-5pm Oct-May) is in a 17th-century Venetian fortress on a hill in the old town's centre. The meagre exhibits deal mostly with the maritime history of Pula, but the views from the citadel walls are worth a stop.

BEACHES

Pula is surrounded by a half-circle of rocky beaches, each one with its own fan club. Like bars or nightclubs, beaches go in and out of style. The most tourist-packed are undoubtedly those surrounding the hotel complex on the **Verudela Peninsula**, although some locals will dare to be seen at the small turquoise-coloured **Hawaii Beach** near the Hotel Park.

For more seclusion, head out to the wild **Rt Kamenjak** (www.kamenjak.hr, in Croatian; pedestrians & cyclists free, per car/scooter 20/10KN; 7am-10pm) on the Premantura Peninsula, 10km south of town. Istria's southernmost point, this gorgeous, entirely uninhabited cape has hills, wildflowers (including 30 species of orchid), low Mediterranean shrubs, fruit trees and medicinal herbs. With 30km of virgin beaches and coves, it's criss-crossed with a maze of gravel roads and paths, making it easy to get around. The views to the island of Cres and the peaks of Velebit are extraordinary. Leave no footprints – be sure to use the plastic bag you get at the entrance for all your rubbish. Watch out for strong currents if swimming off the southern cape.

Stop by the **visitor centre** (575 283; 9am-9pm summer) in the old school building in the centre of Premantura, which has an informative bilingual display about the park's ecosystems. **Windsurf Bar** (091 512 3646; www.windsurfing .hr; Camping Village Stupice) nearby rents bikes and windsurfing equipment (board and sail from 70KN per hour). It also offers trial windsurfing courses from 190KN per hour.

Kolombarica Beach, on the southern end of the peninsula, is popular with daring young men who dive from the high cliffs and swim through the shallow caves at the water's edge. Just above it is a delightful beach bar, **Safari** (snacks 25-50KN; Easter-Sep), half-hidden in the bushes near the beach, about 3.5km from the entrance to the park. A shady place with lush alcoves, found objects and a bar that serves tasty snacks, it's a great place to while away an afternoon.

A fun time to be on Rt Kamenjak is in early November, when **Hallowind** – an extreme sports competition featuring windsurfing, free-climbing and mountain biking – takes place.

Getting to Rt Kamenjak by car is the easiest option, but drive slowly so as not to generate too much dust. A more eco-friendly option is taking city bus 26 from Pula to Premantura (15KN), then renting a bike to get inside the park.

Activities & Tours

There are several diving centres around Pula. At **Orca Diving Center** (224 422; www.orcadiving.hr; Hotel Histria), on the Verudela Peninsula, you can arrange boat, wreck and introductory dives. Alternatively, try **Diving Hippocampus** (www.hip pocampus.hr) at Camping Stoja (right).

In addition to windsurfing courses, **Windsurf Bar** (091 512 3646; www.windsurfing.hr; Camping Village Stupice) in Premantura offers biking (250KN) and kayaking (300KN) excursions.

There's an easy 41km **cycling trail** from Pula to Medulin, following the path of Roman gladiators. Check out **Istria Bike** (www.istria-bike.com), a website run by the tourist board, outlining trails, packages and agencies that offer biking trips. **Edo Sport** (222 207; www.edosport.com; Narodni Trg 9) organises activity-based excursions.

Most agencies listed on p158 offer trips to Brijuni, Limska Draga, Rovinj and inner Istria, but it's often cheaper to book with one of the boats at the harbour. These run regularly and offer fishing picnics (220KN), two-hour 'panorama' excursions to Brijuni (150KN), and a jaunt to Rovinj, Limska Draga and Crveni Otok (250KN). The only ship that goes to Brijuni and actually stops and tours there is **Martinabela** (www.martinabela.hr; tours 250KN); these trips are offered twice daily in summer.

Sleeping

Pula's peak tourist season runs from the second week of July to the end of August. During this period it's wise to make advance reservations. The tip of the Verudela Peninsula, 4km southwest of the city centre, has been turned into a vast tourist complex replete with hotels and apartments. It's not especially attractive, except for the shady pine forests that cover it, but there are beaches, restaurants, tennis courts and water sports. Any travel agency can give you information and book you into one of the hotels, or you can contact **Arena Turist** (529 400; www.arenaturist.hr; Splitska 1a).

The travel agencies listed on p158 can find you private accommodation, but there is little available in the town centre. Count on paying from 250KN to 490KN for a double room and from 305KN to 535KN for a two-person apartment.

Camping Puntižela (517 490; www.puntizela.hr; Puntižela; per adult/tent 40/45KN) This lovely camping ground on a bay 7km northwest of central Pula is open all year. There's a diving centre on site.

Camping Stoja (387 144; www.arenaturist.hr; Stoja 37; per person/tent 52/30KN; Apr-Oct) The closest camping ground to Pula, 3km southwest of the centre, has lots of space on the shady promontory, with a restaurant, diving centre and swimming possible off the rocks. Take bus 1 to Stoja.

ISTRIA

Youth Hostel (☎ 391 133; www.hfhs.hr; Valsaline 4; dm low-high 85-114KN, caravan 103-134KN; 🖳) This hostel overlooks a beach in Valsaline Bay, 3km south of central Pula. There are dorms and caravans split into two tiny four-bed units, each with bathroom and air-con on request (15KN per day). There's bike rental (80KN per day), and campsites (70/15KN per person/tent) are also available. To get here, take bus 2 or 3 to the 'Piramida' stop, walk back towards the city to the first street, then turn left and look for the hostel sign.

Hotel Riviera (☎ 211 166; www.arenaturist.hr; Splitska 1; s low-high 283-354KN, d 464-600KN) There's plenty of old-world elegance at this grand 19th-century building, but the rooms need a thorough overhaul and the carpets a serious scrub. On the plus side, it's in the centre and the front rooms have water views.

Hotel Omir (☎ 218 186; www.hotel-omir.com; Dobrićeva 6; s low-high 324-450KN, d 450-600KN) The best budget option smack in the heart of town, Hotel Omir has modest but clean and quiet rooms. The more expensive units have air-con, and there's a pizzeria downstairs.

Hotel Galija (☎ 383 802; www.hotel-galija-pula.com; Epulonova 3; s low-high 350-498KN, d 500-718KN; 🍴 🖳) A stone's throw from the market in the town centre, this recently built hotel has comfortably outfitted rooms with internet access. Facilities include a sauna, restaurant and even massage on request.

our pick **Hotel Scaletta** (☎ 541 599; www.hotel-scaletta.com; Flavijevska 26; s low-high 398-498KN, d 598-718KN; 🅿) There's a friendly family vibe here, the rooms have tasteful decor and a bagful of trimmings (such as minibars), and the restaurant serves good food. Plus it's just a hop from town.

Hotel Histria (☎ 590 000; www.arenaturist.hr; Verudela; s low-high 400-666KN, d 650-1190KN; 🅿 🍴 🈂) Its concrete behemoth appearance may be off-putting, but the Histria's extensive facilities, balconied rooms and easy beach access make up for the lack of character. There are both indoor and outdoor swimming pools, tennis courts and a casino. It shares facilities with the new, slightly cheaper Hotel Palma (low-high season double 485KN to 935KN) next door.

Eating
CITY CENTRE

There's a number of good eating places in the city centre, although most locals head out of town for better value and fewer tourists. For cheap bites, browse around the central market.

Markat (☎ 223 284; Trg I Svibnja 5; mains from 20KN) As far as self-service spots go, this canteen opposite the central market is worth a stop for its decent cheap grub such as pizza and pasta. You pick what you want and pay at the end of the line.

Jupiter (☎ 214 333; Castropola 42, pizzas 21-37KN) The thin-crust pizza here would make any Italian mama proud; the pasta is yummy, too. There's a terrace upstairs and a 20% discount on Wednesdays.

Vodnjanka (☎ 210 655; Vitezića 4; mains from 30KN; 🕙 closed Sat dinner & Sun) Locals swear by the home cooking here. It's cheap, casual, cash-only and has a small menu that concentrates on simple Istrian dishes. To get here, walk south on Radićeva to Vitezića.

Barbara (☎ 213 501; Kandlerova 5; mains from 45KN) Barbara's food is pretty basic but there's something to it, since the place has been running for 40 years. The location near the harbour is good for people-watching. For 50KN, the daily set menu (fish or meat) is good value.

Kantina (☎ 214 054; Flanatička 16; mains 55-125KN; 🕙 closed Sun) The beamed stone cellar of this Habsburg building has been redone in a modern style. It won't help you fit into your bikini, but you'll appreciate the ravioli Kantina, stuffed with *skuta* (ricotta) and *pršut* (prosciutto) in a cheese sauce.

SOUTH OF THE CITY

Pula's best dining is, fittingly, in the most upmarket part of town, Pješčana Uvala, which lies just east across the bay from Verudela Peninsula.

our pick **Gina** (☎ 387 943; Stoja 23; mains from 60KN) Istrian mainstays such as *maneštra* (a thick vegetable-and-bean soup similar to minestrone) and *fritaja* (omelette), often served with seasonal veggies such as wild asparagus, are prepared with care here, while the pastas are handmade and the veggies picked from the garden. This stylish but low-key eatery near the Stoja camping ground draws in a local crowd. Try the *semifreddo* (semifrozen dessert) with a hot sauce of figs, pine nuts and lavender.

Vela Nera (☎ 219 209; www.velanera.hr; Pješčana Uvala bb; mains from 70KN) A few steps down in the marina, this rival restaurant to Valsabbion has a more subdued decor, an alfresco terrace overlooking the yachts and reliably excellent seafood specialities.

Milan (☎ 300 200; www.milan1967.hr; Stoja 4; mains from 75KN) An exclusive vibe, seasonal specialities, four sommeliers and even an olive oil expert on staff all create one of the city's best dining experiences. The five-course fish menu (195KN) is well worth it. There's also a 12-room hotel in the back (single/double 590/890KN).

Valsabbion (☎ 218 033; www.valsabbion.hr; Pješčana Uvala IX/26; mains 95-175KN) The creative Croatian cuisine conjured up at this award-winning restaurant, one of Croatia's best, is an epicurean delight. The decor is showy but stunning and the menu gimmicky in its descriptions, but the food is tops. Sampling menus range from 395KN to 555KN. It's also a plush 10-room hotel (double 860KN) with a top-floor spa.

Drinking & Entertainment

You should definitely try to catch a concert in the spectacular amphitheatre; the tourist office has schedules and there are posters around Pula advertising live performances. Although most of the nightlife is out of the town centre, in mild weather the cafés on the Forum and along the pedestrian streets Kandlerova, Flanatička and Sergijevaca are lively people-watching spots. To mix with Pula's young crowd, grab some beers and head to the Lungomare coastal strip, where music blasts out of parked cars.

Aruba (☎ 300 535; Šijanska 1a) On the road to the airport, this popular café-bar-disco is a relaxing hang-out during the day and, come night, a hopping venue for live music and parties. The outdoor terrace gets crowded. Wednesday is salsa night.

Rojc (www.rojcnet.hr; Gajeva 3) For the most underground experience, check the program at Rojc, a converted army barracks that now houses a multimedia art centre and art studios with occasional concerts, exhibitions and other events.

ourpick Cabahia (Širolina 4) This artsy hideaway in Veruda has a cosy wood-beamed interior, eclectic decor of old objects, dim lighting, South American flair and a great garden terrace out the back. It hosts concerts and gets packed on weekends. If it's too full, try the more laid-back Bass (Širolina 3), just across the street.

E&D (☎ 89 42 015; Verudela 22) Just above Umbrella Beach on Verudela, you can lounge on the lush outdoor terrace with several levels of seating interspersed with small pools and waterfalls. The sunset views are great and weekend nights are spiced with live DJ tunes.

Pietas Julia (☎ 89 42 015; Riva 20) At this trendy bar right on the harbour, things start to get happening late on weekends, when it stays open till 4am.

Uliks (☎ 219 158; Trg Portarata 1) James Joyce once taught in this apartment building, where you can now linger over a drink at the ground-floor café, pondering *Ulysses* or Pula's pebble beaches.

Getting There & Away

AIR

Pula Airport (☎ 530 105; www.airport-pula.com) is located 6km northeast of town. There are two daily flights to Zagreb (single/return 220/390KN, 40 minutes), one via Zadar. In summer, there are low-cost and charter flights from major European cities. **Croatia Airlines** (☎ 218 909; www.croatiaairlines.hr; Carrarina 8; ☯ 8am-4pm Mon-Fri, 9am-noon Sat) has an office in the city centre.

BOAT

Jadroagent (☎ 210 431; www.jadroagent.hr; Riva 14; ☯ 7am-3pm Mon-Fri) has schedules and tickets for boats connecting Istria with Italy and the islands. It also represents Jadrolinija. For information on connections to Italy, see p309.

Commodore Travel (☎ 211 631; www.commodore -travel.hr; Riva 14, ☯ 8am-8pm Jun-Sep) sells tickets for a catamaran between Pula and Zadar (100KN, five hours), which runs five times weekly from July through early September and twice weekly in June and the rest of September. It also offers a Wednesday boat service to Venice (370KN, 3½ hours) between June and September.

BUS

From the Pula **bus station** (☎ 500 012; Trg 1 Istarske Brigade bb), there are buses heading to Rijeka (86KN to 91KN, two hours) almost hourly. In summer, reserve a seat a day in advance and be sure to sit on the right-hand side of the bus for a stunning view of the Kvarner Gulf.

Other domestic bus services departing from Pula:

Destination	Fare (KN)	Duration (hr)	Daily services
Dubrovnik	568	10½	1
Labin	38	1	8
Poreč	54-65	1-1½	13
Rovinj	35	¾	15
Split	360-396	10	3
Zadar	249-257	7	3
Zagreb	210	4-5½	18

TRAIN

There are two daily trains to Ljubljana (133KN, two hours), with a change in Buzet, and four to Zagreb (125KN to 148KN, 6½ hours), but you must board a bus for part of the trip, from Lupoglav to Rijeka.

There are four daily trains to Buzet (47KN, two hours).

Getting Around

An airport bus (29KN) departs from the bus station several times weekly; check at the bus station. Taxis cost about 100KN.

The city buses of use to visitors are 1, which runs to Camping Stoja, and 2 and 3 to Verudela. The frequency varies from every 15 minutes to every half hour (from 5am to 11.30pm). Tickets are sold at *tisak* (newsstands) for 6KN, or 10KN from the driver.

BRIJUNI ISLANDS

The Brijuni (Brioni in Italian) archipelago consists of two main pine-covered islands and 12 islets off the coast of Istria, just northwest of Pula across the 3km Fažana Channel. Only the two larger islands, Veli Brijun and Mali Brijun, can be visited. Covered by meadows, parks and oak and laurel forests – and some rare plants such as wild cucumber and marine poppy – the islands were pronounced a national park in 1983.

Even though traces of habitation go back more than 2000 years, the islands really owe their fame to Tito, the extravagant Yugoslav leader who turned them into his private retreat.

Each year from 1947 until just before his death in 1980, Tito spent six months at his Brijuni hideaway. To create a lush comfort zone, he introduced subtropical plant species and created a safari park to house the exotic animals gifted to him by world leaders. The blue antelope you'll see roaming around was a present from the former Indian prime minister Nehru, the Somali sheep came from

Ethiopia, while a Zambian leader gave a gift of waterbuck.

At his summer playground, Tito received 90 heads of state and a bevy of movie stars in lavish style. Bijela Vila on Veli Brijun was Tito's 'White House': the place for issuing edicts and declarations as well as entertaining. The islands are still used for official state visits, but are increasingly a favourite on the international yachting circuit, and a holiday spot of choice for royalty from obscure kingdoms and random billionaires who love its bygone aura of glamour.

Every summer, theatre aficionados make their way across the channel to the Minor Fort on Mali Brijun for performances by **Ulysses Theatre** (www.ulysses.hr, in Croatian).

Sights

As you arrive on Veli Brijun, after a 15-minute boat ride from Fažana, you'll dock in front of the Hotel Istra-Neptun, where Tito's illustrious guests once stayed. A guide and miniature tourist train take you on a three-hour island tour beginning with a visit to the 9-hectare **safari park**. Other stops on the tour include the ruins of a **Roman country house**, dating from the 1st century BC, an **archaeological museum** inside a 16th-century citadel, and **St Germain Church**, now a gallery displaying copies of medieval frescoes in Istrian churches.

Most interesting is the **Tito on Brijuni exhibit** in a building behind Hotel Karmen. A collection of stuffed animals occupies the ground floor. Upstairs are photos of Tito with film stars such as Josephine Baker, Sophia Loren, Elizabeth Taylor and Richard Burton, and world leaders including Indira Gandhi and Fidel Castro. Outside is a 1953 Cadillac that Tito used to show the island to his eminent guests. These days, you can pay 50KN for a photo op inside or rent it for a measly 3000KN for 30 minutes. Bikes (25KN per three hours) and electric carts (100KN per hour) are a cheaper option, and a great way to explore the island.

Sleeping & Eating

There is no private accommodation on Veli Brijun but there are several luxurious villas available for rent through the national park office. Boat transport to and from the mainland is included in the following hotel prices; both are on Veli Brijun. There are no sleeping options on Mali Brijun, and Veli Brijun's hotel restaurants are the only places to eat.

ISTRIA

Hotel Karmen (☎ 525 807; www.brijuni.hr; s low-high 267-666KN, d 333-1087KN) Designers and architects from Zagreb flock to this spot on the harbour for its authentic communist design – it's trashy, real and feels as if it's still in the 1950s. Let's just hope they don't renovate.

Hotel Istra-Neptun (☎ 525 807; www.brijuni.hr; s low-high 297-716KN, d 463-1215KN) This is the ultimate in communist chic. Even though it's spruced up and comfy, rooms retain their plain utilitarian look. Each comes with a balcony, some with forest views, too. You can just imagine Tito's famous guests lounging here.

Getting There & Away

You may only visit Brijuni National Park with a group. From the Pula waterfront, a number of excursion boats leave for the islands. Instead of booking an excursion with one of the travel agencies in Pula, Rovinj or Poreč, you could take public bus 21 from Pula to Fažana (15KN, 8km), then sign up for a tour at the **national park office** (☎ 525 883; www .brijuni.hr; tours 110-190KN) near the wharf. It's best to book in advance, especially in summer, and request an English-speaking tour guide. In summer, picnic and swimming excursions to Mali Brijun (160KN) are also offered.

Also check along the Pula waterfront for excursion boats to Brijuni. Note that many of the two-hour 'panorama' trips from Pula to Brijuni (150KN) don't actually stop at the islands; *Martinabela* (250KN) does (see p160).

ROVINJ

pop 14,234

Rovinj (Rovigno in Italian) is coastal Istria's star attraction. While it can get overrun with tourists in summer, and residents are developing a sharp eye for maximising profits by upgrading hotels and restaurants to four-star status, it remains one of the last true Mediterranean fishing ports. Fishers haul their catch into the harbour in the early morning, followed by a horde of squawking gulls, and mend their nets before lunch. Prayers for a good catch are sent forth at the massive Church of St Euphemia, with its 60m-high tower punctuating the peninsula. Wooded hills and low-rise hotels surround the old town webbed by steep, cobbled streets and piazzas. The 13 green, offshore islands of the Rovinj archipelago make for a pleasant afternoon away, and you can swim from the rocks in the sparkling water below Hotel Rovinj.

History

Originally an island, Rovinj was settled by Slavs in the 7th century and began to develop a strong fishing and maritime industry. In 1199, Rovinj signed an important pact with Dubrovnik to protect its maritime trade, but in the 13th century the threat of piracy forced it to turn to Venice for protection.

From the 16th to 18th centuries, its population expanded dramatically with an influx of immigrants fleeing Turkish invasions of Bosnia and continental Croatia. The town began to develop outside the walls put up by the Venetians and, in 1763, the islet was connected to the mainland and Rovinj became a peninsula.

Although its maritime industry thrived in the 17th century, Austria's 1719 decision to make Trieste and Rijeka free ports dealt the town a blow. The decline of sailing ships further damaged Rovinj's shipbuilding industry and in the middle of the 19th century it was supplanted by the shipyard in Pula. Like the rest of Istria, Rovinj bounced from Austrian to French to Austrian to Italian rule before finally becoming part of postwar Yugoslavia. There's still a considerable Italian community.

Orientation

The old town of Rovinj is contained within an egg-shaped peninsula, with the bus station just to the southeast. There are two harbours: the northern open harbour and the small, protected harbour to the south. About 1.5km south of the old town is the Punta Corrente Forest Park and the wooded cape of Zlatni Rt (Golden Cape), with its age-old oak and pine trees, and several large hotels. A small archipelago lies just offshore; the most popular islands are Crveni Otok (Red Island), Sveta Katarina and Sveti Andrija.

Information

INTERNET ACCESS

A-mar (☎ 841 211; Carera 26; per 10min 6KN; 🕑 9am-11pm)

LAUNDRY

Galax (☎ 816 130; Istarska bb; per 5kg 70KN; 🕑 7am-8pm)

LEFT LUGGAGE

Garderoba (per hr 1.40KN; 🕑 6.30am-8.15pm Mon-Fri, 7.45am-7.30pm Sat & Sun) At the bus station. Note the three half-hour breaks at 9.15am, 1.30pm and 4.30pm.

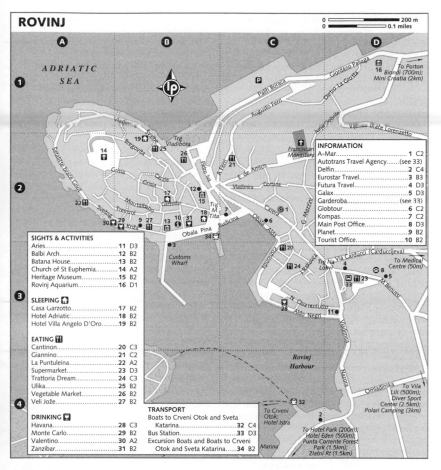

ROVINJ

0 _____ 200 m
0 _____ 0.1 miles

INFORMATION
A-Mar.................................1 C2
Autotrans Travel Agency.......(see 33)
Delfin.................................2 C4
Eurostar Travel....................3 B3
Futura Travel.......................4 D3
Galax.................................5 D3
Garderoba.......................(see 33)
Globtour.............................6 C2
Kompas..............................7 C2
Main Post Office...................8 D3
Planet...............................9 B2
Tourist Office....................10 B2

SIGHTS & ACTIVITIES
Aries.................................11 D3
Balbi Arch..........................12 B2
Batana House......................13 B2
Church of St Euphemia..........14 A2
Heritage Museum.................15 B2
Rovinj Aquarium..................16 D1

SLEEPING
Casa Garzotto.....................17 B2
Hotel Adriatic.....................18 B2
Hotel Villa Angelo D'Oro........19 B2

EATING
Cantinon............................20 C3
Giannino............................21 C2
La Puntuleina......................22 A2
Supermarket.......................23 D3
Trattoria Dream...................24 C3
Ulika.................................25 B2
Vegetable Market.................26 B2
Veli Jože............................27 B2

DRINKING
Havana..............................28 C3
Monte Carlo........................29 B2
Valentino...........................30 A2
Zanzibar............................31 B2

TRANSPORT
Boats to Crveni Otok and Sveta
Katarina.........................32 C4
Bus Station.........................33 D3
Excursion Boats and Boats to Crveni
Otok and Sveta Katarina......34 B2

MEDICAL SERVICES
Medical Centre (☎ 813 004; Istarska bb)

MONEY
There's an ATM next to the bus station entrance, and banks with ATMs all around town. Most travel agencies will change money.

POST
Main post office (Matteo Benussi 4; ⏱ 7am-8pm Mon-Fri, to 2pm Sat) You can make phone calls here.

TOURIST INFORMATION
Tourist office (☎ 811 566; www.tzgrovinj.hr; Pina Budicina 12; ⏱ 8am-10pm Jul & Aug, 8am-9pm Jun & Sep) Just off Trg Maršala Tita, it has plenty of brochures and maps.

TRAVEL AGENCIES
Autotrans Travel Agency (☎ 811 218; Trg Na Lokvi 6; ⏱ 8am-7pm Mon-Fri, to 2pm Sat) Specialises in transfers, excursions and private accommodation. At the bus station.
Eurostar Travel (☎ 813 144; Pina Budicina 1; ⏱ 9am-9pm Mon-Sat, 9am-1pm & 5-8pm Sun) Specialises in boat tickets to Venice and Trieste, and books excursions.
Futura Travel (☎ 817 281; www.futura-travel.hr; Matteo Benussi 2; ⏱ 8.30am-9pm Mon-Sat, 8.30am-1pm & 5-9pm Sun May-Sep) Private accommodation, money exchange, excursions and transfers.
Globtour (☎ 814 130; www.globtour-turizam.hr; Alda Rismonda 2; ⏱ 9am-10pm Jul & Aug, shorter hr rest of year) Excursions, private accommodation and bike rental (60KN per day).

ISTRIA

Kompas (☎ 813 211; www.kompas-travel.com; Trg Maršala Tita 5; ☯ 9am-10pm Jul & Aug, shorter hr rest of year) Daily excursions.

Planet (☎ 840 494; Svetog Križa 1; ☯ 9am-10pm Mon-Sat, 9am-1pm & 5-9pm Sun) Doubles as an internet café (6KN per 10 minutes).

Sights

CHURCH OF ST EUPHEMIA

The town's showcase is this imposing **church** (Sveta Eufemija; ☎ 815 615; Petra Stankovića; ☯ 10am-6pm Jul & Aug, 11am-3pm Sep-Jun), dominating the old town from its hilltop location in the middle of the peninsula. Built in 1736, it's the largest baroque building in Istria, reflecting the period during the 18th century when Rovinj was its most populous town.

Inside the church, look for the marble **tomb of St Euphemia** behind the right-hand altar. Rovinj's patron saint was tortured for her Christian faith by Emperor Diocletian before being thrown to the lions in 304. According to legend, the body disappeared one dark and stormy night only to appear off the coast of Rovinj in a spectral boat. The townspeople were unable to budge the heavy sarcophagus until a small boy appeared with two calves and moved it to the top of the hill, where it still stands in the present-day church. On the anniversary of her martyrdom (16 September), devotees congregate here. Modelled on the belfry of St Mark's in Venice, the 60m **bell tower** is topped by a copper statue of St Euphemia, which shows the direction of the wind by turning on a spindle. You can climb it for 10KN.

HERITAGE MUSEUM

This **museum** (☎ 816 720; www.muzej-rovinj.hr; Trg Maršala Tita 11; adult/concession 15/10KN; ☯ 9am-3pm & 7-10pm Tue-Fri, 9am-2pm & 7-10pm Sat & Sun mid-Jun–mid-Sep, 9am-3pm Tue-Sat mid-Sep–mid-Jun) in a baroque palace contains a collection of contemporary art and old masters from Rovinj and other places in Croatia, as well as archaeological finds and a maritime section.

BALBI ARCH & BACKSTREETS

Nearby is the elaborate Balbi Arch, built in 1679 on the location of the former town gate. The top of the arch is ornamented with a Turkish head on the outside and a Venetian head on the inside. The cobbled street of **Grisia**, lined with galleries where local artists sell their work, leads uphill from behind the arch to St Euphemia.

The winding narrow backstreets that spread around Grisia are an attraction in themselves. Windows, balconies, portals and squares are a pleasant confusion of styles – Gothic, Renaissance, baroque and neoclassical.

Notice the unique *fumaioli* (exterior chimneys), built during the population boom when entire families lived in a single room with a fireplace.

BATANA HOUSE

On the harbour, **Batana House** (☎ 812 593; www .batana.org; Pina Budicina 2; admission free, with guide 15KN; ☯ 10am-1pm & 7-10pm Tue-Sun May-Sep, 10am-1pm Tue-Sun Oct-Apr) is a museum dedicated to the *batana*, a flat-bottomed fishing boat that stands as a symbol of Rovinj's seafaring and fishing tradition. The multimedia exhibits inside this 17th-century townhouse have interactive displays, excellent captions and audio with *bitinada*, which are typical fisher's songs. Check out the *spacio*, the ground-floor cellar where wine was kept, tasted and sold amid much socialising.

ROVINJ AQUARIUM

Great for children, the **aquarium** (☎ 804 712; Giordano Paliaga 5; adult/child 20/10KN; ☯ 9am-9pm Jul & Aug, 9am-8pm Easter-Jun, Sep & Oct) exhibits a good collection of Adriatic marine life. Founded in 1891, it is part of the local centre for maritime research and provides an enlightening lesson on the local sea fauna.

MINI CROATIA

Two kilometres from the town centre on the road to Pazin, **Mini Croatia** (☎ 830 877; Turnina bb; adult/concession 25/10KN; ☯ 9am-9pm Jul & Aug, 10am-6pm Apr-Jun, Sep & Oct) is also popular with kids. It's a theme park with miniature models of Croatia's landmark buildings, monuments, cities and landscapes, and a small zoo with indigenous animals.

PUNTA CORRENTE FOREST PARK

When you've seen enough of the town, follow the waterfront on foot or by bike past Hotel Park to this verdant park, locally known as Zlatni Rt, about 1.5km south. Covered in oak and pine groves and boasting 10 species of cypress, the park was established in 1890 by Baron Hütterott, an Austrian admiral who kept a villa on Crveni Otok. Here you can swim off the rocks or just sit and admire the offshore islands.

Activities

Most people hop aboard a boat for **swimming, snorkelling** and **sunbathing**. A trip to Crveni Otok or Sveta Katarina is easily arranged (see p169). **Diver Sport Center** (☎ 816 648; www.diver.hr; Villas Rubin) is the largest operation in Rovinj, offering boat dives from 210KN with equipment rental. The main attraction is the **Baron Gautsch wreck**, an Austrian passenger steamer, sunk in 1914 by a sea mine, in 40m of water.

There are also 80 **rock-climbing** routes in a former Venetian stone quarry at Zlatni Rt, many suitable for beginners. Bird-watchers can bike to the **ornithological reserve** at Palud Marsh, 8km southwest of Rovinj.

Biking around Rovinj and the Punta Corrente Forest Park is a superb way to spend an afternoon. See p169 for bike rental options.

Tours

Most travel agencies listed on p165 sell day trips to Venice (450KN to 520KN), Plitvice (580KN) and Brijuni (380KN to 420KN). There are also fish picnics (250KN), panoramic cruises (100KN) and trips to Limska Draga Fjord (150KN; see p169). These can be slightly cheaper if booked through one of the independent operators that line the waterfront; **Delfin** (☎ 813 266) is reliable.

There are more exciting options, such as **4WD safaris** in Istria's interior (330KN to 430KN) and **canoe safaris** to the scenic Gorski Kotar region (510KN). To explore the archipelago in a sea kayak, book a trip through **Aries** (☎ 811 659; Obala Vladimira Nazora bb). These 9km jaunts take in two or three islands and a lighthouse for 270KN, lunch included.

Festivals & Events

The city's annual events include various regattas from late April through August. The **Rovinj Summer Festival** is a series of classical concerts that takes place in the Church of St Euphemia and the Franciscan monastery.

The second Sunday in August sees the town's most renowned event, when narrow Grisia becomes an open-air **art exhibition**. Anyone from children to professional painters display their work in churches, studios and on the street.

Sleeping

Rovinj has become Istria's destination of choice for hordes of summertime tourists,

so reserving in advance is strongly recommended. Prices have been rising steadily and probably will continue to do so, as the city gears up to reach elite status.

If you want to stay in private accommodation, there is little available in the old town, where there's also no parking and accommodation costs are higher. Double rooms start at 180KN in the high season, with a small discount for single occupancy; two-person apartments start at 380KN. Out of season, apartments go for 245KN.

The surcharge for a stay of less than three nights is 50% and guests who stay only one night are punished with a 100% surcharge. Outside summer months, you should be able to bargain the surcharge away. You can book directly from one of the travel agencies listed on p165. Planet has some good bargains.

Except for a few private options, most hotels and camping grounds in the area are managed by **Maistra** (www.maistra.com), which unveiled the new Monte Mulini four-star hotel in summer 2008 and is slated to open the even more luxurious Hotel Lone in summer 2009.

Porton Biondi (☎ 813 557; www.portonbiondi.hr; per person/tent 40/23KN; ◔ Apr-Oct) This camping ground that sleeps 1200 is about 700m from the old town.

Polari Camping (☎ 800 501; www.maistra.com; per person/site 57/80KN; ▣ ▨) Right on 2km of beach, it's about 3km southeast of town and has many facilities, such as swimming pools, a supermarket, restaurants, an internet point and playgrounds.

Hotel Istra (☎ 802 500; www.maistra.com; Otok Sv Andrija; s low-high 328-730KN, d 436-976KN; ▨ ▣ ▨) The renowned wellness centre and spa is the chief asset of this four-star complex, a 10-minute boat ride away on Sveti Andrija Island. There's also a restaurant in an old castle.

Vila Lili (☎ 840 940; www.hotel-vilalili.hr; Mohorovičića 16; s low-high 333-385KN, d 505-730KN; ▨ ▣) Bright rooms have all the three-star perks, including air-con and minibars, in a small modern house a short walk out of town. There are also a couple of pricier suites.

Hotel Park (☎ 811 077; www.maistra.com; IM Ronjgova bb; s low-high 343-589KN, d 454-784KN; ▣ ▨ ▣ ▨) It's conveniently close to the ferry dock for Crveni Otok and has such crowd-pleasing amenities as two outdoor pools and a sauna.

Hotel Adriatic (☎ 815 088; www.maistra.com; Pina Budicina bb; s low-high 392-589KN, d 522-784KN; ▨ ▣)

The location right on the harbour is excellent and the rooms spick and span and well equipped, but on the kitschy side. The pricier sea-view rooms have more space.

our pick **Casa Garzotto** (☎ 811 884; www.casa-garzotto.com; Via Garzotto 8; s low-high 510-760KN, d 650-1015KN; P ⛱ 🖳) Each of the four nicely outfitted studio apartments here have original details, a stylish touch and up-to-the-minute amenities. The historic townhouse couldn't be better placed. Bikes are complimentary.

Hotel Eden (☎ 800 400; www.maistra.com; Luja Adamovića bb; s low-high 533-917KN, d 626-1078KN; P ⛱ 🖳 🖳) While it's no quiet hideaway – there are 325 rooms in the complex – the Hotel Eden features sports grounds, a gym, a sauna and indoor and outdoor pools. There's plenty to do in all weather and the wooded location is a plus.

Hotel Villa Angelo D'Oro (☎ 840 502; www.angelodoro.hr; Vladimira Švalbe 38-42; s low-high 619-990KN, d 1005-1762KN; P ⛱) In a renovated Venetian townhouse in the town centre, the 24 plush rooms and (pricier) suites of this boutique hotel have lots of antiques plus mod cons aplenty. There's a sauna, a jacuzzi and a lush interior terrace, a great place for a drink amid ancient stone.

Eating

Picnickers can get supplies at the supermarket next to the bus station or at one of the Konzum stores around town. For a cheap bite, pick up a *burek* (greasy pastry stuffed with meat or cheese) from one of the kiosks near the vegetable market.

Most of the restaurants that line the harbour offer the standard fish and meat mainstays at similar prices. For a more gourmet experience, you'll need to bypass the water vistas. Note that many restaurants shut their doors between lunch and dinner.

Cantinon (☎ 816 075; Alda Rismonda 18; mains 29-74KN) A fishing theme runs through this high-ceilinged canteen that specialises in fresh seafood at low prices. The Batana fish plate for two is great value.

Veli Jože (☎ 816 337; Svetog Križa 3; mains from 35KN) Graze on good Istrian standards, either in the eclectic interior crammed with knick-knacks or at the outdoor tables with water views.

Giannino (☎ 813 402; Augusto Ferri 38; mains from 45KN) Tasty old-school Mediterranean staples are served in the spacious two-level interior or on a small pavement terrace.

Trattoria Dream (☎ 830 613; Joakima Rakovca 18; mains from 75KN) Tucked away in the maze of narrow streets, with its two earthy-coloured outdoor terraces, this stylish trattoria does flavourful dishes, such as salt-baked sea bass, and some global favourites, including chili con carne and chicken curry.

La Puntuleina (☎ 813 186; Svetog Križa 38; mains 100-160KN) Sample creative Med cuisine on three alfresco terraces, from traditional recipes, such as *žgvacet* (a type of stew) of calamari, to revamped ones, including truffle-topped fish fillet. Pasta dishes are more affordable (from 55KN). At night, grab a cushion and sip a cocktail on the rocks below this converted townhouse. Reservations recommended.

Ulika (Vladimira Švalbe 34) For an evening snack of local cheese, cured meats and tasty small bites, head to this place, a tiny tavern a few doors down from Angelo D'Oro. Opening hours vary, but in the high season (July and August) it's usually open from 6pm to 11pm.

Drinking

Havana (Aldo Negri bb) Tropical cocktails, Cuban cigars, straw parasols and the shade of tall pine trees make this open-air cocktail bar a popular spot to chill and watch the ships go by.

Monte Carlo (☎ 830 683; Svetog Križa 21) More quiet and down to earth than its showy neighbour, Valentino, this low-key café-bar has great views of the sea and Sveta Katarina across the way.

Zanzibar (☎ 813 206; Pina Budicina bb) Indonesian wood, palms, wicker lounge chairs and subdued lighting on the huge outdoor terrace of this cocktail bar create a tropical and definitely upmarket vibe.

Valentino (☎ 830 683; Svetog Križa 28) Premium cocktail prices on the terrace of this high-end spot include fantastic sunset views, on the water's edge.

Getting There & Away

There are buses from Rovinj to Pula (35KN, 40 minutes, 13 daily), Dubrovnik (593KN, 16 hours, one daily), Labin (69KN, two hours, two daily), Poreč (37KN, one hour, eight daily), Rijeka (112KN, 3½ hours, four daily), Zagreb (173KN to 255KN, five hours, four daily) and Split (417KN, 11 hours, one daily). For info on connections to Italy, see p309.

The closest train station is at Kanfanar, 20km away on the Pula–Divača line; buses connect Kanfanar and Rovinj.

Getting Around

You can rent bicycles at many agencies around town, including Globtour (p165) for 60KN per day. The cheapest bike rental (5KN per hour) is at the old town entrance, by the Vladibora parking lot and market.

AROUND ROVINJ

A popular day trip from Rovinj is a boat ride to lovely **Crveni Otok** (Red Island). Only 1900m long, the island includes two islets, Sveti Andrija and Maškin, connected by a causeway. In the 19th century, Sveti Andrija became the property of Baron Hütterott who transformed it into a luxuriantly wooded park. The Hotel Istra complex now dominates **Sveti Andrija**, but its small gravel beaches and playground make it popular with families. **Maškin** is quieter, more wooded and with plenty of secluded coves, making it a winner with naturists. Bring a mask for snorkelling around the rocks.

Right across the peninsula is Sveta Katarina, a small island forested by a Polish count in 1905 and now home to **Hotel Katarina** (☎ 804 100; www.maistra.com; Otok Sveta Katarina; s low-high 533-664KN, d 626-943KN; ☒).

In summer, there are 18 boats daily to Sveta Katarina (return 15KN, five minutes) and on to Crveni Otok (return 15KN, 15 minutes). They leave from just opposite Hotel Adriatic and also from the Delfin ferry dock near Hotel Park.

The **Limska Draga Fjord** (Limski Kanal) is the most dramatic sight in Istria. About 10km long, 600m wide and with steep valley walls that rise to a height of 100m, the inlet was formed when the Istrian coastline sank during the last Ice Age, allowing the sea to rush in and fill the Draga Valley. The deep-green bay has a hillside cave on the southern side where the 11th-century hermit priest Romualdo lived and held ceremonies. Fishing, oyster and mussel farming, and excursion boating are the only activities in the fjord.

At the fjord, you'll find souvenir stands and two waterside restaurants that serve up superbly fresh shells, right from the source. Of the two, **Viking** (☎ 448 223; Limski Kanal 1; mains from 55KN) is the better option, where you can get oysters (9KN per piece), great scallops (22KN per piece) and mussels, or fish priced by the kilo on a terrace overlooking the fjord. There's also a picnic area and a swimming cove behind the other restaurant (named Fjord).

Small excursion boats will take you on a one-hour boat ride for 60KN per person (negotiable); these run frequently in July and August, and sporadically in June and September. To get to the fjord, you can take an excursion from Rovinj, Pula or Poreč or follow the signs to Limski Kanal past the village of Sveti Lovreč.

POREČ

pop 17,000

Poreč (Parenzo in Italian; Parentium in Roman times) and the surrounding region are entirely devoted to summer tourism. The ancient Roman town of Poreč is the centrepiece of a vast system of tourist resorts that stretches north and south along the west coast of Istria. The largest is Zelena Laguna, with a full range of facilities and accommodation.

These holiday villages and tourist camps offer a rather industrialised experience, with too much concrete and plastic and too many tour buses for some tastes. The hotels, restaurants, tourist offices and travel agencies, however, are almost universally staffed by friendly, multilingual people who make a real effort to welcome visitors. While this is not the place for a quiet getaway (unless you come out of season), there's a World Heritage–listed basilica, well-developed tourist infrastructure and the pristine Istrian interior within easy reach.

History

The coast of Poreč measures 37km, islands included, but the ancient town is confined to a peninsula 400m long and 200m wide. The Romans conquered the region in the 2nd century BC and made Poreč an important administrative centre from which they were able to control a sweep of land from the Limska Draga Fjord to the Mirna River. Poreč's street plan was laid out by the Romans, who divided the town into rectangular parcels marked by the longitudinal Dekumanus and the latitudinal Cardo.

With the collapse of the Western Roman Empire, Poreč came under Byzantine rule, which lasted from the 6th to 8th centuries. It was during this time that the Euphrasian Basilica, with its magnificent frescoes, was erected. In 1267, Poreč was forced to submit to Venetian rule.

The Istrian plague epidemics hit Poreč particularly hard, with the town's population dropping to about 100 in the 17th century.

ISTRIA

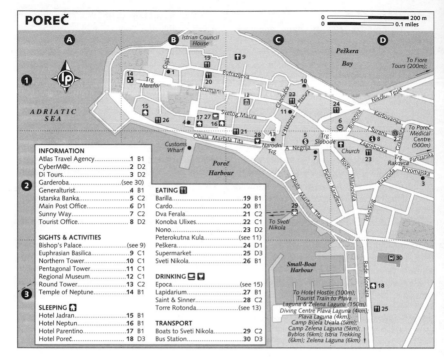

POREČ

INFORMATION
Atlas Travel Agency..................1 B1
CyberM@c.............................2 D2
Di Tours...............................3 D2
Garderoba.........................(see 30)
Generalturist........................4 B1
Istarska Banka.......................5 C2
Main Post Office....................6 D1
Sunny Way............................7 C2
Tourist Office.........................8 D2

SIGHTS & ACTIVITIES
Bishop's Palace....................(see 9)
Euphrasian Basilica..................9 C1
Northern Tower......................10 C1
Pentagonal Tower...................11 C1
Regional Museum...................12 C1
Round Tower........................13 C2
Temple of Neptune.................14 B1

SLEEPING 🏠
Hotel Jadran.........................15 B1
Hotel Neptun........................16 B1
Hotel Parentino.....................17 B1
Hotel Poreč..........................18 D3

EATING 🍴
Barilla.................................19 B1
Cardo.................................20 B1
Dva Ferala...........................21 C2
Konoba Ulixes.......................22 C1
Nono..................................23 D2
Peterokutna Kula................(see 11)
Peškera...............................24 D1
Supermarket.........................25 D3
Sveti Nikola..........................26 B1

DRINKING 🍸
Epoca.............................(see 15)
Lapidarium...........................27 B1
Saint & Sinner.......................28 C2
Torre Rotonda...................(see 13)

TRANSPORT
Boats to Sveti Nikola................29 C2
Bus Station...........................30 D3

With the decline of Venice, the town oscillated between Austrian and French dominance before the Italian occupation that lasted from 1918 to 1943. Upon the capitulation of Italy, Poreč was occupied by the Germans and damaged by Allied bombing in 1944 before becoming part of postwar Yugoslavia and, more recently, Croatia.

Orientation

The compact old town is squeezed onto the peninsula and packed with thousands of shops and agencies. The ancient Roman Decumanus, with its polished stones, is still the main street running through the peninsula's middle. Hotels, travel agencies and excursion boats are on the quayside Obala Maršala Tita, which runs from the small-boat harbour to the tip of the peninsula. The bus station is just outside the old town, behind Rade Končara.

Information

INTERNET ACCESS
CyberM@c (☎ 427 075; Mire Grahalića 1; per hr 42KN; ☽ 8am-10pm) A full-service computer centre.

LEFT LUGGAGE
Garderoba (per day 22KN; ☽ 7am-9pm) At the bus station.

MEDICAL SERVICES
Poreč Medical Centre (☎ 451 611; Maura Gioseffija 2)

MONEY
You can exchange currency at any of the many travel agencies or banks, including **Istarska Banka** (Alda Negrija 2). There are ATMs all around town.

POST
Main post office (Trg Slobode 14; ☽ 8am-noon & 6-8pm Mon-Sat) Has a telephone centre.

TOURIST INFORMATION
Tourist office (☎ 451 293; www.to-porec.com; Zagrebačka 9; ☽ 8am-10pm Mon-Sat, 9am-1pm & 6-10pm Sun Jul & Aug, 8am-4pm Mon-Sat Sep-Jun)

TRAVEL AGENCIES
Atlas Travel Agency (☎ 434 933; www.atlas-croatia .com; Eufrazijeva 63; ☽ 9am-2pm & 6-9pm) Books excursions.

Di Tours (☎ 432 100; www.di-tours.hr; Prvomajska 2; ☺ 9am-10pm Jul & Aug, to 9pm Jun & Sep) Finds private accommodation.

Fiore Tours (☎ 431 397; www.fioretours.com; Mate Vlašića 6; ☺ 8am-10pm Jul & Aug, to 9pm Jun & Sep) Also handles private accommodation.

Generalturist (☎ 451 188; www.generalturist.com; Obala Maršala Tita 19; ☺ 8am-7pm Mon-Fri, to 1pm Sat) Books excursions, transfers and villa accommodation in Istria's interior.

Sunny Way (☎ 452 021; sunnyway@pu.t-com.hr; Alda Negrija 1; ☺ 9am-9pm Jul & Aug) Specialises in boat tickets and excursions to Italy and around Croatia.

Sights

The main reason to visit Poreč is to see the 6th-century **Euphrasian Basilica** (☎ 431 635; Eufrazijeva bb; admission free, to climb belfry 10KN; ☺ 7am-8pm Apr–mid-Oct, or by appointment), a World Heritage – listed site and one of Europe's finest intact examples of Byzantine art. Built on the site of a 4th-century oratory, the sacral complex includes a church, atrium and baptistery. What packs in the crowds are the glittering wall **mosaics** in the apse. These 6th-century masterpieces feature Biblical scenes, archangels and Istrian martyrs. Notice the group to the left, which shows Bishop Euphrasius, who commissioned the basilica, with a model of the church in his hand. The **belfry**, accessed through the octagonal baptistery, affords an invigorating view of the old town.

Also worth a visit is the adjacent **Bishop's Palace** (admission 10KN; ☺ 9am-7pm Apr–mid-Oct, or by appointment), which contains a display of ancient stone sculptures, religious paintings and 4th-century mosaics from the original oratory.

Trg Marafor is where the Roman forum used to stand and public gatherings took place; the original pavement has been preserved along the northern row of houses on the square. West of this rectangular square, inside a small park, are the ruins of the 2nd-century **Temple of Neptune**, dedicated to the god of sea. Northwest of the square are the remains of a large temple from the beginning of the 1st century.

Continue east of Trg Marafor along Decumanus and you'll see a medley of Gothic and Romanesque buildings, as well as the baroque Sinčić Palace. The palace houses the **Regional Museum** (www.muzejporec.hr; Decumanus 9), which is currently under renovation.

There are three 15th-century towers that date from the Venetian rule and once formed the city walls: the gothic **Pentagonal Tower** at the beginning of Decumanus; the **Round Tower** on Narodni Trg; and the **Northern Tower** on Peškera Bay.

From May to October there are passenger boats (15KN) travelling to **Sveti Nikola**, the small island that lies opposite Poreč harbour. They depart every 30 minutes to an hour from the wharf on Obala Maršala Tita.

Activities

Nearly every activity you might want to enjoy is outside the town in either Plava Laguna or Zelena Laguna. Most of the sports and recreational centres – there are 20 – are affiliated with hotels and have tennis, basketball and volleyball courts, windsurfing, rowing, bungee jumping, paintball, golf, water-skiing, parasailing, boat rentals, go-carting and canoeing. If the weather turns bad, you can always work out in the fitness centre or get a massage at one of the spas. For details, pick up the yearly *Poreč Info* booklet from the tourist office, which lists all the recreational facilities in the area.

The gentle rolling hills of the interior and the well-marked paths make **cycling** and **hiking** a prime way to explore the region. The tourist office issues a free map of roads and trails stemming from Poreč, along with suggested routes. You can rent a bike at many places around town; try the outlet just below the **Hotel Poreč** (☎ 098 335 838) for 70KN per day.

There is also horse riding in Zelena Laguna at **Istra Trekking** (☎ 091 885 8403; www.istratrekking .com; Zelena Laguna bb). It offers hour-long rides (140KN) and weeklong tours around Istria, sleeping in different agritourism places (700KN per person per day).

There is good diving in and around shoals and sandbanks in the area, as well as at the nearby *Coriolanus*, a British Royal Navy warship that sank in 1945. At **Diving Centre Plava Laguna** (☎ 098 367 619; www.plava-laguna -diving.hr), boat dives start at 100KN (more for caves or wrecks) or 220KN for full equipment rental.

Festivals & Events

During July and August there's **Poreč Annale**, one of the oldest Croatian contemporary art exhibitions, curated around a single theme. The **Street Art Festival**, held for a week in August, attracts international artists who perform anything from acrobatics to theatre and music in the old town squares and streets. **Classical music concerts** take place at the basilica during July and August several times a week at 9pm; tickets (50KN) can be purchased one hour before the concert at the venue. There are **jazz concerts** (www.jazzinlap.com) between late June and early September, held once a week in the courtyard of the regional museum, beside Lapidarium (opposite). Free concerts take place on Trg Slobode as part of **Poreč Summer**. The tourist office publishes a free *Poreč Day by Day* booklet that lists seasonal events.

Sleeping

Accommodation in Poreč is plentiful but gets booked ahead of time, so advance reservations are essential if you come in July or August.

There is a handful of hotels in the old town but most of the camping grounds, hotels, apartment complexes and resorts spread along the coast north and south of Poreč. The major tourist complexes are in Brulo, 2km south of town, Plava Laguna, 4km south of the old town, and Zelena Laguna, 2km further. North of Poreč are the tourist settlements of Borik and Špadići. Some 20 hotels and a dozen apartment complexes are planted in these wooded areas. Most hotels are managed by **Valamar Hotels & Resorts** (☎ 465 100; www.valamar.com) or **Plava Laguna** (☎ 410 101; www.plavalaguna.hr). All hotels are open from May to October; only a few remain open all year. For stays of less than three nights, expect a 20% surcharge during summer.

If you want to find private accommodation, consult the travel agencies listed on p170. Expect to pay between 200KN and 250KN for a double room in the high season or 280KN to 350KN for a two-person apartment, plus a 30% surcharge for stays of less than four nights. There is a limited number of rooms available in the old town, where there's no parking. Look for the *Domus Bonus* certificate of quality in private accommodation.

Camp Zelena Laguna (☎ 410 700; www.plavalaguna .hr; per adult/site 55/75KN; ☒ Apr-Sep) Well equipped for sports, this camping ground 5km from the old town can house up to 2700 people. It has access to many beaches, including a naturist one.

Camp Bijela Uvala (☎ 410 551; www.plavalaguna .hr; per adult/site 55/75KN; ☒ Apr-Sep; ☒) It can be crowded, as it houses up to 6000, but there are two outdoor pools and the facilities of Zelena Laguna are a stone's throw away.

Hotel Poreč (☎ /fax 451 811; www.hotelporec.com; Rade Končara 1; s low-high 285-495KN, d 395-730KN; ☒) While the rooms inside this concrete box have

uninspiring views over the bus station and the shopping centre opposite, they're acceptable and an easy walk from the old town. It's open all year and has a small spa.

our pick **Hotel Hostin** (☎ 408 800; www.hostin .hr; Rade Končara 4; s low-high 300-650KN, d 395-920KN; ☒ ☒ ☒ ☒) Each of the 39 well-equipped rooms comes with balconies at this charming little place in verdant parkland just steps from the bus station. An indoor swimming pool, fitness room, Turkish bath and sauna are nice perks, as is the pebble beach only 70m away.

Hotel Neptun (☎ 400 800; www.valamar.com; Obala Maršala Tita 15; s low-high 370-515KN, d 500-785KN; ☒) While this is the best of the harbour-front hotels, the rooms are unspectacular (and slated for renovation). If you pay extra for sea vistas, you'll also get noise from the promenade below. It has two cheaper annexes further down the waterfront: Hotel Jadran (double low-high 250KN to 670KN) has spacious twins, some with balconies, while Hotel Parentino (265KN to 740KN) has no-frills doubles in a high-ceilinged 19th-century building.

Eating

Peškera (☎ 432 890; Nikole Tesle bb; meals 35-60KN; ☒ 10am-9pm) Seemingly stuck in the socialist era, this self-service canteen serves simple, cheap meals such as fried chicken and grilled calamari. Just outside the northeastern corner of the old city wall, it has a sea-facing terrace.

Nono (☎ 435 088; Zagrebačka 4; pizzas 45-80KN) Nono serves the best pizza in town, with puffy crusts and toppings such as truffles. Other dishes are tasty, too.

Barilla (☎ 452 742; Eufrazijeva 26; mains from 45KN) Comforting Italian concoctions in all shapes and forms – penne, tagliatelle, fusilli, tortellini, gnocchi and so on. There are tables on the square and a quieter patio out the back. Try the spaghetti with shellfish (170KN for two). Across the square is its sister restaurant, Cardo (Carda Maximusa 8; mains from 55KN), which serves up meat, fish and international standards.

our pick **Dva Ferala** (☎ 433 416; Obala Maršala Tita 13a; mains from 50KN) Savour well-prepared Istrian specialities, such as *istarski tris* for two – a copious trio of homemade pastas (110KN) – on the terrace of this pleasant *konoba* (tavern).

Peterokutna Kula (☎ 451 378; Decumanus 1; mains from 65KN) Inside the medieval Pentagonal Tower, this upmarket restaurant has an alfresco terrace in a stone vault, where a full spectrum of fish and meat can be yours to taste. The oven-baked sea bass is particularly good.

Konoba Ulixes (☎ 451 132; Decumanus 2; mains from 75KN) The fish and shellfish are par excellence at this tavern with a patio just off Decumanus. The Poseidon plate for two (140KN) is good value, or try the pasta with scampi and champagne (100KN).

Sveti Nikola (☎ 423 018; Obala Maršala Tita 23; meals from 80KN) Culinary innovation is part of the deal at this elegant restaurant by the water. You can't go wrong with the set menus for lunch (meat/fish 80/95KN) and dinner (105/120KN). The fish fillet with asparagus and black truffles is a sumptuous experience.

A large supermarket and department store are situated next to Hotel Poreč, near the bus station.

Drinking & Entertainment

Saint & Sinner (☎ 434 390; Obala Maršala Tita 12) A B&W plastic theme runs through this latest opening on the waterfront, where the young ones sip chococcinos during the day and strawberry caipiroskas at night.

Epoca (Hotel Jadran, Obala Maršala Tita 24) Kick back and watch the sun go down by the water, grab a quickie espresso or have a leisurely nightcap cocktail at this café-bar.

Torre Rotonda (Narodni Trg 3a) Take the steep stairs to the top of the historic Round Tower and grab a table at the open-air café to watch the action on the quays.

Lapidarium (Svetog Maura 10) Gorgeous bar with a large courtyard in the back of the regional museum and a series of antique-filled inner rooms. Wednesday is jazz night in summer, with alfresco live music.

Byblos (www.byblos.hr; Zelena Laguna bb) On Fridays, celeb guest DJs such as David Morales and Eric Morillo crank out house tunes at this humongous open-air club, one of Croatia's hottest places to party. Boogie to a mixed bag of dance music on Saturday nights.

Getting There & Away

For information on boat connections to Italy, inquire at Sunny Way travel agency (p171) and see p310. Sunny Way sells tickets for the fast catamaran to Venice, which runs daily in season (single/return 430/520KN), as well as to Trieste with **Ustica Lines** (www.usticalines .it), which runs daily except Monday (single/ return 150/280KN, two hours).

There are daily buses from the **bus station** (☎ 432 153; Rade Končara 1) to Rovinj (38KN, 40 minutes, seven), Zagreb (217KN, five hours, seven), Rijeka (81KN, two hours, 11) and Pula (50KN, one to 1½ hours, 11). Between Poreč and Rovinj the bus runs along the Limska Draga Fjord. To see it clearly, sit on the right-hand side if you're southbound, or the left if you're northbound.

The nearest train station is at Pazin, 37km to the east. There are about 10 buses daily from Poreč (34KN, 30 minutes).

Getting Around

From March to early October, a tourist train operates regularly from Šetalište Antuna Štifanića by the marina to Plava Laguna (10KN) and Zelena Laguna (15KN). There's a passenger boat (25KN) that makes the same run from the ferry landing every hour from 8.30am till midnight. The frequent buses to Vrsar stop at Plava Laguna, Zelena Laguna and the other resorts south of the city.

THE ISTRIAN INTERIOR

Head inland from the Istrian coast and you'll notice that crowds dissipate, hotel complexes disappear and what emerges is an unspoiled countryside of medieval hilltop towns, pine forests, fertile valleys and vineyard-dotted hills. The pace of daily life slows down considerably, defined less by the needs of tourists and more by the demands of harvesting grapes, hunting for truffles, picking wild asparagus and cultivating olive groves. Farmhouses are opening their doors to visitors looking for an authentic holiday experience, rustic taverns in the middle of nowhere serve up slow-food delights, and Croatia's top winemakers provide tastings in their cellars. Remote hilltop villages that once seemed doomed to ruin are attracting colonies of artists and artisans as well as well-heeled foreigners. While many compare the region to Tuscany and the Italian influence can't be denied, it's a world all its own – unique, magnetic and wholesome.

You'll need a car to explore this area, as the bus and train connections are very sporadic. Good news – you're never far from the sea!

LABIN
pop 9000

Perched on a hilltop just above the coast, Labin is the undisputed highlight of eastern Istria,

---

ISTRIA'S OTHER HIGHLIGHTS

A single chapter of a guidebook doesn't fit Istria's many highlights, so here's a rundown of what else awaits you should you wish to explore more.

Novigrad is an attractive old town crammed onto a peninsula, only 20 minutes north of Poreč. It has one of Istria's best restaurants, **Damir i Ornella** (☎ 758 134; Zidine 5), famous for its raw fish specialities. The fishing village of **Savudrija** is Croatia's westernmost point and home to Istria's oldest lighthouse, built in 1818. The **lighthouse** (www.lighthouses-croatia.com) is now available for weekly rentals. **Vrsar**, located roughly between Rovinj and Poreč, is a delightful fishing town rising on a hilltop in a jumble of medieval buildings. It's quieter than its neighbours and has an outdoor sculpture park of renowned Croatian sculptor Dušan Džamonja.

In the interior, art aficionados should head to **Beram**, near Pazin, to take in the amazing 15th-century frescoes in the Church of Saint Mary of Škriljine; the Pazin tourist office (p177) has details. Within easy reach of Poreč is the **Baredine Cave** (www.baredine.com), with subterranean chambers replete with stalagmites and stalactites; various agencies offer excursions. Near Labin is Istria's youngest town, **Raša**, a showcase of modernist functionalist architecture that sprang up under Mussolini's rule in the 1930s. While here, check out the **Liburna Reserve** (www.rezervatliburna.hr) a few kilometres out, which aims to preserve indigenous breeds of donkeys and has an ethnographic museum.

The ancient stone town of **Bale** in the southwest is one of Istria's hidden gems. Here the artsy bar and restaurant **Kamene Priče** (www.kameneprice.com) draws in a bohemian crowd for its jazz fest in early August, delicious food and various offbeat events. On a hilltop north of Motovun is **Oprtalj**, less developed than its neighbour, with cypress trees and fantastic views of the surrounding scenery. Here you'll find the rustic shop-resto **Loggia** (www.loggia.hr), the place to sample Istrian snacks such as *ombolo* (boneless pork loin), pancetta and sheep's cheese. Don't miss the abandoned ancient village of **Kotli**, located 1.5km from the main road between Hum and Roč on the Mirna River. This protected rural complex has preserved courtyards, outer staircases, arched passages and picturesque chimneys.

---

and its historical and administrative centre. The showcase here is the old town, a beguiling potpourri of steep streets, cobblestone alleys and pastel houses festooned with stone ornamentation. What surrounds it below is a grubby new town that has sprouted as a result of the coal mining industry. Labin was the mining capital of Istria until the 1970s, its hill mined so extensively that the town began to collapse. Mining stopped in 1999, the necessary repairs were undertaken and the town surfaced with a new sense of itself as a tourist destination.

It has plenty to offer for a day-long visit. The labyrinth of its old town hides an unusual museum in a loggia, a wealth of Venetian-inspired churches and palaces, and a sprinkling of craft shops. The coastal resort of Rabac, 5km southwest of Labin, is overdeveloped with tightly packed holiday houses, hotels and apartment blocks, but its beaches are decent and it can be a nice way to spend an afternoon.

Orientation

Labin is divided into two parts: the hilltop old town with most of the sights and attractions; and Podlabin, a much newer section below the hill, with most of the town's shops, restaurants and services. Buses stop at Trg 2 Marta in Podlabin, from where you can catch a local bus to the old town. This bus continues on to Rabac in the peak season.

Information

Health service (☎ 855 333; Kature Nove bb)

Main tourist office (☎ /fax 855 560; www.rabac-labin .com; Aldo Negri 20; ☯ 7am-3pm Mon-Fri) The main tourist office is just below the old town.

Post office (Titov Trg bb; ☯ 7am-8pm Mon-Fri, to 2pm Sat) In the old town.

Privredna Banka (Trg 2 Marta bb) At the bus stop; has an ATM.

Tourist office annexe (☎ /fax 852 399; Titov Trg 10; ☯ 8am-9pm Mon-Sat, 10am-1pm & 6-9pm Sun Jun-Sep, 8am-3pm Mon-Fri Oct-May) At the entrance to the old town.

Veritas (☎ 852 758; www.istra-veritas.hr; Ulica Sv Katarine 4; ☯ 8am-3pm & 5-8pm Mon-Fri, 8.30am-1pm & 5-8pm Sat, 9am-noon & 5-8pm Sun) The only travel agency in the old town; specialises in private accommodation.

Sights

Wandering the streets of Labin is the highlight. The **Town Museum** (Gradski Muzej; ☎ 852 477; 1 Maja 6; adult/concession 15/10KN; ☒ 10am–1pm & 6-8pm Mon-Sat, 10am–1pm Sun Jul Sep, 10am–3pm Mon-Fri Oct-Jun) is housed in the baroque 18th-century Battiala-Lazzarini Palace. The ground floor is devoted to archaeological finds, upstairs is a collection of musical instruments with some fun interactive features, while the top floor has a contemporary art gallery. The museum is over a coal pit that has been turned into a realistic re-creation of an actual coal mine. As you make your way through the claustrophobic tunnels, you'll understand why miners preferred other employment.

Take a look at the **Church of the Birth of the Blessed Virgin Mary** (Ulica 1 Maja; ☒ Mass only), a mixture of Venetian Gothic and Renaissance styles featuring a finely carved Venetian lion over the portal. To the right, notice the 15th-century Renaissance **Scampicchio Palace**, with its inner courtyard, and the 1550 **loggia** (Titov Trg), which served as the community centre of Labin in the 16th century. News and court verdicts were announced here, fairs were held and waywards were punished on the pillar of shame.

The highest point in Labin is the **fortress** (*fortica*) at the western edge of town. You can walk along Ulica 1 Maja or take the long way around by following Šetalište San Marco along the town walls. What unfolds below you is a sweeping view of the coast, the Učka mountain range and Cres Island.

Festivals & Events

Labin Art Republic (Labin Art Republika; http://united festival.com) takes over this artsy town – there are over 30 artists living and working here – every July and August. During the festival, the town comes alive with street theatre, concerts, plays, clown performances and open studios. Also worth catching is **Rabac Summer Festival** (www .rabacsummerfestival.com), which pulls in house and techno music fans for its roster of internationally known DJs; performances are held at Park Dubrova, 2km from Labin, and at Girandella Beach in Rabac.

Sleeping

There are no hotels in Labin itself but if you want to stay, choices abound just below in Rabac. Most of the lodging is of the large hotel-resort kind, with a few smaller properties. **Valamar** (www .valamar.com) manages eight hotels here, including two deluxe options (Valamar Sanfior Hotel and Valamar Bellevue Hotel & Residence), five three-star properties, three apartment complexes and a camping ground. Peak season (read August) prices range greatly, from 860KN in a double room at a four-star hotel (half-board), to 615KN at a two-star hotel. There are two-person studios available from 385KN and four-person villas from 725KN. A 20% surcharge is applied for stays under three nights.

Another hotel chain is **Maslinica** (☎ 884 150; www.maslinicarabac.com), which has three midrange properties in Maslinica Bay: Hotel Narciso, Hotel Hedera and Hotel Mimosa. Doubles start at 775KN for half-board; singles go for 500KN. It also manages **Camping Oliva** (☎ 872 258; Rabac bb; per site 75KN), right on Rabac beach in front of the big hotels.

The two independent hotels with more character are **Hotel Amfora** (☎ 872 222; www.hotel -amfora.com; Rabac bb; s low-high 195-510KN, d 290-740KN), in town, and the posh **Villa Annette** (☎ 884 222; www.villaannette.hr; Raška 24; d low-high 668-1268KN; ☒), up on a hill slope; the latter has an outdoor pool overlooking the bay. For stays under four nights at Villa Annette, add a daily half-board supplement of 225KN per person.

Veritas travel agency (opposite) finds double rooms/apartments for 180/285KN in the old town of Labin.

Eating

Labin is known for its truffles cooked with pasta or eggs, which are generally priced well. Rabac has plenty of restaurants serving seafood standards, but most cater to the unfussy tourist crowds.

Gostiona Kvarner (☎ 852 336; Šetalište San Marco bb; mains from 35KN) Just steps from Titov Trg, this restaurant has a terrace overlooking the sea, good food and a loyal following of locals. The *fuži* (hand-rolled pasta) with truffles is a measly 80KN, which is a bargain considering the expense of truffle-hunting.

Getting There & Away

Labin is well connected with Pula (38KN, one hour, 15 daily) by bus. In summer, the bus to Rabac (7KN), via the old town, leaves every hour between 6am and midnight.

VODNJAN

pop 3700

Connoisseurs of the macabre can't miss Vodnjan (Dignano in Italian), located 10km north of Pula. Lying inside a sober church in this sleepy town are the **'mummies'** that constitute Vodnjan's primary tourist attraction. These desiccated remains of centuries-old saints, whose bodies mysteriously failed to decompose, are considered to have magical powers.

There's not much going on in the rest of the town, which has Istria's largest Roma population. The centre is Narodni Trg, composed of several neo-Gothic palaces in varying stages of decay and restoration. It contains the **tourist office** (☎ 511 700; tz-vodnjan-dignano@pu.t-com.hr; Narodni Trg 3; ⏰ 8am-2pm & 7-9pm summer, 8am-2pm Mon-Fri rest of year).

The mummies' resting place is just a few steps away from Narodni Trg in **St Blaise's Church** (Crkva Svetog Blaža; ☎ 511 420; Župni Trg; ⏰ 9am-7pm Mon-Sat, 2-6pm Sun Jun-Sep, sporadic hr Oct-May). This handsome, neobaroque church was built at the turn of the 19th century when Venice was the style-setter for the Istrian coast. With its 63m-high **bell tower** as high as St Mark's in Venice, it's the largest parish church in Istria and is worth a visit for its magnificent altars alone.

The mummies are in a curtained-off area behind the **main altar** (28KN). In the dim lighting, the complete bodies of Nikolosa Bursa, Giovanni Olini and Leon Bembo resemble wooden dolls in their glass cases. Assorted body parts of three other saints complete the display. As you examine the skin, hair and fingernails of these long-dead people, a tape in English narrates their life stories. Considered to be Europe's best-preserved mummy, the body of St Nikolosa is said to emit a 32m bio-energy circle that has caused 50 miraculous healings.

If the mummies have whetted your appetite for saintly relics, head to the **Collection of Sacral Art** (Zbirka Sakralne Umjetnosti; admission incl mummies 45KN) in the sacristy. Here there are hundreds of relics belonging to 150 different saints, including the casket with St Mary of Egypt's tongue. Less grisly exhibits include a masterful 14th-century polyptych of St Leon Bembo by Paolo Veneziano.

Vodnjan's other attraction is **Vodnjanka** (☎ 511 435; Istarska bb; mains from 50KN; ⏰ closed Sun lunch), an excellent regional restaurant with several rustic rooms, lots of style and personal service. The specialities include *fuži* topped with truffles, *maneštra,* various kinds of *fritaja* and prosciutto. For dessert, try *kroštule* (fried

dough with sugar). The terrace has pretty views of the old town rooftops and church spire.

Vodnjan is well connected with Pula by bus (20KN, 20 minutes, 18 to 20 daily).

SVETVINČENAT
pop 300

Lying halfway between Pazin and Pula in southern Istria, Svetvinčenat (also known as Savičenta) is an endearing little town. First settled by Benedictines, it centres on the Renaissance town square. With its surrounding tall cypress trees, harmoniously positioned buildings and laid-back ambience, it's a delightful place for a wander.

The north part of the square is occupied by the 13th-century **Grimani Castle**, a beautifully preserved palace that had a Venetian makeover in the 16th century, with the addition of towers that served as a residence and prison. The site held feasts, parades, fairs and witch burnings (Marija Radoslović was allegedly tortured and burnt at the stake here on charges of sorcery, but was in fact killed for having an improper love affair with one of the Grimanis). The east side of the square has the parish **Church of Mary's Annunciation**, with a trefoil Renaissance facade made of local cut stone, and five elaborate Venetian marble altars in the interior.

The time to be in Svetvinčenat is mid-July, during the annual **Dance Festival & Nonverbal Theater Festival** (www.svetvincenatfestival.com). The festival features contemporary dance pieces, street theatre, circus and mime acts, and various other nonverbal forms of expression. This international event hosts performers from Croatia and Europe, its acts ranging from Finnish hip hop to Brazilian capoeira.

The seasonal **tourist office** (☎ 560 349; www .svetvincenat.hr; Svetvinčenat 20; ⏰ 9am-2pm & 7-8pm Mon-Sat, 10am-1pm Sun Jun-Oct) on the main square has information about private accommodation in and around town.

Sleeping & Eating
Stancija 1904 (☎ 560 022; www.stancija.com; Smoljanci 2-3; s 480KN, d/ste 645/720KN) In the village of Smoljanci, just 3km from Svetvinčenat on the road to Bale, this rural hotel is one of Istria's best. Sophisticated, surrounded by fragrant herb gardens and shaded by tall old-growth trees, a traditional stone Istrian house has been stylishly converted by a Swiss-Croatian family. They offer excellent meals (150KN for a three-course dinner), elaborate

breakfasts (100KN) served till noon, and cooking courses.

Kod Kaštela (☎ 560 012; Savičenta 53; mains from 45KN) Right at the heart of town, with great views of the castle and square, this regional restaurant serves homemade pastas and tasty *pršut*. There are private rooms to rent above; inquire at the restaurant.

PAZIN
pop 5200

Most famous for the gaping chasm that inspired Jules Verne and for its medieval castle, Pazin is a workaday provincial town in central Istria. It deserves a stop mainly for the chasm and castle, but part of the appeal is its small-town feel and the lack of fashionable foreigners stomping its streets. Most of the town centre is given over to pedestrian-only areas, while rolling Istrian countryside surrounds the slightly unsightly outskirts.

Lying at the geographic heart of Istria, Pazin is the county's administrative seat and excellently connected by road and rail to virtually every other destination in the region. The hotel and restaurant pickings in town are skimpy, so you're better off visiting on a day trip since you're within an hour of most other Istrian towns. However, the countryside around Pazin offers plentiful activities, such as hiking, free climbing, biking and visiting local honey makers.

Orientation & Information

The town is relatively compact, stretching little more than a kilometre from the train station on the eastern end to the Kaštel on the western end, which is at the edge of Pazin Cave. The bus station is 200m west of the train station and the old part of town comprises the 200m leading up to the Kaštel.

The best source of information about Pazin is the **tourist office** (☎ 622 460; www.tzpazin.hr; Franine i Jurine 14; ⌚ 8.30am-6pm Jul & Aug, 8am-3pm Mon-Fri Sep-Jun), which also manages the entire central Istrian region. It distributes a map of hiking trails and honey spots (you can visit bee-keepers and taste their delicious acacia honey), and a brochure about wine cellars around Pazin. Another useful stop is **Futura Travel** (☎ /fax 621 045; www.futura-travel.hr; 25 Rujna 42; ⌚ 9am-7pm Mon-Fri, to 2pm Sat), which changes money, books excursions and provides regional information.

Sights

Pazin's most renowned site is undoubtedly the **Pazin Chasm** (☎ 622 220; www.pazinska-jama.com; ⌚ 10am-6pm Tue-Sun mid-May–mid-Oct, 10am-3pm Tue-Thu, noon-5pm Fri, 11am-5pm Sat & Sun mid-Oct–mid-May), a deep abyss of about 100m through which the Pazinčica River sinks into subterranean passages forming three underground lakes. Its shadowy depths inspired the imagination of Jules Verne (see boxed text, below), as well as numerous Croatian writers. Visitors can walk the 1200m path inside the abyss; there are two entrances, one by Hotel Lovac and one by the footbridge that spans the abyss 100m from the castle. Between October and May, entrance to the cave is free but there are no staff on site, so walking the trail is at your own risk; at other

---

MATHIAS SANDORF & THE PAZIN CHASM

The writer best known for going around the world in 80 days, into the centre of the earth and 20,000 leagues under the sea found inspiration in the centre of Istria. The French futurist-fantasist Jules Verne (1828–1905) set *Mathias Sandorf* (1885), one of his 27 books in the series Voyages Extraordinaires, in the castle and chasm of Pazin.

In the novel, later made into a movie, Count Mathias Sandorf and two cohorts are arrested by Austrian police for revolutionary activity and imprisoned in Pazin's castle. Sandorf escapes by climbing down a lightning rod but, struck by lightning, he tumbles down into the roaring Pazinčica River. He's carried along into the murky depths of the chasm, but our plucky hero holds on fast to a tree trunk and (phew!) six hours later the churning river deposits him at the tranquil entrance to the Limska Draga Fjord. He walks to Rovinj and is last seen jumping from a cliff into the sea amid a hail of bullets.

Verne never actually visited Pazin – he spun Sandorf's adventure from photos and travellers' accounts – but that hasn't stopped Pazin from celebrating it at every opportunity. There's a street named after Jules Verne, special Jules Verne days and a website for the Pazin-based **Jules Verne Club** (www.ice.hr/davors/jvclub.htm).

times of the year, admission costs 30/15KN per adult/concession. You can enter the cave with an expert speleologist (100KN), if arranged in advance through the tourist office. If the trip into the abyss doesn't appeal, there's a **viewing point** just outside the castle.

Looming over the chasm, Pazin's **Kaštel** (Trg Istarskog Razvoda 1) is the largest and best-preserved medieval structure in all Istria. First mentioned in 983, it is a medley of Romanesque, Gothic and Renaissance architecture. Within the castle, there are two museums. The **town museum** (☎ 622 220; adult/concession 15/8KN; ☺ 10am-6pm Tue-Sun mid-Apr–mid-Oct, 10am-3pm Tue-Thu, noon-5pm Fri, 11am-5pm Sat & Sun mid-Oct–mid-Apr) has a collection of medieval Istrian church bells, an exhibition about slave revolts and torture instruments in the dungeon. The **Ethnographic Museum** (☎ 622 220; www.emi.hr; adult/concession 15/8KN; ☺ 10am-6pm Tue-Sun mid-Apr–mid-Oct, 10am-3pm Tue-Thu, noon-5pm Fri, 11am-5pm Sat & Sun mid-Oct–mid-Apr) has about 4200 artefacts portraying traditional Istrian village life, including garments, tools and pottery.

Festivals & Events

The first Tuesday of the month is **Pazin Fair**, featuring products from all over Istria. The **Days of Jules Verne** in the last week of June is Pazin's way of honouring the writer that put Pazin on the cultural map. There are races, re-enactments from his novel, and journeys retracing the footsteps of Verne's hero Mathias Sandorf.

Sleeping & Eating

The tourist office helps arrange private accommodation, which is generally reasonably priced. Count on spending from about 100KN per person for a room.

Hotel Lovac (☎ /fax 624 324; tisadoo@inet.hr; Šime Kurelića 4; s/d 240/420KN; P) The late-1960s architecture of Pazin's only hotel, on the western edge of town, could be a hit, if only the rooms were done up right. Request a room with a valley view. The hotel restaurant serves acceptable food – especially as there are no notable restaurants in Pazin itself.

Getting There & Away

From the **bus station** (☎ 624 364; Šetalište Pazinske Gimnazije), there are services to Motovun (27KN, 40 minutes, two each weekday, none on weekends), Poreč (34KN, 45 minutes, seven daily), Pula (41KN, one hour, six daily), Rijeka

(53KN, one hour, nine daily), Rovinj (37KN, one to 1½ hours, five daily) and Zagreb (170KN to 195KN, three to four hours, 10 daily). Services are reduced on weekends. There's also a daily bus to Trieste (60KN to 70KN, two hours), except on Sundays.

Pazin **train station** (☎ 624 310; Od Stareh Kostanji 3b) has services to Buzet (20KN, 50 minutes, three daily), Ljubljana (107KN, 3½ to 4½ hours, two daily), with a transfer in Buzet or Divača, Pula (30KN, one hour, nine daily) and Zagreb (111KN to 127KN, five to eight hours, three daily). The Zagreb journey has a bus portion from Lupoglav to Rijeka. Services are reduced on weekends.

AROUND PAZIN
Gračišće

Gračišće is a sleepy medieval town and one of Istria's best-kept secrets, just 7km southeast of Pazin. Surrounded by rolling hills, its collection of ancient buildings includes the Venetian-Gothic **Salamon Palace** from the 15th century, the Romanesque **Church of St Euphemia**, and the **Church of St Mary** from 1425.

Most of these buildings are unrestored (although some work is being done) and the town is tiny. You won't need more than 30 minutes to circle it, but the ambience is truly lovely and you won't be treading on many people's trails. If you're feeling active, there's an 11.5km **hiking trail** that leads from here, which is well marked with signs.

Another reason to visit are the homemade Istrian specialities at **Konoba Marino** (☎ 687 081; mains from 35KN; ☺ closed Wed). It dishes out copious portions of *fuži* with game, *ombolo* (boneless pork loin) with cabbage, and a variety of truffle dishes in a cosy tavern. The same friendly owners run **Poli Luce** (☎ 687 081; www.konoba-marino-gracisce.hr; r per person 125KN, breakfast 25KN; P), a lovingly restored townhouse with charming rustic rooms.

BUZET
pop 500

It may not be the most fascinating town around, but in sleepy Buzet you get a whiff of the timeless grace of old Istria. Lying 39km northeast of Poreč over the Mirna River and first settled by the Romans, Buzet achieved real prominence under the Venetians who endowed it with walls, gates and several churches. With its grey-stone buildings in various stages of decay and renovation,

---

MAGIC MUSHROOMS?

The truffle trade is less like a business than a highly profitable cult. It revolves around an expensive, malodorous, subterranean fungus allegedly endowed with semimagical powers, which is picked in dark woods and then sent across borders to be sold for a small fortune. Devotees claim that once you've tasted this small, nut-shaped delicacy, all other flavours seem insipid.

There are 70 sorts of truffles in the world, of which 34 come from Europe. The traditional truffle-producing countries are Italy, France and Spain, but Istrian forests boast three sorts of black truffles as well as the big white truffle – one of the most prized in the world, at 34,000KN per kilo. Croatia's largest exporter of Istrian truffles is Zigante Tartufi, whose share of the overall Croatian export market is about 90%. In 1999 the company's owner Giancarlo Zigante, along with his dog Diana, found the world's largest truffle in Istria, weighing 1.31kg and making it into the *Guinness Book of World Records*.

The Istrian truffle business is relatively young. In 1932, when Istria was occupied by Italy, an Italian soldier from the truffle capital of Alba allegedly noticed vegetational similarities between his region and Istria. He returned after his military service with specially trained dogs who, after enough sniffing and digging, eventually uncovered the precious commodity.

Because no sign of the truffle appears above ground, no human can spot it, so dogs (or, traditionally, pigs) are the key to a successful truffle hunt. Istrian truffle-hunting dogs *(breks)* may be mongrels, but they are highly trained. Puppies begin their training at two months, but only about 20% of them go on to have fully fledged careers as truffle trackers.

The truffle-hunting season starts in October and continues for three months, during which time at least 3000 people and 9000 to 12,000 dogs wander around the damp Motovun forests. The epicentre of the truffle-growing region is the town of Buzet (opposite).

Some people believe truffles are an aphrodisiac, though scientific research has failed to prove this. Conduct your own experiment: have a truffle feast, dim the lights, put on some nice music and see what happens.

---

and the cobblestone streets nearly deserted (most of Buzet's residents resettled at the foot of the hill in the unbecoming new part of town long ago), the old town is a quiet but atmospheric place.

In addition to a quick wander around the maze of Buzet's narrow streets and squares, the other reason to come here is the glorious truffle. Self-dubbed the city of truffles, Buzet takes its title seriously. Lying at the epicentre of the truffle-growing region, it offers a variety of ways to celebrate the smelly fungus, from sampling it at the old town's excellent restaurant to various truffle-related activities. The best event is the **Festival of Subotina** on the second Saturday in September. Marking the start of the white truffle season (which lasts through November), the pinnacle of this event is the preparation of a giant truffle omelette (with over 2000 eggs and 10kg of truffles!) in a 1000kg pan.

Orientation & Information

Most commerce is in the new Fontana section of town at the foot of the hilltop old town. Trg Fontana is the small central square, with a few

cafés and shops. If you have wheels, you must park your car by the cemetery on the hill and make the 10-minute walk up to the old town.

The **tourist office** (☎ /fax 662 343; www.tz-buzet.hr; Trg Fontana 7/1; ⏱ 8am-3pm Mon-Fri, 9am-2pm Sat) has info about accommodation, plentiful maps and brochures about wine, olive oil and truffle roads throughout the region, and information on various activities such as hiking and biking. There's an ATM at **Erste Banka** (Trg Fontana 8).

Sights & Activities

The main sight in Buzet is the **Regional Museum** (Zavičajni Muzej Buzet; ☎ 662 792; Ulica Rašporskih Kapetana 5; adult/child 10/5KN; ⏱ 11am-3pm Mon-Fri, by appointment Sat & Sun), housed inside a 17th-century palace. The museum displays a collection of prehistoric and Roman artefacts as well as some ethnological items such as field tools and folk costumes.

On a square a few metres north of the museum is an exquisite **baroque well**, which was restored in 1789 and sports a Venetian lion relief. Other sights to check out, all well marked with English plaques, are the **man- neristic portal** from the 17th century and the

ISTRIA

parish **Church of the Blessed Virgin Mary** at the town's entrance.

Stock up on truffles in various shapes and forms – whole, hand-sliced, puréed, with olives or mushrooms – at the **Zigante Tartufi** (☎ 663 340; www.zigantetartufi.com; ☒ 9am-9pm Jun-Aug) shop on Trg Fontana.

If you want to experience truffle-hunting, contact the friendly **Karlić family** (☎ 667 304; Paladini 14), who can arrange such a trip; request a tour in English ahead of time. The tour includes a story about truffles, cheese and truffle tasting, and then a hunt in the forest that lasts up to two hours (150KN per person).

Sleeping & Eating

A number of farmhouses have rooms and apartments to rent surround Buzet. The tourist office has details and contact information; prices start at 100KN per person. There is only one hotel in town.

Hotel Fontana (☎ 662 615; www.hotelfontanabuzet .com; Trg Fontana 1; s/d 280/400KN; **P**) Housed in a 1970s concrete box of a building, the carpeted rooms here call for some serious love and care. At least all (but three) have balconies and the red-and-white decor cheers things up a bit.

Stara Oštarija (☎ 694 003; Petra Flega 5; mains from 55KN; ☒ closed Tue) This is the place to try truffles in the old town, with truffle dishes starting at 130KN. For a splurge, order a slow-food truffle menu of six courses (645KN for two). It even has ice cream with olive oil and truffles! The classy place has views of the valley below.

Getting There & Away

Buzet is connected by bus with Poreč (41KN to 69KN, 1½ hours, two daily), Rijeka (48KN, one hour, five daily) and Pula (60KN, two hours, two daily). There is no bus station in town, but buses stop by the first streetlight in Fontana, on Riječka; the tourist office has schedules.

The **train station** (☎ 662 899) is 6km east of the town centre, but there's no public transport so you'll have to find your own way on foot or by taxi. There is a train to Pula (47KN, two hours, six daily) and Ljubljana (88KN, 2½ to three hours, two daily). All services are reduced on weekends.

AROUND BUZET

The rolling hills, woods, pastures and vineyards southeast of Buzet make for a memorably scenic drive. Off the main road lie two villages worth a visit. Small and sleepy **Roč**,

8km southeast of Buzet, is snug within its 15th-century walls. A meander will reveal the Romanesque **Church of St Anthony** (Crkva Svetog Antuna), a 15th-century **Renaissance house** in the square next to the church, and a **Roman lapidarium** within the town gate. The **tourist office** (☒ 10am 5pm Sat & Sun Easter Jun, 10am 7pm Tue-Sun Jul-Sep) has keys to all the town's churches, if you want to see the interiors.

Roč slumbers most of the year, roused only by the annual **Accordion Festival** on the second weekend in May, which gathers accordion players from Croatia, Italy and Slovenia.

One of the town's stone buildings houses a regional restaurant, **Ročka Konoba** (☎ 666 451; mains from 35KN; ☒ closed Mon). With an interior fireplace and outdoor tables overlooking a wooded valley, you can discover Istrian specialities such as *fuži*, homemade sausages and *maneštra*.

Outside Roč is **Glagolitic Alley**, a series of 11 outdoor sculptures placed along the road commemorating the area's importance as a centre of the Glagolitic alphabet. Running for 7km to the southwest, the lane ends in **Hum**, a beautifully preserved place that bills itself as the world's smallest town, with a permanent population of 17. Legend has it that the giants who built Istria had only a few stones left over and they used them to build Hum.

In summer, this tiny and adorable town gets a steady stream of visitors who come to meander around the narrow lanes and to visit the **Town Museum** (Gradski Muzej; ☎ 660 054; admission free; ☒ 11am-7pm Jun-Sep, sporadic hr Oct-May), which displays some old village tools but serves more as a souvenir shop. It takes just 30 minutes to see the town on a self-guided tour, as each church and building is marked with informative multilingual plaques. If the town gates happen to be closed, just push them to get in. Don't miss the 12th-century frescoes in the Romanesque **Chapel of St Jerome** (Crkvica Svetog Jerolima), which depict the life of Jesus with unusually vivid colours. The chapel, by the cemetery outside the town gates, is locked, but you can get the key at the town inn, Humska Konoba.

That very inn is reason enough to come to Hum. **Humska Konoba** (☎ 660 005; Hum 2; mains 25-38KN; ☒ closed Mon Nov-Mar) not only serves first-rate Istrian mainstays, but also has a lovely outdoor terrace offering panoramic views. Start with a shot of sweet *biska* (white mistletoe grappa made according to an ancient Celtic recipe), then go on to *maneštra od bobića* (bean and fresh maize soup) and continue with truffle-topped *fuži* (70KN). Then have another shot of *biska*, and if you like the stuff, stock up at the Imela shop run by the restaurant owners; it lies where the village ends.

our pick **Toklarija** (☎ 663 031; Sovinjsko Polje 11; 6-course meal 500KN; ✿ closed Tue) Foodies shouldn't miss a slow-food meal here. It's in the hamlet of Sovinjsko Polje, up in the hills off the road from Buzet to Istarske Toplice (follow the signs for about 4km). At this beautifully converted 600-year-old olive mill, owner Nevio Sirotić serves delectable, homemade Istrian fare. A meal can take up to four hours in a well-timed string of delicate courses; the menu changes daily and features dried Istrian ham, porcini mushrooms, asparagus salad, truffles and juicy meats. Even the bread and pasta are homemade, and it's all paired with local wines such as *teran* and *malvazija*. Eat under the shade of cedar trees outside or ask for the cosy private room by the fireplace. And definitely reserve at least a few days ahead.

You really need your own wheels to explore this region. Roč is on the Pula–Buzet rail line, but the train station is 1500m east of the village. Hum is on the same line, but its train station is 5km away.

MOTOVUN
pop 590

Motovun is a captivating little town perched on a 277m-high hill in the Mirna River Valley, about 25km northeast of Poreč. It was the Venetians who decided to fortify the town in the 14th century, building two sets of thick walls. Within the walls, an atmospheric cluster of Romanesque and Gothic buildings now houses a smattering of artists studios. Newer houses have sprung up on the slopes leading to the old town, but you won't even notice, especially if you come for the popular film festival that takes place in Motovun every summer.

A Venetian lion scowls down from the outer gate, after which sprawls a terrace with a baroque loggia and a café's outside tables, perfect for watching the sun go down below the valley. A cheerier lion adorns the inner gate, which holds a long-running restaurant. Beyond the inner gate is a tree-shaded square with the town's only hotel, an old well and the Church of St Stephen.

Orientation & Information

If you come by car, there are three parking spots. The first one is at the foot of the village,

from where it's a steep 1km hike up to the city gates. Another parking area is 300m below the old town. The last one is for residents and hotel guests. Unless you're staying at the hotel, there's a 15KN charge per day from June to September at the other two parking lots.

The hotel's **tourist agency** (☎ 681 607; Trg Andrea Antico 8; ✿ 7.30am-3.30pm Mon-Fri) acts as the source of information about Motovun, since there is no official tourist office. There's an ATM just after the town entrance on the right.

Montana Tours (☎ 681 970; www.montonatours.com; Kanal 10; ✿ 4-7pm) is another great source of info; it can help with accommodation in central Istria, rural stays and private apartments.

Sights & Activities

The town highlight is the Renaissance **Church of St Stephen** (Svetog Stjepana; Trg Andrea Antico). Designed by Venetian artist Andrea Palladio, it's currently under long-term renovation. Along the inner wall that encloses the old town rises a 16th-century **bell tower** (admission 5KN; ✿ 10am-5pm), which you can climb for a magnificent view.

Be sure to walk on the outer walls of the ramparts for memorable vistas over vineyards, fields and oak woods below. There are a number of galleries and shops before you enter the old town and between the town gates, including a wine-tasting shop and another Zigante food store.

The nearby **Motovun Ranch** (☎ 098 411 404; www.motovun-ranch.com) offers horse-riding lessons (125KN per 50 minutes), two-hour rides along the Mirna River (100KN) and longer excursions through Istria's interior.

Festivals & Events

The **Motovun Film Festival** (www.motovunfilm festival.com) presents a roster of independent and avant-garde films in late July/early August. Over the 10 years since its inception, this small event has grown pretty popular and now attracts quite a crowd, with nonstop outdoor and indoor screenings, concerts and parties.

Sleeping & Eating

Hotel Kaštel (☎ 681 607; www.hotel-kastel-motovun .hr; Trg Andrea Antico 7; s low-high 308-352KN, d 506-594KN; Ⓟ 🖳) The town's only hotel is in a restored stone building with 28 simply furnished rooms. For 100KN more, get room 202 with a balcony overlooking the leafy square. There's a good restaurant offering truffles and Istrian wines, and a wellness centre is being built.

ISTRIA'S TOP RURAL RETREATS

Agritourism is an increasingly popular accommodation option in Istria's interior. Some of these residences are actual farms engaged in producing wine, vegetables and poultry, some are upmarket country houses with rustic rooms to let, while others are plush modern villas with swimming pools. Whatever you choose, the highlights are wholesome food, and hiking and biking opportunities.

The Istrian tourist office has issued a brochure with photos and information about rural holidays throughout Istria; you can also consult www.istra.com/agroturizam. For most of these lodgings, you'll need your own car, as many are located in the middle of nowhere. There's often a supplement for stays under three nights.

At **Agroturizam Ograde** (☎ 693 035; www.agroturizam-ograde.hr; Katun Lindarski 60; per person 140KN), in the village of Katun Lindarski, 10km south of Pazin, you'll hang out with horses, sheep, chickens, ducks and donkeys. Accommodation is simple, with shared bathrooms, and the food a real-deal affair in a dark and cool *konoba* with veggies from the garden, home-cured meats and wine from the cellar. There's a newer building out the back, with two apartments and a pool.

Agroturizam San Mauro (☎ 779 033; Sv Mauro 157; per person 165KN), near the hilltop town of Momjan, 5km from Buje, specialises in tastings of its award-winning wines (40KN), truffle dishes (the sweet *tartufone* cake is a delight!) and homemade jams, honeys and juices that you get to sample for breakfast. Some of the rooms have sea vistas and terraces. The two pigs that roam around, Jack and Gigi, are truffle-hunting retirees.

At the higher end of the scale sits **San Rocco** (☎ 725 000; www.san-rocco.hr; Srednja Ulica 2; d low-high 860-1000KN; P X 🖳 🖳), a top boutique hotel in the village of Brtonigla near Buje. This beautifully designed rural hideaway has 12 stylish rooms – no two are alike, but all are equipped with modern conveniences and graced with original detail. There's an outdoor swimming pool, a top-rated restaurant and a small spa.

Casa Romantica Parenzana (☎ 777 460; www.parenzana.com.hr; Volpia 3; s low-high 270-307KN, d 468-540KN; P 🖳) is another notable rural hotel, 3km from Buje in the village of Volpia. It features 16 rooms with rustic wood and stone decor, and a *konoba* (closed Tuesday), popular for its Istrian food such as *čripnja* (roast meat or fish cooked with potatoes in a cast-iron pot over an open fire). There's wireless internet, bike rental (70KN per day) and tours on request.

Stancija 1904, near Svetvinčenat, also fits the bill as a top rural retreat; see p176.

Mondo (☎ 681 791; Barbacan 1; mains from 55KN; 🕑 closed Tue) Just before the outer town gate, this little tavern had a loyal following in its former guise as Barbacan. It's since lost some of its allure, but the Istrian mainstays are still decent quality. Try the polenta with cheese and truffles.

Pod Voltom (☎ 681 923; Trg Josefa Ressela 6; mains from 55KN; 🕑 closed Wed) In a vaulted space within the town gates, just below the hotel, this wood-beamed place serves simple down-home Istrian cuisine and pricier truffle dishes. Try the steak carpaccio with fresh truffles.

Restaurant Zigante (☎ 664 302; www.zigantetartufi .com; Livade 7, Livade; mains from 160KN) Gourmets from afar come to this destination restaurant, repeatedly named one of Croatia's top 10, a few kilometres below Motovun in the village of Livade. Expect five-star fancy dining, with truffles as the showcase – celery and black truffles cappuccino, pigeon with black truffles, even tiramisu with black truffles… Set menus range from 440KN

to 715KN. The complex also has a few luxury rooms to rent, and a shop next door.

Getting There & Away

It's not easy to visit Motovun without your own car, but there are bus connections, on weekdays only, from Pazin (27KN, 40 minutes, two daily) and Poreč (29KN, 45 minutes, one daily).

ISTARSKE TOPLICE

Dating from the Roman era, **Istarske Toplice** (www.istarske-toplice.hr) is one of Croatia's oldest and most scenic thermal spas. Beneath an 85m-high cliff and surrounded by greenery, the complex features a concrete-box-style hotel and a new wellness centre. The rotten-egg smell is due to the large outdoor pool with a high sulphur content, where temperatures reach 34°C. The thermal waters are said to help rheumatism, skin diseases and respiratory tract disorders. Stressed-out folks can take advantage of acupuncture (125KN), saunas (60KN), various massages – from aromatherapy (300KN per hour) to hydro-massage (150KN per 30 minutes) – and beauty treatments (from 40KN), or just paddle around in the pool (25KN).

Hotel Terme Mirna (☎ 603 000; www.istarske-toplice.hr; Svetog Stjepana 60; s/d 290/500KN; **P**) doesn't boast much character in its spruced-up rooms, but it does offer a variety of good-value, all-inclusive packages. There are also hiking, biking and climbing opportunities in the surrounding forest and various excursions to nearby villages.

There's no public transport, but the spa is easily accessible by road, only 10km north of Motovun and 11km south of Buzet on the main road that connects the two towns.

GROŽNJAN
pop 193

Until the mid-1960s, Grožnjan, 27km northeast of Poreč, was slipping towards oblivion. First mentioned in 1102, this hilltop town was a strategically important fortress for the 14th-century Venetians. They created a system of ramparts and gates, and built a loggia, a granary and several fine churches. With the collapse of the Venetian empire in the 18th century, Grožnjan suffered a decline in its importance and population.

In 1965 sculptor Aleksandar Rukavina and a small group of other artists 'discovered' the crumbling medieval appeal of Grožnjan and began setting up studios in the abandoned buildings. As the town crawled back to life, it attracted the attention of Jeunesses Musicales International, an international training program for young musicians. In 1969 a summer school for musicians, Jeunesses Musicales Croatia, was established in Grožnjan and it has been going strong ever since. Each year there are music, orchestra and ballet courses and recitals. Throughout the entire summer, concerts and musical events are held almost daily, and you can overhear the musicians practising while you browse the many craft shops and galleries.

Orientation & Information
The tiny town is a jumble of crooked lanes and leafy squares. Near the centre is the **tourist office** (☎ 776349; www.tz-groznjan.hr; Umberta Gorjana 3; 8am-4pm Mon-Fri), which provides a list of private accommodation options in and around town and a small map with a list of galleries.

Sights & Activities
The Renaissance **loggia** is immediately to the right of the town gate by the tourist office. Keep going and on your right you'll see the baroque Spinotti Morteani Palace, its patio taken over by the outdoor tables of the **Zigante Tartufi** (☎ 721 998; www.zigantetartufi.com; Umberta Gorjana 5) shop and its adjacent wine bar. Next on the right comes the **Kaštel**, where many concerts are held. The town is dominated by the yellow sandstone bell tower of the **Church of St Vitus, St Modest & St Crescentia**, which was built in the 14th century and renovated in baroque style in 1770.

There are over 30 galleries and studios scattered around town; most are open daily from May to September. **City Gallery Fonticus** (Gradska Galerija Fonticus; ☎ 776349; www.gallery-fonticus-groznjan.net; Trg Lođe 3; 10am-1pm & 5-8pm Tue-Sun) promotes recent work of Croatian and some international artists. It also has a small display of heraldic paraphernalia that includes helmets, insignia and escutcheon.

Festivals & Events
Summer music concerts are organised by the **International Cultural Centre of Jeunesses Musicales Croatia** (☎ 776 223; www.hgm.hr, in Croatian). The concerts are free and no reservations are necessary. They are usually held in the church, main square, loggia or Kaštel.

Sleeping & Eating
There are no hotels in Grožnjan, but the tourist office can put you in touch with private room owners. Count on spending about 100KN per person.

Bastia (☎ 776 370; 1 Svibnja 1; mains from 45KN) The town's oldest restaurant sits on the verdant main square. The decor is bright and cheerful; the menu extensive and heavy on truffles.

Café Vero (Trg Cornera 3) This café-bar at the end of the village has a terrace with wooden tables offering marvellous valley views below.

Getting There & Away
Buses to Grožnjan only coincide with school terms, so there aren't any direct buses from late June to early September when most kids are on school holidays. If you're driving from Motovun, do not take the first marked turn-off for Grožnjan as it's unpaved and takes a lot longer. Continue along the road for another kilometre or so until you get to another sign for Grožnjan – this is a far better approach.

ISTRIA

Northern Dalmatia

The Zadar and Šibenik regions make up northern Dalmatia, an area that's ideal for the discerning traveller, and those wanting to discover a part of the coast that's less of a victim to hordes of seasonal tourists. This is also great off-the-beaten-track territory, with the islands of Pag and Dugi Otok remaining tranquil even in the busiest of summer seasons. Check out the beauty of Krka National Park where the dry karstic interior is divided by the Krka River, connecting the coastal bay with the splendid Krka waterfalls, and feel like a true explorer on the remote and unvisited Kornati Islands – aside from excellent swimming, both destinations have fantastic hiking opportunities. Croatia's two major national parks are here, too. Paklenica National Park is the best in the country for hiking and rock climbing, while the waterfalls and lakes of Plitvice Lakes National Park are a watery, verdant heaven.

On the urban side there's the town of Zadar, a fascinating coastal city filled with museums, Roman ruins, good dining and excellent nightlife. Its relative lack of tourism means that this is a coastal town that still lives and breathes for its inhabitants. Nearby, Šibenik is up and coming with a vengeance, flaunting an extraordinary Renaissance centre, interesting new museums and some great gastronomy, and finally shedding its postwar melancholy.

Northern Dalmatia is a great mix of nature, beaches, good cities and tonnes of exploring opportunities that'll satiate the most ravenous of hungers for new parts of Croatia.

HIGHLIGHTS

- Discovering **Zadar** (opposite), one of the coast's loveliest and most underrated towns
- Partying at **the Garden** (p194), a fantastic venue if ever there was one
- Listening to Zadar's haunting **Sea Organ** (p189)
- Diving from **Sali** (p202), on Dugi Otok
- Taking a wet walk through **Plitvice Lakes National Park** (p195) or swimming in a lake in **Krka National Park** (p212)
- Visiting the village and beaches of **Primošten** (see boxed text, p213)

Plitvice Lakes National Park ★

★ Zadar

Krka National Park ★

Sali ★

Primošten ★

■ TELEPHONE CODE: 022, 023

ZADAR REGION

The Zadar region is a great place to get to know a different side of Croatia. There's the beautiful town itself, the amazing national parks of Plitvice and Paklenica, and the gorgeous island of Ugljan.

ZADAR

☎ 023 / pop 69,200

It's hard to solve the mystery of why Zadar (ancient Zara), the main city of northern Dalmatia, is an underrated tourist destination. Is it because it has a compact, marble, traffic-free old town that follows the old Roman street plan and contains Roman ruins and medieval

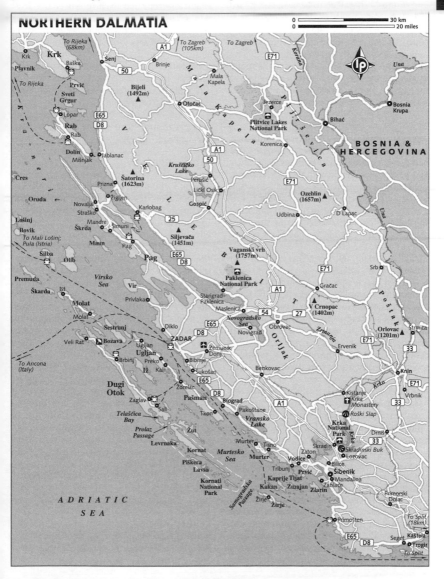

NORTHERN DALMATIA

churches? Or could it be because it's recently been dubbed Croatia's 'city of cool' for its clubs, bars and festivals run by international music stars? Perhaps it's the lively street life, one of Dalmatia's best markets, the busy cafés and good food? Or maybe it's the unusual attractions such as the incredible Sea Organ and the Sun Salutation, a pair of sights – and sounds – that need to be seen and heard to be believed.

Zadar is a city to behold on the Dalmatian coast. Its cultural and entertainment offerings are growing by the year, and with one of Europe's biggest budget airlines (Ryanair) starting to fly into its airport, it's safe to say that Zadar is not going to remain off the beaten track for much longer.

History

Zadar was inhabited by the Illyrian Liburnian tribe as early as the 9th century BC. At the end of the 3rd century BC, the Romans began their 200-year-long struggle with the Illyrians and, by the 1st century BC, Zadar had become a Roman colony. It wasn't a particularly important town for the Romans, but when the Empire was divided Zadar became the capital of Byzantine Dalmatia. The Slavs settled in the city in the 6th and 7th centuries, and Zadar eventually fell under the authority of Croatian-Hungarian kings.

The rise of the Venetian empire in the mid-12th century meant that for the next 200 years Zadar was subjected to relentless assault by Venetians seeking to expand their hold on Adriatic trading interests. There were four unsuccessful citizens' uprisings in the 12th century, but in 1202 the Venetians managed to sack the city and expel its citizens with the help of French Crusaders. The people of Zadar continued to rebel throughout the 13th and 14th centuries, with the help of Croatian-Hungarian kings, but the city was finally sold to Venice in 1409 along with the rest of Dalmatia.

Zadar's economic growth declined under Venetian rule because of Turkish attacks and frequent Veneto-Turkish wars, the result of which was the building of the city walls in the 16th century. With the fall of Venice in 1797, the city passed to Austrian rule. The Austrians imported more Italians to co-administer the city with Zadar's Italianised ruling aristocracy. Italian influence endured well into the 20th century, with Zadar being excluded from the Kingdom of Serbs, Croats and Slovenes and remaining an Italian province. When Italy capitulated to the Allies in 1943, the city was occupied by the Germans and then bombed to smithereens by the Allies; almost 60% of the old town was destroyed. The city was rebuilt following the original street plan.

History repeated itself in November 1991 when Yugoslav rockets launched an attack on Zadar, keeping it under siege for three months. The city's residents were virtually imprisoned in their homes with insufficient food and water. Although the Serb gunners were pushed back by the Croatian army in 1993, the city remains receptive to nationalists and flag-wavers.

No war wounds are visible, however, and Zadar's narrow, traffic-free marble streets are again full of life.

Orientation

Zadar occupies a long peninsula (4km long and only 500m wide), which separates Jazine Harbour on the east from the Zadarski Channel on the west. The old town lies on the northwestern part of the peninsula and encompasses the port and Jazine Bay.

Within the old town, you'll find all of the city's museums, churches and monuments. Most travel agencies are along the town's main commercial street, Široka. The Jadrolinija boats are lined up on the northeastern harbour, which is connected by a footbridge across Jazine Harbour to Obala Kneza Branimira. Continuing northeast you'll come to the marina and then the 'tourist zone' of Borik, with the youth hostel and lots of hotels, about 3km from the old town. The train and bus stations are a 15-minute walk southeast of the harbour and old town. From the train and bus stations take either Kralja Dmitra Zvonimira or Zrinsko-Frankopanska to the old town.

Information

INTERNET ACCESS

Arsenal (☎ 253 833; www.arsenalzadar.com; Trg Tri Bunara 1; per hr 30KN)

Internet Spot (Varoška 3; per hr 30KN)

LEFT LUGGAGE

Garderoba (per day 15KN) bus station (☺ 6am-10pm Mon-Fri); Jadrolinija dock (☺ 7am-8pm Mon-Fri, to 3pm Sat); train station (☺ 24hr)

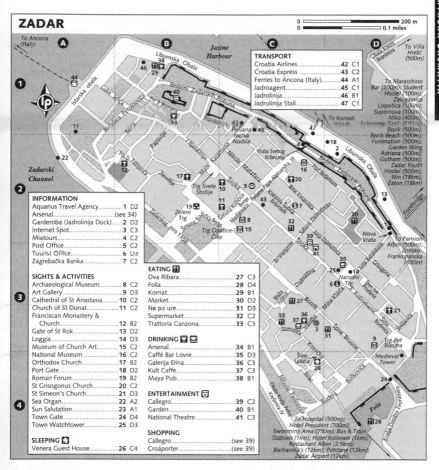

ZADAR

MEDICAL SERVICES

Hospital (☎ 315 677; Bože Peričića 5)

MONEY

Travel agencies also change money and there's an exchange office and ATM at the bus station. There are plenty of ATMs in town, with one at **Zagrebačka Banka** (Knezova Šubića Bribirskih 4), where you can also change money.

POST

Post office (Poljana Pape Aleksandra III; ☽ 8am-7pm Mon-Sat, to 2pm Sun) You can make phone calls here.

TOURIST INFORMATION

Tourist office (☎ 316 166; www.tzzadar.hr; Mihe Klaića 5; ☽ 8am-8pm Mon-Sat, to 1pm Sun Jun-Sep, 8am-6pm Mon-Sat Oct-May) The main information centre. Ask for the free *Zadar City Guide*.

TRAVEL AGENCIES

Aquarius Travel Agency (☎ /fax 212 919; www .juresko.hr; Nova Vrata bb; ☽ 8am-7pm) Books accommodation and excursions.

Miatours (☎ /fax 212 788; www.miatours.hr; Vrata Svetog Krševana; ☽ 8am-7pm Mon-Sat) Arranges accommodation and excursions.

Sights
CITY WALLS

A tour of the city walls provides a good insight into Zadar's history. Start with the eastern walls near the footbridge, the only remains of the ancient Roman and early medieval fortifications (most of the walls were built under Venetian rule). Nearby are four old city gates – northwest is the **Gate of St Rok**, then the **Port Gate**. The latter was built in 1573, and still sports the Venetian lion and part of a Roman triumphal arch, and has a memorial inscription of the 1571 Battle of Lepanto in which the Austrians delivered a decisive blow to the Turkish navy. In the southeast is the **Town Gate**, the most elaborate of all and built under the Venetian administration in 1543. Its Renaissance-style decorations include St Krževan on horseback, the Venetian lion, inscriptions and coats of arms. The fourth gate is at Trg Pet Bunara.

TRG PET BUNARA

Trg Pet Bunara or 'Five Wells Sq', behind St Simeon's Church, was built in 1574 on the site of a former moat and contains a cistern with five wells that supplied Zadar with water until 1838. Its smaller cousin, **Trg Tri Bunara** (Three Wells Sq), sits right on the other side of town and sports the excellent Arsenal (p193). This refurbished shipping warehouse lay in ruins for years before being turned into a cultural centre containing a bar, restaurant, several shops (music, food, wine), a tourist office and a stage that hosts theatre, live music and any number of shows. Just off the square is the Garden bar and club (p194), making this area a mini cultural hub.

ST SIMEON'S CHURCH

This **church** (Crkva Svetog Šime; ☎ 211 705; Trg Šime Budinica; ✹ 8am-noon & 6-8pm Jun-Sep) was reconstructed in the 16th and 17th centuries on the site of an earlier church. The sarcophagus of St Simeon is a masterpiece of medieval goldsmith work. Commissioned in 1377, the coffin is made of cedar and covered inside and out with finely executed gold-plated silver reliefs. The middle relief showing Christ's presentation in the Temple is a copy of Giotto's fresco from *Capella dell'Arena* in Padua, Italy. Other reliefs depict scenes from the lives of the saints and King Ludovic's visit to Zadar. The lid shows a reclining St Simeon.

NARODNI TRG

Narodni Trg was traditionally the centre of public life. The western side of the square is dominated by the late-Renaissance **Town Watchtower**, dating from 1562. The clock tower was built under the Austrian administration in 1798. Public proclamations and judgments were announced from the **loggia** across the square, which is now an exhibition space. Several hundred metres northwest of Narodni Trg is the **Orthodox Church**, behind which is a small Serbian neighbourhood.

CATHEDRAL OF ST ANASTASIA

The Romanesque **Cathedral of St Anastasia** (Katedrala Svete Stošije; ☎ 251 708; Trg Svete Stošije), near the Church of St Donat, was built in the 12th and 13th centuries on the site of an older church. Behind the richly decorated facade is an impressive three-nave interior marked by 13th-century wall paintings in the side apses. Notice the fresco of a gateway in the southern apse, which was used as a model for the door frame of the main portal. On the altar in the left apse is a marble sarcophagus containing the relics of St Anastasia, commissioned by Bishop Donat in the 9th century. The presbytery contains choir stalls lavishly carved by the Venetian artist Matej Morozon in the 15th century. The cathedral was badly bombed during WWII and has since been reconstructed.

CHURCH OF ST DONAT & ROMAN RUINS

The main places of interest are near the circular **Church of St Donat** (Crkva Svetog Donata; ☎ 250 516; Šimuna Kožičića Benje; admission 10KN; ✹ 9.30am-2pm & 4-6pm Mar-Oct), one of the most outstanding monuments in Dalmatia. Dating from the beginning of the 9th century, it was named after Bishop Donat who allegedly had it built following the style of early Byzantine architecture. The unusual circular ground plan is especially visible on the southern side because the southern annexe is missing. The church was built over the **Roman forum**, which was constructed between the 1st century BC and the 3rd century AD. A few architectural fragments are preserved and two complete pillars are built into the church. The original floors were removed, and now slabs from the ancient forum are clearly visible. Notice the Latin inscriptions on the remains of the Roman sacrificial altars.

Outside the church on the northwestern side is a pillar from the Roman era that served as a 'shame post' in the Middle Ages, where wrongdoers were chained and publicly humiliated. The western side of the church has more Roman remains, including pillars with reliefs of the mythical figures Jupiter, Amon and Medusa. Underneath, you can see the remains of the altars used in pagan blood sacrifices. It is believed that this area was a temple dedicated to Jupiter, Juno and Minerva, and dates from the 1st century BC.

ARCHAEOLOGICAL MUSEUM

The **Archaeological Museum** (Arheološki Muzej; ☎ 250 516; Trg Opatice Čike 1; ⏰ 9am-1pm & 5-7pm Mon-Fri, 9am-1pm Sat) was closed for refurbishment at the time of research. It holds pottery fragments dating back to the Neolithic Age; bronze swords, jewellery and pottery from the Liburnian era; a model of Zadar as it existed in Roman times; and statues of emperors Tiberius and Augustus.

MUSEUM OF CHURCH ART

The outstanding **Museum of Church Art** (☎ 211 545; Trg Opatice Čike bb; adult/student 20/10KN; ⏰ 10am-12.30pm & 5-8.30pm Mon-Sat, 10am-12.30pm Sun) in the Benedictine monastery opposite the Church of St Donat offers an impressive display of reliquaries and religious paintings. Along with the goldsmiths' works in the first hall, notice the 14th-century painting of the Madonna. She features again in the second hall, where the most notable works of her are a marble sculpture and Paolo Veneziani's painting. On the 2nd floor you'll find 15th- and 16th-century sculptures and embroidery, and six pictures by the 15th-century Venetian painter Vittore Carpaccio.

ST GRISOGONUS CHURCH

This **church** (Crkva Svetog Krševana; Brne Krnarutića; ⏰ Mass only) is another beautiful structure, formerly part of a 12th-century Benedictine monastery that was destroyed by Allied bombs in 1944. It has a baroque altar constructed in 1701 and Byzantine frescoes on the northern wall and in the northern apse; unfortunately the frescoes in the southern apse are poorly preserved.

NATIONAL MUSEUM & ART GALLERY

The **museum** (Narodni Muzej; ☎ 251 851; Poljana Pape Aleksandra III; admission 10KN; ⏰ 9am-1pm Mon, Tue, Thu & Fri, 9am-1pm & 5-7pm Wed), in the Benedictine monastery of St Krževan's Church, is an excellent historical repository. It features scale models of Zadar from different periods, and old paintings and engravings of many coastal cities. The admission ticket will also get you into the local **Art Gallery** (☎ 211 174; Smiljanića; ⏰ 9am-noon & 5-8pm Mon-Fri, 9am-1pm Sat), which has a changing series of exhibitions highlighting local artists.

FRANCISCAN MONASTERY AND CHURCH

The **Franciscan Monastery & Church** (Samostan Svetog Frane; ☎ 250 468; Zadarskog mira 1358; admission free; ⏰ 7.30am-noon & 4.30-6pm) is the oldest Gothic church in Dalmatia. It was consecrated in 1280 and the interior has a number of Renaissance features such as the lovely Chapel of St Anthony, which contains a 15th-century wooden crucifix. In the sacristy a memorial tablet commemorates a seminal event in Zadar's history: the 1358 treaty under which Venice relinquished its rights to Dalmatia in favour of the Croatian-Hungarian king, Ludovic. The large Romanesque painted crucifix in the treasury behind the sacristy is worth seeing.

SEA ORGAN & SUN SALUTATION

Zadar's incredible (and the world's only) **Sea Organ** (Morske Orgulje), designed by local architect Nikola Bašić, is bound to be one of the more memorable sights you'll see in Croatia. Set within the perforated stone stairs that descend into the sea is a system of pipes and whistles that exudes wistful sighs when the movement of the sea pushes air through it. The effect is utterly unique and hypnotic and the 'music' is the loudest when a boat or ferry passes by. You can swim from the steps off the promenade and listen to the sound of the Sea Organ.

Right next to it is the **Sun Salutation** (Pozdrav Suncu), another wacky and wonderful Bašić creation. It's a 22m circle cut into the pavement, filled with 300 multilayered glass plates that collect the sun's energy during the day and, together with the wave energy that makes the Sea Organ's sound, produce a trippy light show from sunset to sunrise that's meant to simulate the solar system. Thanks to Croatia's many sunny days, the Sun Salutation is now collecting enough energy to power the entire seafront lighting system.

Activities

A great way to cross from the old town peninsula onto the mainland is to take the small wooden boats across the water, experiencing an ancient Zadar tradition, the *barkarioli* (see boxed text, p190) in the process.

There's a **swimming area** with diving boards, a small park and a café on the coastal promenade off Kralja Dmitra Zvonimira. Bordered by pine trees and small parks, the promenade takes you to a beach in front of Hotel Kolovare and then winds on for about a kilometre along the coast.

A BOAT TRIP DOWN MEMORY LANE *Vesna Marić*

The transporting of people on small wooden boats between Zadar's two ports is an 850-year-old tradition that's become somewhat redundant since the completion of the footbridge, but the boatmen, or *barkarioli* as they are locally known, aren't giving up their profession easily. And they don't have to: it is still the locals' favourite form of public transport. It's a short ride – some 80m in length, lasting only a few minutes – and cheap (4KN), and it beats the smelly bus. More than anything, it's romantic.

Seventy-year-old Karlo Sindičić has been a *barkariolo* all his life. He is tanned and sports aviator sunglasses and a little black sailor hat. I ask if he would tell me about his job and he nods an affirmative, helping me onto the rocking boat. I place my 4KN onto a little heap of coins and we sit, waiting for more passengers to get on so that Karlo can start rowing and, hopefully, talking. He looks a little like a rock star, aloof beneath the green-tinted shades. Then he says, 'I've been interviewed by all the big global media houses. CNN talked to me all the way back in Yugoslav times. It was their first ever program about Zadar and I was on it. Me and a nun.' I am impressed. I ask him if he thinks there's a future for the *barkarioli*. 'Oh yes,' he says, 'there are two young men lined up to start this summer.' What does it take to be a *barkariolo*? 'You've got to have at least one foreign language,' he says. 'I speak four myself. Foreigners take the boat sometimes and you've got to know how to chat to them.' Is the demand for crossing on a boat big? 'People still like it though it's not as popular as it was when I was younger. Now everyone drives around.' We get to the other side.

As I step off the boat, I notice the wind is up and I ask if they cross in all kinds of weather. He says that if it's too windy or rainy they stay put. 'It's too much risk; you don't want people tumbling into the water. Plus we'd get too wet on the boat all day. But we do work until midnight in the summer; it's lovely under the stars. We stop at six in the evening on winter days, though. But no matter what the season is, if the sea is calm, we're here at 6am every day!' he says, sitting down again and grabbing the oars. I thank Karlo and watch him row back to the other side of the harbour, feeling as though I've just tasted a slice of history.

You can rent a bike from **Supernova** (☎ 311 010; Obala Kneza Branimira 2a; ☻ 8.30am-12.30pm & 4.30-7.30pm Mon-Fri, 8.30am-1pm Sat) and see Zadar or any of the islands and surrounding national parks while pedalling.

Tours

Any of the many travel agencies around town can supply information on the tourist cruises to Telašćica Bay (p203) and the beautiful Kornati Islands (p214), which include lunch and a swim in the sea or a salt lake. As this is about the only way to see these 101 barren, uninhabited islands, islets and cliffs, it's worthwhile if you can spare the cash. Check with **Aquarius Travel Agency** (☎ /fax 212 919; www.juresko.hr; Nova Vrata bb; ☻ 8am-7pm) or **Miatours** (☎ /fax 212 788; www.miatours.hr; Vrata Svetog Krševana; ☻ 8am-7pm Mon-Sat), or go down to Liburnska Obala from where the excursion boats leave.

From Zadar you can also take an excursion to Paklenica National Park (p198), Krka National Park (p212) or Plitvice Lakes National Park (p195).

Festivals & Events

July to mid-August is a good time to be in Zadar. The **Zadar Dreams** (Zadar Snova; www.zadar snova.hr) theatrical festival takes over Zadar's parks and squares with offbeat theatrical happenings between 7 and 14 August.

The **Garden Festival** (www.thegardenzadar.com) has been running since 2006 in nearby Petrčane, and it's fast becoming one of the most beloved dance-music festivals in Croatia. According to the website, it focuses on 'quality rather than big names' and takes place in Barbarella's nightclub (p194), where you can swim, sunbathe or sit in the pine shade when you're not dancing to thumping music. It's held from 4 to 6 July.

Try to catch the **Full Moon Festival** on the night of the full moon in August. The quays are lit with torches and candlelight, while stalls sell local delicacies and the boats lining the quays become floating fish markets. It's something to see.

Other events include **Musical Evenings** (July) in the Church of St Donat and the **Choral Festival** (October).

Sleeping

There is one small guest house in town and a few private rooms available, but most visitors are dispatched to the 'tourist settlement' at Borik on the Puntamika bus (every 40 minutes from the bus station); here there are hotels, a hostel, a camping ground and many *sobe* (rooms available) signs. Most Borik hotels cater to package tourists, particularly families who flock to the all-inclusive family resort, Funimation (right), complete with an aqua park, tennis courts and more. Most are managed by the Austria-based **Falkensteiner group** (www.falkensteiner.com).

The travel agencies listed on p187 find private accommodation. Expect to pay about 150/200KN per person for a room with a shared/private bathroom. Very little is available in the old town, but you can find some decent deals in Borik.

Do not expect women advertising *sobe* to approach you as you disembark the bus, train or ferry.

BUDGET

Autocamp Borik (☎ 332 074; per adult low-high 36–53KN; per site 90–135KN; ☿ May-Oct) Steps away from Borik Beach, this camping ground is shaded by tall pines and has decent facilities. It's a better option than Zaton if you want to savour city pleasures.

Zaton (☎ 280 280; www.zaton.hr; Nin; per adult low-high 36–68KN; ☿ May-Sep) This is a huge campsite development on a sandy beach 16km northwest of Zadar in Nin, with a 5000-person capacity. It's not attractively landscaped – the terrain is flat and uninteresting – but the facilities are top notch and there are also apartments and mobile homes to rent. There are eight daily buses marked 'Zaton' from the bus station (fewer on weekends), which drop you off in Zaton village, about 1km from the grounds.

Zadar Youth Hostel (☎ 331 145; zadar@hfhs.hr; Obala Kneza Trpimira 76; per person €13; ☐) A great option for backpackers, with plain but clean rooms. Some have wooden floors that creak comfortingly. Many were renovated in 2006 and are quite modern. The service is friendly and multilingual and Borik Beach is just minutes away. There's internet access at 5KN for 15 minutes.

Student Hostel (☎ 224 840; Obala Kneza Branimira bb; dm 103KN; ☿ Jul & Aug) This student dormitory turns into a hostel in July and August. Its location is good – right across the footbridge and an easy trudge to the ferries and old town –

but do note its limited opening times for travellers. The three-bed rooms are clean, though a little cheerless.

MIDRANGE

Venera Guest House (☎ 214 098; www.hotel-venera-zd.hr; Šime Ljubića 4a; d low-high 300-450KN) Venera – also known as the Jović Guest House – is the centre's only option. Although the rooms are miniscule, have oversized wardrobes and no numbers on the doors, all have en suite bathrooms, the beds are good and the atmosphere is pretty relaxed. The price does not include breakfast. If you can't reach Gojko, the owner, you can book through Aquarius Travel Agency (p187).

Pansion Albin (☎ 331 137; www.albin.hr; Put Dikla 47; s low-high 324-390KN, d 432-580KN; **P** ⚡ ⚡) You'll find plenty of warmth and hospitality in this friendly, family-run *pension* (guest house). All the rooms are different and some have balconies. There's a gorgeous little pool surrounded by greenery and the in-house restaurant is decent. The beach is just a 15-minute walk away. It's great value.

our pick Villa Hrešć (☎ 337 570; www.villa-hresc.hr; Obala Kneza Trpimira 28; s low-high 550-650KN, d 750-850KN; **P** ⚡ ⚡) Zadar's loveliest midrange choice is in a cheery pink building on a bay. The stylish rooms are in pastel colours, the beds are luxurious dreaming spots, and as you lounge by the swimming pool you can admire views of the old town. The suites are excellent value, some with massive terraces. It's within walking distance of Zadar's restaurants, sights and nightlife.

Funimation (☎ 206 100; www.falkensteiner.com; Majstora Radovana 7; s low-high €77-177, d €112-234; ⚡ ⚡) With so many spa offerings at this large hotel, your skin will start to resemble a sea creature after you've tried all the steam rooms, saunas and pools – let alone the wonders of the 16 different thalassotherapy treatment rooms. The hotel is open year-round for spa lovers, but it really comes into its own in the summer months when the 'Falky Land' complex opens and kids' activities start up – there's tennis, volleyball, windsurfing and pool madness. So if you're after a family resort that caters to both kids and their (exhausted) parents, Funimation may just be the place for you.

TOP END

Hotel Kolovare (☎ 203 200; www.hotel-kolovare-zadar.t-com.hr; Bože Peričića 14; s low-high 550-750KN, d 760-1200KN; (P) (🏊)) A renovated old-socialist mammoth, the Kolovare has 230 unexciting but comfortable rooms, a swimming pool and a gym. It's near the beach, a 20-minute walk from town and close to the train and bus stations.

Hotel President (☎ 333 464; www.hotel-president .hr; Vladana Desnice 16; r per person low-high €125-400; (P) (❌) (🖳)) The plushest place in town is also the classiest in the traditional sense, with cherry wood furniture, gilded details and grown-up sophistication all round. The hotel restaurant, Vivaldi, is adorned with music scores from the 'Four Seasons'. It's very close to the beach and all the rooms have balconies.

ourpick Garden Wing Adriana (☎ 206 637; www .falkensteiner.com; Majstora Radovana 7; s low-high €144-204, d €216-312; (🕑) mid-May–Oct; (P) (❌) (🏊)) All the rooms in this gorgeously restored 19th-century villa, which was formerly known as Hotel Adriana Select, are termed 'junior suites' and they deliver on their promise of luxury. It's a super-relaxing place in Borik, with white furniture, rattan details, aromatic candles and tonnes of spa treatments. Oh, and there's a pool, four tennis courts and a wonderful beach at the end of the verdant garden. The staff are friendly and discreet.

Eating

Zalogajnica Ljepotica (☎ 311 288; Obala Kneza Branimira 4b; mains from 35KN) The cheapest place in town prepares three to four dishes a day at knock-out prices in a setting that would fit well in a Kaurismäki movie – you know, a rugged, lonesome diner with a pot-bellied chef/waiter who brings you a steaming dish with a somnolent look on his face. The food is great and home cooked, and the dishes are usually squid-ink risotto, tomato and seafood pasta, plus something meaty.

Trattoria Canzona (☎ 212 081; Stomorića 8; mains 40KN) A great little trattoria in the old town, with red-and-white chequered table cloths, friendly waiters and tonnes of locals who love the menu of daily specials. Try the delicious *pašticada* (beef stewed in wine and spices), which comes with juicy gnocchi, and accompany it with a crunchy green salad.

Na po ure (☎ 312 004; Špire Brusine 8; mains from 40KN) From shark to sardines, if it swims this unpretentious *konoba* (simple family-run restaurant) will grill it and serve it up with potatoes and fresh vegetables. You can also get a mean *pašticada*.

Dva Ribara (☎ 213 445; Blaža Jurjeva 1; mains from 40KN) Though it's been refurbished in a minimalist, cool style, away from its former 'fisherman's diner' look, the Two Fishermen still remains an old-school eatery when it comes to the menu. There's a wood-fired pizza oven – much appreciated by the locals – and meaty options dominate, though there are some fish and pasta dishes. There's a decent wine list, too.

Restaurant Albin (☎ 331 137; www.albin.hr; Put Dikla 47; mains 40-100KN) Local people usually head out to Borik when they want to eat out, and this fish restaurant, on the road to Borik at Pansion Albin, is one of the most popular establishments, with a spacious outdoor terrace.

Niko (☎ 337 888; www.hotel-niko.hr; Obala Kneza Domagoja 9; mains from 60KN) A real Zadar institution, Niko is loved for its daily fresh fish (grilled and sprinkled with smooth, aromatic olive oil), the long wine list, and its pasta and seafood dishes. A large terrace overlooks the shimmering Adriatic. Niko is in Puntamika, on the Borik peninsula.

ourpick Kornat (☎ 254 501; Liburnska Obala 6; mains from 70KN) This is without a doubt Zadar's best restaurant. It's elegant and spiffy, with wooden floors and modern furnishings, and the service is excellent, but it's the food that's the real knockout. There's the smooth Istrian truffle monkfish, a creamy squid and salmon risotto, and fresh fish (around 350KN per kilo) that's prepared with simple ingredients to maximum deliciousness. The house wine, Babić, is fantastic, and do leave room for a dessert – try the pistachio and caramel cheesecake.

ourpick Foša (☎ 314 421; Kralja Dmitra Zvonimira 2; mains from 80KN) Foša looks out on the narrow channel that runs alongside the city walls and takes its name from it. The restaurant also pays tribute to the Foša channel by serving fantastic fish caught in its waters, and the small stone terrace is one of Zadar's most gorgeous places to eat. The interior is slick and elegant and the service attentive and discreet. A great find.

SELF-CATERING

It's safe to say that Zadar's **market** ((🕑) 6am-3pm) is one of Croatia's best. If you're staying somewhere you can cook, you're in for a real treat of seasonal, local produce at cheap prices. Spring and early summer see gorgeous bunches of wild asparagus, while summers are cooled with juicy watermelons, cucumbers and bursting tomatoes. There's also mountains of peppery rocket, and the women who

---

WHAT'S THIS MARASCHINO, THEN?

You'll see its name so often around Zadar and there's no way you'll miss the beautiful distillery – a major city landmark – so you'll be forgiven for asking this question. Maraschino, you'll be glad to hear, is a very delicious drink, and something all locals will no doubt prompt you to try.

Maraschino's story started with the birth of the Dalmatian sour cherry – otherwise known as *maraska* – brought, some say, from the areas surrounding the Caspian Sea. The *maraska* is said to be sweeter, fleshier and more nutritious than any other cherry around, and it took keenly to growing by the Adriatic. It was originally used as a medicinal liquor and was first bottled by Dominican monks in the 16th century, but it soon caught on as a proper tipple and commercial distillation developed over the following two centuries.

But the real revolution happened in the 18th century, with the collapse of the Venetian republic. Zara (Zadar) became the capital of Dalmatia, and the Austrians, who took over, brought consuls and representatives from all over Europe. The consular representative for Sardinia, Girolamo Luxardo, arrived in Zadar and, with his wife, tasted the *maraska* liquor for the first time. Captivated by its taste, Luxardo's wife decided to try and perfect it, and her recipe was so successful that the couple established the first Luxardo distillery in 1821 – the famous Maraschino building. The third generation of Luxardos built a modern distillery, while the original old building, which is opposite the old town, was converted into office space.

During Yugoslav times, the Maraschino business was incorporated into the state, while the only surviving Luxardo family member moved his business to Veneto, in Italy. Today, Maraschino is privatised again, reaffirming its role as a major source of local employment. Despite the battering the production received during the recent war, there are once again hundreds of thousands of cherry trees blossoming in Zemunik, near Zadar airport, and the Maraschino tastes better than ever.

---

sell the stuff are keen to bargain. You'll find Pag cheese here, too (at around 80KN per half kilo), and inside the fish market you'll get the day's catch and more. Even if you're not self-catering, check it out just to store some delicious food memories.

There's also a **supermarket** (cnr Široka & Sabora Dalmatinske) that keeps long hours.

Drinking

There are plenty of places to drink in Zadar, from pavement cafés to cool bars, and most are full at all times in the summer. Don't miss tasting the local Maraschino cherry liquor (see boxed text, above).

our pick **Arsenal** (☎ 253 833; www.arsenalzadar.com; Trg Tri Bunara 1) A renovated shipping warehouse now hosts this brilliant cultural centre, with a large lounge-bar/restaurant/concert hall in the centre that has a small stage for live music and shows. Shops surround the central space, and people come in and out all day long, with young Zadrians frequenting the bar in the evenings. It's a great place for breakfast, too.

Galerija Đina (Varoška 2) Just off the main square, Đina's is an arty hang-out that serves good cocktails to a trendy crowd. It's electro music all the way, and a great place to start the night.

Kult Caffe (Stomorića 4) The Kult Caffe draws a young hip hop, heavy metal, rock'n'roll, hippy, punk – you name it – crowd, that hangs out on the shady terrace outside.

Maya Pub (☎ 251 716; Liburnska Obala 6) This is a real chill-out bar, with a hippie-ish decor and quiet electro music in the background. There's an imposing sculpture of Shiva that keeps an eye on the live concerts or the DJ, depending on who's got the stage for the night. It serves Guinness and Kilkenny beer, too.

Maraschino Bar (☎ 211 250; Obala Kneza Branimira 6) Sitting by the sport harbour, 100m east of the old town–mainland footbridge, and overlooking the sea, this is a relatively new bar with a spanking retro interior, cheerful clientele and friendly service. It serves croissants for breakfast, and the terrace is a great place to enjoy a coffee in the sun.

Caffé Bar Lovre (☎ 212 678; Narodni Trg 1) A gorgeous little café with a huge terrace on Narodni Trg (which mingles with some of the neighbouring cafés' terraces), Lovre has the advantage of having the remains of the 12th-century Church of St Lovre at the back. You can enter and wander around it, before or after your coffee. Croissants and other pastries make it perfect for a central breakfast or break from sightseeing.

Entertainment

NIGHTCLUBS

our pick **Garden** (☎ 450 907; www.thegardenzadar.com; Bedemi Zadarskih Pobuna; ☷ late May-Oct) One of the reasons many of Croatia's youngsters rate Zadar as 'a really cool place' is because it offers nightlife options unlike anywhere else – basically, it has the Garden. It's owned and run by UB40's producer Nick Colgan and drummer James Brown, who came to Zadar and liked it so much they decided to buy this traditional walled garden, install a superior sound system and invite their DJ friends to enliven the city's nightlife. They've never looked back. In fact, they've only looked forward and opened Barbarella's, the Garden's more isolated and therefore more rowdy sister. Daytimes here are relaxed, with board games and lots of lounging on the outdoor beds, while night time is when the fun really begins. Don't miss it if you're in town.

our pick **Barbarella's** (☎ 450 907; www.thegarden zadar.com; Punta Radman Put 8, Petrčane) Opened in May 2008, this is a more ambitious and spacious project for the Garden's owners, serving as the setting for the Garden Festival (p190) in July and lots of beach clubbing all through the summer. It's basically a 1970s retro structure that has been carefully refurbished and fitted with sound systems, beach bars and plenty of party space. The festival's Argonaut boat parties sell out sooner than you can say Barbarella's. There's also a hotel adjacent, incase you want to stay awhile.

Gotham (☎ 200 289; Marka Oreškovića 1; ☷ closed Mon) A 20-something crowd comes here for the go-go dancers, tropical fantasy and '70s nights.

THEATRE & CINEMA

National Theatre (☎ 314 552; Široka; ☷ 9am-5pm Mon-Fri) The box office sells tickets to the cultural programs advertised on posters outside.

Callegro (☎ 204 900; www.callegro.com; Široka 18; tickets 20-25KN) A brand new miniplex consisting of three cinema screens, Callegro is a favourite of Zadar's film lovers. You can see art-house films as well as Hollywood blockbusters at fantastically cheap prices in a sleek modern cinema. Films are in the original language, with Croatian subtitles.

Shopping

Callegro (above) is also a shopping centre, housing outlets for Lacoste, Calvin Klein and Ralph Lauren, as well as a **Croáporter** (www.cro-a -porter.hr) boutique, which promotes young Croatian designers. There's a café downstairs, too, with tables on Široka.

Getting There & Away

AIR

Zadar's airport is about 12km east of the town centre. The Croatia Airlines bus (20KN) meets all arrivals. A taxi costs about 175KN.

Croatia Airlines (☎ 250 101; www.croatiaairlines .hr; Poljana Natka Nodila 7; ☷ 8am-4pm Mon-Fri, 9am-noon Sat) has daily flights to Zagreb, and services internationally.

Ryanair (www.ryanair.com) flies to Zadar from London Stansted and Dublin airport.

BOAT

On the harbour, **Jadrolinija** (☎ 254 800; Liburnska Obala 7) has tickets for all local ferries, or you can buy ferry tickets from the Jadrolinija stall on the Jadrolinija dock. Buy international tickets from **Jadroagent** (☎ 211 447; jadroagent -zadar@zd.t-com.hr; Poljana Natka Nodila 4), just inside the city walls.

For information on boat connections to Italy, see p310.

BUS

Croatia Express (☎ 250 502; croatiae@zd.t-com.hr; Široka 14) sells tickets to Zagreb, Split and Trieste (Italy), plus many German cities.

The **bus station** (☎ 211 035; www.liburnija-zadar .hr, in Croatian) is a 10-minute walk from the centre and has buses to Zagreb (100KN to 140KN, 3½ to seven hours, 20 daily), Rijeka (145KN, five hours, six daily), Split (around 100KN, three hours, eight daily) and Dubrovnik (170KN to 210KN, eight hours, seven daily).

TRAIN

The **train station** (☎ 212 555; www.hznet.hr; Ante Starčevića 3) is adjacent to the bus station. There are five daily trains to Zagreb – two fast trains (150KN, seven hours) and three slower ones (134KN, 9¾ hours) that change at Knin – but the fast bus to Zagreb is quicker.

Getting Around

Buses run frequently from the bus station to the harbour and Borik. Buses marked 'Poluotok' run to the harbour and those marked 'Puntamika' (5) run to Borik. Tickets are 6KN and you can buy them at any newsstand or from the driver.

AROUND ZADAR
Ugljan
☎ 023

The island of Ugljan is easily accessible by boat from Zadar, making it a popular getaway for the locals and a kind of residential suburb for people who work in the city. The 50-sq-km island is densely populated, housing about 7500 people, and it can get crowded on summer weekends. There are few forests but many *macchia* (shrubs), some pines and a good deal of farmland with vegetable gardens, olive groves and vineyards. The eastern coast is the most indented and most developed part of the island, while the west is relatively deserted.

The port of entry is **Preko**, directly across from Zadar, with two small harbours and a ferry port. Although there's a town beach, the best beach is on the little island of **Galovac**, only 80m from the town centre. Small, pretty and wooded, Galovac has a Franciscan monastery dating from the 15th century. If you have your own car, you could visit **Ugljan village**, positioned on an indented bay with a sandy beach, the fishing village of **Kali** and the nearby islet of **Ošljak**, which is covered with pine and cypress trees.

Jadrolinija (www.jadrolinija.hr) runs hourly ferries between 5.30am and 11pm from Zadar to Preko (17KN, 25 minutes) year-round.

PLITVICE LAKES NATIONAL PARK
☎ 053

Plitvice Lakes National Park lies midway between Zagreb and Zadar. The 19.5 hectares of wooded hills enclose 16 turquoise lakes, which are linked by a series of waterfalls and cascades. Wooden footbridges follow the lakes and streams over, under and across the rumbling water for an exhilaratingly damp 18km. In 1979, Unesco proclaimed the Plitvice Lakes a World Heritage site, and the lakes and forests are carefully regulated to ensure their continued preservation.

The extraordinary natural beauty of the site merits at least a three-day visit, but you can experience a lot simply on a day trip from Zadar or Zagreb. There's no bad time to visit: in the spring the falls are flush with water, in summer the surrounding hills are greener, and in autumn there are fewer visitors and you'll be treated to the changing colours of leaves.

The lake system is divided into the upper and lower lakes. The upper lakes lying in a dolomite valley are the most impressive, surrounded by dense forests and interlinked by several gushing waterfalls. The lower lakes are smaller and shallower, surrounded only by sparse underbrush. Most of the water comes from the Bijela and Crna (White and Black) Rivers, which join south of Prošćansko Lake, but the lakes are also fed by underground springs. In turn, water disappears into the porous limestone at some points only to re-emerge in other places. All the water empties into the Korana River near Sastavci Falls.

The upper lakes are separated by dolomite barriers, which expand with the mosses and algae that absorb calcium carbonate as river water rushes through the karst. The encrusted plants grow on top of each other, forming travertine barriers and creating waterfalls. The lower lakes were formed by cavities created by the water of the upper lakes. They undergo a similar process, as travertine is constantly forming and reforming itself into new combinations so that the landscape is ever changing. This unique interaction of water, rock and plant life has continued more or less undisturbed since the last Ice Age.

The colours of the lakes also change constantly. From azure to bright green, deep blue or grey, the colours depend upon the quantity of minerals or organisms in the water, whether rain has deposited mud, and the angle of sunlight.

The luxuriant vegetation of the national park is another delight. The northeastern section of the park is covered with beech forests while the rest of it is covered with beech, fir, spruce and white pine dotted with patches of whitebeam, hornbeam and flowering ash, which change colour in autumn.

History
After prehistoric settlements, the first recorded inhabitants in the region were the Thracians who arrived in the 1st millennium BC, followed by the Illyrians and then the ubiquitous Romans who visited in 59 BC and stayed for 600 years. Slavs migrated to the area in the 7th century and were eventually organised into the feudal system that dominated the early Middle Ages. The Turks seized power in 1528 and when they were driven out 150 years later, the Austrians tried to attract new settlers by making it a feudal-free zone. The area became part of the Military Frontier (Vojna Krajina) and was settled by Vlachs and Morlachs who followed the Serbian Orthodox faith.

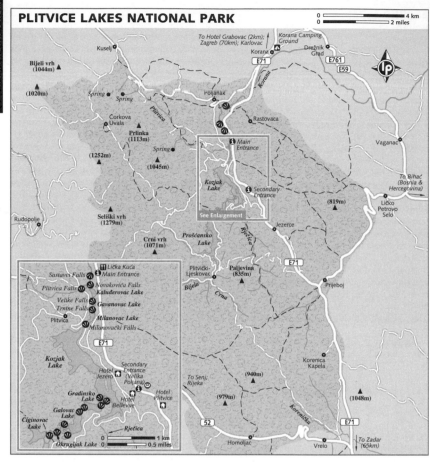

The tourism potential of the lakes was apparent even as early as 1896, when the first hotel was built. A preservation society founded in 1893 ensured the protection of the lake environment well into the 20th century. The boundaries of the national park were set in 1951 with a view towards minimising degradation and maximising tourism. Before the recent 1991 war, the lakes were a major tourist attraction, but their presence within the Serb-dominated Krajina region meant trouble was inevitable when former Yugoslavia began to crack up.

The civil war in former Yugoslavia actually began in Plitvice on 31 March 1991, when rebel Serbs from the Krajina region took control of the park headquarters. The murdered Croatian police officer Josip Jović became the first casualty of the ruthless war that Easter Sunday. Rebel Serbs held the area for the war's duration, turning hotels into barracks and plundering park property. When the Croatian army finally retook the park in August 1995, they found the natural beauty intact but the hotels and facilities completely gutted. All has since been repaired and tourists are flocking to one of Croatia's most wondrous sights.

Wildlife

Animal life flourishes in the unspoiled conditions. The stars of the park are bears and wolves, but there are also deer, boar, rabbits, foxes and badgers. There are more than 120 different species of bird such as hawks, owls, cuckoos, thrushes, starlings, kingfishers, wild ducks and herons. You might occasionally see black storks and ospreys, and flocks of butterflies flutter throughout the park.

Orientation & Information

The **tourist office** (☎ 751 015; www.np-plitvicka-jezera.hr; adult/student Apr-Oct 110/50KN, Nov-Mar 70/35KN; ⏰ 7am-8pm) has its main entrance on Plitvički Jezera, and a secondary entrance at Velika Poljana, near the hotels. At either entrance you can buy tickets and pick up brochures and a map to walk you around the lakes. The admission ticket includes the boats and buses you need to see the lakes. An easy way to see them is to take a bus to Okrugljak Lake at the top and then walk down. There are well-marked trails throughout the park and a system of wooden walkways that allows you to appreciate the beauty of the landscape without disturbing the environment.

Try to get to the lakes before 8am, especially in summer, to avoid the hordes.

The post office is near the hotels and there's an ATM near Hotel Bellevue. Luggage can be left at the tourist information centre at the park's main entrance or at one of the hotels.

Sights

The lower lakes string out from the main entrance and are rich in forests, grottoes and steep cliffs. **Novakovića Falls** is nearest the entrance and is followed by **Kaluđerovac Lake**, near two caves – the Blue Cave and Šupljara. Next is **Gavanovac Lake** with towering waterfalls and last is **Milanovac Lake**, notable for colours that are variously sky-blue, azure or emerald green.

Kozjak Lake is the largest lake and forms a boundary between the upper and lower lakes. Three kilometres long, the lake is surrounded by steep, forested slopes and contains a small oval island, composed of travertine. Past the hotels, you'll see **Gradinsko Lake** bordered by reeds that often harbour nesting wild ducks. A series of cascades links Gradinsko to **Galovac Lake**, considered the most beautiful lake of all. An abundance of water has formed a series of ponds and falls. A set of concrete stairs over the falls, constructed long ago, has eventually been covered by travertine, forming even more falls in a spectacular panorama. Several smaller lakes are topped by the larger **Okrugljak Lake**, supplied by two powerful waterfalls.

Continuing upwards you'll come to **Ciginovac Lake** and finally **Prošćansko Lake**, surrounded by thick forests.

Sleeping

The Zagreb buses drop you off just outside the camping ground while the hotels are clustered on Velika Poljana overlooking Kozjak Lake. There are many *sobe* signs along the road from Korana village to the national park. The tourist office in the park or its branch in Zagreb can refer you to rooms in nearby villages, including Rastovača, about 400m from the entrance. Expect to pay 200KN to 225KN for a double room.

All of the following hotels are in the old Yugo-style (think largeish, with lots of browns and beiges, and retro wood and glass), though a couple have been renovated and are of a pretty good standard. You can book all of them at www.np-plitvicka-jezera.hr.

Korana Camping Ground (☎ 751 015; per adult all incl €9; ⏰ May-Oct) This large, well-equipped autocamp is about 6km north of the main entrance on the main road to Zagreb.

Hotel Grabovac (☎ 751 999; s low-high €40-52, d €54-70) About 10km north of the entrance on the road to Zagreb, this is a large, modern hotel with bland but functional rooms.

Hotel Bellevue (☎ 751 700; Velika Poljana; s low-high €40-55, d €54-74) The rooms are small and a bit sad at this large hotel; you get little in the way of decoration, and the quilts and curtains are faded, but rooms do have en suites and the beds are firm. It's fine if everywhere else is full.

Hotel Plitvice (☎ 751 100; Velika Poljana; s low-high €50-72, d €65-96; Ⓟ) A comfortable modern hotel with spacious, well-equipped rooms, each with TV, phone and minibar. There are more expensive rooms that are larger and have views.

Hotel Jezero (☎ 751 400; jezero@np-plitvicka-jezera.hr; Velika Poljana; s low-high €61-83, d €86-118; Ⓟ 🛎) This is by far the most comfortable and best-appointed hotel in the park, though it's by no means a boutique delight. There's a sauna and swimming pool.

Eating

There's an inexpensive self-service cafeteria next to the tourist office, at the second entrance, as well as a café that sells sandwiches, pastries and roast chicken, and a minimarket for picnic supplies.

NORTHERN DALMATIA

Lička Kuća (☎ 751 024; mains from 55KN) Just across from the main entrance, this sprawling place is usually crowded with tourists who come for the local sausages and roast-meat dishes. Vegetarians will appreciate the *đuveč* (stew of rice, carrots, tomatoes, peppers and onions), as well as the fine local cheese.

Getting There & Away

The Zagreb–Zadar buses that don't use the new motorway road (ie the ones that drive between Zagreb and Zadar in over three hours) stop at Plitvice (check www.akz.hr for more details). The journey takes three hours from Zadar (80KN) and 2½ hours from Zagreb (60KN).

PAKLENICA NATIONAL PARK
☎ 023

Rising high above the Adriatic, the stark peaks of the Velebit Massif stretch for 145km in a dramatic landscape of rock and sea. Paklenica National Park covers 36 sq km of the Velebit Range, extending in a rough circle from the park entrance in the village of Marasovići. For everyone from Sunday strollers to rock climbers and hikers, the park offers a wealth of opportunities to trek across steep gorges, crawl up slabs of stone, or meander along shady paths next to a rushing stream. The panorama inside the park is ever changing and much greener than you would think when looking at the chalky mountains from the sea.

The national park circles around two deep gorges, Velika Paklenica (Great Paklenica) and Mala Paklenica (Small Paklenica), which scar the mountain range like hatchet marks, with cliffs over 400m high. The dry limestone karst that forms the Velebit Range is highly absorbent, but several springs in the park's upper reaches provide a continuous source of water, which explains the unusually lush vegetation. About half the park is covered with forests, mostly beech and pine followed by white oak and varieties of hornbeam. The vegetation changes as you ascend, as does the climate, which progresses from Mediterranean to continental to subalpine. The lower regions, especially those with a southern exposure, can be fiercely hot in the summer, while the *bura* (cold northeasterly wind) that whips through the range in winter brings rain and sudden storms.

Animal life is scarce but you may see Egyptian vultures, golden eagles, striped eagles and peregrine falcons, which nest on the cliffs of the two gorges. If you've forgotten what they look like, there's an illustrated sign at the park's entrance. Rumour has it that bears and wolves live in the park's upper regions, but your chances of seeing any are minuscule.

The best time to visit the park is in May, June or September. In late spring the park is greenest, the streams become torrents and there are few other visitors. In July and August you'll still find the trails uncrowded, since most people come to the region for the sun and sea, but it might be too hot to hike comfortably. In September the weather is mild during the day and cool at night, making it perfect hiking weather, plus you can still finish off a day on the trails with a refreshing swim.

Orientation

The best base for exploring the park is Starigrad (p200). It is the site of the national park office and has the most possibilities for restaurants and accommodation. It's also near the entrance to Velika Paklenica, which offers the most varied walks and climbs. The entrance to the national park is in the village of Marasovići, which is about 2km southeast of Starigrad. The road to the entrance is not particularly interesting, so a lot of people drive to the car park past the reception area. The entrance to Mala Paklenica is on the far side of Seline village, about 2.5km southeast of Starigrad on the road to Zadar. Follow the road opposite St Mark's (Sveti Marko) church towards the canyon. Trails throughout the park are marked by small white and red waymarkers.

Information

The **Paklenica National Park office** (☎ /fax 369 202; www.paklenica.hr; Starigrad; adult/student 40/20KN Apr-Oct, 30/20KN Nov-Mar; ☼ office 8am-3pm Mon-Fri Apr-Oct, park daily 6am-8.30pm year-round) sells booklets and maps, and is in charge of maintaining the park. The *Paklenica National Park* guide gives an excellent overview of the park and suggests various walks. Rock climbers should talk to one of the guides employed by the park administration who can provide detailed advice on climbing routes and their difficulty.

The **Croatian Mountaineering Association** (☎ 01-48 24 142; www.plsavez.hr; Kozaričeva 22, 10000 Zagreb) also has up-to-date information and publishes a useful map of the park with clearly marked routes. It's on sale at larger bookstores in Zagreb.

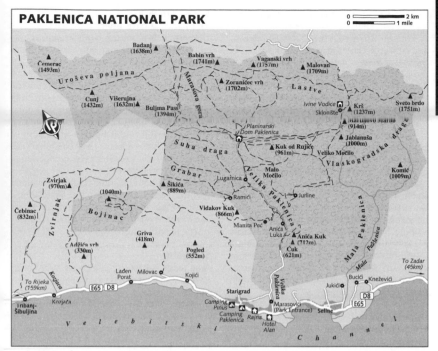

PAKLENICA NATIONAL PARK

Activities
HIKING
Most hikes in the park are one-day affairs from 'base camp' at Starigrad or Seline, or from one of the mountain huts.

Mala Paklenica to Velika Paklenica
Mala Paklenica is smaller and less visited than Velika Paklenica. The karst formations are outstanding in Mala Paklenica, but the trail can get slippery in spring and autumn, and you may have to cross Mala Paklenica stream a few times. You follow the stream through rocks and boulders for the first four hours or so and then zigzag uphill to about 680m. Take the left-hand path marked Starigrad and Jurline. You'll pass through fields and pastures before descending to a rocky gully that leads to the valley floor. You'll arrive at Velika Paklenica, enjoy a marvellous view and then follow the path through the gorge with **Anića Kuk** (712m) on your left down to the valley floor.

Starigrad to Planinarski Dom
Immediately after the park's entrance you'll reach the floor of Velika Paklenica gorge, with

grey-stone massifs looming on either side. In July and August, you're sure to find rock climbers making their way up the cliffs. About 200m up from the car park on the left you'll enter **tunnels** (admission free; ☉ Sun Jul & Aug) that contain well-lit, neat halls and rooms carved out of the rock by the federal Yugoslav army before the 1990s war.

When you pass a rock fall with a stream on your right you'll be at **Anića Luka**, a green, semicircular plateau. In another kilometre or so there's a turn-off to the cave of **Manita Peć** (admission 10KN; ☉ 10am-1pm Jul & Aug, 10am-1pm Wed & Sat Jun & Sep). Take the steps down from the antehall to the centre of the cave, which has a wealth of stalagmites and stalactites enhanced by strategically placed lighting. The area is 40m long and reaches a height of 32m. It's about a two-hour walk from the car park and must be visited with a guide.

From the cave you can follow the trail to **Vidakov Kuk**, which takes 1½ hours. The ascent up the 866m peak is fairly rugged, but on a clear day you'll be rewarded with an unforgettable view over the sea to Pag. You can continue on an easy trail to **Ramići** and then head east to the main trail up to the shelter, Planinarski Dom Paklenica (right).

You can also bypass the Manita Peć detour and continue up to the game warden's hut in the **Lugarnica** area (about two hours' walk from the car park), which is open daily from June to September. You can buy snacks and drinks in the hut before continuing on up to Planinarski Dom Paklenica. You'll pass beech and pine forests before coming to the shelter.

In another route to the hut, take the right path after Anića Luka past the little farmhouse at Jurline. The left fork leads to the black-pine forests of **Malo Močilo**, but you can also continue straight ahead to **Veliko Močilo** and rest beside a spring of drinkable water (three hours from the car park). From here you can take the right fork to the Ivine Vodice hut (right), or at **Martinovo Marilo** (914m) you can take the left path along the southern slope of the upper Velika Paklenica valley, following the Velika Paklenica River to Planinarski Dom Paklenica (about 1½ hours from Veliko Močilo).

Upper Velebit

From Planinarski Dom Paklenica you'll easily reach any of the Velebit peaks in a day, but you'd need about a week to explore all of them. The highest point in the Velebit Range is **Vaganski vrh** (1757m). From the flat, grassy top you have a view of up to 150km inland over the Velebit peaks on a clear day. It may be a long, hard day (depending on your fitness level), but it can be reached with enough time to return to the shelter by nightfall.

Another popular destination is **Babin vrh** (Grandmother's Peak; 1741m). Follow the trail with the Brezimenjača stream on the left to the pass of Buljma (1394m) and then continue to Marasova gora through deciduous forest. There's a small lake at the foot of Babin vrh that never dries up (but the water has been polluted by sheep).

It's also possible to reach all the peaks along the Velebit ridge from Mala Paklenica, but make sure you have survival equipment, a map and the assurance that both huts are open. Past **Sveti Jakov** in Mala Paklenica take the right path to the Ivine Vodice hut. Marked trails lead past **Sveto** brdo (1751m), **Malovan** (1709m), Vaganski vrh and Babin vrh before descending to the Planinarski Dom Paklenica shelter.

ROCK CLIMBING

The national park offers a tremendous variety of rock-climbing routes from beginners' level to borderline suicidal. The firm, occasionally sharp limestone offers graded climbs, including 72 short sports routes and 250 longer routes. You'll see the beginners' routes at the beginning of the park with cliffs reaching about 40m, but the best and most advanced climbing is on Anića Kuk, which offers over 100 routes up to a maximum of 350m. Nearly all routes are well equipped with spits and pitons, except for the appropriately named **Psycho Killer** route.

The most popular climbs here are **Mosoraški** (350m), **Velebitaški** (350m) and **Klin** (300m). Spring is the best climbing season as summers can be quite warm and winters too windy. A rescue service is also available.

Sleeping

Ivine Vodice (Sklonište; ☾ daily Jun-Sep, Sat & Sun Oct-May) East of Planinarski Dom Paklenica, this hut has no beds or running water, but can host 10 people with sleeping bags. It's free and it's not necessary to reserve in advance.

Planinarski Dom Paklenica (Mountain Lodge Paklenica; ☎ 213 792; dm 65KN; ☾ daily Jun-Sep, Sat & Sun Oct-May) This is the most convenient mountain hut. There's no hot water or electricity, but you can reach the highest peaks of Velebit from here. It has 45 beds in four rooms; a sleeping bag is advisable since the lodge provides blankets but no sheets. Reservations are recommended for weekends from June to September.

Getting There & Away

The best way to get to Paklenica (unless you're driving, that is) is to get on one of the Rijeka–Zadar buses (see www.autotrans.hr, in Croatian), all of which stop at Starigrad (28KN, 45 minutes from Zadar, around four daily). The best place to get off the bus is at Hotel Alan.

STARIGRAD

☎ 023 / pop 1160

Starigrad is on either side of the main coastal road from Rijeka to Zadar, and is the best base for exploring Paklenica National Park (p198). It's also referred to as Starigrad-Paklenica, to differentiate it from another Starigrad near Senj (which has nothing to do with the national park). All buses from Rijeka or Zadar stop in front of Hotel Alan and in the centre of town.

The **tourist office** (☎ /fax 369 255; www.rivijera -paklenica.hr; ⏰ 8am-9pm Jul & Aug, to 2pm Mon-Sat Sep-Jun) is in the town centre on the main road across from the small harbour. HVB Splitska Banka is between the tourist office and Hotel Alan. It has an ATM.

Sleeping & Eating

Although camping is not permitted in the national park, there are numerous camping grounds in and around Starigrad. In addition to the larger camping grounds listed here, there are small, private camping grounds stationed along the main road leading into and out of town. The tourist office can put you in touch with them. Starigrad also offers a few hotels.

Private accommodation is abundant in and around Starigrad. Although no agency 'officially' finds accommodation, the tourist office makes it its business to connect people looking for rooms or apartments with the many residents offering them. Prices range from 150KN to 250KN for a double and 275KN to 400KN for a studio. Breakfast is another 18KN to 30KN. Full board and larger apartments are also available. You can find accommodation for yourself by walking along the main road and checking out the many *sobe* signs.

Camping Pinus (☎ 658 652; www.camping-pinus.com; Dr Franje Tuđmana bb; per adult low-high €2.80-4.50; ⏰ Apr-Oct) Around 3km out of town on the road to Rijeka, this is a great place for relaxing in between hikes and expeditions into Paklenica. Swimming is off rocky coves. It's signposted, so if you're using public transport, try asking the driver to drop you off at the entrance.

Camping Paklenica (☎ 209 062; www.paklenica .hr; Dr Franje Tuđmana bb; per adult low-high 30-40KN; ⏰ Apr-Oct) Next to Hotel Alan, this is one of the largest camping grounds. It overlooks a pebble beach only 50m from the road leading to the national park's entrance. Reservations are highly recommended during the summer season.

Rajna (☎ 369 130; www.hotel-rajna.com; Dr Franje Tuđmana 105; s low-high 277-297KN, d 307-347KN; 🍴 🖥) The closest hotel to the park entrance is a favourite meeting spot for climbers and hikers (and those needing a much-deserved break). It's warm, homely and well maintained; the food is good as well.

Hotel Vicko (☎ /fax 369 304; www.hotel-vicko.hr; Jose Dokoze bb; s low-high €42-75, d €56-100; P 🍴 🖥) A nice, comfortable hotel with bright rooms, some of which have balconies. It's only 50m from the beach and it's family friendly (with a kiddies' playground).

Hotel Alan (☎ 209 050; www.bluesunhotels.com; Dr Franje Tuđmana 14; s low-high €82-103, d €128-166; ⏰ mid-Mar–mid-Nov; P 🍴 🖥) Part of the Croatia-wide chain Bluesun Hotels, Hotel Alan sports modern rooms with views over the sea or the mountains. There's also an outdoor pool, tennis courts, a wellness centre and many other comforts to relax you after you've walked around Paklenica all day. Full board is available in the high season.

Getting There & Away

Starigrad is about 51km from Zadar and 165km from Rijeka. All buses between these cities stop in town (www.autotrans.hr, in Croatian; 28KN, 45 minutes from Zadar, around four daily). Buses stop outside Hotel Alan and in the centre of town.

DUGI OTOK

☎ 023 / pop 1800

Dugi Otok is all about natural, unspoilt beauty, so if you're seeking a peaceful, relaxing holiday, you'll find your paradise here. Do note that there is a brief high season in the first three weeks of August, when Italian vacationers come over on the ferry from Ancona or on private vessels, but before and after that, all is quiet for another year. The cluster of small islands on Telašćica Bay nature park is a must-see, while the nearby saltwater Lake Mir (Peace), sandy Sakarun Bay and a panoramic drive along the rocky, indented coast are real delights. All you'll be able to do here is swim, dive and enjoy the spectacular scenery – it's a bit like Mljet Island (p277).

The name Dugi Otok means 'long island'. Stretching northwest to southeast, the island is 43km long and 4km wide. The southeastern coast is marked by steep hills and cliffs, while the northern half is cultivated with vineyards, orchards and sheep pastures. In between is a series of karstic hills rising to 338m at Vela Straža, the island's highest point.

Most people base themselves in either Sali on the southeastern coast or Božava on the northeastern coast. Sali has more opportunities for private accommodation, while Božava offers more of a resort experience.

Roughly in the middle is Brbinj, the main ferry stop.

History

Ruins on the island reveal early settlement by Illyrians, Romans and then early Christians, but the island was first documented in the mid-10th century. It later became the property of the monasteries of Zadar. Settlement expanded with the 16th-century Turkish invasions, which prompted residents of Zadar and neighbouring towns to flee to the island.

Dugi Otok's fortunes have largely been linked with Zadar as it changed hands between Venetians, Austrians and the French, but when northern Dalmatia was handed over to Mussolini the island stayed within Croatia. Old-timers still recall the hardships they endured when the nearest medical and administrative centre was in Šibenik, a long, hard boat ride along the coast.

Economic development of the island has always been hampered by the lack of any freshwater supply – drinking water must be collected from rainwater or, in the dry summers, brought over by boat from Zadar. As on many Dalmatian islands, the population has drifted away over the last few decades, leaving a few hardy souls to brave the dry summers and *bura*-chilled winters.

Getting There & Away

Jadrolinija (www.jadrolinija.hr) has daily ferries all year from Zadar to Brbinj (24KN, 1½ hours, 9am, 12.30pm, 4.30pm and 8pm), Zaglav and Sali (18KN, 45 minutes to 1½ hours, 5.30am, 10am, 3.30pm and 8pm).

Getting Around

There is little public bus transport throughout the island, only a weekly bus taking Božava villagers to Sali and back.

If you're entering the island at Brbinj without your own transport, you may have little choice but to head to Božava. There are no buses between Brbinj and Sali, but buses to Božava from Brbinj (14km) meet all ferries except the one from Ancona that docks at 6am on Sunday.

SALI

pop 1190

As the island's largest town and port, Sali is a positive metropolis when compared with the rest of the towns and villages scattered around Dugi Otok. Named after the salt works that employed villagers during the medieval period, the town has a rumpled, lived-in look that is comfortable and low-key. Sali maintains its relaxed appeal despite the yachts and small passenger boats that dock in town during summer on their way to and from Telašćica Bay and the Kornati Islands. Although the town is tantalisingly close to these natural wonders, you'll need to join a tour or rent your own boat to visit them.

Orientation & Information

The town centres on the port on Porat Bay, where you'll find restaurants, cafés and offices. West of the town centre is sparkling Šašćica Bay, tucked between two hills with swimming coves. From the foot of the port, a path and stairs lead to the Upper Town, surrounded by small vineyards and fields.

The **tourist office** (☎ /fax 377 094; www.dugiotok.hr; Obala Kralja Tomislava; ☼ 8am-10pm Jul & Aug, to noon Mon-Fri Sep-Jun) is the source of all information about Sali. It finds private accommodation, books excursions and distributes the few brochures and maps available.

There is no bank but there is an ATM on the harbour and you can change money or get cash on your MasterCard or Diners Club card at the **post office** (Obala Petra Lorinija; ☼ 8am-2pm & 5-8pm Mon-Sat).

Sights & Activities

Sightseeing within the town is limited, but there is the interesting **St Mary's Church** (Crkva Svete Marije; ☎ 377 041; Svete Marije; ☼ Mass only), built in the 15th century on the site of an earlier church. It is especially notable for the wooden altar and several Renaissance paintings.

The town's proximity to the underwater marine park at the Kornati Islands makes it an excellent base for diving. Hotel Sali has a **dive shop** (☎ 377 079; www.dive-kroatien.de) that runs courses and dive trips around Dugi Otok and to the Kornati Islands.

Diving in the Kornati Islands is marked by steep drop-offs and numerous caves because of the islands' position facing the open sea. There are also possibilities for **cave diving** on the northern side of Dugi Otok; the caves are relatively shallow and large, making them suitable for beginners.

The tourist office can book you on **boat trips** that include a leisurely tour of Telašćica Bay and a stop on one of the Kornati Islands for about 350KN.

Festivals & Events

The weekend before the Assumption (15 August), the island hosts the **Saljske Užance Festival**, which draws visitors from the entire region. Highlights are the donkey races and the candlelight procession of boats around the harbour. Men and women don traditional costumes, play instruments devised from cow horns and perform traditional village dances.

Sleeping

There are no camping grounds on the island. Private accommodation is reasonable in Sali, especially out of the high season, and the tourist office can connect you with some wonderful, out-of-the-way places, including a house on its own little island. In the high season you can expect to find a room for 180KN to 220KN, usually with a shared bathroom. The price is based on double occupancy, so if you're travelling solo you may have to pay the price of a double. In the off season you have a lot more bargaining power and may be able to push the price down by 20% to 30%. Check out www.sali-dugiotok.com (in Croatian) for apartment referrals.

A fully equipped studio runs from 280KN to 300KN and a two-room apartment is priced at 385KN. All prices are based on a three-night minimum stay with a 30% surcharge for fewer nights. The surcharge is usually waived in the off-season.

If you're visiting in summer, it would be a wise idea to ask the proprietor if there are any restrictions placed on the use of water. There also might be an 'excess water' charge. But even if nothing is spelled out, the chances are that long, luxurious showers will not be appreciated.

Hotel Sali (☎ 377 049; www.hotel-sali.hr; s low-high €31-45, d €46-74; Apr-Nov;) This hotel is well located, in excellent condition and offers good value for money. It overlooks swimming coves and is painted in white and marine blue. All rooms have modern bathrooms, satellite TV and balconies, many with views over the sea. The hotel restaurant is also very good.

Eating

There are a few restaurants along Obala Kralja Tomislava. There's also a supermarket located near the Jadrolinija dock.

Grill Tamaris (☎ 377 377; mains from 35KN; Apr-Oct) This is the best restaurant on the street. It offers spaghetti with mixed seafood and freshly grilled shrimp and fish at reasonable prices.

Bife Bočac (☎ 377 322; mains from 35KN) Offering a similar menu to Grill Tamaris, the food here is not bad and you can eat outdoors on a shaded terrace.

TELAŠĆICA BAY

The southeastern tip of Dugi Otok is split in two by the deeply indented Telašćica Bay, dotted with five small islands and five even tinier islets. In fact, the 8200m-long bay contains five smaller bays, which form an indented coastline of 28km and one of the largest and most beautiful natural harbours in the Adriatic.

The Kornati Islands (p214) extend nearly to the edge of Telašćica Bay and the topography of the two island groups is identical – stark white limestone with patches of brush. The tip of the western side of the island faces the sea where the wind and waves have carved out sheer cliffs dropping 166m. There are no towns, settlements or roads on this part of Dugi Otok, only a couple of restaurants on **Mir Bay** catering to the boaters who spend days or even weeks cruising the islands.

Next to Mir Bay is the saltwater **Mir Lake**, fed by underground channels that run through the limestone to the sea. The lake, which is clear but with a muddy bottom, is surrounded by pine forests and the water is much warmer than the sea. Like most mud in unusual places it's supposed to be very good for you, curing ailments and keeping you young.

BOŽAVA
pop 115

Božava is an old town on a harbour that has sprouted a number of comfortable hotels and guest houses. The town is overgrown with lush, flowering trees and there are lovely shady paths along the coast. The harbour has many opportunities for swimming and strolling on pine-shaded paths.

If you arrive by bus, walk downhill from the bus stop to the tiny town centre where you'll find the **tourist office** (☎ /fax 377 607; turisticko -drustvo-bozava@zd.t-com.hr; 8am-noon & 6-8pm Jun-Sep). It can arrange bike, scooter and car rental and can find you private accommodation (150/100KN with/without private facilities).

Veli Rat is a village on the northwestern point of the island on scenic Čuna Bay, about 6km northwest of Božava. Although the area is lovely, there's no transport. Unless you come with your own wheels, you'll be relegated to hitching, walking or paying a resident to drive you out there.

The **Božava Hotel complex** (☎ 291 291; www.hoteli -bozava.hr) includes the three-star Hotel Lavanda (low-high season room per person €31 to €85) and Hotel Agava (€35 to €108), and the luxurious four-star Hotel Maxim (€45 to €82). All rooms are modern with satellite TV, refrigerators, telephones and balconies overlooking the sea, though the Maxim, most recently done up, boasts a more swanky feeling. You'll have access to a sauna, a gym and massage services, along with easy access to the sea.

PAG ISLAND

Pag is like something you'd find in a 1950s Italian film, perfect for a broody B&W Antonioni set – it's barren, rocky, sepia coloured, with vast empty landscapes stretching across the horizon. The Adriatic is steel-coloured around it, and when the sky is stormy it's the most dramatic-looking place in the whole of Croatia. Basically, it's gorgeous. Pag Town has unique architecture that's as stern and basic as the island's appearance. The great 15th-century architect, Juraj Dalmatinac, designed neat streets and a stunning, blindingly white marble town square.

The island has been known for its distinct produce and culture for centuries. Islanders farm the miserly soil and produce the decent domestic white wine, *Šutica*. The tough local sheep graze on herbs and salty grass, lending their milk a distinctive flavour and producing *paški sir* (Pag cheese – soaked in olive oil and aged in stone; see p206), a prized speciality of Croatian cuisine. Intricate Pag lace is famed and framed on many a Croat's wall. But modernity is reaching Pag too: as is often the case with isolated spots, it's become known as a great party location, and Zrće beach, a few kilometres from Novalja, is getting a reputation as the 'Croatian Ibiza', which, depending on your taste, is either a good or bad thing.

History
The island was inhabited by the Illyrians before falling to the Romans in the 1st century BC. The Romans constructed forts and aqueducts. The Slavs settled around Novalja in the 7th century AD and began building churches and basilicas. In the 11th century a new settlement called Stari Grad emerged in the south of the island, 2km south of today's Pag, near the salt works that became the foundation of the island's economy. The next centuries were turbulent for the island as it competed with Zadar and Rab over the salt trade. Zadar launched brutal attacks on the island in the 13th and 14th centuries, but in 1409 it was sold to Venice along with Zadar and the rest of Dalmatia.

Orientation
The 63km karstic island is a strange moonscape defined by two mountain ridges, patches of shrubs and a dozen or so villages and hamlets. There are peaceful coves and bays for swimming in around the main towns of Pag and Novalja, as well as the smaller settlements of Šimuni, Mandre and Straško on the southwestern coast, but the island is never overrun by tourists. Pag Town is roughly in the centre of the island on the southeastern coast of the large Pag Bay (Paški Zaljev), while Novalja is 20km northwest on a small cove. The island is linked to the mainland by Pag Bridge in the southeast.

Getting There & Away
BOAT
There's a catamaran service running from Rijeka to Novalja (40KN, two hours) that passes through Rab (35KN, 50 minutes); it operates daily in summer and three times weekly from October to May. If you're travelling up the coast by car, note that there are regular car ferries (12KN) from Žigljen on the northeast coast to Prizna on the mainland, which run roughly hourly in winter and nonstop from June to September.

BUS
There are three buses a day between Pag and Zadar with **Antonio Tours** (www.antoniotours.hr). Buses leave Zadar for Pag (39KN, one hour) at 10.15am, 2pm and 8pm, and go back to Zadar from Pag Town at 6.20am, 12.20pm and 6.20pm. They leave Novalja at 5.50am, 11.50am and 5.50pm. From Pag Town two buses a day go to Rijeka (100KN, three hours, 5am and noon) from Monday to Saturday and one on Sunday, passing Novalja on the way; one bus a day goes to Split (100KN, two hours,

2pm); and there are two daily buses to Zagreb (100KN, three hours, 5am and 8am).

Getting Around

There are six buses a day that make the 30-minute trip between Pag Town and Novalja (20KN, 5am, 11.15am, noon, 3pm, 6pm and 9pm).

Pag's flat landscape makes bike riding a breeze. Rent bikes from **Jadranka** (☎ 098 306 602) in Pag Town or at the travel agencies listed on p206 for about 30/120KN per hour/day. There are about 115km of bike paths taking you all around the island.

PAG TOWN

☎ 023 / pop 2420

Pag Town is a tiny collection of narrow streets and low stone houses. Life spills out onto the streets from spring to autumn – locals repair appliances and make lace on stools outside their houses, and the lovely white marble square is a socialising hot spot. The small-town ambience is captivating and intimate. There are pebble beaches to relax upon after a morning of lace shopping.

In the early 15th century, the prosperous salt business prompted the construction of Pag Town when nearby Stari Grad could no longer meet the demands of its burgeoning population. The Venetians engaged the finest builder of the time, Juraj Dalmatinac, to design a new city and the first cornerstone was laid in 1443. In accordance with what were then the latest ideas in town planning, the main streets and the cross streets intersect at right angles and lead to four city gates. In the centre, there's a square with a cathedral, St Mary's Church (Crkva Svete Marije), a ducal palace and a bishop's palace, which remained unfinished because Pag never succeeded in having its own bishop. In 1499, Dalmatinac began working on the city walls but only the northern corner, with parts of a castle, remains.

Orientation

The old town, bordered by Vangrada and Podmir, is a pedestrian zone that retains the original simplicity of its architecture. Everyone congregates around the cafés and benches on the main square, Trg Kralja Krešimira IV. Outside the old town there's

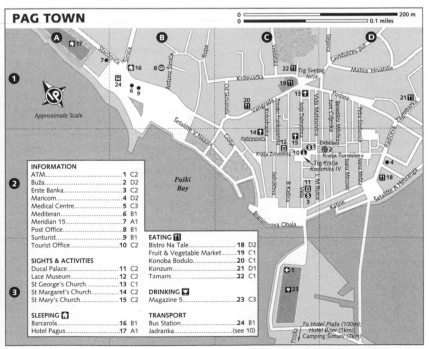

PAG TOWN

INFORMATION	
ATM	1 C2
Buža	2 D2
Erste Banka	3 C2
Maricom	4 D2
Medical Centre	5 C3
Mediteran	6 B1
Meridian 15	7 A1
Post Office	8 B1
Sunturist	9 B1
Tourist Office	10 C2

SIGHTS & ACTIVITIES	
Ducal Palace	11 C2
Lace Museum	12 C2
St George's Church	13 C1
St Margaret's Church	14 C2
St Mary's Church	15 C2

SLEEPING	
Barcarola	16 B1
Hotel Pagus	17 A1

EATING	
Bistro Na Tale	18 D2
Fruit & Vegetable Market	19 C1
Konoba Bodulo	20 C1
Konzum	21 D1
Tamaris	22 C1

DRINKING	
Magazine 5	23 C3

TRANSPORT	
Bus Station	24 B1
Jadranka	(see 10)

NORTHERN DALMATIA

PAG CHEESE

There's no other cheese quite like the distinctive *paški sir* – Pag cheese. Salty and sharp, its flavour easily recalls the island that makes it. As sea winds whip through the low slopes of Pag Island, a thin deposit of salt permeates the ground and the flora it sprouts. The free-range sheep of Pag Island graze freely on the salty herbs and plants, transmitting the flavour to their meat and milk.

The milk for Pag cheese is gathered in May when the flavour is at its peak. It is left unpasteurised, which allows a stronger flavour to emerge during the fermentation process. When the cheese finally ferments, it's rubbed with sea salt, coated with olive oil and left to age for anywhere from six months to a year. The result is a tangy, firm cheese that ripens into an aromatic, dry, crumbly cheese as it ages. As a starter, it's served in thin slices with black olives but it can also be grated and used as a topping instead of Parmesan cheese.

---

a newer section with a couple of hotels, narrow beaches on the bay, travel agencies and restaurants. The bus station (no left-luggage) is next to Hotel Jadran, just outside the old town – it's really just an area where you wait for the bus, and you buy tickets on the bus itself. A bridge across the bay to the southwest leads to a residential quarter, with the large hotels, bigger beaches and most private accommodation.

Information

INTERNET ACCESS
Buža (☎ 600 384; Kralja Tomislava 5; per hr 20KN; ☾ 8am-9pm) A bar with one terminal; the only internet spot in town.

MEDICAL SERVICES
Medical centre (☎ 611 001; Gradska Plaža bb)

MONEY
ATM (Trg Kralja Krešimira IV)
Erste Banka (Vela 18) Changes money.

POST
Post office (Antuna Šimića; ☾ 8am-9pm Mon-Sat) Change money and access cash using MasterCard or Diners Club card.

TOURIST INFORMATION
Tourist office (☎ /fax 611 286; www.pag-tourism .hr; Trg Kralja Krešimira IV 1; ☾ 7am-midnight mid-Jun–mid-Sep, 7am-noon & 6pm-midnight May–mid-Jun & mid-Sep–Oct) Friendly and reasonably equipped.

TRAVEL AGENCIES
Travel agencies are open daily May to September, and Monday to Saturday only for the rest of the year (hours vary).

Maricom (☎ /fax 611 331; www.pag-tourist-service.hr; Stjepana Radića 8)
Mediteran (☎ /fax 611 238; www.mediteran-pag.com; Vladimira Nazora 12)
Meridian 15 (☎ 612 162; www.meridijan15.hr; Ante Starčevića 1) Near the Hotel Pagus.
Sunturist (☎ 612 040; www.sunturist-pago.hr; Vladimira Nazora bb)

Sights & Activities

The simple, Gothic **St Mary's Church** (Crkva Svete Marije; ☎ 611 576; Trg Kralja Krešimira IV; ☾ 9am-noon & 5-7pm May-Sep, Mass only Oct-Apr), built by Juraj Dalmatinac, is in perfect harmony with the modest structures surrounding it. The lunette over the portal shows the Virgin with women of Pag in medieval blouses and headdresses, and there are two rows of unfinished sculptures of saints. Completed in the 16th century, the interior was renovated with baroque ceiling decorations in the 18th century. The wooden crucifix on the altar dates from the 12th century and there is a variety of gold and silver liturgical objects in the church's treasury.

Other notable churches include **St Margaret's Church** (Crkva Svete Margarite; ☎ 611 069; Felicinovića 1; ☾ Mass only), with a Renaissance-baroque facade and a treasury with paintings and reliquaries, and **St George's Church** (Crkva Svetog Jurja; Trg Svetog Jurja; ☾ exhibits 8-10pm), which houses changing art exhibits. Notice also the elaborate portal over the **Ducal Palace** (Kneževa Palača), attributed to a disciple of Dalmatinac.

No visit to Pag would be complete without a look at the small **Lace Museum** (Kralja Dmitra Zvonimira; admission 5KN; ☾ 8am-11pm mid-Jun–mid-Sep) off the main square, which gives a good overview of the island's most famous craft.

Festivals & Events

The last day of July is the **Pag Carnival**, a good opportunity to see the traditional *kolo* (a lively Slavic circle dance) and appreciate the elaborate traditional dresses of Pag. The main square is filled with dancers and musicians, and a theatre troupe presents the traditional folk play *Paška robinja* (The Slave Girl of Pag).

Sleeping

Hotels in Pag have a wide price range, but generally provide good value for money. Most close between October and May.

If there are no women waiting at the bus station to offer *sobe*, you'll find a lot of signs advertising *sobe* on Prosika across the bridge. Any of the travel agencies on opposite will find you private accommodation for about 150/250KN for a single/double and 340KN for a studio.

Camping Šimuni (☎ 697 441; www.camping-simuni .hr; Šimuni; per adult low-high €2.90-7.80; ☯ Apr-Sep) This is on a gorgeous cove with a gravel beach on the southwestern coast, about halfway between Pag Town and Novalja, near the port of Šimuni. All buses from Pag to Novalja stop here.

Barcarola (☎ 611 239, 091 585 4076; Vladimira Nazora 12; d low-high €30-40; ☯ Apr-Nov; ☒) Three double rooms above a *konoba*, this new place is perfect for couples on a budget who want to be close to the old town. All rooms have balconies and en suite bathrooms, along with basic decor (think 1980s technicolour linen).

Hotel Biser (☎ 611 333; www.hotel-biser.com; Matoša 8; s low-high €35-58, d €48-73; ☐P ☒ ☐) This 24-room hotel has comfortable enough rooms with satellite TV and balconies, although the outside has a boxy look that is all too prevalent in Croatia. It's around 1km from the old town (across the water), but close to the beach.

Hotel Pagus (☎ 611 310; www.coning-turizam.hr; Starčevića 1; s low-high €38-74, d €72-144; ☐P ☒ ☒) A four-star beauty, the Pagus was fully renovated in 2007 and now drips with comfort. The classically furnished rooms are elegant and stylish, the balconies overlook the sea, and the wellness centre is a real treat. The hotel is on a narrow beach in the bay, a few minutes' walk from the old town.

Hotel Plaža (☎ 600 855; www.plaza-croatia.com; Marka Marulića 14; s low-high €40-57, d €80-114; ☐P ☒ ☐ ☒) Another four-star place, though further from the old town, the Plaža has lovely rooms with balconies and an excellent restaurant. It's on the beach, so it's perfect for comfort and relaxation.

Eating

Most restaurants offer a little bit of everything – pizza, pasta, fish, meat and salads. Curiously, the price of a starter of Pag cheese isn't much cheaper than anywhere else on the coast, but the quality is bound to be better.

Bistro Na Tale (☎ 611 194; Radićeva 2; mains from 30KN) Immensely popular, it has meat (try the Pag lamb) and seafood dishes, though you can get pizza and pasta, too. Ask what the fresh fish of the day is – it's prepared simply but deliciously.

Tamaris (☎ 612 277; Križevačka bb; mains from 30KN) Pizza, fresh pasta and fried calamari are prepared for a local crowd at a reasonable price. The green pasta with scampi is a particularly good dish.

Konoba Bodulo (☎ 611 989; Vangrada 19; mains from 30KN) At this family-run spot you can dine on country-fresh ingredients under a grapevine.

Self-caterers can pick up fruit, vegetables and local cheese at the daily morning fruit and vegetable market; head to the Konzum supermarket for more elaborate supplies.

Drinking & Entertainment

Magazine 5 (☯ from 11pm Jul & Aug, from 11pm Sat & Sun Sep-Jun) In a former salt warehouse just over the bridge, this is the only disco in town and a good place to research Pagian party habits.

Shopping

Pag offers the most distinctive products in all Croatia. It would be a shame to leave the island without buying lace, since the prices are relatively cheap and buying a piece helps keep the tradition alive. A small circle or star about 10cm in diameter costs about 120KN, but it takes a good 24 hours to make. Larger pieces cost from 200KN to 300KN. The best way to buy lace is to walk down Kralja Tomislava or Kralja Dmitra Zvonimira in the morning while the women are lace-making and buy from them directly. Prices are marked on a card and bargaining is usually futile.

Pag cheese is not as easy to find, although you should be able to get it at the morning market. Otherwise, look out for homemade 'Paški Sir' signs posted outside a house on a remote road somewhere. The asking price for a kilogram is usually 100KN, but you

NORTHERN DALMATIA

THE CROATIAN IBIZA

Despite the overwhelming sense of calm on Pag Island, there's a pocket of wild partying on its beaches every year. Zrće, Caska, Straško and Trinčel beaches are on lovely, wide shallow coves, and, while families bring their kids to play and swim in the day, the big kids hit the same spots at night for Croatia's biggest summer club scene. The most popular is **Zrće beach**, just before the entrance to Novalja. Awarded Blue Flag status, this is where three big clubs, **Aquarius, Kalypso** and **Papaya**, start their 24-hour parties from June to September (for details on events see http://novaljapag.com). Numerous YouTube videos attest to the vigorous arse-shaking, prolific beer and cocktail drinking, and hundreds of nearly naked gyrating bodies clustered together at these clubs. Locals complain about all the sex and drugs and rock'n'roll (well, in this case, techno), but the clubbers are having the time of their lives.

can often bargain down to 70KN or 80KN a kilogram.

NOVALJA
☎ 023 / pop 1900

Although Novalja lacks the unique charm of Pag Town, its beaches, especially Zrće beach, have sparked a thriving tourist business through huge summer nightclubs (see boxed text, above). On the northwestern coast of the island, the town, port and bay are protected from the winds that can buffet Pag Town.

Orientation & Information
The town centre is compact with the tourist office, post office and all shops and services within a few blocks of each other. The bus stop is on the eastern edge of town. Follow the harbour road straight ahead to find travel agencies and shops.

Chery (☎ 662 174; B Radić) Finds private accommodation and has boat information.

Novalja Tourist Board (☎ 663 570; www.tz-novalja .hr; Šetalište Hrvatskih Mornara 1; ⊗ 8am-8pm Jul & Aug, to 3pm Mon-Fri Sep-Jun) Will find private accommodation.

Sleeping & Eating
The tourist office or any travel agency can help find private accommodation. You'll pay from 75KN to 100KN per person.

Hotel Loža (☎ 663 381; www.turno.hr; Trg Loža; s low-high 203-356KN, d 406-712KN; P) The rooms and design here are pretty much standard issue, but you won't be uncomfortable. Some rooms have balconies and views over the sea, and the hotel is in the town centre.

Hotel Liburnija (☎ 661 328; www.turno.hr; Šetalište Hrvatskih Mornara bb; s low-high 137-316KN, d 274-632KN; P) A few hundred metres southeast of the town centre, this hotel is right next to a beach.

Stara i More (☎ 662 423; Braće Radić; mains from 40KN) On the quay, this seafood restaurant serves up the right stuff without fuss or pretension.

ŠIBENIK-KNIN REGION

Spreading over several hills at the centre of a 10km bay, Šibenik makes an excellent base to explore this region. The Kornati Islands are a Mediterranean heaven, and Krka National Park is brimming with swimming and hiking opportunities.

ŠIBENIK
☎ 022 / pop 41,012

Despite the fact that Šibenik often gets overlooked by visitors to northern Dalmatia, the city has really been coming into its own in the last few years. There are exciting new sights, restaurants and bars opening every year and the town is abuzz with new energy. Find a place to stay in town (avoiding the restaurants and hotels scattered among the coastal tourist complexes) and stroll along the harbour and through the steep back streets and alleys. Šibenik has one of the most remarkable cathedrals in Croatia and a network of curving streets and sunny squares from the 15th and 16th centuries. This is a true 'rough diamond'.

The city also makes an excellent base for exploring two beautiful national parks (especially the waterfalls at Krka National Park), which can both be visited without booking an organised tour.

History
Unlike many other Dalmatian coastal communities, Šibenik was settled first by Croat tribes, not Illyrians or Romans.

First mentioned in the 11th century by the Croatian king Krešimir IV, the city was conquered by Venice in 1116 but was tossed around between Venice, Hungary, Byzantium and the Kingdom of Bosnia until Venice seized control in 1412 after a three-year fight. At the end of the 15th century, the Ottomans burst into the region as part of their struggle against Venice.

Over the course of the succeeding two centuries, they periodically attacked the town, disrupting trade and agriculture. The fortresses that were built by the Venetians in defence of the town are still visible, most notably the fortress of St Nikola at the entrance to the Šibenski Channel. The Ottoman threat receded with the 1699 Treaty of Karlowitz, but the city continued to suffer from Venetian rule until it passed into the hands of Austria in 1797, where it remained until 1918.

Šibenik fell under attack in 1991 from the Yugoslav federal army, and was subject to shelling until its liberation as part of 'Operation Storm' by the Croatian army in 1995. Little physical damage is visible, but the city's aluminium industry, which was an important part of the regional economy, was shattered. Šibenik has started to make a serious comeback in the past few years.

Orientation

The city spreads like an amphitheatre from the harbour uphill to the surrounding hills. The main road is Kralja Zvonimira and the old town lies between it and the harbour, which is in a large bay. The entire old town is a pedestrian area and contains the cathedral and several notable churches.

The oldest part of the town is on Zagrebačka and the streets running north. The bus station is in a modern jumble of concrete blocks in the city's southern corner. The main commercial street is Ante Starčevića (then Ante Šupuka) east of the old town, with the train station lying southeast.

Information

The post office, travel agencies and Croatia Express change money. There's an ATM on Kralja Zvonimira and a Zagrebačka Banka with an ATM on Ante Šupuka, among other places.

Atlas Travel Agency (☎ 330 232; Trg Republike Hrvatske 2; ⏰ 8.30am-6pm Mon-Fri, 9am-noon Sat) Changes money and books excursions.

Hospital (☎ 334 421; Stjepana Radića 83)

NIK Travel Agency (☎ /fax 338 540; www.nik.hr; Ante Šupuka 5; ⏰ 9am-6pm Mon-Fri, to noon Sat) The largest travel agency in town. It finds private accommodation and sells international bus and air tickets.

Post office (Vladimira Nazora 51; ⏰ 8am-7pm Mon-Fri, 9am-noon Sat) You can make calls and change money here.

Tourist information centre (☎ 214 441; www .sibenik-tourism.hr; Obala Franje Tuđmana 5; ⏰ 8am-9pm Mon-Sat, 0am-2pm Sun mid-Jun–mid-Sep, 0am-3pm Mon-Fri mid-Sep–mid-Jun)

Sights

CATHEDRAL OF ST JAMES

The **Cathedral of St James** (Katedrala Svetog Jakova; Trg Republike Hrvatske; ⏰ 8am-noon & 6-8pm May-Oct, Mass only Nov-Apr) is Juraj Dalmatinac's masterpiece. The crowning glory of the Dalmatian coast, the cathedral, a World Heritage site, is worth a considerable detour to see. Its most unusual feature is the frieze of 71 heads on the exterior walls of the apses. These portraits in stone are vivid character studies of ordinary 15th-century citizens. Placid, annoyed, proud or fearful, their expressions convey the timelessness of human emotion through the centuries.

Dalmatinac was not the first (and nor the last) sculptor to work on the cathedral. Construction began in 1431, but after 10 years of toying around with various Venetian builders, the city appointed the Zadar native Dalmatinac, who increased the size and transformed the conception of the church into a transitional Gothic-Renaissance style.

In addition to the exterior frieze, other examples of Dalmatinac's style include the two aisle staircases descending into the sacristy on one side and the exquisite baptistery on the other, in which three angels support the baptismal font. The latter was carved by Andrija Aleši after Dalmatinac's designs. Other interior artworks worth noting are the crypt of Bishop Šižigorić (by Dalmatinac), who supported the building of the cathedral; the altar painting of St Fabijan and St Sebastijan (by Zaniberti); the painting *The Gift of the Wise Men* (by Ricciardi); and, next to it, two marble reliefs of angels (by Firentinac). Note also the *Lion's Portal* on the northern side, created by Dalmatinac and Bonino da Milano, in which two lions support columns containing the figures of Adam and Eve, who appear to be excruciatingly embarrassed by their nakedness.

ŠIBENIK

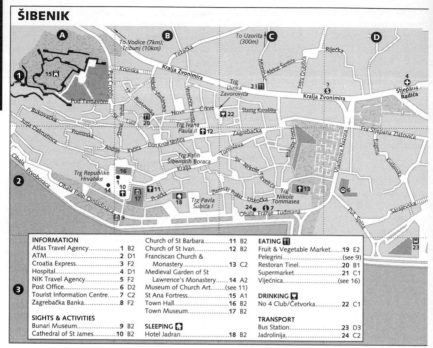

INFORMATION			
Atlas Travel Agency	**1** B2	Church of St Barbara	**11** B2
ATM	**2** D1	Church of St Ivan	**12** B2
Croatia Express	**3** F2	Franciscan Church &	
Hospital	**4** D1	Monastery	**13** C2
NIK Travel Agency	**5** F2	Medieval Garden of St	
Post Office	**6** D2	Lawrence's Monastery	**14** A2
Tourist Information Centre	**7** C2	Museum of Church Art	(see 11)
Zagrebačka Banka	**8** F2	St Ana Fortress	**15** A1
		Town Hall	**16** B2
SIGHTS & ACTIVITIES		Town Museum	**17** B2
Bunari Museum	**9** B2		
Cathedral of St James	**10** B2	**SLEEPING**	
		Hotel Jadran	**18** B2

EATING		
Fruit & Vegetable Market	**19** E2	
Pelegrini	(see 9)	
Restoran Tinel	**20** B1	
Supermarket	**21** C1	
Vijećnica	(see 16)	
DRINKING		
No 4 Club/Cetvorka	**22** C1	
TRANSPORT		
Bus Station	**23** D3	
Jadrolinija	**24** C2	

The cathedral was constructed entirely of stone quarried from the islands of Brač, Korčula, Rab and Krk, and is reputed to be the world's largest church built completely of stone without brick or wood supports. The unusual domed-roof complex was completed after Dalmatinac's death by Nikola Firentinac, who continued the facade in a pure Renaissance style. The church was completed in 1536.

TOWN HALL

Across the square from the cathedral is the town hall, a harmonious Renaissance arrangement of columns and a balustrade, which was constructed between 1533 and 1546. Destroyed during an Allied air attack in 1943, the building was completely rebuilt to its original form.

MEDIEVAL GARDEN OF ST LAWRENCE'S MONASTERY

This is the hottest new attraction in town. The **medieval garden** (Vrt Svetog Lovre; ☎ 212 515; www.cromovens.hr; Trg Republike Hrvatske 4; adult/ student 15/10KN) has been fully restored after

an entire century, and opened in late 2007. Designed and completed by Dragutin Kiš (an award-winning landscape artist), the garden has patches of medicinal plants, water fountains and some pretty pathways. There's also a café and a good restaurant, plus music events during the summer months. Opening hours vary, so it's best to phone ahead.

BUNARI MUSEUM

Another excellent addition to Šibenik's sights is the **Bunari Museum** (☎ 485 055; Obala Palih Omladinaca 2; adult/student 15/10KN; ⏱ 8am-midnight). It's an interactive affair set inside the old water reservoir complex, with children having most of the fun (there are many games to be played), while adults get to learn about Šibenik's past from text boards and videos. The museum hosts the restaurant Pelegrini (p212) on its roof terrace.

TOWN MUSEUM

On the eastern side of the cathedral is the **Town Museum** (Gradski Muzej; ☎ 213 880; www.muzej-sibenik .hr; Gradska Vrata 3; admission free; ⏱ 10am-1pm & 7-10pm

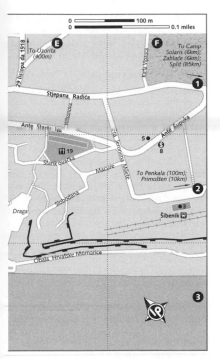

Apr-Sep, 10am-1pm Oct-Mar), which was closed for refurbishment at the time of research, but is looking to re-open in 2009.

OTHER CHURCHES
The town has a wealth of beautiful churches but many are only open for Mass. The **Church of St Ivan** (Crkva Svetog Ivana; Trg Ivana Paula II) is a fine example of Gothic-Renaissance architecture dating from the end of the 15th century. The **Franciscan Church & Monastery** (Franjevački Samostan; Ćulinovića), which dates from the end of the 14th century, has 14th- and 15th-century frescoes and an array of Venetian baroque paintings.

The Church of St Barbara (Crkva Svete Barbare) houses the **Museum of Church Art** (Kralja Tomislava; admission 10KN; 9am-1pm Mon-Fri). The museum exhibits paintings, engravings and sculptures from the 14th to the 18th centuries.

ST ANA FORTRESS
You can climb to the top of St Ana Fortress in the northwest for a magnificent view over Šibenik and the surrounding region.

Festivals & Events
Šibenik hosts a renowned **International Children's Festival** during the last week of June and the first week of July. There are craft workshops, along with music, dance, children's film and theatre, puppets and parades.

Sleeping
Most private accommodation is in neighbouring villages such as Primošten, Tribunj and Vodice along the coast, which are easily reached by bus from Šibenik. In July and August, you may be met by women at the bus or train station offering *sobe* at much lower prices. NIK Travel Agency (p209) has private rooms from about 250KN and studios from about 425KN.

Commercial accommodation possibilities are largely confined to the resort centre **Solaris** (363 951; www.solaris.hr), 6km southwest of town. It's an enormous complex on the beach with six hotels, two highly populous camping grounds and a few self-contained apartments.

Zablaće (/fax 354 015; Solaris; per adult/site 39/65KN) A smaller and cheaper camping option than Camp Solaris.

Camp Solaris (364 450; www.solaris.hr; Solaris; per adult/site 42/75KN; mid-Mar–Oct;) This elaborate camping ground comes complete with a sea-water pool, sports facilities and restaurants.

Hotel Jadran (212 644; www.rivijera.hr; Obala Oslobođenja 52; s low-high 380-470KN, d 760-940KN) This modern hotel conveniently located along the harbour is the only one in town. It's somewhat impersonal but in excellent condition and rooms are equipped with satellite TV. The hotel can be warm in summer, so try to get a room overlooking the harbour to get some breezes.

Eating
Like the rest of the Dalmatian coast, the menus in Šibenik restaurants lean heavily towards fish and are influenced by the pastas and risottos of Italy.

Penkala (219 869; Fra Jeronima Milete 17; mains from 25KN; closed Sun) Popular with the locals and very good, this neighbourhood spot serves up homespun cooking with a focus on hearty meat stews.

Uzorita (213 660; Bana Josipa Jelačića 50; mains from 60KN) This is the oldest restaurant in Šibenik, dating from 1899. It has a shady terrace and a menu featuring fish and meat dishes with a nod to bean-eaters.

our pick Pelegrini (☎ 485 055; Obala Palih Omladinaca 2; mains from 60KN) Sitting on the top of the Bunari Museum (p210) and opened in 2007, this is the suavest new restaurant in Šibenik. The interior is stylish and Mediterranean minimalist, while the menu is full of creamy risottos (try the summer risotto of courgettes, mint and bacon), fresh fish and perfectly prepared pasta. The wine list has the best of Croatia.

Vijećnica (☎ 213 605; Trg Republike Hrvatske; mains from 70KN) On the ground floor of the town hall, across from the cathedral, the terrace and stunning interior offer a fine setting and there are many cosmopolitan dishes on the menu.

Restoran Tinel (☎ 331 815; Trg Puckih Kapetana 1; mains from 75KN) This two-floor restaurant offers some of the finest dining in town with an excellent wine list. Try the wonderful *brodet* (mixed stewed fish with polenta) accompanied by an Istrian *malvazija* (type of white wine).

Self-caterers can stock up at the **supermarket** (Kralja Zvonimira) or the **fruit & vegetable market** (btwn Ante Starčevića & Stankovačka).

Drinking
The seafront area along Obala Prvoboraca is full of bars and youngsters congregating in the summer months.

No 4 Club/Četvorka (☎ 217 517; Trg Dinka Zavorovića 4) Young trendies down cocktails on the ground floor and snack upstairs.

Getting There & Away
Jadrolinija (☎ 213 468; Obala Franje Tuđmana 8; ☽ 9am-6pm Mon-Fri) has tickets for ferry sailings.

Šibenik is well connected by bus to local and international destinations:

Destination	Fare (KN)	Duration (hr)	Daily services
Dubrovnik	217	6	8
Murter	24	¾	9
Osijek	325	8½	1
Primošten	16	½	6
Pula	220	8	3
Rijeka	176	6	13
Split	80	1¾	24
Zadar	60	1½	48
Zagreb	160	6½	15

There's one overnight train (149KN, seven hours, 10.55pm) and two daily trains (6½ hours, 7.40am and 3.15pm) between Zagreb

and Šibenik, plus six trains a day between Šibenik and Split (43KN, two hours), dropping to four on Sunday. Book your ticket in advance, as they can sell out fast on weekends.

KRKA NATIONAL PARK
☎ 022

From the western foot of the Dinaric Range into the sea near Šibenik, the 72.5km Krka River and its wonderful waterfalls define the landscape of the Šibenik-Knin region and are the focus of the Krka National Park. Like Plitvice Lakes (p195), the Krka waterfalls are a karstic phenomenon. The river water formed a deep canyon (up to 200m) through the limestone and brought calcium carbonate with it. Mosses and algae retain the calcium carbonate and encrust it in their roots. The material is called tufa and is formed by billions of plants growing on top of one another. The growths create barriers in the river that produce waterfalls. Unlike Plitvice Lakes, the volume of water rushing through the canyon is much greater, averaging 55 cu metres of water per second at the last cascade, Skradinski Buk, making the spectacle even more dramatic.

Orientation
The main entries to the park are located at the Skradin and Lozovac entrances, which lie on the western and eastern banks respectively.

Park Entry
Park **entry fees** (adult/concession Jul-Aug 80/65KN, Apr-Jun, Sep & Oct 65/50KN, Nov-Mar 25/15KN) is paid at Skradin. The ticket includes a boat or bus ride to Skradinski Buk.

Information
The Skradin **tourist office** (☎ 771 306; www.skradin .hr, in Croatian; Trg Male Gospe 3; ☽ 8am-9pm Jul & Aug, 9am-1pm & 5-8pm Sep-Jun) is along the harbour and will put you in touch with owners of private accommodation. The **Krka National Park office** (☎ 217 720; www.npkrka.hr; Trg Ivana Pavla II, Skradin; ☽ 9am-5pm Mon-Fri) has information and can arrange excursions.

Sights & Activities
The landscape of rocks, cliffs, caves and chasms is a remarkable sight, but the national park also contains several important cultural landmarks. Near its northernmost point there is an Orthodox monastery; it's sometimes called Aranđelovac (Holy Archangel), or

EXCURSIONS FROM ŠIBENIK

Šibenik is easily connected by ferry to several small islands that can be explored in a day trip (or overnight, if you so desire). There's also **Primošten**, on the mainland, by far the most attractive town within reach of Šibenik; it's about 20km south of the town centre. This small village of medieval streets is dominated by a large belfry and neatly contained within a peninsula, making it resemble the Istrian town of Rovinj. Across the bay is another peninsula thickly wooded with pines and bordered by pebbly beaches. The hotels are discrete enough not to spoil the landscape.

Zlarin is only 30 minutes by boat from Šibenik and is known for the coral that used to be abundant before it was torn from the sea and sold for jewellery. Because there are no cars allowed on the island, it makes a tranquil retreat from Šibenik and boasts a sand beach, pine woods and a spacious port.

Only 15 minutes further on from Zlarin, **Prvić** contains two villages, Prvić Luka and Šepurine (another 10 minutes on the ferry), which retain the flavour of simple fishing settlements.

Murter is 29km northwest of Šibenik, separated from the mainland by a narrow channel. The steep southwestern coast is indented by small coves, most notably the cove of **Slanica**, which is the best for swimming. Murter village is in the northwest and has a good harbour and not-so-good beach. The **tourist office** (☎ /fax 434 995; www.murter.com; Rudina 2; ◷ 7.30am-9.30pm mid-Jun–mid-Sep, 8am-noon mid-Sep–mid-Jun) can provide further information on the island.

Although Murter village is unremarkable, it is an excellent base from which to explore the Kornati Islands (p214). Booking an excursion to these islands from Murter will allow you to see more of the archipelago than if you were to come from Šibenik or Zadar, since Murter is much closer. **Coronata** (☎ 435 933; www.coronata.hr; Žrtava Ratova 17) is one of several agencies that run full-day excursions to the Kornati Islands (250KN) from Murter.

If you'd like to stay on an island, **KornatTurist** (☎ 435 855; www.kornatturist.hr; Hrvatskih Vladara 2, Murter) arranges private accommodation. It will cost about €600 per week for a two-person cottage including the boat transfer, a twice-weekly food delivery, gas for lighting and the admission fee for the Kornati National Park. You can also rent a motorboat for €190 per week.

Keep in mind that Murter inhabitants are the owners of the Kornati Islands and visit them occasionally by private boat to tend their land. Asking around town may put you in touch with someone who will run you out there and arrange for you to stay overnight in their cottage for less money.

often simply referred to as the **Krka monastery**. First mentioned in 1402 as the endowment of Jelena Šubić, the sister of Emperor Dušan of Serbia, it was built and rebuilt until the end of the 18th century. The monastery has a unique combination of Byzantine and Mediterranean architecture and had a valuable inventory dating back to the 14th century, some of which was destroyed during the recent war.

Below the monastery the river becomes a lake created by the **Roški Slap** barrier downstream and the valley narrows into a 150m gorge. Roški Slap is a 650m-long stretch that begins with shallow steps and continues in a series of branches and islets to become 27m-high cascades. On the eastern side of the falls you can see water mills that used to process wheat.

The first kilometre of the lake is bordered by reeds and bulrushes sheltering marsh birds. Next downstream is the **Medu Gredama gorge**

with cliffs 150m high cut into a variety of dramatic shapes. Then the gorge opens out into Lake Visovac with **Samostan Visovac**, its lovely island monastery. In the 14th century hermits built a small monastery and church, which they abandoned under threat from the Turks in 1440. They were succeeded by Bosnian Franciscans in 1445, who remained throughout Turkish rule until 1699. The church on the island dates from the end of the 17th century and the bell tower was built in 1728. On the western bank is a forest of holm oaks and on the eastern bank is a forest of white oaks.

Six kilometres downstream you come to the largest waterfall, **Skradinski Buk**, with an 800m-long cascade covering 17 steps and rising to almost 46m. As at Roški Slap, water mills used to grind wheat, mortars pounded felt and huge baskets held rugs and fabrics. The mills are deserted now but Venetians used to collect a small fortune in taxes from the Krka mills. Downstream from Skradinski Buk is less interesting due to the construction of the Jaruga power plant in 1904. It takes about an hour to walk around Skradinski Buk and see the waterfalls. Bring a swimsuit because it is possible to swim in the lower lake.

Sleeping & Eating

There are several restaurants and grocery stores along the harbour. Skradinski Buk has a few snack places and inexpensive restaurants, plus there's one hotel in Skradin.

Hotel Skradinski Buk (☎ 771 771; www.skradin skibuk.hr; Burinovac bb, Skradin; s low-high 275-372KN, d 363-575KN; P ✖ ⌨) This hotel is fairly standard issue in terms of decoration, but it has rooms that are nicely outfitted with satellite TV and internet access. Some of the rooms can be quite cramped.

Getting There & Around

Although several agencies sell excursions to the falls from Šibenik, Zadar and other cities, it is possible, and certainly more interesting, to visit the falls independently if you base yourself in Šibenik.

There are six daily buses from Šibenik that make the 30-minute run to Skradin. The bus drops you outside Skradin's old town. You pay the park admission fee here, which allows you to board a boat to Skradinski Buk. It's about a 45-minute walk if you don't want to wait for a boat. If you take one of the five daily buses to Lozovac, you can take a bus to Skradinski Buk (also included in the park admission price), but you miss out on the boat ride through the canyon that you can enjoy from Skradin.

From Skradinski Buk, there are three boats daily from April to October going to Visovac (adult/concession 70/40KN) and Roški Slap (100/60KN). From Roški Slap, there's a boat to the Krka monastery (70/40KN).

At other times of the year, you should first call the Krka National Park office (p212) or ask at the tourist office in Šibenik (p209) about the boat schedule.

KORNATI ISLANDS

Composed of 147 mostly uninhabited islands, islets and reefs covering 69 sq km, some of which are a national park, the Kornati Islands are the largest and densest archipelago in the Adriatic. Typically karst terrain, the islands are riddled with cracks, caves, grottoes and rugged cliffs. Since there are no sources of fresh water on the islands, they are mostly barren, sometimes with a light covering of grass. The evergreens and holm oaks that used to be

---

KNIN & THE INTERIOR

The interior of the Šibenik-Knin region includes part of the Military Frontier (Vojna Krajina) established by the Austrians in the 16th century as protection from the Turks. It was settled by Vlachs and Morlachs belonging to the Orthodox Church and thus developed a large Serbian population. Upon the Croatian declaration of independence in 1990, the Krajina Serbs, with the help of arms from Belgrade, established their own state and made Knin its capital. When Croatia retook the territory in 1995, virtually the entire Serbian population was expelled, leaving a landscape of smashed buildings and ruined villages. Although the physical damage has been repaired, the economy is in tatters and few Serbs are returning. As a result, many of the formerly thriving small towns in the interior remain underpopulated.

Located on a historical hot seat on the borders of Dalmatia and Bosnia, Knin was an important trading centre in the Middle Ages at the intersection of roads running between Slavonia, Bosnia and the Dalmatian coast. When Croatia was ruled by Croatian kings in the 10th century, Knin was the capital and the seat of the Croatian aristocracy. Realising their vulnerability, they erected the fortress that still looms over the town from steep Spas hill. When the Croatian kings fell, Knin was battered by a series of would-be occupiers until the Ottomans snatched it in 1522. Later, Venice swept in followed by Austria, France and then Austria again.

The huge Croatian flag flying from the top of the fortress is more to do with recent events than medieval history, though the town's economy evaporated along with the expelled Serbs in 1995. Although there's not much for travellers to do besides climb up the fortress, a visit would help the local economy. There's one homely hotel, the **Hotel Mihovil** (☎ 022-664 444; www.zivkovic .hr, in Croatian; Vrpolje bb; d 200KN) with friendly owners and decent rooms. Enjoy the mountain views towards Bosnia and Hercegovina from the café on top of the fortress.

found on some islands were long ago burned down in order to clear the land. Far from stripping the islands of their beauty, the deforestation has highlighted startling rock formations, whose stark whiteness against the deep blue Adriatic is an eerie and wonderful sight.

Information

The **Kornati National Park office** (☎ 434 662; www .kornati.hr; Butina 2; 🕑 8.30am 5pm Mon Fri) in Murter village on the island of Murter has all the information you may need on the park.

Sights

The Kornati Islands form themselves into four series running northwest to southeast. The first two series of islands lie closer to the mainland and are known locally as Gornji Kornat. The largest and most indented of these islands is **Žut**.

The other two series of islands, facing the open sea, comprise the **Kornati National Park** (adult/child 50/25KN) and are the most dramatically indented. **Kornat Island** is by far the largest island in the park, extending 25km in length but only 2.5km in width. Both the land and sea are within the protection of the national park. Fishing is strictly limited in order to allow the regeneration of fish shoals that have been severely overfished. Groper, bass, conger eel, sea bream, pickerel, sea scorpion, cuttlefish, squid, octopus and smelt are some of the fish trying to make a comeback in the region.

The island of **Piškera**, also within Kornati National Park, was inhabited during the Middle Ages and served as a collection and storage point for fish. Until the 19th century the islands were owned by the aristocracy of Zadar, but about a hundred years ago peasant ancestors of the present residents of Murter and Dugi Otok bought the islands, built many kilometres of rock walls to divide their properties and used the land to raise sheep.

The islands remain privately owned: 90% belong to Murter residents and the remainder to residents of Dugi Otok. Although there are no longer any permanent inhabitants on the islands, many owners have cottages and fields that they visit from time to time to tend the land. Olive trees account for about 80% of the land under cultivation, followed by vineyards, orchards and vegetable gardens. All told, there are about 300 buildings on the Kornati Islands, mostly clustered on the southwestern coast of Kornat.

Getting There & Away

The best way to visit the islands is by boat, especially your own. The largest marina is on the island of Piškera, on the southern part of the strait between Piškera and Lavsa. There's another large marina on Žut and a number of small coves throughout the islands where boaters can dock.

Otherwise, you can book an excursion from Zadar, Šibenik, Split and other coastal cities or arrange private accommodation from Murter (see boxed text, p213). There is no ferry transport between the Kornati Islands and the mainland.

Split & Central Dalmatia

Central Dalmatia is the most action-packed, sight-rich and diverse part of Croatia, with dozens of castles, fascinating islands, spectacular beaches, dramatic mountains, quiet ports and an emerging culinary scene, not to mention Split's Diocletian Palace and medieval Trogir (both Unesco World Heritage sites). In short, this part of Croatia will grip even the most picky visitor.

The region stretches from Trogir in the northwest to Ploče in the southeast. Split is its largest city and a hub for bus and boat connections along the Adriatic coast. The rugged 1500m-high Dinaric Range provides the dramatic background to the region.

Diocletian's Palace is a sight like no other (a Roman ruin and the living soul of Split) and it would be a cardinal Dalmatian sin to miss out on the sights, bars, restaurants and general buzz inside it. The Roman ruins in Solin are altogether a more quiet, pensive affair, while Trogir is a tranquil city that's preserved its fantastic medieval sculpture and architecture. Then there is Hvar Town, the region's most popular destination, richly ornamented with Renaissance architecture, good food, a fun atmosphere and tourists – who are in turn ornamented with deep tans, big jewels and shiny yachts.

Let's not forget the coastline: you can choose from the slender and seductive Zlatni Rat on Brač, wonderful beaches in Brela on the Makarska Riviera, secluded coves on Brač, Šolta and Vis, or gorgeous (and nudie) beaches on the Pakleni Islands off Hvar. Best of all is that Dalmatia is always quite a bit warmer than Istria or the Gulf of Kvarner, and you can plunge into the crystalline Adriatic from the beginning of May right up until the end of September.

HIGHLIGHTS

- Discovering the wonders and nightlife in Diocletian's Palace in **Split** (p220)
- Getting to know **Vis** (p240), Croatia's most remote island
- Stretching out on Croatia's sexiest beach, Zlatni Rat, in **Bol** (p247)
- Taking in the glamour in **Hvar Town** (p251) and getting into your birthday suit on the beaches of the **Pakleni Islands** (p254)
- Hiking up dramatic **Mount Biokovo** (p237) and getting views of Italy from the top

- TELEPHONE CODE: 021

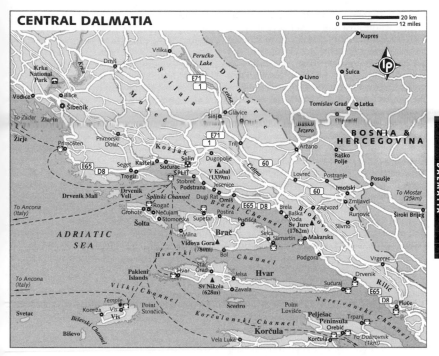

CENTRAL DALMATIA

SPLIT

pop 173,700

The second-largest city in Croatia, Split (Spalato in Italian) is a great place to see Dalmatian life as it's really lived. Free of mass tourism and always buzzing, this is a city with just the right balance of tradition and modernity. Step inside Diocletian's Palace (a Unesco World Heritage site and one of the world's most impressive Roman monuments) and you'll see dozens of bars, restaurants and shops thriving amid the atmospheric old walls where Split life has been going on for thousands of years. Split's unique setting and exuberant nature make it one of the most delectable cities in Europe. The dramatic coastal mountains are the perfect backdrop to the turquoise waters of the Adriatic and you'll get a chance to appreciate the gorgeous Split cityscape when making a ferry journey to or from the city.

Split is often seen mainly as a transport hub to the hip nearby islands (which, indeed, it is), but the city has been sprucing itself up and attracting attention by renovating the old Riva

(seafront) and replacing the former cement strolling ground with a shiny, new marble look. Even though the modern transformation hasn't pleased all the locals, the new Riva is a beauty. The growing tourist demand also means that Split's city authorities are under pressure to expand the city's transport resources, and there's talk that in the near future the currently very handy bus station may be moved further out to make way for the harbour expansion (for big, shiny yachts and monstrous cruisers?) and luxury hotels.

HISTORY

Split achieved fame when the Roman emperor Diocletian (AD 245–313), noted for his persecution of early Christians, had his retirement palace built here from 295 to 305. After his death the great stone palace continued to be used as a retreat by Roman rulers. When the nearby colony of Salona (now Solin) was abandoned in the 7th century, many of the Romanised inhabitants fled to Split and barricaded themselves behind the high palace walls, where their descendants live to this day.

First the Byzantine Empire and then Croatia controlled the area, but from the 12th to the 14th centuries medieval Split enjoyed a large measure of autonomy, which favoured its development. The western part of the old town around Narodni Trg, which dates from this time, became the focus of municipal life, while the area within the palace walls continued as the ecclesiastical centre.

In 1420 the Venetians' conquering of Split led to its slow decline. During the 17th century, strong walls were built around the city as a defence against the Ottomans. In 1797 the Austrians arrived; they remained until 1918, with only a brief interruption during the Napoleonic Wars.

ORIENTATION

The bus, train and ferry terminals are clustered on the eastern side of the harbour, a short walk from the old town (see Map p220). Obala Hrvatskog Narodnog Preporoda – commonly known as Riva (the waterfront promenade) – is your best central reference point in Split. Most of the large hotels and the best restaurants, nightlife and beaches lie east of the harbour along Bačvice, Firule, Zenta and Trstenik Bays. The wooded Marjan Hill (123m) dominates the western tip of the city and has many beaches at its foothills.

See p293 for more information on the use of street names in Split.

INFORMATION
Bookshops
Algoritam (Map p220; Bajamontijeva 2; ☾ 9am-7pm Mon-Fri, to 4pm Sat) A good English-language bookshop.
International Bookshop (Map p220; Obala Hrvatskog Narodnog Preporoda 21; ☾ 9am-7pm Mon-Fri, to 4pm Sat) Doesn't really sell any books but it has international magazines and periodicals.

Cultural Centres
Alliance Française (Map p220; ☎ 347 290; Marmontova 3; ☾ 9am-6pm Mon-Fri) The centre of French cultural life in Split.

Internet Access
Internet Games & Books (Map p220; ☎ 338 548; Obala Kneza Domagoja 3; per hr 25KN; ☾ 9am-7pm) Also sells used books, offers luggage storage and provides information for backpackers.
Mriža (Map p220; ☎ 321 320; Kružićeva 3; per hr 20KN; ☾ 8am-10pm Mon-Sat, 9am-4pm Sun)

Laundry
Modrulj (Map p220; ☎ 315 888; www.modrulj.com; Šperun 1; ☾ 8am-8pm Apr-Oct, 9am-5pm Mon-Sat Nov-Mar) A sparkling laundrette with coin-operated washing machines (wash/dry 25/20KN), which also has internet access (5KN per 15 minutes).

Left Luggage
Garderoba bus station (Map p220; per hr 3KN; ☾ 6am-10pm); train station (Map p220; per hr 3KN; ☾ 6am-10pm)
Internet Games & Books (Map p220; ☎ 338 548; Obala Kneza Domagoja 3; per day 10KN; ☾ 9am-7pm)

Medical Services
KBC Firule (Map p219; ☎ 556 111; Spinčićeva 1) Split's hospital.

Money
You can change money at travel agencies or the post office. There are ATMs around the bus and train stations and throughout the city.

Post
Main post office (Map p220; Kralja Tomislava 9; ☾ 7am-8pm Mon-Sat, 8am-1pm Sun)

Telephone
There's a telephone centre at the main post office.

Tourist Information
Croatian Youth Hostel Association (Map p219; ☎ 396 031; www.hfhs.hr; Domilijina 8; ☾ 9am-6pm Mon-Fri, to 4pm Sat) Sells HI cards and has information about youth hostels all over Croatia.
Internet Games & Books (Map p220; ☎ 338 548; Obala Kneza Domagoja 3; ☾ 9am-7pm) Information for backpackers. Also has used books, internet connection and luggage storage.
Tourist office (Map p220; ☎ /fax 342 606; www .visitsplit.com; Peristil; ☾ 9am-8.30pm Mon-Sat, 8am-1pm Sun) Has information on Split and sells the Split Card (36KN), which offers free and discounted admissions to Split attractions.

SPLIT CARD

Not a bad deal at all – get the Split Card for 36KN for one day and you can use it for three days without paying anything extra. You get free access to most of the city museums, half-price discounts to many galleries, and tons of discounts on car rental, restaurants, shops and hotels.

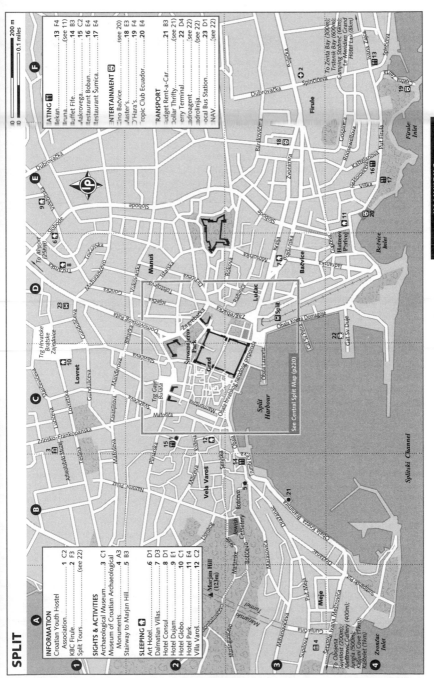

SPLIT & CENTRAL DALMATIA

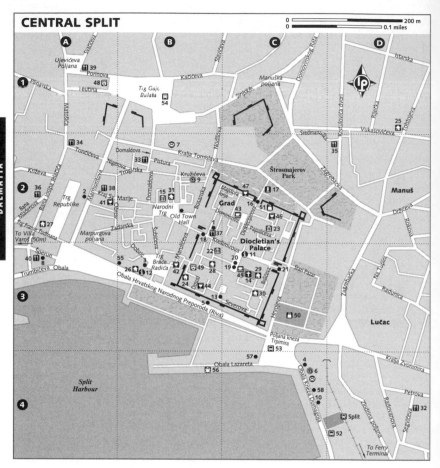

CENTRAL SPLIT

Turist Biro (Map p220; ☎ /fax 342 142; www.turist biro-split.hr; Obala Hrvatskog Narodnog Preporoda 12; ⏰ 9am-7pm Mon-Fri, to 4pm Sat) Best for arranging private accommodation; sells guidebooks and the Split Card.

Travel Agencies

Atlas Travel Agency (Map p220; ☎ 343 055; Trg Braće Radića 6; ⏰ 9am-6pm Mon-Fri) Also the American Express representative.

Daluma Travel (Map p220; ☎ /fax 338 484; www .daluma.hr; Obala Kneza Domagoja 1; ⏰ 8.30am-7pm Mon-Fri, to 5pm Sat) Arranges private accommodation.

Split Tours (Map p219; ☎ 352 553; www.splittours.hr; Gat Sv Duje bb; ⏰ 9am-7pm Mon-Fri, to 4pm Sat) In the ferry terminal, it handles tickets between Ancona (Italy), Split and Hvar, and finds private accommodation.

Touring (Map p220; ☎ 338 503; Obala Kneza Domagoja 10; ⏰ 9am-7pm Mon-Sat) Near the bus station, it represents Deutsche Touring and sells tickets to German cities.

SIGHTS
Diocletian's Palace

Facing the harbour, Diocletian's Palace (Map p220) is one of the most imposing Roman ruins in existence and the place you'll spend most of your time while in Split. Don't expect a palace though, nor a museum – this palace is the living heart of the city, and its labyrinthine streets are packed with people, bars, shops and restaurants. The narrow streets hide passageways and courtyards, some deserted and eerie, others thumping with music from bars and cafés, while the local residents hang out their washing to dry

SPLIT & CENTRAL DALMATIA

overhead, kids play football amid the ancient walls, and grannies sit in their windows watching the action below. It's an enchanting place.

Although the original structure was modified in the Middle Ages, the alterations have only served to increase the allure of this fascinating site. The palace was built from lustrous white stone from the island of Brač and construction lasted 10 years. Diocletian spared no expense, importing marble from Italy and Greece, and columns and sphinxes from Egypt. A military fortress, imperial residence and fortified town, the palace measures 215m from east to west (including the square corner towers) and is 181m wide at the southernmost point. The walls at their highest measure 26m and the entire structure covers 31,000 sq metres.

Each wall has a gate named after metals: at the northern end is the **Golden Gate**, while the southern end has the **Bronze Gate**; the eastern gate is the **Silver Gate** and to the west is the **Iron Gate**. From the eastern to the western gate there's a straight road (Krešimirova; also known as Decumanus), which separates the imperial residence on the southern side, with its state rooms and temples, from the northern side, once used by soldiers and servants. The Bronze Gate, in the southern wall, led from the living quarters to the sea. Two of the gates, the Bronze and Golden, are fronted by city landmarks: **Meštrović sculptures** of literary scholar Marko Marulić and the medieval bishop Grgur Ninski.

There are 220 buildings within the palace boundaries, home to about 3000 people as well as housing shops, cafés and restaurants. Each street has small signs at its beginning and end marking what you'll find upon it – bars, cafés, restaurants, shops, museums. It makes moving around much easier, though one of the best things you can do is get lost in the palace – it's small enough that you'll always find your way out easily. In any case, once you enter the palace, forget about street names.

The best way to see the palace's main sights is to follow our Walking Tour; see p222.

Archaeological Museum

Although it's north of the town centre, the **Archaeological Museum** (Arheološki Muzej; Map p219; ☎ 329 340; www.mdc.hr/split-arheoloski; Zrinsko-Frankopanska 25; adult/student 20/10KN; ☽ 9am-2pm Tue-Fri, to 1pm Sat & Sun) is worth the walk. The emphasis is on the Roman and early Christian period, with exhibits devoted to burial sculpture and excavations at Salona. The quality of the sculpture is high, and there are interesting reliefs based on Illyrian mythical figures. There's also jewellery, ceramics and coins on display.

Museum of Croatian Archaeological Monuments

This **museum** (Muzej Hrvatskih Arheoloških Spomenika; Map p219; ☎ 323 901; www.mhas-split.hr, in Croatian; Stjepana

---

PICIGIN

For a bit of fun, join the locals at the beach and play the very Dalmatian sport of *picigin*. The rules are simple: stand in the water up to your knees/waist and pass a small ball (the size of a squash ball) to other players at a rather high speed by whacking it with the palm of your hand. The idea is to keep the ball from falling and touching the water's surface. It is imperative to throw yourself about and into the water as much as possible. It's also advised to splash all the people standing around you and display your sporting vigour freely.

Check out the *picigin* 'headquarters' page at www.picigin.org (in Croatian only, but the photos should be illustrative enough) or the several YouTube videos demonstrating *picigin* techniques (which vary between Split, Krk and other parts of the coast). Have a go at the special New Year's eve *picigin* game if you think you're tough enough.

Gunjače bb; adult/student 10/5KN; ⊗ 9.30am-4pm Mon-Fri, to 1pm Sat) concentrates on medieval Croatian rulers, with inscribed stone fragments, parts of altars and furniture, late medieval tombstones, swords and jewellery. Captions are in Croatian, however, which makes it difficult to identify the exhibits.

Ethnographic Museum

In the centre of town is the mildly interesting **Ethnographic Museum** (Etnografski Muzej; Map p220; ☎ 343 108; www.etnografski-muzej-split.hr; Narodni Trg 1; adult/student 10/5KN; ⊗ 9am-2pm & 5-8pm Mon-Fri, 9am-1pm Sat Jun-Sep, 9am-2pm Mon-Fri, 9am-1pm Sat Oct-May), which has a collection of photos of old Split, traditional costumes and memorabilia of important citizens. Captions are in Croatian.

Meštrović Gallery & Kaštelet

Split's finest art museum is the **Meštrović Gallery** (Galerija Meštrović; off Map p219; ☎ 358 719; Šetalište Ivana Meštrovića 46; adult/student incl Kaštelet 30/15KN; ⊗ 9am-2pm Tue-Fri, to 1pm Sat & Sun). You'll see a comprehensive, well-arranged collection of works by Ivan Meštrović, Croatia's premier modern sculptor, who built the gallery as a personal residence from 1931 to 1939. Although Meštrović intended to retire here, he emigrated to the USA soon after WWII.

Don't miss the nearby **Kaštelet** (off Map p219; ☎ 358 185; Šetalište Ivana Meštrovića 39; admission by Meštrović Gallery ticket or adult/student 20/10KN; ⊗ 9am-9pm Tue-Sun mid-May–Sep, 9am-4pm Tue-Sat, 10am-3pm Sun Oct–mid-May), the fortress that Meštrović bought and restored to house his powerful *Life of Christ* wood reliefs.

ACTIVITIES

A flourishing beach life gives Split its aura of insouciance in summer. The most popular beach is **Bačvice** – awarded with a Blue Flag – on the eponymous inlet. It's a biggish pebbly beach with good **swimming** and a lively ambience, and is where you'll find *picigin* games galore (see above). There are showers and changing rooms at both ends of the beach. Bačvice is also a popular summer bar and club area, so head out here at night-time, too. The other choice is to follow Šetalište Ivana Meštrovića west, past the Meštrović Gallery, to the quieter **Kašjuni cove**.

From the Meštrović Gallery it's possible to hike straight up **Marjan Hill** (123m). Go up Tonća Petrasova Marovića on the western side of the gallery and continue straight up the stairway to Put Meja. Turn left and walk west to Put Meja 76. The trail begins on the western side of this building. Otherwise, you can start the walk closer to the centre, from the stairway that sits less than 100m west of Buffet Fife (Map p219), on Dražanac. Marjan Hill offers **trails** through the forest, **lookouts** and old **chapels**.

WALKING TOUR: DIOCLETIAN'S PALACE

Begin the walk just outside the palace at the imposing statue of **Gregorius of Nin** (**1**; Grgur Ninski), the 10th-century Croatian bishop who fought for the right to use old Croatian in liturgical services. Sculpted by Ivan Meštrović, this powerful work is one of the defining images of Split. Notice that his left big toe has been polished to a shine – it's said that rubbing the toe guarantees that you'll come back to Split.

To the west of the statue you'll see the well-preserved corner tower of the palace. Between the statue and the tower are the remains of the pre-Romanesque church of St Benedict with the 15th-century **Chapel of Arnir** (**2**). Peer through the protective glass and you'll see the altar slab and altar sarcophagus carved by the early Renaissance master Juraj Dalmatinac.

WALKING TOUR: DIOCLETIAN'S PALACE

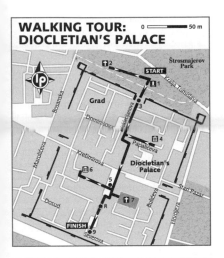

WALK FACTS

Start Statue of Gregorius of Nin
Finish Basement Halls
Distance 1km
Duration Two hours

The statue is right outside the **Golden Gate** (**3**; Zlatna Vrata or Northern Palace Gate), which was once the starting point for the road to Solin. From the fragments that remain, it's possible to visualise the statues, columns and arches that once decorated the gate. Turn left at Papalićeva and at No 5 is **Papalić Palace (4)** with a courtyard, loggia and external staircase. Built by Dalmatinac for one of the many noblemen who lived within the palace in the Middle Ages, it is considered a fine example of late-Gothic style with an elaborately carved entrance gate that proclaimed the importance of its original inhabitants.

The exterior of the palace is closer to its original state than the interior, which has been thoroughly restored to house the **Town Museum** (Muzej Grada Splita; ☎ 341 240; www.mdc.hr/splitgr; Papalićeva 5; adult/concession 10/5KN; ☼ 9am-9pm Tue-Fri, 10am-1pm Sat & Sun Jun-Sep, 10am-5pm Tue-Fri, 10am-1pm Sat & Sun Oct-May). Captions are in Croatian, but wall panels in a variety of languages provide a historical framework for the exhibits. The museum has three floors, with drawings, heraldic coats of arms, 17th-century weaponry, fine furniture, coins and documents from as far back as the 14th century.

Return to Dioklecijanova, turn left and you'll see the Peristil, the ceremonial entrance court to the imperial quarters, measuring 35m by 13m and three steps below the level of the surrounding streets. The longer side is lined by six granite columns, linked by arches and decorated with a stone frieze. The southern side is enclosed by the **Protiron (5)**, which is the entrance into the imperial quarters. The square has an outdoor café and the ancient stones provide handy seats to relax and people-watch in this popular meeting place.

Turn right (west) onto the narrow street of Kraj Sveti Ivana, which leads to what used to be the ceremonial and devotional section of the palace. Although the two temples that once flanked the streets have long since disappeared, you can still see parts of columns and a few fragments. At the end of the street is the **Temple of Jupiter (6)**, later converted into a baptistery. The temple once had a porch supported by columns, but the one column you see dates from the 5th century. The headless sphinx in black granite guarding the entrance was imported from Egypt at the time of the temple's construction in the 5th century. The walls of the temple support a barrel-vaulted ceiling and there's a decorative frieze around the other three walls. Below the temple is a crypt, which was once used as a church.

Returning to the Peristil, go up the eastern stairs to the **Cathedral of St Domnius (7**; Katedrala Svetog Duje; ☎ 342 589; Kraj Svetog Duje 5; adult/student incl Treasury 10/5KN; ☼ 7am-noon & 4-7pm), originally built as Diocletian's mausoleum. The original octagonal form of the mausoleum, encircled by 24 columns, has been almost completely preserved. The domed interior is round with two rows of Corinthian columns and a frieze showing Emperor Diocletian and his wife, Prisca.

The oldest monuments in the cathedral are the remarkable scenes on the wooden entrance doors from the life of Christ. Carved by Andrija Buvina in the 13th century, the scenes are presented in 28 squares, 14 on each side, and recall the fashion of Romanesque miniatures of the time.

Notice the right altar carved by Bonino da Milano in 1427 and the vault above the altar decorated with murals by Dujam Vušković. To the left is the altar of St Anastasius (Sveti Staš; 1448) by Dalmatinac, with a relief of *The Flagellation of Christ*, which is one of the finest sculptural works of its time in Dalmatia. The main altar dates from the 13th century and the vault is ornamented with paintings by Matija Pončun.

The choir is furnished with 13th-century Romanesque seats that are the oldest in Dalmatia. Cross the altar and follow the signs to the **Treasury** (8am-noon Sun Jul & Aug, 10am-noon Sun Jun & Sep, 11am-noon Sun Oct-May), rich in reliquaries, icons, church robes, illuminated manuscripts and documents in Glagolitic script.

Part of the same structure, the Romanesque **belfry** (admission 5KN; 7am-noon & 4-7pm Jul & Aug, 8am-noon Jun & Sep) was constructed between the 12th and 16th centuries and reconstructed in 1908 after it collapsed. Notice the two lion figures at the foot of the belfry and the Egyptian black-granite sphinx dating from the 15th century BC on the right wall. South of the mausoleum, there are remains of the Roman baths, a Roman building with a mosaic and the remains of the imperial dining hall in various stages of preservation.

Immediately to the west of the cathedral are the massive steps leading down through the Protiron into the **vestibule (8)**, which is the best-preserved part of the imperial residence. The circular ground floor is topped by a cupola once covered in mosaics and marble, although the centre of the dome has disappeared. Today, the cellars are filled with stands selling souvenirs and handicrafts. To the left is the entrance to the **basement halls (9**; adult/concession 6/3KN; 10am-6pm) of the palace. Although mostly empty, the rooms and corridors emit a haunting sense of timelessness that is well worth the price of the ticket. The cellars open onto the southern gate.

TOURS

Atlas Travel Agency (p220) runs excursions to the waterfalls at Krka National Park (p212) and Zlatni Rat beach (p247) on the island of Brač, as well as other day trips. If you're after more of a party kind of tour, check out Split Hostel Booze & Snooze (opposite) for booze cruises (120KN) and more sober rafting (280KN) and Krka National Park (280KN) tours.

Also check if your hotel organises excursions and activities.

FESTIVALS & EVENTS

Most festivals in Split take place along the Riva. The tourist office can give you more info about all the festivals listed here.

The traditional February **Carnival** sees locals dressing up and dancing in the streets; it's great fun. There's also the **Feast of St Duje** (7 May), otherwise known as Split Day, when there's much singing and dancing. There is a **Flower Show** in May, and from June to September a variety of evening entertainment is presented in the old town, usually around the Peristil. The four-day **Festival of Popular Music** is held around the end of June. The **Split Summer Festival** (www.splitsko-ljeto.hr, in Croatian), from 14 July to 14 August, features opera, drama, ballet and concerts on open-air stages. The summer concert season usually starts off with the **Split Jazz Festival** in late July. Split also has a **Film Festival** (www.splitfilmfestival.hr), which focuses on new international films and lots of art-house movies. It's held from 13 to 20 September.

SLEEPING

Good budget accommodation is quite thin on the ground in Split, unless you're looking to sleep in dorms. Private accommodation is the best option and in the summer you may be deluged at the bus station by women offering *sobe* (rooms available). Make sure you are clear about the exact location of the room or you may find yourself several bus rides from the town centre. The best thing to do is to book through the Turist Biro (p220) or Daluma Travel (p220), but there is little available within the heart of the old town.

Expect to pay between 145KN and 220KN for a double room where you will probably share the bathroom with the proprietor. If you have your own wheels and don't mind staying out of town, you will find a wealth of *pensions* (guest houses) along the main Split–Dubrovnik road just south of town.

Also consider **Dalmatian Villas** (Map p219; 340 680; www.dalmatinskevile.hr; Kralja Zvonimira 8; r low-high per week €250-450, apt €350-1000), where you can rent rooms or apartments in renovated stone villas. It has accommodation on the islands, too, and rents both rooms and apartments on a daily basis out of the high season.

Budget

Camping Stobreč (off Map p219; 325 426; www.camping split.com; Sv Lovre 6, Stobreč; per adult low-high €3.60-4.60, site €2.90-4.50; Apr-Nov;) This is a great place to pitch your tent and enjoy Split and Solin (it's around 6km away from each), as well as the beach. It's a well-equipped place, with two

KLAPA YOUR HANDS! *Vesna Marić*

There won't be a visitor to Croatia who hasn't heard the dulcet tones of a *klapa* song. This music involves a bunch of hunky men in a circle, singing tear-jerkers about love, betrayal, patriotism, death, beauty and other life-affirming subjects in honeyed multitonal harmonies (see p46 for more on *klapa*).

I happened upon a *klapa* rehearsal in the midst of Diocletian's Palace one spring evening. After listening for a while and being overcome with a multitude of emotions, which this macho-yet-sensitive music often inspires, I seized an opportunity to talk to the first tenor, Branko Tomić, a man whose high-toned voice complements the basses and baritones that accompany him.

'I've sung with the Filip Devič *klapa* for 35 years,' he says. 'It's a passion of mine. I started singing in high school and I loved it.' I wonder how someone who grew up in the 1960s, with all the rock'n'roll and free love, opted to sing in a *klapa* rather than a rock band. 'We sing about so many different things: we serenade, we sing traditional songs, sentimental songs about missing your family or your home town. It's a gentler, more companionship-based experience, though the new generations are starting to prefer our covers of pop songs. That's a really big thing in Croatia nowadays.' Apparently, though, the tourists still like the traditional stuff. 'I don't mind,' he says, 'as long as we can carry on singing and someone is listening.'

With this he has to leave – their performance in a local club is about to start. A few seconds later, all that's left on the old street is the sound of their voices and me, reminiscing about love and life as I order an ice cream.

beaches (one sandy and great for kids), three bars, a restaurant, shop, internet café, you name it. You can also organise excursions from here, and a gazillion activities are on offer, including horse riding and rafting. If you don't have a tent of your own, you can rent one.

Hostel Split Mediterranean House (Map p220; ☎ 098 987 1312; www.hostel-split.com; Vukasovićeva 21; dm from 100KN; ☒) It's a 10-minute walk from the Golden Gate and Grgur Ninski to this friendly, family-run hostel set in a lovely old stone building. There are two six-bed dorms and some newer en suite three-bed dorms. You get to use a kitchen and the lovely courtyard. Check-in is between 9am and 8pm.

Split Hostel Booze & Snooze (Map p220; ☎ 342 787; www.splithostel.com; Narodni Trg 8; dm low-high 110-180KN; ☒) A great new addition to Split's backpacker scene, this hostel is run by Aussie Croats and does exactly what it says on the tin. It's a party place, with 23 beds to snooze in and a nice terrace, and it's right in the centre of town. The two women who run the place are super-friendly, and, of course, English-speaking. They organise several tours around town, including a 'booze cruise', more liver-friendly day trips to Krka National Park and rafting on the Cetina River. It's the backpackers' favourite in the city.

Hotel Jupiter (Map p220; ☎ 344 801; www.hotel-jupiter.info; Grabovčeva Širina 1; r per person low-high 200-250KN; ☒) Hotel Jupiter advertises itself as 'the cheaper place to stay in Split' and while this is vaguely the case, it's also very frill-free for the price. All the bathrooms are shared, the beds are low, the lighting is weak and dreary, and the service is torpid at times. The best things about it are the location, the air-con and, well, the price.

Midrange

our pick B&B Kaštel 1700 (Map p220; ☎ 343 912; www.kastelsplit.com; Mihovilova Širina 5; s low-high 290-510KN; d 400-660KN; ☒ ☐) Among Split's best value-for-money places, this is right by the Southern Gate, within the palace walls. It's near the bars, overlooks Radićev Trg and has sweet and tidy rooms and friendly, efficient service. There are also triples, and apartments have small kitchens. Book in advance.

Hotel Dujam (Map p219; ☎ 538 025; www.hoteldujam.com; Velebitska 27; s low-high 370-490KN, d 500-660KN; ☒ ☒) A bit of a hike out of the centre (a 20-minute walk), Hotel Dujam sits in an apartment block of a quiet residential area. The carpeted rooms are clean and bright with en suite bathrooms, air-con and satellite TVs. If you don't fancy walking, take bus 9 from the port.

our pick Villa Varoš (Map p219; ☎ 483 469; www.villavaros.hr; Miljenka Smoje 1; d high-low 400-500KN; ☒) Midrangers are getting a better deal in Split nowadays with places such as Villa Varoš around. Owned by a New Yorker Croat, Villa Varoš is central (in the Varoš neighbourhood), the rooms are simple, bright and airy, the three apartments are excellent (with a well-equipped kitchen) and the price is most commendable.

Hotel Bellevue (Map p220; ☎ 345 644; www .hotel-bellevue-split.hr; Bana Josipa Jelačića 2; s low-high 513-610KN, d 703-830KN) The Bellevue is an atmospheric old classic that has sure seen more polished days, but it still remains one of the more dreamy hotels in town. It's all regal patterned wallpaper, dark-brown wood, art deco elements, billowing gauzy curtains and faded but well-kept rooms. Don't stay here if you want modern-day luxury, but do spend a night if you fancy feeling like you're stepping back in time.

Hotel Adriana (Map p220; ☎ 340 000; www.hotel -adriana.com; Obala Hrvatskog Narodnog Preporoda 9; s low-high 550-650KN, d 750-900KN; ⌘) Good value, excellent location. The rooms are not massively exciting, with their navy curtains and beige furniture, but some have sea views, which is a real bonus in Split's old town. If you're catching a bus/ferry/train out of town in the evening, you can rent a room here for the day at 50% of the normal price. The downstairs restaurant is popular with local families for big celebratory lunches or dinners.

Hotel Consul (Map p219; ☎ 340 130; www.hotel -consul.net; Tršćanska 34; s low-high 620-650KN, d 850-920KN; ⓟ ⌘) The Consul is a good 20-minute walk from the centre, with rooms that have worn-out green carpets and little in the way of decoration save for some flat-screen TVs. Still, it's quiet, there's a large leafy terrace and some of the rooms have jacuzzis. This place may suit travellers with their own wheels who want to spend one night in Split. If you're on foot, go up Držićev Prilaz off Ulica Domovinskog Rata.

Top End

Split is getting some very swanky hotels indeed. If you fancy lazing in a jacuzzi or an aromatic wellness centre after you've been lazing by the Adriatic all day long, well here's your chance.

Hotel Globo (Map p219; ☎ 481 111; www.hotelglobo .com; Lovretska 18; s low-high €98-107, d €119-135; ⓟ ⌘) Renovated in 2007 and geared towards business travellers, this is a lovely, swish four-star hotel with elegantly decorated rooms, high ceilings and luxurious beds. The spacious

bathrooms have baths. It's a 15-minute walk from the centre of town.

our pick **Hotel Peristil** (Map p220; ☎ 329 070; www .hotelperistil.com; Poljana Kraljice Jelene 5; s low-high 700-1000KN, d 900-1200KN; ⌘ ⌘) The loveliest hotel in Split also has the best location: it overlooks the bell tower of the Cathedral of St Domnius and the Peristil, gazes at the square where people sip coffee and souvenirs are sold, and is basically at the heart of it all, in the midst of Diocletian's Palace. The owner, Mile Čaktaš, is proud of his co-op set-up, where all the staff have a share in running the hotel, so you'll find the service sincerely warm. The rooms are absolutely gorgeous – all have wooden floors, antique details, smooth linen and good views. Room 304 even has a small cove in the corner with a bit of the palace's ancient wall exposed *and* it overlooks the Peristil. A roof terrace was being built at the time of research, to be completed by 2009, so expect to have the most spectacular future location for eating breakfasts and sighing over sunsets.

Hotel Park (Map p219; ☎ 406 400; www.hotelpark -split.hr; Hatzeov Perivoj 3; s low-high €113-137, d €143-189; ⓟ ⌘ ⌘) The Park has been one of Split's top upmarket hotels for years and its popularity isn't waning. This must be thanks to the good, comfy rooms, the central location (behind Bačvice), the gorgeous palm-fringed terrace, the wellness centre and amazing buffet breakfasts. The hotel's restaurant, Bruna (p228), is a coveted place to splash out on supper.

Art Hotel (Map p219; ☎ 302 302; www.arthotel.hr; Ulica Slobode 41; s/d from €119-160; ⓟ ⌘ ⌘) In a renovated factory building, the Art Hotel sits between boutique and business, with plush beds, pretty rooms, a gym and aerobics classes.

Le Meridien Grand Hotel Lav (off Map p219; ☎ 500 500; www.lemeridien.com; Grljevačka 2A; r from €120; ⓟ ⌘ ⌘ ⌘) The daddy of all Split hotels, this five-star giant sits 8km south of Split, at Podstrana, with 800m of beach, four interlinking buildings and 381 beautifully designed rooms. Think lots of reds, whites and blacks, endless sea views, the longest swimming pool in history, luscious gardens, a new marina for your yacht, a diving centre, an amazing restaurant and free access to Split's art collections. It really is something else. Check out its excellent internet weekend rates.

Hotel Vestibul Palace (Map p220; ☎ 329 329; www .vestibulpalace.com; Iza Vestibula 4; s low-high €120-160, d €140-390; ⌘ ⌘) The poshest in the palace, with seven stylish rooms, all with exposed ancient walls, leather and wood.

EATING
Budget
Burek Bar (Map p220; Domaldova 13) Just down from the main post office, Burek Bar serves a good breakfast or lunch of *burek* (pastry stuffed with ground meat or cheese) and yoghurt for about 12KN.

Black Cat (Map p220; ☎ 490 284; Segvićeva 1; mains from 20KN) If you get tired of Croatian food and crave a taco, quesadilla or any other Mexican delight, head straight for this little bistro, five-minutes' walk from the seafront and bus station. There's lots for vegetarians and the chef does some excellent homemade desserts. The little terrace is covered and heated in winter.

Galija (Map p220; Tončićeva 12; pizzas from 26KN) Galija has been the most popular place on Split's pizza scene for several decades now. It's the sort of joint that locals take you to for an unfussy but good lunch or dinner, where everyone relaxes on the wooden benches with the leftovers of a *quattro stagioni* or *margherita* in front of them and several emptied carafes of wine.

Kod Joze (Map p220; ☎ 347 397; Sredmanuška 4; mains from 40KN) A die-hard faction of locals keeps this informal *konoba* (simple family-run establishment) alive and kicking. It's Dalmatian all the way – ham, cheese and green tagliatelle with seafood.

Makrovega (Map p219; ☎ 394 440; www.makrovega.hr; Leština 2; mains from 40KN; ☑ 9am-7pm Mon-Fri, to 4pm Sat; ☒) What a difference a decade makes! Vegans and vegetarians were an unknown species in Croatia some years ago, forced to eat the potatoes on the side of the lamb shank, but this is no more. Makrovega is a meat-free haven with a clean, spacious (nonsmoking!) interior and delicious buffet and à la carte food that alternates between macrobiotic and vegetarian. Choose from wild rice with vegetables, pea and mint soup and excellent cakes.

Buffet Fife (Map p219; ☎ 345 223; Trumbićeva Obala 11; mains around 40KN) Dragomir presides over a motley crew of sailors and misfits who drop in for his simple, home cooking, especially the *pašticada* (beef stew with wine and spices), and own brand of grumpy but loving hospitality.

☐ our pick Konoba Trattoria Bajamont (Map p220; ☎ 091 253 7441; Bajamontijeva 3; mains from 50KN) This is possibly Split's most characterful *konoba*, and we mean that literally: the number of local characters who hang out in this tiny place within the palace walls make it one of the most authentic places to drop in and eat. It's a one-room joint with four or five tables on one side and a heavily leaned-on bar on the other; there's no sign above the door and the menu is written out in marker pen and stuck in an inconspicuous spot by the entrance. The food is excellent and the menu usually features things such as small fried fish, squid-ink risotto, octopus salad and *brujet* (fish/seafood stew with wine, onions and herbs, served with polenta; called *brodet* elsewhere in Croatia). It's all fresh and made on a daily basis. The loyal bar-proppers bring a guitar from time to time and everyone gets merry and sings along.

Midrange
Restaurant Boban (Map p219; ☎ 543 300; Hektorovićeva 49; mains from 60KN) This has been Split's favourite restaurant since 1973, and you'll know why when you sink your teeth into the fresh seafood and juicy fish that's seared and served with some imaginative sauces. It's a family-run place that likes to innovate and keep its reputation high. In the Firule area.

Šperun (Map p220; ☎ 346 999; Šperun 3; mains from 70KN) A sweet little restaurant decked out with rustic details and exposed stone walls, Šperun is a favourite among the foreigners – possibly because the waiters seem to speak every language under the sun. The food is classic Dalmatian, with a decent *brujet*, fresh mussels in a tomato and parsley sauce, or grilled tuna with capers. There is also a good buffet and daily menu.

Bekan (Map p219; ☎ 389 400; Ivana Zajca 1; mains from 70KN) Bekan serves an array of seafood prepared Dalmatian style. It's not cheap (unless you order the spaghetti with seafood for 52KN), but you can sample a savoury shrimp *buzara* (a sauce of tomatoes, white wine, onions and breadcrumbs) on an airy terrace overlooking the sea.

Restaurant Šumica (Map p219; ☎ 389 897; Put Firula 6; mains from 70KN) For a splurge you can't do better than this place. Homemade pasta is combined with salmon or other fish in imaginative sauces. The grilled scampi is perfection, but you pay a steep 380KN per kilogram. Before your meal you'll be served a dish of homemade fish pâté with bread to whet your appetite. Meals are served on an open-air terrace under pine trees with a view of the sea.

Konoba Hvaranin (Map p220; ☎ 091 767 5891; Ban Mladenova 9; mains from 70KN) A mother-father-son business that feeds Split's journalists and writers, the Hvaranin is a long-standing favourite of the city's creatives. Mum and dad cook great fish and seafood, bake their own bread and stew their own tomato sauce, and the regulars adore their traditional basics such as *pašticada* and risottos. This is a good place to try *rožata* (Croatian crème brûlée) – it's fresh and homemade.

Top End

Noštromo (Map p220; ☎ 091 405 6666; www.restoran-nostromo.hr; Kraj Sv Marije 10; mains from 80KN) Sitting on the side of the fish market, Noštromo is one of Split's poshest restaurants. The locals love it because it prepares fish bought daily at the market and because tradition is all; there are no culinary surprises, just fresh, well-prepared and wonderfully presented food and delectable wines.

Bruna (Map p219; ☎ 406 425; Hatzeov Perivoj 3; mains from 80KN) This is Hotel Park's (p226) restaurant and a place that's kept its head chef and excellent reputation for the last 30 years. It's all seasonal produce here; depending on when you're around, you can choose from truffles, wild asparagus or mushroom dishes.

Self-Catering

The vast **supermarket** (Map p220; Svačićeva 1) stocks a wide selection of meat and cheese for sandwiches and nearly everything else you might want for a picnic. Sit around the square and eat your goodies.

DRINKING

Split is great for nightlife, especially (or more so) in the spring and summer months. The palace walls are generally throbbing with loud music on Friday and Saturday nights, and you can spend the entire night going around the mazelike streets, discovering new places. Note that palace bars close at 1am (as people live within the palace walls). The entertainment complex of Bačvice has a multitude of open-air bars and clubs that stay open till the wee hours. Daytime coffee sipping is best along the Riva or on one of the squares inside the palace walls.

Buža (Map p220; Priora Petra 7) Every Dalmatian town has a place named 'Buža' (literally 'Hole') and they are usually of a similar nature: simple, basic and friendly. Split's Buža is in a small palace courtyard and it plays rock'n'roll, fast and slow.

Teak Caffe (Map p220; Majstora Jurja 11) On a busy square, the Teak's terrace is super-popular for coffees and chats during the day. It's busy in the evenings, too, and a great place to check out the locals.

Le Porta (Map p220; Majstora Jurja) Next door to Teak Caffe, Le Porta is renowned for its cocktails. On the same square – Majstora Jurja – are Kala, Dante, Whisky Bar and Na Kantunu, all of which end up merging into one when the night gets busy, so remember your waiter!

Galerija (Map p220; Dominisova 9) Parallel to Majstora Jurja is Dominisova, another street that's full of fun bars. Galerija is quieter than others, catering to smooching lovers or those wanting to catch up with friends without blasting music drowning out the conversation. The interior is granny-chic, with pretty floral sofas and armchairs, paintings on the walls and little lamps dotted everywhere. Try any of the many types of tea.

Mosquito Bar (Map p220; Dominisova) If you've had enough tea at Galerija, head next door to Mosquito Bar, where you can sit on the big terrace, grab a cocktail, listen to music and hang out with the Splićani.

Ghetto Club (Map p220; ☎ 346 879; Dosud 10) Head for Split's most bohemian bar in an intimate courtyard amid flowerbeds, a trickling fountain, great music and a friendly atmosphere.

Luxor Bar (Map p220; Kraj Sv Ivana 11) Having coffee in the courtyard of the cathedral may be the most touristy thing to do, but it's also one of the best: little cushions are laid out on the steps, you've got Sv Duje on one side, the Peristil on the other, people are snapping photos all round, and the locals are going about their business.

Red Room (Map p220; ☎ 459 231; Carrarina Poljana 4) Tropical colours, a leopard-spotted bar and the DJ music here drag young Splićani in by the hundreds. Open till midnight and a great pre-clubbing spot.

Café Puls (Map p220; Mihovilova Šira) and **Café Shook** (Map p220; Mihovilova Šira) are pretty much indistinguishable late on Friday or Saturday night, when the dozen steps that link these two bars are chock-a-block with youngsters. It's an area that's hard to miss if you enter the palace from the Riva, and its popularity hasn't waned in a decade. Great for people watching and cocktail drinking.

ENTERTAINMENT
Nightclubs
After all the bars go quiet at 1am, head over to Bačvice for some clubbing under the stars. The best sources of information about Split's clubs are www.clubbing-scene.com and the *Splitski Navigator* or *Scena* brochures (both available in tourist offices). Alternatively, look out for flyers in any of the late-night bars.

Obojena Svjetlost (off Map p219; ☎ 358 280; Šetalište Ivana Meštrovića 35) Tons of live and DJ music, a wide seafront terrace and a massive interior make Obojena Svjetlost (Coloured Light) one of the best places to go out in Split. It's by Kasuni beach so you can watch the sunrise while dipping your toes in the sea.

Master's (Map p219; ☎ 536 983; Osječka) Split's most popular club and the one where such big-name DJs head – this is where you, too, should go if you want a proper night's clubbing. It's 60KN to get in when big names are booked.

Tropic Club Ecuador (Map p219; Bačvice bb) Palm trees and fruity cocktails, DJ house music, the lapping of the Adriatic, hanging out at the beach under the stars – top ingredients for a top night out.

Jungla (off Map p219; ☎ 091 571 3099; Šetalište Ivana Meštrovića bb) Jungla fell on hard times for a while but is fortunately up again, hosting good electro nights for a young, fun crowd.

O'Hara's (Map p219; ☎ 098 364 262; Cvjetna Zenta 3; ☼ Jun-Sep) A waterfront terrace means alfresco clubbing in the summer months. Head here if you're a house-music fan.

Puls 2 (Map p220; Buvinina 1) Hip and sleek, this bar pulsates on summer nights. Friday night is live music and Saturday is disco night.

Cinemas
Kino Bačvice (Map p219; ☎ 091 500 214; Bačvice bb) The after-dark entertainment zone of Bačvice is a perfect venue for the open-air cinema that runs nightly in summer.

Theatre
Croatian National Theatre (Map p220; ☎ 515 999; Trg Gaje Bulata) During winter, opera and ballet are presented here. The best seats cost about 60KN and tickets for the same night are usually available. Erected in 1891, the theatre was fully restored in 1979 in the original style; it's worth attending a performance for the architecture alone.

SHOPPING
Shopaholics will find their habit hard to kick in Split – this is the place with the most shoe shops in Croatia. The Diocletian Palace walls are packed with shops – small boutiques and international chains alike. Marmontova is equally popular among the locals for shopping.

Diocletian's Cellars (Map p220) is part of the palace's basement halls (p224). It is a market for crafted jewellery, reproductions of Roman busts, silver cigarette cases, candlestick holders, wooden sailing ships, leather goods and other odds and ends. Prices aren't too steep and you might find the perfect lightweight item to fulfil back-from-a-trip, gift-giving obligations.

There's a daily market (Map p220) above Obala Lazareta where you can buy fruit, vegetables, shoes, confectionery, clothing, flowers, souvenirs and other products. If you can't find what you're looking for in this market, the chances are it doesn't exist in Split.

Zlatna Vrata (Map p220; ☎ 360 122; Carrarina Poljana 1) Antiques and junk lovers will delight in the knick-knacks at Zlatna Vrata – old Yugoslav clocks, antique ceramics, vintage socialist phones and who knows what else can be found with a bit of digging around.

GETTING THERE & AWAY
Air
Croatia Airlines (Map p220; ☎ 362 997; www.croatiaairlines.hr; Obala Hrvatskog Narodnog Preporoda 9; ☼ 8am-8pm Mon-Fri, 9am-noon Sat) operates one-hour flights to and from Zagreb up to four times a day and there's a daily flight to Dubrovnik.

Easyjet (www.easyjet.com) has started flying to Split, too, making flights from the UK more affordable.

The airport is 25km west of town.

Boat
Jadrolinija (Map p219; ☎ 338 333, 355 399; Gat Sv Duje bb), in the large ferry terminal opposite the bus station, handles the coastal ferry line that runs from Rijeka to Dubrovnik, stopping at Stari Grad on Hvar (92KN, 1½ hours) and Korčula (102KN, five hours). However, the local car ferry is cheaper (38KN, 1½ hours), and there's a fast passenger boat, the **Krilo** (www.krilo.hr), that goes to Hvar Town (40KN, one hour) daily in July and August (four to five times a week from September to June) and then on to Korčula, as well as a passenger boat

(22KN, two hours) that goes on to Vela Luka (27KN, 3¼ hours).

The schedules and tickets for all lines from Split to Italy are available from **Jadroagent** (Map p219; ☎ 338 335) in the ferry terminal. At **SNAV** (Map p219; ☎ 322 252; ⌚ 9am-7pm Mon-Fri, to 4pm Sat), also in the ferry terminal, you can book a four-hour connection to Ancona and Pescara in Italy. For more on boats to Italy, see p310.

Car ferries and passenger lines depart from separate docks; the passenger lines leave from Obala Lazareta (Map p220) and car ferries from Gat Sv Duje (Map p219). You can buy tickets from either the main Jadrolinija office in the large ferry terminal opposite the bus station, which handles all car ferry services that depart from the docks around the ferry terminal, or at one of the two stalls near the docks (Map p220). In summer it's usually necessary to reserve at least a day in advance for a car ferry and you are asked to appear several hours before departure. There is rarely a problem obtaining a ticket off-season, but reserve as much in advance as possible in July and August.

Bus

Advance bus tickets with seat reservations are recommended. There are buses from the main **bus station** (Map p220; ☎ 060 327 327; www.ak-split.hr, in Croatian) beside the harbour to the following destinations, among others:

Destination	Fare (KN)	Duration (hr)	Daily services
Dubrovnik	105-166	4½	12
Makarska	60	11½	12
Međugorje*	120	3	5
Mostar*	120	2-4	4
Pula	331	10	1
Rijeka	250-380	7½	10
Sarajevo*	200	7	11
Zadar	120	3	8
Zagreb	195	5-9	27

*Bosnia & Hercegovina

Bus 37 goes to Split airport and Trogir (15KN, half hourly), also stopping at Solin; it leaves from a local bus station on Domovinskog Rata, 1km northeast of the city centre, but it's faster and more convenient to take an inter-city bus heading north to Zadar or Rijeka.

Note that Split–Dubrovnik buses pass briefly through Bosnian territory, so keep your passport handy for border-crossing points.

Car

If you want to rent a car in Split, try one of the following:

Budget Rent-a-Car (Map p219; ☎ 345 700; www .budget.hr; Hotel Marjan, Obala Kneza Branimira 8)

Dollar Thrifty (Map p219; ☎ 339 000; Hotel Marjan, Obala Kneza Branimira 8)

ITR (Map p220; ☎ 343 070; Obala Lazareta 2)

Train

There are two fast trains a day between Split **train station** (Map p220; ☎ 338 525; www.hznet.hr; Obala Kneza Domagoja 9) and Zagreb (175KN, six hours) and one overnight train (168KN, 8½ hours). From Monday to Saturday there are six daily trains between Šibenik and Split (60KN, two hours) and four trains on Sunday. There are also seven trains a day from Split to Zadar (82KN, 4½ hours).

GETTING AROUND
To/From the Airport

The bus to Split airport (30KN) leaves from Obala Lazareta 3 about 90 minutes before flight times, or you can take bus 37 from the local bus station on Domovinskog Rata (15KN, 50 minutes). Croatia Airlines buses meet all Croatia Airlines flights; passengers on other flights are also welcome to take them. A taxi will cost about 125KN.

Bus

Local buses connect the town centre and the harbour with outlying districts. A one-zone ticket costs 9KN for one trip in central Split and buses run about every 15 minutes from 5.30am to 11.30pm.

AROUND SPLIT
Šolta

This lovely, wooded island (just 59 sq km) is a popular getaway for Split inhabitants escaping the sultry summer heat. The island's only entry point is Rogač, where ferries from Split tie up in front of the **tourist office** (☎ /fax 654 491; www .solta.hr; ⌚ 8am-7pm Mon-Sat Jul & Aug, 8am-3pm Mon-Fri Sep-Jun) on the edge of a large bay. A shady path leads around the bay to smaller coves with rocky beaches and a small road leads uphill to a market. **Nečujam** is 7km from Rogač; set on a curving beach, it has a hotel, snack bar and outdoor shower. There is only one ATM on the island, in Stomorska, so bring enough cash.

Three to five daily car ferries run between Split and Rogač (28KN, one hour).

Solin (Salona)

The ruins of the ancient city of Solin (Roman Salona), among the vineyards at the foot of mountains just northeast of Split, are the most archaeologically important in Croatia.

Although Solin is today surrounded by noisy highways and industry, it was first mentioned in 119 BC as the centre of the Illyrian tribe. The Romans seized the site in 78 BC and under the rule of Augustus it became the administrative headquarters of the Roman Dalmatian province.

When Emperor Diocletian built his palace in Split at the end of the 3rd century AD, it was the proximity to Solin that attracted him. Solin was incorporated into the Eastern Roman Empire in the 6th century, but was levelled by the Slavs and Avars in 614. The inhabitants fled to Split and neighbouring islands, leaving Solin to decay.

SIGHTS

A good place to begin your visit to the city is at the main entrance near Caffe Bar Salona. There's a small **museum & Information centre** (☎ 211 538; admission 10KN; ⏱ 9am-6pm Mon-Sat Jun-Sep, 9am-1pm Mon-Sat Oct-May) at this entrance. **Manastirine**, the fenced area behind the car park, was a burial place for early Christian martyrs prior to the legalisation of Christianity. The excavated remains of **Kapljuč Basilica** – one of the early Christian cemeteries in Salona and the place where cemeterial basilicas were built – and the 5th-century **Kapjinc Basilica** that sits inside it are highlights, although this area was outside the ancient city itself. Overlooking Manastirine is **Tusculum Museum**, an archaeological museum with interesting sculpture embedded in the walls and in the garden.

The Manastirine/Tusculum complex is part of an **archaeological reserve**. Pick up a brochure at the information centre if it's open at the time of your visit.

A path bordered by cypresses runs south to the northern city wall of Solin. Notice the **covered aqueduct** located south of the wall. It was probably built around the 1st century AD and supplied Solin and Diocletian's Palace with water from the Jadro River. The ruins you see in front of you as you stand on the wall were an early Christian site; they include

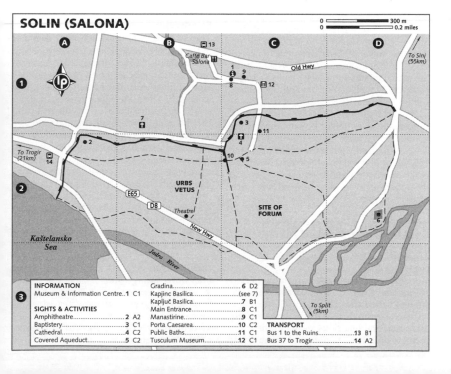

SOLIN (SALONA)

0 — 300 m
0 — 0.2 miles

To Sinj (55km)

Caffe Bar Salona

Old Hwy

To Trogir (21km)

URBS VETUS

E65

D8   Theatre

SITE OF FORUM

New Hwy

Kaštelansko Sea

Jadro River

To Split (5km)

INFORMATION			
Museum & Information Centre..1	C1	Gradina................................6	D2
		Kapjinc Basilica.....................(see 7)	
SIGHTS & ACTIVITIES		Kapljuč Basilica.......................7	B1
Amphitheatre...........................2	A2	Main Entrance..........................8	C1
Baptistery...............................3	C1	Manastirine..............................9	C1
Cathedral................................4	C2	Porta Caesarea........................10	C2
Covered Aqueduct...................5	C2	Public Baths............................11	C1
		Tusculum Museum....................12	C1
		TRANSPORT	
		Bus 1 to the Ruins....................13	B1
		Bus 37 to Trogir.......................14	A2

a three-aisled, 5th-century **cathedral** with an octagonal **baptistery**, and the remains of **Bishop Honorius' Basilica** with a ground plan in the form of a Greek cross. **Public baths** adjoin the cathedral on the east.

Southwest of Solin's cathedral is the 1st-century eastern city gate, **Porta Caesarea**, later engulfed by the growth of the city in all directions. Grooves in the stone road left by ancient wheels can still be seen at this gate. South of the city gate was the centre of town, the forum, with temples to Jupiter, Juno and Minerva, none of which are visible today.

At the western end of Solin is the huge 2nd-century **amphitheatre**, destroyed in the 17th century by the Venetians to prevent it from being used as a refuge by Turkish raiders. At one time it could accommodate 18,000 spectators, which gives an idea of the size and importance of this ancient city.

The southeastern corner of the complex contains the **Gradina**, a medieval fortress around the remains of a rectangular early Christian church.

GETTING THERE & AWAY

The ruins are easily accessible on Split city bus 1 (15KN), which goes directly to Caffe Bar Salona (look out for the yellow bus shelter on the left-hand side) every half-hour from Trg Gaje Bulata. Alternatively, you can catch most Sinj-bound buses (15KN, 10 daily) from the main bus station to take you to Solin, or catch the 37 that leaves from Split's local bus station on Domovinskog Rata.

From the amphitheatre at Solin it's easy to continue on to Trogir by catching a westbound bus 37 from the nearby stop on the adjacent highway (buy a four-zone ticket for 15KN in Split if you plan to do this). If, on the other hand, you want to return to Split, use the underpass to cross the highway and catch an eastbound bus 37.

TROGIR & AROUND

TROGIR

pop 1600

Gorgeous and tiny Trogir (formerly Trau) is beautifully set within medieval walls, its streets knotted and mazelike. It's fronted by a wide seaside promenade that's lined with bars and cafés, and luxurious yachts in the summer. Trogir is unique among Dalmatian towns

for its profuse collection of Romanesque and Renaissance architecture (which flourished under Venetian rule); this, along with its magnificent cathedral, earned it World Heritage status in 1997.

Trogir is an easy day trip from Split and a relaxing place to spend a few days, taking a trip or two to nearby islands.

History

Backed by high hills in the north, the sea to the south and snug in its walls, Trogir (Tragurion to the Romans) proved an attractive place to settlers. The early Croats settled the old Illyrian town by the 7th century. Its defensive position allowed Trogir to maintain its autonomy throughout Croatian and Byzantine rule, while trade and nearby mines ensured its economic viability. In the 13th century sculpture and architecture flourished, reflecting a vibrant, dynamic culture. When Venice bought Dalmatia in 1409, Trogir refused to accept the new ruler and the Venetians were forced to bombard the town into submission. While the rest of Dalmatia stagnated under Venetian rule, Trogir continued to produce great artists who enhanced the beauty of the town.

Orientation

The old town of Trogir occupies a tiny island in the narrow channel between Čiovo Island and the mainland, just off the coastal highway. Most sights can be seen on a 15-minute walk around this island. The nearest beach is 4km west at the Hotel Medena.

The heart of the old town is divided from the mainland by a small channel, and is a few minutes' walk from the bus station. After crossing the small bridge near the station, go through the North Gate. Turn left (east) at the end of the square and you'll come to Trogir's main street, Gradska. Trogir's finest sights are around Trg Ivana Pavla II, straight ahead. The seafront, Obala Bana Berislavića, is lined with bars, restaurants and cafés, overlooking Čiovo Island. The old town is connected to Čiovo Island to the south by a drawbridge.

Information

Atlas Travel Agency (☎ 881 374; www.atlas-trogir .hr; Obala Kralja Zvonimira 10; ☺ 8.30am-7pm Mon-Fri, to 4pm Sat) Arranges private accommodation and runs excursions.

Garderoba (per day 13KN; ☺ 9am-10pm) Left-luggage office in the bus station.

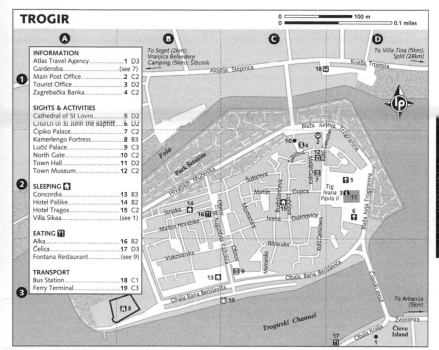

TROGIR

0 ———— 100 m
0 ————— 0.1 miles

INFORMATION
Atlas Travel Agency.................1 D3
Garderoba..........................(see 7)
Main Post Office.....................2 C2
Tourist Office........................3 D2
Zagrebačka Banka..................4 C2

SIGHTS & ACTIVITIES
Cathedral of St Lovro...............5 D2
Church of St John the Baptist....6 D2
Čipiko Palace.........................7 C2
Kamerlengo Fortress...............8 B3
Lučić Palace..........................9 C3
North Gate...........................10 C2
Town Hall............................11 D2
Town Museum......................12 C2

SLEEPING
Concordia............................13 B3
Hotel Pašike.........................14 B2
Hotel Tragos........................15 C2
Villa Sikaa.........................(see 1)

EATING
Alka.................................16 B2
Ćelica...............................17 D3
Fontana Restaurant..............(see 9)

TRANSPORT
Bus Station.........................18 C1
Ferry Terminal......................19 C3

To Seget (2km);
Vranjica Belvedere
Camping (5km), Šibenik

To Villa Tina (5km);
Split (28km)

To Arbanija
(5km)

Čiovo
Island

Trogirski Channel

Main post office (Kralja Tomislava 9; 9am-6pm Mon-Fri, to 2pm Sat) There's a telephone centre here.
Tourist office (881 412; www.dalmacija.net/destination/trogir; Trg Ivana Pavla II 1; 8am-9pm Jun-Aug, 9am-2pm Mon-Fri Sep-May) Another good source of information; also arranges private accommodation.
Zagrebačka Banka (Gradska Vrata) There's an ATM outside.

Sights

Even though it's a pocket-sized town, there's plenty to see in Trogir. The town has retained many intact and beautiful buildings from its age of glory – between the 13th and 15th centuries. As you enter, notice the Renaissance **North Gate**, with the statue of the town protector, St Ivan Orsini, hovering overhead. As you proceed down Kohl-Genscher, you may wish to visit the **Town Museum** (Gradski Muzej; 881 406; Kohl-Genscher 49; admission 10KN; 9am-1pm & 5-9pm Mon-Sat Jun-Sep, 9am-2pm Mon-Fri, 9am-noon Sat Oct-May), housed in the former Garanjin-Fanfogna palace. The five rooms exhibit books, documents, drawings and period costumes from Trogir's long history.

The glory of the town is the three-naved Venetian **Cathedral of St Lovro** (Katedrala Svetog Lovre; 881 426; Trg Ivana Pavla II; admission 15KN; 8am-noon & 4-7pm Jun-Aug, 8am-noon Sep-May), built from the 13th to 15th centuries and one of the finest architectural works in Croatia. Note first the **Romanesque portal** (1240) by Master Radovan. The sides of the portal depict lion figures (the symbol of Venice) with Adam and Eve above them, the earliest example of the nude in Dalmatian sculpture. The outer pilasters show saints, the centre scenes represent the calendar months and the small posts feature hunting scenes. Overhead is the Nativity of Christ. At the end of the portico is another fine piece of sculpture – the **baptistery** sculpted in 1464 by Andrija Aleši. Enter the building through an obscure back door to see the richly decorated **Renaissance Chapel of St Ivan**, created by the masters Nikola Firentinac and Ivan Duknović from 1461 to 1497. Within the **sacristy** there are paintings of St Jerome and John the Baptist. Be sure to take a look at the **treasury**, which contains an ivory triptych and several medieval illuminated manuscripts.

A sign informs you that you must be 'decently dressed' to enter the cathedral, which means that men must wear tops (women too, of course) and shorts are a no-no. You can even climb the 47m cathedral **tower** (if it's open) for a delightful view. To be sure of getting into the cathedral, it's best to come in the morning. Its hours can be irregular and it is often closed in the afternoon.

Before leaving the square, look at the 15th-century **town hall** opposite the cathedral, with a Gothic yard decorated with coats of arms and a stone head. Next to the cathedral is the **Čipiko Palace**, with its stunning carved triforium, the work of Firentinac and Aleši.

Southeast of the cathedral, look at the magnificent carved portal on the **Church of St John the Baptist** representing the mourning of Christ. Inside, you can see 14th- to 17th-century paintings and statues in the gallery.

Walk along the waterfront and notice the portal and courtyard of the Renaissance **Lučić Palace**, next to the Fontana Restaurant. If you keep walking you'll come to the **Kamerlengo Fortress**, which looks exactly as a medieval fortress should. Once connected to the city walls, the fortress was built around the 15th century. At the furthest end, you'll see an elegant gazebo built by the French Marshal Marmont during the Napoleonic occupation of Dalmatia, where he used to sit and play cards amid the waves. At that time, the western end of the island was a lagoon; the malarial marshes were not drained until the 20th century. The fortress is now an **open-air cinema** during summer, showing movies at 9pm.

Festivals & Events

Every year from mid-June to mid-August, Trogir hosts a **summer music festival**, with classical and folk concerts presented in churches and open squares. Posters advertising the concerts are all around town.

Sleeping

Atlas Travel Agency (p232) can arrange private rooms from 220KN a double, studios for 440KN, and two-, three- and four-room apartments. Check out the offerings at www.trogir-online.com.

Seget (☎ /fax 880 394; www.kamp-seget.hr; Hrvatskih Žrtava 121, Seget Donji; per adult low-high 24-33KN; per site 80-115KN; ☼ mid-Apr–Oct) Closer to Trogir (2km)

than the Vranjica camping ground, Seget is also smaller. There's a small shingle beach and a cemented diving point. It offers tennis, cycling, windsurfing and numerous other activities.

Vranjica Belvedere Camping (☎ 894 141; www .vranjica-belvedere.hr; Seget Vranjica, Seget Donji; per adult low-high €4-5; ☼ mid-Apr–Oct) Lying just off the highway to Zadar 5km west of Trogir, this camping ground offers tennis, biking, windsurfing, water-skiing, sailing and horse riding. Take bus 24 from the bus station.

Villa Tina (☎ 888 305; www.vila-tina.hr; Arbanija; d low-high €30-46; P ☒) Tastefully decorated, with spacious and bright rooms, Villa Tina is excellent if you want to relax and swim. It's about 5km east of Trogir, right on the coast, near the beach. Enjoy the views from the terrace as you wind down.

Concordia (☎ 885 400; www.concordia-hotel.net; Obala Bana Berislavića 22; s low-high 400-450KN, d 550-680KN; P ☒) Right on the seafront, the somewhat faded rooms here are clean but pretty basic, though the service and location are lovely. Try to get a room with sea views, as this may mitigate the lacklustre decoration.

Hotel Tragos (☎ 884 729; www.tragos.hr; Budislavićeva 3; s low-high 450-600KN, d 600-800KN; ☼ closed Nov-Feb; ☒ ☐) This medieval family house has been exquisitely restored, its sleek, beautifully decorated rooms outfitted with satellite TV, minibars and internet access. Even if you don't stay here, come for the wonderful home cooking served in the hotel restaurant (mains around 80KN).

Villa Sikaa (☎ 881 223; www.vila-sikaa-r.com; Obala Kralja Zvonimira 10; s low-high 520-600KN, d 550-650KN; ☒ ☐) Villa Sikaa has lovely rooms with fantastic views of the old town – it's on Čiovo Island. The seven large rooms have big bathrooms, double-glazed windows and satellite TVs, while some are equipped with a sauna and massage shower.

our pick **Hotel Pašike** (☎ 885 185; www.hotel pasike.com; Sinjska bb; s low-high 550-600KN, d 700-800KN; ☒ ☐) The most gorgeous hotel in Trogir (and wider Dalmatia), Hotel Pašike has eight rooms full of 19th-century furniture, while the hotel itself is in a 15th-century house. The rooms are painted in vivid colours that beautifully set off the heavy walnut and wrought-iron beds (covered with antique knitted throws). The friendly and professional staff wear traditional outfits, you get a satellite TV and wi-fi in each room, and there is a lovely two-table roof terrace. A potent glass of *rakija* (brandy), champagne and lemon awaits each guest upon arrival, sweetened by *rafioli*, a traditional Trogir almond cake. Book in advance. If you're here in October or from November to April, you get a 20% or 30% discount respectively. The restaurant is also good.

Eating

Ćelica (☎ 882 344; Obala Kralja Zvonimira; mains 65-100KN) This boat-restaurant offers a highly agreeable ambience on the channel. The menu centres on seafood, of course.

Fontana Restaurant (☎ 884 881; Obrov 1; mains around 80KN) When locals want to have a night out they usually head to the Fontana with its large waterfront terrace. You can get almost anything here, from inexpensive pizza and omelettes to pricier grilled fish and meat, but the speciality is fish.

Alka (☎ 881 856; Bl Augustina Kažotića 15; mains around 80KN) Alka is another popular choice with similar prices to Fontana Restaurant; it also has an outdoor terrace.

Getting There & Away

Southbound intercity buses from Zadar (130km) and northbound buses from Split (28km) will drop you off in Trogir. Getting buses from Trogir to Zadar can be more difficult, as they often arrive full from Split.

City bus 37 from Split leaves half-hourly throughout the day, with a stop at Split airport en route to Trogir, but it leaves from the local bus station and takes longer than the intercity bus. You can buy the four-zone ticket from the driver in either direction.

There's also a ferry once a week from Split (11KN) that docks in front of the Concordia hotel.

AROUND TROGIR

Although there are beaches to the west of Trogir, it's a much better idea to head to the beaches on Drvenik Mali and Drvenik Veli islands, an easy boat trip from town. Boats leave from the ferry terminal in front of the Concordia hotel. Both islands are sparsely inhabited and idyllic getaways.

In addition, there is the beautiful Kaštela area, with seven ports and several castles built by the Dalmatian nobility some 500 years ago.

Drvenik Mali & Drvenik Veli

The smaller island, Drvenik Mali has olive trees, a population of 56 and a sandy beach that curves around the cove of Vela Rina. Drvenik Veli has secluded coves and olive trees plus a few cultural highlights to get you off the beach: the **Church of St George** dates from the 16th century and houses baroque furniture and a Venetian altarpiece. Outside Drvenik Veli village is the unfinished 18th-century **Church of St Nicholas**, whose builder never quite got past the monumental front.

To get to the islands from Trogir, get on a **Jadrolinija ferry** (www.jadrolinija.hr). These cost 13KN and take one hour to get to Drvenik Veli, and one hour 20 minutes to Drvenik Mali. Three ferries operate daily; from Monday to Saturday they leave Trogir at 9am, 3pm and 8.30pm, returning from the islands at 6am, noon and 7pm. On Sunday the times are 9am, 6pm and 9pm from Trogir, and 7am, 4pm and 7.20pm from the islands. Always check Jadrolinija's website or with the local tourist office for up-to-date schedules, especially in the off-season months. If you're interested in spending more time on the islands, the tourist office in Trogir can find you private accommodation.

Kaštela

If you're looking to snuggle down in safety, you can't do much better than have the mountains behind you and the sea in front of you. At least that's what the Dalmatian nobility thought when they looked at the invading Ottomans in the 15th and 16th centuries. The 20km stretch of coast between Trogir and Split, backed by long, low Kozjak hill, looked like the perfect place to relax in a well-fortified castle. One after the other, rich families from Split filed down to Kaštela bay to build their mansions. The Turks never reached them and the castles remain today.

Kaštela is the name given to the seven little ports around these coastal fortified castles and visiting it is a delightful day trip from Split or Trogir. Starting in the west, from Trogir, you'll come first to **Kaštel Štafilić**, a castle on an islet connected to the mainland by a drawbridge. There's also a Renaissance church in town. Next is **Kaštel Novi**, built in 1512, and then **Kaštel Stari**, built in 1476 and the oldest in the bay. An arcaded cloister stands in the middle. Further on is the **Kaštel Lukšić**, the most impressive of all. Built in a transitional Renaissance-baroque style in 1487, it now houses municipal offices, a small museum and the tourist office of the region. It's also the site of a rather involved tale of thwarted lovers who were married and buried here. Continue east to the **Kaštel Kambelovac**, the only purely local castle, and then on to **Kaštel Gomilica**, built by Benedictine nuns and surrounded by shallow, sandy beaches. Finish at the **Kaštel Sućurac**, then take the path that runs past the cemetery, climbing to the refuge at Putalj (480m) where you can climb to the ridge of Kozjak.

For details on accommodation in Kaštela, contact the **tourist office** (☎ 227 933; www.dalmacija .net/kastela.htm; Kaštela Lukšić; ☒ 8am-7pm Mon-Sat, 8am-1pm Sun Jul & Aug, 9am-5pm Mon-Fri Sep-Jun).

To get to Kaštela, take bus 37 from Split to Trogir (15KN, half-hourly) – this bus stops in all the towns along the bay. You can also go on the faster but less regular Kaštela buses – there are four daily to Kaštel Novi and Kaštel Štafilić (6am, noon, 2pm and 4pm) and seven to Kaštel Stari (6am, 7am, noon, 1pm, 2pm, 3pm and 4pm). These buses leave from the main bus station on Obala Kneza Domagoja.

MAKARSKA RIVIERA

The Makarska Riviera is a 50km stretch of coast at the foot of the Biokovo Range, where a series of cliffs and ridges forms a dramatic backdrop to a string of beautiful pebble beaches. The foothills are protected from harsh winds and covered in lush Mediterranean greenery, including pine forests, olive groves and fruit trees.

MAKARSKA
pop 15,000

Makarska is a pretty port town, with a limestone centre that turns a peachy orange at sunset. It's an active place – there's an abundance of hiking, climbing, windsurfing and swimming opportunities – and it has a spectacular natural setting, backed by the gorgeous Mt Biokovo (peaking at 1762m at Sveti Jure). There is a long pebbly town beach, filled with a feast of activities, from beach volleyball to screaming children's games. Makarska is favoured by tourists from neighbouring Bosnia and Hercegovina, who descend upon the town in huge numbers during July and August. The high season is pretty raucous and a lot of fun for those with children. If you're after hanging around beach bars, playing beach volleyball and generally lounging about with perfect beach bodies, you'll like Makarska. Outside the high season, things are pretty quiet.

Being the largest town in the region, Makarska has very good transport connections, making it a good base for exploring the coast and neighbouring Bosnia and Hercegovina. Don't miss venturing up Mt Biokovo.

History

Makarska owes its name to the Roman settlement of Muccurum, which probably existed in the village of Makar about 2km north of Makarska. Excavations on Sveti Petar Peninsula, however, revealed that there was another linked settlement along the coast, called Inaronia, that served as a way station between Solin (Salona) and the important trading town of Narona down the coast. Both settlements were allegedly destroyed in 548 by Totila, king of the Eastern Goths.

The region was populated by migrating Slavs in the 7th century who eventually set up a booming piracy business that disrupted Venetian shipping. The Venetian warships that sailed into Makarska in 887 were severely trounced in battle and the Venetians were thereafter forced to pay for the right to sail past the settlement. In the 11th century, Makarska came under the rule of the Croatian-Hungarian kings, which lasted until 1324 when it fell to the Bosnian ruler Kotromanić. In 1499, the town was taken by the Ottomans who were pushing against the Venetians for control of the Adriatic coast. During the 150 years that Makarska was under Turkish rule, it became an important port for the salt trade from Bosnia and Hercegovina.

The Venetians took over the town in 1646 and held it until the end of their empire in 1797. Trade prospered and a new aristocracy built baroque mansions to the east and west of the town. After the fall of Venice, Makarska was then subject to Austrian, French and Austrian rule again before becoming part of the Kingdom of Yugoslavia.

Orientation

Makarska is located on a large cove bordered by Cape Osejava in the southeast and the Sveti Petar Peninsula in the northwest.

The bus station is on Ante Starčevića, about 300m uphill from the centre of the old town. Take Kralja Zvonimira from the bus station downhill to Obala Kralja Tomislava and you'll be on the main promenade of the old town with travel agencies, shops and restaurants.

The long pebble town beach stretches from the Sveti Petar park at the beginning of Obala Kralja Tomislava northwest along the bay. This is where you'll find most of the large hotels. The southeastern side of town is rockier – and the rocks are often inhabited by nudists – but it's a good place to swim.

Information

There are many banks and ATMs along Obala Kralja Tomislava and you can change money at the travel agencies on the same street.

Atlas Travel Agency (☎ 617 038; www.atlas-croatia .com; Kačićev Trg 8; ☼ 9am-7pm Mon-Fri, to 2pm Sat) At the far end of town; finds private accommodation.

Biokovo Active Holidays (☎ 679 655; www.biokovo .net; Kralja Petra Krešimira IV 7b; ☼ 9am-7pm Mon-Fri, to 2pm Sat) A fount of information on Mt Biokovo and organises hiking, biking, rafting and kayaking trips.

Garderoba (per day 15KN; ☼ 6am-10pm) Left-luggage at the bus station.

Internet Club Master (☎ 612 466; Jadranska 1; per hr 30KN; ☼ 9am-10pm) Internet access; behind Hotel Biokovo.

Mariva Turist (☎ 616 010; www.marivaturist.hr; Obala Kralja Tomislava 15a; ☼ 9am-7.30pm Mon-Fri, to 3pm Sat) Has money exchange facilities and books excursions and private accommodation along the whole Makarska coast, including in Brela.

Post office (Trg 4 Svibnja 533; ☼ 9am-7pm Mon-Fri, to 2pm Sat) You can change money, make phone calls or withdraw cash on MasterCard.

Tourist office (☎ /fax 612 002; www.makarska-info .hr; Obala Kralja Tomislava 16; ☼ 7am-9pm Jun-Sep, 7am-2pm Mon-Fri Oct-May) Publishes a useful guide to the city with a map that you can pick up here or at any of the travel agencies.

Turist Biro (☎ 611 688; www.turistbiro-makarska.com; Obala Kralja Tomislava 2; ☼ 9am-7pm Mon-Fri, to 4pm Sat) Finds private accommodation and books excursions.

Zagrebačka Banka (Trg Tina Ujevića 1) Has an ATM.

Sights

Makarska is more renowned for its natural beauty than its cultural highlights, but on a rainy day you could check out the **Town Museum** (Gradski Muzej; ☎ 612 302; Obala Kralja Tomislava 17; admission free; ☼ 7am-3pm Mon-Fri, 9am-noon Sat), which traces the town's history in a less-than-gripping collection of photos and old stones.

More interesting is the **Franciscan monastery** (Franjevački Samostan; Franjevački Put 1; ☼ Mass only), built in 1400 and restored in 1540 and 1614. The single-nave church is worth visiting for the **shell collection** (☎ 611 256; admission 15KN; ☼ 11am-noon) in the cloister and a painting of the Assumption by the Flemish artist Pieter de Coster (1760). The 18th-century **St Mark's Church** (Crkva Svetog Marka; ☎ 611 365; Kačićev Trg; ☼ Mass only) features a baroque silver altar from 1818 and a marble altar from 18th-century Venice.

Activities

The roads and trails that criss-cross the limestone massif of Mt Biokovo are irresistible to hikers. Rising behind the city, the mountain, which is administered and protected by **Biokovo National Park** (☎ 616 924; Trg Tina Ujevića 1; park admission adult/student 30/15KN; ☼ 8am-4pm Apr–mid-May & Oct–mid-Nov, 7am-8pm mid-May–Sep), offers wonderful hiking opportunities. If you're hiking independently (ie not part of an organised hiking excursion), you have to enter the park at the beginning of 'Biokovo Rd' – basically the only road that runs up the mountain and impossible to miss – and buy an admission ticket there.

Vošac peak (1422m) is the nearest target for hikers, only 2.5km from the city. From St Mark's Church on Kačićev Trg, you can walk or drive up Put Makra, following signs to the village of Makar, where a trail leads to Vošac. From Vošac, a good marked trail leads to **Sveti Jure** (four hours), the highest peak at 1762m, from where you can get spectacular views of the Croatian coast, and, on a clear day, the coast of Italy on the other side of the Adriatic. Take plenty of water, sunscreen, a hat and waterproof clothes – the weather on top is always a lot colder than by the sea.

For **rock climbers**, Makarska has a decent climbing area on Osejava, to the east of the centre, just behind Šetalište Fra Jure Radića. It's popular in the summer months.

Another popular destination is the **Botanical Garden** (near the village of Kotišina), which can be reached by a marked trail from Makar that passes under a series of towering peaks. Although once a major regional highlight, the garden has fallen into decay.

Biokovo Active Holidays (left) is an excellent source of hiking and other information about Mt Biokovo. For diving, try **More Sub** (☎ 611 727; Hotel Dalmacija, Kralja Krešimira bb).

SPLIT & CENTRAL DALMATIA

Tours

Biokovo Active Holidays (p237) offers guided walks and drives on Mt Biokovo for all levels of physical exertion. You can go part of the way up the mountain by minibus and then take a short hike to Sveti Jure peak, take a 5½ hour hike through black pine forests and lush fields, or enjoy an early drive to watch the sun rise over Makarska.

Sleeping

There's a rather overwhelming blandness to Makarska's hotels, so be prepared for nothing special, though comfortable beds and good views are reliable in the more upmarket spots.

All of the travel agencies listed on p237 can find private rooms. Count on spending from 200KN to 300KN for a double room. There are plenty available in the centre of town as well as on the outskirts.

Baško Polje (☎ 612 329; per adult/tent 40/60KN; ☯ May-Oct) Between Makarska and Baška Voda, this is a lovely autocamp, close to town and on the beach, amid thick pines.

Hotel Makarska (☎ /fax 616 622; www.makarska -hotel.com; Potok 17; s low-high €42-47, d €70-78; P ☒) A bit like what you might get if you stay with a very welcoming local family, Hotel Makarska has fluffy linen, long net curtains and friendly hosts. It's in town, about 200m from the beach, and the rooms are comfortable, with satellite TV and minibars.

Hotel Dalmacija (☎ 615 777; www.hoteli-makar ska.hr; Kralja Krešimira bb; s low-high €49-72, d €98-144; P ☒ ☯) A huge block of a hotel with 190 rooms and an enclosed private beach. As you may expect, it's not the cosiest of places, but many like it for its range of facilities. The rooms are comfortable but bland.

Hotel Biokovo (☎ 615 244; www.hotelbiokovo.hr; Obala Kralja Tomislava bb; s low-high €60-96, d €90-134; P ☒) Swanky Hotel Biokovo is regarded as one of the better hotels in town. The rooms are spacious (all have balconies) and the beds comfortable. It's right in the centre, on the promenade, and if you get a sea-view room you'll have excellent views of the town and all the summer buzz. Fortunately, the double-glazed windows keep out noise at night.

Hotel Meteor (☎ 602 600; www.hoteli-makarska .hr; Šetalište Donja Luka 1; s low-high €62-86, d €120-164; P ☒ ☯) This three-star hotel 400m west of the town centre on a pebble beach is the most luxurious. Each of the 280 rooms is

air-conditioned and has a balcony with a sea view. There are indoor and outdoor swimming pools, shops and tennis courts. Don't expect much of a discount in room rates outside the high season.

Hotel Porin (☎ 613 744; www.hotel-porin.hr; Marineta 2; d low-high €90-117; P ☒) A decent choice in the town centre. The soundproofed rooms have good beds and satellite TVs, though little in the way of cosiness or decoration. The price goes down around 10% for stays over two nights.

Eating

Pizzeria Lungo Mare (☎ 615 244; Obala Kralja Tomislava bb; pizzas from 30KN) Next to the Hotel Biokovo, this place serves hearty pizzas and there's a comfortable outdoor terrace.

Riva (☎ 616 829; Obala Kralja Tomislava 6; mains 40-90KN) A lovely restaurant just off the main drag, in a quiet leafy courtyard. The food is decent, with the usual choice of fish, seafood and meat. Some of the pasta dishes can be too creamy and heavy, so try a risotto or a fish and seafood platter.

Susvid (☎ 612 732; Kačićev Trg; meals from 45KN) Right on the main square and massively popular, Susvid claims to be a 'health food' restaurant, which may simply mean that pleasure is good for your health. There are excellent vegetarian and fish dishes.

Ivo (☎ 611 257; Starčevića 41; mains around 60KN) Away from the main drag and the beach, Ivo is a true find. Fish and meat dishes are cooked to perfection and expertly seasoned.

Picnickers can get supplies at the fruit and vegetable market next to St Mark's Church or at the **supermarket** (Obala Kralja Tomislava 14).

RIDING THE RAILS TO MOSTAR

A great way to beat the crowds and do something different is to take a train from Ploče to Mostar in Bosnia and Hercegovina. The train is a slow and huffy thing that leaves Ploče twice a day (29KN, 70 minutes, 6am and 5pm), travelling through the gorgeous Dalmatian and Hercegovinian landscape, often tracing the upstream flow of the Neretva River. All Dubrovnik-bound buses that stop in Makarska pass Ploče (around 50KN). EU, US, Australian and Canadian citizens don't need visas to enter Bosnia and Hercegovina; other nationalities should check with their relevant embassy.

Entertainment

Grotta (☎ 091 569 4657; Sveti Petar bb) On Sveti Petar Peninsula just after the port, this popular disco tucked into a cave welcomes local DJs plus an array of jazz, blues and rock bands.

Deep Night Bar (Osejava bb) What is it about caves and Makarska? Here's another one at the other end of town. This one attracts a super-trendy set to sip cocktails, with a DJ spinning the latest beats in the background.

Getting There & Away

In summer there are three to five ferries a day between Makarska and Sumartin on Brač (30KN, 30 minutes), reduced to two a day in winter. The **Jadrolinija stall** (☎ 338 333; Obala Kralja Tomislava) is near the Hotel Biokovo.

From the **bus station** (☎ 612 333; Ante Starčevića 30) there are 10 buses daily to Dubrovnik (129KN, three hours), 11 buses daily to Split (64KN, 1¼ hours), three daily to Rijeka (307KN, nine hours) and 10 a day to Zagreb (110KN to 142KN, eight hours). There's also a daily bus to Mostar (100KN, three hours) and Sarajevo (160KN, six hours) in Bosnia and Hercegovina.

BRELA

The tiny town of Brela, 14km northwest of Makarska, has the longest and loveliest coastline in Dalmatia stretching through it. Six kilometres of pebble beaches curve around coves thickly forested with pine trees and largely unmarred by ugly tourist developments. The sea is beautifully clear and the sunsets are fantastic. A shady promenade lined with bars and cafés winds around the coves. If you're after a week's lounging on a beach and 100% relaxation, Brela is the perfect place.

Orientation

The bus stop (no left-luggage office) is behind Hotel Soline, a short walk downhill to Obala Kneza Domagoja, the harbour street and town

centre. Beaches and coves are on both sides of the town, but the longest stretch is the 4km coast west of the town centre. The best beach is **Punta Rata**, a stunning pebble beach about 300m southwest of the town centre.

Information

Bonavia Travel Agency (☎ 619 019; www.bonavia -agency.hr; Obala Kneza Domagoja 18; ☒ 8.30am-8.30pm Mon-Fri, 9am-4pm Sat) Finds private accommodation, changes money and books excursions.

Tourist office (☎ 618 455, 618 337; www.brela.hr; Trg Alojzija Stepinca bb; ☒ 8am-9pm mid-Jun–mid-Sep, 8am-2pm Mon-Fri mid-Sep–mid-Jun) Provides a town map and a cycling map for the region. Has an ATM outside.

Sleeping

The closest camping is at Baško Polje (opposite). For private accommodation you'll pay from 100/190KN a single/double.

There are no cheap hotels in Brela, but much of the private accommodation on offer from the tourist office or travel agencies is really small *pensions*. The four large hotels are managed by **Blue Sun Hotels** (☎ 603 190; www.bluesunhotels.com).

Hotel Berulia (☎ 603 599; Frankopanska bb; s 257-684KN, d 514-1236KN; ▣ ⌘ ⌘) About 300m east of the town centre, this four-star hotel has spacious but quite bland rooms. It is a little more secluded than the other Blue Sun hotels, but not as luxurious as Hotel Soline, the other four-star place in town.

Hotel Marina (☎ 608 608; s low-high 287-625KN, d 442-1088KN; ▣ ⌘) The Marina is the most affordable of the Blue Sun hotels, with basic but comfortable rooms and a wall of pine trees that separates the hotel from the luxuriant Brela beach.

Hotel Soline (☎ 603 207; s low-high 316-750KN, d 544-1368KN; ▣ ⌘ ⌘) A four-star luxury hotel with plush, spacious rooms overlooking the beach. There's a fragrant wellness centre and

SPLIT & CENTRAL DALMATIA

RAFTING ON THE CETINA RIVER

The Cetina is the longest river in central Dalmatia, stretching 105km from the eponymous village. It flows over the Dinara mountains, through the fields of Sinj and gathers steam until it pours into a power plant around Omiš. It is an extraordinarily scenic journey as the limpid, blue river is bordered by high rocky walls, thick with vegetation. Rafting is possible from spring to autumn, but the rapids can become quite fast after heavy rains. Rafting in the summer is best for inexperienced rafters. It usually takes three to four hours to raft the Cetina. To organise a trip, try **Biokovo Active Holidays** (☎ 679 655; www.biokovo.net; Kralja Petra Krešimira IV 7b, Makarska; ☒ 9am-7pm Mon-Fri, to 2pm Sat), which organises a day's rafting, canyoning or canoeing on the Cetina for €54.

if you're here in winter, you can swim in the indoor pool. Soline is close to the centre.

Eating & Drinking

Konoba Feral (☎ 618 909; Obala Domagoja 30; mains from 40KN) Every Dalmatian place has its *konoba*, and this is Brela's local. It's friendly, with wooden tables and good seafood and fish. The line-caught squid (280KN per kg) is deliciously grilled with garlic and parsley. Combine it with a summer salad and some crisp local white wine and you've got heaven on your table.

ourpick Southern Comfort Beach Bar (Ikovac Beach) Apart from fabulous beaches, Brela hides one of Croatia's best beach bars, too. Southern Comfort prepares killer cocktails (the Margaritas are divine) plays good music, has comfy chairs by the sea and torch light at night, and stays open pretty much all day and night. To get here, walk past Hotel Berulia, towards Baska Voda. The bar is around 200m down – you'll spot the torches.

Getting There & Away

All buses running between Makarska and Split stop at Brela, making it an easy day trip from either town.

VIS ISLAND

pop 5000
Of all the Croatian islands, Vis is the most mysterious – even to the locals. The furthest of the main central Dalmatian islands from the coast, Vis spent much of its recent history serving as a military base for the Yugoslav National army, cut off from foreign visitors from the 1950s right up until 1989. The isolation preserved the island from tourist development (and development in general) and drove the work-seeking population of Vis to move elsewhere in Croatia, leaving it underpopulated for many years.

But as has happened with impoverished islands across the Mediterranean, Vis' lack of development has become its very drawcard as a tourist destination. International and local travellers alike flock to Vis nowadays, seeking authenticity, nature, peace and quiet, and, gourmet delights. Vis produces some of Croatia's best known wines – *vugava* (white) and *plavac* (red) – and you'll see miles of vineyards across the island. You'll also taste

some of the freshest fish here, thanks to a still thriving fishing tradition.

Vis is divided between two small towns at the foot of two large bays: Vis Town (in the northeast) and Komiža (southwest). The rugged coast is dotted with gorgeous coves, caves and a couple of sand beaches. The island's remnants of antiquity displayed in the Archaeological Museum and elsewhere around Vis Town are a fascinating additional insight into the complex character of this tiny island.

History

Inhabited first in Neolithic times, the island was settled by the ancient Illyrians who brought the Iron Age to Vis in the 1st millennium BC. In 390 BC a Greek colony was formed on the island, known then as Issa, from which the Greek ruler Dionysius the Elder controlled other Adriatic possessions. The island eventually became a powerful city-state and established its own colonies on Korčula and at Trogir and Stobreč. Allying itself with Rome during the Illyrian wars, the island nonetheless lost its autonomy and became part of the Roman Empire in 47 BC. By the 10th century Vis had been settled by Slavic tribes and was sold to Venice along with other Dalmatian towns in 1420. Fleeing Dalmatian pirates, the population moved from the coast inland.

With the fall of the Venetian Empire in 1797, the island fell under the control of Austria, France, Great Britain, Austria again and then Italy during WWII as the Great Powers fought for control of this strategic Adriatic outpost. The island was an important military base for Tito's Partisans. Tito established his supreme headquarters in a cave on Hum Mountain, from which he coordinated military and diplomatic actions with Allied forces and allegedly made his legendary statement: 'We don't want what belongs to others, but we will not give up what belongs to us.'

Getting There & Around

Vis Town is best reached by daily car ferry from Split, but note that day trips outside of the summer season are basically impossible due to boat schedules aimed at commuters and not tourists. In July and August, however, there are boats (47KN, two hours 20 minutes) departing at 9am on Friday,

Saturday and Sunday, coming back from Vis at 6pm. Other days the ferry leaves at 9.30am from Split but doesn't come back in the afternoon.

The local **Jadrolinija office** (☎ 711 032; www .jadrolinija.hr; Šetalište Stare Isse; ☿ 8.30am-7pm Mon-Fri, 9am-noon Sat) is in Vis Town. For connections to Italy, see p310.

The only island bus transport connects Vis Town with Komiža. The bus meets the Jadrolinija ferries at Vis Town and leaves for Komiža. The connections are prompt in July and August, but you may have to wait off-season.

VIS TOWN

On the northeastern coast of the island, at the foot of a wide, horseshoe-shaped bay, lies the ancient town of Vis, the first settlement on the island. In only a short walk you can see the remains of a Greek cemetery, Roman baths and an English fortress. Ferry arrivals give spurts of activity to an otherwise peaceful town of coastal promenades and crumbling 17th-century buildings.

Orientation

The town is on the southern slope of Gradina hill and is a merger of two settlements: Luka on the northwestern part of the bay and Kut in the southeast. The ferry ties up at Luka and a harbourside promenade runs from Luka to Kut. Most beaches are along this promenade, while the ancient ruins and another beach in front of the Hotel Issa are a short walk north along the coast.

Information

You can change money at the bank, post office or any travel agency.

Bilba (☎ 717 475; Radojevića Prolaz 1; per hr 20KN; ☿ 8am-10pm Mon-Sat) Internet access.

Hospital (☎ 711 633; Poljana Sv Duha 10)

HVB Splitska Banka (Obala Svetog Jurja 34) There's an ATM.

Ionios Travel Agency (☎ 711 532; fax 711 356; Obala Svetog Jurja 36; ☿ 8.30am-7pm Mon-Fri, 9am-noon Sat) Finds private accommodation, changes money, rents cars, bikes and scooters, and runs excursions.

Post office (Obala Svetog Jurja 25; ☿ 9am-6pm Mon-Fri, to noon Sat)

Tourist office (☎ 711 017; www.tz-vis.hr; Šetalište Stare Isse 2; ☿ 8am-1pm & 6-8pm Jul & Aug, 8am-noon Mon-Fri Sep-Jun) Right next to the Jadrolinija ferry dock.

Sights & Activities

The **Archaeological Museum** (Arheološki Muzej; ☎ 711 729; Gospina Batarija Fortress, Šetalište Viški Boj 12; adult/child 10/5KN; ☿ 9am-1pm & 5-7pm Tue-Sun Jun-Aug, 9am-1pm Tue-Sun Sep-May) has extensive archaeological exhibitions, but it also has a healthy ethnographic collection, including the lowdown on the island's fishing, wine-making, shipbuilding and recent history. The 2nd floor has the largest collection of Hellenistic artefacts in Croatia, with Greek pottery, jewellery and sculpture, including an exquisite 4th-century bronze head of a Greek goddess that could be either Aphrodite or Artemis. A leaflet gives an overview of the exhibits, the history of Vis and a useful map showing the locations of the ruins around town.

Walk north from the dock about 100m and, behind the tennis court, you can see remains of a **Greek cemetery** next to remains of **Greek walls**. A few metres further along the coastal road, you'll see remains of **Roman baths** behind a fence – the site is still being researched. During their four-year rule over the island through the Napoleonic Wars (1811–15), the British built several **fortresses** on hills around the bay; the one on the northern corner is the most prominent.

Scenic **coastal roads** with dramatic cliffs and hairpin turns make it worth renting your own wheels for a day. You can hire scooters/ mountain bikes for 300/100KN a day (12 hours), or 200/50KN per half day (six hours) from Ionios Travel Agency (left) in Vis Town or Darlić & Darlić Travel Agency (p242) in Komiža.

Diving is excellent in the waters around Vis. Fish are plentiful and there's a **wreck** of an Italian ship dating from the 1866 naval battle between Austria and Italy. **Dodoro Diving Centre** (☎ 711 913; www.dodoro-diving.com; Trg Klapavica 1, Vis Town) and **Issa Diving Centre** (☎ 091 201 2731; www .scubadiving.hr; Hotel Biševo, Komiža) have extensive diving programs.

Tours

The island and its surroundings are best appreciated by boat. Ionios (left) and Darlić & Darlić (p242) travel agencies both offer boat trips that visit the Blue Grotto (p242), the Green Grotto and other great spots.

Sleeping

There are no camping grounds in Vis Town and only a few hotels, but you should have no trouble finding private accommodation, either rooms or apartments. **Navigator** (☎ 717 786; www.navigator.hr; Šetalište Stare Isse; ☻ 8am-10.30pm) can find private accommodation. You'll pay between 150KN and 200KN per person for a room with shared bathroom and between 350KN and 400KN for a small studio with a kitchenette and bathroom.

Hotel Tamaris (☎ 711 350; www.vis-hoteli.hr; Svetog Jurja 30; s low-high €36-62, d €54-110; P ❄) The Tamaris is a good deal; its 54 rooms are comfortable, with air-conditioning, phones and TVs. It is set in an attractive old building and is only about 100m southeast of the ferry dock.

Hotel Paula (☎ 711 362; www.hotelpaula.com; Petra Hektorovića; r per person low-high 359-572KN; P ❄) A gorgeous and original little hotel, the Paula is family-run, with individually decorated rooms, some with kitchenettes. The hotel is in Kut, the old part of Vis in the southeastern area of the bay. It also houses an excellent seafood restaurant, and a wine bar, too.

our pick Kuća Visoka (☎ in the UK 44-7944 315 949; www.thisisvis.com; house low-high €85-130; P) An entire house, just for you. The UK-owned Kuća Visoka is a renovated stone house with wooden beams, four floors, three tasteful, airy and bright bedrooms, two bathrooms, a gorgeous ground-floor kitchen, a spacious living room, a verandah, and a DVD and stereo room. It's absolutely perfect for a longer stay, which is just as well since there's a four-day minimum on rentals.

Eating

Restaurant Val (☎ 711 763; Don Cvjetka Marasovića 1; mains from 50KN) The Val (Wave) is set in an old stone house, and its shady terrace overlooks the sea. The seasonal menu has an Italian twist; try the offerings of wild asparagus in spring time, wild boar and mushrooms in winter, and lots of fish and fresh, sunny vegetable dishes in summer.

Villa Kaliopa (☎ 711 755; V Nazora 32; mains from 65KN) In the exotic gardens of the 16th-century Gariboldi mansion, Villa Kaliopa is an upmarket restaurant full of yachting enthusiasts. Palm trees, bamboo and classical statuary provide the setting for a menu of Dalmatian specialities that are pricey but manageable if you choose carefully.

KOMIŽA

On the western coast at the foot of Hum mountain, Komiža is a captivating small town on a bay, with sand and pebble beaches on the eastern end. Narrow back streets lined with tawny 17th- and 18th-century houses twist uphill from the port, which has been used by fisher folk at least since the 12th century. East of town is a 17th-century church on the site of a Benedictine monastery, and at the end of the main wharf is a Renaissance citadel dating from 1585.

The bus from Vis stops at the edge of town next to the post office and a few blocks away from the citadel. Walking all the way around the harbour, you'll come to the municipal **tourist office** (☎ /fax 713 455; www.tz-komiza.hr; Riva 1; ☻ 8am-7pm Jul & Aug, 9am-noon Mon-Fri Sep-Jun).

Sleeping & Eating

Next door to the tourist office, **Darlić & Darlić Travel Agency** (☎ 713 760; www.darlic -travel.hr; Riva Svetog Mikule 13) can find private accommodation.

Villa Nonna (☎ 098 380 046; www.villa-nonna.com; Ribarska 50; d low-high €35-70; ❄) A lovely old townhouse with seven renovated apartments, each with wooden floors, kitchens and some with balconies. The owners also have a gorgeous old house, Casa Nono, that can sleep six to nine people (from €80 to €200 per day), with a lovely garden and self-catering facilities.

Hotel Biševo (☎ 713 095; modra.spilja@st.t-com.hr; Ribarska 72; s/d from 370/610KN; ❄) Facilities are modest, but it's right near the beach. Try to get one of the renovated rooms.

Bako (☎ 713 008; Gundulićeva 1; mains from 50KN; ☻ dinner Jun-Sep) Bako has a fabulous seaside terrace and excellent food – try the lobster *brodet* (seafood stew with polenta) or the very local *pogača* (fish-filled, homemade bread). The cool stone interior contains a fish pond and a collection of Greek and Roman amphorae.

Konoba Jastožera (☎ 713 859; Gundulićeva 6; mains around 100KN) Scaly delicacies are cooked to perfection here. Meat dishes complete the menu at this unique restaurant where you eat on planks over the water.

AROUND KOMIŽA
Biševo

The tiny islet of Biševo has little other than vineyards, pine trees and a spectacular **Blue Grotto** (Modra Špilja). Between 11am and noon the sun's rays pass through an underwater opening in this coastal cave to bathe the interior in an unearthly blue light. Beneath the crystal-blue water, rocks glimmer in silver and pink to a depth of 16m. The only catch is that the water can be too choppy to enter the cave outside the summer months or when the *juga* (southern wind) is blowing. When the tourist season is at its peak in July and August, the cave can be woefully crowded and the line of boats waiting to get in discouragingly long. Outside of the high season, you may be able to swim here. There's a regular boat from Komiža to Biševo (30KN) that leaves daily throughout July and August at 8am, returning at 6pm, or you can book an excursion through one of the travel agencies. Another alternative is to rent a boat from one of the agencies and go on your own (admission 20KN).

our pick **Natural Holiday** (☎ 098 173 1673; www .bisevo.org; Salbunara Bay; bungalows per week low-high €466-728) is one of the best places to stay in this part of Croatia. This is an eco-friendly and luxury camping ground that doesn't feature tents; instead it has bungalows, of sorts, though the owners call them 'shelters'. They are basically like Bedouin tents, only with super-comfy beds inside, an outdoor area and a private bathroom with 50L of water per shelter. It's great for socialising or being alone, there's a communal kitchen and you can spend hours swimming and exploring the island. As good as it gets.

BRAČ ISLAND

pop 13,824

Brač is famous for two things: its radiant white stone, which Diocletian's Palace in Split and the White House in Washington DC (oh, yes!) are made from, and Zlatni Rat, the long pebbly beach at Bol that sticks out lasciviously into the Adriatic and adorns 90% of Croatia's tourism posters. It's the largest island in central Dalmatia, with two towns, several sleepy villages and a dramatic Mediterranean landscape of steep cliffs, inky waters and pine forests. The interior of the island is full of piles of rocks – the result of backbreaking labour of women, who, over hundreds of years, gathered the rocks in order to prepare the land for the cultivation of vineyards, olive orchards, figs, almonds and sour cherries.

The tough living conditions on the island have meant that a lot of people moved to the mainland in search of work, leaving the interior nearly deserted. Driving around and exploring Brač's stone villages is one of the loveliest experiences. The two main centres,

Supetar and Bol, differ greatly from one another: Supetar has the appearance of a transit town, while luxurious Bol revels in its more exclusive appeal.

History

Remnants of a Neolithic settlement have been found in Kopačina cave near Supetar, but the first recorded inhabitants were the Illyrians, who built a fort in Škrip to protect against Greek invasion. The Romans arrived in 167 BC and promptly set to work exploiting the stone quarries near Škrip and building summer mansions around the island. Slavs settled the island in the 9th century, gathering in the interior to escape the notorious Dalmatian pirates. During the four centuries of Venetian rule (1420–1797), the interior villages were devastated by plague and the inhabitants moved to the 'healthier' settlements along the coast, revitalising the towns of Supetar, Bol, Sumartin and Milna. After a brief period under Napoleonic rule, the island passed into Austrian hands. Wine cultivation expanded until the phylloxera epidemic at the turn of the 20th century ravaged the island's vines and people began leaving for North and South America, especially Chile. The island endured a reign of terror during WWII when German and Italian troops looted and burned villages, imprisoning and murdering their inhabitants.

Although the tourism business took a hit in the mid-1990s, it has rebounded well and the island is crowded in summer.

Getting There & Away

AIR

Brač's **airport** (☎ 631 370; www.airport-brac.hr) is 14km northeast of Bol and 32km southeast of Supetar. There are weekly flights from Zagreb to the Brač airport from April to October, but there's no transport from the airport to Supetar so you'll need to take a **taxi** (☎ 098 522 4379, 098 781 377), which costs about 300KN.

BOAT

There are 13 car ferries a day between Split and Supetar in summer (30KN, one hour) and seven a day at other times of the year. The ferry drops you off in the centre of town, only steps from the bus station. Make bookings at **Jadrolinija** (☎ 631 357; www.jadrolinija.hr; Hrvatskih Velikana bb, Supetar), about 50m east of the harbour.

BRAČ ISLAND

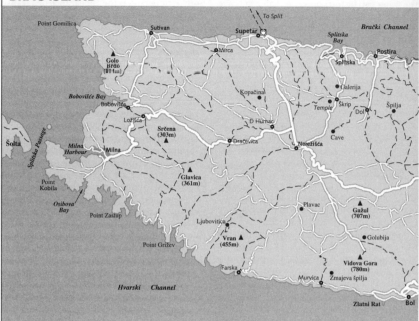

There's a Jadrolinija catamaran in summer between Split and Bol (50KN, 50 minutes) that goes on to Jelsa on Hvar. There are also three to five daily summer car ferries between Makarska and Sumartin (30KN, 30 minutes), reduced to two a day in winter. Note that you may have to wait an hour or two in Sumartin for a bus connection to Supetar (see below for bus times).

Getting Around

Public transport to the island's highlights is sparse so you may wish to have your own wheels if you want to see a few sites in a short time. You can hire cars from travel agencies on the island or bring them from the mainland.

Supetar is the hub for bus transport around the island. There are several buses running Monday to Saturday that connect Supetar with Bol (40 minutes); these leave Supetar at 5am, 10.25am, 12.40pm and 3.15pm, returning from Bol at 6am, 11.20am and 4.35pm. There are only two services on Sunday. Four buses a day (only two on Sunday) connect Sumartin and Supetar (1½ hours), leaving Sumartin at 5.45am, 7.55am, 12.50pm and 3.50pm.

SUPETAR

Supetar is not a great beauty – it feels more like a transit town than a living place in itself. However, it's a great hub for transport and a short stroll around the town will reveal some nice stone streets and a pretty church and square.

The pebbly beaches are an easy stroll from the town centre and there are a couple of good restaurants here, too.

Orientation

Supetar is easy to navigate since most offices, shops and travel agencies are on the main road that radiates roughly east–west from the harbour. Called Porat at the harbour, the road becomes Hrvatskih Velikana in the east and Vlačica on to Put Vele Luke as it travels west. There are five pebbly beaches on the coast. Vrilo beach is about 100m east of the town centre. Walking west, you'll come first to Vlačica then Banj beach, lined with pine trees. Next is Bili Rat, site of the water-sports centre, then if you cut across St Nikolaus Cape you come to Vela Luka beach. The bus

SPLIT & CENTRAL DALMATIA

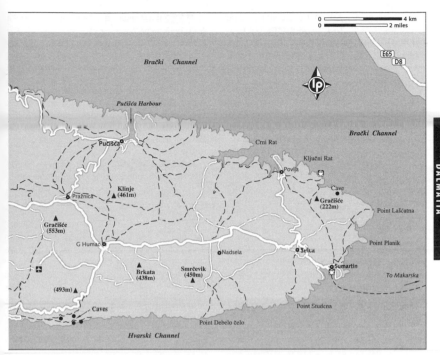

SPLIT & CENTRAL DALMATIA

station (no left-luggage office) is next to the Jadrolinija office.

Information

There's an ATM outside Privredna Banka Zagreb (at the dock) and another outside the Jadrolinija office.

Atlas Travel Agency (☎ /fax 631 105; Porat 10; ☺ 8.30am-7pm Mon-Fri, 9am-noon Sat) It's near the harbour and holds mail for Amex clients.

Hospital (☎ 640 000; Mladena Vojdonovića)

Maestral (☎ 631 258; www.travel.maestral.hr; Kovačića 3; ☺ 8.30am-7pm Mon-Fri, 9am-1pm Sat) Finds private accommodation.

Main post office (Vlačica 13; ☺ 9am-6pm Mon-Fri, to 2pm Sat) You can change money or withdraw cash on MasterCard.

Supetar Travel (☎ 631 520; Bračka 2; ☺ 8.30am-7pm Mon-Fri, 9am-noon Sat) Finds private accommodation, books hotels and changes money.

Tourist office (☎ /fax 630 551; www.supetar.hr; Porat 1; ☺ 8am-10pm Jul & Aug, to 4pm Mon-Fri Sep-Jun) Only a few steps east of the harbour, it has a full array of brochures on the activities and sights available in Supetar, as well as up-to-date bus and ferry timetables.

Sights & Activities

The baroque **Church of the Annunciation** (☺ Mass only), west of the harbour, was built in 1733. Although the exterior is plain, except for the semicircular entrance staircase, the interior is painted in cool, minty pastels and contains an interesting set of altar paintings, particularly the painting of the Annunciation from the school of Giambattista Pittoni.

The cemetery is at the tip of St Nikolaus Cape and you can't miss the monumental **Mausoleum of the Petrinović family**. The sculptor Toma Rosandić from Split incorporated elements of Byzantine style into this impressive structure dominating the tip of the cape.

The best diving on the island is found off the southwestern coast between Bol and Milna, making Bol a better base for divers, but you can book dives, take a diving course and rent equipment at **Hotel Kaktus** (☎ 631 133; www .watermanresorts.com; Put Vele Luke 4) in Supetar.

Festivals & Events

The **Supetar Summer Cultural Festival** lasts from June through to September, when folk music, dances and classical concerts are presented several times a week in public spaces and churches. Tickets to festival events are usually free or cost very little, and there are also frequent art exhibitions around town.

Sleeping

Most of the big hotels are in a tourist complex a few kilometres west of the port on Vela Luka bay. For a sprawling development of this kind, the landscaping is surprisingly pleasant, with pine trees, shrubbery and a nearby beach.

During the summer, women often meet the ferries offering *sobe* (rooms) at a good price but without the quality control of an agency. Travel agencies can find you good-quality rooms, often with private bathrooms. Check www.supetar.hr for details of rooms and villas available.

BUDGET

Camping Supetar (☎ 630 088; www.camp-supetar.com; per adult low-high 20-22KN) A mid-sized autocamp about 300m east of town, which has access to a small rocky beach.

Pansion Opačak (☎ 630 018; Šibnja 15; per person low-high 120-146KN; 🔀) Simpler than Pansion Palute (and without TVs) but also pleasant and family run. Breakfast is 45KN extra.

Pansion Palute (☎ /fax 631 541; palute@st.t-com.hr; Put Pašika 16; per person 160KN; 🔀) Open year-round, this is a small, family-run *pension* with clean and tidy rooms, wooden floors, TVs, balconies and a voluble proprietor. Outstanding homemade jam is served with breakfast. Walk all the way down Put Vele Luke (15 minutes) until you get to 1 Svibnja; turn into 1 Svibnja and you'll see Palute on the corner.

MIDRANGE & TOP END

Hotel Villa Britanida (☎ 631 038; www.supetar.hr /britanida; Hrvatskih Velikana 26; per person low-high €41-55) This is a small hotel and restaurant on the eastern end of town across the street from the Autocamp Babura and a narrow, rocky beach. All rooms are pleasantly furnished in a Mediterranean style with phones and satellite TV. Try to get one of the rooms facing the sea for the view and cool breeze.

Velaris Tourist Resort (☎ 606 606; www.velaris.hr; Put Vele Luke 10; per person low-high 330-540KN; P 🔀) This resort complex is spread out in a series of small buildings. Some rooms have balconies and park-view rooms are cheaper (low-high season 285KN to 482KN per person), but all are near the sea.

our pick Hotel Amor (☎ 606 606; www.velaris.hr; Put Vele Luke 10; per person low-high 365-585KN; P 🔀 🍸) A new development and part of the Velaris Tourist Resort, Amor is a small four-star, 50-room hotel that specialises in everything that is comfortable. The rooms have lovely wooden floors and are decked out in yellows, olives and bright greens, and there's an opulent spa area, a pool and wi-fi. It's surrounded by peaceful olive and pine woods, the service is super-friendly and it's also close to the beach.

Hotel Villa Adriatica (☎ 343 806; www.villaadri atica.com; Put Vele Luke 31; per person low-high 365-610KN; P 🔀 🍸) This pretty hotel with palm trees and a garden is only 100m from the beach. All of the artfully decorated rooms have balconies and the hotel restaurant has good vegetarian platters. It's not as good as Hotel Amor when it comes to value for money, although it is closer to the centre of town.

Hotel Kaktus (☎ 631 133; www.watermanresorts.com; Put Vele Luke 4; s low-high €54-121, d €92-158; P 🔀 🍸) Plush and all in virginal white, with a wellness centre, and indoor and outdoor swimming pools. Great for major relaxing.

Eating

Bistro Palute (☎ 631 730; dishes 32-47KN) On the harbour next to Atlas Travel Agency, Bistro Palute specialises in grilled meat, but the fish dishes are also good. Dining is casual.

Restaurant Punta (☎ 631 507; Punta 1; mains from 50KN) This is a fabulously located restaurant, with a beach terrace overlooking the sea. Choose from excellent fish and seafood, dive into some meat or just have a pizza as you watch the waves and windsurfers play around.

our pick Vinotoka (☎ 630 969; Jobova 6; mains 60KN) One of the best places in town, Vinotoka is inside a renovated traditional stone house, decorated with simple, marine-inspired pieces. The food is excellent – go for a fish or cuttlefish *brodet*, one of the yummiest you'll try anywhere and best accompanied by some local white. Fresh fish starts from 350KN per kilo.

Entertainment

Summer Club Luna (www.summerclubluna.hr; Sv Roka; admission 40KN; 🕐 Jul-Oct) is a new summer venue where you dance under the stars, while **XXL** (☎ 630 699; Put Vele Luke) is an old favourite, by the beach and near to the centre.

AROUND SUPETAR

One of the more interesting sites is the village of **Škrip**, the oldest settlement on the island, about 8km southeast of Supetar. Formerly a refuge of the ancient Illyrians, the fort was taken over by the Romans in the 2nd century BC, followed by inhabitants of Solin fleeing 7th-century barbarians and eventually early Slavs. Remains of the **Illyrian wall** are visible around the citadel in the southeastern corner. The most intact Roman monument on the island is the mausoleum at the base of **Radojkovic's tower**, a fortification built during the Venetian-Turkish wars; the tower is now a museum. Sarcophagi from the early Christian period are near **Cerinics citadel**, with a nearby quarry containing a relief of Hercules from the 3rd or 4th century. You can catch an early morning bus here from Supetar and an early afternoon bus back.

The port of **Milna**, 20km southwest of Supetar, is the kind of lovely, intact fishing village that in any other part of the world would have been long ago commandeered by package tourists. The 17th-century town is set at the edge of a deep natural harbour that was used by Emperor Diocletian on the way to Split. Paths and walks take you around the harbour, which is studded with coves and rocky beaches that are usually deserted. Besides the picture-perfect setting, there's the 18th-century **Church of Our Lady of the Annunciation**, with a baroque front and early-18th-century altar paintings.

The **Illyrian Resort** (☎ /fax 636 566; www.illyrian -resort.hr; apt low-high €68-125; P 🐕 🏊), right on Milna beach, provides an extraordinary level of modernity, style and comfort. There are plenty of water sports on offer if lazing around the pool becomes too soporific.

Milna is an easy day trip from Supetar, with a morning bus to the town and an afternoon bus back to Supetar. During the summer, the early evening hydrofoil from Bol stops at Milna before going on to Split.

BOL
pop 1480

The old town of Bol is popular and attractive, with small stone houses and winding streets dotted with pink and purple geraniums. Bol's real highlight is Zlatni Rat, the seductive pebbly beach that 'leaks' into the Adriatic and draws crowds of swimmers and windsurfers in the summer months. A long coastal promenade, lined with pine trees,

connects the beach with the old town, and along it are most of the town's hotels. It's a great, buzzing place in summer – one of Croatia's favourites.

Orientation

The town centre is a pedestrian area that stretches east from the bus station. Zlatni Rat beach is 2km west of town and in between are Borak and Potočine beaches. Behind them are several hotel complexes, including Hotel Borak, Elaphusa and Bretanide.

Information

There's an ATM outside both banks. There are also many money changers in the port area and you can get cash advances on MasterCard and change money at the post office.

Atlas Travel Agency (☎ 635 233; fax 635 707; Rudina 12; 🕙 8.30am-7pm Mon-Fri, 9am-noon Sat) Here you can rent a boat, scooter or bike, and book private accommodation.

Bol Tours (☎ 635 693; www.boltours.com; Obala Vladimira Nazora 18; 🕙 9am-6.30pm Mon-Fri, to noon Sat) Books excursions and finds private accommodation.

HVB Splitska Banka (Riva Frane Radića)

Interactiv (☎ 092 134 327; Rudina 6; per hr 30KN; 🕙 10am-1pm & 4.30-7pm May-Nov) A dozen fast computers. The only place to check your email on the island.

Post office (Uz Pjacu 5; 🕙 8.30am-5.30pm Mon-Fri, 9am-2pm Sat) You can make phone calls here.

Tourist office (☎ 635 638; www.bol.hr; Porat Boskih Pomoraca; 🕙 8.30am-10pm Jul & Aug, 8.30am-2pm & 5-8pm Mon-Sat, 9am-noon Sun Sep-Jun) A good source of information on town events.

Zagrebačka Banka (Uz Pjacu 4)

Sights

Most people come to Bol to soak up the sun or windsurf at **Zlatni Rat** beach, which extends like a tongue into the sea for about 500m from the western end of town. It's a gorgeous stretch, made up of smooth white pebbles, and the shape of the tip is shuffled by the wind and waves. Pine trees provide shade and rocky cliffs rise sharply behind the beach, making the setting one of the loveliest in Dalmatia. Note, though, that it does get packed in the high season.

East of the town centre on the Glavica Peninsula is the **Dominican monastery** (Dominikanski Samostan; ☎ 635 132; Anđelka Rabadana 4; 🕙 Mass only) and the **Church of Our Lady of Mercy** (Crkva Gospe od Milosti; ☎ 635 132; Anđelka Rabadana 4; 🕙 Mass only).

SPLIT & CENTRAL
DALMATIA

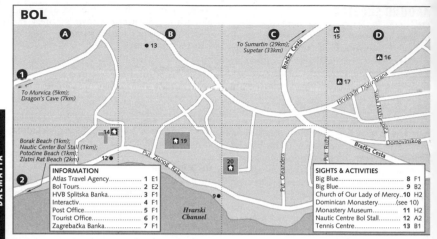

BOL

To Sumartin (29km);
Supetar (33km)

To Murvica (5km);
Dragon's Cave (7km)

Borak Beach (1km);
Nautic Center Bol Stall (1km);
Potočine Beach (1km);
Zlatni Rat Beach (2km)

Put Zlatnog Rata

Hvarski
Channel

INFORMATION		
Atlas Travel Agency	1	E1
Bol Tours	2	E2
HVB Splitska Banka	3	F1
Interactiv	4	F1
Post Office	5	F1
Tourist Office	6	F1
Zagrebačka Banka	7	F1

SIGHTS & ACTIVITIES		
Big Blue	8	F1
Big Blue	9	B2
Church of Our Lady of Mercy	10	H2
Dominican Monastery	(see 10)	
Monastery Museum	11	H2
Nautic Centre Bol Stall	12	A2
Tennis Centre	13	B1

The monastery and church were built in 1475 on the site of a 12th-century Episcopal palace. The late-Gothic church is notable for a late-16th-century altar screen, as well as ceiling paintings by the Croatian baroque painter Tripo Kikolija. The church is partly paved with tombstones, some of which have initials of various monastic orders or inscriptions in Glagolitic script.

Nearby is the **Monastery Museum** (☎ 635 132; Anđelka Rabadana 4; admission 10KN; ☽ 10am-noon & 5-8pm Apr-Oct), presenting prehistoric items excavated from the Kopačina cave, a collection of ancient coins, amphorae and church vestments. The highlight of the collection is the altar painting *Madonna with Child and Saints* attributed to Tintoretto, for which the museum retains the original invoice of 270 Venetian ducats.

You can go by foot to **Dragon's Cave**, an extremely unusual set of reliefs believed to have been carved by an imaginative 15th-century friar. Carved angels, animals and a gaping dragon decorate the walls of this strange cave in a blend of Christian and Croat pagan symbols. First you walk 5km to Murvica, and from there it's a one-hour walk to the cave. The cave is closed to the public but the tourist office occasionally organises guided excursions at a cost of 100KN.

Activities

Bol is undoubtedly the **windsurfing** capital of Croatia and most of the action takes place at Potočine beach, west of town. Although the *maestral* (strong, steady westerly wind)

blows from April to October, the best time to windsurf is at the end of May and the beginning of June, and at the end of July and the beginning of August. The wind generally reaches its peak in the early afternoon and then dies down at the end of the day. **Big Blue** (☎ /fax 635 614; www.big-blue-sport.hr) is a large operation that rents windsurfing boards (€50 per half-day) and offers beginners' courses (eight hours €150). It is situated next to the tourist office.

You can dive (from €45) with another company named **Big Blue** (☎ 306 222; www.big-blue-diving.hr; Hotel Borak, Zlatni Rat) – the two Big Blues used to be one company but have parted ways, though both, confusingly, still use the same name. There are no wrecks to dive but there are some coral reefs at 40m and a large cave; boats go out regularly during the high season. The Hotel Borak Big Blue rents **mountain bikes** (per hour/half-day €3/8) and **kayaks** (per hour/half-day €4/10), too.

There are professional-quality clay tennis courts at the **Tennis Centre** (☎ 635 222; Zlatni Rat; per hr low-high 40-60KN) along the road to Murvica. Depending on the time of day, a tennis pro can help you work on your serve (or whatever) for 90/130KN per one/two people per hour. Rackets and balls can be rented.

You can rent boats from the **Nautic Center Bol stall** (☎ 098 361 651; www.nautic-center-bol.com; Potočine beach; per day from €60), which sits opposite the Bretanide hotel during the day. In the evening you can find the stall at the harbour, where it moves to attract more customers.

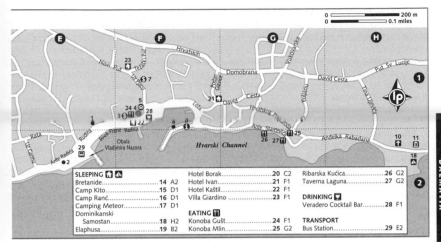

SPLIT & CENTRAL DALMATIA

SLEEPING 🏠 🏕		EATING 🍴		Ribarska Kućica..............**26** G2
Bretanide.............................**14** A2	Hotel Borak..........................**20** C2	Konoba Gušt.......................**24** F1	Taverna Laguna..................**27** G2
Camp Kito............................**15** D1	Hotel Ivan............................**21** F1	Konoba Mlin.......................**25** G2	
Camp Ranč..........................**16** D1	Hotel Kaštil..........................**22** F1		DRINKING 🍸
Camping Meteor..................**17** D1	Villa Giardino **23** F1		Veradero Cocktail Bar...........**28** F1
Dominikanski				
Samostan...........................**18** H2			TRANSPORT
Elaphusa..............................**19** B2			Bus Station..........................**29** E2

If you fancy hiking, a good two-hour walk is up to **Vidova Gora** (780m), the area's highest peak. The local tourist office can give you the basic info on this hike.

Festivals & Events

There's a **Summer Cultural Festival** in Bol during which dancers and musicians from around the country perform in churches and open spaces. The festival is held in July and August.

The patron saint of Bol is Our Lady of Carmel; on her **feast day** (5 August), there's a procession with residents dressed up in traditional costumes, as well as music and feasting on the streets.

Sleeping

The camping grounds are near town and are relatively small. There are few small hotels but several large tourist complexes, which, surprisingly, blend in well with the landscape. Several hotels are 'all-inclusive'. Reservations for most hotels are handled by **Blue Sun Hotels** (☎ 306 206; www.bluesunhotels.com).

Bol Tours (p247) finds private accommodation at around 150KN per person with private bath. A four-person equipped apartment costs around 600KN in the high season and there are other sizes available.

BUDGET

Camping grounds in Bol are small and familial. West of town and near the big hotels you'll find **Camping Meteor** (☎ 635 630; Hrvatskih Domobrana; per adult/site 42/45KN; ☽ May-Oct), **Camp**

Ranč (☎ 635 635; Hrvatskih Domobrana; per adult/site 45/35KN; ☽ May-Oct), which is behind a restaurant of the same name, and **Camp Kito** (☎ 635 551; kamp_kito@inet.hr; Bračka Cesta; per adult/site 53/30KN; ☽ mid-Apr–mid-Sep). They are all well kept and placed in scenic spots.

Another camping ground, **Dominikanski Samostan** (☎ 635 132; Anđelka Rabadana; per adult/site 40/44KN; ☽ May-Oct), is east of town near the Dominican monastery. The tourist office can direct you to a few others.

MIDRANGE

Hotel Borak (☎ 635 210; www.bluesunhotels.com; Zlatni Rat; r per person half-board low-high €37-90; 🅿 🗶 🗎) Close to Zlatni Rat beach and the sporting activities, this four-star place lacks character

---

TOP FIVE CENTRAL DALMATIAN BEACHES

- Zlatni Rat (p247) – the famous beach finger that appears in nearly all of Croatia's publicity

- Brela (p239) – a string of palm-fringed sandy coves

- Pakleni Islands (p254) – rocky islands near Hvar with clothing-optional coves

- Šolta (p230) – quiet, rocky coves not far from noisy Split

- Milna (p247) – usually deserted beaches on the busy island of Brač

thanks to its size. It is, however, a comfortable place to relax after your windsurfing, diving, mountain biking, kayaking, swimming (we could go on).

Hotel Kaštil (☎ 635 995; www.kastil.hr; Riva Frane Radića 1; s low-high 330-710KN; d 480-1040KN; P ✿) All rooms have sea views in this lovely central hotel. The decor is crimson, the bathrooms granite-coloured and paintings adorn the rooms.

Villa Giardino (☎ 635 286; villa.giardino@st.t-com.hr; Novi Put 2; d low-high €89-98; P) An iron gate opens onto a luxuriant garden at the end of which is this old white house. The tastefully restored rooms are furnished with antiques and some overlook the garden. It's an oasis of peace.

Hotel Ivan (☎ 640 888; www.hotel-ivan.com; David Cesta 11a; apt from 850KN; P ✿ 🖥 🛋) In a spruced-up stone building with a large pool at the front, the Ivan has small studios and big apartments, all in whites and blues; a number have balconies and sea views. There's also a spa downstairs that has dozens of therapeutic options.

TOP END

Elaphusa (☎ 635 210; www.bluesunhotels.com; Zlatni Rat; r per person half-board low-high from €50-65; P ✿ 🖥 🛋) Enormous and glistening, this four-star hotel feels like the inside of a cruise ship. It's all smooth interiors, glass partitions, salt-water pools, big conference halls and slick rooms. If you like your accommodation to be glam and glitz (and quite soulless), this is it.

Bretanide (☎ 740 140; www.bretanide.com; Zlatni Rat; s low-high €66-121, d €96-160; P ✿ 🛋) Sitting on the hill, Bretanide is the closest to Zlatni Rat beach and offers a comprehensive sport and wellness program. Certain beauty and wellness treatments cost extra, but even if you just use the basic services you'll emerge beautiful and well.

Eating

Bol's restaurant scene is good thanks to the healthy competition between establishments. Expect fresh fish and creative cooking.

Konoba Gušt (☎ 635 911; Riva Frane Radića 14; mains 48-90KN) This restaurant offers good, informal dining in a setting of burnished wood, old photos and knick-knacks. The seafood and meat dishes are prepared simply but well; try the fried calamari with vegetables and potatoes.

Konoba Mlin (☎ 635 376; Ante Starčevića 11; mains from 50KN; ◷ 5pm-midnight Jun-Nov) A summer affair next to a 19th-century mill, this place has a lovely leafy terrace above the sea. The chef griddles the seafood local style.

Taverna Laguna (☎ 635 692; Ante Starčevića 9; mains from 65KN) This place is in a romantic spot next to a quiet lagoon that would make the restaurant a stand-out even if the food was mediocre. The pasta and seafood dishes are far better than average.

Ribarska Kućica (☎ 635 033; www.ribarska-kucica .com; Ante Starčevića bb; mains from 90KN; ◷ Jun-Nov) A lobster extravaganza is in order at this seaside restaurant (A Fisherman's Little House), where you sit above the water under straw sun umbrellas and gorge on top-class seafood.

Entertainment

Veradero Cocktail Bar (Riva Frane Radića; cocktails 45-55KN; ◷ May-Nov) An open-air cocktail bar on the seafront where you can sip coffee and fresh OJ during the day and come back in the evening for fab cocktails, DJ music and lounging on wicker sofas and armchairs.

SUMARTIN

Sumartin is a quiet, pretty port with a few rocky beaches and little to do, but it makes a nice retreat from the busier tourist centres of Bol and Supetar. The bus station is in the centre of town next to the ferry, and there are a number of *sobe* signs around the tiny town if you decide to stay.

Sumartin is the entry point on Brač if you're coming from Makarska. See Boat on p243 for information on ferry connections between the two towns, and Getting Around, p244, to find out about bus times between Sumartin and Supetar.

HVAR ISLAND

pop 11,459

Hvar is the number-one carrier of Croatia's superlatives: it's the most luxurious island, the sunniest place in the country (2724 sunny hours each year) and, along with Dubrovnik, the most popular tourist destination. Hvar Town, the island's capital, is all about swanky hotels, elegant restaurants, trendy bars and clubs, posh yachters and a general sense that, if you care about seeing and being seen, this is the place to be. Stari Grad and Jelsa are the cultural and historical centres of the island and make up the more quiet and discerning spots.

Hvar is also famed for its verdancy and lilac lavender fields, as well as other aromatic plants such as rosemary and heather. You'll find that some of the really luxe hotels use skin-care products made out of the gorgeous smelling herbs.

History

The island was first settled by the Illyrians, who fought numerous battles with Greek colonisers in the 4th century BC. The Greeks won and established the colony of Faros on the site of present-day Stari Grad. The Romans conquered the island in 219 BC, but it was not an important outpost for the Romans and there are few remains from that period. With the collapse of the Roman Empire, Hvar came under Byzantine rule. In the 7th and 8th centuries Slavic tribes settled the island, and in the 11th century it became part of Croatia under King Petar Krešimir. After several centuries in which Venice, Byzantium and Croatian-Hungarian kings ruled the island, in 1331 it opted for the most powerful of the lot – Venice – as protection against the notorious pirates of Omiš. The island staged several serious rebellions that were ruthlessly crushed by Venice's superior forces.

Getting There & Away

The local car ferry from Split calls at Stari Grad (42KN, 1½ hours) three times a day (five times daily in July and August). **Krilo** (www.krilo.hr), the fast passenger boat, travels five times a day between Split and Hvar Town (22KN, one hour) in the summer months; it also goes to Korčula (33KN, 1½ hours). You can buy tickets at **Split Tours** (Map p219; ☎ 352 553; www.splittours.hr; Gat Sv Duje bb) in Split, **Marko Polo Tours** (Map p284; ☎ 715 400; www.korcula.com; Biline 5) in Korčula or **Pelegrini Tours** (Map p254; ☎ /fax 742 250; www.pelegrini-hvar.hr; Riva bb) in Hvar.

There are at least 10 shuttle ferries (fewer in the off-season) running from Drvenik, on the mainland, to Sućuraj (13KN, 25 minutes) on the tip of Hvar Island. The **Jadrolinija agency** (☎ 741 132; www.jadrolinija.hr) is beside the landing in Stari Grad.

Besides the local ferries that run from Split to Hvar, there are connections to Italy (see p310) in the summer season. The Jadrolinija ferries that operate between Rijeka and Dubrovnik call at Hvar twice

a week during winter and four times a week from June to early September, stopping in Stari Grad before continuing on to Korčula.

Getting Around

Buses meet most ferries that dock at Stari Grad and go to Hvar Town (15KN, 50 minutes) and Jelsa. There are six buses a day between Stari Grad and Hvar Town in the summer months, but services are reduced on Sunday and in the low season. A taxi costs from 150KN to 200KN. **Radio Taxi Tihi** (☎ 098 338 824) is cheaper if there are a number of passengers to fill up the minivan. It's easy to recognise with a picture of Hvar painted on the side.

If you're driving from Stari Grad to Hvar Town, be aware that there are two routes: the scenic route, which is a narrow road winding through the interior mountains, and the direct route, which is a modern roadway (2960) that gets you to town rapidly.

HVAR TOWN

The island's hub and busiest destination, Hvar Town is estimated to draw around 30,000 people a day in the high season. It's odd that they can all fit in the small bay town where 13th-century walls surround beautifully ornamented Gothic palaces and traffic-free marble streets, but fit they do. Visitors wander along the main square, explore the sights on the winding stone streets, swim on the numerous beaches or pop off to get into their birthday suits on the Pakleni Islands, but most of all they party at night. There are several good restaurants here and a number of great hotels, but thanks to the island's penchant for well-heeled guests, the prices can be somewhat astronomical. Don't be put off if you're on a lower budget though, as private accommodation and a couple of hostels cater to a younger, more diverse crowd.

Orientation

Hvar is such a small, easily manageable town that it doesn't even use street names. The main street is the long seaside promenade, dotted with small, rocky beaches, sights, hotels, bars and some restaurants. The town square is called Trg Svetog Stjepana and the bus stop is minutes away from here. On the northern slope above the square and within the old ramparts are the remains of some palaces that belonged to the Hvar aristocracy. From the bus station

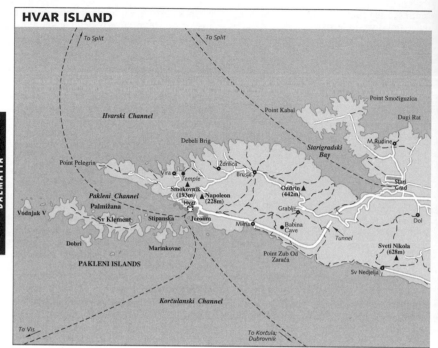

HVAR ISLAND

to the harbour, the town is closed to traffic, which preserves the medieval tranquillity.

Information

Atlas Travel Agency (☎ 741 670; www.atlas-croatia .com; ☼ 8.30am-7pm Mon-Fri, 9am-noon Sat) On the western side of the harbour, this travel agency finds private accommodation and books excursions.

Clinic (☎ 741 300; Sv Katarine) Medical clinic about 700m from the town centre, past Hotel Pharos.

Fontana Tours (☎ 742 133; www.happyhvar.com; Riva 16) Finds private accommodation, runs excursions and handles rentals.

Garderoba (per day 15KN; ☼ 7am-midnight) Left-luggage facilities are available in the bathroom next to the bus station.

HVB Splitska Banka (Riva) Has an ATM.

Internet Leon (☎ 741 824; Riva; per hr 42KN; ☼ 8.30am-10pm Mon-Fri, 9am-4pm Sat & Sun) Internet access next to the Hotel Palace.

Pelegrini Tours (☎ /fax 742 250; www.pelegrini-hvar .hr; Riva bb; ☼ 8.30am-7pm Mon-Sat, 9am-noon Sun) Also finds private accommodation.

Post office (Riva; ☼ 8.30am-7pm Mon-Sat, 9am-noon Sun) You can make phone calls here.

Privredna Banka (Fabrika) Changes money.

Tourist office (☎ /fax 742 977; www.tzhvar.hr; ☼ 8am-1pm & 5-9pm Mon-Sat, 9am-noon Sun Jun-Sep, 8am-2pm Mon-Sat Oct-May) On Trg Svetog Stjepana.

Sights

Don't organise your stay around the opening hours of the museums and churches as they tend to be highly irregular. The hours given following are for the summer season, which runs roughly from June to September, as well as the week between Christmas and New Year and Holy Week. Off-season, Hvar's highlights are open mornings only.

The centre of town is the main square, **Trg Svetog Stjepana**, which was formed by filling in an inlet that once stretched out from the bay. At 4500 sq metres, it's one of the largest old squares in Dalmatia. The town first developed in the 13th century to the north of the square and later spread south of the square in the 15th century. Notice the **well** at the northern end of the square, which was built in 1520 and has a wrought-iron grill dating from 1780.

On the southern side of the square is the **Arsenal**, which was built in 1611 to replace a previous building destroyed by the Ottomans.

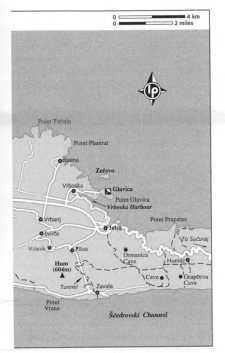

Mentioned in Venetian documents as 'the most beautiful and the most useful building in the whole of Dalmatia', the Arsenal once served as a repair and refitting station for war galleons. The northern side of the building was used to store food, and in 1612 a **Renaissance theatre** was built that is reported to be the first theatre in Europe open to plebeians and aristocrats alike. The theatre remained a regional cultural centre throughout the centuries, and plays were still staged here right up until 2008 when it was decided the old building was too unstable to support crowds; it was being thoroughly refurbished at the time of research.

Another landmark building in Hvar Town is the **Cathedral of St Stjepan** (Katedrala Svetog Stjepana; Trg Svetog Stjepana; twice daily, 30min before Mass), which forms a stunning backdrop to the square. The bell tower rises four levels, each more elaborate than the last. The cathedral was built in the 16th and 17th centuries at the height of the Dalmatian Renaissance on the site of a previous cathedral destroyed by the Turks. Parts of the older cathedral are visible in the nave and in the carved 15th-century choir stalls, but most of the interior dates from the 16th and 17th centuries.

The **Bishop's Treasury** (Riznica; ☎ 741 269; admission 15KN; 9am-noon & 5-7pm), behind the tower and adjoining the cathedral, houses the cathedral treasury of silver vessels, embroidered Mass robes, numerous Madonnas, a couple of 13th-century icons and an elaborately carved sarcophagus.

Northwest of the square is the unfinished Gothic **Hektorović Mansion**. Go up a few stairs to the **Benedictine monastery** (☎ 741 052; admission 10KN; 10am-noon & 5-7pm), which has a re-creation of a Renaissance house and a collection of lace painstakingly woven by the nuns from dried agave leaves. Nearby is the 16th-century **loggia** in front of the Hotel Palace. In front of it is an 18th-century column **Standarac**, from which governmental decisions used to be announced. The same road will take you to the remains of the Dominican **Church of St Marko**, which was destroyed by the Turks in the 16th century. In the apse there is a small **Archaeological Museum** (☎ 741 009; admission 10KN; 10am-noon Jun-Sep), which has some Neolithic weapons and ceramics on display.

The **Main Town Gate**, northwest of the square, leads to a network of tiny streets with small palaces, churches and old houses. From there you can climb up through a park to the **Španjol** (☎ 718 936; admission 15KN; 8am-midnight Jun-Aug), a citadel built on the site of a medieval castle to defend the town from the Turks. The Venetians strengthened it in 1557 and then the Austrians renovated it in the 19th century by adding barracks. Inside is a tiny collection of ancient amphorae recovered from the sea bed, and the view over the harbour is magnificent.

Back in town, visit the 15th-century **Franciscan monastery & museum** (☎ 741 193; admission 15KN; 10am-noon & 5-7pm), which overlooks a shady cove. The elegant **bell tower** was built in the 16th century by a well-known family of stonemasons from Korčula. The Renaissance cloister leads to a **refectory** containing lace, coins, nautical charts and valuable documents, such as an edition of Ptolemy's *Atlas*, printed in 1524. Your eye will immediately be struck by *The Last Supper*, an 8m by 2.5m work by the Venetian Matteo Ingoli dating from the end of the 16th century. The cypress in the **cloister garden** is said to be more than 300 years old. The adjoining church, named **Our Lady of Charity**, contains more fine paintings such as the three

SPLIT & CENTRAL DALMATIA

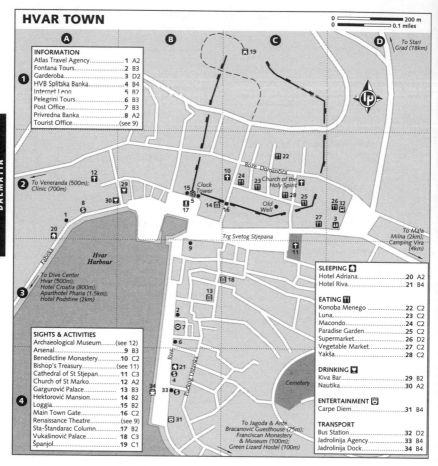

HVAR TOWN

INFORMATION	
Atlas Travel Agency	1 A2
Fontana Tours	2 B3
Garderoba	3 D2
HVB Splitska Banka	4 B4
Internet Leon	5 B2
Pelegrini Tours	6 B3
Post Office	7 B3
Privredna Banka	8 A2
Tourist Office	(see 9)

SIGHTS & ACTIVITIES	
Archaeological Museum	(see 12)
Arsenal	9 B3
Benedictine Monastery	10 C2
Bishop's Treasury	(see 11)
Cathedral of St Stjepan	11 C3
Church of St Marko	12 A2
Gargurović Palace	13 B3
Hektorović Mansion	14 B2
Loggia	15 B2
Main Town Gate	16 C2
Renaissance Theatre	(see 9)
Sta-Štandarac Column	17 B2
Vukašinović Palace	18 C3
Španjol	19 C1

SLEEPING	
Hotel Adriana	20 A2
Hotel Riva	21 B4
EATING	
Konoba Menego	22 C2
Luna	23 C2
Macondo	24 C2
Paradise Garden	25 C2
Supermarket	26 C2
Vegetable Market	27 C2
Yakša	28 C2
DRINKING	
Kiva Bar	29 B2
Nautika	30 A2
ENTERTAINMENT	
Carpe Diem	31 B4
TRANSPORT	
Bus Station	32 D2
Jadrolinija Agency	33 B4
Jadrolinija Dock	34 B4

polyptychs created by Francesco da Santacroce in 1583, which represent the summit of this painter's work, and the *Cruxifixion* by Leandro Bassano on the altar. Below the altar is the tomb of Hanibal Lučić, the 16th-century author of *Female Slave,* the first nonreligious drama in Croatia. The Renaissance relief over the portal, *Madonna with Child,* is a small gem created by Nikola Firentinac in 1470.

After your visit, stroll through the old streets and notice the **Vukašinović Palace** with its seven balconies and monumental entrance, and the 15th-century **Gargurović Palace**.

Activities

In front of the Hotel Amfora, **Dive Center Hvar** (☎ 742 490; www.divecenter-hvar.com) is a large operation that offers a certification course, dives and all sorts of water sports (banana boating, snorkelling, waterskiing), as well as hotel packages. You can rent scooters at **Pelegrini Tours** (☎ /fax 742 250; www.pelegrini-hvar.hr; Riva bb) for between 250KN and 300KN per day.

There are coves around the hotels Amfora and Dalmacija for swimming, but most people head to the **Pakleni Islands** (Pakleni Otoci), which got their name from Paklina, the resin that once coated boats and ships. Taxi boats (15KN, 30 minutes) leave regularly during the high season from in front of the Arsenal to the islands of **Jerolim** and **Stipanska**, which are popular naturist islands (although nudity is not mandatory), and then continue on to **Ždrilica** and **Palmižana**, the latter being a sandy beach.

Tours

Atlas Travel Agency (p252) and Pelegrini Tours (p252) organise tours of the island, trips to the surrounding islands and rafting excursions.

Festivals & Events

Hvar's **Summer Music Festival** includes classical concerts in the Franciscan monastery and occasional concerts at Camping Vira.

Sleeping

As Hvar is one of the Adriatic's most popular resorts, don't expect many bargains. Most Hvar hotels are managed by **Sunčani Hvar Hotels** (☎ 750 750; www.suncanihvar.hr) and many have undergone a total transformation.

Accommodation in Hvar is extremely tight in July and August even though many, many houses have been renovated or constructed to accommodate the crush of tourism. Try the travel agencies (p252) for help. If you arrive without a reservation, you will be offered rooms at the ferry dock and there are many *sobe* signs in town. If you rent a room or apartment from someone at a dock, make sure that their house sports a blue *sobe* sign. Otherwise, they are renting illegally and you'll be unprotected in case of a problem. Get a business card if possible. It is amazingly easy to get lost in the warren of unnamed streets hanging over and around the old town and you may need to call the owner for help. Expect to pay from 250/400KN per single/double with private bathroom in the town centre. Outside the high season you can negotiate a much better price.

BUDGET

Camping Vira (☎ 741 803; www.suncanihvar.hr; per person low-high €6-8) Belonging to Sunčani Hvar and therefore of a predictably high standard, this camping ground is located on a beautiful, wooded bay and is one of the best in Dalmatia. There's a gorgeous beach, a lovely café and restaurant, and a volleyball pitch, and the facilities are well kept and good quality.

Mala Milna (☎ 745 027; per adult/site 66/100KN; ☺ May-Sep) The closest camping ground to town is this site, 2km southeast of the centre. It's small but beautifully situated on Milna Bay and it's best reached with your own wheels, as there are few buses.

Jagoda & Ante Bracanović Guesthouse (☎ 741 416, 091 520 3796; www.geocities.com/virgilye/hvar-jagoda .html; Poviše Škole; s low-high 100-120KN, d 190-220KN) The Bracanović family has turned a traditional stone building into a small *pension*. Rooms come with balconies, private bathrooms and access to a kitchen, and the family goes out of its way for guests. It's a great deal for the price.

Green Lizard Hostel (☎ 742 560; www.greenlizard.hr; Lučića bb; dm 110KN, d per person 135KN; ☺ Apr-Nov) This privately run hostel is a welcome and most necessary budget option on Hvar. Rooms are simple and immaculately clean, there's a communal kitchen and there are a few doubles available with private and shared facilities.

MIDRANGE

Hotel Croatia (☎ 742 400; www.hotelcroatia.net; Majerovica bb; per person low-high 245-575KN; P) Only a few steps from the sea, this medium-sized, rambling 1930s building is among gorgeous, peaceful gardens. The rooms are simple and fresh, many with balconies overlooking the gardens and the sea.

Aparthotel Pharia (☎ 778 080; www.orvas-hotels .com; Majerovica bb; s low-high 280-460KN, d 506-844KN, apt 595-992KN; P ✿) This sparkling complex is only 50m from the water in a quiet neighbourhood slightly west of the town centre. All the rooms and apartments have balconies, some with views over the water. For a small hotel, you couldn't do better.

TOP END

Hotel Podstine (☎ 740 400; www.podstine.com; s low-high 550-2050KN, d 600-2150KN; ✿) Just 2km southwest of the town centre on the secluded Podstine cove lies this family-run hotel (yes, that means not part of the Sunčani Hvar empire) with its own private beach. The landscaping and decor are cheerful and the hotel has regular transfers to and from town, or you can rent a bike, scooter or motorboat. The cheapest rooms have no sea view.

Hotel Riva (☎ 750 750; www.suncanihvar.hr; Riva bb; s low-high €176-380, d €187-391; ✿ ▣) Now the luxury veteran on the Hvar Town hotel scene, the Riva is a picture of success. The 100-year-old hotel has rooms that play with blacks, reds and whites, with glass walls between the bedroom and bathroom, and each room features large B&W posters of movie stars. The location is right on the harbour, perfect for watching the yachts glide up and away.

ourpick Hotel Adriana (☎ 750 200; www.suncani hvar.hr; Fabrika bb; per person from €300; ✿ ▣ ▣)

Opened in June 2007, this is Croatia's only place classified by The Leading Small Hotels of the World, which gives you some idea of the world of comfort you'll find here. All of the glorious rooms overlook the sea and medieval town, and there's a comprehensive spa, a gorgeous roof top heated pool next to the roof-top bar, wi-fi, a plush restaurant, excursions, you name it.

Eating

Hvar's eating scene is good, though as with the hotels, restaurants often target affluent diners.

Paradise Garden (☎ 741 310; mains from 50KN) This eatery, up some stairs on the northern side of the cathedral, serves up a memorable spaghetti with seafood, as well as the usual excellent assortment of grilled or fried fish. Tables are outdoors on an enclosed patio.

Konoba Menego (☎ 742 036; mains from 70KN) On the stairway and steep street above the Church of the Holy Spirit, this is a rustic old house kept as simple and authentic as possible. Everything is decked out in Hvar antiques, the staff wear traditional outfits, the service is unobtrusive but informative, and the marinated meats, cheeses and vegetables are prepared the old-fashioned Dalmatian way. Try the cheese and fig desserts and some local wine.

Luna (☎ 741 400; mains from 70KN) With its brightly painted walls and 'stairway to heaven' (you have to guffaw) to the rooftop terrace, Luna is a slightly wacky place, which is a refreshing change from all those traditional and high-class Hvar restaurants. The menu is good, with dishes such as gnocchi with truffles, and seafood and wine pasta.

Yakša (☎ 277 0770; www.yaksahvar.com; mains from 80KN) This top-end restaurant is where many come not just for the food but also for its reputation as the place to be seen in Hvar. There is a lovely garden at the back and the food is excellent, with lobster (250KN) being a popular choice.

Macondo (☎ 741 851; mains from 90KN) In a narrow alley over the main square, Macondo turns out wonderful fish dishes. The cold mixed plate offers two fish pâtés, octopus salad and salted anchovies, which makes either a tasty opening to the main meal or a good light meal in itself.

Self-caterers can head to the supermarket next to the bus station, or pick up fresh supplies at the next-door vegetable market.

Drinking & Entertainment

Hvar has some of the best nightlife on the Adriatic coast, mostly centred on the harbour.

Nautika (Fabrika) With the latest cocktails and nonstop dance music – ranging from techno to hip hop – this place is an obligatory stop on Hvar's night-crawl circuit.

Kiva Bar (Fabrika) Just up the street, the place to chill out and talk between dance numbers.

Carpe Diem (☎ 742 369; www.carpe-diem-hvar.com; Riva) Look no further. You have arrived at the mother of Croatia's coastal clubs. From a groggy breakfast to late-night cocktails, there is no time of day when this swanky place is dull. The music is smooth, the drinks aplenty, and there's lots of dancing on the tables in bikinis.

Veneranda (☒ from 9.30pm) A former fortress on the slope above Hotel Delfin, Veneranda alternates star DJs with live bands, while the punters groove on a dance floor surrounded by a pool.

Shopping

Lavender, lavender and more lavender is sold in small bottles, large bottles or flasks, or made into sachets. Depending on the time of year, there will be anywhere from one to 50 stalls along the harbour selling the substance, its aroma saturating the air. Various herbal oils, potions, skin creams and salves are also hawked.

STARI GRAD

Stari Grad (Old Town), on the island's northern coast, is a more quiet, cultured and altogether sober affair than its stylish and stunning sister. If you're not after pulsating nightlife and thousands of people crushing each other along the streets in the high season, head for Stari Grad and enjoy Hvar at a more leisurely pace.

History

Road signs around Stari Grad note a secondary name ('Faros'), a reference to the Greek colony that was founded here in 385 BC. The local population resisted Greek rule but the Greek navy from Issa (present-day Vis) defeated the islanders in one of the oldest historically confirmed naval battles. The Romans ousted the Greeks in 219 BC, and razed the town. Later, Slavs settled it and it became the political and cultural capital of the island until 1278, when the bishopric moved to Hvar Town.

The town occupied itself with navigation and shipbuilding, and in the 16th century the poet Petar Hektorović built a mansion here, which has become the highlight of a visit to Stari Grad.

Orientation

Although most ferries connecting the island to the mainland list Stari Grad as their port of call, the town is, in fact, a couple of kilometres northeast of the ferry dock. Stari Grad lies along a horseshoe-shaped bay with the old quarter on the southern side of the horseshoe. The bus station (no left-luggage office) is at the foot of the bay and the northern side is taken up by residences, a small pine wood and the sprawling Helios hotel complex.

Information

HVB Splitska Banka (Riva 12) ATMs.
Post office (Trg Tvrdalj; ☼ 9am-6pm Mon-Fri, to noon Sat) On the main square.
Tourist office (☎/fax 765 763; www.stari-grad-faros.hr; Noa Riva 2; ☼ 8am-10pm mid-Jun–mid-Sep, to 2pm Mon-Fri mid-Sep–mid-Jun) Distributes a good map and has ATMs outside.

Sights

Tvrdalj (☎ 765 068; Trg Tvrdalj; admission 10KN; ☼ 10am-noon Jun-Sep) is Petar Hektorović's 16th-century fortified castle. The leafy fish pond reflects the poet's love for fish and fishermen. His poem *Fishing and Fishermen's Chat* (1555) paints an enticing portrait of his favourite pastime. The castle also contains quotes from the poet's work inscribed on the walls in Latin and Croatian.

Another highlight of Stari Grad is the old **Dominican monastery** (Dominikanski Samostan; admission 10KN; ☼ 10am-noon & 6-8pm Jun-Sep), which was founded in 1482, damaged by the Turks in 1571 and later fortified with a tower. In addition to the library and archaeological findings in the monastery museum, there is a 19th-century church with *The Interment of Christ* attributed to Tintoretto, and two paintings by Gianbattista Crespi.

Sleeping

The only agency finding private accommodation is **Mistraltours** (☎/fax 765 281; Grofa Vranjicanija 2), near the bus station, which will find singles/doubles with private facilities for 150/250KN in July and August.

Kamp Jurjevac (☎ 765 843; Predraga Bogdanića; per adult/site 37/80KN; ☼ Jun-Sep) Near swimming coves off the harbour just east of the old town.

Helios (☎ 765 865; www.hoteli-helios.hr; s low-high €35-60, d €50-90; [P]) This modern two-star hotel is part of a large complex that has commandeered the northern wing of the town. There are apartments available.

Other hotels situated in the Helios complex are the three-star **Arkada** (☎ 765 555; s low-high €45-70, d €65-105) and **Lavanda** (☎ 306 330; s low-high €45-70, d €70-110).

JELSA

Jelsa is a small town, port and resort 27km east of Hvar Town, surrounded by thick pine forests and high poplars. Although it lacks the Renaissance buildings of Hvar, the intimate streets and squares are pleasant and the town is within easy reach of swimming coves and sand beaches. Hotel accommodation is cheaper than in Hvar Town and the town has become the island's most popular second choice.

History

Jelsa emerged in the 14th century as a port for the inland village of Pitve and spread around the churches of Sts Fabian and Sebastian and St John in the Field. In the 16th century a fort was erected over the town to protect it from the Turks and by the 19th century Jelsa had grown into a prosperous fishing village.

In the middle of the 19th century the marshes around the coast were drained and the town gradually spread out. In 1868 the public library became the first public reading room in the Dalmatian islands, and in 1881 it became the centre of Matica Hrvatska, a celebrated Croatian literary circle.

Orientation

Jelsa is wrapped around a bay with several large hotels on each side and the old town at the foot of the harbour. A promenade stretches from the west end of the bay and rises up the hill on the eastern side leading to a sandy cove. The bus station is on the edge of the main road leading into town (no one bothers with street names). As you proceed into town you'll come to the post office.

Information

You can change money at any travel agency and there's an ATM at Privredna Banka on the main square.

Atlas Travel Agency (☎ 761 038; www.atlas-croatia .com; Riva bb; ☼ 9am-7pm Mon-Fri, to noon Sat) At the harbour. Helps find private accommodation.

HVB Splitska Banka (Trg Tome Gamulina) On the eastern side of the harbour.

Tourist office (☎ 761 918; www.jelsa-online.com; Riva bb; ☼ 7.30am-noon & 6.30-8.30pm Mon-Sat, 9am-noon Sun) Across the street from Atlas and along the quay. Also helps find private accommodation.

Sights & Activities

In the **Church of Sts Fabian & Sebastian** (Crkva Sv Fabijana i Sebastijana; ☼ Mass only), 30 minutes before a service, you can see a 17th-century baroque altar by wood carver Antonio Porri and a wooden statue of the Virgin Mary brought by refugees from the village of Čitluk, near Sinj, who were fleeing the Turks in the 16th century.

In addition to the **sand beach** near the Hotel Mina, there is a daily taxi boat (25KN) to the naturist beaches of **Zečevo** and **Glavica**, or you can rent wheels and head across the hill to the coves surrounding the village of **Zavala**. The hair-raising road is superbly scenic and takes you through the tiny village of **Pitve**, before descending to a number of isolated coves.

The **Island Travel Agency** (☎ 761 404; www.hvar -jelsa.net) on the road to Mina rents out scooters

for 240KN a day and motorcycles for 300KN a day.

For diving, the place to go to is **Dive Center Jelsa** (☎ /fax 761 822; www.tauchinjelsa.de; Hotel Jadran).

Tours

Atlas Travel Agency (left) offers more or less the same program as in Hvar Town (see p255), but the prices sometimes differ.

Sleeping

Atlas Travel Agency finds private rooms from 120KN per person in the high season.

Grebišće (☎ 761 191; www.grebisce.hr; per adult low-high €4.40-4.60; ☼ Apr-Sep) A camping ground 5km east of Hotel Mina, Grebišće has access to a beach. There are also a few four-person bungalows available for rent (€75 to €90 depending on the season).

Pansion Murvica (☎ /fax 761 405; www.murvica.net; r per person low-high €25-30; ☒) This lovely little *pension* is on a side street that runs parallel to the main road leading into town. The comfortable studios are attractively decorated and the shady terrace restaurant serves up delicious meals.

Hotel Hvar (☎ 761 122; www.dalmacia-holiday.com; d low-high €65-175) Part of a three-hotel resort, this is a 206-room place with pleasant rooms with balconies, some of which overlook the sea. It's close to the beach, too.

Dubrovnik & Southern Dalmatia

What can you say about Dubrovnik that hasn't already been said? Lord Byron's 'jewel of the Adriatic' has been quoted endlessly, and Bernard Shaw's 'paradise on Earth' is a well-worn saying. Dubrovnik leaves most people speechless; its beauty is gobsmacking, its setting a knockout. Not that it's a secret, quite the contrary: too many people know of its beauty and thousands of tourists walk squashed along the main street throughout the year, gazing, gasping, snapping. It's one of the world's hottest tourist destinations.

Dubrovnik is also a great launching place for expeditions to the surrounding region, which is equally, though less famously, gorgeous. There is an array of lush islands, including Korčula (the largest), which produces excellent white wines, *pošip* and *grk*; a flurry of smaller unpopulated and paradisaical islands; and the idyllic national park on Mljet. The mountainous Pelješac Peninsula is famous for its *postup* and *dingač* reds, the legendary seafood of Ston and the gorgeous gardens at Trsteno.

Steeped in sunshine and bathed in mild sea breezes, the coastal belt stretches from Ploče in the north to the Montenegrin border in the south. With the exception of Korčula Island, the county largely follows the borders of the old independent Republic of Ragusa (Dubrovnik).

The lure of Dubrovnik has given a boost to the entire region as hotels spread outwards from the walled city, creating a 'Dubrovnik Riviera'. Unlike other parts of the Adriatic coast, however, there are no mega-resorts or sprawling tourist settlements, which has discouraged mass tourism but makes individual travel especially rewarding.

DUBROVNIK & SOUTHERN DALMATIA

HIGHLIGHTS

- Revelling in the most lovely and touristy of activities: seeing **Dubrovnik** (p267) from its city walls
- Having a drink and watching the open sea from one of Dubrovnik's **Bužas** (p274)
- Escaping the crowds and sunbathing at **Lokrum** (p276)
- Spending a few days on **Mljet** (p277), as close as Croatia gets to a verdant paradise
- Trying the oysters in **Ston** (p290)

- TELEPHONE CODE: 020

SOUTHERN DALMATIA

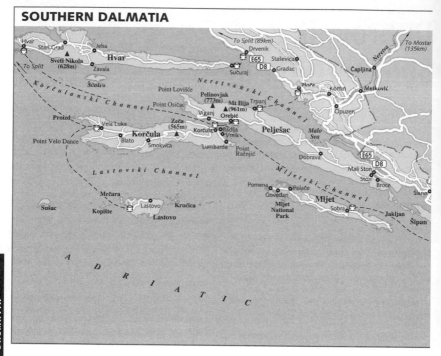

DUBROVNIK

pop 45,800

Regardless of whether you are visiting Dubrovnik for the first time or you're returning again and again to this marvellous city, the sense of awe and beauty when you set eyes on the Stradun never fades. It's hard to imagine anyone, even the city's inhabitants, becoming jaded by its marble streets and baroque buildings, or failing to be inspired by a walk along the ancient city walls that once protected a civilised sophisticated republic for five centuries, and that now look out onto the endless shimmer of the peaceful Adriatic.

Although the shelling of Dubrovnik in 1991 horrified the world, the city has bounced back with characteristic vigour to again enchant its visitors. The hedonistic can pamper themselves in one of the city's fine hotels or enjoy a refreshing plunge into the sea. History buffs can trace the rise and fall of Dubrovnik's commercial empire in museums replete with art and artefacts. A local symphony orchestra and a busy concert season delight music-lovers. Whether it's the relaxed Mediterranean lifestyle, the interplay of light and stone, the fresh sea breezes or the remarkable history, Dubrovnik is suffused with an ineffable magic that makes it one of the world's great destinations.

HISTORY

The story of Dubrovnik begins with the 7th-century onslaught of barbarians that wiped out the Roman city of Epidaurum (site of present-day Cavtat). The residents fled to the safest place they could find, which was a rocky islet separated from the mainland by a narrow channel. Building walls was a matter of pressing urgency due to the barbarian invasions; the city was well fortified by the 9th century when it resisted a Saracen siege for 15 months.

Ragusa had help from the powerful Byzantine Empire, under whose protection it remained from the 7th to the 12th century. Meanwhile, another settlement emerged on the mainland, stretching from Zaton in the north to Cavtat in the south, and became known as Dubrovnik, named after the *dubrava* (holm oak) that carpeted the region.

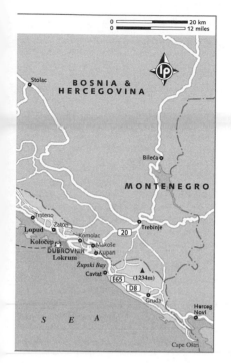

The two settlements merged in the 12th century, and the channel that separated them was paved over to become Placa.

By the end of the 12th century, Dubrovnik had become an important trading centre on the coast, providing an important link between the Mediterranean and Balkan states. From the hinterlands, cattle and dairy products, wax, honey, timber, coal, silver, lead, copper and slaves were exported, along with Dubrovnik products such as salt, cloth, wine, oil and fish.

Dubrovnik came under Venetian authority in 1205, finally breaking away from its control in 1358. Although the city thereafter acknowledged the authority of the Croatian-Hungarian kings and paid them tribute, it was largely left alone to do what it did best – make money.

By the 15th century the Respublica Ragusina (Republic of Ragusa) had extended its borders to include the entire coastal belt from Ston to Cavtat, having previously acquired Lastovo Island, the Pelješac Peninsula and Mljet Island. It was now a force to be reckoned with. The city turned towards sea trade and established a fleet of its own ships, which were dispatched to Egypt, Syria, Sicily, Spain, France and later Turkey. Through canny diplomacy the city maintained good relations with everyone – even the Ottoman Empire, to which Dubrovnik began paying tribute in the 16th century.

Centuries of peace and prosperity allowed art, science and literature to flourish. Marin Držic (1508–67) was a towering figure in Renaissance literature, best known for his comic play *Dundo Maroje*. Ivan Gundulić (1589–1638) was another Dubrovnik poet-dramatist whose greatest work was the epic *Osman*. To the world of science, Dubrovnik gave Ruđer Bošković (1711–87), who produced a seminal work in the field of theoretical physics, as well as numerous tomes on optics, geography, trigonometry and astronomy. Composers, poets, philosophers and painters turned Dubrovnik into a major cultural centre on the Adriatic.

Tragically, most of the Renaissance art and architecture in Dubrovnik was destroyed in the earthquake of 1667, which killed 5000 people and left the city in ruins, with only the Sponza Palace and the Rector's Palace surviving. The city was rebuilt in a uniform baroque style with modest dwellings in rows and shops on the ground floor. The earthquake also marked the beginning of the economic decline of the town, accentuated by the opening of new trade routes to the east and the emergence of rival naval powers in Western Europe.

The final coup de grâce was dealt by Napoleon whose troops entered Dubrovnik in 1808 and announced the end of the republic. The Vienna Congress of 1815 ceded Dubrovnik to Austria, where the city maintained its shipping but succumbed to social disintegration. It remained a part of the Austro-Hungarian Empire until 1918 and then slowly began to develop its tourism industry.

Caught in the cross-hairs of the war that ravaged former Yugoslavia, Dubrovnik was pummelled with some 2000 shells in 1991 and 1992, suffering considerable damage. All of the damaged buildings have now been restored.

ORIENTATION

The city extends about 6km from the mouth of the Rijeka River in the west to the cape of Sveti Jakov in the east, and includes the promontory of Lapad.

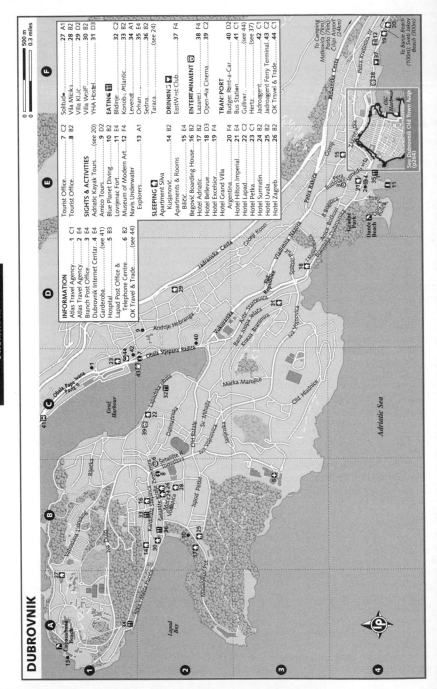

DUBROVNIK: DESTRUCTION & RECONSTRUCTION

Many remember the incredible TV footage of the shelling of Dubrovnik. Although now in the past, the memory of the city's year at war is still fresh in the minds of locals – you'll see reminders of it on the several plaques through the old town.

Shells struck 68% of the 824 buildings in the old town, leaving holes in two out of three tiled roofs. Building facades and the paving stones of streets and squares suffered 314 direct hits and there were 111 direct hits on the great wall. Nine historic palaces were completely gutted by fire, while the Sponza Palace, Rector's Palace, St Blaise's Church, Franciscan Monastery and the carved fountains, Amerling and Onofrio, sustained serious damage. The total destruction was estimated at US$10 million. It was quickly decided that the repairs and reconstruction would be done with traditional techniques, using traditional materials whenever feasible.

Dubrovnik has since regained most of its original grandeur. The great town walls are once again intact, the gleaming marble streets are smoothly paved and famous monuments such as the 15th-century Onofrio Fountain and the Clock Tower have been lovingly restored. Damage to Sponza Palace, Rector's Palace, St Blaise's Church, the cathedral and various 17th-century residences has been repaired with the help of an international brigade of specially trained stoneworkers.

This leafy residential suburb with rocky beaches contains the hostel and most of the town's hotels. The old walled town lies southeast of Lapad at the foot of Srđ Hill, halfway between Gruž Harbour and the cape of Sveti Jakov. The entire old town is closed to cars and is divided nearly in half by the wide street Placa, also referred to as Stradun.

Pile Gate is the western entrance to the old town and the last stop for local buses from Lapad and Gruž. The eastern gate is Ploče, which leads to the town beach and several luxury hotels along Frana Supila. The Jadrolinija ferry terminal and the bus station are a few hundred metres apart at Gruž, which is about 2km northwest of the old town. To get to the old town from the bus station take buses 1a, 1b, 3 or 8. To get to Lapad take bus 7.

The city boundaries also include the Elafiti Islands (Šipan, Lopud, Koločep, Olipe, Tajan and Jakljan).

INFORMATION

Bookshops

Algebra (Map p264; ☎ 323 217; Placa 9; ⏰ 9.30am-8pm Mon-Sat) Books and souvenirs and souvenir books, plus English-language guides to the city and region.
Algoritam (Map p264; ☎ 322 044; www.algoritam .hr; Placa 8; ⏰ 9am-8.30pm Mon-Fri, to 3pm Sat) A good selection of English-language books.

Internet Access

Dubrovnik Internet Centar (Map p262; ☎ 311 017; Dubrovačkih Branitelja 7; per hr 20KN; ⏰ 9am-9pm)
Netcafé (Map p264; ☎ 321 125; www.netcafe.hr; Prijeko 21; per hr 30KN; ⏰ 9am-11pm) A wonderfully friendly café with a fast connection and good services: CD/DVD burning, wi-fi, photo printing and transferring, and so on.

Left Luggage

Garderoba (per day 15KN; ⏰ 5.30am-9pm) At the bus station.

Medical Services

Hospital (Map p262; ☎ 431 777; Dr Roka Mišetića)

Money

You can change money at any travel agency or post office. There are numerous ATMs in town, and near the ferry terminal and bus station.

Post

Branch post office (Map p262; Dubrovačkih Branitelja 2; ⏰ 9am-6pm Mon-Sat)
Lapad Post Office & Telephone Centre (Map p262; Šetalište Kralja Zvonimira 21; ⏰ 9am-6pm Mon-Sat)
Main post office (Map p264; cnr Široka & Od Puča; ⏰ 9am-6pm Mon-Sat) In the old town.

Tourist Information

Tourist office (www.tzdubrovnik.hr; ⏰ 8am-8pm Jun-Sep, 8am-3pm Mon-Fri, 9am-2pm Sat Oct-May) bus station (Map p262; ☎ 417 581; Obala Pape Ivana Pavla II 44a); Gruž Harbour (Map p262; ☎ 417 983; Obala Stjepana Radića 27); Lapad (Map p262; ☎ 437 460; Šetalište Kralja Zvonimira 25); old town (Map p264; ☎ 323 587; Široka 1); old town 2 (Map p264; ☎ 323 887; Ulica Svetog Dominika 7); Pile Gate (Map p264; ☎ 427 591; Dubrovačkih Branitelja 7) Maps, information and the indispensable *Dubrovnik Riviera* guide.

DUBROVNIK & SOUTHERN DALMATIA

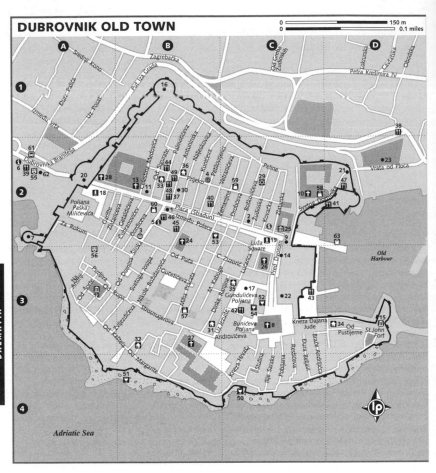

DUBROVNIK OLD TOWN

DUBROVNIK & SOUTHERN DALMATIA

Travel Agencies
Atlas Travel Agency (www.atlas-croatia.com; ⊙ 9am-6pm Mon-Sat, to 1pm Sun) Gruž Harbour (Map p262; ☎ 418 001; Obala Papa Ivana Pavla II 1); Pile Gate (Map p262; ☎ 442 574; Sv Đurđa 1) In convenient locations, this agency is extremely useful for general information, excursions and finding private accommodation.
OK Travel & Trade (Map p262; ☎ 418 950; okt-t@du
.t-com.hr; Obala Stjepana Radića 32; ⊙ 9am-6pm Mon-Sat, to 1pm Sun) Near the Jadrolinija ferry terminal.

SIGHTS
The Old Town
Due to its confined space and neat street grid, Dubrovnik's old town naturally lends itself to a walking tour. We've listed points of interest in a logical way here so that you can wander

at your own pace and discover the city at your leisure.

PILE GATE
The natural starting point to any visit to Dubrovnik, this fabulous city gate (Map p264) was built in 1537. Crossing the drawbridge at the gate's entrance, imagine that this was once actually lifted every evening, the gate closed and the key handed to the prince. Notice the statue of St Blaise, the city's patron saint, set in a niche over the Renaissance arch. As you pass through the outer gate you come to an inner gate dating from 1460, and soon after you're struck by the gorgeous view of the main street, **Placa**, or as it's commonly known, **Stradun**, Dubrovnik's pedestrian promenade. It

stretches right down to the end of the old town and at its eastern end it widens out into **Luža Square**, formerly used as a marketplace.

ONOFRIO FOUNTAIN

One of Dubrovnik's most famous landmarks, **Onofrio Fountain** (Map p264) was built in 1438 as part of a water-supply system that involved bringing water from a well 12km away. Originally, the fountain was adorned with sculpture, but it was heavily damaged in the 1667 earthquake and only 16 carved masks remain with water gushing from their mouths into a drainage pool.

ST SAVIOUR CHURCH

This **church** (Crkva Svetog Spasa; Map p264; Placa) was built between 1520 and 1528 and was one of the few buildings to have survived the earthquake of 1667. It's open for occasional exhibitions and concerts.

FRANCISCAN MONASTERY & MUSEUM

Over the door of the **Franciscan Monastery & Museum** (Muzej Franjevačkog Samostana; Map p264; ☎ 321 410; Placa 2; adult/concession 20/10KN; ☯ 9am-6pm) is a remarkable pietà sculpted by the local masters Petar and Leonard Andrijić in 1498. Unfortunately, the portal is all that remains of the richly decorated church that was destroyed in the 1667 earthquake. Inside the monastery complex is the mid-14th-century **cloister**, one of the most beautiful late-Romanesque structures in Dalmatia. Notice how each capital over the dual columns is topped by a different figure, portraying human heads, animals and floral arrangements.

Further inside you'll find the third-oldest functioning pharmacy in Europe, which has been in business since 1391. The pharmacy may have been the first pharmacy in Europe open to the general public. Before leaving, visit the monastery museum with its collection of relics, liturgical objects, paintings, gold work and pharmacy items such as laboratory gear and medical books.

WAR PHOTO LIMITED

One of the better photography galleries you're likely to come across in your gallery life, **War Photo Limited** (Map p264; ☎ 326 166; www.warphotoltd .com; Antuninska 6; admission 30KN; ☯ 9am-9pm May-Sep, 10am-4pm Tue-Sat, 10am-2pm Sun Oct & Apr) has changing exhibitions that are curated by the gallery owner and former photojournalist Wade Goddard. The gallery is open from April to October and has up to three exhibitions over that period relating to the subject of war seen

DUBROVNIK & SOUTHERN DALMATIA

from various perspectives. The 2008 season saw Ron Haviv's powerful and disturbing images of the Yugoslav war in 'Blood & Honey', Bruce Connew's Myanmar exhibitions 'On the Way to An Ambush' and 'Child Soldier', and many other collections by award-winning international photographers. Highly recommended.

SERBIAN ORTHODOX CHURCH & MUSEUM
Dating from 1877, the **Serbian Orthodox Church & Museum** (Muzej Pravoslavne Crkve; Map p264; ☎ 323 283; Od Puča 8; adult/concession 10/5KN; ⏱ 9am-2pm Mon-Sat) is a fascinating collection of icons dating from the 15th to 19th century. In addition to portraits of the biblical family originating in Crete, Italy, Russia and Slovenia, there are several portraits by the illustrious Croatian painter Vlaho Bukovac.

ETHNOGRAPHIC MUSEUM
Sitting in the 16th-century Rupe Granary, the **Ethnographic Museum** (Etnografski Muzej; Map p264; ☎ 323 013; Od Rupa; adult/student 35/15KN; ⏱ 9am-2pm Sun-Fri) contains exhibits relating to agriculture and local customs.

SYNAGOGUE
The oldest Sephardic and second-oldest **synagogue** (Sinagoga; Map p264; ☎ 321 028; Žudioska 5; admission 10KN; ⏱ 10am-8pm Jun-Sep, 9am-3pm Mon-Fri Oct-May) in Europe dates back to the 15th century. Inside is a museum that exhibits religious relics, documentation on the local Jewish population and WWII remains.

ORLANDO COLUMN
The Orlando Column (Roland's Column; Map p264) is a popular meeting place that used to be the place where edicts, festivities and public verdicts were announced. Carved in 1417, the forearm of this medieval knight was the official linear measure of the Republic – the ell of Dubrovnik, which measures 51.1cm.

CLOCK TOWER
The Clock Tower (Map p264) dominates Luža Sq and makes an elegant punctuation point at the end of Placa. First built in 1444, it was restored many times, most recently in 1929, and is notable for the two bronze figures in the bell tower that ring out the hours.

SPONZA PALACE
The 16th-century Sponza Palace (Map p264) was originally a customs house, then a minting house, a state treasury and a bank. Now it houses the **State Archives** (Državni Arhiv u Dubrovniku; ☎ 321 032; admission 15KN; ⏱ 8am-3pm Mon-Fri, to 1pm Sat), which contain a priceless collection of manuscripts dating back nearly a thousand years. This superb structure is a mixture of Gothic and Renaissance styles beginning with an exquisite Renaissance portico resting on six columns. The 1st floor has late-Gothic windows and the 2nd-floor windows are in a Renaissance style, with an alcove containing a statue of St Vlaho. Also inside is the **Memorial Room of the Defenders of Dubrovnik** (⏱ 10am-10pm Mon-Fri, 8am-1pm Sat), a heartbreaking collection of portraits of young people who perished between 1991 and 1995.

LITTLE ONOFRIO FOUNTAIN
On Luža Sq, this **fountain** (Map p264) is part of the same water project as its larger cousin to the west. It was built to supply water to the square's marketplace.

ST BLAISE'S CHURCH
This imposing **church** (Crkva Svetog Vlahe; Map p264; Luža Sq; ⏱ morning & late-afternoon Mass Mon-Sat) is one of Dubrovnik's most prominent. Built in 1715 to replace an earlier church destroyed in the earthquake, it was constructed in a baroque style following the church of St Mauritius in Venice. The ornate exterior contrasts strongly with the sober residences surrounding it. The interior is notable for its marble altars and a 15th-century silver gilt statue of the city's patron, St Blaise, who is holding a scale model of pre-earthquake Dubrovnik.

RECTOR'S PALACE
The Gothic-Renaissance **Rector's Palace** (Map p264; ☎ 321 437; Pred Dvorom 3; adult/student 35/15KN; audio guide 30KN; ⏱ 9am-6pm) was built in the late 15th century and adorned with outstanding sculptural ornamentation. It retains a striking compositional unity despite being rebuilt many times. Notice the finely carved capitals and the ornate staircase in the atrium, which is often used for concerts during the Summer Festival (p268). Also in the atrium is a statue of Miho Pracat, who bequeathed his wealth to the Republic and was the only commoner in the 1000 years of the Republic's existence to be honoured with a statue (1638). We may assume that the bequest was considerable. The palace was built for the rector who governed Dubrovnik, and it contains the

rector's office, his private chambers, public halls and administrative offices. Interestingly, the elected rector was not permitted to leave the building during his one-month term without the permission of the senate. Today the palace has been turned into a **museum** with artfully restored rooms, portraits, coats of arms and coins, evoking the glorious history of Dubrovnik.

CATHEDRAL OF THE ASSUMPTION OF THE VIRGIN

Built on the site of a 7th-century basilica that was enlarged in the 12th century, the **Cathedral of the Assumption of the Virgin** (Stolna Crkva Velike Gospe; Map p264; Poljana M Držića; ☾ morning & late-afternoon Mass) was supposedly the result of a gift from England's King Richard I, the Lionheart, who was saved from a shipwreck on the nearby island of Lokrum. Soon after the earlier cathedral was destroyed in the 1667 earthquake, work began on this new cathedral, which was finished in 1713 in a purely baroque style. The cathedral is notable for its fine altars, especially the altar of St John Nepomuk made of violet marble. The cathedral **treasury** (Riznica; ☎ 411 715; adult/child 10/5KN; ☾ 8am-5.30pm Mon-Sat, 11am-5.30pm Sun) contains relics of St Blaise as well as 138 gold and silver reliquaries largely made in the workshops of Dubrovnik's goldsmiths between the 11th and 17th centuries. Among a number of religious paintings, the most striking is the polyptych of the Assumption of the Virgin, made in Titian's workshop.

ST IGNATIUS CHURCH & AROUND

Built in the same style as the cathedral and completed in 1725, the **St Ignatius Church** (Crkva Svetog Ignacija; Map p264; Uz Jezuite; ☾ late-evening Mass) has frescoes displaying scenes from the life of St Ignatius, founder of the Jesuit society. Abutting the church is the **Jesuit College** at the top of a broad flight of stairs leading down to Gundulićeva Poljana, a bustling **morning market** (Map p264; ☾ 6am-1pm). The monument in the centre is of Dubrovnik's famous poet, Ivan Gundulić. The reliefs on the pedestal depict scenes from his epic poem, *Osman*.

DOMINICAN MONASTERY & MUSEUM

If you return to the Sponza Palace and follow Ulica Svetog Dominika to Ploče Gate, you'll find the **Dominican Monastery & Museum** (Muzej Dominikanskog Samostana; Map p264; ☎ 322 200; off Ulica Svetog Dominika 4; adult/child 20/10KN; ☾ 9am-5pm). It's a real architectural highlight of a transitional Gothic-Renaissance style and has a rich trove of paintings. Built at the same time as the city walls in the 14th century, the stark exterior resembles a fortress more than a religious complex. The interior contains a graceful 15th-century cloister constructed by local artisans after the designs of the Florentine architect Massa di Bartolomeo, and a large, single-naved church with an altarpiece by Vlaho Bukovac. The eastern wing contains the monastery's impressive art collection, which includes paintings from Dubrovnik's finest 15th- and 16th-century artists. Notice the works of Nikola Božidarević, Dobrić Dobričević and Mihajlo Hamzić.

The City Walls & Forts

No visit to Dubrovnik would be complete without a leisurely walk around the powerful **city walls** (Gradske Zidine; Map p264; adult/child 50/20KN; ☾ 9am-7.30pm Apr-Oct, 10am-3.30pm Nov-Mar), the finest in the world and Dubrovnik's main claim to fame. Built between the 13th and 16th centuries, they are still intact today.

The first set of walls to enclose the city was built in the 13th century. In the middle of the 14th century the 1.5m-thick walls were fortified with 15 square forts. The threat of attacks from the Turks in the 15th century prompted the city to strengthen the existing forts and add new ones, so that the entire old town is now contained within a curtain of stone over 2km long and up to 25m high. The walls are thicker on the land side – up to 6m – and range from 1.5m to 3m on the sea side. The round **Minčeta Tower** (Map p264) protects the northern edge of the city from land invasion, while the western end is protected from land and sea invasion by the detached **Lovrjenac Fort** (Map p262). Pile Gate is protected by the **Bokar Tower** (Map p264), and the **Revelin Fort** (Map p264) protects the eastern entrance.

The views over the town and sea are great, so be sure to make this walk the high point of your visit. The entrance to the walls is immediately to the left of Pile Gate when you enter the city. You can also enjoy Shakespeare's plays, which are staged on the Lovrjenac Fort terrace during the Summer Festival.

The **Maritime Museum** (Map p264; ☎ 323 904; adult/child 35/15KN; ☾ 9am-6pm), inside St John

Fort, traces the history of navigation in Dubrovnik with ship models, maritime objects and paintings.

East of the Old Town
MUSEUM OF MODERN ART
The Museum of Modern Art (Map p262; ☎ 426 590; Frana Supila 23; admission free; ☒ 10am-7pm Tue-Sun) is great for those interested in contemporary Croatian artists, particularly the local painter Vlaho Bukovac.

ACTIVITIES
Swimming
It's tough to know where to swim in Dubrovnik, what with all those walls and harbours. There are several city beaches, but many take a boat to the Elafiti Islands (p276).

Banje Beach (Map p262) is the main town beach, just beyond the 17th-century Lazareti (p274), outside Ploče Gate. Although many people rent lounge chairs and parasols from the nearby EastWest Club, there's no problem with just flinging a towel on the beach. A nearby beach is **Sveti Jakov** (Map p262), a 20-minute walk down Vlaho Bukovac or a quick ride on bus 5 or 8 from Frana Supila at the old town's northern end. It's a good, local beach that doesn't get rowdy or too busy, and has showers, a bar and a restaurant.

Beaches past Pile Gate include the pebbly **Šulići** (Map p262) and the rocky **Danče** (Map p262). There are also two tiny **coves**, one right next to Orhan restaurant (p273) and the other a two-minute walk from the restaurant, down the beach-level narrow streets.

Another excellent place for swimming is below the two Buža bars (p274), on the outside of the city walls. Diving is off the rocks, there are steps to help you get in and out, and there's some cemented space between the rocks for sunbathing. It's a very atmospheric place but there's not much shade here, so bring a hat and strong sun protection.

Lapad Bay (Map p262) is brimming with hotel beaches that you can use without a problem. The largest public beach on Lapad is outside the Hotel Kompas. A little further on is **Copacabana Beach** (Map p262) on Babin Kuk peninsula, a good shallow beach with a toboggan for kids. If you're a naturist, head down to **Cava** (Map p262), signposted near Copacabana Beach.

Diving & Boating
The waters around Dubrovnik offer excellent diving opportunities.

Navis Underwater Explorers (Map p262; ☎ 099 350 2773; www.navisdubrovnik.com; Copacabana Beach) offers a full range of dives, courses and diving services. The main diving site is the wreck of the *Taranto*. **Blue Planet Diving** (Map p262; ☎ 091 899 973; www.blueplanetdiving.com; Masarykov Put 20) is inside Hotel Dubrovnik Palace and offers the same services.

Whether you're just dipping into the sport or you're an experienced kayaker, **Adriatic Kayak Tours** (Map p262; ☎ 091 722 0413; www.adriatickayaktours.com; Zrinsko Frankopanska 6) has a kayak tour for you. There are multiday tours available that cover Lokrum Island and the Elafiti Islands; you can also go white-water rafting on the Tara River canyon and kayaking in Kotor Bay in Montenegro. The main office is in Gruž, and it also has a booking office on Banje Beach during the summer months.

TOURS
Dubrovnik Walks (☎ 095 806 4526; www.dubrovnikwalks.com) conducts 1½-hour guided walks of the old town in English daily at 10am and 5pm (90KN). It also offers 1½-hour walks of Dubrovnik's walls and forts daily at 9.30am and 3.30pm (140KN), also in English. The meeting place is in front of the Latino Club Fuego (p274) and no reservation is necessary. A combination ticket for both tours costs 200KN.

Amico Tours (Map p262; ☎ 418 248; www.amico-tours.com; Od Skara 1) offers day trips to Mostar and Međugorje (390KN), Montenegro (390KN), Albania (990KN), Korčula and Pelješac (390KN), and the Elafiti Islands (250KN), as well as numerous kayaking, rafting and jeep-safari day trips (590KN).

FESTIVALS & EVENTS
The **Dubrovnik Summer Festival** (Map p264; ☎ 326 100; www.dubrovnik-festival.hr; Od Sigurate 1) is the most prestigious summer festival in Croatia and has taken place every year since 1950. For five weeks in July and August, a program of theatre, concerts and dance is presented on open-air stages throughout the city. The opening ceremony takes place on Luža Sq and usually includes fireworks and a band. In addition to attracting the best national artists and regional folklore ensembles, the program usually

includes one or two big-name international artists. Theatre productions feature the plays of Marin Držić, Shakespeare, Moliére and the Greek tragedians. Tickets range from 50KN to 300KN and are available from the festival office on Placa or on site one hour before the beginning of each performance. You can also reserve and buy them online.

Libertas Film Festival (www.libertasfilmfestival.com) takes place between 29 June and 4 July with films being screened in the open air at old town venues. A real treat. Check the website for the program.

The **Feast of St Blaise** (3 February) is another citywide bash marked by pageants and processions. **Carnival** festivities heralding the arrival of Lent in February are also popular.

SLEEPING

Most of Dubrovnik's hotels are gathered in the Lapad and Ploče areas, though there are a few gorgeous (and pricey) places to stay in the old town. The more expensive resort hotels are located east of town.

Private Rooms

If you're on a budget, you'll have little choice but to go for private accommodation, but beware of the scramble of private owners at the bus station or Jadrolinija ferry terminal: some provide what they say they offer, others are scamming. Try to pin down the location in advance or you could wind up staying a considerable distance from town. If the ones listed here are all booked up, it's a good idea to try booking through any of the travel agencies (p264) or the tourist office (p263). If you rent a room or apartment from someone at the bus station, make sure that their house sports a blue *sobe* (rooms available) sign. Otherwise, they are renting illegally and you are unprotected in case of a problem.

Expect to pay about 200KN to 220KN for a room in the high season. There are also apartments available starting at about 500KN for a studio. It's a very good idea to book in advance, especially in the summer season.

Begović Boarding House (Map p262; ☎ 435 191; http://begovic-boarding-house.com; Primorska 17; dm low-high €14-19, s €25-32, d €32-40; 🖵) This is one of Dubrovnik's favourite private room options, mainly because of the wonderful hospitality offered by the Begović family. The rooms are basic and comfortable, there's a lovely communal terrace and garden, and you're close

to all that Lapad has to offer. It's a 20- to 25-minute walk to the old town. The owners will pick you up for free from the bus station and by arrangement from the airport. Breakfast is not included, but is available at extra cost, and internet access is free. The family also organises fishing picnics (250KN), which are a wonderful way to spend the day.

Apartments Silva Kusijanović (Map p262; ☎ 435 071; 098 244 639; antonia_du@hotmail.com; Kardinala Stepinca 62; per person 100KN) Sweet Silva has four large apartments that can hold four to eight beds. All have terraces with gorgeous views and it's possible to barbecue.

Apartments & Rooms Biličić (Map p264; ☎ 417 152; www.geocities.com/apartments_bilicic; Privežna 2; s low-high €18-25, d €36-50, apt €50-100; 🞥) One of the few options near the old town, this is a great place to stay. The rooms are bright, clean and pleasant, with TVs and views of the gorgeous garden, which has a lovely open-air kitchen where you can make your own breakfast. The private bathrooms are across the hall from the rooms. There is a four-person apartment, too. It's a 15-minute walk to Pile Gate. The friendly owner, Marija, is a good source of local information.

Rooms Vicelić (Map p264; ☎ 098 979 0843; www .dubrovnik-online.com/rooms_vicelic; Antuninska 9 & 10; r low-high €50-80) Two houses sit on a stepped alley within the heart of the old town. The location is the real charmer here; the rooms are modern or a bit ramshackle but cute. Most rooms in number 9 have high ceilings and a straightforward modern decor, with comfy beds, TVs and en suite shower, toilet and kitchenette. Those in number 10 are more shabby-chic; note that one ground-floor room has an upstairs bathroom, no real windows and bang-your-head concrete beams, while all share a mid-floor kitchenette and a two-seat sitting area.

Villa Klaić (Map p262; ☎ 411 144; www.hostelworld .com/hosteldetails.php/VillaKlaic-Dubrovnik-14432; Šumetska 11; d from €200; 🞥 🖳) Many of Dubrovnik's hundreds of homestays have friendly owners, but few are as wise, interesting and worldly as Milo Klaić, the owner of excellent Villa Klaić. This must be the only budget accommodation in Dubrovnik to offer guests a private outdoor swimming pool. Although high above the centre, the old city is just 15 minutes' walk away. All rooms have good private bathrooms; room No 7, with sheepskin-style throw carpets and a great shower, sits aloof near the pool.

Camping

Solitudo (Map p262; ☎ 448 200; www.camping-adriatic .com; per person/site 49/55KN; ⦿ mid-May–mid-Oct) This pretty and renovated camping ground is on Lapad promontory within walking distance of the beach.

CampIng Matkovića (off Map p262; ☎ 485 067; Mlini; per adult/site 40/50KN; ⦿ May-Oct) is next to **Porto** (off Map p262; ☎ 487 078; Mlini; per adult/site 45/55KN; ⦿ May-Oct), 7km south of Dubrovnik. Both are small, near a quiet cove. It's best to call first. To get here, take bus 10 or 16 to Srebreno, which will leave you almost at the gate to both grounds.

Old Town & Around

our pick **Fresh Sheets** (Map p264; ☎ 091 799 2086; beds@igotfresh.com; Sv Šimuna 15; per person €25; 🖳) A brand new place run by Jon and Sanja from Fresh (p272), Fresh Sheets offers one double room and four individually decorated apartments – Lavender, Rainforest, Sunshine and Heaven – with each sleeping two to four people. The decoration ranges from brightly painted walls and colourful bed-throws to pristine and airy white interiors. The atmosphere is lively and the hosts cater mainly to backpackers and party-loving people. The location is excellent – very close to Buža (p274) – and you get free internet and wi-fi and, when the Fresh bar's kitchen is open, a free smoothie every day.

Apartments Amoret (Map p264; ☎ 091 530 4910; www.dubrovnik-amoret.com; Dinke Ranjine 5 & Restićeva 2; apt €50-120; 🅿) Six artistically appointed apartments and rooms are tucked away within two old town houses (Amoret 1 and Amoret 2) that date back to the 16th century. Each is different but all are lovingly decorated to create some of the most charming accommodation anywhere in Dubrovnik.

our pick **Karmen Apartments** (Map p264; ☎ 323 433, 098 619 282; www.karmendu.com; Bandureva 1; apt €55-145; 🅿) One of the best accommodation choices in the whole of Dubrovnik, this collection of apartments is run by Marc Van Bloemen, an Englishman who has lived in Dubrovnik since the age of 11 and is therefore a fount of information on the city. Set inside an old stone house in the middle of the old town, the four apartments are beautifully decorated with original artwork and imaginative use of recycled materials, all made by Marc's artist mother. There are small, one- to two-person apartments, as well as two for three or four people; apartment No 1 has views of the harbour. Book well in advance because it all gets booked up by June.

Hotel Stari Grad (Map p264; ☎ 322 244; www .hotelstarigrad.com; Palmotićeva; s low-high 650-1180KN, d 920-1580KN; 🅿) Staying in the heart of the old town in a lovingly restored stone building is an unmatchable experience. The eight rooms here are elegantly and tastefully furnished to feel simple and luxurious at the same time. There is a marvellous view over the town from the rooftop terrace, where you can have your breakfast. Book in advance in the summer and note that there is a 10% extra charge for one-night stays.

Pucić Palace (Map p264; ☎ 326 222; www.thepucic palace.com; Od Puča 1; s low-high €206-315, d €290-505; 🅿 🅿) Right in the heart of the old town and inside what was once a nobleman's mansion, this five-star hotel is Dubrovnik's most exclusive and hottest property. There are only 19 rooms, all exquisitely decorated and featuring Italian mosaics, Egyptian cotton and baroque beds. Many flush couples wed at the 1st-floor terrace's tiny chapel. The rooftop restaurant Defne (p273) is one of the city's finest, and the Café Royal downstairs serves breakfast à la carte.

Hotel Hilton Imperial (Map p262; ☎ 320 320; www .hilton.com; Marjana Blazića 2; d from €250; 🅿 🅿 🖳 🅿) The luxury Hilton is a restoration of the 19th-century Hotel Imperial, Dubrovnik's finest establishment when the city was part of the Austro-Hungarian Empire. Located right outside Pile Gate, the hotel offers decor that is modern but warm and inviting, with cheerful Mediterranean colours. Business travellers to Dubrovnik will appreciate the conference rooms, secretarial services and audiovisual equipment, while leisure travellers can take advantage of the fitness room, indoor pool and fine dining offered at the hotel's Restaurant Porat.

our pick **Hotel Bellevue** (Map p262; ☎ 330 000; www.hotel-bellevue.hr; Petra Čingrije 7; d from €250; 🅿 🖳 🅿) A five-minute walk west from Pile Gate, Hotel Bellevue's location – on a cliff that overlooks the open sea and the lovely bay underneath – is pretty much divine. The rooms are beautifully designed, the balconies overlook said sea and bay, and the breakfast, which can be eaten on your balcony, is wonderful. Despite being closed for much of 2007, Bellevue is once again (since reopening in June 2008) top dog in Dubrovnik's high-end hotel scene. Its restaurant, Vapor, is top notch, too, with excellent seasonal products, fish, meat and a wide range of Croatian wines.

Lapad

Most of the less-expensive hotels are in Lapad, as well as a few more luxurious establishments. It's quite a pleasant place to stay, away from the droves of tourists that flood the old town. It's also a mixed residential and tourist neighbourhood, and weekends are full of strolling locals and their kids, so you really get the feeling of being part of the city. The main road is Šetalište Kralja Tomislava, while the pedestrian tree-lined Šetalište Kralja Zvonimira makes a lovely stroll past stalls and outdoor cafés. Nika i Meda Pucića is a cliffside path, shaded by a pine forest and dotted with cafés and bars. It's prime strolling ground on Sunday.

A walk along the coast past the Hotel Kompas leads to lots of spots for stretching out along the rocks and taking a swim. After about 1km you'll come to the Hotel Neptune and a series of package-tour hotels. Bus 6 runs between Pile Gate and the bus stop in Lapad near the post office, though you can walk it easily in 20 minutes.

YHA Hostel (Map p262; ☎ 423 241; dubrovnik@hfhs.hr; Vinka Sagrestana 3; per person low-high 85-120KN) Basic in decor, the YHA Hostel is clean and, as travellers report, a lot of fun. If you are allowed to choose a bed (rare), the best dorms are rooms 31 and 32. They cost the same as any other but share a 'secret' roof terrace with a refreshingly lovely view. Rates include breakfast. To get here head up Vinka Sagrestana from Bana Josipa Jelačića 17.

Vila Micika (Map p262; ☎ 437 332; www.vilamicika .hr; Mata Vodapića; s low-high 150-210KN, d 300-420KN; P) This is a simple, well-run establishment. The rooms are painted in soft colours and equipped with TVs and modern bathrooms. There's a pleasant outdoor terrace, and it's only 200m to the Lapad beaches. Micika has a few clauses: prices do not include breakfast (€8 per person extra), and add 30% to stays shorter than three days and 73KN for air-con.

Hotel Adriatic (Map p262; ☎ 437 302; www.hoteli maestral.com; Masarykov Put 9; s low-high €40-80, d €68-140) This large hotel has simple but serviceable rooms and is close to the beach. Front rooms are more expensive and overlook the sea but could be noisy.

Hotel Sumratin (Map p262; ☎ 438 930; www .hotels-sumratin.com; Šetalište Kralja Zvonimira 31; s low-high 290-460KN, d 460-760KN; P) The socialist-style reception (large, brightly lit and decked out in dark wood) gives way to pretty decent rooms with terracotta carpets and spacious beds. Many rooms have small balconies, too. The Sumratin is well located on the main Lapad drag near all of the beaches.

our pick **Hotel Zagreb** (Map p262; ☎ 430 930; www.hotels-sumratin.com; Šetalište Kralja Zvonimira 27; s low-high 400-660KN, d 700-1060KN;) Under the same ownership as Hotel Sumratin, Hotel Zagreb is the more stylish sister, set inside a lovely, salmon-coloured, 19th-century building. The rooms are large, the beds comfy, and there are flat-screen TVs, paintings with marine motifs, and large creamy bathrooms.

Hotel Uvala (Map p262; ☎ 433 580; www.hoteli maestral.com; Masarykov Put 6; d €120-170; P) A newly renovated four-star hotel that's decked out with a lovely reception, indoor and outdoor pools and a comprehensive spa. The service is friendly and it's a comfortable place, very close to the beach. It's unfortunate, however, that the rooms are a bit of a let-down, with their glum browns and whites.

Hotel Lapad (Map p262; ☎ 432 922; www.hotel -lapad.hr; Lapadska Obala 37; d from €130; Jun–mid-Oct;) Renovated in 2008, Hotel Lapad is inside a lovely old limestone building, with swanky new rooms that are all sharp corners, sleek lines and modern furnishings. There's no beach access but the hotel runs a daily boat to a remote beach near Zaton for a small charge.

our pick **Villa Wolff** (Map p262; ☎ 438 710; www .villa-wolff.hr; Nika i Meda Pucića 1; s low-high 1533-1879KN, d 1606-1898KN; P) A gorgeous boutique hotel right on the lovely seaside promenade, Villa Wolff only has six rooms, all beautifully outfitted, bright and airy. The suites have their own balconies and there is a verdant garden that guests use for sunbathing.

Gruž Harbour

Hotel Petka (Map p262; ☎ 410 500; www.hotelpetka .com; Obala Stjepana Radića 38; s low-high €55-106, d €80-144; P) Hotel Petka is opposite the Jadrolinija ferry terminal, with 104 business-oriented rooms, each with TV, phone and minibar. It's good if you need to catch an early morning ferry.

Ploče

The best luxury establishments are east of the old town along Frana Supila within walking distance of the city centre.

Hotel Grand Villa Argentina (Map p262; ☎ 440 555; www.gva.hr; Frana Supila 14; d from €200; P ⌧ ⌕) This is a large hotel accompanied by two villas: Villa Orsula and the recently built Villa Sheherezade. The latter is presented in fully blown Arabian Nights style, with golds and crimsons, tonnes of patterns and carved wood. Villa Orsula is a more classic affair, but richly decorated nonetheless. The main hotel offers luxury suites as well as sleek, well-serviced modern rooms, some of which overlook the sea. There's an indoor and outdoor swimming pool, but the swimming is excellent from the rocks next to the hotel.

Hotel Excelsior (Map p262; ☎ 353 353; www.hotel-excelsior.hr; Frana Supila 12; s/d from 1640/1890KN; P ⌧ ⌕) This is possibly Dubrovnik's biggest hotel extravaganza. Recently closed for a €10 million refit, the legendary Excelsior opened again in 2008 to many bated breaths. Like Argentina, there is now an adjacent boutique villa, Villa Odka, whose rooms are gorgeously understated (as are those in the main building). There is also an indoor and outdoor swimming pool and a palm-tree terrace.

EATING
Old Town & Around

You have to choose carefully when it comes to the old town's restaurants. Many ride on the assumption that you're here just for a day (as many of the big cruiser passengers are) and that you won't be coming back. Rather than looking for somewhere to eat on the Stradun, go to the side streets, where you'll find plenty of good places to eat and snack (see our recommendations following). Also be highly discerning when choosing to eat on Prijeko, where many of the offerings can be overpriced.

Smuuti Bar (Map p264; ☎ 091 896 7509; Palmotićeva 5; smoothies 18-25KN) Perfect for breakfast smoothies and nice big mugs of coffee (at a bargain 10KN), this is the breakfast sister of Nishta (right). The friendly staff speak English.

Buffet Skola (Map p264; ☎ 321 096; Antuninska 1; snacks from 20KN) For a quick bite between sightseeing spots, you can't do better. Fresh cheese, local tomatoes and local ham are some of the ingredients stuffed into the heavenly homemade bread here.

Fresh (Map p264; ☎ 091 896 7509; www.igotfresh.com; Vetranićeva 4; wraps from 20KN) A mecca for young travellers who gather here for the smoothies, wraps and other healthy snacks, as well as drinks and music in the evening (see p274).

Nishta (Map p264; ☎ 091 896 7509; Prijeko 30; mains from 30KN) When this 100% vegetarian restaurant opened in Dubrovnik (an unprecedented case), the baffled locals asked the owners what they served. 'Everything except meat', they said, and the locals concluded that they must be serving nothing. Hence the name Nishta, which means 'nothing' in Croatian. Alas, you're in the Balkans, what do you expect? Head here for a refreshing gazpacho, a heartwarming miso soup, Thai curries, veggies and noodles, and many more nonmeat delights.

Pizzeria Baracuda (Map p264; ☎ 323 160; Nikole Božidarevića 10; mains from 35KN) A Dubrovnik oldtimer, this is a friendly pizzeria near the Orthodox Church, with tables outside on a quiet courtyard. Don't expect Italian-style pizza perfection, but it's cheap, the portions are generous, and with a crisp, cold beer in your hand it's a real treat.

Kamenice (Map p264; ☎ 421 499; Gundulićeva Poljana 8; mains from 40KN) It's been here since the 1970s and not much has changed; not the socialist-style waiting uniforms, nor the simple interior and the massive portions of mussels, grilled or fried squid, griddled anchovies and *kamenice* (oysters). And the owners have, incredibly, seen no need to up their prices. The terrace is on one of Dubrovnik's most gorgeous squares.

ourpick Lokanda Peskarija (Map p264; ☎ 324 750; Ribarnica bb; mains from 40KN) Located on the Old Harbour right next to the fish market, this is undoubtedly one of Dubrovnik's best eateries. It satisfies on every level: the quality of the seafood dishes is unfaltering, the prices are good and the location is gorgeous. Locals queue along with tourists for the wonderful baby squid, the substantial risottos and the juicy mussels. Sip a glass of *dingač* and try the *rožata,* a Croatian version of crème brûlée, while you watch the boats bob on the silky waters.

dub (Map p264; ☎ 426 319; www.dub-loungebar.hr; Brsalje 1; breakfast from 50KN) If you fancy a big breakfast while overlooking the city walls and Pile Gate from a breezy terrace, dub is the place. Vegetarian, meaty and eggy breakfasts come with salads, fresh juices and coffee or tea, but only before noon. The lounge

DUBROVNIK & SOUTHERN DALMATIA

chairs and sofas are very comfortable, so you can come here for an afternoon snack or an evening cocktail, too.

Orhan (Map p262; ☎ 414 183; Od Tabakarije 1; mains from 50KN) Orhan is beautifully located on a rocky cove, overlooking the city walls. It specialises in fish and seafood, but the quality of the cooking has suffered from restingonitslaurelsitis in the last few years, so opt for something simple and enjoy the view.

Revelin (Map p264; ☎ 322 164; Ulica Svetog Dominika bb; mains from 60KN) There are few places in Dubrovnik with such a wonderful location and good prices as the Revelin. A restaurant and bar in the summer, and bar and club in the winter, this place has a terrace spreading under an old pine tree by Ploče Gate, overlooking the harbour. It serves good pastas (try the crayfish tagliatelle with a tangy tomato sauce) and meat dishes, such as veal medallions and lamb shanks.

Wanda (Map p264; ☎ 098 944 9317; www.wandarestaurant.com; Prijeko 8; mains from 70KN) Single-handedly saving the reputation of Prijeko restaurants, Wanda is truly one you can go to for reliably good upmarket dining. The menu is Italian, with wonderful dishes such as zucchini stuffed with prawns, osso bucco and saffron risotto, and a heady stew of prawns, scallops, lobster, clams, mussels and fish. The ingredients are fresh, local and seasonal, and the setting elegant and relaxed.

Defne (Map p264; ☎ 326 200; Od Puča 1; mains from 70KN) Pucić Palace's (p270) top-floor restaurant is one of the old town's classiest. The Turkish chef makes sure you get some good kebabs on the menu (posh kebabs, that is, with fresh mint and lavender sauces), but he mainly focuses on Dalmatia's fish and seafood. Try the octopus carpaccio starter, served with black *tagliolini* and truffle – a piece of heaven in your mouth – or the gorgeous lobster with white risotto. The wine list is impeccable.

Proto (Map p264; ☎ 323 234; www.esculap-teo.hr; Široka 1; mains from 80KN) Sister restaurant to the painfully classy Nautika, Proto is an equally elegant affair with understated flavours and simple fresh ingredients. The fish is top-notch (try the fish soup) and the lobster is a feast. The sauces are light and balance the dishes perfectly. Book in advance.

Gil's (Map p264; ☎ 322 222; www.gilsdubrovnik.com; Ulica Svetog Dominika bb; mains from 120KN) Uber-posh, super-expensive and gloriously glitzy, Gil's is a Russo-French affair of, you guessed it,

Russian dosh and French taste. As such, it's aimed at Dubrovnik's creamiest tourists (and locals) who want to dine on Sevruga caviar (360KN), seashell *panna cotta*, exquisite black truffle risotto with veal glacé, raw red tuna julienne, black ravioli with lobster sauce, and other dizzyingly delectable dishes. The wine cellar is the chef's pride and joy, with 6000 carefully chosen bottles, and the setting is the best in Dubrovnik – overlooking the harbour from within the walls, with a gorgeous terrace upstairs. If you've got the dough, this is the place to spend it.

Self-caterers have the privilege to use the local food **market** (Map p264; Gundulićeva Poljana; ☎ 6am-1pm), which sells fresh local and seasonal products every morning.

Lapad

Lapad's main drag, Šetalište Kralja Tomislava, is packed with cafés, bars and restaurants. Some restaurants are tourist traps, so check the menu well before you commit, though most are decent places much enjoyed by the locals.

Sedna (Map p262; ☎ 352 000; www.hotel-kompas.hr; Petra Čingrije 7; pizzas from 26KN, omelettes 30-35KN) The Hotel Kompas bar-pizzeria is a great and unpretentious spot for breakfast, lunch or dinner. You can sit on a terrace overlooking the beach and Lapad Bay, while the locals buzz around, drinking coffees and chatting on sunny mornings and afternoons.

Konoba Atlantic (Map p262; ☎ 435 726; Kardinala Stepinca 42; mains from 45KN) It's not terribly atmospheric at the outdoor tables here, since it's next to a bus stop. Install yourself indoors, however, and you can sample superb homemade pastas, vegetarian lasagne and gnocchi with rabbit sauce.

our pick Levanat (Map p262; ☎ 435 352; Nika i Meda Pucića 15; mains 45-120KN) One of the best spots in the whole city, Levanat overlooks the sea from the pine-laden hill between Lapad Bay and Babin Kuk. The food is innovative and equally gorgeous, with seafood and unusual sauces, fresh ingredients and delicious vegetarian options.

Taraca (Map p262; Šetalište Kralja Zvonimira; mains from 50KN; ☼ Jun-Sep) Under Hotel Sumratin, in the pine-shaded courtyard, this is a large-scale people's restaurant that grills everything: meat, fish and vegetables. Sit on one of the plastic chairs, let your kids run wild, and enjoy the lively atmosphere.

Blidinje (Map p262; ☎ 358 794; Lapadska Obala 21; mains from 70KN) A great local that's not frequented by many tourists, Blidinje has fabulous views of Gruž Harbour from its terrace. The food is aimed primarily at carnivores, so use the opportunity to taste lamb or veal slow-cooked under hot coals – but make sure you ring in and order at least two hours in advance. Then, order some good red wine and settle in for the evening.

Ploče

Chihuahua Cantina Mexicana (Map p264; ☎ 424 445; Hvarska 6; mains from 30KN) No matter how good the local cuisine is, sometimes you just want to bury your face in a plate of empanadas. This is a lively, young place and the punters come for the quesadillas, tacos and enchiladas, as well as a cool bottle of Corona.

DRINKING

Summer in Dubrovnik is a fabulous time. You sit under the stars, sipping beer, cocktails or wine, everyone's dressed up and ready to stay up, and there's a great buzz in town. Most people head for the old town; Lapad is a place for families and quieter fun, but pleasant nonetheless.

Troubadur (Map p264; ☎ 412 154; Bunićeva Poljana 2) A legendary Dubrovnik venue, you've got to have at least one drink at the Troubadur. There are live jazz concerts in the summer on most nights – often (though not always) played by Marko, the owner, and his jazz band. The atmosphere is excellent and anyone who's anyone in town comes to hang out here.

our pick **Buža** (Map p264; Ilije Sarake) Another must-have-drink place, the Buža (literally 'hole') started out as just a simple place on the outside of the city walls, facing out onto the open sea. It served drinks in plastic cups to blissful punters, with only a white metal fence and a straw awning to protect you from the elements. It's stayed pretty much the same (though it now has real glasses), but it's become a city attraction, with increased prices to match. Find it by following the 'cold drinks' sign along the city walls.

our pick **Buža II** (Map p264; Crijevićeva 9) Sister to the more frazzled original Buža, this one is lower on the rocks, with a snazzier look and good swimming from the rocks. A great place to spend the day.

Fresh (Map p264; ☎ 091 896 7509; www.igotfresh.com; Vetranićeva 4; cocktails from 35KN) All of Dubrovnik's backpackers head over to Fresh in the evening, when the smoothies and wraps are replaced by cocktails, beers (lots of two-for-ones), music and a great party atmosphere.

Karaka Irish Bar (Map p264; ☎ 324 014; Između Polača 7) The Emerald Isle is well represented here with Irish draught beer on tap, Irish music in the evenings and a happy hour from 3pm to 7pm. You can even watch UK sporting events beamed in by satellite.

EastWest Club (Map p262; ☎ 412 220; Frana Supila bb) By day this outfit on Banje Beach rents out beach chairs and umbrellas and serves drinks to the bathers who come here to relax and rehydrate. When the rays lengthen, the cocktail bar opens and a smart-casual set admires the sunset over a long, cool drink.

Hemingway Cocktail Bar (Map p264; Pred Dvorom) A massively popular venue opposite the Rector's Palace, Hemingway's has the longest cocktail list in Dubrovnik – old Ernest would have been proud! Dressed-up youngsters like to hang out here and it gets pretty packed on weekend nights.

ENTERTAINMENT
Nightclubs

Latino Club Fuego (Map p264; Pile Brsalje 11) Despite the name, you'll find a range of dance music that includes techno and pop. The atmosphere is relaxed with no glowering bouncer and no rigid dress code.

Lazareti (Map p262; ☎ 324 633; Frana Supila 8) Dubrovnik's best art and music centre, Lazareti hosts cinema nights, club nights, live music, masses of concerts and pretty much all the best things in town.

Cinemas

Sloboda Cinema (Map p264; ☎ 321 425; clock tower) This is the most centrally located cinema in Dubrovnik. Posters outside advertise the nightly showings.

Open-Air Cinema (Map p262; Kumičića, Lapad) In two locations, it is open nightly in July and August with screenings starting after sundown (9pm or 9.30pm). Also at Za Rokom in the old town (Map p264).

Lazareti (Map p262; ☎ 324 633; Frana Supila 8) Come here for the free art-film seasons hosted by a group of local film enthusiasts throughout the year. International and local films are projected onto the 19th-century walls of the Lazareti complex, once a quarantine barracks.

Live Music

St Blaise's Church (Map p264; Luža Sq; admission free) Open-air folklore shows are conducted in front of the church at 11am on Sundays through May, June and September.

Dubrovnik Orchestra (☎ 417 101) The orchestra regularly gives concerts in the atrium of the Rector's Palace and at various other sites around town.

Dubrovnik String Quartet (Map p264; St Saviour Church, Placa) The quartet gives concerts throughout autumn on Monday night in St Saviour Church. Look for posters around town or ask at the tourist office.

SHOPPING

You'll find souvenir stores all over Stradun, selling Dalmatian marine details, stripy tops, anchors and the like.

Maria (Map p264; ☎ 321 330; www.maria-dubrovnik .hr; Ulica Svetog Dominika bb) Take a few deep breaths before you step into this shop, for you are sure to swoon at the sight of soft Miu Miu leather bags, lacquered Alexander McQueen shoes and gorgeous Marni dresses. The prices are international, of course, and the service is friendly, too, which is always a pleasant surprise.

Sheriff & Cherry (Map p264; ☎ 324 888; www.sheriff -andcherry.com; Đorđićeva 4; ✆ 10am-5pm Mon-Fri, to 3pm Sat) One of the few trendy boutiques in town, this Zagreb-based shop stocks all the major fashion labels, such as Paul & Joe, Cheap Mondays, Anya Hindmarch and Dries Van Noten, among many, many others.

Photo Gallery Carmel (Map p264; ☎ 091 577 7157; www.phototgallerycarmel.com; Zamanjina 10; ✆ 9am-4pm Mon-Sat) A newly opened photography gallery that hosts work by local and international artists. Prints are for sale.

Djardin (Map p264; ☎ 324 744; Miha Pracata 8; ✆ 9.30am-6pm Mon-Fri, to 12.30pm Sat) A sprawling jewellery shop where you can get lost for hours.

GETTING THERE & AWAY
Air

Daily flights to and from Zagreb are operated by **Croatia Airlines** (Map p264; ☎ 413 777; www .croatiaairlines.hr; Brsalje 9; ✆ 8am-4pm Mon-Fri, 9am-noon Sat). The one-way fare is about 400KN but can run higher in peak season. There are

also nonstop flights to Rome, London and Manchester from April to October.

Boat

In addition to the **Jadrolinija** (Map p262; ☎ 418 000; www.jadrolinija.hr; Gruž Harbour) coastal ferry north to Hvar, Split, Zadar and Rijeka, there's a local ferry that leaves Dubrovnik for Sobra and Polače on Mljet (50KN, 2½ hours) throughout the year. In summer there are two ferries a day. There are several ferries a day year-round to the outlying Elafiti Islands of Koločep, Lopud and Šipan.

Ferries also go from Dubrovnik to Bari, in southern Italy; there are six a week in the summer season (346KN to 477KN, nine hours, 11pm Friday to Wednesday) and two (Friday at 3.30pm and Monday at 11pm) in the winter months.

Jadroagent (Map p262; ☎ 419 000; Obala Stjepana Radića 32) books ferry tickets and has information.

Bus

Daily buses from Dubrovnik include the following:

Destination	Fare (KN)	Duration (hr)	Daily services
Korčula	95	3	1
Mostar*	100	3	2
Orebić	80	2½	1
Rijeka	400	13	2
Sarajevo*	200	5	1
Split	120	4½	14
Zadar	250	8	7
Zagreb	250	11	7-8

*Bosnia & Hercegovina

For international buses, see p308. In a busy summer season and on weekends, buses out of Dubrovnik **bus station** (Map p262; ☎ 060 305 070; Obala Pape Ivana Pavla II 44a) can be crowded, so book a ticket well before the scheduled departure time.

Split–Dubrovnik buses pass briefly through Bosnian territory, so keep your passport handy for border-crossing points.

GETTING AROUND
To/From the Airport

Čilipi international airport is 24km southeast of Dubrovnik. The Croatia Airlines airport buses (30KN) leave from the main bus

CROSS-BORDER JAUNTS

Dubrovnik is an easy bus ride away from Montenegro's gorgeous towns of Kotor, Herceg Novi and Budva. All three have wonderful old town centres, with curving marble streets and pretty architecture, while Kotor is on one of Europe's largest fjords, Kotor Bay. If you really want to take your time and explore the region, you should rent a car, but there's a daily 11am bus to the Montenegrin border, from where a bus takes you to Herceg Novi (80KN, two hours) and on to Kotor (120KN, 2½ hours) and Bar (150KN, three hours), stopping at Budva on the way. EU, US, Australian, New Zealand and Canadian citizens don't need a visa to enter Montenegro; other nationalities should check with their relevant embassy.

There are also buses to Mostar (see p275), giving you a chance to glance at Mostar's Old Bridge and dip your toe into the world of Bosnia and Hercegovina. It's quite difficult to go for a day on public transport, but Amico Tours (p268) organises day trips.

station 1½ hours before flight times. A taxi costs about 220KN.

Bus

Dubrovnik's buses run frequently and generally on time. They make an excellent alternative to hassling with Dubrovnik's increasingly burdened traffic and parking scene. The fare is 10KN if you buy from the driver, but only 8KN if you buy a ticket at a *tisak* (newsstand). Timetables are available at the station and at www.libertas dubrovnik.hr.

Car

The entire old town is a pedestrian area so a car is mainly valuable for trips out to Lapad and throughout the region. Bear in mind that traffic on the roads leading to the old town can be heavy in summer. Car-rental companies include the following:

Budget Rent-a-Car (Map p262; ☎ 418 998; www.budget.hr; Obala Stjepana Radića 24)
Gulliver (Map p262; ☎ 313 313; Obala Stjepana Radića 31)
Hertz (Map p262; ☎ 425 000; www.hertz.hr; Frana Supila 9)
OK Travel & Trade (Map p262; ☎ 418 950; okt-t@du.t-com.hr; Obala Stjepana Radića 32) Near the Jadrolinija ferry terminal.

AROUND DUBROVNIK

Dubrovnik is an excellent base for day trips into the surrounding region. You can hop over to the Elafiti Islands for a day of peaceful sunbathing, head to the beautiful islands of Korčula and Mljet for some good food and wine, and check out the heady smell of Trsteno's gardens. Cavtat is a

quieter alternative to Dubrovnik, good for a lovely day's worth of sights, swimming and yummy food.

LOKRUM ISLAND

A ferry shuttles half-hourly in summer to lush Lokrum Island (80KN return), a Unesco-protected national park. It's a beautiful, peaceful place, where most visit to get away from the hustle of Dubrovnik. Note that no one can stay overnight. The rocky **nudist beach** (marked FKK) is a delight for naturists, and there is a **botanical garden** and the ruins of a **medieval Benedictine monastery**. You can swim off numerous rocks. It's heavenly.

Snack at **Lacroma** (snacks from 20KN), a bar two minutes' walk uphill from the harbour. There is live guitar music, too, so you can chill out with a coffee before the boat arrives. More substantial food can be had at **Konoba Lokrum** (mains from 50KN), the Benedictine monastery restaurant, where you eat among the old ruins. The food is the usual combo of seafood, meat, pastas and risottos.

ELAFITI ISLANDS

A day trip to one of the islands in this archipelago northwest of Dubrovnik makes a perfect escape from the summer crowds. The most popular islands are **Koločep**, **Lopud** and **Šipan**, which are accessible by daily Jadrolinija (www.jadrolinija.hr) car ferry. From Dubrovnik you can take a fast boat to Koločep (11KN, 20 minutes), Lopud (11KN, 35 minutes) or Šipan (16.50KN, 1¼ hours) on Saturday mornings. A good way to see all three islands in one day is to take the 'Three Islands & Fish Picnic' tour offered by Amico Tours (p268).

Koločep is the nearest island and is inhabited by a mere 150 people. There are several sand-and-pebble beaches, steep cliffs and sea caves, as well as centuries-old pine forests, olive groves, and orange and lemon orchards.

Lopud is 25 minutes further and has a number of interesting churches and monasteries dating from the 16th century, when the inhabitants' seafaring exploits were legendary. Lopud village is composed of stone houses surrounded by exotic gardens. You can walk across the spine of the island to beautiful and sandy **Šunj beach**; there is a little bar there that serves griddled sardines and other types of fish. No cars are allowed on the island.

Šipan is the largest of the islands and was a favourite with the Dubrovnik aristocracy, who built houses there in the 15th century. The boat lands in **Šipanska Luka** in the northwest of the island, which has the remains of a Roman villa and a 15th-century Gothic duke's palace. Eat at **Kod Marka** (☎ 758 007; Šipanska Luka; mains from 50KN), where you'll have gloriously prepared seafood.

MLJET ISLAND
pop 1237

Of all the Adriatic islands, Mljet (mil-yet) may be the most seductive. Much of the island is covered by forests and the rest is dotted with fields, vineyards and small villages. The northwestern half of the island has been named **Mljet National Park**, where the lush vegetation and gentle coves are unmarred by development schemes, large resorts or virtually any other tourism trappings. It's an unspoiled oasis of tranquillity that, according to legend, captivated Odysseus for seven years. We're sure he didn't regret a moment.

History

Ancient Greeks called the island 'Melita' or 'honey' for the many bees humming in the forests. It appears that Greek sailors came to the island for refuge against storms and to gather fresh water from the springs. At that time the island was populated by Illyrians, who erected hill forts and traded with the mainland. They were conquered by the Romans in 35 BC, who expanded the settlement around Polače by building a palace, baths and servants' quarters.

The island fell under the control of the Byzantine Empire in the 6th century and was later subjected to the 7th-century invasions of Slavs and Avars. After several centuries of regional rule from the mainland, Mljet was

given to the Benedictine order in the 13th century, which constructed a monastery in the middle of Veliko Jezero. Dubrovnik formally annexed the island in 1410.

Although Mljet's fortunes were thereafter tied to those of Dubrovnik, the inhabitants maintained their traditional activities of farming, viticulture, husbandry and seafaring. Except for seafaring, the traditional activities are still the foundation of the economy. Establishing the national park in 1960 helped bring tourism to Mljet, but the islanders are content to keep visitors down to manageable levels. Priorities here are peace and quiet.

Orientation & Information

The island is 37km long, and has an average width of about 3km. The main points of entry are Pomena and Polače, two tiny towns about 5km apart. Tour boats from Korčula and the Dubrovnik catamarans arrive at Polače wharf in the high season. There's a good map of the island posted at Polače's wharf. Pomena is the site of the island's only conventional hotel, Hotel Odisej. Jadrolinija ferries stop only at Sobra.

Govedari, the national park's entry point, is between Pomena and Polače. The **national park** (adult/concession 90/30KN) measures 54 sq km and the entry price includes a bus and boat transfer to the Benedictine monastery. If you stay overnight on the island you only pay the park admission once.

The **tourist office** (☎ 744 186; www.mljet.hr; ☽ 8am-8pm Mon-Sat, to 1pm Sun Jun-Sep, 8am-1pm & 5-8pm Mon-Fri Oct-May) is in Polače and there is an ATM next door. There's another ATM at the Hotel Odisej in Pomena.

The administrative centre of the island is at Babino Polje, 18km east of Polače, where there is another **tourist office** (☎ /fax 745 125; www.mljet .hr; ☽ 9am-5pm Mon-Fri) and a post office.

Sights

The highlights of the island are **Malo Jezero** and **Veliko Jezero**, the two lakes on the island's western end connected by a channel. Veliko Jezero is connected with the sea by the Soline Canal, which makes the lakes subject to tidal flows.

In the middle of Veliko Jezero is an islet with a **Benedictine monastery**. The monastery was originally built in the 12th century but has been rebuilt several times, adding Renaissance and baroque features to the Romanesque structure. It contains the **Church of St Mary**

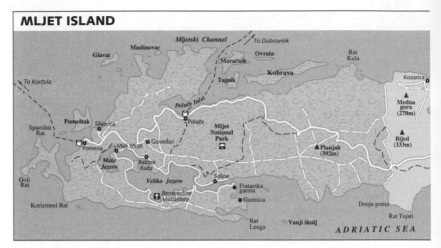

MLJET ISLAND

DUBROVNIK & SOUTHERN
DALMATIA

(Crkva Svete Marije), which was built around the same time. In addition to building the monastery, the Benedictine monks deepened and widened the passage between the two lakes, taking advantage of the rush of sea water into the valley to build a **mill** at the entrance to Veliko Jezero. The monastery was abandoned in 1869 and the mill housed the government's forest-management offices for the island until 1941. It was then converted into a hotel, which was trashed during the 1990s war. Now it contains a pricey but atmospheric restaurant.

There's a boat from Mali Most (about 1.5km from Pomena) on Malo Jezero that leaves for the island monastery every hour at 10 minutes past the hour. It's not possible to walk right around the larger lake as there's no bridge over the channel connecting the lakes to the sea. If you decide to swim it, keep in mind that the current can be strong.

Polače features a number of remains dating from the 1st to 6th centuries. Most impressive is the **Roman palace**, probably dating from the 5th century. The floor plan was rectangular and on the front corners are two polygonal towers separated by a pier. On a hill over the town you can see the remains of a late-antique **fortification** and northwest of the village are the remains of an early **Christian basilica** and a 5th-century **church**.

Activities

Renting a bicycle is an excellent way to explore the national park. You can rent from a **private operator** (☎ 098 428 074) in Mali Most, at the

Hotel Odisej in Pomena or at the harbour in Polače. The price is 20/100KN per hour/day. If you plan to cycle the 5km between Pomena and Polače, be aware that the two towns are separated by a steep mountain. The bike path along the lake is an easier and very scenic pedal, but it doesn't link the two towns. You can also get a **Mini Brum** (☎ 745 084), a small electric car, from Sobra, Polače and Pomena. Prices start at 260KN for five hours.

You can rent a **paddle boat** and row over to the monastery, but beware you'll need quite strong arms.

The island offers some unusual opportunities for **diving**. There's a Roman wreck dating from the 3rd century in relatively shallow water. The remains of the ship, including amphorae, have calcified over the centuries and this has protected them from pillaging. There's also a German torpedo boat from WWII and several walls to dive. Contact **Kronmar Diving** (☎ 744 022; Hotel Odisej).

Tours

See p264 (Dubrovnik) and p283 (Korčula) for agencies offering excursions to Mljet. Tours last from about 8.30am to 6pm and include the park entry fee.

Sleeping

The Polače tourist office arranges private accommodation for 250KN per double, but it is essential to make arrangements before arrival in the peak season. There are more *sobe* signs around Pomena than Polače, and practically

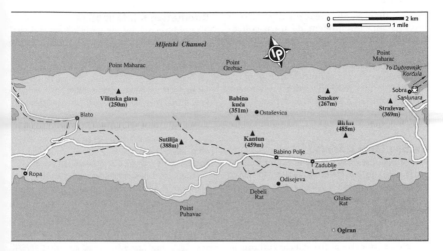

none at all in Sobra. A number of the restaurants listed on right rent out rooms.

There's no camping permitted inside the national park but there are two camping grounds outside it.

Marina (☎ 745 071; Ropa; per person/site 25/47KN; ⊙ Jun-Sep) A small camping ground in Ropa, about 1km from the park.

Camping Mungos (☎ 745 300; Babino Polje; per person/site 30/62KN; ⊙ May-Sep) Not very shady but well located, this camping ground is not far from the beach and the lovely grotto of Odysseus (Odisejeva pećina).

Stermasi (☎ 098 939 0362; Saplunara; apt low-high €30-45; ☒) An excellent choice for those wanting to self-cater and get away from it all. Seven well-equipped, bright apartments sleep two to four people; two have their own terrace and the rest have a private balcony. Saplunara is pretty isolated, though, on the eastern side of the island, but you get the bonus of being near the only sandy beaches on Mljet. There's also an excellent restaurant attached (see right).

Soline 6 (☎ 744 024; www.soline6.com; Soline; d low-high €45-75) This hotel is a more interesting choice. It's the only accommodation within the national park and is designed with waterless toilets, solar heating and organic waste composting. You'll have to do without electricity though.

Hotel Odisej (☎ 744 022; www.hotelodisej.hr; Pomena; s low-high 354-599KN; d 436-820KN; ☒) The only conventional hotel option on the island, this is a modern structure in Pomena, which has decent enough rooms and offers a range of activities.

Eating

The restaurants on Mljet serve good quality fish and seafood, but also the unexpected surprise of kid and lamb. A lot of dishes are done 'under the bell' – cooked from top and bottom under hot coals. Fresh fish costs about 300KN per kilogram. A tip for boaters: you can moor at any of the restaurants for free if you eat there.

our pick Stermasi (☎ 098 939 0362; Saplunara; mains from 50KN) Phone Stermasi two hours in advance and head over to Saplunara for a dinner or lunch you'll remember for the rest of your life. Octopus and kid under the bell (200KN and 260KN respectively) are possibly the most delicious, sticky, aromatic and juicy you'll ever taste. Alternatively, you can just turn up and order the spaghetti with lobster (280KN) or, if that's not delicious enough, try the heavier option of wild boar with gnocchi. Then go and digest it all on the nearby sandy beach.

Melita (☎ 744 145; www.mljet-restoranmelita.com; St Mary's Island, Veliko Jezero; mains from 60KN) A more romantic (and touristy) spot can't be found on the island – this is the restaurant attached to the church on the little island in the middle of the big lake. The menu is packed with the usual fish, seafood and meat dishes, but it's the setting that counts.

Triton (☎ 745 131; Sršenović 43, Babino Polje; mains from 70KN) Another place for under-the-bell meat, Triton mainly focuses on kid, though there is also veal on offer. Don't miss its amazing homemade spirit collection (though beware if you're driving – it's potent stuff!).

Mali Raj (☎ 744 115; Babine Kuće 3, Goveđari; mains from 80KN) Lovely and simple, Mali Raj serves more kid under the bell (order a day in advance), plus fish and seafood in a lovely setting by the sea. It's in Goveđari, near the Polače harbour.

Getting There & Around

Jadrolinija ferries stop only at Sobra (32KN, two hours) but the **Melita catamaran** (☎ 313 119; www.gv-line.hr; Vukovarska 34, Dubrovnik) goes to Polače (70KN) after Sobra (50KN) in the summer months, leaving Dubrovnik at 9.45am daily and returning from Polače at 4.55pm, making it ideal for a day trip. Tour boats from Korčula also arrive at the Polače harbour in the high season.

Boat tickets are sold at the **tourist office** (Map p262; ☎ 417 983; Obala Stjepana Radića 27, Dubrovnik) at Gruž Harbour or on board, but it's wise to buy in advance as the boats fill up quickly.

From Sobra, you can get to Pomena (1½ hours) on a bus; from Polače you can either cycle or walk to Pomena.

CAVTAT
pop 1930

If it weren't for little Cavtat, there'd be no Dubrovnik. Well, at least not the Dubrovnik we know and love. The inhabitants of this originally Greek settlement fled from the Slavs and set up shop in Dubrovnik, establishing the city in 614. But Cavtat is interesting in itself. A lot more 'local' than Dubrovnik – read, not flooded by tourists on a daily basis – it's lively and has a charming beauty. Wrapped around a pretty harbour that's bordered by beaches, it's a great place to stay.

History

Originally a Greek settlement called Epidaurus, Cavtat became a Roman colony around 228 BC and was later destroyed during the 7th-century Slavic invasions. Throughout most of the Middle Ages it was part of the Dubrovnik republic and shared the cultural and economic life of the capital city. Cavtat's most famous personality was the painter Vlaho Bukovac (1855–1922), one of the foremost exponents of Croatian modernism.

Orientation & Information

The old town is by the harbour; several gargantuan tourist complexes lie on the eastern edge, along the town's best beach.

Atlas Travel Agency (☎ 479 031; www.atlas-croatia .hr; Trumbićev put 2; 🕙 9am-6pm Mon-Sat, to 1pm Sun) For excursions and private accommodation.

Post office (Kneza Domagoja 4; 🕙 9am-6pm Mon-Sat) Near the bus station.

Teuta (☎ 479 778; Trumbićev put 3) Changes money, books excursions and finds private accommodation. Also offers internet access.

Tourist office (☎ 479 025; www.tzcavtat-konavle .hr; Tiha 3; 🕙 8am-6pm Jul & Aug, 8am-3pm Mon-Fri, 9am-noon Sat & Sun Sep-Jun)

Sights

Several sights make the city well worth a stop. The Renaissance **Rector's Palace** (☎ 478 556; Obala Ante Starčevića 18; adult/student 10/5KN; 🕙 9am-1pm Mon-Fri), near the bus station, houses a rich library (which belonged to 19th-century lawyer and historian Baltazar Bogišić), as well as lithographs and a small archaeological collection. Next door is the baroque **St Nicholas Church** (Crkva Svetog Nikole; admission 5KN; 🕙 10am-1pm) with wooden altars.

The **birth house of Vlaho Bukovac** (Rodna Kuća Vlahe Bukovca; ☎ 478 646; Bukovca 5; admission 20KN; 🕙 10am-1pm & 4-8pm Tue-Sun), Cavtat's most famous son, is at the northern end of Obala Ante Starčevića. The early-19th-century architecture provides a fitting backdrop to the mementos and paintings of Croatia's most renowned painter. Next door is the **Monastery of Our Lady of the Snow** (Samostan Snježne Gospe; Bukovca), which is worth a look for some notable early Renaissance paintings.

A path leads uphill from the monastery to the cemetery, which contains the **mausoleum** (admission 5KN; 🕙 10am-noon) of the Račić family, built by Ivan Meštrović. The elaborate monument reflects the sculptor's preoccupation with religious and spiritual concerns.

Sleeping & Eating

For private accommodation try Atlas (above) or one of the other travel agencies around the town centre.

Villa Kvaternik (☎ 479 800; www.hotelvillakvaternik .com; Kvaternikova 3; r low-high €85-178, ste €127-193; 🐾) Five stylish rooms and a suite make this one of the loveliest places to stay in Cavtat. The hotel is in a 15th-century villa in the centre of town.

Hotel Cavtat (☎ 478 246; www.iberostar.com; Tiha bb; s/d 640/910KN; P ⊠) The Cavtat has 94 rooms in the town centre overlooking the beach. The warmly decorated rooms are in very good condition and have satellite TV.

Restaurant Kolona (☎ 478 269; Put Tihe 2; mains 60-110KN) A verdant terrace and the freshest fish in town. Order the mussels *buzara* (a sauce of tomatoes, white wine and herbs).

Leut (☎ 478 477; Trumbićev put 13; mains from 60KN) and **Galija** (☎ 478 566; Vuličelićeva 1; mains from 60KN) are the top-end, high-flyer favourites, boasting innovative cuisine and the most exquisite seafood and fish. Galija has some well-priced and mighty tasty pastas. Book in advance.

Getting There & Away
Bus 10 runs hourly to Cavtat (15KN, 45 minutes) from Dubrovnik's bus station, or you can take a boat (return 80KN, three daily) from the Lokrum boat dock, near Ploče Gate.

TRSTENO
Just 13km northwest of Dubrovnik sits Trsteno, a verdant haven that once served as Dubrovnik's aristocratic gardening grounds. Trsteno came into its own during the 16th century, when Dubrovnik's noblesse paid extra attention to the appearance of their gardens both in the city and here, and Ivan Gučetić, a Dubrovnik aristocrat, planted the first seeds of his garden and the Trsteno gardening trend. Sadly, many of Dubrovnik's gardens haven't survived the ages, except for those remaining in Trsteno.

Ivan Gučetić's descendants maintained their garden throughout the centuries, until the land was taken over by the (former Yugoslav and now Croatian) Academy of Sciences, which turned it into an **arboretum** (☎ 751 019; admission 12KN; ☯ 8am-8pm Jun-Sep, to 5pm Oct-May). The garden has a gorgeous Renaissance layout with a set of geometric shapes made with Mediterranean plants and bushes (lilac lavender, green rosemary, fuchsia bougainvillea), while citrus orchards perfume the air. It is only partially landscaped, though – quite a bit of it is just wonderfully wild. You'll notice a section that's burned down – this is the result of a Yugoslav army shell falling onto the garden in 1991, and of a summer fire in 2000. Don't miss the two **plane trees** at the entrance to Trsteno – each is over 400 years old and around 500m high and has a 15m diameter.

You can stay at the local camping ground, **Autocamp Trsteno** (☎ 751 060; www.trsteno.hr/camping .htm, per person/tent 25/20KN), which is well equipped and has a nice bar, too. The beach is rocky and small, though there are coves to be found if you explore.

To get to Trsteno, take any bus (40 minutes, 12 daily) bound for Split from Dubrovnik's bus station. Buses stop at the plane trees.

KORČULA ISLAND
pop 17,038
Korčula is rich in vineyards, olive groves, small villages and hamlets. The island's dense woods led the original Greek settlers to call the island Korkyra Melaina (Black Korčula). Its main settlement, Korčula Town, is a gorgeous grid of marble streets and impressive architecture. The steep southern coast is dotted with quiet coves and small beaches, while the flatter northern shore is rich in natural harbours. Tradition is alive and kicking on Korčula, with age-old religious ceremonies, folk music and dances still being performed to an ever-growing influx of tourists. Oenophiles will adore visiting Korčula and sampling its wine, especially the dessert wine made from the *grk* grape cultivated around Lumbarda.

Korčula is separated from the Pelješac Peninsula by a narrow channel. It is the sixth-largest Adriatic island, reaching nearly 47km in length and 5km to 8km in width.

History
A Neolithic cave (Vela Špilja) near Vela Luka, on the island's western end, points to the existence of a prehistoric settlement on the island, but it was the Greeks who first began spreading over the island in the 6th century BC. Their most important settlement was in the area of today's Lumbarda around the 3rd century BC. Romans conquered the island in the 1st century, giving way to the Slavs in the 7th century. The island was conquered by Venice in AD 1000 and then passed under Hungarian rule. It was briefly part of the Republic of Dubrovnik before again falling under Venetian rule in 1420, where it remained until 1797. Under Venetian rule, the island became known for its stone, which was quarried and cut for export by skilled local artisans. Shipbuilding also flourished despite Venetian attempts to restrict competition with its own shipyards.

DUBROVNIK & SOUTHERN DALMATIA

KORČULA ISLAND & PELJEŠAC PENINSULA

After the Napoleonic conquest of Dalmatia in 1797, Korčula's fortunes followed those of the region, which changed hands among the French, Austro-Hungarians and English before becoming a part of Yugoslavia in 1921.

Getting There & Around

BOAT

The island has two major entry ports – Korčula Town and Vela Luka. All the Jadrolinija ferries between Split and Dubrovnik stop in Korčula Town. Jadrolinija runs a passenger boat daily from June to September from Split to Vela Luka (27KN, two hours), stopping at Hvar. There's also a fast boat, the **Krilo** (www.krilo.hr), running from Split to Korčula (55KN, 2¾ hours), stopping at Hvar. It leaves daily in summer and three to five times a week between October and May. It also leaves from Prigradica, near Blato. For further information, contact **Marco Polo Tours** (Map p284; ☎ 715 400; www.korcula.com; Biline 5) in Korčula or **Split Tours** (Map p219; ☎ 352 553; www.splittours.hr; Gat Sv Duje bb) in Split.

There's a regular afternoon car ferry between Split and Vela Luka (35KN, three hours) that stops at Hvar most days (although cars may not disembark at Hvar). Six daily buses link Korčula Town to Vela Luka (28KN, one hour), but services from Vela Luka are reduced on the weekend.

You can also take a car ferry from Ploče to Trpanj (103KN, 30 minutes, three or four daily), then drive across the Pelješac Peninsula to get the car ferry from Orebić to Dominče

(58KN, 15 minutes). Prices are for a car and driver.

From Orebić, look out for the passenger launch (15KN, 15 minutes, at least four daily Monday to Friday year-round), which will drop you off near Hotel Korčula right below Korčula Town's towers. The car ferry is the only option on weekends. On Saturday, the ferry connects with the bus from Lumbarda, but on Sunday it only meets the morning bus from Korčula Town.

BUS

There's one bus every day to Dubrovnik (87KN, three hours) and Zagreb (195KN, 12 hours). The bus to Dubrovnik can fill up in the summer; an advance reservation is recommended.

KORČULA TOWN

pop 3000

Loved by holidaying families for its peaceful atmosphere, Korčula Town is a thing of beauty. The marble streets are dotted with Renaissance and Gothic architecture and its fascinating fish-bone layout was cleverly designed for the comfort and safety of its inhabitants: the western streets were built straight in order to open the city to the refreshing summer *maestral* (strong, steady westerly wind), while the eastern streets were curved to minimise the force of the winter *bura* (cold northeasterly wind). The town cradles a harbour, overlooked by round defensive towers and a compact cluster of red-roofed houses.

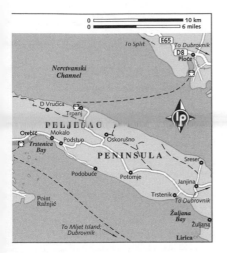

There are rustling palms all around and several beaches are an easy walk from town, though, this being a favourite family island, you'll want to get out of town to more remote beaches if you want some peace. Korčula Town is the best place to base yourself for day trips to Lumbarda, the islet of Badija, the town of Orebić on the Pelješac Peninsula, and Mljet Island.

History
Although documents indicate that a walled city existed on this site in the 13th century, it wasn't until the 15th century that the current city was built. Construction of the city coincided with the apogee of stone-carving skills on the island, lending the buildings and streets a distinctive style. In the 16th century, carvers added decorative flourishes such as ornate columns and coats of arms on building facades, which gave a Renaissance look to the original Gothic core. People began building houses south of the old town in the 17th and 18th centuries as the threat of invasion diminished and they no longer needed to protect themselves behind walls. The narrow streets and stone houses in the 'new' suburb attracted merchants and artisans, and this is still where you'll find most commercial activity.

Orientation
The big Jadrolinija car ferry usually drops you off below the walls of the old town of Korčula in the eastern harbour unless there's too much wind, in which case the ferry ties up

in the western harbour in front of the Hotel Korčula and the tourist office. The passenger launches to Orebić also tie up in the western harbour. The bus station (no left-luggage office) is south of town past the marina, on the way to the large hotels.

Most people head to the beaches of Orebić, but the waters around town are clean enough to swim from any point. There's a small cove next to the large Governor's Gate, and rocky beaches around the hotels and around the Sveti Nikole promenade southwest of the old town.

Information
There's an ATM at HVB Splitska Banka. You can change money there, at the post office or at any of the travel agencies.

Atlas Travel Agency (☎ 711 231; 🕒 9am-6pm Mon-Fri, to 4pm Sat) There are a couple of these agencies in town, and they use the same phone number. It represents American Express, runs excursions and finds private accommodation.

Eterno (☎ 716 538; www.eternotravel.com; Put Sv Nikole bb; 🕒 9am-10pm Mon-Fri, to 4pm Sat & Sun) This friendly agency finds private accommodation, organises excursions and has internet access (25KN per hour).

Hospital (☎ 711 137; Kalac bb) About 1km past the Hotel Marko Polo.

Kantun Tours (☎ 715 622; www.kantun-tours.com; Plokata 19 Travnja bb; 🕒 9am-7pm Mon-Fri, to 6pm Sat, to 1pm Sun) Organises private accommodation and excursions and also has internet access (25KN per hour).

Marko Polo Tours (☎ 715 400; www.korcula.com; Biline 5; 🕒 9am-9pm Mon-Fri, to 6pm Sat & Sun) Organises accommodation and excursions.

Post office (🕒 7.30am-7pm Mon-Fri, 8am-noon Sat) Hidden next to the stairway up to the old town; there are telephones here.

Tino's Internet (☎ 091 509 1182; Tri Sulara; per hr 30KN; 🕒 9am-10pm Mon-Sat, to 4pm Sun) Tino's has another outlet at the ACI Marina, also open long hours.

Tourist office (☎ 715 701; www.korcula.net; Obala Franje Tuđmana bb; 🕒 8am-3pm & 5-9pm Mon-Sat, 8am-3pm Sun Jun-Sep, 8am-1pm & 5-9pm Mon-Sat Oct-May) On the west harbour; an excellent source of information.

Sights
Take a closer look at the remaining walls and towers that make the sea approach to the town particularly striking. On the western harbour, the **Tower of the West Sea Gate** has an inscription in Latin from 1592 stating that Korčula was founded after the fall of Troy. Nearby are the conical **Large Governor's Tower** (1483) and the

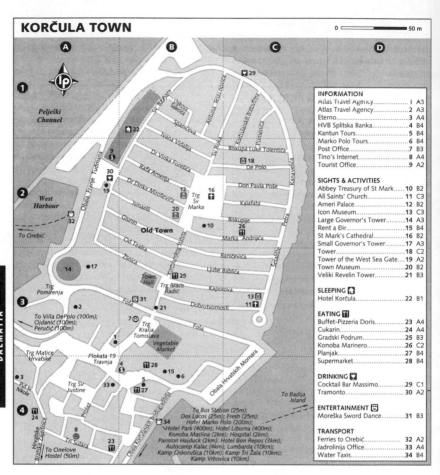

KORČULA TOWN

0 ━━━━━━━━ 50 m

Small Governor's Tower (1449) that protected the harbour and the Governor's Palace, which used to stand next to the town hall.

The entrance to the old city is through the **Veliki Revelin Tower** southern land gate. Built in the 14th century and later extended, the tower is adorned with coats of arms of the Venetian doge and Korčulan governors. There was originally a wooden drawbridge here, but it was replaced in the 18th century by the wide stone steps that give a sense of grandeur to the entrance. The only remaining part of the town walls stretch west of this tower.

Other sightseeing is centred on **Trg Svetog Marka** (St Mark's Sq), dominated by the magnificent **St Mark's Cathedral** (Katedrala Svetog Marka; Statuta 1214; 9am-9pm Jul & Aug, Mass only Sep-Jun).

This 15th-century cathedral was built from Korčula limestone in a Gothic-Renaissance style by Italian and local artisans. Over the solemn portal, the triangular gable cornice is decorated with a two-tailed mermaid, an elephant and other sculptures. The **bell tower** that rises from the cathedral over the town is topped by a balustrade and ornate cupola, beautifully carved by the Korčulan Marko Andrijić.

The interior of the cathedral features modern sculptures in the **baptistery**, including a pietà by Ivan Meštrović. The ciborium was also carved by Andrijić and behind it is the altarpiece painting *Three Saints* by Tintoretto. Another painting attributed to Tintoretto or his workshop, *The Annunciation,* is on the baroque altar of St Antony. Other noteworthy works include a bronze statue of St Blaise by Meštrović near the altar on the northern aisle, and a painting by the Venetian artist Jacopo Bassano in the apse of the southern aisle.

The **Abbey Treasury of St Mark** (☎ 711 049; Statuta 1214; admission 15KN; ✹ 9am-8pm Mon-Sat May-Nov) in the 14th-century Abbey Palace next to the cathedral is also worth a look. Past the anteroom with its collection of icons, you enter the **hall of Dalmatian art** with an excellent selection of 15th- and 16th-century Dalmatian paintings. The most outstanding work is the polyptych of *The Virgin* by Blaž Trogiranin. There are also liturgical items, jewellery, furniture and ancient documents relating to the history of Korčula.

The **Town Museum** (Gradski Muzej; ☎ 711 420; Statuta 1214; admission 15KN; ✹ 9am-9pm Jun-Aug, 9am-1pm Mon-Sat Sep-May) is in the 16th-century Gabriellis Palace opposite the treasury. It traces the history and culture of Korčula throughout the ages, beginning with a tablet recording the Greek presence on the island in the 3rd century BC. The stone-carving collection follows the development of that craft with sculptures and stonemason tools, and the shipbuilding hall displays tools and models of local ships. There's also an archaeology collection with prehistoric objects, and an art collection with furniture, textiles and portraits. Explanations are in English.

Before leaving the square, notice the elegantly ornamented **Arneri Palace** next door to the museum and extending west down the narrow street of the same name.

It's said that Marco Polo was born in Korčula in 1254 and, for a small fee, you can climb the **tower** (Ulica De Polo; admission 15KN; ✹ 9am-9pm Jul & Aug) of the house that is supposed to have been his. A planned restoration will turn it into a museum. There's also an **Icon Museum** (Trg Svih Svetih; admission 10KN; ✹ 10am-noon & 5-7pm Mon-Sat). It isn't much of a museum, but it has some interesting Byzantine icons painted on wood on gold backgrounds, and 17th- and 18th-century ritual objects. Visitors are let into the beautiful old **All Saints' Church** (Crkva Svih Svetih) next door as a bonus. This 18th-century baroque church features a carved and painted 15th-century rood screen and a wooden late-18th-century pietà, along with a wealth of local religious paintings.

In the high season, water taxis at the Jadrolinija port collect passengers for visits to various points on the island as well as **Badija Island**, which has a 15th-century Franciscan monastery and a naturist beach.

Activities
You can rent a bike at Kantun Tours (p283) or a motorcycle (200KN for 24 hours) or boat (540KN per day) from **Rent a Đir** (☎ 711 908; www.korcula-rent.com; Biline 5). For some beach activity, head to Orebić (p288).

Tours
The agencies on p283 can set you up on an island tour, a trip to Mljet, a rafting tour and a handful of other excursions.

Festivals & Events
Holy Week celebrations are particularly elaborate in Korčula. Beginning on Palm Sunday, the entire week before Easter is devoted to ceremonies and processions organised by the local religious brotherhoods dressed in traditional costumes. The townspeople sing medieval songs and hymns, Biblical events are re-enacted and the city gates are blessed. The most solemn processions are on Good Friday when members of all the brotherhoods parade through the streets. A schedule of events is available at the tourist office, but keep in mind that these are religious events and spectators are expected to be discreet about photos.

Sleeping
CAMPING GROUNDS
There's one large and several small camping grounds. The largest camping ground, **Autocamp Kalac** (☎ 711 182; fax 711 146; per person/site 50/46KN; ✹ Jun-Sep), is an attractive site behind Hotel Bon Repos in a dense pine grove near the beach.

About 10km west of town near Račišće are three small camping grounds that offer more privacy and access to uncrowded beaches. They are all open from June to mid-September and cost about 90KN per person, including a tent and car:
Kamp Oskorušica (☎ 710 747)
Kamp Tri Žala (☎ 721 244; trizala@vip.hr)
Kamp Vrbovica (☎ 721 311)

HOSTELS
Onelove Hostel (☎ 716 755; www.korculabackpacker .com; Hrvatske Bratske Zajednice 6; dm 100KN) Prepare for hedonism at this South African/Croatian-run hostel, where, according to travellers,

good-looking girls and heavy boozers get priority bookings. It's all grog, dance, stay up all night and party, so don't say you haven't been warned.

HOTELS

Korčula's hotel scene is on the bulky and resort side, but the hotels listed here are decent. Overhauls may happen during the lifespan of this book. The following are all owned by **Korčula Hotels** (www.korcula-hotels.com).

Hotel Park (☎ 726 004; per person low-high €28-47; P) This concrete behemoth would never win any architectural prizes, but it boasts its own beach and many of its rooms come with balconies and sea views.

Hotel Bon Repos (☎ 726 800; per person low-high €45-60; P ☒) Outside town on the road to Lumbarda, it has manicured grounds and a large pool overlooking a small beach. The hotel complex is so large you could get lost trying to find the reception, but the rooms are quite comfortable.

Hotel Korčula (☎ 711 078; Obala Franje Tuđmana 5; per person low-high €55-80; P ☒) Positioned on the western harbour, it has the most character of all the hotels and a wide terrace where you can linger over coffee. The mediocre rooms vary in size; try to get one with a sea view. There's no lift and you'll have to carry your bags to your room.

Hotel Liburna (☎ 726 006; Put Od Luke 17; per person low-high €55-88; P ☒) There's a pool, tennis courts and opportunities to windsurf from the concrete beach here, but the rooms are fairly bland.

PRIVATE ROOMS

If you don't fancy staying in any of the big hotels, a more personal option is a guest house. Atlas Travel Agency and Marko Polo Tours (see p283) arrange private rooms for around 250KN to 350KN for a double, or you could try one of the following.

Villa DePolo (☎ /fax 711 621; tereza.depolo@du.t-com.hr; d low-high 240-290KN; ☒) In the residential neighbourhood close to the old town and 100m west of the bus station, this guest house has four modern, clean rooms, some with sea views. Note that there is a 30% extra charge on one-night stays.

Pansion Hajduk (☎ 711 267; olga.zec.@du.t-com.hr; d from €40; ☒ ☒) It's a couple of kilometres from town on the road to Lumbarda, but you get a warm welcome, air-conditioned rooms

with TVs and even a swimming pool. If you're going on foot, go past the Hotel Marko Polo for about 1km, passing the fire station, and you'll see it on the right. The hotel restaurant is also worth the walk.

Other guest houses nearby for about the same price include **Peručić** (☎ /fax 715 930; tonci .perucic@du.t-com.hr), with great balconies, and the homely **Ojdanić** (☎ /fax 711 708; roko-taxi@du.t-com. hr). The owner of the latter, Ratko Ojdanić, also has a water taxi and lots of experience with fishing trips around the island.

Eating

You can pick up picnic and other basic supplies at the supermarket.

Cukarin (☎ 711 055; Hrvatske Bratske Zajednice; cakes from 10KN) You've got to try Korčula's pastries such as *cukarini* (sweet biscuit), *klajun* (walnut pastry), *amareta* (round, rich cake with almonds) and *harubica* (carob biscuit) – they're all prepared on site, explaining the long queues in the mornings.

Fresh (☎ 091 799 2086; www.igotfresh.com; 1 Kod Kina Liburne; snacks from 20KN) Right across from the bus station, Fresh is fab for breakfast smoothies, lunch wraps, or beers and cocktails in the evening. It's sister to Dubrovnik's Fresh (p272).

Buffet-Pizzeria Doris (☎ 711 596; Tri Sulara; mains from 35KN) Simple but tasty dishes are served up indoors or outdoors on a shaded terrace. The grilled vegetable platter is a welcome vegetarian treat.

Planjak (☎ 711 015; Plokata 19 Travnja; mains from 50KN) Meat lovers should head here for the mixed grill and proper Balkan dishes, served on a covered terrace.

Konoba Marinero (☎ 711 170; Marka Andrijića; mains from 50KN) Right in the heart of the medieval old town, the friendly and marine-themed Marinero is family-run and cosy. The sons catch the fish and the parents prepare it according to a variety of traditional recipes.

Konoba Maslina (☎ 711 720; Lumbarajska cesta bb; mains from 50KN) It's well worth the walk out here for the authentic Korčulan home cooking. The multibean soup is a standout. It's about a kilometre past the Hotel Marko Polo on the road to Lumbarda, but you can often arrange to be picked up or dropped off in town.

Gradski Podrum (☎ 711 222; Kaporova; mains from 70KN) Situated just inside the southern gate, this restaurant serves fish Korčula style (poached with potatoes and topped with a

---

SWORD DANCES

One of the island's most colourful traditions is the Moreška sword dance, performed in Korčula since the 15th century. Although the dance is probably of Spanish origin, Korčula is now the only place it is performed. It tells the story of two kings – the White King (dressed in red) and the Black King – who fight for a princess abducted by the Black King. In the spoken introduction the princess declares her love for the White King and the Black King refuses to relinquish her. The two armies draw swords and 'fight' in an intricate dance accompanied by a band. Enthusiastic townspeople perform the dance, which takes place outside the southern gate. Although traditionally performed only on Korčula's town day, 29 July, the dance now takes place every Monday and Thursday evening in July and August (and sometimes in June and September, too).

Kumpanija dances are also held around the island regularly, in Pupnat, Smokvica, Blato and Čara. This dance also involves a 'fight' between rival armies and culminates in the unfurling of a huge flag. It's accompanied by the *mišnice* (a local instrument like a bagpipe) and drums.

---

fresh tomato sauce). Pasta and seafood dishes are also reasonable.

Drinking

Cocktail Bar Massimo (☎ 718 878; Šetalište Petra Kanavelića) It's original, you have to grant them that. This bar is lodged in a turret and accessible only by ladder; the drinks are brought up by pulley. You get a lovely view of the cathedral.

Fresh (☎ 091 799 2086; www.igotfresh.com; 1 Kod Kina Liburne; snacks from 20KN) A party atmosphere develops at this little kiosk in the evenings, when happy hours and two-for-one offers kick in.

Tramonto (☎ 098 192 1048; Ismaelli 12) Fantastic sunsets are to be savoured as you sip cocktails at this terrace bar. It's popular with locals, tourists and yachters alike. The music is relaxed and the vibe easygoing.

Dos Locos (☎ 091 528 8971; Šetalište Frana Kršinića 14) The craziest place in town (as the name suggests), as well as the youngest, with loud music and music videos projected on the side of a building. Just behind the bus station.

Entertainment

Every visitor to Korčula in summer inevitably winds up at the Moreška sword dance (see boxed text, above), held at 9pm Monday and Thursday in July and August by the old town gate. Tickets cost 100KN and can be purchased on the spot or from any travel agency. If you can work out the transport, the Kumpanija dances in the villages of Pupnat, Smokvica, Blato and Čara make a fun night out, but as yet there's no bus that makes the run.

Getting There & Away

For information on getting to and from Korčula Town, see p282. There's a **Jadrolinija office** (☎ 715 410) about 25m down from the West Harbour.

LUMBARDA

Surrounded by vineyards and coves, Lumbarda is a laid-back village around a harbour on the southeastern end of Korčula Island. The sandy soil is perfect for the cultivation of grapes, and wine from the *grk* grape is Lumbarda's most famous product. Greeks were the first to settle the island, followed by Romans. In the 16th century, aristocrats from Korčula built summer houses around Lumbarda, and it remains a bucolic retreat from the more urbanised Korčula Town. The town beaches are small but sandy. A good beach (Plaza Pržina) is on the other side of the vineyards beyond the supermarket.

Information

The post office is next door to the **tourist office** (☎ /fax 712 005; www.lumbarda.hr; 🕒 8am-noon & 4-8pm mid-Jun–Jul, 8am-10pm Jul–mid-Sep, 8am-noon & 4-8pm mid-Sep–Oct, 8am-2pm Mon-Fri Oct–mid-Jun), which is up the street from the bus stop and finds private accommodation.

Sleeping & Eating

There are several small, inexpensive camping grounds up the hill from the bus stop.

Pansion Marinka (☎ 712 007, 098 344 712; marinka .milina-bire@du.t-com.hr; d low-high 150-230KN) This is a working farm and winery situated in a beautiful setting within walking distance of the beach. The owners turn out excellent wines and liqueurs, catch and smoke their own fish and are happy to explain the processes to their guests, who are invited to participate if they like. They rightly bill their farm as 'a place where you can forget all your problems'.

Hotel Borik (☎ 712 215; www.hotelborik.hr; s/d 300/570KN) This hotel is set back from the road on a small hill in the centre of town and is definitely quiet. Rooms are simple.

More (☎ 712 068; mains from 70KN) A lovely seafront restaurant, More has a terrace thick with vine leaves and a kitchen that produces the island's best lobster and other seafood.

Getting There & Away

In Korčula Town, water taxis wait around the Jadrolinija port for passengers to Lumbarda. You'll only pay about 50KN depending on the number of passengers. Buses to Lumbarda (10KN, 15 minutes) run about hourly until mid-afternoon, but there's no service on Sunday. The bus stops in the town centre.

VELA LUKA

Vela Luka, at the western end of Korčula, is a simple, sober port town that has little of interest for visitors. If you do decide to stay, know that there are no beaches around town, but small boats can take you to the idyllic offshore islands of Proizd and Osjak.

Surrounded by hills covered with olive trees, most of the town is engaged in the production and marketing of Korčula's famous olive oil. Because of the town's large sheltered harbour, the fishing industry also thrives.

Orientation & Information

Most of the town and nearly all commercial activity is clustered around the harbour.

Atlas Travel Agency (☎ 812 078; www.atlas-velaluka .com; Obala 3; ⏰ 9am-6pm Mon-Fri, to noon Sat) On the quay and near the bus station; finds accommodation.

Tourist office (☎ /fax 813 619; www.tzvelaluka .hr; Ulica 41; ⏰ 8am-9pm Mon-Sat Jun-Sep, 8am-3pm Mon-Fri Oct-May) Coming from Korčula Town, it's at the entrance to town.

Sights & Activities

There isn't a lot to see at Vela Luka, but if you have some time to kill you should take a look at the Neolithic **Vela Špilja** (admission 5KN) cave, which is spacious enough to make cave-dwelling seem like a viable accommodation option. Signs from town direct you to the cave, which overlooks the town and

harbour. Opening hours for the cave vary, so check with the tourist office first.

For a total veg-out at the beach, nothing beats the offshore islands of **Proizd** and **Osjak**. The clear, blue water and white stones of Proizd are dazzling, while Osjak, the larger island, is known for its forest. Bring plenty of sunscreen as there is little shade. There are inexpensive eating options on both islands. Several small boats leave each morning in July and August and pick you up in the afternoon. The bay of **Gradina**, 5km northwest of Vela Luka, is another lovely, peaceful spot graced with a few beaches. You'll need your own wheels though.

Sleeping & Eating

Camp Mindel (☎ 813 600; www.mindel.hr; per adult/ site 25/40KN; ⏰ May-Sep) There's no bus service to this camping ground 5km west of Vela Luka so you'll need your own transport.

Hotel Dalmacija (☎ /fax 812 022; www.humhotels.hr; Obala bb; s/d 460/615KN) This is one of several hotels in Vela Luka managed by Hum Hotels. Rooms have cool Mediterranean colours and it's on the waterfront.

Pod Bore (☎ 813 069; Obala 5; mains from 60KN) This spacious restaurant with an outdoor terrace offers a pleasant view over the harbour, and the food isn't bad either.

Getting There & Away

For information on getting to and from Vela Luka, see p282.

PELJEŠAC PENINSULA

OREBIĆ

pop 1489

Orebić, on the southern coast of the Pelješac Peninsula (Map pp282–3) between Korčula and Ploče, has the best beaches in southern Dalmatia – wide, sandy coves bordered by groves of tamarisk and pine. Only 2.5km across the water from Korčula, it's a perfect day trip from Korčula or an alternative place to stay. After enough lazing on the beach, you can take advantage of some excellent hiking up and around Mt Ilija (961m) or poke around in a couple of churches and museums. Mt Ilija protects the town from harsh northern winds, allowing Mediterranean vegetation to flourish. The temperature is usually a few degrees warmer than Korčula; spring arrives earlier and summer leaves later.

History

Orebić and the Pelješac Peninsula became part of Dubrovnik in 1333 when it was purchased from Serbia. Until the 16th century, the town was known as Trstenica (the name of its eastern bay) and was an important maritime centre. In fact, the town is named after a family of sea captains who, in 1658, built a citadel as a defence against the Turks. Many of the houses and exotic gardens built by prosperous sea captains still grace Orebić and its surroundings. The height of Orebić seafaring occurred in the 18th and 19th centuries when it was the seat of one of the largest companies of the day: the Associazione Marittima di Sabioncello. With the decline of shipping, Orebić began exploiting its tourist attractions to bolster the local economy.

Orientation & Information

The ferry from Korčula ties up in the town centre, just steps from the tourist office. The bus stop (no left-luggage office) is at the end of the ferry dock, and the main commercial street, Bana Josipa Jelačića, runs parallel to the port. There's a beach west of the dock, but the best beach is the long stretch at Trstenica cove, about 500m east of the dock along Šetalište Kneza Domagoja.

Orebić Tours (☎ 713 367; www.orebic-tours.hr; Bana Josipa Jelačića 84a; ☼ 9am-5.30pm Mon-Fri, to noon Sat) Finds private accommodation, changes money and books excursions.

Post office (Trg Mimbeli bb) Next door to the tourist office.

Tourist office (☎ /fax 713 718; www.tz-orebic.com; Trg Mimbeli bb; ☼ 8am-8pm Jul & Aug, 8am-1pm & 5-8pm Mon-Fri Sep-Jun) Also finds private accommodation, changes money and dispenses information.

Sights & Activities

The **Maritime Museum** (☎ 713 009; Obala Pomoraca; admission 10KN; ☼ 10am-noon & 6-9pm Mon-Fri, 7-9pm Sat), next to the tourist office, is interesting enough for a peek. There are paintings of boats, boating memorabilia, navigational aids and prehistoric finds from archaeological excavations in nearby Majsan. Explanations are in English.

Orebić is great for **hiking**, so pick up a map of the hiking trails from the tourist office. A trail through pine woods leads from Hotel Bellevue to a 15th-century **Franciscan monastery** (admission 5KN;

> ### THE RIGHT KIND OF WIND
>
> If you're into windsurfing, head over to Viganj, a village that sits on the southwestern end of Pelješac and faces Korčula Island. It has some of the best windsurfing in Croatia. The village is a tiny thing, with few visitors except for those who are affected by the windsurfing frenzy. There are several places where you can rent out equipment in the village and tons of beach bars come alive during the summer. Try **Karmela 2** (☎ 719 097) for bizarre frolics and beach parties.

☼ 8am-noon & 5-7pm) on a ridge 152m above the sea. From their vantage point, Dubrovnik patrols could keep an eye on the Venetian ships moored on Korčula and notify the authorities of any suspicious movements. The village of **Karmen** near the monastery is the starting point for walks to picturesque upper villages and the more daring climb to the top of **Mt Ilija**, the bare, grey massif that hangs above Orebić. Your reward is a sweeping view of the entire coast. On a hill east of the monastery is the **Lady of Karmen Church** (Gospa od Karmena), next to several huge cypresses, as well as a baroque **loggia** and the **ruins** of a duke's castle.

Sleeping & Eating

The tourist office or Orebić Tours find private rooms (from 150KN per person) as well as studios and apartments.

All the modern resort complexes are west of town and run by **HTP Orebić** (www.orebic-htp.hr). There's one good camping ground.

Glavna Plaža (☎ 713 399; www.glavnaplaza.com; Trstenica; per adult/site 25/50KN; ☼ Apr-Sep) This family-run camping ground overlooks the long, sandy Trstenica beach and there are also apartments available (375KN).

Hotel Bellevue (☎ /fax 713 148; www.orebic-htp.hr; Svetog Križa 104; r per person from 400KN; Ⓟ ⓡ) On a rocky beach, it's the closest resort to town. Facilities include tennis courts and water sports on the hotel beach.

Restoran Amfora (☎ 713 719; Kneza Domagoja 6; mains from 50KN) This family-run restaurant is a local favourite for its fantastic seafood dishes.

Getting There & Away

If you're coming from the mainland, there are three or four daily ferries (seven in summer) from Ploče to Trpanj, which connect with a bus to Orebić. Korčula buses to Dubrovnik, Zagreb and Sarajevo stop at Orebić. For more bus and ferry information, see p282.

STON & MALI STON
pop 740

The two settlements of Ston and Mali Ston are 59km northwest of Dubrovnik on an isthmus that connects the Pelješac Peninsula with the mainland. Formerly part of the Republic of Dubrovnik, Ston was and is an important salt-producing town. Its economic importance to the Republic of Dubrovnik led, in 1333, to the construction of a 5.5km wall, the longest fortification in Europe. The walls are still standing, sheltering an appealing cluster of medieval buildings in the town centre. Mali Ston, a little village and harbour situated about 1km northeast of Ston, was built along with the wall as part of the defensive system and is now known for the oyster beds along its bay. Both Ston and Mali Ston are major gastronomic highlights, turning out the best seafood in Croatia.

Orientation & Information
The bus stop is located in the centre of Ston, near the tourist office, bank and post office. The **tourist office** (☎ /fax 754 452; www.tzo-ston.hr; Peljestki put 1; ☉ 7am-1pm & 5-7pm Mon-Fri, 7am-1pm Sat Jul & Aug, 7am-3pm Mon-Fri Sep-Jun) has a small selection of brochures and can arrange private accommodation.

Sights & Activities
The major sight in Ston is the 14th-century **walls** (admission free; ☉ 10am-dusk) that stretch from the town far up the hill. The clear Pelješac air allows for magnificent views out over the peninsula.

There are no beaches in town but it's an easy walk to Camping Prapratno, 4km southwest of town, where there's a cove and a **pebble beach**.

Sleeping & Eating
Each of the hotels listed here has an excellent restaurant, but there are also a few other possibilities for sampling the superb seafood.

Camping Prapratno (☎ 754 000; fax 754 344; per adult/site 28/48KN; ☒) This camping ground 4km southwest of Ston is right on Prapratno Bay and offers tennis and basketball courts as well as swimming facilities.

Vila Koruna (☎ 754 359; www.vila-koruna.hr; s/d 500/660KN; ℗ ☒) In an old house on the harbour of Mali Ston, this six-room hotel provides warm, personal service and comfortable rooms with TV and phone, as well as a restaurant downstairs.

Ostrea (☎ 754 555; www.ostrea.hr; s/d half board 800/1200KN; ℗ ☒ ☒) Rooms are on a grander scale in this harbourside hotel in Mali Ston, containing modern bathrooms, computer terminals and minibars.

ourpick Kapetanova Kuća (☎ 754 452; mains from 75KN) Near the Ostrea hotel, this is one of the most venerable seafood restaurants in the region. The oysters and mussels are to die for.

Bella Vista (☎ 753 110; mains from 75KN) On a cliff overlooking Prapratno Bay, this friendly restaurant serves up delicious seafood platters and has a marvellous view of the bay.

Getting There & Away
Three daily buses go from Dubrovnik to Orebić, stopping at Ston and Mali Ston (59KN, 1½ hours). The one daily Dubrovnik–Korčula bus also travels via Mali Ston and Ston (67KN, two hours).

Directory

CONTENTS

ACCOMMODATION

In this book, budget accommodation includes camping grounds, hostels and some guest houses, and costs up to 500KN for a double. Midrange accommodation costs 500KN to 900KN a double, while top-end starts from 900KN and can go as high as 4000KN per double. Reviews are listed in budget order.

Along the coast, accommodation is priced according to four seasons, which vary from place to place. November to March are the cheapest months. There may only be one or two hotels open in a coastal resort but you'll get great rates – often no more than 350KN for a double in a good three-star hotel and 250KN in a lesser establishment. Generally, April, May and October are the next cheapest months and June and September are the

shoulder season. In July and August count on paying top price, especially in the peak period, which starts in mid-July and lasts until mid- or late August.

Prices quoted in this book range from the lowest to the highest season. Note that many establishments add a 30% charge for less than three-night stays and include 'residence tax', which is 7.50KN per person per day. Prices in this book do not include the residence tax. Accommodation is generally cheaper in Dalmatia than in Kvarner or Istria, but in July and August you should make arrangements in advance wherever you go.

This book provides the phone numbers of most accommodation facilities. Once you know your itinerary it pays to start calling around to check prices and availability. Most receptionists speak English.

It's becoming difficult to get a confirmed reservation without a deposit, particularly in the high season. Hotels are equipped to reserve accommodation using a credit-card number. Some guest houses might require a SWIFT wire transfer (where your bank wires directly to their bank). Unfortunately, banks charge fees for the transaction, usually in the range of US$15 to US$30. The only way around it is to book online through an agency.

Camping

Nearly 100 camping grounds are scattered along the Croatian coast. Most operate from mid-April to mid-September only, although a few are open March to October. In spring and autumn, it's best to call ahead to make sure that the camping ground is open before beginning the long trek out. Don't go by the opening and closing dates you read in travel brochures

---

BOOK YOUR STAY ONLINE

For more accommodation reviews and recommendations by Lonely Planet authors, check out the online booking service at www.lonelyplanet.com. You'll find the true, insider lowdown on the best places to stay. Reviews are thorough and independent. Best of all, you can book online.

PRACTICALITIES

■ Widely read newspapers include *Večernji List, Jutarnji List, Slobodna Dalmacija* and the *Feral Tribune*. The most respected daily is the state-owned *Vjesnik*. The most popular weeklies are *Nacional* and *Globus*. The Croatian edition of *Metro* was launched in 2006.

■ The most popular radio station is Narodni radio, which airs only Croatian music. Croatian Radio broadcasts news in English four times daily (8am, 10am, 2pm and 11pm) on FM frequencies 88.9, 91.3 and 99.3 between June and September.

■ Bills include a service charge, but it's common to round up the bill.

■ Electrical supply is 220V, 50Hz AC. Croatia uses the standard European round-pronged plugs.

■ Croatia uses the metric system (see conversion chart on the inside front cover).

■ The video system is PAL.

or even this book, as these can change. Even local tourist offices can be wrong.

Many camping grounds in Istria are gigantic 'autocamps' with restaurants, shops and row upon row of caravans, but in Dalmatia the camping grounds are smaller and often family owned. Expect to pay up to 100KN for the site at some of the larger establishments. Most camping grounds charge from 40KN to 60KN per person per night. The tent charge is sometimes included in the price, but occasionally it's an extra 10KN to 15KN. The vehicle charge is sometimes included; it may be an extra 10KN to 50KN. If you bring a caravan you'll pay about 30% more for a site; then there's an electricity charge that may be included or may cost an extra 15KN per night. The residence tax costs about an extra 7KN per person per night, depending on the season and the region. Prices in this book are per adult and site, which includes a tent and car.

Although small, family-owned camping grounds are starting to pop up, most grounds are still autocamps. If you want a more intimate environment, the town tourist office should be able to refer you to smaller camping grounds, but you may have to insist upon it. Naturist camping grounds (marked FKK) are among the best because their secluded locations ensure peace and quiet. However, bear in mind that freelance camping is officially prohibited. A good website for camping information and links is www.camping.hr.

The Camping Card International (CCI; formerly the Camping Carnet) is a camping ground ID that can be used instead of a passport when checking into a camping ground; it includes third-party insurance. As a result, many camping grounds offer a small discount (5% to 10%) if you sign in with one. CCIs are issued by automobile associations and camping federations. In the USA, the AAA issues them for US$20. In the UK, the AA no longer sells CCIs, but AA members can get one from the Caravan Club by calling ☎ 01342 327 410 and quoting their AA membership number.

Hostels

The **Croatian YHA** (Map pp74-5; ☎ 01-48 47 472; www.hfhs .hr; Dežmanova 9, Zagreb) operates youth hostels in Rijeka, Dubrovnik, Punat, Zadar, Zagreb and Pula. Nonmembers pay an additional 10KN per person per day for a stamp on a welcome card; six stamps entitle you to membership. Prices given in this book are for the high season in July and August; prices fall the rest of the year. The Croatian YHA can also provide information about private youth hostels in Krk, Zadar, Dubrovnik and Zagreb. Most hostels are now open in winter but may not be staffed all day. It's wise to call in advance.

Hotels

Tourism really started to take off in Croatia (then part of Yugoslavia) in the 1970s and 1980s, which was when most of the hotels along the coast were built. At the time, the idea was to market the coast to package tourists and then send them to 'tourist settlements', usually far from town and along a stretch of beach. Since they were all state-owned and built at the same time with the same idea, it's unsurprising that they all look alike. There is nothing particularly Istrian or even Croatian in an Istrian hotel complex to distinguish it from a Dalmatian or Spanish hotel complex.

The advantage of this approach is that it left the historic old towns more or less alone, free of a lot of the tourist trappings that would have been present if tourists had commandeered the towns for the summer. The disadvantage is the lack of small family-owned hotels where the owner's taste and personality are reflected in the rooms. For a more personal experience, you have to stay in private accommodation. Many family-run establishments that used to rent rooms through the local travel agency are proclaiming themselves *pensions* (guest houses). Since the owners usually have decades of experience in catering to travellers, these private *pensions* offer excellent value. Some *pensions* are included in this book, but as more and more pop up each season it pays to ask the local tourist office about them. Don't go by the printed brochures as these often cover only the larger hotels.

Zagreb and other big cities have at least one grand old hotel built in the 19th century when the railway came through. Opatija was a popular resort in the Austro-Hungarian Empire and has a conglomeration of elegant, European-style hotels that retain a certain faded splendour.

Private entrepreneurs and European hotel chains are changing the top end of the hotel scene in Croatia. There are more and more completely overhauled hotels along the coast that offer a high standard of amenities and service. You'll find that even the older hotels are clean, serviceable and fairly efficient. Double rooms, if not singles, are a good size, and nearly all rooms in Croatian hotels have private bathrooms.

The majority of hotels in Croatia fall into the moderate range – around 800KN for a double in the summer along the coast, dropping to around 450KN in late spring or early autumn. At that price you can get a clean, pleasant but unexceptional room equipped with a private bathroom, a telephone and sometimes a TV with a satellite hook-up. Since there's usually no surcharge for a short stay, hotels can be a better deal than private accommodation if you're only staying a night or two. Apartments are self-contained units that include equipped kitchens, a bed or beds, and a bathroom.

Most hotels offer the option of half board. In a 'tourist settlement' far from town, half board may be the only dining possibility within reach. Sometimes half board is only a marginal increase over the B&B rate, making it worth considering even if you only plan to take a few meals at the hotel. Except in luxury establishments, the meals centre on cheaper cuts of meat, although some hotels are starting to offer a vegetarian menu.

Croatian hotels are rated according to a star system that is not terribly helpful. One-star hotels are rare, two-star hotels have private bathrooms but do not have satellite TV, and five-star hotels offer clearly luxurious rooms and facilities (gym, sauna, swimming pool etc), but otherwise the stars are awarded too inconsistently to provide much indication as to the quality of the establishment. The distinction between three- and four-star hotels seems particularly whimsical.

Private Accommodation

The best value for money in Croatia is a private room or apartment, often within or attached to a local home – the equivalent of small private guest houses in other countries.

STREET NAMES

Particularly in Zagreb and Split, you may notice a discrepancy between the names used in this book and the names you'll actually see on the street. In Croatian, a street name can be rendered either in the nominative or possessive case. The difference is apparent in the name's ending. Thus, Ulica Ljudevita Gaja (street of Ljudevita Gaja) becomes Gajeva ulica (Gaja's street). The latter version is the one most commonly seen on the street sign and used in everyday conversation. The same principle applies to a *trg* (square), which can be rendered as Trg Petra Preradovića or Preradovićev trg. Some of the more common names are Trg Svetog Marka (Markov trg), Trg Josipa Jurja Strossmayera (Strossmayerov trg), Ulica Andrije Hebranga (Hebrangova), Ulica Pavla Radića (Radićeva), Ulica Augusta Šenoe (Šenoina), Ulica Nikole Tesle (Teslina) and Ulica Ivana Tkalčića (Tkalčićeva). Be aware also that Trg Nikole Šubića Zrinjskog is almost always called Zrinjevac.

In an address the letters 'bb' following a street name (such as Placa bb) stand for *bez broja* (without number), which indicates that the building has no street number.

Not only is private accommodation cheaper than a hotel, the service is also likely to be friendlier and more efficient, and the food better. Such accommodation can be arranged by travel agencies or by dealing with proprietors who meet you at the local bus or ferry station. You can also knock on the doors of houses with *sobe* or *zimmer* (rooms available) signs.

Dealing with an agency gives you the assurance that the accommodation has been professionally vetted. Also, you have someone to complain to if things go wrong and you can complain in English rather than bumble around in Croatian, German or Italian. If you stay for fewer than four nights, the agencies will add at least a 30% surcharge and some will insist on a seven-night minimum stay in the high season.

If you choose the knocking-on-doors approach, start early in the day since proprietors may be out on errands in the afternoon. You'll be more comfortable and in a better position to negotiate a price if you leave your luggage in a *garderoba* (left-luggage office) before trudging around town.

Whether you rent from an agency or rent from the owners privately, don't hesitate to bargain, especially if you're staying for a week. In the high season along the coast it may be impossible to find a proprietor willing to rent you a room for one night only. Single rooms are scarce. Showers are always included but often breakfast is not, so ask about the breakfast charge.

If possible, it may be worthwhile to take a half-board option and stay with a family. Most families on the coast have a garden, a vineyard and access to the sea. You could find yourself beginning your evenings with a homemade aperitif before progressing on to a garden-fresh salad, home-grown potatoes and grilled fresh fish, all washed down with your host's very own wine.

Travel agencies classify private accommodation according to a star system. The most expensive rooms are three-star and include a private bathroom. In a two-star room, the bathroom is shared with one other room and, in a one-star room, the bathroom is shared with two other rooms or with the owner. Studios with cooking facilities can be a good deal, costing little more than a double room, but remember that self-catered meals are not cheap in Croatia. If you're travelling in a small group, it may be worthwhile to get an apartment.

THINGS TO AVOID WITH PRIVATE RENTALS

If you decide to go with proprietors (usually women) at the bus or ferry station, try to pin them down on the location or you could get stuck way out of town. Clarify whether the price is per person or per room. Nail down the exact number of days you plan to stay and when in the day you plan to check out so you don't get stuck with a surcharge. If you land in a room or apartment without a blue *sobe* or *apartmani* sign outside, the proprietor is renting to you illegally (ie not paying residence tax). They will probably be reluctant to provide their full name or phone number and you'll have absolutely no recourse in case of a problem.

Under no circumstances will private accommodation include a telephone, but satellite TV is becoming increasingly common.

Accommodation rates are usually fixed by the local tourist association and don't vary from agency to agency, although some agencies may not handle rooms in the cheapest category. Some prefer to only handle apartments. In legally rented accommodation there is often a 'registration tax' to register you with the police.

The prices quoted in this book assume a four-night stay in the high season. Prices fall dramatically outside July and August.

ACTIVITIES
Diving

The varied underwater topography of the Croatian coast has spurred a growing diving industry. From Istria to Dubrovnik, nearly every coastal resort has a dive centre, usually German-owned. Although there's a little bit of everything along the coast, the primary attractions are shipwrecks and caves. The porous karstic stone that forms the coastal mountains has created an astonishing variety of underwater caves all along the coast, but especially in the Kornati Islands (p214). Shipwrecks are also a common sight, most notoriously the *Baron Gautsch* wreck near Rovinj (p167). Remains of Roman wrecks with 1st-century amphorae can be found within reach of Dubrovnik (p268), but special permission is necessary since they are protected cultural monuments. Diving from

Lošinj Island (p133) offers a good mixture of sights – sea walls, caves and wrecks.

The marine life is not as rich as it is in the Red Sea or the Caribbean, for example, but you'll regularly see gropers, eels, sardines and snails. Sponges and sea fans are common sea flora, but coral reefs tend to lie in deep water – around 40m – since the shallower coral has already been plundered. The waters around Vis Island (p241) are richest in marine life because the island was an off-limits military base for many years and the sea was not overfished. Most of the coastal and island resorts mentioned in this book have dive shops. See the following websites for further information:

Croatian Diving Federation (www.diving-hrs.hr, in Croatian)

Pro Diving Croatia (www.diving.hr)

Hiking

The steep gorges and beech forests of Paklenica National Park (p198), 40km northeast of Zadar, offer excellent hiking. Starigrad, the main access town for the park, is well connected by hourly buses from Zadar. Hotels, private accommodation and a camping ground are available in Starigrad.

Risnjak National Park (p128) at Crni Lug, 12km northwest of Delnice between Zagreb and Rijeka, is a good hiking area. Due to the chance of heavy snowfalls, hiking is advisable only from late spring to early autumn. It's a 9km, 2½-hour climb from the park entrance at Bijela Vodica to Veliki Risnjak (1528m).

For a great view of the barren coastal mountains, climb Mt Ilija (961m) above Orebić, opposite Korčula, or Sv Jure (1762m) on Biokovo, above Makarska (p237).

Kayaking

There are countless possibilities for anyone carrying a folding sea kayak, especially among the Elafiti and Kornati Islands (take the ferry from Zadar to Sali). River kayaking is also popular and centres on the four rivers of Karlovac. Zagreb-based **Huck Finn** (☎ 01-61 83 333; www.huck-finn.hr; Vukovarska 271) is a good contact for sea and river kayaking packages.

Rafting

The network of Croatian rivers provides wonderful opportunities for rafting adventures. In the interior, Karlovac (p92) is Croatia's rafting centre as it lies on the confluence of four rivers. The Kupa River originating in Risnjak

---

RESPONSIBLE DIVING

Please consider the following tips when diving and help preserve the ecology and beauty of reefs:

- Never use anchors on the reef, and take care not to ground boats on coral.
- Avoid touching or standing on living marine organisms or dragging equipment across the reef. Polyps can be damaged by even the gentlest contact. If you must hold on to the reef, only touch exposed rock or dead coral.
- Be conscious of your fins. Even without contact, the surge from fin strokes near the reef can damage delicate organisms. Take care not to kick up clouds of sand, which can smother organisms.
- Practise and maintain proper buoyancy control. Major damage can be done by divers descending too fast and colliding with the reef.
- Take great care in underwater caves. Spend as little time within them as possible as your air bubbles may be caught within the roof and thereby leave organisms high and dry. Take turns to inspect the interior of a small cave.
- Resist the temptation to collect or buy corals or shells or to loot marine archaeological sites (mainly shipwrecks).
- Ensure that you take home all your rubbish and any litter you may find as well. Plastics in particular are a serious threat to marine life.
- Do not feed fish.
- Minimise your disturbance of marine animals. *Never* ride on the backs of turtles.

DIRECTORY

LINKS FOR THE ACTIVE TRAVELLER

Adriatic Croatia International Club (www.aci-club.hr) Manages 21 coastal marinas.

Cro Challenge (www.crochallenge.com) Extreme sports association.

Croatian Aeronautical Federation (www.caf.hr) Parachuting club.

Huck Finn (www.huck-finn.hr) Zagreb-based outfit handling canoeing, kayaking, rafting and hiking tours.

Outdoor (www.outdoor.hr) Adventure and incentive travel.

Riverfree (www.riverfree.hr, in Croatian) Rafting and canoeing club.

National Park and the Korana River flowing from the Plitvice lakes are best in early spring or after heavy rains. The Dobra River and the cascade-spotted Mreznica River are good year-round. The most scenic river along the coast is the Cetina River (p239), whose rocky banks are dense with vegetation. Rafting the Krka River is the best way to explore the magnificent Krka National Park (p212). The Una River, which forms the border between Croatia and Bosnia, can offer an exciting white-water ride when the water level is high. The Zrmanja has high water in the springtime but the summers are too dry for anything but canoes and kayaks. The grade for most rivers is 3, but rises to 4 on the Dobra and Una Rivers.

Rock Climbing

The karstic stone of Croatia's coast provides excellent climbing. Paklenica National Park (p198) has the widest range of routes – nearly 400 – for all levels of experience. Spring, summer and autumn are good seasons to climb, but in winter you'll be fighting the fierce *bura* (cold northeasterly wind). Another popular climbing spot is the rocks surrounding Baška (p147) on Krk Island, which can be climbed year-round (and if you come in summer, you can combine climbing with a beach holiday). Makarska (p237) also allows climbing and beach-bumming, but in winter there's a strong *bura*. For details, contact the **Croatian Mountaineering Association** (☎ 01-48 24 142; www.plsavez.hr, in Croatian; Kozaričeva 22, 10000 Zagreb).

Windsurfing

Although most coastal resorts offer windsurfing courses and board rentals, serious windsurfers gravitate to the town of Bol (p248) on Brač Island. The *maestral* (strong, steady westerly wind) blows from April to October, and the wide bay catches the wind perfectly. The best windsurfing is in late May, early June, late July and early August. The wind generally reaches its peak in the early afternoon and then dies down at the end of the day.

Another good spot to windsurf is Viganj (see boxed text, p289) on the Pelješac Peninsula, not far from Orebić, which has windsurfing schools and hosts various windsurfing championships.

Yachting

There's no better way to appreciate the Croatian Adriatic than by boat. The long, rugged islands off Croatia's mountainous coast all the way from Istria to Dubrovnik make this a yachting paradise. Fine, deep channels with abundant anchorage and steady winds attract yachties from around the world. Throughout the region there are quaint little ports where you can get provisions, and yachts can tie up right in the middle of everything.

There are 40 marinas along the coast, some with more facilities than others. Every coastal town mentioned in this book has a marina, from little Sali on Dugi Otok to the large marinas in Zadar, Split and Dubrovnik. Most marinas are open throughout the year, but it's best to check first. A good source of information is the **Association of Nautical Tourism** (Udruženje Nautičkog Turizma; ☎ 051-209 147; fax 051-216 033; Bulevar Oslobođenja 23, 51000 Rijeka), which represents all Croatian marinas. You could also try **Adriatic Croatia International** (ACI; ☎ 051-271 288; www.aci-club.hr; M Tita 51, Opatija), which represents about half the marinas.

Although you can row, motor or sail any vessel up to 3m long without authorisation, for larger boats you'll need to get authorisation from the harbour master at your port of entry, which will be at any harbour open to international traffic. Come equipped with a boat certificate, documents proving your sailing qualifications, insurance documents and money.

Yachting enthusiasts may wish to charter their own boat. Experienced sailors can charter a yacht on a 'bareboat' basis, or you can pay for the services of a local captain for a 'skippered' boat. **Sunsail** (☎ in UK 0870-777 0313, in USA 888-350 3568; www.sunsail.com) is an international operator offering bareboat and skippered charters from Dubrovnik, the Kornati Islands and Kremik, south of Šibenik. In the UK, you could also try **Cosmos Yachting** (☎ 0800-376 9070; www.cosmosyachting.com), which offers charters out of Dubrovnik, Pula, Rovinj, Split, Trogir, Lošinj, Punat and other destinations, or **Nautilus Yachting** (☎ 01732-867 445; www.nautilus -yachting.com), which offers rentals from Pula, Split, Dubrovnik and the Kornati Islands. The price depends upon the size of the boat, the number of berths and the season.

BUSINESS HOURS

Official office hours are from 8am to 4pm Monday to Friday; this is when you'll find all banks open. Post office hours are generally 7.30am to 7pm on weekdays and 8am to noon on Saturday. Many shops are open 8am to 7pm on weekdays and until 2pm on Saturday. Supermarkets are open 8am to 8pm Monday to Friday, 8am to 6pm Saturday and 8am to 1pm Sunday. Croats are early risers; by 7am there will be lots of people on the street and many places already open. Along the coast, life is more relaxed; shops and offices frequently close around noon for an afternoon break and reopen at about 4pm.

Restaurants are open long hours, often from noon to midnight, with Sunday closings out of peak season. Cafés are usually open daily from 8am to midnight, and bars are open from 9am to midnight. In Zagreb and Split discos and nightclubs are open year-round, but many places along the coast are only open in summer. Cybercafés are also open long hours – usually seven days a week.

Reviews throughout this book only list business hours where they differ from the standard hours outlined here.

CHILDREN

Successful travel with young children requires planning and effort. Don't try to overdo things by packing too much into the time available. Involve the kids in the planning, and balance that visit to the art museum with a trip to the zoo or time spent in a playground. Lonely Planet's *Travel with Children* offers a wealth of tips and tricks to make travelling with tots child's play.

In Croatia, children's discounts are widely available for everything from museum admissions to hotel accommodation. The cut-off age is often nine. Hotels may have children's cots, but numbers are usually limited. For greater comfort, look into renting an apartment. There's much more space for the same price as a hotel room, and a kitchen can be handy for preparing kids' meals.

Disposable nappies are easy to find, particularly American Pampers and German Linostar. Look for supermarkets such as Konzum, and the pharmacy DM. Very few restaurants or public restrooms have nappy-changing facilities. Keep in mind that electric sterilisers are expensive and hard to find. Breast-feeding in public is uncommon, but generally accepted if done discreetly.

Kids love the beach, but choose your sites carefully, as many 'beaches' are rocky with steep drop-offs. Sandy beaches are more kid-friendly. Try Baška on Krk Island, Brela along the Makarska coast, Copacabana beach near Dubrovnik, the beaches surrounding Orebić and the narrow stretch of shingle beach on Crveni Otok near Rovinj.

CLIMATE CHARTS

The climate varies from Mediterranean along the Adriatic coast to continental further inland (see climate charts, p298). The sunny coastal areas experience hot, dry summers and mild, rainy winters, while the interior regions are warm in summer and cold in winter.

In spring and early summer, the *maestral* keeps the temperature down along the coast. It generally starts blowing at around 9am, increases until early afternoon and dies down in the late afternoon. This strong, steady wind makes good sailing weather.

Winter weather is defined by two winds. The southeasterly sirocco from the Sahara Desert brings warm, moist air to the mainland and can produce a heavy cloud cover and the steady winds that sailors love. The northeasterly *bura* blows from the interior to the coast in powerful gusts, bringing dry air and blowing away clouds.

Sun-lovers note that the island of Hvar gets 2715 hours of sun a year, followed by Split (2697), Korčula Island (2671) and Dubrovnik (2584). The lack of rainfall along the coast, and especially on islands further removed from the mainland, has produced severe water shortages in Dalmatia throughout its history. Summer dry periods can last up to 100 days. For the best time of year to visit Croatia, see p17.

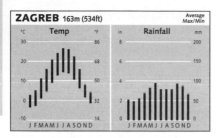

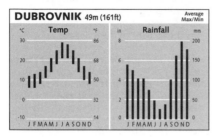

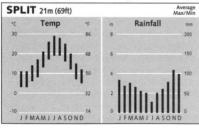

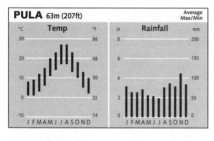

CUSTOMS REGULATIONS

Travellers can bring their personal effects into the country, along with 1L of liquor, 1L of wine, 500g of coffee, 200 cigarettes and 50mL of perfume. The import or export of kuna is limited to 15,000KN per person. Camping gear, boats and electronic equipment should be declared upon entering the country. For information about taxes and refunds, see p301.

There is no quarantine period for animals brought into the country, but you should have a recent vaccination certificate. Otherwise, the animal must be inspected by a local veterinarian, who may not be immediately available.

DANGERS & ANNOYANCES

Personal security, including theft, is generally not a problem in Croatia. However, the former confrontation line between Croat and federal forces was heavily mined in the early 1990s, and over a million mines were laid in eastern Slavonia around Osijek, and in the hinterlands north of Zadar. Although the government has invested heavily in demining operations, it's a slow job. In general, the mined areas are well signposted with skull-and-crossbones symbols and yellow tape, but don't go wandering off on your own in sensitive regions before checking with a local. Never go poking around an obviously abandoned and ruined house.

Croatia is not unduly burdened with biting or stinging creatures, but mosquitoes do abound in eastern Slavonia, and sea urchins are nearly everywhere along the coast.

DISCOUNT CARDS

Most museums, galleries, theatres and festivals in Croatia offer student discounts of up to 50%. An International Student Identity Card (ISIC) is the best international proof of your student status. People under the age of 26 who are not students qualify for the International Youth Travel Card (IYTC).

Both the ISIC and IYTC carry basic accident and sickness insurance, and cardholders have access to a worldwide hotline for help in medical, legal or financial emergencies.

Croatia is a member of the **European Youth Card Association** (www.euro26.hr), which offers reductions in shops, restaurants and libraries in participating countries. The card can be used at around 1400 places of interest in Croatia.

STA Travel (www.statravel.com), an international company specialising in youth travel, offers all of the cards discussed here. In Croatia, contact **Dali Travel** (Map pp74-5; ☎ 01-48 47 472; travelsection@hfhs .hr; Dežmanova 9, 10000 Zagreb; ✆ 9am-5pm Mon-Fri).

EMBASSIES & CONSULATES

The following are all in Zagreb (Map pp74–5):
Albania (☎ 01-48 10 679; Jurišićeva 2a)
Australia (☎ 01-48 91 200; Kaptol Centar, Nova Ves 11)
Bosnia & Hercegovina (☎ 01-48 19 420; Pavla Hatza 3)
Bulgaria (☎ 01-46 46 609; Gornje Pekrižje 28)

Canada (☎ 01-48 81 200; Prilaz Ðure Deželića 4)
Czech Republic (☎ 01-61 77 239; Savska 41)
France (☎ 01-48 93 680; Andrije Hebranga 2)
Germany (☎ 01-61 58 105; Avenija Grada Vukovara 64)
Hungary (☎ 01-48 90 900; Pantovčak 255-257)
Ireland (☎ 01-63 10 025; Miramarska 23)
The Netherlands (☎ 01-46 84 880; Medvešćak 56)
New Zealand (☎ 01-65 20 888; Avenija Dubrovnik 15)
Poland (☎ 01-48 99 444; Krležin Gvozd 3)
Romania (☎ 01-45 77 550, Mlinarska ul 43)
Serbia (☎ 01-45 79 067; Pantovčak 245)
Slovakia (☎ 01-48 48 941; Prilaz Ðure Deželića 10)
Slovenia (☎ 01-63 11 000; Savska 41)
UK (☎ 01-60 09 100; I Lučića 4)
USA (☎ 01-66 12 200; Ul Thomasa Jeffersona 2)

FESTIVALS & EVENTS
February
Carnival For the best costumes, dancing and revelry in this pre-Lent celebration, head to Rijeka, Samobor or Zadar.

March
Days of Croatian Film Short features and animated films are shown in Zagreb theatres, followed by awards.
Vukovar Puppet Spring Festival In the last week of March, Vukovar becomes a puppet town with workshops, demonstrations and performances.

April
Queer Zagreb FM Festival In the last week of April, this festival hosts gay-themed films and music.
Zagreb Biennial of Contemporary Music In odd-numbered years, Zagreb hosts this prestigious musical event. By 'contemporary', do not read 'pop'.

May
Dance Week Festival (www.danceincroatia.com) Zagreb hosts experimental dance companies from around the world in the last week of May.

June
Festival of Animated Films In even-numbered years, this Zagreb festival honours animated films.
International Children's Festival This Šibenik festival presents puppets, theatre and workshops to children.
International Festival of New Films Films, videos, installations and workshops for experimental filmmakers.

July
Dubrovnik Summer Festival (www.dubrovnik-festival .hr) From mid-July to mid-August, Dubrovnik hosts local and national classical musicians.
International Folklore Festival Zagreb becomes a whirlwind of colour and music as costumed fiddlers and dancers descend on the capital from all over the world.

Motovun Film Festival (www.motovunfilmfestival.com) This is probably Croatia's most glamorous film festival.
Poreč Annale This month-long series of exhibits in Poreč showcases the finest young Croatian artists.

September
Varaždin Baroque Evenings Baroque music in the baroque city of Varaždin.

FOOD
Restaurant listings in this book are given in order of price: budget (under 80KN), midrange (80KN to 150KN) and top end (over 150KN). The majority of Croatian eateries are midrange and offer excellent value for money.

If you're self-catering, bear in mind that groceries are not cheap in Croatia. There are good deals on fresh produce, but anything in a bottle or a can is no cheaper than anywhere in Western Europe. Special and tasty local ham, sausage, cold cuts and cheese can be pricey. You can get good deals on fish out of season, but during summer the best fish goes to the restaurants. For more on Croatian cuisine, see p51.

GAY & LESBIAN TRAVELLERS
Homosexuality has been legal in Croatia since 1977 and is tolerated, but not welcomed with open arms. Public displays of affection between same-sex couples may be met with hostility, especially beyond the major cities. Exclusively gay clubs are a rarity outside Zagreb, but many of the large discos attract a mixed crowd. Raves are also a good way for gays to meet.

On the coast, gays gravitate to Rovinj, Hvar, Split and Dubrovnik, and tend to frequent naturist beaches. In Zagreb, the last week in April is the **Queer Zagreb FM Festival** (www.queer zagreb.org) and the last Saturday in June is Gay Pride Zagreb day. Gay-friendly venues are listed throughout this book.

Most Croatian websites devoted to the gay scene are in Croatian only, but a good starting point is http://travel.gay.hr. Otherwise, there's **LORI** (www.lori.hr, in Croatian), the lesbian organisation based in Rijeka.

HOLIDAYS
Croats take their holidays very seriously. Shops and museums are shut and boat services are reduced. On religious holidays, the churches are full; it can be a good time to check out the artwork in a church that is usually closed.

Holidays falling in the milder months are often marked by street spectacles that include dancing and bands. Easter and Holy Week are especially good times to catch local celebrations. In and around Dubrovnik, palm or olive twigs are decorated with flowers, blessed and placed in homes on Palm Sunday. Holy Week preceding Easter is celebrated with processions on Hvar, Brač and Korčula Islands. Central Croatia celebrates Holy Week with *krijes* (bonfires), and painted eggs are given as Easter gifts.

Croatian public holidays are as follows:

New Year's Day 1 January
Epiphany 6 January
Easter Monday March/April
Labour Day 1 May
Corpus Christi 10 June
Day of Antifascist Resistance 22 June; marks the outbreak of resistance in 1941
Statehood Day 25 June
Homeland Thanksgiving Day 5 August
Feast of the Assumption 15 August
Independence Day 8 October
All Saints' Day 1 November
Christmas 25 & 26 December

INSURANCE

A travel-insurance policy to cover theft, loss and medical problems is a good idea. You should check your existing insurance policies at home before purchasing travel insurance, as some may already provide worldwide coverage. Some credit cards also offer limited accident insurance.

A good travel agent should be able to guide you in choosing the right policy. There's a variety of policies available, so check the small print. Some policies specifically exclude 'dangerous activities', which can include diving, motorcycling and even trekking. A locally acquired motorcycle licence is not valid under some policies.

You may prefer a policy that pays doctors or hospitals directly rather than you having to pay on the spot and claim later. If you have to claim later, make sure you keep all documentation. Some policies ask you to call (reverse charges) a centre in your home country where an immediate assessment of your problem is made. Check that your policy covers ambulances and an emergency flight home.

Worldwide travel insurance is available at www.lonelyplanet.com/bookings. You can buy, extend and claim online any time – even if you're already on the road.

For additional insurance information, see Health (p315) and Transport (p313).

INTERNET ACCESS

Cybercafés are listed under Information in the regional chapters of this guide; internet access costs around 30KN per hour. The local tourist office should have the latest on the scene. In smaller towns, the tourist office may let you quickly check your email on their computer if you ask nicely. Public libraries usually have internet access, but their hours can be limited. Most travellers make constant use of internet cafés and free web-based email such as **Yahoo** (www.yahoo.com) or **Hotmail** (www.hotmail.com). If you need to access another nonweb-based account, you'll need to know your incoming (POP or IMAP) mail-server name, your account name and your password.

Upmarket hotels are almost always equipped with wi-fi, as are business-geared hotels. Some private guest houses also have wi-fi, though you shouldn't count on it.

For a selection of useful websites about Croatia, see p21.

LEGAL MATTERS

Although it is highly unlikely that you'll be hassled by the police, you should keep identification with you at all times as the police have the right to stop you and demand ID. By international treaty, you have the right to notify your consular official if arrested. Consulates can normally refer you to English-speaking lawyers, although they will not pay for one.

MAPS

Freytag & Berndt publishes a series of country, regional and city maps. Its 1:600,000 map of Croatia, Slovenia and Bosnia and Hercegovina is particularly useful if you're travelling in the region. Others include *Croatia, Slovenia* (1:800,000) by GeoCenter and *Hrvatska, Slovenija, Bosna i Hercegovina* (1:600,000) by Naklada Naprijed in Zagreb. Regional tourist offices often publish good regional driving maps showing the latest roads. Apart from Zagreb, Split, Zadar, Rijeka and Dubrovnik, there are few top-quality city maps. Local tourist offices usually publish helpful maps.

MONEY

Croatia uses the kuna (KN). Commonly circulated banknotes come in denominations of 500, 200, 100, 50, 20, 10 and five kuna, bearing images of Croat heroes such as Stjepan Radić and Ban Josip Jelačić. Each kuna is divided into 100 lipa. You'll find silver-coloured 50- and 20-lipa coins, and bronze-coloured 10-lipa coins.

The kuna has a fixed exchange rate tied to the euro. To amass hard currency, the government makes the kuna more expensive in summer when tourists visit. You'll get the best exchange rate from mid-September to mid-June. Otherwise, the rate varies little from year to year. International boat fares are priced in euros, not kuna, although you pay in kuna. In this book, we list prices for hotels, camping and private accommodation in kuna and in euros, depending on how an establishment quotes them. For more information about expenses, see p17; for exchange rates, see the table on the inside front cover.

ATMs

Automatic teller machines are prevalent nearly everywhere in Croatia and can be a convenient way of changing money. Most are tied in with Cirrus, Plus, Diners Club and Maestro. Privredna Banka usually has ATMs for cash withdrawals using American Express cards. Most other ATMs also allow you to withdraw money using a credit card, but you'll start paying interest on the amount immediately, in addition to paying the withdrawal fee. All post offices will allow you to make a cash withdrawal on MasterCard or Cirrus, and a growing number work with Diners Club as well.

Cash

There are numerous places to change money in Croatia, all offering similar rates; ask at any travel agency for the location of the nearest exchange. Post offices change money and keep long hours. Most places deduct a commission of 1% to 1.5% to change cash, but some banks do not. Travellers cheques may be exchanged only in banks. Kuna can be converted into hard currency only at a bank and only if you submit a receipt of a previous transaction. Hungarian currency (the forint) is difficult to change in Croatia. If you can't get to an exchange operation, you can pay for a meal or small services in euros, but the rate is not as good. You can pay for most private accommodation in euros as well.

Credit Cards

Credit cards (Visa, MasterCard, Diners Club, American Express) are widely accepted in

hotels but rarely accepted in any kind of private accommodation. Many smaller restaurants and shops do not accept credit cards.

Amex card holders can contact Atlas travel agencies in Dubrovnik, Opatija, Pula, Poreč, Split, Zadar and Zagreb for the full range of Amex services, including cashing personal cheques and holding clients' mail. Privredna Banka is a chain of banks that handles many services for Amex clients.

Following is the Zagreb contact information for the major credit-card companies:

American Express (☎ 01-61 24 422; www.american express.hr; Lastovska 23)
Diners Club (☎ 01-48 02 222; www.diners.hr; Praška 5)
Eurocard/MasterCard (☎ 01-37 89 620; www.zaba .hr; Zagrebačka Banka, Samoborska 145)
Visa (☎ 01-46 47 133; www.splitskabanka.hr; Splitska Banka, Tuškanova 28)

Taxes & Refunds

Travellers who spend more than 500KN in one shop are entitled to a refund of the value-added tax (VAT), which is equivalent to 22% of the purchase price. In order to claim the refund, the merchant must fill out the *Poreski ček* (required form), which you must present to the customs office upon leaving the country. Mail a stamped copy to the shop, which will then credit your credit card with the appropriate sum. There is also a service called Global Refund System, which will give you your refund in cash at the airport or at participating post offices. Post offices in Zagreb, Osijek, Dubrovnik, Split, Korčula and a few dozen other towns participate in the system. For a complete list, see www.posta.hr.

PHOTOGRAPHY

Though most people use digital cameras nowadays, you can still find colour-print film produced by Kodak and Fuji in photo stores and tourist shops. It's fairly expensive in Croatia compared with a lot of other countries, so stock up ahead of time. If you choose to develop your photos in Croatia, remember that the standard size for prints is only 9cm x 13cm. Digital-imaging techniques are available in Zagreb and other large cities, but few places develop APS film. One-hour developing is not widely available. Slide film is widely available in major cities and tourist centres, but can be scarce in out-of-the-way places.

If you're shooting in one of Croatia's steamy summer months, remember that film should be kept cool and dry after exposure. The intense summer light can wash out colour between mid-morning and late afternoon, and the overcast skies of winter may dictate the use of a fairly fast film.

As in any country, politeness goes a long way when taking photos; ask permission before photographing people. Military installations may not be photographed, and you may have a lot of angry naked people after you if you try to take pictures in a naturist resort.

POST

HPT Hrvatska, recognised by its red, white and blue sign, offers a wide variety of services, from selling stamps and phonecards to sending faxes. If you want to avoid a trip to the post office and just want to send a few postcards, you can buy *pismo* (stamps) at any *tisak* (newsstand) and drop your mail into any of the yellow postboxes on the street. It takes anywhere from five days (Europe) to two weeks (North America and Australia) for a card or letter to arrive at its destination.

Domestic mail costs 2.80KN for up to 20g, and 5KN for up to 100g. Postcards are 1.80KN. For international mail, the base rate is 3.50KN for a postcard, 5KN for a letter up to 20g, and 15KN for a letter up to 100g. Then, add on the airmail charge for every 20g: 2KN for Europe, 3KN for North America, 3.20KN for Africa and Asia, and 4KN for Australia.

If you have an Amex card or are travelling with Amex travellers cheques, you can have your mail addressed to branches of Atlas travel agencies in Dubrovnik, Opatija, Poreč, Pula, Split, Zadar and Zagreb; mail will be held at the office for up to two months.

SHOPPING

The finest artisans' product from Croatia is the intricate lace from Pag Island, part of a centuries-old tradition that is still going strong. Although you'll sometimes see it in handicraft shops in Zagreb and Dubrovnik, it's more fun to take a trip out to Pag where you can buy the patches of lace directly from the women who make them.

Embroidered fabrics are also featured in many souvenir shops. Croatian embroidery is distinguished by the cheerful red geometric patterns set against a white background, which you'll see on tablecloths, pillowcases and blouses.

Lavender and other fragrant herbs made into scented sachets or transmuted into oils make popular and inexpensive gifts. You can find them on most central Dalmatian islands, but especially on Hvar Island, which is known for its lavender fields.

Brač Island is known for its lustrous stone. Ashtrays, vases, candlestick holders and other small but heavy items carved from Brač stone are on sale throughout the island.

Samples of local food, wine and spirits also make great gifts or souvenirs. In Samobor, pick up some mustard or *bermet* (liqueur). In Pag you can buy savoury homemade cheese, but be aware that customs regulations in many countries forbid the importation of unwrapped cheese. *Cukarini* (sweet biscuits) from Korčula keep for a while if they are wrapped in cellophane. Local brandies, often with herbs inside the bottle, can conjure up the scents and flavours of each region, since it seems that almost every town produces its own special brandy.

A recent addition to the Croatian shopping scene are the jewellery shops that are cropping up in cities and towns. They are usually run by immigrants from Kosovo who have a centuries-old tradition in silver working. Although the shops also sell gold, the workmanship on silver filigree earrings, bracelets and *objets d'art* is often of astonishingly high quality.

SOLO TRAVELLERS

The joy of travelling solo is that it is a compromise-free trip. You do what you want when you want to do it, but you will pay for the privilege. Guest houses or private accommodation often don't have special rates for singles, although you may be able to knock a few kuna off the double-room price if you visit out of season.

If you want to meet other travellers and sample the local life, it's best to stay away from large resort-style hotels, as they tend to be frequented by families and couples. They are also isolated from community life. It's much better to stay in guest houses that have a few rooms where you can meet other travellers. To mix with the locals, try to find a place in the centre of town where you can go out to cafés and bars. Internet cafés are also good places to meet both travellers and locals. The staff at internet cafés often speak excellent English.

If you find that dining out alone is a forlorn experience, make lunch the main meal of your day, when the dining room is more likely to contain solo business or pleasure diners.

TELEPHONE
Mobile Phones
If you have a 3-G phone (which most people now do) and if it's unlocked, you can buy a SIM card for about 50KN, which includes 20 minutes of connection time – the cheapest is Tomato card. You can also buy a packet (mobile and phonecard) at any telecom shop for about 500KN, which includes 30 minutes of connection time. Mobile-phone rental is not widely available in Croatia.

Phone Codes
To call Croatia from abroad, dial your international access code, then ☎ 385 (the country code for Croatia), then the area code (without the initial 0) and the local number. To call from region to region within Croatia, start with the area code (with the initial zero); drop it when dialling within the same code. Phone numbers with the prefix ☎ 060 are either free or charged at a premium rate, so watch out for the small print; phone numbers that begin with ☎ 09 are mobile phone numbers, which are billed at a much higher rate than regular numbers (figure on about 6KN per minute).

Phonecards
There are few coin-operated phones in Croatia, so you'll need a phonecard to use public telephones. Phonecards are sold according to *impulsa* (units), and you can buy cards of 25 (15KN), 50 (30KN), 100 (50KN) and 200 (100KN) units. These can be purchased at any post office and most tobacco shops and newspaper kiosks. Many phone boxes are equipped with a button on the upper left with a flag symbol. Press the button and you get instructions in English. If you don't have a phonecard, you can call from a post office.

Calls placed from hotel rooms are much more expensive. For local and national calls, the mark-up is negligible from cheaper hotels but significantly more from four-star establishments. Private accommodation never includes a private telephone, but you may be able to use the owner's for local calls.

A three-minute call from Croatia using a phonecard will cost around 12KN to the UK and Europe and 15KN to the USA or Australia. Local calls cost 0.80KN whatever

the time of day, although owners of a fixed line get cheaper rates from 7pm to 7am.

TIME
Croatia is on Central European Time (GMT/UTC plus one hour). Daylight saving comes into effect at the end of March, when clocks are turned forward an hour. At the end of September they're turned back an hour.

For a rundown of world times, see the World Time Zone map (pp342-3).

TOURIST INFORMATION
The **Croatian National Tourist Board** (Map pp74-5; ☎ 01-45 56 455; www.htz.hr; Iblerov Trg 10, Importanne Gallerija, 10000 Zagreb) is a good source of information. There are regional tourist offices that supervise tourist development, and municipal tourist offices that have free brochures and good information on local events. Some arrange private accommodation. Contact information for local tourist offices is listed in the regional chapters.

Following is contact information for regional tourist offices:

Dubrovnik-Neretva County (☎ 020-324 222; www.visitdubrovnik.hr; Cvijete Zuzorić 1/1, 20000 Dubrovnik)

Istria County (☎ 052-452 797; www.istra.com; Pionirska 1a, 52440 Poreč)

Krapina-Zagorje County (☎ 049-233 653; tzkzz@kr.htnet.hr; Zagrebačka 6, 49217 Krapinske Toplice)

Osijek-Baranja County (☎ 031-675 897; www.obz.hr; Sunčana 39, 31222 Bizovac)

Primorje-Gorski Kotar (Kvarner) County (☎ 051-272 988; www.kvarner.hr; N Tesle, 251410 Opatija)

Šibenik-Knin County (☎ 022-219 072; www.sibenik-knin.com; Fra N Ružića bb, 22000 Šibenik)

Split-Dalmatia County (☎ 021-490 032; www.dalmatia.hr; Prilaz Braće Kaliterna 10/1, 21000 Split)

Zadar County (☎ 023-315 107; www.zadar.hr; Š Leopolda B Mandića 1, 23000 Zadar)

Zagreb County (☎ 01-48 73 665; www.tzzz.hr; Preradovićeva 42, 10000 Zagreb)

Tourist information is also dispensed by commercial travel agencies such as **Atlas Travel Agency** (www.atlas-croatia.com) and **Generalturist** (www.generalturist.com), which also arrange private accommodation, sightseeing tours etc. Ask for the schedule for local ferries and then ask how to read it.

Croatian tourist offices abroad include the following:

Austria (☎ 01-585 3884; office@kroatien.at; Kroatische Zentrale für Tourismus, Am Hof 13 1010 Vienna)

Czech Republic (☎ 02-2221 1812; infohtz@iol.cz; Hrvatska Turistiška Zajednica OS, Krakovská 25, 11000 Prague)
France (☎ 01 45 00 99 55; croatie.ot@wanadoo.fr; 48 Ave Victor Hugo, 75016 Paris)
Germany Frankfurt (☎ 069-238 5350; kroatien-info@gmx.de; Kroatische Zentrale für Tourismus, Kaiserstrasse 23, D-60311); Munich (☎ 089-223 344; kroatien-tourismus@t-online.de; Kroatische Zentrale für Tourismus, Rumfordstrasse 7, D-80469)
Hungary (☎ 01-266 6505; www.horvatinfo@axelro.hu; Horvát Idegenforgalmi Közösség Magyar u 36, 1053 Budapest)
Italy Milan (☎ 02-86 45 44 97; info@enteturismocroato.it; Ente nazionale Croato per il turismo, Piazzete Pattari 1/3, 20123); Rome (☎ 06-32 11 03 96; officeroma@enteturismocroato.it; Via dell' Oca 48 00186)
The Netherlands (☎ 20-661 6422; kroatie-info@planet.nl; Nijenburg 25, Amsterdam 1081)
UK (☎ 020-8563 7979; info@cnto.freeserve.co.uk; Croatian National Tourist Office, 2 Lanchesters, 162-4 Fulham Palace Rd, London W6 9ER)
USA (☎ 212-279 8672; cntony@earthlink.net; Croatian National Tourist Office, Suite 4003, 350 Fifth Ave, New York, NY 10118)

TRAVELLERS WITH DISABILITIES

Due to the number of wounded war veterans, more attention is being paid to the needs of disabled travellers in Croatia. Public toilets at bus stations, train stations, airports and large public venues are usually wheelchair accessible. Large hotels are wheelchair accessible, but very little private accommodation is. Bus and train stations in Zagreb, Zadar, Rijeka, Split and Dubrovnik are wheelchair accessible, but the local Jadrolinija ferries are not. For further information, get in touch with **Savez Organizacija Invalida Hrvatske** (☎ /fax 01-48 29 394; Savska 3, 10000 Zagreb).

VISAS

Citizens of the EU, USA, Canada, Australia, New Zealand, Israel, Ireland, Singapore and the UK do not need a visa for stays of up to 90 days. South Africans must apply for a 90-day visa in Pretoria. Contact any Croatian embassy, consulate or travel agency abroad for information.

If you want to stay in Croatia longer than three months, the easiest thing to do is cross the border into Italy or Austria and return.

Croatian authorities require all foreigners to register with the local police when they arrive in a new area of the country, but this is a routine matter normally handled by the hotel, hostel, camping ground or agency securing your private accommodation. That's why they need to take your passport away for the night.

If you're staying elsewhere (eg with relatives or friends), your host should take care of it for you. See opposite for information about passports and entering the country.

WOMEN TRAVELLERS

Women face no special danger in Croatia. There have been cases, however, of some lone women being harassed and followed in large coastal cities, though you'd have to be pretty unlucky for this to happen.

It's important to be careful about being alone with an unfamiliar man, since claims of 'date rape' are not likely to be taken very seriously.

Croatian women place a high priority on good grooming and try to buy the most fashionable clothes they can afford. Topless sunbathing is tolerated, but you're better off on one of the numerous nudist beaches.

Transport

GETTING THERE & AWAY

Getting to Croatia is becoming ever easier, especially if you're arriving in summer. Low-cost carriers are finally establishing routes to Croatia, and a plethora of bus and ferry routes shepherd holidaymakers to the coast. Flights, tours and rail tickets can be booked online at www.lonelyplane t.com/bookings.

ENTERING THE COUNTRY
With an economy that depends heavily on tourism, Croatia has wisely kept red tape to a minimum for foreign visitors. The most serious hassle is likely to be long lines at immigration checkpoints.

Passport
A valid passport is necessary to enter Croatia. To avoid problems, it's best to ensure that your passport will remain valid for the entire course of your stay. Always make a photocopy of your passport and keep the photocopy in a separate place.

In the case that your passport is lost or stolen, being able to produce a photocopy of the original at your embassy or consulate will greatly facilitate its replacement. If your passport disappears right before your departure, take your airline tickets to your embassy or consulate and you will normally get a temporary passport enabling you to at least re-enter your home country. See opposite for information about visas.

AIR
Airports & Airlines
Major airports in Croatia:
Dubrovnik (airport code DBV; ☎ 020-773 377; www .airport-dubrovnik.hr)
Pula (airport code PUY; ☎ 052-530 105; www.airport -pula.com)
Rijeka (airport code RJK; ☎ 051-842 132; www.rijeka -airport.hr)
Split (airport code SPU; ☎ 021-203 506; www.split -airport.hr)
Zadar (airport code ZAD; ☎ 023-313 311; www.zadar -airport.hr)
Zagreb (airport code ZAG; ☎ 01-62 65 222; www .zagreb-airport.hr)

Dubrovnik has direct flights from Brussels, London (Gatwick), Manchester, Hannover, Frankfurt, Cologne, Stuttgart and Munich. Pula has nonstop flights from Manchester, London (Gatwick), Glasgow and Edinburgh. Rijeka has flights from Hanover, Cologne, Stuttgart, Munich and London (Luton).

Split has direct connections to London, Frankfurt, Munich, Cologne, Prague and Rome. Zagreb has direct flights to all European capitals, plus Hamburg, Stuttgart and Cologne.

Note that there are no direct flights from North America to Croatia.

Croatia Airlines (airline code OU; Map pp74-5; ☎ 01-48 19 633; www.croatiaairlines.hr; Zrinjevac 17, Zagreb; 🕒 8am-8pm

---

CLIMATE CHANGE & TRAVEL

Climate change is a serious threat to the ecosystems that humans rely upon, and air travel is the fastest-growing contributor to the problem. Lonely Planet regards travel, overall, as a global benefit, but believes we all have a responsibility to limit our personal impact on global warming.

Flying & Climate Change

Pretty much every form of motorised travel generates CO_2 (the main cause of human-induced climate change), but planes are far and away the worst offenders, not just because of the sheer distances they allow us to travel, but also because they release greenhouse gases high into the atmosphere. The statistics are frightening: two people taking a return flight between Europe and the US will contribute as much to climate change as an average household's gas and electricity consumption over a whole year.

Carbon Offset Schemes

Climatecare.org and other websites use 'carbon calculators' that allow travellers to offset the level of greenhouse gases they are responsible for with financial contributions to sustainable travel schemes that reduce global warming – including projects in India, Honduras, Kazakhstan and Uganda.

Lonely Planet, together with Rough Guides and other concerned partners in the travel industry, supports the carbon offset scheme run by climatecare.org. Lonely Planet offsets all of its staff and author travel.

For more information check out our website: lonelyplanet.com.

Mon-Fri, 9am-noon Sat) is the sole domestic carrier, connecting Zagreb with Dubrovnik, Pula, Rijeka, Split and Zadar. All internal flights pass through Zagreb.

The following are the major airlines flying into the country (all contact phone numbers given are for Zagreb):

Adria Airways (airline code JP; ☎ 01-48 10 011; www .adria-airways.com)

Aeroflot (airline code SU; ☎ 01-48 72 055; www .aeroflot.ru)

Air Canada (airline code AC; ☎ 01-48 22 033; www .aircanada.ca)

Air France (airline code AF; ☎ 01-48 37 100; www .airfrance.com)

Alitalia (airline code AZ; ☎ 01-48 10 413; www.alitalia.it)

Austrian Airlines (airline code OS; ☎ 01-62 65 900; www.aua.com)

Croatia Airlines (airline code OU; ☎ 01-48 19 633; www.croatiaairlines.hr)

ČSA (airline code OK; ☎ 01-48 73 301; www.csa.cz)

Delta Airlines (airline code DL; ☎ 01-48 78 760; www .delta.com)

Easyjet (airline code EZY; www.easyjet.com)

Germanwings (airline code GWI; www.germanwings.com)

Hapag Lloyd Express (airline code HLX; www.hlx.com)

KLM-Northwest (airline code KL; ☎ 01-48 78 601; www.klm.com)

Lot (airline code LOT; ☎ 01-48 37 500; www.lot.com)

Lufthansa (airline code LH; ☎ 01-48 73 121; www .lufthansa.com)

Malev Hungarian Airlines (airline code MA; ☎ 01-48 36 935; www.malev.hu)

Ryanair (airline code RYR; www.ryanair.com)

SNBrussels (airline code SN; www.flysn.com)

Turkish Airlines (airline code TK; ☎ 01-49 21 854; www .turkis hairlines.com)

Wizzair (airline code W6; www.wi zzair.com)

Tickets

With a bit of research (ringing around travel agencies, checking out internet sites and perusing the travel ads in newspapers) you can often get yourself a good travel deal. Start early, as some of the cheapest tickets need to be bought well in advance and popular flights can sell out.

Full-time students and people under 26 years (under 30 in some countries) have access to better deals than other travellers. You have to show a document proving your date of birth or a valid International Student Identity Card (ISIC) when buying your ticket and boarding the plane.

The best ticket prices are generally found by booking over the internet. Many airlines, both full service and no frills, offer some excellent fares to Web surfers. They may sell seats by auction or simply cut prices to reflect the reduced cost of electronic selling.

Many travel agencies around the world have websites, which can make the internet a quick and easy way to compare prices. There is also an increasing number of agents that operate only on the internet.

Online ticket sales work well if you are doing a simple one-way or return trip on specified dates. Online super fact fare generators, however, are no substitute for a travel agent who knows all about special deals, has strategies for avoiding layovers, and can offer advice on everything from which airline has the best vegetarian food to the best travel insurance.

You may find that the cheapest flights are advertised by obscure agencies. Such firms are usually honest and solvent, but there are some rogue fly-by-night outfits around. Paying by credit card generally offers protection, as most card issuers provide refunds if you can prove you didn't get what you paid for. Similar protection can be obtained by buying a ticket from a bonded agent, such as one covered by the **Air Travel Organiser's Licence** (ATOL; www.atol.org.uk) scheme in the UK. Agents who accept only cash should hand over the tickets straight away and not tell you to 'come back tomorrow'. After you've made a booking or paid your deposit, call the airline and confirm that the booking was made. It's generally not advisable to send money (even cheques) through the post unless the agent is very well established – some travellers have reported being ripped off by fly-by-night mail-order ticket agencies.

If you purchase a ticket and later want to make changes to your route or get a refund, you need to contact the original travel agent. Airlines issue refunds only to the purchaser of a ticket – usually the travel agent who bought the ticket on your behalf. Many travellers change their routes halfway through their trips, so think carefully before you buy a ticket that is not easily refunded.

Travellers with Special Needs

If they're warned early enough, airlines can often make special arrangements for travellers with special needs, providing things such as wheelchair assistance at airports or vegetarian meals on the flight. Children under two years of age travel for 10% of the standard fare (or free on some airlines) as long as they don't occupy a seat. They don't get a baggage allow-

ance. 'Skycots', baby food and nappies should be provided by the airline if requested in advance. Children aged between two and 12 can usually occupy a seat for half to two-thirds of the full fare, and do get a baggage allowance.

The disability-friendly website www.allgo here.com has an airline directory that provides information on the facilities offered by various airlines.

Asia

Although most Asian countries are now offering fairly competitive airfare deals, Bangkok, Singapore and Hong Kong are still the best places to shop around for discount tickets. A one-way fare from Bangkok to Zagreb starts at US$800. Hong Kong's travel market can be unpredictable, but some excellent bargains are available if you are lucky.

The reliable **STA Travel** (www.statravel.com) has branches in Hong Kong, Tokyo, Singapore, Bangkok and Kuala Lumpur; check the website for contact details.

Australia

Two well-known agencies for cheap fares are **STA Travel** (☎ 134 782; www.statravel.com.au) and **Flight Centre** (☎ 133 133; www.flightcentre.com.au). STA Travel has offices in all major cities and on many university campuses. Flight Centre also has dozens of offices throughout Australia. Flights from Sydney or Melbourne will be via another European city such as London, Rome or Frankfurt. Return fares start at A$1800.

Canada

Canada's main student travel organisation is **Travel Cuts** (☎ 1866 246 9762; www.travelcuts.com), with offices in Toronto and Montreal. Online you can also check out www.expedia.ca or www.travelocity.ca. Return fares from Toronto to Zagreb cost from C$1500.

Continental Europe

Though London is the travel discount capital of Europe, there are several other cities in which you will find a range of good deals to Zagreb.

In Amsterdam, try **NBBS Reizen** (☎ 900 10 20 300; www.nbbs.nl); special offers can be found for as low as €139.

In Paris, recommended travel agencies include **OTU Voyages** (☎ 01 55 82 32 32; www.otu.fr) and **Nouvelles Frontières** (☎ 08 25 00 07 47; www.nouvelles-frontieres.fr). On the internet, there's

Lastminute (☎ 08 92 70 50 00; www.fr.lastminute.com). Return fares to Zagreb start from around €325 with Croatia Airlines.

In Italy, a recommended travel agency in Rome is **CTS Viaggi** (☎ 06-462 0431; www.cts .it). A return fare from Rome to Zagreb costs around €250.

In Germany, a recommended agency is **STA Travel** (☎ 030-310 0040; www.statravel.de). Fares can be found for as low as €139.

New Zealand

A good place to start price shopping is the travel section of the *New Zealand Herald,* which carries adverts from travel agencies. **Flight Centre** (☎ 0800 243 544; www.flightcentre.co.nz) has a large central office in Auckland and many branches throughout the country. **STA Travel** (☎ 0508 782 872; www.statravel.co.nz) has offices throughout New Zealand.

The cheapest fares to Europe are generally routed through the USA. Otherwise, you can fly from Auckland to pick up a connecting flight in Melbourne or Sydney. A return flight from New Zealand would cost around NZ$1800.

UK

London is one of the best centres in the world for discounted air tickets. For students or travellers under 26 years, popular travel agencies in the UK include **STA Travel** (☎ 0870 160 0599; www.statravel.co.uk) and **Trailfinders** (☎ 0845 058 58 58; www.trailfinders.com). Trailfinders produces a lavishly illustrated brochure that includes airfare details. The weekend editions of national newspapers sometimes have information on cheap fares. In London, also try the *Evening Standard, Time Out* and *TNT,* a free weekly magazine ostensibly for antipodeans. Fare checking on internet travel sites can turn up some good deals. Try the following:

Cheapest Flights (www.cheapestflights.co.uk)
Online Travel (www.travelocity.co.uk) Good deals on flights from more than a dozen British cities.

USA

Discount travel agencies in the USA are known as consolidators (although you won't see a sign on the door saying 'Consolidator'). San Francisco is the ticket consolidator capital of America, although some good deals can also be found in Los Angeles, New York and other big cities. When shopping around check out the following websites:

Cheap Tickets (☎ 888-922 8849; www.cheaptickets .com)
Expedia (☎ 800-397 3342; www.expedia.msn.com) Microsoft's travel site.
Flight Centre International (☎ 866-967 5351; www .flightcentre.us)
Orbitz (☎ 888-656 4546; www.orbitz.com)
STA Travel (☎ 800-777 0112; www.statravel.com)
Travelocity (☎ 888-872 8356; www.travelocity.com)

LAND
Car & Motorcycle

The main highway entry and exit points for crossing between Croatia and Hungary are Goričan (between Nagykanizsa and Varaždin), Gola (23km east of Koprivnica), Terezino Polje (opposite Barcs) and Donji Miholjac (7km south of Harkány). There are 29 border-crossing points to and from Slovenia – way too many to list here. And there are dozens of border crossings into Bosnia and Hercegovina, Serbia and Montenegro, including the main Zagreb–Belgrade highway. Major destinations in Bosnia and Hercegovina, such as Sarajevo, Mostar and Međugorje, are all accessible from Zagreb, Split, Osijek and Dubrovnik.

For information on car and motorcycle travel within Croatia, see p312.

Austria
BUS

Eurolines operates bus services from Vienna to Zagreb (€35, six hours, two daily), Rijeka (€53, 8¼ hours, twice weekly), Split (€56, 15 hours, weekly) and Zadar (€45, 13 hours, weekly).

TRAIN

There are two daily and two overnight trains between Vienna and Zagreb (€69, 6½ to 13 hours) and three go on to Rijeka (€79, 11½ to 16½ hours).

Belgium
BUS

Eurolines operates a twice-weekly service all year from Brussels to Zagreb (€115, 22 hours), and another weekly bus to Split (€120, 28 hours), stopping at Rijeka.

Bosnia & Hercegovina
BUS

There are daily connections from Sarajevo (€18, five hours, daily), Međugorje (€18, three hours, two daily) and Mostar (€15, three hours, two daily) to Dubrovnik; from Sarajevo to Split (€19, seven hours, five daily), which stop at Mostar; and from Sarajevo to Zagreb (€18, eight hours, three daily) and Rijeka (€35, 10 hours, daily).

TRAIN
There's a daily train service to Zagreb from Sarajevo each morning (260KN, eight hours), a daily train to Osijek (113KN, 8½ hours) and a daily service to Ploče (310KN, 10 hours) via Mostar, Sarajevo and Banja Luka.

Germany
BUS
As Croatia is a prime destination for Germans on vacation and Germany is a prime destination for Croatian workers, the bus services between the two countries are good. All buses are handled by **Deutsche Touring GmbH** (☎ 069-79 03 50; www.deutsche-touring.de; Am Romerhof 17, Frankfurt) and fares are cheaper than the train. There are no Deutsche Touring offices in Croatia, but numerous travel agencies and bus stations sell its tickets. There are buses between Zagreb and Berlin, Cologne, Dortmund, Frankfurt, Main, Mannheim, Munich, Nuremberg and Stuttgart; buses depart four times a week from Berlin, and daily from the others. There's a weekly bus to Istria from Frankfurt and two buses a week from Munich.

The Dalmatian coast is also served by daily buses from German cities and there's a twice-weekly bus direct from Berlin to Rijeka and on to Split.

TRAIN
There are three trains daily from Munich to Zagreb (€88, nine hours) via Salzburg and Ljubljana. Reservations are required southbound but not northbound.

Hungary
BUS
There are two daily Eurolines buses to Osijek (125KN to 160KN, 2½ hours) via Mohács (1½ hours) from Budapest.

TRAIN
There are four daily trains from Zagreb to Budapest (€60, 5½ to 7½ hours).

Italy
BUS
Trieste is well connected with the Istrian coast. There are around three buses a day

to Rijeka (96KN, two to three hours), plus buses to Rovinj (177KN to 195KN, 3½ hours, one daily), Poreč (170KN to 210KN, 2¼ hours, one daily) and Pula (170KN to 230KN, 3¾ hours, four daily). There are fewer buses on Sunday.

To Dalmatia there's a daily bus that leaves at 5.30pm and stops at Rijeka (60KN, 2½ hours), Zadar (120KN to 140KN, 7½ hours), Split (195KN, 10½ hours) and Dubrovnik (250KN, 15 hours).

There's also a bus from Padua that passes Venice and Trieste, Monday to Saturday, and then goes on to Poreč (€25, 2½ hours), Rovinj (€27, three hours) and Pula (€29, 3¼ hours). For schedules, see www.saf.ud.it.

TRAIN
Between Venice and Zagreb (€60, 6½ to 7½ hours), there are two daily direct connections and several more that run through Ljubljana.

Montenegro
BUS
The border between Montenegro and Croatia is open to visitors, allowing Americans, Australians, Canadians and Brits to enter visa-free. There's a daily bus from Kotor to Dubrovnik (120KN, 2½ hours) that starts at Bar and stops at Herceg Novi.

Serbia
BUS
There are six daily buses from Zagreb to Belgrade (€20, six hours). At Bajakovo on the border, a Serbian bus takes you on to Belgrade.

TRAIN
Five daily trains connect Zagreb with Belgrade (€25, seven hours).

Slovenia
BUS
Like Italy, Slovenia is well connected with the Istrian coast. There is one weekday bus that runs between Rovinj and Koper (87KN, three hours) stopping at Piran, Poreč and Portorož (41KN, 1½ hours), as well as a daily bus from Rovinj to Ljubljana (94KN, 5½ hours). There are also buses from Ljubljana to Zagreb (110KN, three hours, two daily), Rijeka (84KN, 2½ hours, one daily) and Split (310KN, 10½ hours, one daily).

TRANSPORT

TRAIN

There are up to 11 trains daily between Zagreb and Ljubljana (€16, 2¼ hours) and four between Rijeka and Ljubljana (93KN, three hours).

SEA

Regular boats from several companies connect Croatia with Italy and Slovenia. Passengers in cabin class have breakfast included, otherwise the price is about €3.50. There is no port tax if you are leaving Croatia by boat. All of the boat-company offices in Split are located inside the ferry terminal.

Jadrolinija (☎ in Ancona 071-20 71 465, in Bari 080-52 75 439, in Rijeka 051-211 444; www.jadrolinija.hr), Croatia's national boat line, runs car ferries from Ancona to Split (346KN to 477KN depending on the season, 10 hours, three to seven weekly) and Zadar (325KN to 448KN, seven hours, three to four weekly), a line from Bari to Dubrovnik (346KN to 477KN, nine hours, two to six weekly), a year-round ferry from Pescara to Split (346KN to 477KN, 10 hours, twice weekly) and a summer ferry from Pescara to Hvar (346KN to 477KN, nine hours, once weekly). Prices listed are for a deck seat; bringing a car costs an extra 50%. Couchettes and cabins are more expensive; check the website for details.

Split Tours (☎ in Ancona 071-20 40 90, in Split 021-352 553; www.splittours.hr) runs the Blue Line car ferries connecting Ancona with Zadar and Split, and continuing on to Stari Grad (Hvar) for the same prices as Jadrolinija. It also connects Ancona with Vis in the summer.

SNAV (☎ in Ancona 071-20 76 116, in Naples 081-76 12 348, in Split 021-322 252; www.snav.com) has a fast car ferry that links Split with Pescara (€36 to €90, 4¾ hours, daily) and Ancona (€36 to €90, 4½ hours, three to seven weekly), and Pescara with Hvar (€36 to €90, 3¼ hours, daily). **Sanmar** (www.sanmar.it) handles the same route for a similar price.

Venezia Lines (☎ 041-52 22 568; www.venezialines .com; Santa Croce 518/A, Venice 30135) runs passenger boats from Venice to the following destinations once, twice or three times weekly, depending on the destination and the month:

DEPARTURE TAX

There is an embarkation tax of €4 from Italian ports that is included in the price of the tickets.

FLIGHT-FREE TRAVEL

To learn how to get to Zagreb from London without having to fly, log on to www.seat61 .com and search under 'Croatia'. You'll get instructions on how to get to Zagreb from the UK capital via bus and rail (it gives you departure times and all!).

Pula (low-high season €50 to €55, three hours), Rovinj, (€48 to €53, 3¾ hours) and Poreč (€48 to €53, 2½ hours). The company also covers other Istrian destinations and runs some routes from Rimini and Ravenna.

Emilia Romagna Lines (www.emiliaromagnalines.it) is another company that runs summer passenger boats (14 April to 30 September) from Italy to Croatia. Routes run from Cesenatico, stopping at Rimini and Pesaro, to Rovinj (low-high season €57 to €62, 3¼ hours), Lošinj (Lussino in Italian; €62 to €72, four hours), Zadar (€72 to €82, 4½ hours) and Hvar (€71 to €82, 5½ hours).

In Croatia, contact **Jadroagent** (☎ 052-210 431; jadroagent-pula@pu.t-com.hr; Riva 14) in Pula and **Istra-Line** (☎ 052-451 067; www.istraline.hr; Šetalište 2) in Poreč for information and tickets on boats between Italy and Croatia.

GETTING AROUND

AIR

Croatia Airlines (airline code OU; Map pp74-5; ☎ 01-48 19 633; www.croatiaairlines.hr; Zrinjevac 17, Zagreb) is the one and only carrier for flights within Croatia. Fares depend on the season and you get better deals if you book ahead. Seniors, children under 12 and people aged under 26 get discounts. There are daily flights between Zagreb and Dubrovnik, Pula, Split and Zadar. In addition to the standard airport security measures, note that all batteries must be removed from checked luggage when leaving from any airport in Croatia.

BICYCLE

Cycling can be a great way to explore the islands, and bicycles are easy to rent along the coast and on the islands. Relatively flat islands such as Pag, Mljet and Mali Lošinj offer the most relaxed biking, but the winding, hilly roads on other islands offer spectacular views. Some tourist offices, especially in the Kvarner and Istria regions, have maps of routes and can refer you to local bike-rental agencies. Cycling on the coast or the mainland requires caution, as most roads are busy two-lane highways with no bicycle lanes.

BOAT
Coastal Ferries
Year-round, Jadrolinija car ferries operate along the Bari–Rijeka–Dubrovnik coastal route, stopping at Split and the islands of Hvar, Korčula and Mljet several times a week. Services are less frequent in winter. The most scenic section is Split to Dubrovnik, which all Jadrolinija ferries cover during the day. Ferries are a lot more comfortable than buses, though somewhat more expensive. From Rijeka to Dubrovnik the deck fare is 190/228KN in the low/high season, with high season running from about the end of June to the end of August, and there's a 20% reduction on the return portion of a return ticket. Cabins should be booked a week ahead, but deck space is usually available on all sailings. You must buy tickets in advance at an agency or a Jadrolinija office, since they are not sold on board. Bringing a car means checking in two hours in advance.

Meals in the restaurants aboard Jadrolinija ships are about 100KN for a fixed-price menu of somewhat mediocre food. All the cafeteria offers is ham-and-cheese sandwiches for 30KN. Coffee is cheap in the cafeteria, but wine and spirits tend to be expensive. Breakfast in the restaurant costs about 30KN but is included in the price of a cabin ticket. Do as the Croatians do: bring some food and drink with you.

Local Ferries
Local ferries connect the bigger offshore islands with each other and with the mainland, but you'll find many more ferries going from the mainland to the islands than from island to island. On most lines, service is less frequent between October and April. Passenger and car tickets must be bought in advance, as there are no ticket sales on board.

Taking a bicycle on these services incurs a small charge and taking a vehicle aboard obviously incurs a larger charge. The car charge is calculated according to the size of your vehicle and begins at about four times the price of a passenger ticket. In summer, ferries to the islands fill up fast, so you should reserve as far in advance as possible if you're bringing your car. Some of the ferries operate only a couple of times a day and, once the vehicular capacity is reached, the remaining motorists must wait for the next available service. Even with the reservation, you will have to show up several hours before boarding.

On some of the shorter routes, such as Jablanac to Mišnjak or Drvenik to Sućuraj, the ferries run nonstop in the summer and an advance reservation is unnecessary. If there's no Jadrolinija office in town, you can buy the ticket at a stall near the ferry stop that usually opens 30 minutes before departure. In summer you'll be told to arrive one to two hours in advance for ferries to the more popular islands even if you've already bought your ticket. Foot passengers and cyclists should have no problem getting on.

There is no meal service on local ferries although you can buy drinks and snacks on board. Most locals bring their own food.

Extra passenger boats are added in the summer and are usually faster, more comfortable and more expensive than the car ferries. Boats connecting Split and Zadar with Italy usually make stops on the islands of Hvar, Brač or Vis. See opposite for more information.

BUS
Bus services are excellent and relatively inexpensive. There are often a number of different companies handling each route so prices can vary substantially, but the prices in this book should give you an idea of costs (unless otherwise noted, all bus prices are for one-way fares). Luggage stowed in the baggage compartment under the bus costs extra (7KN a piece, including insurance). Following are some prices for the most popular routes, but it's generally best to call or visit the bus station to get the complete schedule and compare prices.

Route	Fare (KN)	Duration (hr)	Daily services
Dubrovnik-Rijeka	400	12	2
Dubrovnik-Split	120	4½	14
Dubrovnik-Zadar	250	8	7
Zagreb-Dubrovnik	250	11	79
Zagreb-Korčula	224	12	1
Zagreb-Pula	130-230	7	9
Zagreb-Split	195	5-9	27

TRANSPORT

ROAD DISTANCES (KM)

	Dubrovnik	Osijek	Rijeka	Split	Zadar	Zagreb
Dubrovnik	---					
Osijek	495	---				
Rijeka	601	459	---			
Split	216	494	345	---		
Zadar	340	566	224	139	---	
Zagreb	572	280	182	365	288	---

Phone numbers and websites (if they exist) are listed in the regional chapters, but the companies listed here are among the largest:

Autotrans (☎ 051-660 360; www.autotrans.hr) Based in Rijeka. Connections to Istria, Zagreb, Varaždin and Kvarner.

Brioni Pula (☎ 052-502 997; www.brioni.hr) Based in Pula. Connections to Istria, Trieste, Padua, Split and Zagreb.

Contus (☎ 023-315 315; www.contus.hr) Based in Zadar. Connections to Split and Zagreb.

Croatiabus (☎ 01-23 31 566; www.croatiabus.hr) Connecting Zagreb with towns in Zagorje and Istria.

At large stations, bus tickets must be purchased at the office, not from drivers; try to book ahead to be sure of a seat, especially in the summer. Departure lists above the various windows at bus stations tell you which window sells tickets for your bus. On Croatian bus schedules, *vozi svaki dan* means 'every day' and *ne vozi nedjeljom i blagdanom* means 'no service Sunday and holidays'.

Some buses travel overnight, saving you a night's accommodation, but don't expect to get much sleep, as the inside lights will be on and music will be blasting the whole night. Don't complain – it keeps the driver awake. Take care not to be left behind at meal or rest stops, which usually occur about every two hours.

CAR & MOTORCYCLE

Croatia has recently made a major investment in infrastructure, the highlight of which is a new and badly needed motorway connecting Zagreb with Split. The 'autoroute' is expected to reach Dubrovnik in a few years. Zagreb and Rijeka are now connected by motorway and an Istrian motorway has shortened the travel time to Italy considerably. Although the new roads are in excellent condition, there are stretches where service stations and facilities are few and far between.

Along the coast, the spectacular Adriatic highway from Italy to Albania hugs the steep slopes of the coastal range, with abrupt drops to the sea and a curve a minute. You can drive as far south as Vitaljina, 56km southeast of Dubrovnik, and then cross the border into Montenegro.

Any valid driving licence is sufficient to drive legally and rent a car; an international driving licence is not necessary. The **Hrvatski Autoklub** (HAK; Croatian Auto Club; Map pp74-5; ☎ 01-46 40 800; www.hak.hr; Draškovićeva 25, Zagreb) offers help and advice. You can also contact the nationwide **HAK road assistance** (Vučna Služba; ☎ 987).

Petrol stations are generally open from 7am to 7pm and often until 10pm in summer. Petrol is Eurosuper 95, Super 98, normal or diesel. See www.ina.hr for up-to-date fuel prices; petrol per litre currently costs around 9.65KN.

You have to pay tolls on all motorways, to use the Učka tunnel between Rijeka and Istria, to use the bridge to Krk Island, and on the road from Rijeka to Delnice. For general news on Croatia's motorways and tolls, see www.hac.hr.

The radio station HR2 broadcasts traffic reports in English every hour on the hour from July to mid-September.

Hire

In order to rent a car, you must be 21 and have a major credit card. Independent local companies are often much cheaper than the international chains, but the big companies have the advantage of offering one-way rentals that allow you to drop the car off at any one of their many stations in Croatia free of charge.

Major car-rental companies include the following:

Avis (Map pp74-5; ☎ 01-46 73 603; www.avis.com.hr; Hotel Sheraton, Kneza Borne 2, Zagreb)

Budget Rent-a-Car (Map pp74-5; ☎ 01-45 54 936; www.budget.hr; Hotel Sheraton, Kneza Borne 2, Zagreb)

Hertz (Map pp74-5; ☎ 01-48 46 777; www.hertz.hr; Vukotinovićeva 1, Zagreb)

Sometimes you can get a lower car-rental rate by booking the car from abroad. Tour companies in Western Europe often have fly-drive packages that include a flight to Croatia and a car (two-person minimum). Bear in mind that if you rent a car in Italy, many insurance companies will not insure you for a trip into Croatia. Border officials know this and may refuse you entry unless permission to drive into Croatia is clearly marked on the insurance documents. Most car-rental companies in Trieste and Venice are familiar with this requirement and will furnish you with the correct stamp. Otherwise, you must make specific inquiries.

Insurance
Third-party public liability insurance is included by law with car rentals, but make sure your quoted price includes full collision insurance, known as a collision damage waiver (CDW). Otherwise, your responsibility for damage done to the vehicle is usually determined as a percentage of the car's value beginning at around 2000KN.

Road Rules
In Croatia you drive on the right, and use of seatbelts is mandatory. Unless otherwise posted, the speed limits for cars and motorcycles are 50km/h in the built-up areas, 80km/h on main highways and 130km/h on motorways. On any of Croatia's winding two-lane highways, it's illegal to pass long military convoys or a line of cars caught behind a slow-moving truck. In a desperate measure to get a handle on the country's high accident rate, the government passed a 'zero tolerance' law, making it illegal to drive with any alcohol whatsoever in the blood. You are required to drive with your headlights on even during the day.

HITCHING
Hitching is never entirely safe in any country in the world, and we don't recommend it. Travellers who decide to hitch should understand that they are taking a small but potentially serious risk. People who do choose to hitch will be safer if they travel in pairs and let someone know where they are planning to go.

Hitching in Croatia is a gamble. The coast is used to hitchhikers and you can get a lift on the islands, but in the interior you'll notice that cars are small and usually full.

LOCAL TRANSPORT
Zagreb and Osijek have a well-developed tram system as well as local buses, but in the rest of the country you'll only find buses. Buses in major cities such as Dubrovnik, Rijeka, Split and Zadar run about once every 20 minutes, less on Sunday. A ride is usually around 8KN, with a small discount if you buy tickets at a *tisak* (newsstand). Small medieval towns along the coast are generally closed to traffic and have infrequent links to outlying suburbs. Bus transport within the islands is also infrequent since most people have their own cars. Whatever transport exists is scheduled for the workday needs of the inhabitants, not the holiday needs of tourists. To get out and see the islands, you'll need to rent a bike, boat, motorcycle or car.

TOURS
Atlas Travel Agency (www.atlas-croatia.com) Dubrovnik Gruž Harbour (Map p262; ☎ 020-418 001; Obala Papa Ivana Pavla II 1); Dubrovnik Pile Gate (Map p262; ☎ 020-442 574; Sv Đurđa 1) offers a wide variety of bus tours, fly-drive packages and 'adventure' tours, which feature bird-watching, canoeing, caving, cycling, diving, fishing, hiking, riding, sailing, sea kayaking and white-water rafting.

A German company, **Inselhüpfen** (☎ 7531-942 3630; www.island-hopping.de), combines boating and biking and takes an international crowd through southern Dalmatia, Istria or the Kvarner islands, stopping every day for a bike ride.

Katarina Line (☎ 051-272 110; www.katarina-line.hr; Maršala Tita 75, 51410 Opatija) offers week-long cruises from Opatija to Split, Mljet, Dubrovnik, Hvar, Brač, Korčula, Zadar and the Kornati Islands on an attractive wooden ship.

TRAIN
Zagreb is the hub for Croatia's less-than-extensive train system. You'll notice that no trains run along the coast and only a few coastal cities are connected with Zagreb. For travellers, the main lines of interest are: Zagreb–Rijeka–Pula; Zagreb–Zadar–Šibenik–Split; Zagreb–Varaždin–Koprivnica; and Zagreb–Osijek. The system is being modernised as exemplified by the high-speed 'tilting train' connection between Zagreb and Split, which has cut travel time by a third.

Trains are less frequent than buses but more comfortable. Domestic trains are either 'express' or 'passenger' (local). Express trains have smoking and nonsmoking as well as 1st- and 2nd-class cars. A reservation is advisable and they are more expensive than passenger trains, which offer only unreserved 2nd-class seating. Prices in this book are for unreserved 2nd-class seating.

There are no couchettes available on any domestic services, but there are sleeping cars on the overnight trains between Zagreb and Split. Baggage is free on trains and most train stations have left-luggage offices charging about 15KN apiece per day (passport required).

EU residents who hold an InterRail pass can use it in Croatia for free travel, but it is unlikely that you would take enough trains in the country to justify the cost.

For information about schedules, prices and services, contact **Croatian Railways** (Hrvatske Željeznice; ☎ 060-333 444; www.hzn et.hr).

Some terms you might encounter posted on timetables at train stations include the following:

brzi – fast train
dolazak – arrivals
polazak – departures
ne vozi nedjeljom i blagdanom – no service Sunday and holidays
poslovni – business-class train
presjedanje – change of trains
putnički – economy-class/local train
rezerviranje mjesta obvezatno – compulsory seat reservation
svakodnevno – daily

Health

CONTENTS

Travel health depends on your predeparture preparations, your daily health care while travelling and how you handle any medical problem that does develop. The standard of medical care in Croatia is high, and all foreigners are entitled to emergency medical aid at the very least.

BEFORE YOU GO

Prevention is the key to staying healthy while abroad. A little planning before departure, particularly for pre-existing illnesses, will save trouble later: see your dentist before a long trip, carry a spare pair of contact lenses and glasses, and take your optical prescription with you. Bring medications in their original, labelled containers. A letter from your physician describing your medical conditions and medications, including generic names, is also a good idea. If you are carrying syringes, be sure to have a physician's letter with you documenting their necessity.

It's usually a good idea to consult your government's travel health website before departure, if one is available:
Australia www.smartraveller.gov.au
Canada www.travelhealth.gc.ca
United Kingdom www.dh.gov.uk
United States www.cdc.gov

INSURANCE

If you're an EU citizen, you will be covered for most emergency medical care except for emergency repatriation home. Citizens from other countries should find out if there is a reciprocal arrangement for free medical care between their country and Croatia. If you do need health insurance, strongly consider a policy that covers you for the worst possible scenario, such as an accident requiring an emergency flight home. Find out in advance if your insurance plan will make payments directly to providers or if it will reimburse you later for any overseas health expenditures. The former option is generally preferable, as it doesn't require you to pay out of pocket in a foreign country.

RECOMMENDED VACCINATIONS

The World Health Organization (WHO) recommends that all travellers should be covered for diphtheria, tetanus, measles, mumps, rubella and polio, regardless of their destination. Since most vaccines don't produce immunity until at least two weeks after they're given, visit a physician at least six weeks before departure.

INTERNET RESOURCES

The WHO's publication *International Travel and Health* is revised annually and is available online at www.who.int/ith. Other useful websites include the following:
www.ageconcern.org.uk Advice on travel for the elderly.
www.fitfortravel.scot.nhs.uk General travel advice for the layperson.
www.mariestopes.org.uk Information on contraception and women's health.
www.mdtravelhealth.com Travel-health recommendations for every country; updated daily.

IN TRANSIT

DEEP VEIN THROMBOSIS (DVT)

Blood clots may form in the legs during plane flights, chiefly due to prolonged immobility.

HEALTH

The longer the flight, the greater the risk. The chief symptom of DVT is swelling of or pain in the foot, ankle or calf, which is usually, but not always, on just one side. When a blood clot travels to the lungs, it may cause chest pain and breathing difficulties. Travellers with any of these symptoms should immediately seek medical attention.

To prevent the development of DVT on long-distance flights you should walk about the aircraft cabin, contract the leg muscles while sitting, drink plenty of fluids and avoid alcohol.

JET LAG & MOTION SICKNESS

To avoid jet lag (which is common when crossing more than five time zones) try drinking plenty of nonalcoholic fluids and eating light meals. Upon arrival, get exposure to natural sunlight and readjust your schedule (for meals, sleep and so on) as soon as possible.

Antihistamines such as dimenhydrinate (Dramamine) and meclizine (Antivert, Bonine) are usually the first choice for treating motion sickness. A herbal alternative is ginger.

IN CROATIA

AVAILABILITY & COST OF HEALTH CARE

Good health care is readily available in Croatia, and for minor illnesses pharmacists can give valuable advice and sell over-the-counter medication. They can also advise when more specialised help is required and point you in the right direction. The standard of dental care is usually good, but it is sensible to have a dental check-up before a long trip.

INFECTIOUS DISEASES

Tick-borne encephalitis is spread by tick bites. It is a serious infection of the brain and vaccination is advised for those in risk areas who are unable to avoid tick bites (such as campers and hikers). Two doses of vaccine will give a year's protection; three doses up to three years'.

TRAVELLER'S DIARRHOEA

If you develop diarrhoea, be sure to drink plenty of fluids, preferably an oral rehydration solution (eg dioralyte).

A few loose stools don't require treatment, but if you start having more than four or five loose stools per day, you should start taking an antibiotic (usually a quinolone drug) and an antidiarrhoeal agent (such as loperamide).

If diarrhoea is bloody, persists for more than 72 hours, or is accompanied by fever, shaking, chills or severe abdominal pain, you should seek medical attention.

ENVIRONMENTAL HAZARDS
Heat Exhaustion & Heatstroke

Heat exhaustion occurs following excessive fluid loss with inadequate replacement of fluids and salt. Symptoms include headache, dizziness and tiredness. Dehydration is already happening by the time you feel thirsty – aim to drink sufficient water to produce pale, diluted urine. To treat heat exhaustion, replace lost fluids by drinking water and/or fruit juice, and cool the body with cold water and fans. Treat salt loss with salty fluids such as soup or Bovril, or add a little more table salt to foods than usual.

Heatstroke is much more serious, resulting in irrational and hyperactive behaviour and eventually loss of consciousness and death. Rapid cooling by spraying the body with water and fanning is ideal. Emergency fluid and electrolyte replacement by intravenous drip is recommended.

Sea Urchins

Watch out for sea urchins around rocky beaches; if you get some of their needles embedded in your skin, olive oil will help to loosen them. If they are not removed, they could become infected. As a precaution wear rubber shoes while walking on the rocks or bathing.

Snake Bites

To avoid getting bitten by snakes, do not walk barefoot or stick your hands into holes or cracks. Half of those bitten by venomous snakes are not actually injected with poison (envenomed). If bitten by a snake, do not panic. Immobilise the bitten limb with a splint (eg a stick) and apply a bandage over the site firmly, similar to a bandage over a sprain. Do not apply a tourniquet, or cut or suck the bite. Get medical help as soon as possible so that antivenene can be administered if necessary.

TRAVELLING WITH CHILDREN

All travellers with children should know how to treat minor ailments and when to seek medical treatment. Make sure the children are up to date with routine vaccinations, and discuss possible travel vaccines well before departure, as some vaccines are not suitable for children under a year.

In hot moist climates any wound or break in the skin is likely to let in infection. The area should be cleaned and kept dry.

Remember to avoid contaminated food and water. If your child is vomiting or has a bout of diarrhoea, lost fluid and salts must be replaced. It may be helpful to take rehydration powders for reconstituting with boiled water.

Children should be encouraged to steer clear of dogs and other mammals because of the risk of rabies and other diseases. Any bite, scratch or lick from a warm-blooded, furry animal should be thoroughly cleaned straight away. If you think there is any possibility that the animal is infected with rabies, immediate medical assistance should be sought.

HEALTH

Language

CONTENTS

Croatian belongs to the western group of the South Slavic language family. Other languages in this group are Serbian, Bosnian and Montenegrin.

Croatia's break from former Yugoslavia in 1991 has had an impact on the language. Though it's now referred to as Croatian, in linguistic terms it's not actually a separate language from Serbian, Bosnian or Montenegrin (all formerly known as 'Serbo-Croatian'). The four languages are so similar that they are actually dialects of the one language, with only slight variations in pronunciation and vocabulary.

For information on food and dining, including lots of useful words and phrases to help you when eating out, check out p51.

PRONUNCIATION

The Croatian writing system is phonetically consistent, meaning that every letter is pronounced and its sound will not vary from word to word. With regard to the position of stress, only general rules can be given: the last syllable of a word is never stressed, and in most cases the accent falls on the first vowel in the word. You don't need to worry about this though, as the stressed syllable is indicated with italics in our pronunciation guides.

Croatian is written in the Roman alphabet and many letters are pronounced as in English. The following lists some specific Croatian letters and pronunciations, plus their closest English-letter equivalents (as used in our guides to pronunciation).

c	ts	as the 'ts' in 'cats'
ć	ch	as the 'tu' in 'future'
č	ch	as the 'ch' in 'church'
đ	j	as the 'j' in 'jury'
dž	j	as the 'dj' in 'adjust'
j	y	as the 'y' in 'young'
lj	ly/l'	as the 'lli' in 'million'
nj	ny/n'	as the 'ny' in 'canyon'
š	sh	as the 'sh' in 'hush'
ž	zh	as the 's' in 'pleasure'

ACCOMMODATION

I'm looking for a ...

Tražim ...	tra·zheem ...
camping ground	
kamp	kamp
guesthouse	
privatni smještaj	pree·vat·nee smyesh·tai
hotel	
hotel	haw·tel
youth hostel	
prenoćište za mladež	pre·naw·cheesh·te za mla·dezh

Where's a (cheap) hotel?

Gdje se nalazi (jeftin) hotel?	gdye se na·la·zee (yef·teen) haw·tel

What's the address?

Koja je adresa?	kaw·ya ye a·dre·sa

Could you write it down, please?

Možete li to napisati?	maw·zhe·te lee taw na·pee·sa·tee

Do you have any rooms available?

Imate li slobodnih soba?	ee·ma·te lee slaw·bawd·neeh saw·ba

Do you have a ...?

Imate li ...?	ee·ma·te lee ...
bed	
krevet	kre·vet
single room	
jednokrevetnu sobu	yed·naw·kre·vet·noo saw·boo
double/twin bedroom	
dvokrevetnu sobu	dvaw·kre·vet·noo saw·boo
room with a bathroom	
sobu sa kupaonicom	saw·boo sa koo·pa·aw·nee·tsawm

MAKING A RESERVATION

(for written and phone inquiries)

From ...	*Od ...*	awd ...
To ...	*Do ...*	daw ...
Date	*Datum*	da·toom
credit card	*kreditna karta*	kre·deet·na kar·ta
number	*broj*	broy
expiry date	*rok važenja*	rawk va·zhe·nya

I'd like to book ...
Želim rezervirati ...
zhe·leem re·zer·vee·ra·tee ...
In the name of ...
Na ime ...
na ee·me ...
Please confirm availability and price.
Molim potvrdite ima li slobodnih soba i cijenu.
maw·leem pawt·vr·dee·te ee·ma lee
slaw·bawd·neeh saw·ba ee tsye·noo

How much is it ...?
Koliko košta ...?   kaw·lee·kaw kawsh·ta ...
  per night
  za noć   za nawch
  per person
  po osobi   paw aw·saw·bee

May I see it?
Mogu li je vidjeti?   maw·goo lee ye vee·dye·tee
Where is the bathroom?
Gdje je kupaonica?   gdye ye koo·pa·aw·nee·tsa
Where is the toilet?
Gdje je toalet?   gdye ye taw·a·let
I'm leaving today.
Ja odlazim danas.   ya awd·la·zeem da·nas
We're leaving today.
Mi odlazimo danas.   mee awd·la·zee·maw da·nas

CONVERSATION & ESSENTIALS

Hello.	*Bog.*	bawg
Goodbye.	*Zbogom.*	zbaw·gawm
See you later.	*Doviđenja.*	do·vee·jen·ya
Yes.	*Da.*	da
No.	*Ne.*	ne
Please.	*Molim.*	maw·leem
Thank you.	*Hvala.*	hva·la
You're welcome.	*Nema na čemu.*	ne·ma na che·moo
Excuse me.	*Oprostite.*	aw·praw·stee·te
Sorry.	*Žao mi je.*	zha·aw mee ye
Just a minute.	*Trenutak.*	tre·noo·tak

Where are you from?
Odakle ste/si? (pol/inf)   aw·da·kle ste/see
I'm from ...
Ja sam iz ...   ya sam eez ...

What's your name?
Kako se zovete/   ka·kaw se zaw·ve·te/
zoveš? (pol/inf)   zaw·vesh
My name is ...
Zovem se ...   zaw·vem se ...
I (don't) like ...
Ja (ne) volim ...   ya (ne) vaw·leem ...

DIRECTIONS

Where is ...?
Gdje je ...?   gdye ye ...
Go straight ahead.
Idite ravno naprijed.   ee·dee·te rav·naw na·pree·yed
Turn left/right.
Skrenite lijevo/desno.   skre·nee·te lee·ye·vaw/des·naw
at the corner
na uglu   na oo·gloo
at the traffic lights
na semaforu   na se·ma·faw·roo

SIGNS

Ulaz	Entrance
Izlaz	Exit
Otvoreno	Open
Zatvoreno	Closed
Zabranjeno	Prohibited
Zahodi	Toilets/WC
Muškarci	Men
Žene	Women

---

behind	*iza*	ee·za
in front of	*ispred*	ee·spred
far (from)	*daleko (od)*	da·le·kaw (awd)
near	*blizu*	blee·zoo
next to	*pored*	paw·red
opposite	*nasuprot*	na·soo·prawt

beach	*plaža*	pla·zha
bridge	*most*	mawst
castle	*zamak*	za·mak
cathedral	*katedrala*	ka·te·dra·la
church	*crkva*	tsr·kva
island	*otok*	aw·tawk
lake	*jezero*	ye·ze·raw
main square	*glavni trg*	glav·nee trg
old city (town)	*stari grad*	sta·ree grad
palace	*palača*	pa·la·cha
quay	*kej*	key
riverbank	*riječna obala*	ree·yech·na aw·ba·la
ruins	*ruševine*	roo·she·vee·ne
sea	*more*	maw·re
square	*trg*	trg
tower	*kula*	koo·la

LANGUAGE

EMERGENCIES

Help!
Upomoć!
oo-paw-mawch
There's been an accident!
Desila se nezgoda!
de-see-la se nez-gaw-da
I'm lost.
Izgubio/Izgubila sam se. (m/f)
eez-goo-bee-aw/eez-goo-bee-la sam se
Leave me alone!
Ostavite me na miru!
aw-sta-vee-te me na mee-roo
Call a doctor!
Zovite liječnika!
zaw-vee-te lee-yech-nee-ka
Call the police!
Zovite policiju!
zaw-vee-te paw-lee-tsee-yoo

HEALTH

I'm ill.
Ja sam bolestan/   ya sam baw-le-stan/
bolesna. (m/f)   baw-le-sna
It hurts here.
Boli me ovdje.   baw-lee me awv-dye

I'm ...
Ja imam ...
ya i-mam ...

asthmatic	astmu	ast-moo
diabetic	dijabetes	dee-ya-be-tes
epileptic	epilepsiju	e-pee-lep-see-yoo

I'm allergic to ...
Ja sam alergičan/alergična na ... (m/f)
ya sam a-ler-gee-chan/a-ler-geech-na na ...

antibiotics	antibiotike	an-tee-bee-aw-tee-ke
penicillin	penicilin	pe-nee-tsee-leen
bees	pčele	pche-le
nuts	razne orahe	raz-ne aw-ra-he
antiseptic	antiseptik	an-tee-sep-teek
aspirin	aspirin	as-pee-reen
condoms	kondomi	kawn-daw-mee
contraceptive	sredstva za	sreds-tva za kawn-
	kontracepciju	tra-tsep-tsee-yoo
diarrhoea	proljev	praw-lyev
medicine	lijek	lee-yek
nausea	mučnina	mooch-nee-na
sunscreen	krema za	kre-ma za
	sunčanje	soon-cha-nye
tampons	tamponi	tam-paw-nee

LANGUAGE DIFFICULTIES

Do you speak (English)?
Govorite/Govoriš li (engleski)? (pol/inf)
gaw-vaw-ree-te/gaw-vaw-reesh lee (en-gle-skee)
Does anyone here speak (English)?
Da li itko govori (engleski)?
da lee eet-kaw gaw-vaw-ree (en-gle-skee)
What's this called in Croatian?
Kako se ovo zove na hrvatskom?
ka-kaw se aw-vaw zaw-ve na hr-vat-skawm
What does ... mean?
Što znači ...?
shtaw zna-chee ...
I (don't) understand.
Ja (ne) razumijem.
ya (ne) ra-zoo-mee-yem
Could you write it down, please?
Možete li to napisati, molim vas?
maw-zhe-te lee taw na-pee-sa-tee maw-leem vas
Can you show me (on the map)?
Možete li mi to pokazati (na karti)?
maw-zhe-te lee mee taw paw-ka-za-tee (na kar-tee)

NUMBERS

0	nula	noo-la
1	jedan	ye-dan
2	dva	dva
3	tri	tree
4	četiri	che-tee-ree
5	pet	pet
6	šest	shest
7	sedam	se-dam
8	osam	aw-sam
9	devet	de-vet
10	deset	de-set
11	jedanaest	ye-da-na-est
12	dvanaest	dva-na-est
13	trinaest	tree-na-est
14	četrnaest	che-tr-na-est
15	petnaest	pet-na-est
16	šesnaest	shes-na-est
17	sedamnaest	se-dam-na-est
18	osamnaest	aw-sam-na-est
19	devetnaest	de-vet-na-est
20	dvadeset	dva-de-set
21	dvadeset jedan	dva-de-set ye-dan
22	dvadeset dva	dva-de-set dva
30	trideset	tree-de-set
40	četrdeset	che-tr-de-set
50	pedeset	pe-de-set
60	šezdeset	shez-de-set
70	sedamdeset	se-dam-de-set
80	osamdeset	aw-sam-de-set
90	devedeset	de-ve-de-set
100	sto	staw
1000	tisuću	tee-soo-choo

LANGUAGE

PAPERWORK

name	*ime*	*ee*·me
nationality	*nacionalnost*	na·tsee·awn·*nal*·nawst
date of birth	*datum rođenja*	*da*·toom raw·*je*·nya
place of birth	*mjesto rođenja*	mye·staw raw·*je*·nya
sex/gender	*spol*	spawl
passport	*putovnica*	poo·*tawv*·nee·tsa
visa	*viza*	vee·za

QUESTION WORDS

Who?	*Tko?*	tkaw
What?	*Što?*	shtaw
What is it?	*Što je?*	shtaw ye
When?	*Kada?*	ka·da
Where?	*Gdje?*	gdye
Which?	*Koji/Koja/*	*kaw*·yee/*kaw*·ya/
	Koje? (m/f/n)	*kaw*·ye
Why?	*Zašto?*	za·shtaw
How?	*Kako?*	ka·kaw
How much?	*Koliko?*	kaw·*lee*·kaw

SHOPPING & SERVICES

I'm just looking.
Ja samo razgledam.
ya *sa*·maw *raz*·gle·dam

I'd like to buy (an adaptor plug).
Želim kupiti (utikač za konverter).
zhe·leem koo·pee·tee (oo·*tee*·kach za kawn·*ver*·ter)

May I look at it?
Mogu li to pogledati?
maw·goo lee taw *paw*·gle·da·tee

How much is it?	*Koliko košta?*	kaw·*lee*·kaw *kawsh*·ta
It's cheap.	*To je jeftino.*	taw ye *yef*·tee·naw
That's too expensive.	*To je preskupo.*	taw ye pre·skoo·paw
I like it.	*Sviđa mi se.*	*svee*·ja mee se
I'll take it.	*Uzeću ovo.*	oo·ze·choo *aw*·vaw

Do you accept ...?
Da li prihvaćate ...?
da lee *pree*·hva·cha·te ...

credit cards	*kreditne*	*kre*·deet·ne
	kartice	*kar*·tee·tse
travellers cheques	*putničke*	*poot*·neech·ke
	čekove	*che*·kaw·ve

more	*više*	*vee*·she
less	*manje*	*ma*·nyc
enough	*dosta*	*daws*·ta
bigger	*veći/veća/*	ve·chee/ve·cha/
	veće (m/f/n)	ve·che
smaller	*manji/manja/*	*ma*·nyee/*ma*·nya/
	manje (m/f/n)	*ma*·nye

Where's ...?	*Gdje je ...?*	gdye ye ...
a bank	*banka*	*ban*·ka
the church	*crkva*	*tsrk*·va
the city centre	*centar grada*	*tsen*·tar *gra*·da
the ... embassy	*... ambasada*	... am·ba·*sa*·da
the hospital	*bolnica*	*bawl*·nee·tsa
the market	*tržnica*	*trzh*·nee·tsa
the museum	*muzej*	*moo*·zey
the police	*policija*	paw·*lee*·tsee·ya
the post office	*pošta*	*pawsh*·ta
a public phone	*javni telefon*	*yav*·nee te·*le*·fawn
a public toilet	*javni zahod*	*yav*·nee za·hawd
the tourist office	*turistički biro*	too·*rees*·teech·kee *bee*·raw

TIME & DATES

What time is it?
Koliko je sati? kaw·*lee*·kaw ye *sa*·tee

It's (one) o'clock.
(Jedan) je sat. (*ye*·dan) ye sat

It's (10) o'clock.
(Deset) je sati. (*de*·set) ye *sa*·tee

in the morning
ujutro oo·*yoo*·traw

in the afternoon
poslijepodne paw·slee·ye·*pawd*·ne

in the evening
navečer na·ve·cher

today	*danas*	*da*·nas
tomorrow	*sutra*	*soo*·tra
yesterday	*jučer*	*yoo*·cher

Monday	*ponedjeljak*	paw·*ne*·dye·lyak
Tuesday	*utorak*	oo·*taw*·rak
Wednesday	*srijeda*	sree·*ye*·da
Thursday	*četvrtak*	chet·*vr*·tak
Friday	*petak*	*pe*·tak
Saturday	*subota*	*soo*·baw·ta
Sunday	*nedjelja*	ne·*dye*·lya

January	*siječanj*	see·*ye*·chan'
February	*veljača*	ve·*lya*·cha
March	*ožujak*	*aw*·zhoo·yak
April	*travanj*	*tra*·van'
May	*svibanj*	*svee*·ban'
June	*lipanj*	*lee*·pan'
July	*srpanj*	*sr*·pan'
August	*kolovoz*	*kaw*·law·vawz
September	*rujanj*	*roo*·yan'
October	*listopad*	*lee*·staw·pad
November	*studeni*	*stoo*·de·nee
December	*prosinac*	*praw*·see·nats

TRANSPORT
Public Transport
What time does the ... leave/arrive?
U koliko sati kreće/stiže ...?
oo kaw·lee·kaw sa·tee kre·che/stee·zhe ...

boat	brod	brawd
bus	autobus	a·oo·taw·hoos
plane	avion	a·vee·awn
train	vlak	vlak
tram	tramvaj	tram·vai

I'd like a ... ticket.
Želio/Željela bih jednu ... kartu. (m/f)
zhe·lee·aw/zhe·lye·la beeh yed·noo ... kar·too

one-way	jednosmjernu	yed·naw·smyer·noo
return	povratnu	paw·vrat·noo
1st class	prvorazrednu	pr·vaw·raz·red·noo
2nd class	drugorazrednu	droo·gaw·raz·red·noo

I want to go to ...
Želim da idem u ...   zhe·leem da ee·dem oo ...
The train has been delayed.
Vlak kasni.   vlak kas·nee
The train has been cancelled.
Vlak je otkazan.   vlak ye awt·ka·zan

the first	prvi	pr·vee
the last	posljednji	paws·lyed·nyee
the next	sljedeći	slye·de·chee
platform number	broj perona	broy pe·raw·na
ticket office	blagajna	bla·gai·na
timetable	red vožnje	red vawzh·nye
train station	željeznička postaja	zhe·lyez·neech·ka paws·ta·ya

Private Transport
I'd like to hire a/an ...
Želio/Željela bih iznajmiti ... (m/f)
zhe·lee·aw/zhe·lye·la beeh eez·nai·mee·tee ...

bicycle	bicikl	bee·tsee·kl
car	automobil	a·oo·taw·maw·beel
4WD	džip	jeep
motorbike	motocikl	maw·taw·tsee·kl

How much for daily/weekly hire?
Koliko stoji dnevni/tjedni najam?
kaw·lee·kaw staw·yee dnev·nee/tyed·nee na·yam
Is this the road to ...?
Je li ovo cesta za ...?
ye lee aw·vaw tse·sta za ...
Where's a service station?
Gdje je benzinska stanica?
gdye ye ben·zeen·ska sta·nee·tsa

Opasno	Danger
Obilaznica	Detour
Ulaz	Entry
Izlaz	Exit
Ulaz Zabranjen	No Entry
Zabranjeno Preticanje	No Overtaking
Zabranjeno Parkiranje	No Parking
Jedan Pravac	One Way
Uspori	Slow Down
Putarina	Toll

Please fill it up.
Pun rezervoar molim.
poon re·zer·vaw·ar maw·leem
I'd like ... litres.
Trebam ... litara.
tre·bam ... lee·ta·ra

diesel		
dizel gorivo		dee·zel gaw·ree·vaw
petrol		
benzin		ben·zeen

(How long) Can I park here?
(Koliko dugo) Mogu ovdje parkirati?
(kaw·lee·kaw doo·gaw) maw·goo awv·dye par·kee·ra·tee
Where do I pay?
Gdje se plaća?
Gdye se pla·cha
I need a mechanic.
Trebam automehaničara.
tre·bam a·oo·taw·me·ha·nee·cha·ra
The car/motorbike has broken down (at ...).
Automobil/Motocikl se pokvario (u ...).
a·oo·taw·maw·beel/maw·taw·tsee·kl se pawk·va·ree·aw (oo ...)
The car/motorbike won't start.
Automobil/Motocikl neće upaliti.
a·oo·taw·maw·beel/maw·taw·tsee·kl ne·che oo·pa·lee·tee
I have a flat tyre.
Imam probušenu gumu.
ee·mam praw·boo·she·noo goo·moo
I've run out of petrol.
Nestalo mi je benzina.
ne·sta·law mee ye ben·zee·na
I've had an accident.
Imao/Imala sam prometnu nezgodu. (m/f)
ee·ma·aw/ee·ma·la sam praw·met·noo nez·gaw·doo

TRAVEL WITH CHILDREN
Are children allowed?
Da li je dozvoljen pristup djeci?
da lee ye dawz·vaw·lyen pree·stoop dye·tsee

Do you mind if I breast-feed here?
Da li vam smeta ako ovdje dojim?
da lee vam *sme*·ta *a*·kaw *awv*·dye *daw*·yeem

Do you have (a/an) ...?
Imate li ...?
ee·ma·te lee ...

  baby change room
  sobu za previjanje beba
  suw·boo za pre·*vee*·ya·nye *be*·ba

  car baby seat
  sjedalo za dijete
  sye·da·law za dee·*ye*·te

  child-minding service
  usluge čuvanja djece
  oo·sloo·ge *choo*·va·nya *dye*·tse

  children's menu
  dječji jelovnik
  dyech·yee ye·*lawv*·neek

  (disposable) nappies/diapers
  pelene (za jednokratnu upotrebu)
  pe·le·ne (za yed·*naw*·krat·noo *oo*·paw·tre·boo)

  (English-speaking) babysitter
  dadilju (koja govori engleski)
  da·dee·lyoo (*kaw*·ya *gaw*·vaw·ree en·gle·skee)

  highchair
  visoku stolicu za bebe
  vee·saw·koo *staw*·lee·tsoo za *be*·be

  infant milk formula
  formulu za bebe
  fawr·moo·loo za *be*·be

  potty
  tutu
  too·too

  pusher/stroller
  dječju hodalicu
  dyech·yoo *haw*·da·lee·tsoo

LANGUAGE

Also available from Lonely Planet:
Croatian Phrasebook

Glossary

amphora (s), **amphorae** (pl) – large, two-handled vase in which wine or water was kept
apse – altar area of a church
autocamps – gigantic camping grounds with restaurants, shops and row upon row of caravans
Avars – Eastern European people who waged war against Byzantium from the 6th to 9th centuries

ban – viceroy or governor
bb – in an address the letters 'bb' following a street name (such as Placa bb) stand for *bez broja* (without number), which indicates that the building has no street number
brek – Istrian truffle-hunting dog
brzi – fast train
bura – cold northeasterly wind

cesta – road
citura – zither
crkva – church

dnevna karta – day ticket
dolazak – arrivals
dom – dormitory, mountain cottage or lodge
drmeš – fast polka danced by couples in small groups
dubrava – holm oak

fortica – fortress
fumaioli – exterior chimneys

galerija – gallery
garderoba – left-luggage office
Glagolitic – ancient Slavonic language put into writing by Greek missionaries Cyril and Methodius
gora – mountain
gostionica – simple family-run restaurant
grad – city

HAK – Hrvatski Autoklub; Croatian Auto Club
HDZ – Hrvatska Demokratska Zajednica; Croatian Democratic Union

Illyrians – ancient inhabitants of the Adriatic coast, defeated by the Romans in the 2nd century BC
impulsi – units (phonecards)

jezero – lake
juga – southern wind

karst – highly porous limestone and dolomitic rock
karta – ticket

kavana – café
kazalište – theatre
kino – cinema
klapa – an outgrowth of church-choir singing
kolo – lively Slavic round dance in which men and women alternate in the circle, accompanied by Roma-style violinists
konoba – the traditional term for a small, intimate dining spot, often located in a cellar; now applies to a wide variety of restaurants; usually a simple, family-run establishment

macchia – shrubs
maestral – strong, steady westerly wind
malo – little
maquis – dense growth of mostly evergreen shrubs and small trees
mišnice – local Korčulan instrument, a bit like bagpipes
morčići – historically, *moretto;* a traditional symbol of Rijeka; the image of a black person topped with a colourful turban made into ceramic brooches and earrings
moretto – historical term for *morčići*
muzej – museum

nave – central part of a church flanked by two aisles
NDH – Nezavisna Država Hrvatska; Independent State of Croatia

obala – waterfront
odlazak – departures; also *polazak*
otok (s), **otoci** (pl) – island

pećina – cave
pension – guest house
pismo – stamp
pivnica – pub
plaža – beach
pleter – plaited ornamentation often found in churches
polazak – departures; also *odlazak*
polje – collapsed limestone area often under cultivation
poskočica – dance featuring couples creating various patterns
poslovni – business-class train
potok – stream
put – path, trail
putnički – economy-class train

restauracija – restaurant
restoran – restaurant

rijeka – river
ris – lynx

sabor – parliament
samoposluživanje – self-service restaurant; cafeteria
šetalište – walkway
slastičarna – pastry shop
sobe – rooms available
sveti – saint
svetog – saint (genitive case – ie of saint, as in the Church of St Joseph)

tamburica – three- or five-string mandolin
tisak – newsstand

toplice – spa
trg – square
turbo folk – version of Serbian music
turistička zajednica – tourist association

ulica – street
uvala – bay

velik – large
vlak – train
vrh – summit, peak

zimmer – rooms available (a German word)

The Authors

VESNA MARIĆ
Coordinating Author, front and back chapters, Zagreb, Northern Dalmatia, Split & Central Dalmatia, Dubrovnik & Southern Dalmatia

Vesna was born in Bosnia and Hercegovina while it was still a part of Yugoslavia, and she has never been able to see Croatia as a foreign country. A lifetime lover of Dalmatia's beaches, pine trees, food and wine, she expanded her knowledge of the region this edition by exploring Zadar and Zagreb, two cities she discovered anew. Researching this book was a true delight.

ANJA MUTIĆ
Food & Drink, Hrvatsko Zagorje, Slavonia, Kvarner Region, Istria

It's been more than 16 years since Anja left her native Croatia. She journeyed to several continents before making New York her base 10 years ago. But the roots are a'calling. She's been returning to Croatia frequently for work and play, intent on discovering a new place on every visit, be it a nature park, an offbeat town or an island. She's happy that Croatia's many beauties are appreciated worldwide, but secretly longs for the time when you could have a leisurely seafront coffee in Hvar without waiting for a table.

CONTRIBUTING AUTHOR

Will Gourlay wrote the History chapter. Will ate his first *ćevapčići* at a child's birthday party at Melbourne's Yugoslav consulate in the mid-1970s. Some 25 years later he had his next serve at Zagreb's Dolac market and he's never looked back. Now firmly fixated on all things Balkan, he has since made repeat trips to Croatia and its neighbours, sometimes with family in tow. A serious travel junky with tertiary degrees in history and editing, Will has worked as a commissioning editor for Lonely Planet for several years. He is now thinking that retiring to Lopud, with his family and a large trunk of books, would be more fun.

LONELY PLANET AUTHORS

Why is our travel information the best in the world? It's simple: our authors are passionate, dedicated travellers. They don't take freebies in exchange for positive coverage so you can be sure the advice you're given is impartial. They travel widely to all the popular spots, and off the beaten track. They don't research using just the internet or phone. They discover new places not included in any other guidebook. They personally visit thousands of hotels, restaurants, palaces, trails, galleries, temples and more. They speak with dozens of locals every day to make sure you get the kind of insider knowledge only a local could tell you. They take pride in getting all the details right, and in telling how it is. Think you can do it? Find out how at **lonelyplanet.com**.

Behind the Scenes

THIS BOOK

This 5th edition of *Croatia* was researched and written by Vesna Marić and Anja Mutić, both of whom positively ooze 'Balkan cred'. Will Gourlay wrote the History chapter. The Health chapter was adapted from material written by Dr Caroline Evans. The first four editions of this book were written by Jeanne Oliver. This guidebook was commissioned in Lonely Planet's Melbourne office, and produced by the following:

Commissioning Editor Will Gourlay
Coordinating Editors Michelle Bennett, Pete Cruttenden
Coordinating Cartographer Ross Butler
Coordinating Layout Designer Cara Smith
Senior Editors Helen Christinis, Katie Lynch
Managing Cartographers Mark Griffiths, Shahara Ahmed
Managing Layout Designer Laura Jane
Assisting Cartographers Fatima Basic, Andy Rojas, Tom Webster
Cover Designer Pepi Bluck
Project Manager Rachel Imeson
Language Content Coordinator Quentin Frayne

Thanks to Jennifer Garrett, Lisa Knights, Michelle Lewis, Darren O'Connell, Trent Paton, Branislava Vladisavljevic

THANKS
VESNA MARIĆ

Hvala to Maja Gilja, my mother, Toni and Marina Ćavar, Ružica, Stipe, Ante, Dana and Loreta Barać. Also *hvala* to Kristina Hajduka, and Janica and Matej. Thanks to Gabriel and all the travellers I chatted to along the way. Thanks also to Anja Mutić and William Gourlay.

ANJA MUTIĆ

Hvala mojim prekrasnim roditeljima – mom for her cooking and laughter, and dad for the drives and encouragement. *Gracias* to the Barcelona family, especially my nephew Biel for his hilarious Croatian pronunciation. *Obrigada* Hoji, for being there before, during and after. A huge *hvala* to my friends in Croatia who gave me endless contacts and recommendations, and whose names would easily fill several pages – this book wouldn't be the same without you. A big thank you goes to my editor William Gourlay for his support and enthusiasm. Finally, to the inspiring memory of my grandmother Mira who still guides my travels.

WILL GOURLAY

Thanks to Vesna and Anja for making this book-length journey so much fun. A special *hvala ljepa*

THE LONELY PLANET STORY

Fresh from an epic journey across Europe, Asia and Australia in 1972, Tony and Maureen Wheeler sat at their kitchen table stapling together notes. The first Lonely Planet guidebook, *Across Asia on the Cheap*, was born.

Travellers snapped up the guides. Inspired by their success, the Wheelers began publishing books to Southeast Asia, India and beyond. Demand was prodigious, and the Wheelers expanded the business rapidly to keep up. Over the years, Lonely Planet extended its coverage to every country and into the virtual world via lonelyplanet.com and the Thorn Tree message board.

As Lonely Planet became a globally loved brand, Tony and Maureen received several offers for the company. But it wasn't until 2007 that they found a partner whom they trusted to remain true to the company's principles of travelling widely, treading lightly and giving sustainably. In October of that year, BBC Worldwide acquired a 75% share in the company, pledging to uphold Lonely Planet's commitment to independent travel, trustworthy advice and editorial independence.

Today, Lonely Planet has offices in Melbourne, London and Oakland, with over 500 staff members and 300 authors. Tony and Maureen are still actively involved with Lonely Planet. They're travelling more often than ever, and they're devoting their spare time to charitable projects. And the company is still driven by the philosophy of *Across Asia on the Cheap*: 'All you've got to do is decide to go and the hardest part is over. So go!'

to Claire, Bridget and Tommy, my best-ever Balkan travel companions. *Sretan put!*

OUR READERS

Many thanks to the travellers who used the last edition and wrote to us with helpful hints, useful advice and interesting anecdotes:

Chiara Abbati, Carol Abel, Declan Alcock, Dvora Baruch, Tad Boniecki, Brian Bowman, Rory Cox, Claire Daley, Monica Davis, Rob Den Exter, Brian Fawcus, Gary Fine, Kate Goldman, Noni Gove, Renata Gukovas, Douglas Hagan, Rachel Harper, Andrew Hedges, Steve Hilton, Anita Hodak, T&B Horn, Neville Horner, Joanna Jeans, Alma Jenkins, Louise Jones, Stefan Kanduymski, Jerome Kenyon, Mirian Kesseler, Hrvoje Korbar, Andrew Lampitt, Kaung Chiau Lew, Chresten Lyng, Mikael Lypinski, Sarah Marshall, Kay McKenzie, Susan Metcalf, Vanessa Mikulic, Marie Miller, Sean Murray, Sinead Murray, Pamela Nelson, Jo & Paul Noakes, Eleanor O'Brien, Liis Parre, W Patson, Suzanne Quartermain, Rebecca Rosen, Ophelia Rubinich, Adam Russell, Virginia Ryan, Oliver Selwyn, Eva Sharpe, Bill Smith, Ed Smith, Mia Šoški, Cathy Spinage, Lisa Spratling, Robert Szabo, Cristy Tapia, Ruby Tuke, Maurice Van Dael, Loeki Vereijken, Stacey Vos, Kylie Webster, Jonathan Wheatley, David Whyman, James Woodward and Philippa Woon.

ACKNOWLEDGMENTS

Many thanks to the following for the use of their content:

Globe on title page ©Mountain High Maps 1993 Digital Wisdom, Inc.

Internal Photographs: p64, p67 (#6), p68 (#1) Andrew Burke; p62 Jon Davison; p63 (#1), p65 (#2) Tim Hughes; p61, p66 Holger Leue; p65 (#3), p67 (#3) Martin Moos; p63 (#6) Witold Skrypazak; p68 (#2) Jochen Tack

SEND US YOUR FEEDBACK

We love to hear from travellers – your comments keep us on our toes and help make our books better. Our well-travelled team reads every word on what you loved or loathed about this book. Although we cannot reply individually to postal submissions, we always guarantee that your feedback goes straight to the appropriate authors, in time for the next edition. Each person who sends us information is thanked in the next edition – and the most useful submissions are rewarded with a free book.

To send us your updates – and find out about Lonely Planet events, newsletters and travel news – visit our award-winning website: **lonelyplanet.com/contact**.

Note: we may edit, reproduce and incorporate your comments in Lonely Planet products such as guidebooks, websites and digital products, so let us know if you don't want your comments reproduced or your name acknowledged. For a copy of our privacy policy visit www.lonelyplanet.com/privacy.

BEHIND THE SCENES

Index

INDEX

INDEX

INDEX

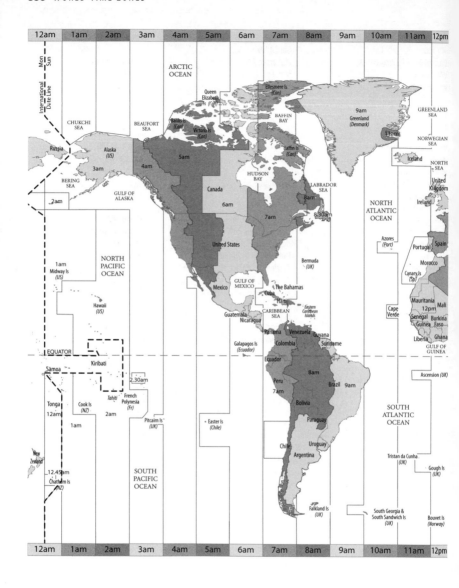

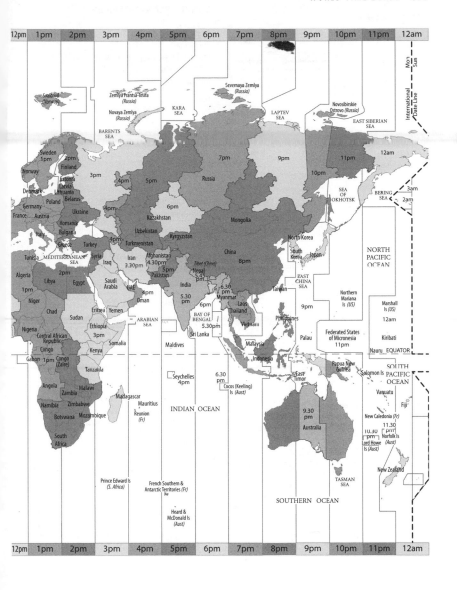

340

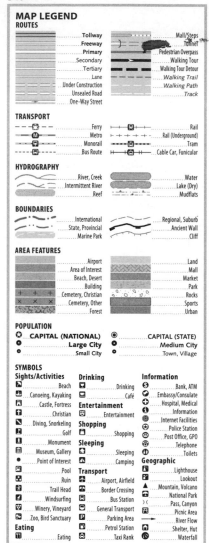

MAP LEGEND
ROUTES
..........Tollway
..........Freeway
..........Primary
..........Secondary
..........Tertiary
..........Lane
..Under Construction
..........Unsealed Road
..........One-Way Street

..........Mall/Steps
..........Tunnel
..Pedestrian Overpass
..........Walking Tour
..Walking Tour Detour
..........Walking Trail
..........Walking Path
..........Track

TRANSPORT
..........Ferry
..........Metro
..........Monorail
..........Bus Route

..........Rail
..Rail (Underground)
..........Tram
..Cable Car, Funicular

HYDROGRAPHY
..........River, Creek
..Intermittent River
..........Reef

..........Water
..........Lake (Dry)
..........Mudflats

BOUNDARIES
..........International
..State, Provincial
..........Marine Park

..........Regional, Suburb
..........Ancient Wall
..........Cliff

AREA FEATURES
..........Airport
..Area of Interest
..Beach, Desert
..........Building
..Cemetery, Christian
..Cemetery, Other
..........Forest

..........Land
..........Mall
..........Market
..........Park
..........Rocks
..........Sports
..........Urban

POPULATION
○ **CAPITAL (NATIONAL)**
● **Large City**
● Small City

◉ ....**CAPITAL (STATE)**
○ ....**Medium City**
○ ....Town, Village

SYMBOLS
Sights/Activities
..........Beach
..Canoeing, Kayaking
..Castle, Fortress
..........Christian
..Diving, Snorkeling
..........Golf
..........Monument
..Museum, Gallery
..Point of Interest
..........Pool
..........Ruin
..........Trail Head
..........Windsurfing
..Winery, Vineyard
..Zoo, Bird Sanctuary
Eating
..........Eating

Drinking
..........Drinking
..........Café
Entertainment
..Entertainment
Shopping
..........Shopping
Sleeping
..........Sleeping
..........Camping
Transport
..Airport, Airfield
..Border Crossing
..........Bus Station
..General Transport
..Parking Area
..Petrol Station
..........Taxi Rank

Information
..........Bank, ATM
..Embassy/Consulate
..Hospital, Medical
..........Information
..Internet Facilities
..Police Station
..Post Office, GPO
..........Telephone
..........Toilets
Geographic
..........Lighthouse
..........Lookout
..Mountain, Volcano
..National Park
..Pass, Canyon
..........Picnic Area
..........River Flow
..........Shelter, Hut
..........Waterfall

LONELY PLANET OFFICES

Australia
Head Office
Locked Bag 1, Footscray, Victoria 3011
☎ 03 8379 8000, fax 03 8379 8111
talk2us@lonelyplanet.com.au

USA
150 Linden St, Oakland, CA 94607
☎ 510 250 6400, toll free 800 275 8555
fax 510 893 8572
info@lonelyplanet.com

UK
2nd fl, 186 City Rd,
London EC1V 2NT
☎ 020 7106 2100, fax 020 7106 2101
go@lonelyplanet.co.uk

Published by Lonely Planet Publications Pty Ltd
ABN 36 005 607 983

© Lonely Planet Publications Pty Ltd 2009

© photographers as indicated 2009

Cover photograph: Korčula Town on Korčula Island, off the southern Dalmatia coast, Rainer Jahns. Many of the images in this guide are available for licensing from Lonely Planet Images: www.lonelyplanetimages.com.

Printed by Fabulous Printers Pte Ltd
Printed in Singapore.

Although the authors and Lonely Planet have taken all reasonable care in preparing this book, we make no warranty about the accuracy or completeness of its content and, to the maximum extent permitted, disclaim all liability arising from its use.